OKLAHOMA

A Guide to the Sooner State

Compiled by Kent Ruth
and the Staff of the
University of Oklahoma Press
With Articles by Leading Authorities
and Photographic Sections Arranged
by J. Eldon Peek

Norman : University of Oklahoma Press

Library of Congress Catalog Card Number: 57–7333

First published in the American Guide Series in 1941
by the University of Oklahoma Press.
Reprinted 1945 and 1947. Revised edition: July, 1957.

Composed and printed at Norman, Oklahoma, U.S.A.,
by the University of Oklahoma Press.

PREFACE

Oklahoma: A Guide to the Sooner State, as compiled and written by Workers of the Writers' Program of the Work Projects Administration in the State of Oklahoma, was first published by the University of Oklahoma Press in 1941 as a part of the American Guide Series, in which all the forty-eight states were represented. The Oklahoma Guide was one of the outstanding achievements of that nationwide project.

This completely revised edition of the Guide to the Sooner State is intended to supply a newer and more comprehensive index to the state of Oklahoma for readers in all parts of America. It has been our aim to present an objective and more contemporary interpretation of the achievements of the Sooner State in industry, education, recreation, literature, and the arts, together with a full appreciation of the state's natural resources and its historical heritage.

The staff of the University of Oklahoma Press has been responsible for the editorial direction and organization of the Guide, including its maps. Mr. Kent Ruth revised and brought up to date the sections on cities and tours. Special articles have been contributed by people of authoritative experience and knowledge in the various fields covered in this survey. We have endeavored to deal in positive terms with what Oklahoma is, rather than with what we might assume or wish it to be. To all readers throughout the United States we hope to convey a realistic conception not only of Oklahoma's pioneer traditions and background, the racial fabric of its population, but also of the modern-day enterprise and the courageous, optimistic spirit of the residents of Oklahoma, a state that has its roots in the frontier of yesterday and a vision commensurate with the requirements of tomorrow.

The Staff of the University of Oklahoma Press.

ACKNOWLEDGMENTS

We wish to acknowledge our indebtedness to Professors Edwin C. McReynolds, John W. Morris, and Harry E. Hoy of the University of Oklahoma for their assistance and advice on the construction of maps for the Oklahoma Guide. The map of Oklahoma surface features was drawn by Professor Hoy and is the first of its kind for this state. We are grateful also to James Webb for valuable data concerning the industrial possibilities of the Sooner State, and to R. G. Miller for his long and continuing stimulus to the understanding of Oklahoma. The Oklahoma Planning and Resources Board, as well as the State Highway Patrol and its employees, and W. D. Hamilton in particular, gave us much helpful assistance and information.

CONTENTS

ILLUSTRATIONS

MAPS

NOTES ON THE CONTRIBUTORS

KENT RUTH, editor and compiler of the sections on cities and tours, is the well-known author of *Western Vacations*, recently published by the University of Oklahoma Press, and travel editor of the *Daily Oklahoman*. He is a resident of Geary, Oklahoma, and a constant traveler throughout Oklahoma and the Trans-Mississippi West.

RALPH HUDSON, native Oklahoman and graduate of the University of Oklahoma, has served as state librarian and archivist for Oklahoma since 1937, except for a period with the United States Army from 1943 to 1946.

STANLEY DRAPER, SR., has been managing director of the Oklahoma City Chamber of Commerce since 1930. He has served for several years on executive committees of the Oklahoma Medical Research Foundation and the Frontiers of Science Foundation of Oklahoma.

SAVOIE LOTTINVILLE has been director of the University of Oklahoma Press since 1938, where supervision of publications has kept him in close touch with the history and development of Oklahoma and the Southwest.

JOHN W. MORRIS, author of *Oklahoma Geography*, published in 1952 by the Harlow Publishing Company, is professor of geography in the University of Oklahoma. Articles by Mr. Morris have appeared in various journals such as *Economic Geography, Southwestern Social Science Quarterly*, and others.

WILLIAM E. BITTLE, professor of anthropology in the University of Oklahoma, is the author of articles published in the *Southwestern Journal of Anthropology, Philosophy of Science*, and *Phylon*. He is currently working on a project concerning the back-to-Africa movement affecting Negro populations in Oklahoma from 1913 to 1916.

EDWIN C. MCREYNOLDS' first interest in Oklahoma history began in 1906, when he collected newspaper reports of the Oklahoma Constitutional Convention being held in Guthrie, Oklahoma. Mr. McReynolds, professor of history in the University of Oklahoma, is the author of *Oklahoma: A History of the Sooner State*, published by the University of Oklahoma Press in 1954.

ARTHUR H. DOERR, associate professor of geography in the University of Oklahoma and author of articles in several geographical journals, is one of the contributors to the *Symposium on the Geography of Puerto Rico*, published by the Waverly Press of Baltimore and University of Puerto Rico Press.

JAMES A. CONSTANTIN, professor of marketing and transportation in the University of Oklahoma, is the author of several articles in scholarly and trade journals. His book, *Water Transportation*, was published by the University of Alabama Press, and another, scheduled for early publication, concerns the problems of motor transportation.

A. E. DARLOW, vice president of Oklahoma Agricultural and Mechanical College and dean of its agricultural school, is a nationally and internationally known livestock authority. A member of the United States Chamber of Commerce Agriculture Committee, he has for years served as one of America's foremost judges of beef cattle, both in this nation and in England.

JEFF GRIFFIN, with fourteen years' experience as reporter for the *Daily Oklahoman* and *Oklahoma City Times*, has served as director of the Oklahoma Department of Public Welfare, and since 1948 he has been director of publicity for the Oklahoma Planning and Resources Board.

FRANK A. BALYEAT has been with the staff of the College of Education in the University of Oklahoma since 1927. His special field of study has been the history of education in Indian Territory. Several of Mr. Balyeat's articles have appeared in the *Chronicles of Oklahoma*.

ROY P. STEWART, former correspondent for *Time*, *Life*, and *Fortune* magazines, has been a staff member of the *Daily Oklahoman* since 1939, serving as reporter, feature writer, city editor, and Washington correspondent. He now writes a daily column dealing with personalities, agriculture, livestock, and history.

Edith Copeland has edited the literary page of the *Sunday Oklahoman* during 1947–49, and since 1953. A graduate of the University of Oklahoma, she has also done graduate work in literature at Louisiana State University, where she studied with Robert Penn Warren and Cleanth Brooks. Mrs. Copeland is a third-generation descendant of Oklahoma pioneers, her grandparents having settled near Ponca City at the time of the opening of the Cherokee Outlet.

John O'Neil, director of the School of Art in the University of Oklahoma, has spent most of his life as an artist-teacher in Oklahoma. His paintings have been shown in many regional and national exhibitions. Mr. O'Neil has taught at New York University and the University of Michigan, and recently has traveled extensively in the Mediterranean countries.

Spencer Norton, pianist-composer, is a professor of music in the University of Oklahoma. He is a graduate of the University of Oklahoma and the Eastman School of Music. Mr. Norton has edited and translated musical works for publication by the University of Oklahoma Press.

J. Stanley Clark is the author of *Open Wider, Please,* an account of the dental profession in Oklahoma, published by the University of Oklahoma Press in 1955. Articles by Mr. Clark have appeared in various magazines, such as the *Mississippi Valley Historical Review, Kansas Historical Quarterly,* and the *Chronicles of Oklahoma.*

J. Eldon Peek, a graduate of Oklahoma Agricultural and Mechanical College at Stillwater, is the owner and president of the Oklahoma Theatre Supply Company. Photography has always been his most active and stimulating hobby.

GENERAL INFORMATION

By Ralph Hudson

Railways: Arkansas Western Ry. (AW) 9.65 m.; the Atchison, Topeka and Santa Fe Ry. (AT&SF) 1,233.13 m.; Beaver, Meade and Englewood R. R. (BM&E) 105.13 m.; the Chicago, Rock Island and Pacific Ry. (CRI&P) 1,062.3 m.; Ft. Smith and Van Buren Ry. (FS&VB) 20.92; Gulf Colorado and Santa Fe Ry. (GC&SF) 133.83 m.; the Kansas City Southern Ry. (KCS) 127.64 m.; Kansas, Oklahoma and Gulf Ry. (KO&G) 310.28 m.; Midland Valley R. R. (MV) 239.62 m.; Missouri–Kansas–Texas R. R. (MKT) 863.38 m.; Missouri Pacific R. R. (MP) 161.91 m.; Oklahoma City–Ada–Atoka Ry. (OCAA) 115.87 m.; Okmulgee Northern Ry. (ON) 9.90 m.; Panhandle and Santa Fe Ry. (P&SF) 91.26 m.; St. Louis–San Francisco Ry. (SL&SF) 1,421.60 m.; and Sand Springs Ry. (SSRy) 13.74 m.

Highways: There are 23 numbered federal highways and 173 numbered state highways in Oklahoma. In addition there are city streets, and county, and farm-to-market roads. The total mileage of highways and roads in the state was 93,557.28 miles as of January 1, 1956.

Traffic Regulations: Maximum speed for passenger vehicles, buses, and light pick-up trucks is 65 mph during daylight hours and 55 mph during nighttime hours. Residents are required to have drivers' licenses. A nonresident whose home state does not require a driver's license must secure an Oklahoma license within 30 days. A nonresident from a state that does require a driver's license may operate a motor vehicle in Oklahoma without securing an Oklahoma license. Cities and towns establish their own traffic regulations. Oklahoma has adopted the Uniform Traffic Code. Gasoline tax (including federal tax) is 9.5 cents per gallon. Inspection of passenger cars is not required. Safety-responsibility insurance is required by law. The Division of Highway Patrol of the Department of Public Safety has a force of 300 men in uniform. Prohibited are acts forbidden by the Uniform Traffic Code or the standard rules of the road.

Air Lines: American Airlines, Inc., Braniff International Airways, Inc., Central Airlines, Inc., Continental Air Lines, Inc., Slick Airways, Inc. (freight only); and Trans World Airlines, Inc. These lines connect the larger cities of the state with all important points throughout the nation.

Air Ports: Oklahoma has 120 air ports and landing fields as of October 1, 1956.

Climate and Travel Equipment: The average annual temperature is 60.5° F. The average temperature for the months of April–September is 74° F. The midsummer season is generally hot. The heaviest annual rainfall (42 in.) is in the southeastern section. Changes in weather may occur with unusual suddenness and out-of-season weather is not rare. The western half of the state is subject to occasional dust storms. Outer coats are usually unnecessary after early April or before late October.

Prohibition of intoxicating liquors: It is illegal to manufacture, sell, or transport any liquors containing more than 3.2 per cent of alcohol by weight.

Poisonous Snakes and Plants: Five varieties of rattlesnakes are found in Oklahoma. Two types are fairly common to the entire state, and the remaining three are in certain sections. All rattlesnakes have rattles. Copperheads are generally found in the southeastern two-thirds of Oklahoma. Cottonmouth moccasins are usually found along streams and in swamp areas in the eastern one-third of the state and along the southern border. The presence of the coral snake in Oklahoma has never been authenticated by herpetologists. Poison ivy is common in all parts of the state, especially in wooded areas. It grows in clusters of three leaves, while all other ivies have five-leaf clusters. The plant may not always be in the form of a vine, but may grow as a bush in fields or among rocks.

State Parks: Alabaster Caverns, 200 acres land, no water; Beavers Bend, 1,300 acres land, 30 acres water; Boiling Springs, 880 acres land, 4 water; Greenleaf Lake, 1,495 acres land, 920 water; Lake Murray, 21,000 acres land, 6,000 water; Lake Wister, 50 acres land, 4,000 water; Osage Hills, 1,005 acres land, 18 water; Quartz Mountain, 10,810 acres land, 6,810 water; Red Rock Canyon, 150 acres land, no water; Robber's Cave, 8,400 acres land, 52 water; Roman Nose, 560 acres land, 20 water; Sequoyah, 3,180 acres land, 19,000 water; Tenkiller, 1,180 acres land, 12,500 water; Texoma, 1,876.5 acres land, 93,080, water.

State Recreation Areas: Clayton Lake and recreation area, 345 acres land, 65 water; Grand Lake (Lake O' the Cherokees) and recreation area, 138.85 acres land, 46,300 water; Heyburn Lake and recreation area, 438.5 acres land, 1,070 water.

Other Park and Recreation Areas: Canton Lake (state and federal), Craterville Park (privately operated), Fort Gibson Reservoir (state and federal) Fort Supply Reservoir (federal), Great Salt Plains Reservoir and Wildlife Refuge (federal), Hulah Dam and Lake (federal), Lake Carl Blackwell (Oklahoma A. and M. College), Ouachita National Forest (federal), Platt National Park (federal), Spavinaw Creek (city of Tulsa), Spavinaw Hills Park and Upper and Lower Lakes (city of Tulsa), Turner Falls Recreation Area (privately operated), Wichita Mountains Wildlife Refuge (federal).

Fish and Game Laws (digest): Licenses are issued by fish and game wardens and by some 3,000 hardware, sporting goods, general merchandise, and drug stores.

All residents 16 years of age or more must have licenses to fish and pay fees to fish. An annual fee of $5.00 is required of nonresidents, but a temporary nonresident license, valid for 10 days, may be secured for $2.25. Resident fishing licenses may be obtained by those who have resided in the state for at least 60 continuous days.

Residents 16 years of age or more must have licenses to hunt and must pay fees of $2.00 each. Nonresidents also are required to secure licenses to hunt. The annual fee is at least $15.00 or more if the nonresident's home state charges a higher fee to nonresidents. Anyone living in the state for 60 or more continuous days may secure a resident hunting license. Nonresidents from states bordering on Red River may acquire special nonresident licenses to hunt migratory waterfowl along that portion of the river bed in Oklahoma for a fee of $2.50. A resident may obtain a combination fishing and hunting license for $3.50. Licenses are required for commercial fishing and trapping and fur dealers and minnow seiners are also required to have licenses.

The hunting season and bag limits for migratory wild fowl is determined by the laws of the United States. The season for quail is November 20–January 1, and they may be hunted only on Tuesdays, Thursdays, and Saturdays. The bag limit for quail is 10 per day and 50 per season, and "pot shooting" is prohibited. The squirrel-hunting season is May 15–January 1, and the limit is 6 per day. Certain fur-bearing animals (badger, civet cat, fox, mink, muskrat, opossum, raccoon, and skunk) may be taken Dec. 1–Jan. 31. Otter or beaver may not be hunted. The Game and Fish Commission sets the season dates and bag limits for antelope, deer, elk, prairie chicken, wild turkey, and other game animals and birds, and establishes the rules and regulations under which this game may be taken. The importation, sale, or possession for sale of the skins or plumage of wild birds, except for scientific purposes, is forbidden. The whooping crane may not be hunted or trapped. It is illegal to take or destroy the nests and eggs of game birds.

The bag limit on fish is 10 bass, 15 catfish, 37 crappie, 10 trout, and 15 bullfrogs. The use of trotlines, nets, and other artificial devices to catch fish is regulated.

The Game and Fish Commission may raise or lower bag limits to a certain extent, may prescribe the dates or time of fishing seasons and may forbid certain game to be taken in a season.

It is prohibited to use a drug, spotlight, explosive, poisonous gas, snare, pitfall, electrical generating device, or similar deleterious substances or mechanical contrivances in taking fish or game. A gun larger than 10-gauge may not be used. Fishing or hunting on land of another without consent is illegal. Meetings may not be disturbed by shooting, nor may guns be fired across highways. Game birds, fish, and animals may not be sold or offered for sale. Possession of any of these, except as provided by law, in a closed season is considered to be evidence that they were taken in the course of such season. Cottontail or swamp rabbits may not be shipped out of the state. Certain game may be shipped, but only in accordance with the law and with the regulations of the Game and Fish Commission.

CALENDAR OF ANNUAL EVENTS

By Stanley Draper

JANUARY

Mid-January	at Oklahoma City	Variety Stores Association Meeting and Trade Show
Mid-January	at Oklahoma City	Meeting of the Oklahoma Farmers Union
Second or third week	at Guthrie	Scottish Rite Reunion
Third and fourth weekends	at Oklahoma City	*Times*' Bowling Championships (men)
Latter part of month	at Oklahoma City	Oklahoma Press Association's Midwinter conference
Last week	at Oklahoma City	State Hi "Y" Model Legislature

FEBRUARY

First part of month	at Oklahoma City	Hardware and Implement Dealers' Meeting and Trade Show
First part of month	at Oklahoma City	40 et 8, Oklahoma Voiture
Third and fourth weekends	at Oklahoma City	*Times*' Bowling Classics (women)
Latter part of month	at Tahlequah	Junior Livestock (Fat Stock) Show
Last Monday	at Pawnee	Pawnee County Junior Livestock Show and Sale
Last week	at Oklahoma City	Interdenominational Choir Concert
Last week	at Oklahoma City	Oklahoma Livestock Marketing Association

MARCH

First week	at Muskogee	Muskogee Junior Livestock Show
First week	at Oklahoma City	Semiannual Oklahoma All-Breed Dog Show
First week	at Pauls Valley	Junior Fat Stock Show
First week	at Pawhuska	Annual 4-H Livestock Show
First or second week	at Lawton	Comanche County Livestock Show and Sale
Second week	at Stillwater	County Livestock Show
Second week	at Ardmore	Southern Oklahoma Junior Livestock Show
Mid-March	at Oklahoma City	State All-Star Games
First half of month	at Frederick	Junior Livestock Show and Sale
Second or third week	at Guthrie	Scottish Rite Reunion
Second and third weekends	at Oklahoma City	State Highschool Basketball Tournament, Sections I and II
Third week	at Oklahoma City	Oklahoma 4-H Clubs and FFA Livestock Show
Third week	at Oklahoma City	Oklahoma Aberdeen Angus Breeders Association Meeting and Sale
Third week	at Oklahoma City	Oklahoma Hereford Breeders Association Meeting and Sale
Third week	at Oklahoma City	Oklahoma Shorthorn Breeders Association Meeting and Sale
Third week	at Oklahoma City	Oklahoma Hampshire Swine Breeders Association Meeting and Sale
Third week	at Oklahoma City	Intercollegiate Livestock Judging Contest
Last three weekends	at Oklahoma City	State Handicap Bowling Tournament (men)
Last Saturday	at Pawnee	Pawnee Parade (High School Band Festival)
Last Saturday	at Tulsa	Square Dance Festival

MARCH OR APRIL

Date indefinite	at Oklahoma City	Greater Oklahoma Home Show
Easter Morning	at Lawton	Wichita Mountains Easter Pageant

APRIL

First week	at Oklahoma City	Oklahoma Rabbit Association Meeting and Show
First part of month	at Waynoka	Waynoka Snake Hunt
First part of month	at Okeene	Rattlesnake Roundup
Tenth–thirteenth	at Ardmore	Carter County Rodeo
Fourteenth	at Oklahoma City	Pan-American Day Observance
Mid-April	at Tulsa	Tulsa Home Builders Association Home Show
Mid-April	at Purcell	Farmer's Day
Mid-April	at Tahlequah	Dogwood Week
Fifteenth–eighteenth	at Bartlesville	Gas and Electric Appliance Show
Twenty-second	at Guthrie	Eighty-Niners' Celebration
Twenty-second	at El Reno	Pioneer Day
Twenty-sixth–twenty-seventh	at Bartlesville	Lions' Carnival
No fixed date	at Cushing	Cushing Breeder Show, Junior
No fixed date	at Sulphur	Redbud Pilgrimage

APRIL OR MAY

Last week of April or first week of May	at Frederick	Farm Women's Dress Review
Last week of April or first week of May	at Muskogee	Muskogee Homes Show
	at Prague	Kolache Festival

MAY

Fifth	at Oklahoma City	Mexican Independence (from Maximilian) Day Celebration

First part of month	at Tahlequah	Cherokee Seminaries Homecoming
First part of month	at Oklahoma City	International Range and Pasture School
First part of month	at Oklahoma City	National Land Judging Contest
First part of month	at Oklahoma City	Oklahoma 4-H Clubs and FFA Land Judging Contest
First part of month	at Oklahoma City	Oklahoma Lamb and Wool Show
First Thursday–Saturday	at Guymon	Pioneer Celebration and Rodeo
Seventh	at Tahlequah	Cherokee (Male and Female) Seminary Reunion
Mid-May	at Oklahoma City	Oklahoma City Charity Horse Show
Mid-May	at Stilwell	Strawberry Festival
Second or third week	at Guthrie	Scottish Rite Reunion
Sixteenth	at Claremore	Opening of Will Rogers Turnpike
Nineteenth	at Oklahoma City	Armed Forces Day Observance
Nineteenth–twenty-second	at Frederick	Old Settlers' Reunion
Third Saturday	at Lawton	Armed Forces Day Observance
Latter part of month	at Tulsa	Tulsa Charity Horse Show
No fixed date	at Tahlequah	Roundup Club Rodeo
No fixed date	at Pawhuska	Osage County Cattlemen's Association Ranch Tour

JUNE

Saturday nights, June 1–July 10	at Lawton	Dramatizations of Old Testament stories at the Holy City in the Wichita Mountains, by the Easter Pageant Association
First part of month	at Sulphur	Hereford Heaven Stampede and Rodeo
First part of month	at Broken Bow	Forest Festival

First or second Sunday–Tuesday	at Oklahoma City	Variety Stores Association Meeting and Trade Show
First/Second week	at Muskogee	Indian Capital Rodeo
Second week	at Lawton	Entertainment, Junior Class, West Point Cadets
Second Sunday	at Blackburn	Drought Survivors Reunion
Mid-June	at Pauls Valley	Pauls Valley Rodeo
Thirteenth–fifteenth	at Okmulgee	Pioneer Powwow
Twenty-eighth–Thirtieth	at Cushing	Cushing Sac and Fox Indian Powwow
Last of month	at Pawhuska	Ben Johnson Memorial Steer Roping
Last of month	at Kellyville	Creek and Euchee Dance Celebration

JULY

First	at Claremore	Opening of Will Rogers Freeway to Tulsa
First–Fifth	at Claremore	Will Rogers Roundup Club Rodeo
First week	at Drumright	Rodeo
July 1–September 1, Thursday nights	at Drumright	Pro and Semipro Sooner Outdoor Variety Show
Third–fifth	at Purcell	Rodeo
Fourth	at Woodward	American Legion Horse Races
Fourth	at Frederick	July Fourth Celebration
Fourth	at Pauls Valley	Fireworks and Show
Fourth–seventh	at Miami	Indian Stomp Dance at Devil's Promenade
Weekend near Fourth	at Tahlequah	Roundup Club Rodeo
Second Week	at Hinton	Hinton Kiwanis Rodeo
Second Friday	at Mangum	Old Greer County Cowboys' Association Reunion-Rodeo
Second weekend	at Pawnee	Pawnee Indian Home-Coming Celebration
Sixteenth–nineteenth	at Chickasha	Rodeo
Seventeenth–twentieth	at Miami	Rodeo

Nineteenth	at Box	Cherokee Sacred Fire Ceremony
Twenty-eighth	at Ardmore	Ardmore's Birthday Celebration
No fixed date	at Pawhuska	Square Dance Festival

AUGUST

First week	at Oklahoma City	Oklahoma Poultry Improvement Meeting and Show
Fifth–ninth	at Miami	Indians' Green Corn Feast
Sixth	at Lawton	Lawton's Birthday Celebration and Pioneer Day
Sixth–ninth	at Lawton	Lawton Rangers' Rodeo
Second Tuesday	at Ada	Rodeo
Second week	at Drumright	Negro Rodeo
Mid-August	at Oklahoma City	Wholesale Druggists' Fall Gift Show
Third week	at Anadarko	American Indian Exposition
July 28–September 1	at Vinita	Will Rogers Memorial Rodeo
Thirty-first	at Wetumka	Sucker Day

SEPTEMBER

First of month	at Woodward	Elk's Rodeo
Five days, ending on Labor Day	at Ponca City	Ponca Indian Powwow
First half of month	at Frederick	Tillman County Fair
Weekend preceding Labor Day	at Tahlequah	Roundup Club Rodeo
Four days, beginning Labor Day	at Elk City	Elk City Rodeo
First Monday–Friday	at Miami	Ottawa County Fair
First Monday–Friday	at Miami	Ottawa County Race Meet
First Wednesday, Thursday and Friday	at Hugo	Choctaw County Fair
On or near Sept. 6	at Tahlequah	Cherokee National Holiday
Fifth–seventh	at Cushing	District Fair
Sixth–eleventh	at Cushing	Southwest Regional Amateur World Series
First or second week	at Lawton	Comanche County Fair

Second Tuesday–Friday	at Guymon	Tri-State Fair
Second week	at Lawton	Entertainment, Artillery and Guided Missile Center
Second week	at Pawnee	Pawnee Free Fair and Old Timers' Reunion
Second week	at Pauls Valley	Garvin County Free Fair
Eleventh–fourteenth	at Woodward	Elks' Rodeo and County Fair
Sixteenth	at Oklahoma City	Mexican Independence (from Spain) Day Festival
Second or third week	at Guthrie	Scottish Rite Reunion
Mid-September	at Tahlequah	Cherokee County Fair
Mid-September	at Ada	Pontotoc County Fair and Exposition
Mid-September	at Oklahoma City	Oklahoma Liquefied Gas Association Meeting
Mid-September	at Bartlesville	Fall Festival
Week including fifteenth	at Bartlesville	County Fair
Sixteenth	at Ponca City	Cherokee Outlet Opening Celebration
Sixteenth	at Cleveland	Pioneer Day
Third week	at Muskogee	Oklahoma Free State Fair
Third week	at Claremore	Rogers County Free Fair
Third week	at Ardmore	County Fair
Third week	at Oklahoma City	Oklahoma County Fair
Third week	at Stillwater	Payne County District Fair
Third week	at Purcell	Annual County Fair
Fourth week	at Oklahoma City	Oklahoma State Fair and Exposition
Last of month	at Cherokee	"Little Juarez" Celebration
Last of month	at Pawhuska Indian Village	Osage Indian Celebration
No fixed date	at Cherokee	Alfalfa County Fair and Rodeo

OCTOBER

First week	at Tulsa	Tulsa State Fair and Exposition
Tenth	at Pryor	Oklahoma Historical Day

Eleventh–twelfth	at Alva	Northwestern State College Homecoming
Latter part of month	at Tahlequah	Northeastern State College Homecoming
Fourth week	at Oklahoma City	Semiannual Oklahoma All-Breed Dog Show
Halloween night	at Frederick	Halloween Carnival
Halloween night	at Pawhuska	Halloween Inc. Parade and Carnival
No fixed date (odd years only)	at Pauls Valley	Golden Trend Oil Show
October 15–April 15	at Hugo	Opening of Circus Season (Winter Zoo)

NOVEMBER

First week	at Oklahoma City	Shrine Circus
First week	at Oklahoma City	Oklahoma Telephone Association Meeting
Fourth	at Claremore	Will Rogers Day
First part of month	at Tahlequah	Foliage Tour (or Week)
Second week	at Oklahoma City	Oklahoma Hall of Fame Dinner
Second week	at Oklahoma City	Oklahoma Farm Bureau Meeting
Second week	at Cleveland	Ninth Annual Farmers' Night
Second week	at Muskogee	Muskogee Kennel Club Unbenched Dog Show
Second or third week	at Guthrie	Scottish Rite Reunion
Thanksgiving week	at Oklahoma City	Oklahoma 4-H Club Congress
Saturday after Thanksgiving	at Oklahoma City	Santa Claus Parade

NOVEMBER OR DECEMBER

Last week of November or first week of December	at Cleveland	Christmas Opening, Special Features
	at Oklahoma City	Oklahoma State School Board Association Meeting

DECEMBER

First week	at Oklahoma City	Oklahoma State Poultry Show
First week	at Frederick	Christmas Opening
First week	at Ardmore	Southern Oklahoma Pecan Show
Second week	at Ardmore	Community Band and Concert Course
Mid-December	at Purcell	Kiddies' Christmas Party
No fixed date	at Ada	Christmas Pageant
Between Christmas and New Year's Day	at Oklahoma City	All-College Basketball Tournament

ALL YEAR

All Year	at Anadarko	Indian City, U.S.A.
All Year	at Hugo	Goodland Indian Orphanage (visitors welcome)

PART I: *The General Background*

THE SPIRIT OF OKLAHOMA

By Savoie Lottinville

Few who have attempted to interpret the claim of a state to the affections of its citizens can have failed to read and remember the late Carl Becker's account of the Kansas schoolgirls who were returning by train to the flat country of their homeland. Looking reverently for perhaps a quarter of an hour at the endless miles of corn, and the sunflowers lining the track, one said to the other, "*Dear old Kansas!*"

Affection may or may not be transferable, but it attaches itself to almost identical objects wherever people have their roots. Oklahoma lies immediately south of Kansas, north of Texas, and is bounded, despite the tendency of Texas to enfold it, also by four other states: Missouri and Arkansas on the northeast and east, and Colorado and New Mexico on the northwest and west. But Oklahomans are, if not a species apart, at least certain of why they want to be where they are. *This is home.*

It is so for reasons which do not always meet the eye or strike the ear—particularly the latter, for to an outsider who has observed the state for more than forty years, Oklahomans are a singularly unboasting race. The loyalties that are bred here are of a subtler kind. Perhaps they come from the intangibles—the familiar patterns of abundant sunshine, a mild climate, and a constantly changing landscape, windswept in spring as the prairie grasses emerge green as far as the eye can see, dazzling in autumn as the red-browns claim the woodlands and meadows, and almost snow free during the short winters.

It has always been a land of opportunity: for the fifty or more Indian tribes who, on being removed here during the nineteenth century, found a new living in the vast region between the Illinois and Grand rivers in the east to the high buffalo plains stretching close to the Rockies in the west. It was the promised land for thousands of whites who spilled eagerly into the near vacuum left by a small Indian population, beginning in 1889 and continuing in successive land rushes until after the turn of the century. It offered a heady challenge to the migrant oil drillers of Pennsylvania, Ohio, and West Virginia as they followed the productive fingers of oil strata extending southward from Kansas more than a decade before statehood. It attracted miners to its rich coal seams in the east, and ranchers and wheat growers and millers to its endless plains in the west. Finally, it provided the opportunity to processors, builders of light and heavy industry, distributors, and to all who supply mankind's needs, as it became populated by more than a million and a half inhabitants in the first twenty years after the opening of the Oklahoma District in 1889.

Nowhere else in America did precisely these forces find free play—nor so late in American national development. They have left an indelible impress upon all who live here. Oklahomans are late-comers—at least they were late in achieving lands, homes, and personal and corporate possessions, in relation both to the older, settled areas of the East and to the great Western migration of the nineteenth century. As such they are characterized by the tolerance and readiness for give-and-take of a people still, spiritually at least, in the pioneering stage. They have found and kept the quality of detachment. This is, in many ways, their most attractive asset. It has freed them of much of the conservatism and many of the inhibitions of an older society. And from a positive point of view, it has made of Oklahoma a fertile field for new ideas, new business and industrial drives, and new concepts of economic and social development, manifested in churches, schools, hospitals, and factories "as new as yesterday."

A common misgiving on the part of those who come to the state for the first time, usually from the North or East, is reflected in a rather odd question, "How can things be so new and clean?"—leaving unstated the unconscious feeling, "I miss the familiar stains and scars of another architectural climate." The answer is obvious: "Everything *is* new!" But there is another reason. Oklahoma is practically smokeless. Its vast supplies of hydrocarbons—natural gas and petroleum—have provided unobtrusive light, heat, and power, with none of the side effects of smog, grime, and atmospheric overcast common under other conditions.

But it would be a mistake to assume from these appearances that Oklahoma "has no past, only a future." The small city of Tahlequah in eastern Oklahoma is nearly a century and a quarter old and conveys almost instantly both its age and something of its rich tradition even to the casual visitor. Up and down the eastern third of the state are towns and cities with melodious Indian names—Talihina, Muskogee, Atoka, Broken Bow, Tulsa, Pawhuska, Eufaula—some dating back a century, a few less than three quarters. They are thus recent but with deep roots in the nineteenth-century movement which brought thousands of "civilized" Indians (Cherokees, Creeks, Seminoles, Choctaws, and Chickasaws) to Oklahoma before white settlers had a legal right to enter. The settlement of central Oklahoma dates from 1889, and the western half of the state, for all practical purposes, was developed after 1900.

Edward Everett Dale, the distinguished professor of history in the University of Oklahoma, is responsible for the metaphor of the red and white threads in Oklahoma citizenship. Much of Oklahoma's rapid progress during a century has been aided by able and discerning red men. Will Rogers, a member of the Cherokee Tribe, delighted not only his contemporary Oklahomans, but the world at large. Lynn Riggs, the playwright from Claremore, was also of that tribe, as was Ed Hicks, as noble a wit as Oklahoma has produced. Thomas Gilcrease, creator of the great museum bearing his name at Tulsa, is a member of the Creek Tribe. Miss Muriel H. Wright, the historian, is a granddaughter of the distinguished Choctaw leader, Allen Wright, who gave the state its name. Examples could be multiplied, but these are some of the obvious ones. Although it is often difficult today to distinguish Oklahoma citizens of Indian blood, it remains that the red thread is there, now firmly woven into the fabric of a democratic society.

While it would be a mistake to assume that Oklahoma is homogeneous, socially, throughout its four sections, north, south, east, and west (wide variations in geography would preclude that), it remains that its racial outlook is much in advance of the times. Perhaps the long association of Indians and whites here has had something to do with this attitude. As one observer has remarked, "You couldn't get anything but tolerance when, during the nineteenth century, many members of the Five Civilized Tribes were reading Greek and Latin, while white traders and trappers couldn't sign their own names."

Oklahoma's Negro population is relatively small—just at 150,000—but the speed with which it has been accorded the benefits of truly equal citizenship has less to do with its size than with the basically just attitude of Oklahomans towards race as such. However great the impact of original white settlement from Southern and so-called Border states, the outlook of the people today is Western in spirit. This outlook has not only set the stage for swift social advance by non-white segments of the Oklahoma population, but has affected vitally, and in most respects beneficially, the thinking of the people as a whole.

For a generation which has been brought up on a beguiling fare of *Green Grow the Lilacs,* the great Oklahoma folk play by the late Lynn Riggs of Claremore, and the perhaps even better-known musical based upon it, *Oklahoma!* by Richard Rodgers and Oscar Hammerstein II, it may be rather difficult to see beyond the delightful fantasy to the fact. But Brooks Atkinson, the New York drama critic, suggests it in the introduction he wrote for Riggs's play, printed for the Limited Editions Club in 1954:

"In 1900 in the Indian Territory Mr. Riggs was hardly old enough for adult observation. . . . By the time he settled down to writing *Green Grow the Lilacs* thirty years later, the Indian Territory was already a legend composed of songs, golden memories, and yarns. Life probably did not seem romantic to the people of the time when such neighbors as Curly, Laurey, and Aunt Eller were wrestling with the harsh realities of farms and cattle lands. But that kind of life had become romantic by the time Mr. Riggs got around to writing about it, all the workaday details gone and happily forgotten, leaving only a residue of love and revelry. That's the way life invariably seems to be when we look back on it from the prosy solidity of a settled civilization. We look romantic even to ourselves, when we are old enough to have escaped from the illusions and anxieties of childhood."

Mr. Atkinson is right about the lyrical base, but there is a further point that needs to be made if we are to understand Oklahomans. Every society carries beyond the period of its actual need certain cautionary baggage. Thus, despite its up-to-dateness, Oklahoma is not so remote from the sod-house frontier that its people do not retain, as half-memory, tradition, sixth sense, or what you will, a certain flinty hardness of spirit. It is as if they were prepared to do what another generation had to do, i. e., wrest from the elements all that was needed for survival.

This attitude is good in itself, and when joined with a residuum of frontier idealism, energy, and the zest for things to come, it portends a happy balance of life. It is, moreover, real and deep-grained, even to a new generation far more familiar with the motor car than with a "surrey with the fringe on top." Students at the University of Oklahoma are "Sooners," taking a leaf from those among their forebears who staked claims to land before legally organized "runs" were to begin. The tradition of grubbing out brush land and rising to ranching affluence in a generation is common, as is also the oil, mineral, or business success from infinitely small beginnings. To seek a net doubling of a city's population or a vast lake system or the power to sway regional finance—there is scarcely anything that the thinking and energy of Oklahomans cannot encompass, once they have set their hearts upon it.

As is suggested elsewhere in this book, education is almost an obsession here. It began early in the nineteenth century, with the arrival of the Five Civilized Tribes, whose members created good to excellent elementary schools, and even academies where higher studies could be pursued. The identification of opportunity with sound educational preparation has been a notable item in the thinking of Oklahomans since territorial days, when society was predominantly rural and agricultural. Today, the eighteen state-supported colleges and universities and the fifteen other institutions of higher learning in Oklahoma enroll just at 50 per cent of the annual graduating high-school classes—perhaps the highest percentage in the nation. In this, the mottoes of the Oklahoma State Regents for Higher Education, "*Vita Abundantior*," and the University of Oklahoma, "*Civi et Reipublicae*," exhibited on their seals, reflect the spirit of their constituencies.

Without attempting to state their position in quite these terms, Oklahomans have nevertheless regarded their environment, whether cultural or physical, as being constantly subject to change in the interest of improvement. As with their aggressive educational ideas, so also with their interest in art, music, the theatre, and books: these aspects of cultural environment have had remarkable attention, not only at the major institutions of higher education in the state, but in many of the larger cities and in countless smaller communities.

From these processes has come a striking export of ideas, particularly during the past quarter of a century, less significant in the areas of oil and agriculture, where they could be expected, than in literature, historical writing, musical composition, drama, folklore, and naval strategy, where they were not. It is impossible in this short essay to pinpoint the emergence and influence of these ideas, but they are easily traced in the hundreds of books published in or from Oklahoma, and in the performances and exhibitions of artistic works here and elsewhere in the world.

The assault of Oklahomans upon their physical environment has taken many forms—in agricultural and municipal development, notably—but it is nowhere so apparent as in their lakes and reservoirs. The state lies partly within the Mississippi drainage system, with fairly good rainfall, partly in the Great Plains, where semiarid conditions prevail. But the pattern of large lakes created here can only be appreciated, first, by reference to a modern map, and, second, by actually seeing what man has wrought. There are times and places when the visitor might imagine that arms of the sea had won their way into the very center of the United States. But for Oklahomans, as for all of their neighbors, the most welcome news is still "Rain!"

It used to be oil, and there is still much talk of the greatest resource, next to agriculture, that the state possesses. The oil industry, however, has long since moved out of the catch-as-catch-can phase into the realm of ordered, large-scale industrial development. It touches just as many lives—perhaps more than a quarter of a century ago—but a combination of its own technological development, the revolution in transportation, and conservation principles has seen the disappearance of the boom town and all that went with it.

Oklahomans are interested in the land, in conservation, livestock, 4-H Clubs, Future Farmers, agricultural contests and fairs. Somehow, Brooks Atkinson comes to mind again. Agricultural employment has steadily declined here during the past twenty years, as urban employment and populations have risen. The trend is entirely in consonance with the new agricultural revolution, which has enormously increased the net product of the soil while exacting fewer man hours. But Oklahomans are still close to the soil—almost every adult has a stake in the land or aspires to it. And again, it is as if they remembered the days when land holding was the guaranty—the only guaranty—of the full life.

These are some of the qualities to be found in most Oklahomans, and their sum accounts, in part, for the spirit of the state. There is one remaining—the essential generosity and friendliness of the people as a whole. It is not in any sense unique, for Americans everywhere are bestirred by the ideas of hospitality, of sharing, and of an open heart, if not always an open mind. Here, however, friendliness is very real and apparently loses no ground as an increasingly urban civilization takes hold of the region. It appears in its most attractive form when an Oklahoman is cast in the role of listener—which is almost always the case—when others are eager to tell of their own commonwealths. "Sounds interesting," says the Oklahoman. "Tell me more."

In this instance, however, the roles are reversed. We are about to tell you more about Oklahoma.

NATURAL SETTING

By John W. Morris

Oklahoma, lying within the transition zone between humid and subhumid climates, varies extensively in regional characteristics. It is frequently said that Oklahoma has four halves: an eastern and western which differ widely in vegetation, rainfall, and land forms, and a northern and southern which vary greatly in length of growing seasons and roughness of local topography. In location, Oklahoma is slightly south of the geographic center of the nation, with a gradual slope decrease from northwest to southeast. The highest elevation, 4,978 feet, is on Black Mesa, in the northwestern corner of Cimarron County; the lowest point, 324 feet, is in the southeastern corner of McCurtain County. The average elevation for the state is 1,300 feet. The principal rivers of the state flow in a general southeasterly direction; the entire drainage is carried to the Mississippi through the Arkansas and Red rivers.

Oklahoma is one of the larger states, ranking seventeenth in size. Its area of 69,919 square miles is larger than that of any state east of the Mississippi. It is bordered by six states, on the north by Colorado and Kansas, on the east by Missouri and Arkansas, on the south by Texas, and on the west by Texas and New Mexico.

GEOGRAPHICAL REGIONS

The state may be said to consist of ten fairly homogeneous regions. The Ouachitas, Arbuckles, Wichitas, and Ozarks constitute the mountain and plateau regions; the Sandstone Hills and the Gypsum Hills form two hilly areas that cross the state from north to south; the High Plains, Red Beds Plains, Red River region, and Prairie Plains make up the more level regions of Oklahoma.

The Ouachita Mountains (pronounced like Washita), in the southeastern corner of the state, have a rougher topography than any other region. These mountains are composed of several high, almost concentric parallel ridges—Winding Stair, Jackfork, Rich, Buffalo, Blue

Bouncer, Kiamichi—which extend in a general east-west direction and were formed by the faulting of thick layers of sandstone. Many of the valleys are narrow, and most have spring-fed streams. The region contains the principal pine forests of Oklahoma as well as some hardwood forests.

In the central and southwestern parts of the state are the Arbuckle and Wichita mountains. The Arbuckles, covering an area of about one thousand square miles, are old mountains, worn down to a height of only six or seven hundred feet above the surrounding plains. They present a remarkable variety of geologic formations—conglomerates, limestone, sandstone, shale, and granite. The limestone formations are largely grass covered, while most of the others are timbered. The Wichitas are formed of rough granite peaks which rise abruptly above the surrounding plains. Like the Arbuckles, they are the tops of buried mountains. Erosion has left little except the bare granite outcroppings.

The Ozark Plateau, extending into Oklahoma from the east, is a region of moderate hills with deep, narrow valleys and numerous clear streams. The base of the plateau is a limestone formation known as the Boone chert; and steep, picturesque bluffs have been formed where the streams have cut it deeply. Timbered with oak, ash, hickory, elm, and other hardwoods, the region is one of great beauty, especially in autumn. The building of the Fort Gibson, Tenkiller Ferry, and Pensacola dams has created three large lakes, the best known of which is the Lake O' The Cherokees (Grand Lake); however, Sequoyah State Park, which has been developed on the eastern shore of the Fort Gibson reservoir, is attracting many tourists to that area.

The Sandstone Hills and the Gypsum Hills are separated from each other by the Red Beds Plains. Both extend north-south across the state and each continues into Kansas. The principal rocks making up the Sandstone Hills are sandstone and shale. The shale weathers rapidly, leaving sandstone hills that often stand 250 to 400 feet above the lowlands. Many parts of this region are covered with blackjack and post oak, thickly wooded areas which are commonly referred to as the Cross Timbers. Much of the early Oklahoma oil development took place in these hills, such fields as the Burbank, Glenn Pool, Seminole, Earlsboro, Bowlegs, St. Louis, Cushing, and others became world famous. In the Gypsum Hills region the rocks are primarily shale and the soil is red clay. Three lines of gypsum hills extend northward through the region. These "gyp hills" are 150 to 200 feet high and are capped with layers of white gypsum fifteen to twenty feet thick. One form of gypsum, selenite, is crystalline and breaks into pieces resembling fragments of glass or mica. The Glass, or Gloss Mountains, an outlier of the

Blaine Escarpment, are so called because their sides are littered with flakes of selenite which glisten in the sun. The salt plains near Cherokee and the sand dunes south of Waynoka are also interesting regional features.

The Red River region, south of the Ouachitas and Arbuckles, is a strip of sandy land, much of which has an elevation of less than five hundred feet. Shale, sandstone, and limestone are the principal rocks forming the base of the region. It was once an excellent agricultural area but because of erosion and poor crop management the land has lost much of its early productivity. The Prairie Plains include the fertile Arkansas valley and the land adjacent to the Ozarks. Agriculture and grazing are the important activities even though this region has vast deposits of good bituminous coal. Both the Prairie Plains and the Red River regions are becoming important stock-producing areas.

The largest of the geographic regions is the Red Beds. Extending north-south through the central part of the state, it is a gently rolling plain which, on the surface, slopes from west to east while the underlying rock formations slope from east to west. This region is the zone of change between eastern and western Oklahoma. The eastern part of the Red Beds region has sufficient rainfall for forest, the Cross Timbers of the Sandstone Hills extending into this region. In the western part, however, grass covers most of the plains and trees grow well only in the stream valleys. Some of the soils of the Red Beds are very fertile. Cotton, broomcorn, melons, and various feed crops are produced in the southern part, while wheat and hay are the chief crops in the northern section. Numerous oil fields are scattered throughout the region.

The High Plains region, which includes the northwestern counties and the Panhandle, is an area of level grassland, treeless except for elms, cottonwoods, and willows along the streams. The area is sparsely populated, the leading industries being wheat production and cattle grazing. Rainfall is low; thus the problem of drought and dust storms is ever present. Two features of special interest in this region are the Antelope Hills, located in a bend of the Canadian River in Roger Mills County, and Black Mesa in Cimarron County. The top of Black Mesa marks the highest elevation in the state.

GEOLOGY

The rocks of Oklahoma are as varied as those of any area of comparable size in the world. Ancient crystalline rocks nearly one billion years old form the core of the Arbuckle Mountains, the axis of the Wichita Mountains, and are exposed at Spavinaw.

The first seas to invade Oklahoma covered the state late in the Cambrian period and remained through the Ordovician. As much as six thousand feet of limestone and dolomite accumulated during this time and the sandstones of the middle Ordovician are the reservoirs of large quantities of petroleum. These rocks form the main part of the Arbuckle Mountains and are in the foothills of the Wichitas. Cambrian (?) and Ordovician rocks occur west of Broken Bow in the core of the Ouachita Mountains and in small areas in northeastern Oklahoma.

In Silurian and Devonian seas sediments accumulated forming the Hunton group of limestones. These rocks have a remarkable abundance of fossils, as is the case in the Haragan marlstone on famous White Mound near Dougherty. The Hunton is the oil pay in such fields as West Edmond and Short Junction. The high-purity limestone at Marble City is a Silurian rock. Black siliceous muds which became platy shale and bedded chert were deposited in late Devonian time. This black rock is the radioactive Woodford formation of southern and central Oklahoma and the Chattanooga shale of northeastern Oklahoma. The novaculite of the Ouachita Mountains is of similar age.

Mississippian rocks are at the surface over much of northeastern Oklahoma in the southwestern segment of the Ozark uplift. Most of the units are cherty and supply the sharp rocks locally called "flint rock," which cover wide areas. The zinc and lead ores of the Miami-Picher district are in this sequence. The thick Stanley shale of the Ouachitas is Mississippian and it contains altered volcanic ash beds.

A third of Oklahoma's present surface has bedrock of Pennsylvanian age. The limestones of the Pawhuska, Tulsa, and Claremore areas are of this age. So are the sandstone hills of eastern Osage, Creek, Okmulgee, Okfuskee, and Hughes counties. The shale valleys and sandstone mesas of the McAlester area and eastward are Pennsylvanian. The Ardmore Basin, the red beds of Pottawatomie and eastern Lincoln counties, and the massive sandstone hills of the Kiamichi Mountains are of this period. Much of the oil production and all of the coal production of the state are from these rocks. During this period thick sediments were laid down in the McAlester, Ardmore, and Anadarko basins. Early in the Pennsylvanian the Wichita Mountains were folded and uplifted and the Ouachita Mountains were thrust northward. Late in the period the Arbuckle Mountains were folded and faulted.

The red rocks of western Oklahoma are Permian in age. These rocks range from the red sandstones and shales of the Oklahoma City area to the gypsum beds of Blaine County and the boulder conglomerates of Caddo County. Fossil remnants of large reptiles have been found near Norman and numerous fossil insects near Perry. The limestone ridges of western Osage, eastern Kay, and western Pawnee counties are early Permian.

Rocks of the Mesozoic era occur in the Panhandle, in buttes in western Oklahoma, and in the belt of Gulf Coastal Plain sediments north of the Red River.

Oklahoma was eroded to a plain in Tertiary time and in the last epoch of the period, the Pliocene, nonmarine sediments accumulated in basins in western Oklahoma and the Panhandle. At that time camels, horses, sabre-toothed cats, and other now-extinct animals lived in the area.

Early in the Pleistocene, river waters poured over Oklahoma from the Rocky Mountains and deposited sand and gravel widely over the state. The ice sheets did not reach Oklahoma, but the cooler intervals of time are recorded in the sediments and fossils. Many fish, snails, and types of beaver, alligator, elephant, and horse lived on the plains. White ash settled over the area from a volcanic explosion in New Mexico. Late in the Pleistocene time rainfall became sparse and streams cut into and through the sands and gravels to establish their present drainage patterns. As the streams cut down to bedrock, some stream courses and valleys were affected by the resistance to erosion of the strata. Some streams flow parallel to tilted resistant layers, others follow the trace of faults.

CLIMATE

Oklahoma, because of its location between 33° and 37° North Latitude and 94° and 103° West Longitude, is in the transition zone between the humid subtropical climates to the south and the colder continental climates to the north. It is also a part of the transition zone between the humid eastern section of the United States and the drier plains areas which border the Rocky Mountains. During the winter the Arctic storms move southward over the plains into Oklahoma causing low temperatures and occasionally disagreeable weather. Air masses form over the Gulf of Mexico and often move inland in a northern and northeastern direction, sometimes bringing with them the moisture so badly needed in most parts of the state. Frequently these contrasting pressure areas meet over Oklahoma. When great differences in temperature and humidity exist between the air masses, squall lines with possible violent storms of hail, tornadoes, and gully-washing rains may form.

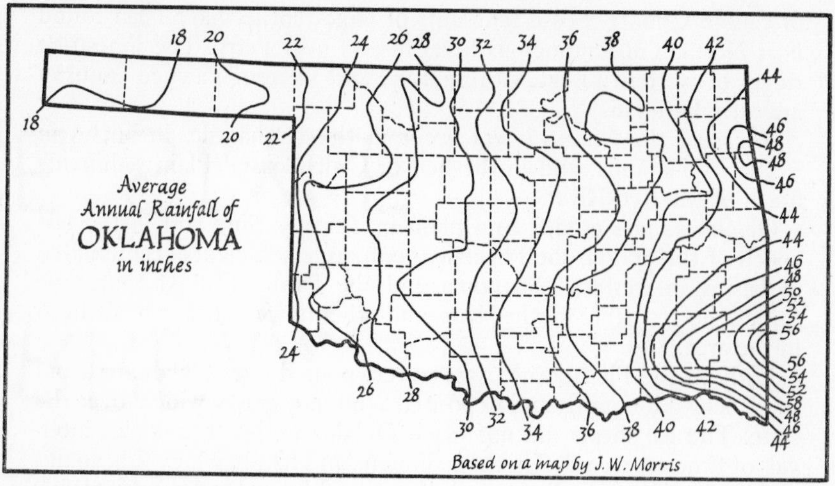

Rainfall varies greatly from east to west across the state. The average annual rainfall over the entire state is about 30 inches. The wettest year in Oklahoma was 1908, with an average total of 47.7 inches; the driest year was 1910, when the average rainfall was 18.9 inches. The greatest annual rainfall reported by any station was 119 inches, which fell at the Kiamichi Mountain tower in 1949; the smallest annual total reported was 8.6 inches at Boise City in 1934. December, January, and February are the months having the lowest average rainfall; May and June have the highest. The Ouachita Mountain region has a greater rainfall than any other region in the state, the steep slopes causing the winds to drop some of their moisture as they start to climb over the mountains. The region having the lowest total annual rainfall is the High Plains. Total average annual rainfall across the state decreases from 56 inches in the southeastern part to less than 18 inches in the northwestern section. In the southeastern area rain can be expected on about one hundred days per year; in the northwestern part rain will fall on only about forty-five days during the year.

Temperature changes in Oklahoma vary widely from day to day. The average annual temperature for the entire state is 60.5° F. This is about the same as the average temperatures for the month of March. July and August are the two hottest months with temperatures that average 81.9° and 81.7° F. However, these two months have had temperatures that averaged as high at 88.0° F. and as low as 74.1° F. January is the coldest month, having an average temperature of 38.3°

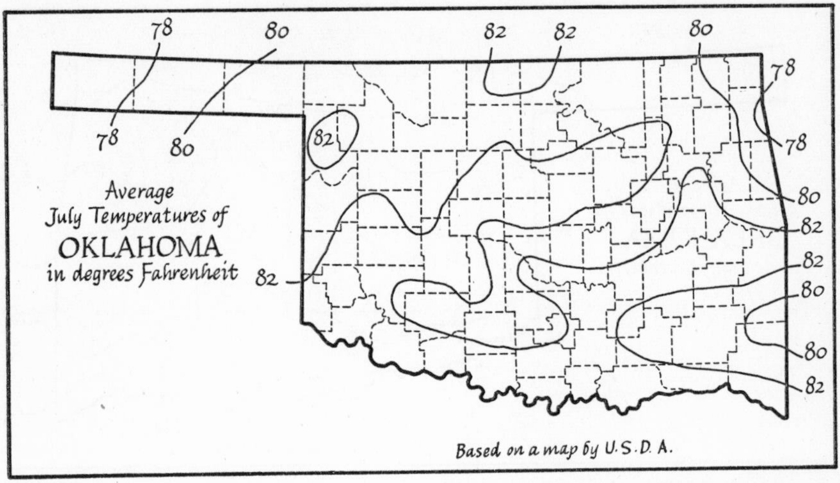

F. December, January, and February may all have monthly temperatures which fall below the freezing mark. The Red River region has the highest average annual temperatures; the lowest are in the western part of the High Plains. Daily temperatures of 100° F. or higher are often recorded during the summer. The highest temperature on record is 120° F. recorded at Alva, Altus, Poteau, and Tishomingo. Temperatures below 0° F. usually occur in the state sometime during each winter. The lowest on record is −27° F., recorded at Vinita during February, 1905, and at Watts in January, 1930.

PLANT AND ANIMAL LIFE

Because of differences in climatic conditions and variations in soils, the natural vegetation of Oklahoma ranges from the short grasses of the Panhandle to the forests of the Ouachita and Ozark regions. Approximately 25 per cent of the total area of the state is covered by forests, forest areas of varying sizes being found in sixty-five of the seventy-seven counties. Grasses, except for a few local areas of shinnery, form the dominant vegetation in the rest of the state.

Oklahoma has 133 varieties of native trees. Longleaf pine, various species of oak, elm, ash, hickory, pecan, walnut, cottonwood, willow, and some magnolia and cypress are characteristic. The two principal types of forest found in southeastern Oklahoma are the oak-pine of the Ouachita Mountains and the tupelo-red gum and cypress forests

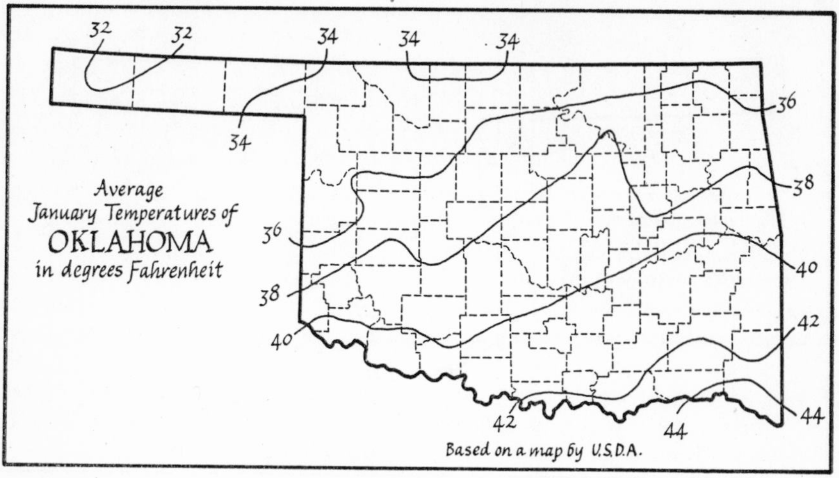

along the wet bottom lands of Red and Little rivers. In the western part of the state, among the canyons of the Red Beds and Gypsum Hills, red cedar, or juniper, is abundant. Along the stream courses cottonwoods are quite numerous. Mesquite is found in the southwest.

West and north of the Ouachita region the oak-pine forests give way to woodlands and park lands. Extensive belts of prairies, especially on limestone and smoother shale areas, exist. Jack oak and post oak are the most common variety of trees, although hickory is dominant in a few areas in the Ozarks. Native pecans thrive in the bottom lands.

North and west of the woodland belt, prairie grasses become dominant where moisture is sufficient. Prairie vegetation, of which the bluestems are the chief varieties, is abundant. West of the Enid-Duncan longitude, bluestem grows in bunches since there is insufficient moisture to form a thick mat or sod. On the sandy soils of Roger Mills, Ellis, and Woodward counties vegetation consists largely of sage, sand grass, and shinnery. Short grasses, including wire grass, grama, mesquite, and buffalo grass characterize the High Plains regions.

The redbud (Judas tree) and dogwood, which bloom in early spring, show masses of bright pink and creamy white along the hillsides and throughout the eastern, central, and most of the southern parts of the state. Violets, including the dogtooth variety, and the primrose, anemone, petunia, spiderwort, verbena, phlox, wild indigo in blue and cream varieties, poppy mallow, goldenrod, and sunflower are commonly seen. Roses thrive in most parts of Oklahoma as do many other garden flowers. Cape jasmine does well in the southern counties and crape myrtle is a favorite shrub in the northern part of the state.

Cottontails and jack rabbits are fairly common on the plains. Coyotes and prairie dogs are also found there. Mink, otter, opossum, gray and fox squirrels, and racoons live in the timbered sections. Deer, although not plentiful, are found in many parts of the state. No buffaloes exist today outside the zoos and game preserves.

The chief species of birds are the meadow lark, mockingbird, dove, swallow, robin, blue jay, and English sparrow. Crows and English starlings are also numerous. Redbirds, blue jays, and quail remain in Oklahoma all year. Prairie chickens are sometimes seen in the western counties, and mallard, teal, and other varieties of duck, as well as wild geese, fly over the state in the spring and fall. Wild turkeys, found in great abundance by the early hunters, are now rare.

There are few poisonous snakes. The copperhead and cottonmouth, or water moccasin, are most common. Rattlesnakes are still found in many places, especially in the Arbuckle Mountains, the Gypsum Hills, and Wichita Mountains regions. Horned toads and other varieties of harmless lizards are widely prevalent.

EARLY OKLAHOMANS

By William E. Bittle

In times before the white man first landed on this continent, the great stretching plains of western Oklahoma and the well-watered woodlands in the east harbored a great variety of Indian cultures. Although no historical document traces the course of these developments, archaeologists, through painstaking analysis and synthesis of far-scattered sites, have been able to piece together something of the nature of these groups and to state the relationships between them.

Sometime shortly after the end of the Pleistocene epoch of geologic time a hunting and gathering group migrated into Oklahoma from the west. This culture, generally known as Folsom, has never been documented in Oklahoma from an excavated site, yet the many distinctive Folsom points which have been recovered, most of them from the western half of the state, attest to its presence. Folsom man was nonagricultural and made no pottery; the principal artifacts recovered are projectile points, flint knives, snub-nosed scrapers, and various choppers and hammerstones, the generalized tools of the hunter.

Dating from a time not long after Folsom are the hunting cultures of Clovis and Plainview. Evidences of similar early hunting horizons have also been found in the eastern portion of Oklahoma. The lack of extensive documentation for these sites in the state reflects only the great need for more archaeological work in this region.

In the Oklahoma Panhandle there are several cave sites which, on excavation in 1929, yielded materials which are suggestive of the well-known Basket Maker people of Arizona and New Mexico. Although relationships are not well established between these cave sites and the culture of the Basket Makers, there is every indication that they are of considerable antiquity. Again, these cave-dwellers were a hunting and gathering group, a seminomadic people, apparently depending for their food upon bison, deer, elk, antelope, jack rabbit, cottontail, coyote, and other animals.

In northeastern Oklahoma a well-documented focus exists which suggests a relationship between some early Oklahoma tribes and the

Ozark Bluff Dwellers of Missouri and Arkansas. This area, called the Grove focus, is known primarily from excavations in caves and bluff shelters, although sites in open fields are also known.

Generally throughout the entire eastern portion of the state numerous well-documented sites bear evidence to the development of an extensive Archaic complex. The representative cultures were, like the earlier ones in the western part, lacking in pottery, and the people were still dependent upon hunting and gathering for subsistence. After the development of this group of cultures several actual migrations of people into the state took place, some from the woodland area to the east, and others from the southeast. Ceramic types were introduced into eastern Oklahoma which point to definite affiliations of these Oklahoma sites with cultural centers in the northern Mississippi Valley and the Southeast.

Subsequent to this period the first development of a well-defined Caddoan archaeological area began, and cultural development reached a climax in this region which was not again equaled. The Gibson aspect, one of the best defined in this period, is characterized by burial mounds containing grave furniture of extreme splendor and great aesthetic achievement. Although trade with other areas of the country was well developed, the Gibson aspect is marked by definite regional specialization which documents it as an indigenous florescence. One principal factor in the evolution of these elaborate related cultures seems to be religious, for along with the burial mounds are found truncated pyramidal structures with temples or ceremonial buildings placed upon them. These religious centers appear to have served village areas for some distance around. The deservedly well-known culture of Spiro in eastern Oklahoma is associated with this general development.

Following the Gibson aspect, there is a general decline in over-all cultural complexity in eastern Oklahoma, although certain industries (e.g., ceramics) continue in their development and achieve a high peak of perfection. One peculiar feature of these post-Gibson cultures is a decrease in their geographical distribution. The Caddoan area literally shrinks in size, a fact which may best be accounted for in terms of pressures from tribes outside the region. Thus, in the northeastern part of the state a cultural complex having strong affiliations with the upper Mississippi region appears, while in the north-central area a culture type with Plains characteristics is evident. It should be stressed that these latter intrusive cultures did not remain isolated from those of the Caddoan area, but rather proved the vehicle for the restriction of the latter and produced a dilution of its characteristics by cultural phenomena originating outside of Oklahoma.

Despite the descriptive tag "Caddoan," archaeological work in the state is as yet so scanty (despite extensive efforts on the part of the University of Oklahoma and other agencies) that one should not conceive of the archaeologically known cultures as being the exact historical precursors to the historically known Caddoan tribes—Wichita, Caddo, Pawnee, etc. At the present time there exists a great time lag between the end of the prehistoric period and the beginning of the historic residence of the Caddoan-speaking peoples. Although certain archaeologically known items are quite suggestive of those possessed by historic peoples, the picture is not yet in focus, and archaeologists have declined to make the link between the prehistoric and historic peoples a definite one. There is little doubt that another ten-year period will provide sufficient additional materials to clarify the relationship.

Little mention has been made of early peoples in eastern and central Oklahoma. This is largely because of the fact that connected sequences for this area are not known. Although there are many well-defined sites in this region, they tend to exist only as isolated units. It appears though, even on the basis of present scanty evidence, that the affiliations of the central and eastern Oklahoma cultures will be with the Plains and the Eastern Woodlands rather than with the Southeast. Some, indeed, like those in the Panhandle, show affiliations with the Southwest.

Of the historic inhabitants of Oklahoma prior to the peopling of the area as Indian Territory, two main categories or types may be recognized: the nomadic, bison-hunting Plains tribes, and the sedentary, agricultural village tribes. The Kiowa, Comanche, and Kiowa-Apache were the principal representatives in Oklahoma of the nomadic tribes. These three groups, speaking entirely different and unrelated languages, occupied the territory known culturally as the Southern Plains and comprising portions of Colorado, Kansas, New Mexico, and Texas. Their principal range was from southern Kansas through western Oklahoma, the eastern portions of New Mexico, into West Texas and the Texas Panhandle. Since they were nomadic, however, they extended at various times over a much larger range.

In terms of superficial culture types these three tribes do not show impressive differences among themselves. The bison constituted the principal game animal, upon which the entire economy of the tribes was based. Not only was this animal used as food, but its hide provided the raw material for almost every manufacture which these tribes produced. The hunting of the bison was accomplished, in pre-horse times, by drives in which hundreds of the animals would be forced over cliffs or driven into a corral and slaughtered. Individual stalking was also employed, but that method could not provide the quantity of meat needed for large groups. When the horse was introduced into the Southern Plains, new techniques of hunting were devised. The one most used was the "surround," a procedure in which groups of mounted men encircled a segment of a bison herd and cut them down with bow and arrow.

Plains culture was singularly well adapted in all of its aspects to the bison hunt. Mobility was the underlying principle of Plains Indian existence, even before the horse was introduced, though of course this latter animal provided greater potential for mobility. In pre-horse times the dog was employed for transporting the impedimenta of the tribes from one hunting area to another. The principal form of dwelling was the tipi, a conical, skin-covered tent which could be erected and disassembled in a matter of minutes. Cooking utensils, articles of war, materials for the preparation of meat and hide were all non-breakable and highly portable.

Although we now speak of tribes when referring to the Comanche, Kiowa, and Kiowa-Apache, these groups did not live together the year round in aboriginal times. The principal political and social unit was the band, and each tribe comprised a number of these bands. The band operated by itself throughout most of the year, its members living together and hunting together. At certain periods, notably in late summer, the entire tribe would come together for a great religious festival, the Sun Dance, and later for the annual buffalo hunt, which was designed to equip the entire tribe with sufficient meat to last through a western Oklahoma winter. The tribe, then, was a sociological unit, not a highly functional political or social one.

Political organization on the Southern Plains was "informal." Chiefs or leaders were not formally appointed, nor did they indeed have great authority. Men revered for their exploits in war or on the hunt, or honored for their wisdom and age, emerged informally as leaders of the band. To these men the people would go for advice, and these individuals maintained only through the consent of the people the influence which they did exercise. Plains political organization was, then, highly democratic, and band membership, which was flexible, provided a check on authority, since a people who found themselves at the mercy of a local autocrat might change bands if they so chose.

Despite the apparent homogeneity of culture on the Southern Plains the three component tribes were not aboriginal to this region. The Kiowa and the Kiowa-Apache were probably northern tribes from the Montana and Rocky Mountain country who migrated to the Black Hills of the southern Dakota regions, and after many years of war with the Cheyenne and the Dakota tribes pressing down from the north finally moved into the Plains country. The Comanche were kinsmen of the Shoshonean-speaking peoples in the Wyoming and Idaho regions and areas west of the Rocky Mountains. They may have been related to the Aztecs of Mexico. The lure of the buffalo was probably the reason for their hunting raids from the Rocky Mountains into the Plains, but the dates of these movements and the routes employed are obscure. When the horse, acquired from the Spaniards, became a basic element of Comanche existence, they probably left their mountain homeland under pressure from the Sioux to the north and became a truly nomadic people. They migrated southward, attacking and displacing other Plains tribes, notably the great Caddoan family, and the Kiowa and the Kiowa-Apache, as well as the Plains Apache of the Arizona-New Mexico region. Following a peace treaty with the United States in 1853, conflicting interests brought on war between the Comanche and the Osage that for a long time endangered the Western frontier.

Among these hunting tribes of early historic times in the Great Plains the Osage held high rank. One of the Siouan linguistic family who, archaeologists believe, migrated in prehistoric times from the west to the Atlantic Coast, the Osage, with many others, reversed their course of migration to settle eventually in the Missouri regions. With the disappearance of the buffalo from the Mississippi Valley after the coming of the white traders, the Osage were forced to make hunting expeditions to the west, into conflict with the Kiowa, Comanche, and Apache tribes of the Plains. These raids extended over wide areas, including parts of what is now Oklahoma. Late in the eighteenth century, under the influence of French traders, some of the Osage settled permanently on the Arkansas River in Oklahoma. The name of the hereditary chief, Clermont, has been perpetuated in the name of the Oklahoma town of Claremore.

The Arapaho were the trading group of the Great Plains region between the Osage, Pawnee, and others on the north, and the Kiowa and Comanche to the south. One of the westernmost tribes of Algonquian stock, their earliest home is placed near Lake Superior. They drifted eastwards to the Plains, becoming a nomadic tribe in conjunction with their allies, the Cheyenne, members of the same linguistic family. Pushed by the Sioux, these two tribes moved from the Black Hills southwestward, in turn driving the Kiowa farther and farther south. They were often at war with the Kiowa, Shoshoni, Ute, and the Pawnee. Both the Cheyenne and Arapaho divided into northern and southern groups, the southern contingents finally locating, after a Medicine Lodge treaty, in what is now northern Oklahoma.

The Utes were a Shoshonean tribe from the Northwest. They once ranged south from the Panhandle on hunting expeditions. Historical records refer to wars in western Oklahoma between them and the Plains tribes. After the last herds of buffalo were killed, they returned to their Rocky Mountain homeland.

The principal sedentary tribes in prehistoric Oklahoma were the Caddoan-speaking peoples, notably the Wichita and the Caddo proper, although the Pawnee, of the same linguistic family, apparently established towns in parts of the state at various times. According to tribal tradition, the Caddoan tribes once lived in the Lower Mississippi Valley. They were the most largely represented linguistic family in Oklahoma during its early historic period. The term "sedentary" should not be taken to imply that these tribes maintained villages in one place for extended periods of time, for there is some evidence that they moved about in various parts of the state in considerable degree. Both exhaustion of the land and devastation by predatory nomadic tribes were constant threats to the sedentary peoples. The mainstay of their economy was agriculture. Corn, beans, squash, indeed the usual agricultural foodstuffs of the North American Indian diet, were the principal crops grown. The basic unit of political organization was the village, an assemblage of semipermanent dwellings, each occupied in most cases by a number of related persons. The village had a chief, and the political organization of the village was quite a formal one by contrast to the Plains situation. Inheritance of the chieftainship was the rule, and certain other class positions were also hereditary.

In contrast to the Plains tribes, the sedentary peoples developed a variety of artifacts, and their utensils had an air of permanence about them. The houses themselves were usually quite large. Some, like those of the Pawnee, were enormous earth structures built into an excavated depression for protection against the winters. The agricultural base of their economy demanded a great variety of tools for growing and harvesting the crops and for preparing food.

But the present status of Oklahoma as a "modern Indian territory" does not come alone from the aboriginal inhabitants of the state. The early policy of the federal government of setting aside a permanent homeland for the American Indian and the implementation of that policy are chiefly responsible for the large Indian population in Oklahoma today. With increasing population pressures in the East and Southeast, and with the growth of huge private ranges in the north,

American Indians were moved into Oklahoma and resettled on reservations. The most extensive of this government resettlement of tribes was the removal of the Five Civilized Tribes in the 1830's from the southeastern part of the United States to reservations in the Oklahoma Territory. These were the Cherokee, Chickasaw, Choctaw, Creek, and Seminole tribes, the first modern occupants of Oklahoma, whose early institutions and customs established before their removal greatly furthered the progress of civilization within the new Territory. Their continued development and achievements, which formed such an integral part of the history of Oklahoma for more than half a century, are dealt with in more detail in the chapter on Oklahoma's history by Edwin C. McReynolds.

Although the Indian reservations in Oklahoma Territory were clearly defined as inviolable by the white man, time and circumstance produced a situation which saw the dissolution of Indian rights to these lands and the allotment of acreages to the tribesmen who had been given priority to them. The Oklahoma Indian today, then, is not a reservation Indian. Each family occupies acreages which were allotted either to members of that family, or to their progenitors. Certain of the modern Indians farm this land, although a more frequent practice, particularly in the western part of the state, is the leasing of such land to white farmers in the area. The role of farmer was not an acceptable one to the nomadic Plains tribes, and even the sedentary farmers of the area were unable to adjust easily to a system which defines the male as the principal hand in the field. For among the Caddoan tribes, the women tilled the fields. Adjustment to the agricultural pattern of the white man was not an easy one for the Oklahoma Indian, and it is an adjustment which he has not yet made.

The modern Indian in Oklahoma has conformed, however, in a remarkable number of ways. There is little left of his aboriginal culture, though he is fiercely proud of his heritage and symbolizes it in powwows and other quasi-ceremonial functions. Perhaps one of the most important integrating ceremonials of the Oklahoma Indian at present is that connected with the Native American Church, an American Indian nativistic movement which has gained in strength and membership since its introduction into the Southern Plains. This ceremonial, which involves the use of the famous plant, peyote, affords the Indian a context in terms of which he may assert his long historical tradition, and further, in terms of which he may seek communion with other Indians in the state. A unique development, called by the late Karl Schmitt pan-Indianism, may be noted in Oklahoma. Although tribal distinctions are maintained by most, intermarriage between the tribes and their frequent social intercourse has led to a leveling of tribal differences. Thus, being an "Indian" is of more importance than being a particular tribal member. Costumes employed in war dancing, indeed the dance steps themselves, have become uniform. Similarly, other modern manifestations of "Indianism" in the state, such as beadwork, moccasins, and the like, have become more general than specific. In spite of this, however, there may still be noted delicate and subtle variations in pattern which are linked to particular tribes. But in general, the "Oklahoma Indian" has become a category unto itself.

Approximately one-third of the nation's Indian population is in Oklahoma. Twenty-nine tribes are officially listed under their tribal identities in the Indian agencies of the state. Smaller tribes or remnants of tribes have merged with these to make a total of sixty-seven different Indian tribal groups represented in Oklahoma, whose name itself is a memorial to the race which, from prehistoric times, has formed so great a part of the background and cultural heritage of the state.

The role of the Indian as a citizen of the state is as yet ambiguous. Many Indians have achieved prominence in social, religious, and political affairs. Indeed, many of our governors have claimed Indian blood. But for the full-blood, the situation is somewhat different. He is a member of a minority group, and one which suffers a degree of economic depression which is perhaps not uncommon for any rural dweller, regardless of ethnic affiliations.

But the future holds a certain promise for the Indian. Participation in industrial activities, voluntary removal from the more or less isolated rural areas to the urban centers, increased educational opportunities in mixed public schools—all of these factors are at present contributing to a sounder acculturation. And despite the romantic approach of many toward the American Indian, acculturation appears at present to be the single alternative for this group. There is no possibility that the Indian may "return" to his aboriginal way of life, nor even to a reasonable facsimile of it. His single path is in the direction the majority in the state are traveling, and the success with which he integrates with the majority will, in large, measure his own progress and be the key to it.

HISTORY

By Edwin C. McReynolds

In Oklahoma, as in Egypt and Mesopotamia, India, Iran, and Greece, there is a record of man's achievement earlier than the literary history. This evidence includes artifacts in quartz, jade, and agate; fine lace and other textiles; beaten copper vessels with intricate designs; ceramics, and implements fashioned from the bones of animals; ceremonial objects, remains of public buildings and grass dwelling houses, and numerous other materials of early peoples. To a great extent these have been found by excavation at Spiro and elsewhere in the state.

The first contacts of Europeans with Caddoan Indians and natives of the Plains who belonged to other linguistic families furnished material for the earliest written records. Spanish travel journals by Pedro de Castañeda, Captain Juan Jaramillo, and Rodrigo Ranjel, bearing the date 1541, are the earliest documents. Before the end of the seventeenth century, French accounts had become an essential part of Oklahoma history; and in the early decades of the nineteenth century, records of expeditions led by United States Army officers took a leading place in the story. James B. Wilkinson, Colonel George C. Sibley, Captain J. R. Bell, Major Stephen H. Long, and Colonel Hugh Glen are among names that appear in the chronicles of this period.

During the clash at arms with England from 1812 to 1815 and the undeclared war against Indian allies of England in Spanish Florida between 1816 and 1818, native tribes destined to play a major part in Oklahoma history in the next decades were involved as friends or foes of the United States. Florida was acquired and the Seminoles became a part of the possessions of the United States. All of the southern tribes were parties to the wars and the treaties that followed.

The volume of written material on Oklahoma steadily expanded. Naturalists, such as Thomas Nuttall, Dr. Edwin James, and Thomas Say, appear among the contributors to source material of peculiar value; traders—including Pierre Melicourt Papin, agent for Pierre Chouteau's American Fur Company, Jacob Fowler, the surveyor from Kentucky who told a colorful story of his adventures in Oklahoma, and

The Setting

Fall Plowing, near Enid.

(*above*) Tilted Rock Strata, Arbuckle Mountains.

(*below*) Washington Oil Pool, near Purcell.

Fort Gibson Lake, Sequoyah State Park near Wagoner.

Lake Murray, near Ardmore.

(*above*) Water Skiing.

(*below*) Snipe Regatta.

(*above*) Fort Gibson Dam and Reservoir, near Muskogee.

(*below*) Tenkiller Dam, near Tahlequah.

(*above*) Skyline Trail, Lake Murray State Park.

(*below*) Skelly Ranch, between Pawhuska and Tulsa.

(*above*) Buffalo Wallow, Wichita Mountains Wildlife Refuge.
(*below*) Quail Hunting, eastern Oklahoma.

(*above*) Fort Sill Military Reservation, near Lawton.
(*below*) Turner Turnpike, between Tulsa and Oklahoma City.

Josiah Gregg, whose journals reveal the connection between Oklahoma and the Santa Fé trade—add their part to a narrative of frontier development; and the missionaries, such as Worcester and Dwight, Isaac McCoy and Alfred Wright, contribute their vital and intimate picture of life in the Indian lands of the Southwest.

Before it reaches the middle of the nineteenth century, the story of Oklahoma's past has made the reader aware of important bonds of interest between the Mississippi Valley and many widely separated parts of the world. Spain, France, and other builders of empire had essential parts in the development of Oklahoma as a part of the great province of Louisiana. After 1803, the most significant outside influences came from Washington, D. C., and from states east of the Mississippi that were intent upon removing their Indians to the west.

The tragic and fascinating story of Indian removal and the struggle of the Five Civilized Tribes to establish permanent homes in Oklahoma during the second quarter of the nineteenth century hold the center of the historian's attention. For the person whose interest lies in analysis of United States Indian policy, the period has unusual appeal.

One significant feature of the era was the progress of Cherokees, Choctaws, Chickasaws, and Creeks in adjusting their own usages to the white man's government by means of basic tribal laws. The Seminoles, with more primitive institutions, did not develop a written constitution; but their tribal citizens who attended schools did come face to face with the problem of fitting Anglo-Saxon law with Indian customs. In the following generations Oklahoma Indians were to demonstrate outstanding talent in representative government.

From the acquisition of Florida in 1819 to the outbreak of war between North and South in 1861, Negro slavery, with the bitter conflict over slave property, was a major issue in the relations of southern tribes with each other and with the United States. Negro slavery, however, had little to do with Indian participation in the war. Geographic location, relative to Union and Confederate states, was the determining factor. Choctaws and Chickasaws, in the southern part of Indian Territory, were strongly Confederate; Creeks, Seminoles, and Cherokees, threatened by northern as well as southern military power, were divided in their support of Confederacy and Union. All of the tribes were concerned primarily with survival, and would have preferred neutrality. Their attitude toward the war was similar in many respects to that of the border state, Kentucky.

The Civil War, with internal strife for three of the five major tribes of the East Side, deeply affected the course of development of the region. Economic stability, for a people who were late in starting their progress in agriculture and commerce, manufacturing and all forms of modern production, was retarded enormously. In every part of the Indian Territory shocking evidence of destruction of human life, property losses, decline of healthy political activity, and lowered levels in morals and education were obvious results of the war. No part of the South or the border region where the actual fighting took place suffered losses more horrible than those of the Indian Territory.

Reconstruction among the Indians of the Five Civilized Tribes meant starting from the bottom in the struggle for economic competence as measured by white men's standards. Fields were neglected, fences destroyed, dwelling places in ruins. Schoolhouses and other public buildings had been burned to the ground. Furthermore, the Indians were required to give up half of the land that had been awarded to them in the process of removal from the region east of the Mississippi. Provision was made for admitting railroad lines into the Indian lands; and the building of railroads, as anticipated by many Indians, was to prove a powerful factor in the final surrender of the natives to the culture developed by the European invaders of North America.

The Northern Drive, by which cattle were moved from Texas to railroad lines in Kansas and Nebraska, was another wedge for opening Indian lands to white settlement. At the end of the Civil War, a fat steer on the Texas range was worth four or five dollars; and at the cattle market within reach of the new railroad lines, the same animal would sell for fifteen or twenty times as much. The cattle drives, beginning before the war and progressing through the final stages of experiment immediately afterward, reached their climax between 1870 and 1880. During that decade the annual movement of cattle along the trails through western Oklahoma varied from 400,000 to 600,000 head.

The period following the Civil War was a time of readjustment for the Plains Indians as well as the red men recently transferred from lands east of the Mississippi River. Officials of the United States government had been compelled to give increased attention to the problem of safe travel for its citizens across the Plains for fifteen years prior to the outbreak of war between the North and the South. The annexation of Texas, war with Mexico, the great Mormon migration, addition of vast territories in the Southwest by the terms of the Treaty of Guadalupe Hidalgo, and discovery of gold in California had all occurred within a brief span of years.

While terms of new agreements were being worked out with the Five Civilized Tribes, and the contest over political reconstruction of the southern states was being waged by President Andrew Johnson against the disgraceful policies of the Fortieth Congress, a notable development was taking place in United States Indian policy. In 1867 the Department of the Interior obtained an appropriation for a peace commission to go among the Plains Indians. It was the hope of far-sighted statesmen to forestall the rising tide of hostility among the western tribes.

Nathaniel G. Taylor, head of the Indian Office, was named chairman of the peace commission. Senator John B. Henderson of Missouri and five officers of the United States Army were the members. In the West, they traveled with their interpreters, clerks, and the newspaper correspondent, Henry M. Stanley, in two ambulances well guarded by three companies of United States cavalry. The final conference was at Medicine Lodge Creek, about thirty miles north of present day Alva, Oklahoma.

Chiefs of the Plains tribes agreed to settle on reservations. Probably they placed their marks on the documents without realizing their full meaning; and certainly the young men of the tribes did not understand that they were expected to settle down to farming on the reservations defined for them. The treaties of Medicine Lodge Creek and the later executive agreements were attempts to settle the Plains tribes of the Southwest on definite territory. The agreements proved to be preludes to a series of wars on the Great Plains.

The trouble began promptly in Oklahoma. In 1868, Custer crushed a band of Southern Cheyennes under Moke-ta-ra-to at the Battle of the Washita; Comanches and Kiowas raided wagon trains across the Red River in Texas, and in some instances were arrested and punished under the white man's law. In February, 1870, Little Raven (Hosa), an Arapaho chief who was a signer of the Medicine Lodge Creek Treaty, settled with his people in the vicinity of Fort Supply. Other bands came in later and settled near the Cheyenne and Arapaho agency at Darlington. Before midsummer, a majority of the two tribes were in camp. However, some of the warriors continued to take part in the Indian uprisings until after the surrender of Quanah Parker and his Quahada Comanches on January 24, 1875. The worst disorders were subsiding on the Southern Plains as the great conflict arose over possession of the Black Hills in the Northwest.

After Custer and most of his men were killed in Montana, the hostile Plains chiefs were worn down and beaten. Both Crazy Horse and Sitting Bull of the Sioux died by violence, and the Indians of the Northwest, like their kinsmen of the Southern Plains and the tribes of the Southeast before the Civil War, yielded to overwhelming numbers and resources.

Political reconstruction of Indian Territory involved drastic changes in the lives of some thousands of Indians and definite revisions of tribal relations with the government. On the economic side, Indians took up the slow and painful work of rebuilding very much as other people did. Indian Territory had suffered more than other areas, but there was ample land for the number of people concerned, and the Indians wasted little time on regrets. Also, the greatest bitterness of partisan strife was ended, and a new era of comparative good order was at hand. After 1875 even the western reservations were areas of peace and progress.

Coal mining, closely associated with early railroad building, began with the activities of Colonel J. J. McAlester in the Choctaw Nation shortly after the Civil War. Later, coal was discovered on Creek and Cherokee lands. In 1906, the year before statehood, Oklahoma mines produced 2,500,000 tons, approximately one per cent of the national total at that time.

Railroad building, together with the operation of coal mines and the activities of the great cattle trails, stimulated the demands of western farmers and other interested persons for the opening of Indian lands to white settlement. The whole country between the Red River and the 37th parallel, west from the boundaries of Arkansas and Missouri to the 100th meridian, with a long "Panhandle" stretching farther to 103 degrees West Longitude, was an unused area much in the public mind; and it was only a question of time until the laws protecting Indians in their tribal rights would yield to the pressure of popular demand.

Between 1870 and 1890 the population of the United States grew from 38,558,000 to 63,000,000—an increase of 63 per cent. In the same period Texas, neighbor to Oklahoma on the south, grew from 819,579 to 2,235,527, almost threefold; and Kansas on the north expanded from a population of 356,399 to 1,428,000, a fourfold increase. Pressure for white occupation of Indian lands kept pace with the growth of population in these adjacent areas.

After 1866 various portions of the land given up by the Five Civilized Tribes in the treaties at Washington were assigned to Indians from Kansas, Nebraska, Idaho, and other states and territories. By 1889 all the land had been assigned except an area less than 2,000,000 acres in extent, formerly the property of Creeks and Seminoles, and approximately 6,000,000 acres of the Cherokee Outlet.

Organized demands for opening Oklahoma began with the work of Elias C. Boudinot soon after the end of the Civil War. He had many influential friends in Washington through his work as an attorney and as clerk of the House Committee on Private Land Claims. His stand in favor of opening Oklahoma Indian lands to settlement was very popular with white settlers in the West, and extremely offensive to a majority of the members of his own tribe. T. C. Sears, attorney for the Missouri, Kansas and Texas Railroad, worked with Boudinot in his campaign of publicity for the opening of Oklahoma.

C. C. Carpenter, in 1879, and David L. Payne, from 1880 to 1884, led bands of Boomers on the border between Kansas and Oklahoma, threatening invasion and settlement of the "Unassigned Lands" south of the Cherokee Outlet. After 1884, William L. Couch was the leader of the Boomers. Payne was the most spectacular of those who organized bands of colonists and demanded entrance; Couch was the most determined and the leader of greatest personal courage. The Indians finally yielded to the pressure for white settlement, Congress authorized the movement, and on April 22, 1889, the first great opening was made by a run of prospective homesteaders into the unassigned Creek and Seminole lands.

It was more than a year later when Congress provided a territorial organization for the American citizens of the newest province. Seven counties were stipulated—six in the region of the run, and a seventh in the Panhandle far to the northwest. An appointed governor and judges, an elected delegate to Congress, and elected members of a two-house legislature were provided. Territorial government had fallen into a well-defined pattern in the United States by 1890, and the Oklahoma Organic Act followed the main features of other recently established territorial governments.

Surrounding the six counties of Oklahoma Territory on all sides and adjoining the seventh county at its east end, on the 100th meridian, were Indian lands, consisting of reservations, the Cherokee Outlet, and the Chickasaw Nation. During the seventeen years of territorial government, one after another of these units was added to Oklahoma by runs, in one notable instance by a gigantic lottery, and simply by assigning tribal lands to the members, in severalty. Greer County, claimed by Texas, was added by Congress in 1896, after a decision by the United States Supreme Court denying the contention of Texas.

Oklahoma Territory contained many poor farmers and laborers among its people because of the conditions of its settlement. Prevented by law from entering the region, through a period of agitation for opening, the settlers who finally broke through the barrier did so by weight of numbers—effective in a land where lack of property was no obstacle to voting. Suddenly the gates had been opened, and the avalanche of landless citizens poured into the region of opportunity.

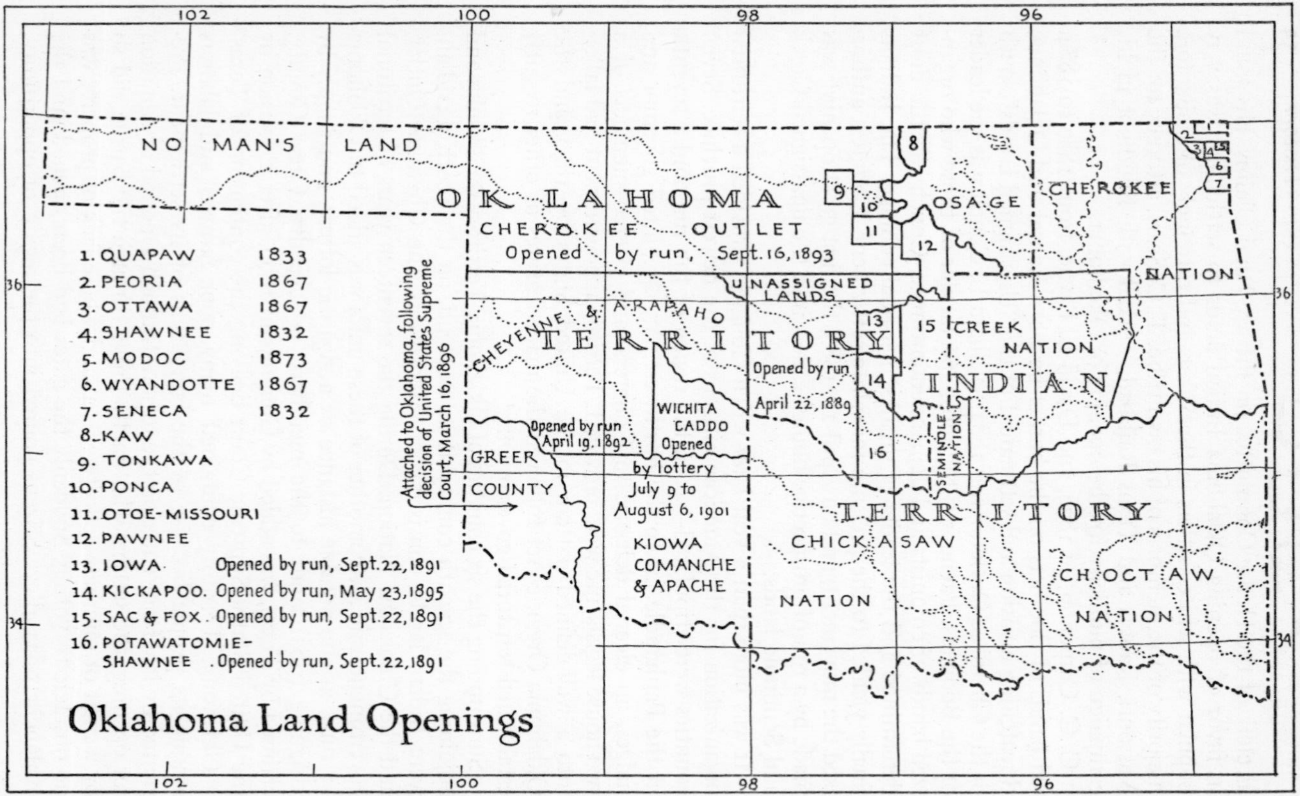
102
100
98
96
NO MAN'S LAND
OKLAHOMA
CHEROKEE OUTLET
Opened by run, Sept. 16, 1893
UNASSIGNED LANDS
CHEYENNE & ARAPAHO
TERRITORY
Opened by run
April 22, 1889
Opened by run
April 19, 1892
WICHITA
CADDO
Opened
by lottery
July 9 to
August 6, 1901
KIOWA
COMANCHE
& APACHE
GREER
COUNTY
Attached to Oklahoma, following decision of United States Supreme Court, March 16, 1896
OSAGE
CHEROKEE
NATION
CREEK
NATION
INDIAN
SEMINOLE NATION
TERRITORY
CHICKASAW
NATION
CHOCTAW
NATION
36
34
1. QUAPAW 1833
2. PEORIA 1867
3. OTTAWA 1867
4. SHAWNEE 1832
5. MODOC 1873
6. WYANDOTTE 1867
7. SENECA 1832
8. KAW
9. TONKAWA
10. PONCA
11. OTOE-MISSOURI
12. PAWNEE
13. IOWA. Opened by run, Sept. 22, 1891
14. KICKAPOO. Opened by run, May 23, 1895
15. SAC & FOX. Opened by run, Sept. 22, 1891
16. POTAWATOMIE-SHAWNEE. Opened by run, Sept. 22, 1891
Oklahoma Land Openings

It was a condition which attracted large resources of human energy ready to labor on the virgin soil, rather than capital for investment in business ventures. Many a man who staked a claim and tried to hold it, and who often did hold it in spite of every hardship, had little capital for livestock, implements, or buildings.

Agricultural discontent was sure to flourish in such a population. Radical views took root easily on the Southwestern Plains in the wake of droughts and low prices on farm products. Agrarian radicalism took organized form in the Southern Alliance of Texas and the Northern Alliance, to which wheat farmers of Kansas, Minnesota, and other northern states were attracted. The Populist party had a large following in Oklahoma when James B. Weaver ran as its candidate for the presidency in 1892 and won the popular vote of Kansas, Colorado, Nevada, and Idaho, polling over a million votes in a national total that was under twelve million. Free silver had a strong appeal four years later when William Jennings Bryan ran against William McKinley and carried every state on the borders of Oklahoma for Populist doctrines.

Oklahoma Territory contained 258,657 inhabitants in 1890—enough for a congressional district, hence enough for statehood. The formation of the State of Oklahoma had to wait for the Enabling Act of June 16, 1906, the convention that followed, and the election of state officers. The first governor elected by the people of the new state took office on November 16, 1907.

Six of the seven territorial governors had been Republicans, appointed by Presidents of their party; but territorial officers as a whole were more equally divided. Three of the elected delegates to Congress were Republicans, one was the candidate of a Democratic-Populist fusion party. The northern part of the territory generally elected Republican local officers, the southern counties, Democratic officers.

The political complexion of the first state elections in Oklahoma was strongly Democratic, with a substantial Republican minority among the voters. As in territorial days, there was a definite trend toward Populist views which encouraged the major parties to bid for the radical vote. The First Legislature elected both Democratic candidates for the United States Senate, Robert L. Owen and Thomas P. Gore; and the voters elected four Democrats and one Republican for the lower house of Congress. Both branches of the legislature had a majority of Democrats—39 out of 44 in the Senate and 93 out of 109 in the House of Representatives. Charles N. Haskell, Democrat, was elected by a substantial majority over his Republican opponent, Frank Frantz, who had served as the last territorial governor. The Democrats had succeeded in gaining a following among the radical voters.

In 1908, Oklahoma took part for the first time in a national election, and gave its seven electoral votes to William Jennings Bryan over William H. Taft. In the elections for the state legislature, the Republicans increased their membership in both houses, and elected three of the five members for the United States House of Representatives: Bird S. McGuire of Pawnee, Dick T. Morgan of Woodward, and Charles E. Creager of Muskogee. The Democrats returned to office C. D. Carter of Ardmore and Scott Ferris of Lawton. In the state elections of 1910, Lee Cruce of Ardmore won the Democratic nomination for governor over William H. Murray and other well-known party leaders. The Republican candidate, Joseph W. McNeal, received 99,527 votes in the general election, to 120,218 for Cruce. The Socialist candidate, J. T. Cumbie, with almost 25,000 votes held the balance between the major party leaders; but in this election no runoff was provided, and Cruce won with a plurality.

Haskell's term was devoted to organization of the state government, strengthening the primary schools, balancing the state institutions of higher learning as to geographic distribution, making a start on establishing a taxing system, and the obvious needs in roads and state buildings. The capital was removed from Guthrie to Oklahoma City in 1910, in violation of a measure inserted by Congress in the Enabling Act. The Supreme Court of the United States upheld the action of the state in determining the location of its own capital.

Primary schools in Oklahoma had been lacking in financial support because a considerable part of the land was not subject to taxation. A few good schools for Indians had been provided by tribal funds, supplemented by federal appropriations and the support of churches; but schools for white children were seriously inadequate. Three months of schooling, outside of the towns, was a limit that was forced upon many children by lack of money for support of education in the western as well as the eastern territory. Frequently, the teacher of a rural school, with a miserably low salary, had academic preparation somewhat less than that provided by a high school. A vast majority of the children, east and west, lived on farms.

Lee Cruce of Ardmore, a Democrat, took office as the second governor in 1911. He had served for three years as chairman of the Board of Regents for the University of Oklahoma. Perhaps the most notable developments of his administration were the results of his interest in education and public highways. The reorganized Board of Education, six members appointed by the governor and working under the chairmanship of an elected superintendent of public instruction, had general supervision of public schools, exercised control over the state colleges with the exception of the Oklahoma Agricultural and Mechanical College, and served as the state textbook commission.

Governor Cruce appointed Sidney Suggs, an Ardmore newspaperman, highway commissioner. Suggs, a man of imagination, was able to grasp the enormous importance of good hard-surfaced roads, and he worked diligently to gain support for his progressive ideas. Oklahoma was badly retarded in road building, and as various parts of the Southwest became adjusted to the age of motor vehicles, Suggs, moving rapidly ahead with appropriations that were necessarily large, insisted upon more and better roads for the new state.

Oklahoma was entitled to eight representatives in Congress, as a result of reapportionment after the Thirteenth Census. Governor Cruce had the choice of calling a special legislative session for redistricting the state, or ordering the election of three representatives-at-large. With results of previous elections in his hands, it was not difficult for Cruce to decide upon the latter method. Republican gains of 1908 had been offset by more recent Democratic recovery; and total pluralities of the Republicans in three districts in 1908, the year of their most successful state election, were smaller than the total Democratic pluralities in two districts. Election-at-large in 1912 resulted in three new Democratic representatives for Oklahoma: William H. Murray of Tishomingo, Claude Weaver of Oklahoma City, and Joseph B. Thompson of Pauls Valley.

The over-all policy of Governor Cruce in Oklahoma was moderate and progressive. His fight for economy was not a miserly program in which essential services were slashed, but rather a steady pressure for efficient control of state expenditures. His aim was for permanent values, good state buildings, roads to meet new transportation needs, and high standards in public education. In later administrations the state schools at times became pawns in the game of politics, a development which was not a necessary outgrowth of Cruce's reorganization, but the inevitable result of mediocrity in high office. More adroit political managers have held the office of governor in Oklahoma, but few executives in any state have worked with greater zeal for the public interest.

Robert L. Williams of Durant defeated J. B. A. Robertson and Al Jennings in the Democratic primary election of 1914. Robertson was an attorney whose home was Chandler, Jennings was a former bandit who had recently completed a federal prison term. In the general election Williams defeated John Fields, a farm-paper editor who had formerly been director of the experiment station at the Oklahoma Agricultural and Mechanical College. Williams had 100,597 votes; Fields, 95,597; and Fred Holt, Socialist, 52,703. The third party also made a strong bid for a seat in the United States Senate, with Thomas P. Gore, Democratic incumbent, receiving 119,442 votes; John H. Buford, Republican, 73,292; and Patrick Nagle, Socialist, 52,229. In the congressional elections the Republicans carried one district, returning Dick Morgan of Woodward for a third term.

Governor Williams was a hard worker, a champion of clean government, and an aggressive advocate of "white supremacy" in politics. An initiated measure added to the Oklahoma Constitution in 1910 provided against the voting of illiterates, unless they were descendants of persons who were eligible to vote before January 1, 1866. This "grandfather clause" was clearly intended to enfranchise illiterate white citizens and to bar illiterate Negroes from the vote; and in 1915 the United States Supreme Court declared the clause unconstitutional, as a violation of the Fifteenth Amendment to the Federal Constitution.

Governor Williams called a special session of the legislature to propose a new Oklahoma amendment concerning Negro suffrage. Obviously he expected to phrase the revised clause in such manner as to defeat the purpose of the Fifteenth Amendment, which was to give the Negroes equality of opportunity in the matter of voting, along with white citizens. By a special election in August, 1916, the voters of Oklahoma were given a chance to pass upon the newly devised Negro suffrage clause. The popular vote was 133,140 against the proposed measure to 90,605 in favor of its adoption. Apparently, toleration had made more progress at this time among the voters than among the lawmakers.

In 1914 work was begun on the state capitol, authorized by the Fourth Legislature. As governor, Williams was ex officio chairman of the Capitol Commission, which consisted of William B. Anthony, Patrick J. Goulding, and Stephen A. Douglas. In 1917 the State University Hospital was provided with an appropriation of $300,000 for construction of a first unit.

Oklahoma voted for Woodrow Wilson over Charles Evans Hughes in the presidential election of 1916, with a margin of 51,000 votes. War had begun in Europe in 1914, and with the entrance of the United States in 1917 the attention of all state officers was centered upon the work of organizing resources for the common task of the nation. As war governor, Robert L. Williams made the greatest contribution of his life. He directed the work of all major councils, drove himself to the limit in the important job undertaken by the Oklahoma Speakers'

Bureau, gave freely of his time to the Red Cross, YMCA, Salvation Army, Knights of Columbus, Liberty Loan drive, and countless related services. He conducted his office in such a way as to make his political opponents, as well as his friends who were annoyed by his prejudices and narrow-minded aggressiveness, admit that Oklahoma had named her ablest citizen chief executive.

Major Eugene M. Kerr directed military recruiting and registration for the draft. Over one-fifth of the 435,688 men who were registered actually entered the armed forces. Of the 90,126 men in military service, over 1,000 were killed in action and 6,286 were listed as killed or wounded. Colonel Roy Hoffman, who had commanded the Oklahoma National Guard in the Mexican expedition of 1916, attained the rank of brigadier general in the European war.

The Socialist party in Oklahoma, as in other parts of the nation, declined as a minor party because of its pacifist members. The "Green Corn Rebellion," which took the form of antidraft agitation among tenant farmers, was clearly related to the agrarian discontent that was a definite factor in early politics of Oklahoma.

The Williams administration cannot be measured solely in terms of Oklahoma's development, because of concentration by state officials upon the war program. Governor Williams has usually been classed as a conservative, although his tax program was fairly progressive. In some respects he was a reactionary. On Negro suffrage his attitude was approximately the same as that of Alabama at the time of his birth—during the bitterness of Reconstruction in the South. His economy was too drastic; some of the state's progress in building received only reluctant support or bare acquiescence from the Governor. His war record was superb, with commendable support for the national government, remarkable efficiency, and tireless effort.

For twelve years after the end of Governor Williams' term of office, impeachment and threats of impeachment became very common in Oklahoma. In addition to one elected governor who was threatened sharply with impeachment proceedings, a president of the Board of Agriculture was impeached, but he was acquitted by the state Senate; three justices of the state Supreme Court were impeached but not removed from office; and two governors were impeached, convicted, and removed. It was an era of impeachments.

Governor J. B. A. Robertson, victorious in the Democratic primary over William H. Murray and in the general election over his Republican opponent, Horace G. McKeever, served in a time of political turmoil throughout the nation. Woodrow Wilson was being defeated in his efforts to use America's power, recently demonstrated in the war with the Central Powers, and her prestige among the democratic peoples of the earth for gaining leadership in the diplomatic struggle for permanent peace. The period had the outward appearance of prosperity when Robertson took office in 1919. The price of oil was high; from $2.25 per barrel in the fall of 1918 it ranged upward to $3.50 by March 1, 1920. Oklahoma pumped from her wells 106,206,000 barrels of crude oil in 1920, which was more than California or Texas produced in that year. Farm prices were high also during the year after the end of the war; but a sharp decline followed, first in cotton and corn, then in wheat. Livestock prices also collapsed; and Oklahoma farmers had a preview of the great depression that was to descend upon the nation in 1929.

Oklahoma voted for Warren G. Harding in 1920, giving its electoral vote to a Republican presidential candidate for the first time. The Eighth Legislature, with a Republican majority in the House and a Democratic majority in the Senate, devoted a great deal of time and energy to party conflict. At the end of the sixty-day regular session the appropriation bills had not been passed, and Governor Robertson called a special session to continue work on them. His proposed bond issue of $50,000,000 for highways had been defeated by the voters, and many of his requests for money were reduced by this legislature. The principle of state aid for weak schools was incorporated in the appropriations, however, with a grant of $100,000. This item was to become a regular factor in Oklahoma school support, with $12,800,000 state aid in 1937 and $29,515,000 per year in 1953–54.

Financial depression in 1920–21 brought hardship to many banks. The Bank of Commerce at Okmulgee was one that failed, and Governor Robertson was held responsible by some of his political opponents. They tried hard to find cause for impeachment in his connection with the bank, but were unable to make a case.

John C. Walton, mayor of Oklahoma City, became the Democratic candidate for governor in 1922. He had the support of the Farmer-Labor Reconstruction League, including many voters who had voted for Warren G. Harding and for Senator John W. Harreld in 1920. John Fields, the Republican candidate, lost to Walton by 50,000.

The impeachment of Governor Walton grew out of his political ineptitude, his ignorance of the law, and, if the charges on which he was convicted were true, his complete disregard for the law. He carried his political battles into the University of Oklahoma, the Agricultural and Mechanical College at Stillwater, the proceedings of a grand jury, and many other institutions and activities of the state. The Ku Klux Klan had become active in Oklahoma; and aware of the fact that many citizens regarded the methods of the organization with disfavor, Walton used his fight with the Klan as an excuse to abuse executive power. The House considered twenty-two charges against Governor Walton, presented by W. E. Disney as chairman of an investigating committee. The Governor was quickly impeached on two charges and suspended by a vote of 38 to 1 in the Senate. Other accusations were sent to the Senate, which adjudged him guilty on eleven counts. The vote was unanimous on the charge that he had made excessive use of the pardoning power.

Lieutenant-Governor Martin E. Trapp, who was serving his third term in that office, took the oath as governor, with more than three years of the term remaining. More or less by political accident, the state had discovered a strong man for governor in a difficult situation. Under the Oklahoma Constitution, Governor Trapp was not eligible to succeed himself, and the Democratic primary named Henry S. Johnston of Perry as the candidate of the party for the office. Johnston defeated Omer K. Benedict by a vote of 213,167 to 170,714.

The impeachment of Governor Johnston was different in many respects from that of John C. Walton. Johnston was an ardent advocate of prohibition, and his political following, somewhat less than a majority of the voters, were disappointed when the Oklahoma delegation accepted Alfred E. Smith as Democratic candidate for President. The Protestant dry voters of the Southwest were opposed to Smith; and the Ku Klux Klan of Oklahoma, along with many advocates of prohibition who were not Klan members but were strongly anti-Catholic, were disappointed in Johnston.

Johnston was impeached on eleven charges and convicted on one—that of incompetency. His administration, like that of John C. Walton, was a low point in Oklahoma politics. There were many able men in public life at the time, but to a great extent their efforts toward progress were nullified by clashing interests, partisan contests, and bungling in state affairs. The Governor was not an able administrator. Some of his activities suggest senility. He showed excessive interest in discussions of the mystic, the occult; and his grasp of the duties of his high office was never strong. He pardoned a murderer who had previously been paroled and had broken his parole. After he had been returned to the penitentiary, Governor Walton had granted him an "informal leave," and he simply remained outside and appeared on the penitentiary records as a fugitive. When Johnston learned details of the fugitive's record, he attempted to revoke the pardon by which he had granted the man his freedom but found that he could not legally withdraw clemency after a complete pardon. The Governor was neither a criminal nor a statesman. His impeachment and conviction, however, were dangerous precedents.

William J. Holloway, who succeeded to the office left vacant by Johnston's removal in the middle of his term, wisely determined to concentrate upon efficiency and economy rather than an extensive building program. He was a quiet and unassuming man, brisk in his manner, courteous and businesslike. His purpose was to erase the deficit; but the financial panic of 1929 and the long depression that followed it make estimates of his success peculiarly difficult. He did not create a satisfactory balance in the state treasury; but he did improve the child-labor restrictions of Oklahoma and took the lead in forming a new coal-mining code. He appointed a Republican, Lew Wentz of Ponca City, as chairman of the state highway commission. Wentz was able and vigorous but handicapped by the necessity of restricted state income during the depression.

William H. Murray, with a long and varied political experience, attained the office of governor in the election of 1930, when he was past sixty. He demonstrated political skill in his contest for the Democratic nomination against Frank Buttram and in his election over Ira Hill. He also showed both skill and courage in his acceptance of the impeachment challenge. "I've heard about your threats," he said to senators who paid him a visit in his office. "I've even been reminded that Jim Ferguson was impeached in Texas for vetoing a university appropriation bill. You fellows go ahead and pass these appropriations as you have them outlined and I'll veto every damned one of them. And if you've got any impeachment ideas in your heads, hop to it. It'll be like a bunch of jack rabbits tryin' to get a wildcat out of a hole."

The stature of William H. Murray is a subject on which there will always be disagreement. To some observers his manners were offensive; to others they were of no consequence, trivial details of a rugged frontier character. He was lacking in polish, deficient in education for the chief executive of a modern state, opinionated, and overconfident. But he had courage, intellectual power, and constructive ability as a party leader. He gave a solid foundation to Oklahoma economy, reversed the low trend of crude-oil prices, and gave common citizens the advantages of more equitable taxation. He broke the Oklahoma legislature of the bad habit of impeaching political nonconformists, a habit which might develop, in the hands of incompetent men, toward complete subjection of the executive power to factional combinations of the House and Senate. Impeachment of Governor Robertson by the Eighth Legislature, discussed but not effected, was preposterous; impeachment of Jack Walton by the Ninth was inevitable and probably the best solution for a bad situation; attempts to impeach Henry S. Johnston by the Eleventh Legislature and his impeachment by the Twelfth were in the nature of political wrongs. The old gentleman would have been happier and the state better off if he had never been put up by political managers as a candidate for governor. His removal on the grounds of incompetency was an admission by Oklahoma of failure to make a written constitution work effectively. But when the Thirteenth Legislature would have strengthened the precedent of impeaching governors who dared to disagree with them by an attack on Bill Murray, they met their match.

After three years of the nation's worst depression, Oklahoma voted in 1932 almost three to one against President Hoover and his party. Both of Oklahoma's members in the United States Senate and all its members in the lower house of Congress were Democrats at the beginning of Franklin D. Roosevelt's first term as President.

Ernest W. Marland was a businessman who made a fortune in Oklahoma oil, lost it during the great depression, and turned to politics after he had spent his greatest energy in private enterprise. He was elected governor over the Republican candidate, W. B. Pine of Okmulgee, in an election that drew more than 500,000 voters to the polls. Marland's majority was more than 100,000; and the congressional district in which he lived, normally Republican, was carried by a Democrat, Ferguson.

Marland was humane and in many respects progressive; but he lacked the energy to fight effectively for his political principles. He laid the foundation, however, for future development in Oklahoma's conservation of oil, state planning, educational progress, and social security. He was followed in office by Leon C. Phillips, one of his principal opponents in the Fifteenth Legislature. On December 7, 1941, Japan's surprise attack at Pearl Harbor involved the United States in World War II.

As in World War I, Oklahoma's part in the gigantic conflict of 1941–45 was creditable. Well over 200,000 men and women from the state served in the various branches of the armed forces. Twenty-eight army camps and thirteen naval bases were established in Oklahoma. Among the important establishments were the Tinker and Will Rogers airfields at Oklahoma City, naval air stations at Clinton and Norman, and air training centers at Miami and Ponca City.

Many officers of high rank emerged from the great conflict. Major General William S. Key, a veteran at the beginning of the war who was placed in command of the Oklahoma National Guard, was joined by many young officers who rose rapidly in rank. Ira C. Eaker, Lucian

K. Truscott, Jr., and Raymond S. McLain became lieutenant generals during the war. Major General Clarence L. Tinker, an Osage Indian, was killed in action in a bombing raid over the Pacific; Patrick J. Hurley, formerly secretary of war, achieved the rank of major general. Mark A. Mitcher became an admiral; J. J. Clark and A. S. Soucek, rear admirals. Many other men and women in the regular army, national guard, and other branches of the armed forces, gained distinction in rank or other recognition for unique service to continue Oklahoma's tradition for outstanding performance in national defense.

In 1942, Robert S. Kerr was elected governor over William J. Otjen, Republican nominee, in a close contest. In the same election, the Democratic senator, Josh Lee, was defeated by E. W. Moore of Tulsa. Governor Kerr, born near Ada, was the first governor who was a native Oklahoman. He had previously served as American Legion commander for Oklahoma and had developed extensive oil properties. As governor, he advocated reform in three fields: education, pardon and parole, and state finances. These were areas in which changes were needed, and Governor Kerr had enough success in dealing with them to lay the foundation for his later election to the United States Senate.

Roy J. Turner, who became governor in 1947, followed Robert S. Kerr's program of reform in some respects. Economy, road building, and reforms intended to remove educational institutions from the field of partisan politics received his greatest attention.

Johnston Murray, son of the former chief executive William H. Murray, was elected governor in 1950. Oklahoma cast its electoral vote for the Republican candidate for the presidency, Dwight D. Eisenhower, in the election of 1952. Adlai Stevenson received the creditable popular vote of 430,939, as compared with the winner's 518,045—a total of 948,984—by far the largest balloting in the state's history. Raymond S. Gary, the present Democratic governor, took office in January, 1955.

In the national elections of 1956, Eisenhower again defeated Stevenson, and carried Oklahoma for the second time. Thus, in thirteen presidential elections since Oklahoma became a state, it has voted for the Republican candidate four times. In each of these shifts to the Republican ranks, Oklahoma voted for the winner: Harding in 1920, Hoover in 1928, and Eisenhower in 1952 and 1956. Each of these Republican candidates carried a substantial part of the South.

Since Governor Kerr's administration (1943–47) Oklahoma has given increased attention to highway building. A notable development in this period was the completion of the Turner Turnpike from Oklahoma City to Tulsa and the extension of the road to a Missouri connection with Joplin. The original 88-mile turnpike cost $38,000,000. Its first year of operation brought a net revenue of $1,599,594; and the legislature authorized sale of bonds for three new projects which are estimated at an aggregate cost of $220,000,000.

Oklahoma generally is lowering its race barriers in compliance with the Supreme Court decision ordering prompt desegregation of the public schools. Geographic concentration of the Negroes, however, in many areas tends to maintain essential segregation in fact, if not actually by law. School integration itself is progressing smoothly and the one-time segregation as to recreational facilities is also breaking down. Oklahoma's biracial tradition of close and harmonious co-operation between Indians and whites has greatly facilitated work in desegregation, and by many observers it is considered a model of progress with respect to racial integration, not only for its own particular region, but perhaps for the entire nation as well.

Rapid progress has been made in Oklahoma in its many fields of material growth; and in education, literature, and the fine arts, its contributions to national culture have advanced steadily. To an even greater extent than in the field of politics, evaluation of these achievements is dependent upon a perspective that time alone can supply.

INDUSTRY AND LABOR

By Arthur H. Doerr

A variety of industries contribute to the whole of Oklahoma's economy. Some of them are robust and show an active growth, others are essentially stable, while a few are showing signs of senility and decay. Oklahoma's most significant enterprises are the mineral industries, agriculture, transportation, utilities, and manufacturing.

THE MINERAL INDUSTRY

Minerals have traditionally occupied a paramount role in the economic life of Oklahoma. Oil and Oklahoma are almost synonymous in the minds of people from outside the state. It should be pointed out, however, that a variety of other minerals are, and for years have been, produced in commercial quantities within the boundaries of the state. Mineral production in Oklahoma had its earliest known beginnings in 1822 when the Chouteaus began producing salt in northeastern Oklahoma. Subsequently, in the interval from 1829 to 1840, some coal was stripped from exposed seams in the state's eastern areas.

Mining in Oklahoma was not commercially significant, however, until the coming of the railroads in 1872. In that year J. J. McAlester began the mining of a four-foot vein of coal in the Choctaw Nation in eastern Oklahoma. By 1889 oil was drilled by Kansas speculators in the Cherokee Nation near Chelsea. In 1890 lead and zinc mining in the Joplin, Missouri district was expanded into Ottawa County, Oklahoma. The years since statehood have seen the steady advance of mining into other fields.

Of all Oklahoma's minerals, however, oil has shown the most dramatic growth, and has captured the imagination of the people of the state and the nation. The Red Fork–Tulsa field, opened in 1901, furnished the first commercially significant quantities of oil in the state. In 1904 there was active exploration and the development of fields around Alluwe, Coody's Bluff, and Cleveland. The Glenn Pool, twelve miles south of Tulsa, opened in 1905, attracted national attention to the oil resources of Oklahoma. Almost every year since 1905 has witnessed the opening of a new and significant petroleum field somewhere within the state. Particularly significant discoveries were those at Cushing, Seminole, Oklahoma City, and in Osage and Okmulgee counties. Exploration and development of petroleum fields is currently taking place in Osage County, at Short Junction near Moore, the north Madill field, and near Laverne. The latter is primarily a gas field.

Oil, natural gas, and natural gas liquids are by far the most important minerals produced in Oklahoma. In 1955 these liquid and gaseous hydrocarbons accounted for 90 per cent of the dollar value of all minerals produced within the state. Total value of oil and associated products amounted to about $666,000,000 in 1955.

Oklahoma's oil production is distributed through fifty-five of the seventy-seven counties. Commercial production of petroleum has grown from the thirty barrels produced in 1891 to 197,000,000 barrels in 1955. Oklahoma is the nation's fourth largest petroleum-producing state, a position which she has maintained after falling from third position approximately a decade ago.

The application of latest scientific information and the utilization of the most modern drilling techniques are responsible for continued exploration in the state's petroliferous beds. Skilled geologists and petroleum engineers trained at the University of Oklahoma, Tulsa University, or Oklahoma Agricultural and Mechanical College are constantly in search of petroleum traps or reservoirs which may be tapped by drilling. And, while it is true that scientists and technological advance have reduced the risk in oil exploration, it is still axiomatic that "oil is where you find it."

After an early period of waste, Oklahoma has settled down to conservative production measures. Spacing of wells, proration of production, exploration of new horizons, and secondary recovery methods have all contributed significantly to an extension of the estimates of oil reserves within the state. No statement as to the state's available petroleum reserves can be accurate, but it is reasonable to assume that oil derricks will continue to be conspicuous features of the Oklahoma landscape, and that oil will continue to be a driving force in the economy of the state.

While oil has shown an over-all increase in production since early discoveries, the other major carboniferous fuel, coal, has suffered violent oscillations in production. When McAlester began mining coal in the Choctaw Nation in 1872, he found a ready market in the expanding railroads of the region. Coal production increased erratically until

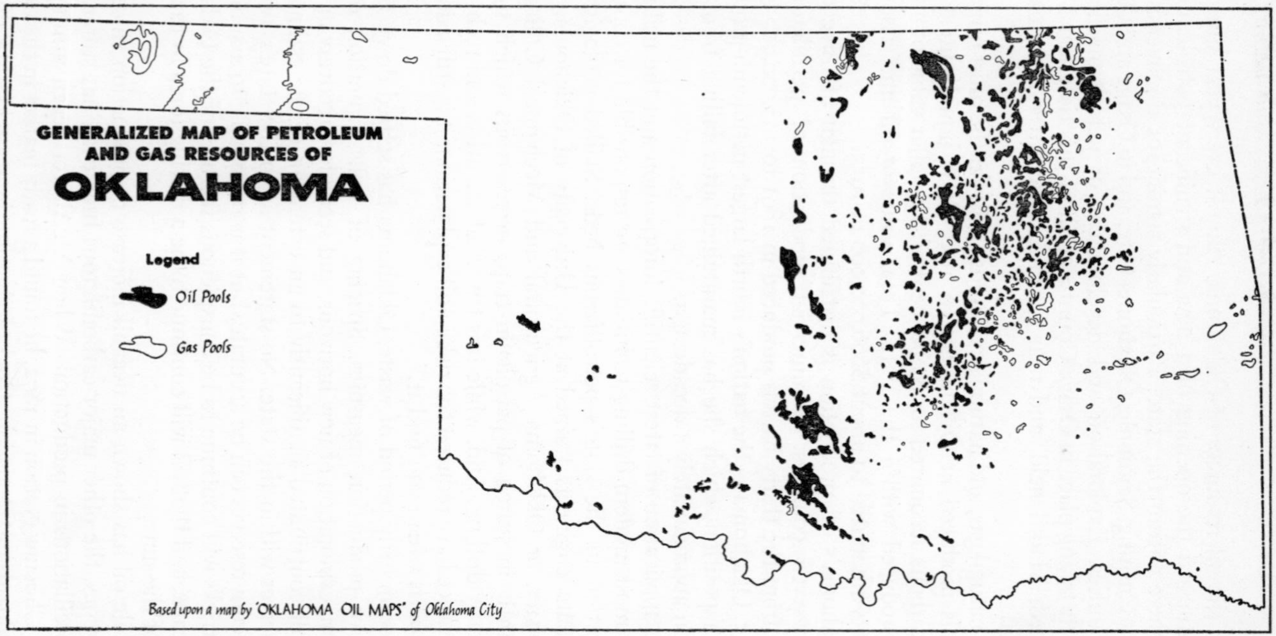
GENERALIZED MAP OF PETROLEUM
AND GAS RESOURCES OF
OKLAHOMA
Legend
Oil Pools
Gas Pools
Based upon a map by "OKLAHOMA OIL MAPS" of Oklahoma City

1903, then suffered a temporary slump until 1910, when more than 2,500,000 tons were mined. In the decade from 1910 to 1920 coal production rose steadily until a peak of almost 5,000,000 tons was produced in 1920. After 1920 coal production declined in the face of increasing competition from cheap oil. The depression was felt in coal mining as in all facets of Oklahoma's industries, and as a result coal production dropped to less than a million tons in 1933. Coal production has fluctuated since the 1930's, but the fuel demands of World War II accounted for a temporary partial recovery. The post–World War II period has seen a decline in coal production, in part, at least, because of the dieselization of the railroads.

In 1955 coal production in Oklahoma was almost 2,000,000 tons, and the output was valued at slightly more than $12,000,000. Thirteen counties produce coal in Oklahoma at the present time, and Okmulgee County is the leading producer. One of the largest mines in the state, the McCurtain Mine of the Lone Star Steel Company, was closed in 1955 because of an underground fire. This same company was planning at that time to open two new mines in southeastern Oklahoma to insure a steady flow of coking coal for their steel works at Lone Star, Texas. Estimated state reserves of over fifty billion tons of coal insure its long-term availability.

Locally, underground mining has resulted in surface subsidence, which has altered the appearance of local terrain. Strip mining has resulted in the destruction of some agricultural and forest land and has created areas of modified hill topography with occasional lakes. Local attempts have been made to revegetate the abandoned strip-mine areas, but there is still much to be done in rehabilitating these stripped regions.

Nonmetallic minerals are the second most important group of minerals produced in Oklahoma, but their combined value accounted for only 5 per cent of the worth of minerals in 1955. The most significant nonmetallic minerals are stone, both crushed and dimension, sand and gravel, clay, and gypsum. Smaller quantities of native asphalt, lime, pumicite, salt, tripoli, and sulphur (obtained as a natural gas by-product) are produced. Workable deposits of nonmetallic minerals are widely distributed over the state. Their estimated value was about $30,000,000 in 1955.

Metallic minerals, chiefly lead and zinc, are the least significant group of minerals produced in Oklahoma. While zinc and lead mining began in Oklahoma in 1890, production was not significant until World War I. New discoveries at that time resulted in a local boom. Production continued at a relatively high level except for a depression dip. Heavy market demands of World War II resulted in a rapid depletion of ores, and zinc and lead production has generally declined since that time. High metal prices enable continued working of normally submarginal ores.

In 1955, Oklahoma produced 15,000 tons of recoverable lead, valued at $4,500,000. In the same year zinc production was 40,570 tons, and was valued at $10,000,000. Small quantities of cadmium, germanium, and indium are recovered from smelter-flue dusts, but it is impossible to ascertain what portion of these minerals come from Oklahoma ores, since all smelters utilize ores from a variety of sources. No traveler through the northeastern corner of Oklahoma can fail to see the imprint of man's hand on the landscape, the result of his efforts to recover zinc from beneath the surface. Tremendous piles of waste rock dot the countryside and are readily observable by any passing motorist. Subsidence has resulted in some spectacular cave-ins at certain localities. Downtown Picher has several square blocks roped off as danger zones because of the collapse of mine pillars.

Oklahoma's minerals will undoubtedly continue to be a most noteworthy aspect of Oklahoma's economy. Several features of the mineral economy are presently apparent, however. Petroleum and related products will continue to be dominant in the mineral picture. Nonmetallic minerals will become relatively more important and the metallic minerals will probably decline in significance in the immediate future.

MANUFACTURING

While the mineral industries continue to dominate Oklahoma's economic base, manufacturing is becoming increasingly significant. During the first quarter of a century after statehood Oklahoma's manufacturing was largely restricted to the processing of a variety of raw materials and the preparation of them for shipment to consumer markets elsewhere. This type of industry included flour milling, meat packing, lumber milling, petroleum refining, and zinc and lead smelting. It is still true that such manufacturing enterprises are of considerable importance, but Oklahoma's industries have expanded and become more diversified in recent years. Examples of this newer type of manufacturing activity are the production of oil-field machinery and equipment, transportation equipment, glass manufacture, and a whole host of others.

The manufacturing industry in Oklahoma has demonstrated an important growth from rather meager beginnings. In 1889 only 2,650 persons were employed in manufacturing in the entire state. In 1956 it was estimated that more than 90,000 persons were so employed.

The most significant industries in Oklahoma in terms of the number of persons they employ are the manufacture of transportation equipment (used in the broadest sense), food processing, petroleum and coal products, machinery, stone, clay, and glass products, fabricated metals, printing and publishing, primary metals, and timber products (except furniture). These industries generally reflect the strong relationship between the availability of raw materials, fuel, and labor.

A consideration of manufacturing activities within the state logically begins with an appreciation of the regional concentration of the major enterprises. The most significant manufacturing nucleus in Oklahoma is in the northeastern part of the state. Tulsa County is the focal point of industry in this region, but Okmulgee, Muskogee, Creek, Washington, Payne, and Kay counties are important as well. This area most nearly approaches the status of a heavy-manufacturing district. Primary metal industries, petroleum refining, oil-field equipment and machinery plants, cement mills, glass factories, and transportation-equipment plants are all of some consequence within the region.

The other major concentration of manufacturing in Oklahoma is in the central part of the state. Oklahoma City, in Oklahoma County, serves as the hub for industries situated in Pottawatomie, Canadian, and Logan counties. Diversified manufactures are characteristic of this region, but food processing, metal fabrication, and transportation equipment and repair are the most significant.

The southwestern part of Oklahoma has a number of relatively small and widely scattered manufacturing plants. The most important enterprise in this section of the state is the processing of cotton and cottonseed. Important cotton gins and/or cotton-oil mills are situated at Altus, Chickasha, Anadarko, Mangum, and Hobart. The dry northwestern part of the state has only a few scattered manufacturing industries. A small number of persons are employed in local feed or grain mills and a carbon-black and natural-gas plant. The one significant manufacturing center in northwestern Oklahoma is Enid, where both flour milling and petroleum refining are important activities.

In southeastern Oklahoma most manufacturing that exists can be related directly to the availability of timber resources in that section of the state. McCurtain, LeFlore, Choctaw, and Pushmataha are the principal lumbering counties, and Broken Bow in McCurtain County is the dominant center.

Three other counties not logically included in the regional groupings already discussed, but nevertheless important in manufacturing, are

Stephens and Pontotoc counties in south-central Oklahoma and Ottawa County in the extreme northeastern part of the state. Duncan in Stephens County merits attention because of its petroleum refineries and production of cement equipment for oil wells. Ottawa County owes its importance to the establishment of a rubber factory at Miami, and Pontotoc County is noteworthy for the manufacture of cement and glass products.

According to the last available *Census of Manufacturing* (1947), ten counties in Oklahoma had more than 1,000 persons employed in manufacturing. Those ten counties together had almost 80 per cent of the wage earners employed in manufacturing in the entire state. In 1950 four counties had more than 2,500 industrial workers and two counties had more than 5,000 so employed. If the number of wage earners employed is deemed to be an adequate criterion of relative manufacturing importance, then Tulsa, Oklahoma, Kay, and Okmulgee counties are the state's pre-eminent industrial counties.

Specific examination of the significant manufacturing enterprises of the state in terms of their areal distribution and characteristics should provide an understanding of Oklahoma's industrial consequence. At present it appears that the transportation-equipment industry employs more persons than any other manufactural activity. The relative rank of this industry is debatable, since the position of employees at Tinker Field, outside of Oklahoma City, is a rather nebulous one. It is presumed that most of the civilian laborers at Tinker Field are in some measure connected with the transportation-equipment industry. Since part of the work is of a classified nature, it is not possible to make a completely accurate analysis. It appears certain, however, that this industry is one of the state's least stable. Periodic oscillations from wartime demand to peacetime lull mean radical variations in the significance of such an industry. To illustrate, aircraft manufacture, the largest component of the transportation-equipment industry has employed as few as 200 persons at times but as many as 50,000 during the period of peak demand in World War II.

If Tinker Field is not considered, a large aircraft company in Tulsa and a smaller one in Oklahoma City employ the lion's share of workers in the transportation-equipment industry. Smaller enterprises in this group include the production of truck bodies and trailers in Oklahoma City and the manufacture of trailers in Tulsa. It is estimated that there are about 30,000 persons employed in the transportation-equipment industry at the present time. A new helicopter plant, very recently established at Altus, will add slightly to this total when it begins full-scale operation.

Food processing, traditionally the most significant type of manufacture in the state, is currently in second place because of the recent ascendancy of the transportation-equipment industry. Currently, approximately 15,000 persons are employed in some phase of food processing. Meat, bakery, and grain-mill products, beverages, and dairy foods are the most important in the food-processing category. Oklahoma City is the dominant center for this type of manufacture, although the food industries have a widespread areal distribution.

With two major exceptions these industries are ubiquitous. Only grain-mill products and meat packing may be considered types not universally encountered. Oklahoma City is the most significant meat-packing center in the state and it has important grain mills as well. Enid and Shawnee are quite important in grain milling.

Petroleum and coal-products manufacturing is third in importance among the industries of the state. Presently more than 11,000 persons are employed in some facet of the coal and petroleum-products industry. Obviously, petroleum refining is the most significant activity within this group. Oil refining is generally concentrated in the north-central and south-central parts of the state. Tulsa in Tulsa County and Ponca City in Kay County are the leading refining centers. Large refineries are located also at Duncan, Enid, and Cushing. Many others are in operation in Osage, Pawnee, Payne, Creek, Garfield, Pontotoc, Okmulgee, Stephens, Caddo, and Garvin counties.

Petroleum refining has had an over-all growth trend in Oklahoma with the exception of the recession decade of 1929–39. Refineries normally possess modern equipment, and refining techniques are comparable to those in any other part of the world. Almost seventy natural-gasoline and cycle plants operate in widely scattered sections of the state. Coal products account for a minimal number of the employees in the petroleum-coal products group. Small quantities of coke and tar are produced.

Machinery, the fourth most important manufacturing industry, and fabricated-metals products, fifth in importance, are discussed jointly because of basic similarities and areal correspondence. Further, both types of activities have developed in primary response to the petroleum industry. Tulsa and Oklahoma counties are the most significant producers of machinery and fabricated metals. Tulsa leads in this type of industry and Oklahoma City ranks second. Enid, Blackwell, Muskogee, and Duncan are of somewhat lesser significance in this regard. The total number of persons employed in the combined machinery and fabricated-metals group totals approximately 17,000.

Stone, clay, and glass products rank fifth in terms of the numbers

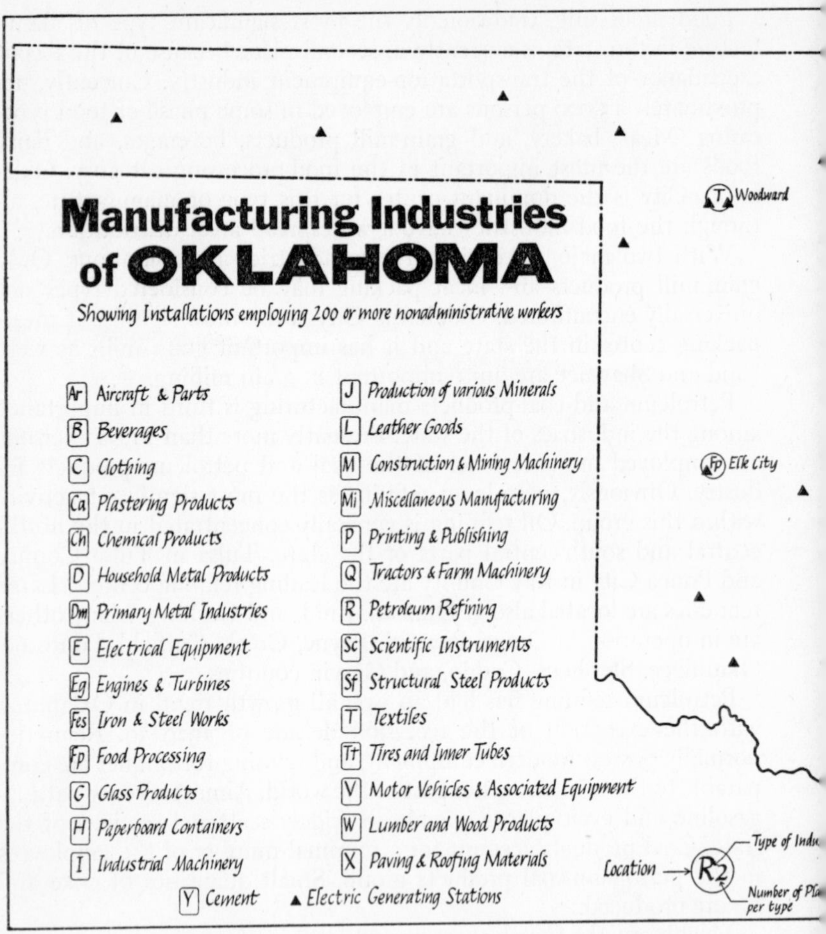

of persons which they employ—more than 6,000 persons. Industries of this group are irrevocably tied to the availability of a variety of raw materials and frequently, also, to cheap fuel. Basic raw materials utilized by these industries are glass sand, clay, gypsum, dolomite, limestone, and small quantities of shale.

Of this group the glass companies provide the largest number of jobs. Glass plants are located in Okmulgee, Creek, Muskogee, Tulsa, and Washington counties. A plant at Blackwell in Kay County was destroyed by a tornado in 1955, and has not been rebuilt. Each of the

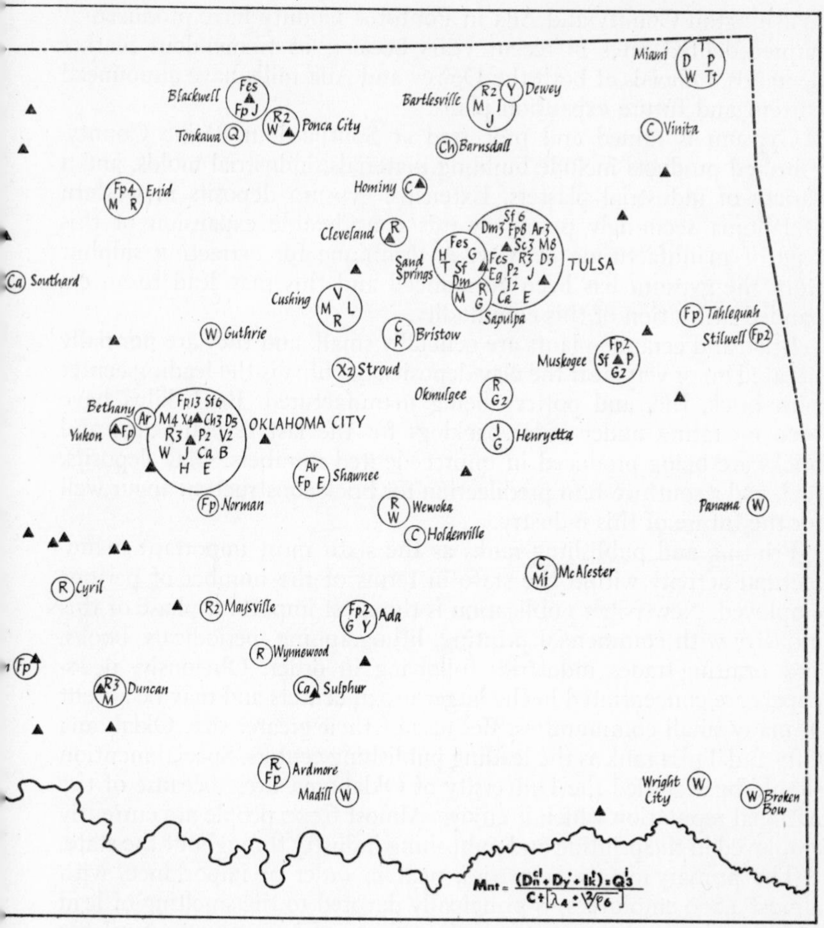

glass factories is located in close proximity to abundant quantities of high-quality glass sand and cheap natural gas. Because of the abundance of high-grade silica, the availability of low-cost fuel, and access to an expanding market Oklahoma is in a particularly advantageous position to increase the number of plants presently operating and to expand operations within existing plants.

Similarly, quantities of limestone, gypsum, clay, and sand, coupled with cheap fuel and a very extensive building program, favor the production of cement in Oklahoma. Cement plants at Dewey in

Washington County and Ada in Pontotoc County have produced at unprecedented rates in recent years because of tremendous market demands. Officials at both the Dewey and Ada mills have announced current and future expansion plans.

Gypsum is mined and processed at Southard in Blaine County. Finished products include building materials, industrial molds, and a variety of industrial plasters. Extensive gypsum deposits in western Oklahoma seemingly point towards considerable expansion of this type of manufacturing activity. A technique for extracting sulphur from the gypsum has been announced and this may lead to an expanded utilization of this commodity.

Brick and ceramic plants are generally small, and they are normally situated on or very near the clay deposits. Sapulpa is the leading center with brick, tile, and pottery being manufactured. Brick kilns have been operating under order backlogs for the last several years, and bricks are being produced in unprecedented numbers. Clay deposits, fuel, and a southwestern predilection for brick construction augur well for the future of this industry.

Printing and publishing ranks as the sixth most important manufactural activity within the state in terms of the number of persons employed. Newspaper publication is the most important phase of this industry with commercial printing, lithographing, periodicals, books, and printing-trades industries following in order. Obviously, newspapers are concentrated in the larger urban centers and may be absent in many small communities. Because of their greater size, Oklahoma City and Tulsa rank as the leading publishing centers. Special mention should be accorded the University of Oklahoma Press because of the national reputation which it enjoys. Almost 6,000 people are currently employed in the printing and publishing industry throughout the state.

The primary-metals industries, next in order of importance, with almost 4,000 employees, is principally devoted to the smelting of lead and zinc ores and the recovery of a variety of by-products. Available fuel plus local ore supplies led to the initial establishment of zinc-lead smelters in the state, although at the present time imported and domestic ores are utilized. Currently, primary-metal processing is carried on in Tulsa, Washington, Okmulgee, and Kay counties. A steel foundry is situated at Sand Springs in Tulsa County, a steel casting plant within the city of Tulsa, and zinc smelters in Bartlesville, Blackwell, and Henryetta. Plans for a tantalum-columbium plant at Muskogee have recently been announced.

Lumber and wood products (other than furniture) hire the smallest number of employees (3,000) among the major manufacturing enterprises. Saw lumber, millwork, and prefabricated wood products constitute the most significant facets of the industry. The southeastern part of the state, with Broken Bow as the hub, is the most significant lumber-producing area of the state. There has been a proposal to erect a paper mill in the area, but the project has not as yet been developed. One large company dominates lumbering within the region, but a number of small transient operators are in business as well. Poor forest practices of the past have been replaced, for the most part, by conservation-wise and sustained-yield forest programs.

There are many other industries of consequence in the state. In Oklahoma City and Guthrie household and office furniture and fixtures, screens, shades, and blinds are manufactured for both local and national markets. The electrical-machinery industry includes the manufacture of storage batteries in Oklahoma City and oil-field electrical equipment in Tulsa. Electronics equipment such as radio and television tubes are manufactured in Shawnee. Envelopes, millinery bags, and set and folding boxes are types of paper products manufactured in Oklahoma City, while Sand Springs produces corrugated boxes. Tulsa manufactures parking meters, taximeters, time bombs, watchmen's clocks, and control instruments. One of the major rubber plants in the southwest produces tires and tubes at Miami. Some of the largest of several apparel plants in Oklahoma are situated at McAlester and Miami. The large chemical plant at Tallant in Osage County produces alcohols, aldehydes, ketones, including methyl-acetone solvents, formaldehyde, methanol, and acetaldehyde. The textile mill at Sand Springs, producing sheeting primarily, is one of the larger textile establishments of the Great Plains. A variety of other manufacturing activities are carried on in Oklahoma, but they are of lesser significance from the standpoint of the number of persons they employ.

A perfunctory examination of the types of manufactures presently situated in Oklahoma suggests that the principal industrial advantages of the state are an abundant and cheap fuel supply, a variety of basic raw materials, a generally adequate labor supply, an adequate transportation network, and a competitive position in an expanding southwestern market. Industrial leaders who have recently established plants in Oklahoma and those currently planning to do so corroborate the preceding statement. In addition, some chose Oklahoma sites because of qualities in the town, or because of the willingness of civic groups to provide a home for the prospective industry.

A comprehensive study of tax totals to be expected in Oklahoma, together with separate tax comparisons with tax structures in other states, puts Oklahoma in a very favorable position from the industrialist's viewpoint. Oklahoma collects no ad valorem or "intangible" tax at the state level, while its effective corporation income tax, after allowable deductions, proves to be lower than that in many of the surrounding states. Machinery to produce for retail trade is exempt from sales and use taxes. Property purchased by a manufacturer, if consumed in the manufacturing process—such as fuel and electric energy—is not subject to sales or use taxes. And Oklahoma's corporation franchise tax rate is levied with a taxable limit on capitalization.

From the point of view of future industrialization, Oklahoma presents large potentials and at the same time a variety of problems which must be surmounted for continued development of the state's resources. Water is the indispensable component of success for many industrial proposals. The heavily forested areas of eastern Oklahoma, once thought of as a handicap to good farming, now offer water in relative abundance, flowing in clear streams through the hilly, timber-covered regions. The rainfall in eastern Oklahoma, amounting to more than 40 inches in average years, contrasts with 18 inches in the western part of the state.

Irrigation probably will not supply the water necessary to develop the full potential of Oklahoma. Solution of the problem has been sought in the creation of reservoirs, and these man-made lakes and ponds have in some measure improved the situation, but aridity is an ever increasing threat which has to be faced, and one to which the people of Oklahoma must give new and deeper thought, as well as concerted and individual action. There must be an understanding of what has to be given back to the soil of Oklahoma before its people can keep on taking from it. The once-rich plains of the western areas, where great herds pastured with only the elements of weather as a threat to sustenance, must be preserved through more scientific treatment and organization.

Oklahoma has been going through an agricultural and industrial revolution in the past forty years—one which has brought heavy shift of population from rural to industrial areas. But the era of violent change is past. The vast mineral wealth of the state has leveled off from the grandiose "strikes" of former years to regulated, stabilized production. Oklahoma now needs only the initial zeal of its citizens to recognize the change in its basic economy and to adapt the immense labor resources of the state to new economic horizons. Close descendants of an enterprising and intelligent breed of men who carved a state from the raw, and who were as insistent for education as they were for the privilege to work, the people of Oklahoma can supply fit man power to meet the industrial needs of their state.

LABOR

Labor organization began in Oklahoma in 1882 when two Illinois coal miners—Dill Carroll and Frank Murphy—established a local assembly of the Knights of Labor in Indian Territory near McAlester. Because of the distrust and overt opposition of mine owners unionization was a slow and difficult process, but by 1894 there were four local assemblies of the Knights of Labor, with an aggregate membership of about fifteen hundred. Three of the locals were mixed assemblies, while the fourth was exclusively a miner's union.

In early days wages in Oklahoma coal mines were higher than elsewhere in the country, and employment was relatively stable, but the advantages were offset by the hazards which gave Indian Territory mines the reputation for being the most dangerous in the world. Company towns and poor working conditions gave rise to labor unrest. The first major strike in Oklahoma came in 1894 in the face of owner's threats to reduce wages by 25 per cent. After a great deal of difficulty and the actual deportation of striking miners, who subsequently returned, the strike was settled with only slight concessions to the union.

By 1898 the Knights of Labor had lost the majority of its influence in Oklahoma, and a new union, the United Mine Workers of America, dominated the coal fields. Late in the winter of 1898 the UMWA began calling local strikes for improved working conditions and wages, and within a year practically every mine was closed or operating on a greatly curtailed schedule. The four-year strike, one of the longest in history was terminated when the owners agreed to the miners' terms in 1903. The miners were granted recognition of the union, an eight-hour day, payment of wages twice a month, and the checkoff (deduction of union dues from the miners' wages by the employers).

Carpenters, painters, plasterers, and hod carriers began active organization during the late 1890's, as did the typographical workers and the building-trades workers. By 1903 practically every active trade in Oklahoma was represented by a union. The Railroad Brotherhoods were among the largest. Early attempts at consolidation of all labor groups were only partially successful, but labor lobbies had a significant effect on the constitutional convention. Most of the union proposals were agreed to by a majority of the members of the convention.

In 1907 the State Federation of Labor established a legislative committee which was credited with securing the creation of the Department of Charities and Corrections; the establishment of an eight-hour day on public works projects; the child labor law, prohibiting the employment of children under sixteen in any occupation injurious to health or morals, or especially hazardous to life and limb; laws requiring factory and boiler inspection; laws prohibiting employers from bringing strikebreakers into the state by using false statements as to conditions of employment; requirement of employers to state in advertisements where there is a strike in progress; prohibition of blacklisting of employees; and the Workmen's Compensation Law. An outstanding achievement is the so-called Labor's Bill of Rights, forestalling any attempt to declare a union illegal.

The Federation's legislative committee also fought the passage of acts such as the Industrial Court Bill, the Conspiracy Bill, the Anti-Picketing Bill, and the proposal to extend the working day on public works. More recently, organized labor has vigorously opposed the Right to Work Bill and the Taft-Hartley Act.

In the early years after statehood labor unions grew in number and membership; the sole exception was the decline of the once-powerful Farmer's Union, primarily because of a court ruling which admitted outsiders to the farmer co-operatives.

In 1914 a militant secret organization known as the Working Class Union sprang up in Arkansas and spread into Oklahoma. It advocated government ownership of public utilities and the abolition of rent, interest, and profit taking; and it proposed revolution as the means to the end. Violence erupted with the coming of the Draft Act in 1917. The so-called "Green Corn Rebellion" was quickly put down and the Working Class Union ceased to be a factor in Oklahoma's labor picture.

Strikes were outlawed either by agreement or legislation during World War I. Immediately after the war, however, strikes occurred in almost every major industry and the unions lost practically every one. In the early postwar years, the Farmer-Labor Reconstruction League attained its greatest influence, drawing its membership from the recently revived Farmer's Union, the Railroad Brotherhoods, and the State Federation of Labor. This group was interested in political action and was successful in electing a governor and numerous other state officials in the election of 1922. Upon the impeachment of the governor the Farmer-Labor Reconstruction League went into eclipse.

Labor organization in Oklahoma during the next decade closely paralleled the national pattern. Organized labor lost ground during the middle and late twenties and picked up sharply after 1930. During the depression years of the mid-thirties the unemployed councils attained a membership of approximately thirty thousand. After the arrest of their leaders in 1934, the councils largely disintegrated and the membership was absorbed into groups with comparable aims, but exercising greater control.

The CIO appeared on the Oklahoma labor scene in 1937, when a heterogeneous group of laborers under the banner of the Oklahoma-Arkansas Industrial Council was granted a charter. Unions have continued to grow in membership and strength in Oklahoma in the past twenty years, but many workers are still unorganized.

The post–World War II years have spawned a number of strikes, as was the case immediately following World War I. After World War II, however, the unions have gained many more valuable concessions. Labor organizers are still attempting to unionize unorganized laborers. In 1956 an unsuccessful attempt was made to organize city employees in Oklahoma City.

Oklahoma's present nonfarm labor force is about 550,000. Four counties in eastern Oklahoma—Muskogee, Pittsburg, LeFlore, and Sequoyah—have substantial labor surpluses. The current labor supply commonly exceeds the demand. One of the attractive factors for outside industry has been an abundant labor supply. Frequently, too, the manufacturers are interested in the relatively cheap female labor available in a number of Oklahoma cities.

While full employment has not yet been obtained in Oklahoma, factory employment more than doubled in the fifteen-year interval from 1940 to 1955. The factory labor force of over 91,000 in 1955 was at an all-time high. A further example of Oklahoma's growth in the labor population was the increase in payrolls covered by the Oklahoma Employment Security Law from about $58,000,000 in 1940 to $314,000,000 in 1954. The largest employers of Oklahoma's workers, in addition to manufacturing, are trade, government, service industries, public utilities, and mining. These industries employ approximately 135,000, 112,000, 59,000, 51,000, and 48,000 respectively.

The mobility of Oklahoma's labor supply is attested to by the fact that a number of permanent Oklahoma residents annually migrate to adjacent states for part-time employment. Similarly, in 1951, when a large aircraft industry announced that a plant would be reopened in the state, 20,000 applications were received, 7,000 of them from out-of-state people, mainly Oklahomans who wished to return.

The state's present labor force is under-utilized as indicated by the fact that 72.7 per cent of the male and 23.7 per cent of the female labor force of work age are employed, compared to like percentages of 78.5 and 28.6 for the nation as a whole. No doubt the labor force will increase slightly as the rural-to-urban trend continues within the state. Hence, a labor reservoir is available and will undoubtedly continue to be available in the immediate future.

An over-all consideration of the future of the state should be based upon the fact that Oklahoma is the very center of that region termed the Southwest, that region which controls the greatest energy resources to be found in the United States—75 per cent of the nation's petroleum and 90 per cent of its natural gas reserves. It is a region with a growth expectancy of thirty-three million people by 1975. There are twelve major rivers running from west to east and pouring into the Mississippi or the Gulf more uncommitted pure water than is available anywhere else in the nation. This area has now advanced to that economic point at which indigenous capital accumulation can predominate in the financing of industrial growth. Other parts of the country have grown rich from the profits of processing and manufacturing, while the Southwest has remained the primary producer—the exporter of its own vast resources.

Oklahoma—as the center of a regional framework of energy development and control—with its billions of cubic feet of natural gas, its tremendous supply of fuel oil, in reserve or readily available, and its millions of tons of coal in still untapped reserves, has only to capture, conserve, and distribute its water power in order to attain an industrial development measured to the full scope of the state's resources.

TRANSPORTATION IN OKLAHOMA

By James A. Constantin

Like many another facet of the state's economy, plans and developments for Oklahoma's transport future are undergoing great changes—some openly dramatic, like highway, water, and air transport; some quietly dramatic, like pipeline and rail transport, the two older carriers, which are performing their jobs and growing in a more sedate manner than the relative newcomers to the field.

HIGHWAYS AND HIGHWAY TRANSPORTATION

The improvements being made on Oklahoma highways are readily apparent to anyone driving in almost any part of the state. It may be disturbing to many to be detoured, slowed down, or stopped on the highway while Oklahoma improves, but construction and reconstruction work on approximately 15,000 miles of pavement is smoothing the way to destiny. Six United States highways, part of the national highway system connecting large centers of population, go through the state. In addition, other federal and state roads provide paved access to practically any place in Oklahoma.

The revival of toll roads in this country and in Oklahoma is fairly new. If completed as authorized, Oklahoma's turnpike system will consist of over three hundred miles of paved highway. The Oklahoma City–Tulsa segment has been in operation since 1952. Other authorized toll roads will connect Tulsa with Joplin, Missouri; Oklahoma City to a point in Oklahoma near Wichita Falls, Texas; Oklahoma City to the Kansas border to meet a Kansas toll road from Wichita. This latter segment will be built as a free road because of the 1956 highway bill and the inability of the Toll Road Authority to sell the bonds. Construction of other free roads in the state has been given considerable impetus by the enactment of the 1956 highway bill.

The rural roads of Oklahoma are used by approximately one hundred trucking companies and twenty bus companies to provide connections for freight and passengers to all points.

AIR TRANSPORTATION

Five passenger airlines and one scheduled freight line serve Oklahoma's air transport needs. In addition, several contract air carriers maintain service for the air force installation at Tinker Field in Oklahoma City. American Airlines and Trans World Airlines are major east-west carriers that operate in the state. American connects the East and West coasts through, generally, the southern portion of the country, while TWA lines cross through the lower central portion. Braniff International Airways is largely a north-south carrier for the mid-continent area and the East Coast. Continental and Central are more regional, covering the Oklahoma, Kansas, Arkansas, and Colorado areas. Slick Airways is an all-freight carrier which provides service between Oklahoma and the large manufacturing centers of the country.

The cities of Oklahoma are very conscious of the importance of air transportation, and are seeking to take advantage of it in all possible ways. The airlines are in process of expanding their operations in terms of frequency of schedules and number of points served. Too, carriers not licensed in Oklahoma are seeking authorization to operate in the state. Airport inadequacy is one of the vital problems in air transport development. Many of the aircraft of the future will not be able to use existing facilities. The major cities of Oklahoma recognize this problem and await only the availability of funds before carrying out expansion plans.

RAILROADS

Oklahoma is blanketed by nearly 6,000 miles of railroad track. Nine Class I and eight other railroads operate in the state. The nine Class I roads serving the state are: Chicago, Rock Island and Pacific; Kansas City Southern; Kansas, Oklahoma and Gulf; Midland Valley; Missouri-Kansas-Texas; Missouri Pacific; Oklahoma City-Ada-Atoka; Atchison, Topeka and Santa Fe; and the St. Louis-San Francisco.

Progress made by the railroads is not so colorful nor so widely publicized as that of other forms of transportation. One reason is that decisions for change, improvements, and enlargement of facilities are made in private conference rooms instead of public meetings. Too, since the public does not participate (through legislation) in financing improvements, they do not become issues of public controversy. In addition, the improvements often are of such a nature that the public does not realize they have been made.

Two types of improvements may possibly be noted by the public: (1) improvement of the roadbed; and (2) newer and more efficient rolling stock. Most people, however, will not realize that modernization is a continuous process with most railroads. For example, crews are constantly working to improve the roadbeds; new devices for controlling traffic are being installed; new techniques for making up trains are being developed; new equipment of all types is being tested and utilized.

The progress in the railroad industry is as great, if not as noticeable, as that of any other transport media. As the economy expands, the demands on railroads increase; so, despite the rapid advancement of its competitors, the future looks bright for the railroads. The fact that they are moving a smaller proportion of all goods moved than previously (even though their total tonnage is up) does not spell doom for the industry. To the contrary, a more effective utilization of the railroad plant results in better service for all.

WATER TRANSPORTATION

The possibility of water transportation in semiarid, land-bound Oklahoma has been offered as a prospect for the future. Of the several projects, the one most likely to reach fruition contemplates a chain of slack-water lakes from a point near Oklahoma City, south and east to a point near Antlers on the Kiamichi River. At Ada, a canal would connect this series of lakes to the Eufaula reservoir. The prime purpose of this project is to supply Oklahoma City with water, but the proposal is of such a nature that barge transportation could be provided.

Other developments that have been considered call for the improvement for navigation purposes of the Arkansas, Canadian, and the North Canadian rivers. The improvement of the Arkansas River is the key to much of the other proposed river projects. If the Arkansas is fully developed for navigation purposes, Tulsa and Muskogee would have access to the Mississippi. Central Oklahoma would have similar access as a result of two different plans. First, proposals contemplate improvement of the Canadian River from the vicinity of Oklahoma City to a point on the Arkansas below Webbers Falls, Oklahoma. Second, the plan for the North Canadian visualizes a development project extending from a point near Oklahoma City to the junction with the Canadian near Eufaula, and thence to the Arkansas and Mississippi rivers. The supposition is that these river developments would be made largely at government expense. Their value is a matter of controversy.

PIPELINES

In 1950 over 168,000,000 barrels of crude oil were moved in Oklahoma by pipeline. Three years later in 1953 (the latest date for which data are available) about 25 per cent more crude was moved—over 208,-000,000 barrels. There was a similar increase of about 25 per cent in the movement of natural gas, from over 482,000,000,000 cubic feet to nearly 600,000,000,000.

The trunk pipelines serving the state are owned largely by major oil companies. They run, roughly, through the central portion of the state from southwest to northeast. Pipeline mileage of both trunk and gathering crude-oil lines as well as products lines has increased in the period 1952–55 from 21,279 miles to 23,322 miles, an increase of nearly 10 per cent. The capacity or pipeline fill has increased to 7,094,000 barrels, about 13 per cent.

AGRICULTURE IN OKLAHOMA

By A. E. Darlow

Agriculture is Oklahoma's biggest industry, with gross receipts from livestock and crops totaling more than $600,000,000 annually. Sixteen major types of farming in the state attest to the wide variety of climate and soils and the diversity of agricultural opportunity. From the high-rainfall belt of the east spring the forest kingdom and fruit and vegetable crops. Cotton is king in the southwest and wheat and beef cattle dominate the west and northwest. The Osage cattle empire of the north is outstanding in the nation for its wealth of cattle maintained on large ranches and native grass pastures.

Leading the parade of agricultural resources is the beef cattle industry which annually brings $235,000,000 to the state. This industry was conceived seventy-five years ago as longhorn cattle grazed the lush grasslands of central Oklahoma on their way to northern markets. The state has shown a rapid and steady growth in number and quality of beef cattle. Today, Oklahoma ranks seventh among the states in beef cattle production.

Improvement has been the watchword of Oklahoma's agriculture almost from the beginning. Wheat replaced cotton as the state's leading cash crop during the drought and depression years of the 1930's. It maintained and strengthened that position during World War II, finally increasing during the postwar years to two and three times the value of cotton. The rolling prairies of western and northern Oklahoma combine with good soil and an ideal climate to make the state one of the leading producers of wheat. The state wheat crop increased in value from $31,000,000 in 1940 to more than $142,000,000 in 1954. Cotton declined almost one million acres from 1940 to 1954. Despite the acreage reduction, returns from cotton increased from $40,000,000 in 1940 to $54,000,000 in 1954.

Farms and ranches are getting bigger but fewer, and frequently more diversified. In 1930 the average-size farm was 165 acres. By 1954 the average farm had grown to about 300 acres, almost doubling in size in twenty-five years. The number of farms decreased during the same

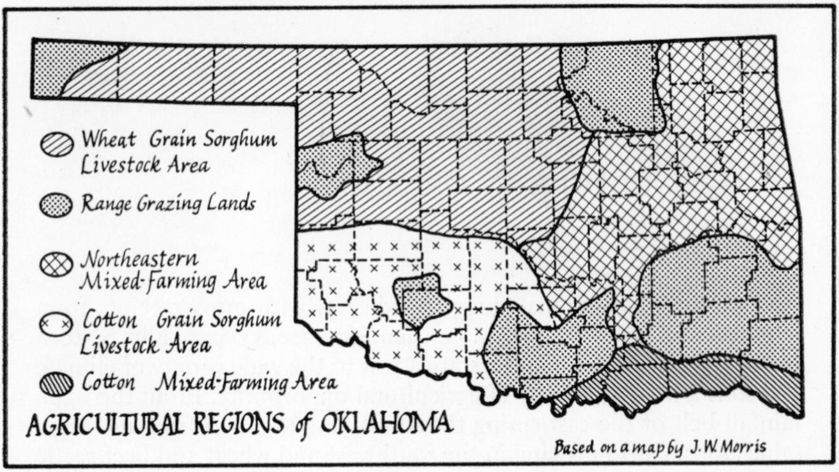

period while the total acreage remained almost without change. From 1930 to 1954 many farmers bought their own land, increasing the number of farm owners by more than 5,000 during that period, while the number of tenant farmers declined from 125,000 to 28,000.

In addition to the principal crops of wheat and cotton, Oklahoma fields turn out grain and forage sorghum, peanuts, sweet potatoes, pecans, spinach, soybeans, oats, rye, barley, and castor beans. Oklahoma ranks first in broomcorn, producing a third of the national supply. The Sooner state also stands first in the production of mung beans and hairy-vetch seed. Oklahoma frequently ranks second and third in wheat production and is among the top three states in the production of grain sorghum, pecans, alfalfa seed, and a number of native grass seeds.

Roughly, the period of land cultivation by the white man in Oklahoma dates from 1890. Varied soil, contrasting topography, and the difference in average rainfall—18 to 20 inches in the northwest to more than 40 inches in the southeast—combine to influence the agricultural patterns that have been established. Farm mechanization, fertilization, irrigation, and improved methods in general have all been influential in bringing about changes for the improvement of farming procedures and results.

In the early days most of the newly broken prairie sod was planted to corn, wheat, and cotton. Cotton and corn remained important during the first quarter of the twentieth century but declined sharply during the next twenty-five years. Of the three crops wheat alone has maintained a strong and increasingly important position in the state's economy.

With change and progress, farming is becoming increasingly scientific. The state Agricultural and Mechanical College at Stillwater provides leadership for this movement through resident instruction, research, and extension activities. Here young men are trained in agricultural methods, and young women in homemaking. They graduate into farm homes, teaching, research, extension service of the college, agricultural industry, and government service. Student enrollment in agriculture ranged between 1,400 and 1,800 from 1950 to 1955. Fields of study include agricultural economics, animal husbandry, agronomy, agricultural education, entomology, etc.

The Oklahoma Agricultural Experiment Station is the research arm of the Division of Agriculture in Oklahoma Agricultural and Mechanical College. The organization of the Agricultural Experiment Station includes the headquarters located on the college campus, and nineteen special stations at various locations in the state. Six of the special stations are jointly operated between the Agricultural Experiment Station and the United States Department of Agriculture. The main station includes farms adjoining the campus plus a farm at Perkins and parts of 20,000 acres of college-owned Lake Carl Blackwell property.

Since 1949 a long-range program of biological research has been carried on at the University of Oklahoma Biological Station, Lake Texoma, near Willis, Oklahoma. Much of the information revealed by this research on native plants and animals is of great value to agriculture and conservation. The Biological Station is a permanent field laboratory designed and operated for study and research in ecology and natural history, and in those phases of taxonomy, evolution, morphology, and physiology that require extensive study of organisms in their natural habitats. It is both a research and instructional unit, containing laboratory facilities for the study of comprehensive collections of plants, insects, and animals. Subjects for study include the plant sciences and many phases of zoology—mammalogy, ornithology, herpetology, entomology, and others. Research is made also into the biological, chemical, and physical features of fresh-water lakes, ponds, and streams, with special emphasis on natural history and plant and animal ecology.

The Agricultural Extension Service is the arm of the Agricultural and Mechanical College which takes research results and better farm and homemaking practices to each of the seventy-seven counties in the state. It administers the Oklahoma 4-H Club program with an annual membership of 75,000 boys and girls, and provides guidance for more than 8,000 volunteer men and women, local leaders who carry educational programs in agriculture and home economics into 119,000 farm and ranch homes each year.

A more informal program of education in the agricultural and livestock field, but one of great value to both adults and young people, is that derived from the extensive list of books published by the University of Oklahoma Press, whose reputation for usefulness in this field of study has extended far beyond the borders of the state to national and international prominence. These publications cover a wide range of agricultural problems, including in the list such subjects as farm management, livestock history, grassland development, and the use, conservation, and nutrition of soils.

In addition to Oklahoma Agricultural and Mechanical College, the state's land-grant college, agriculture is taught in seven other state schools, two four-year colleges and five junior colleges. The four-year colleges are Panhandle Agricultural and Mechanical College at Goodwell and Langston University at Langston. Junior colleges are Cameron State Agricultural College, Lawton; Conners State Agricultural College, Warner; Eastern Oklahoma Agricultural and Mechanical College, Wilburton; Murray State Agricultural College, Tishomingo; and Northeastern Oklahoma Agricultural and Mechanical College, Miami.

In a large measure the proof of Oklahoma's prominence in agriculture is contained in the prize-winning records of individual boys and girls, judging teams, and livestock in competition with the best the rest of the nation has to offer. The outstanding accomplishments of the members of Oklahoma's 4-H clubs and the Future Farmers of America read like fiction stories or fairy tales but they are all true. Oklahoma 4-H Club members consistently rank high or lead the nation in the number of national winners in demonstrated ability and leadership in the several fields of agriculture and homemaking. In 1951, Oklahoma had sixteen national winners, more than any other state has achieved in a single year. Fourteen individuals were national winners in 1956. Club members have won honors in meat and livestock judging at the American Royal Livestock Show in Kansas City and the International Livestock Show in Chicago. These national championships, although indication of individual achievement, are primarily the fruit of well-directed and effective local programs. In addition to paid extension workers in each county, more than 8,000 adult volunteers direct the activities of some 2,000 local clubs in the state.

The Oklahoma organization of the Future Farmers of America is outstanding in the nation. Three times the national FFA president has been an Oklahoma boy. No other state has had more than two. Three boys have been elected Star Farmers of America and three have been elected Regional Star Farmers, making a total of six. This is a national record. Oklahoma also leads on a per capita basis in the number of American Farmer degrees conferred.

Oklahoma Agricultural and Mechanical College and its student teams have an outstanding record in competition. At the International Livestock Show in Chicago, it is the only college to have shown a grand champion fat steer in each of the three main beef breeds, with a record of four champions. Sixteen fat steers from the school's livestock have been either champions or reserve champions of their respective breeds. Since 1923, the College has had more than a dozen first-prize groups of three fat steers. In the collegiate contest, the state Agricultural and Mechanical College has placed thirty-one among the top ten individuals in thirty-two years of competition and has scored a team victory six times. No team from the College has ever placed lower than eleventh. The collegiate meat-judging team has won the first-place trophy six times; the crop-judging team has placed first in nine competitions. The College is the only school to have won more than two collegiate judging contests at the International Livestock Show in the same year. Livestock-judging teams, as well as those in crop and meat judging, scored victories in 1948.

Besides the farm clubs sponsored by the Extension Service of the state Agricultural and Mechanical College, farmers have developed on their own initiative a number of co-operative marketing associations and other effective groups for the promotion of their products and the improvement of agriculture.

SPORTS AND RECREATION

By Jeff Griffin

Oklahoma has been consistently progressive in the development of facilities for sports and outdoor recreation during the half century since the advent of statehood. In state-developed parks, and in hundreds of other public and privately owned recreational areas and playgrounds, the emphasis has been on the wide variety of all-year outdoor activities open to sports enthusiasts in virtually every area of the state.

In recent years Oklahoma athletes have excelled in most collegiate and professional sports—in football, major-league baseball, wrestling, tennis, golf, and as world-famed rodeo performers. Each era, beginning with the triumphs of the immortal Indian athlete, Jim Thorpe, has seen one or more Oklahoma youths rise to outstanding prominence in competitions on a national level.

Oklahoma, meantime, has developed and conserved facilities for hunting and fishing that have elevated the state to top rank as an outdoor recreation center favored by sportsmen specializing in hunting, fishing, speedboating, and aquatic sports. Oklahoma's mild climate enhances the popularity of the region by making outdoor recreation available and enjoyable in any season.

Predominant among the favored sports is the excellent fishing provided and sustained by a continuing state-directed program in which many millions of dollars have been invested to make and keep Oklahoma fishing and other recreational facilities outstanding in the nation. In a current phase of the program the people of Oklahoma have invested $7,200,000 in luxurious lodges and ultramodern cabins at major park resorts, and additional millions of dollars in improving recreation facilities in all areas of the state.

Numerous bodies of "big" water are especially inviting to fishing enthusiasts. These include nine major reservoirs, ranging from hundreds to thousands of acres in extent, and about 100,000 smaller lakes, streams, and ponds that give Oklahoma more than a thousand square miles of water surface.

The popularity of Oklahoma fishing is attested by the excellent catches of black bass, crappie, channel cat, and numerous other species of game fish. Enterprising citizens in helping to make tourist and vacation spending one of the state's major industries have inaugurated heated fishing docks to insure solid comfort for fishing enthusiasts despite temperatures during winter months.

Nature in the beginning endowed Oklahoma with rugged mountains, topped by timber with clear fish-filled streams to make the region a veritable paradise for hunting and fishing. In a progressive program of development the natural environs have been conserved and improved by the state government, and virtually every area abounds with a variety of game.

Emphasizing an invitation that annually brings millions of tourists, vacation travelers, and sports enthusiasts to Oklahoma, the state maintains a network of fourteen state parks aggregating more than 53,000 acres. The recreation centers are situated at advantageous locations making each easily accessible over a widespread system of hard-surfaced roads.

Hunting and expeditions for bird shooting are equally as popular as fishing among the increasing thousands of visitors. State regulations provide for a brief annual season on deer, which are found mainly in the eastern third of the state. The deer season includes special days for hunting with bow and arrows, and other specific days for killing a limited number with firearms. In the counties where deer are numerous the State Game and Fish Department maintains research projects along with a refuge system to protect and increase the number of this game species.

In the forested areas—and Oklahoma has some ten million acres of forests—and along wooded streams squirrels are plentiful. Bobwhite quail shooting probably attracts the greater number of hunters, and such shooting is generally good throughout the state. Prairie chicken are plentiful in some areas, especially in Osage and Ellis counties, but in other sections of the prairie country they have virtually disappeared, and those remaining are given strict protection. Migratory waterfowl afford good hunting along the state's numerous rivers and on waters impounded by the larger reservoirs. Dove hunting, too, apparently becomes more popular each year and offers excellent sport for gunners.

Oklahoma often is considered unique in hunting practices and in other sports. Popular in many sections of the state is the chase of coyotes, 'coon, bobcat, and fox, and the sport is practiced by organized groups. The most unusual sport is the annual international rattlesnake hunt that brings hundreds of enthusiasts to the Okeene and Watonga areas of northwestern Oklahoma each spring. A few years ago Okla-

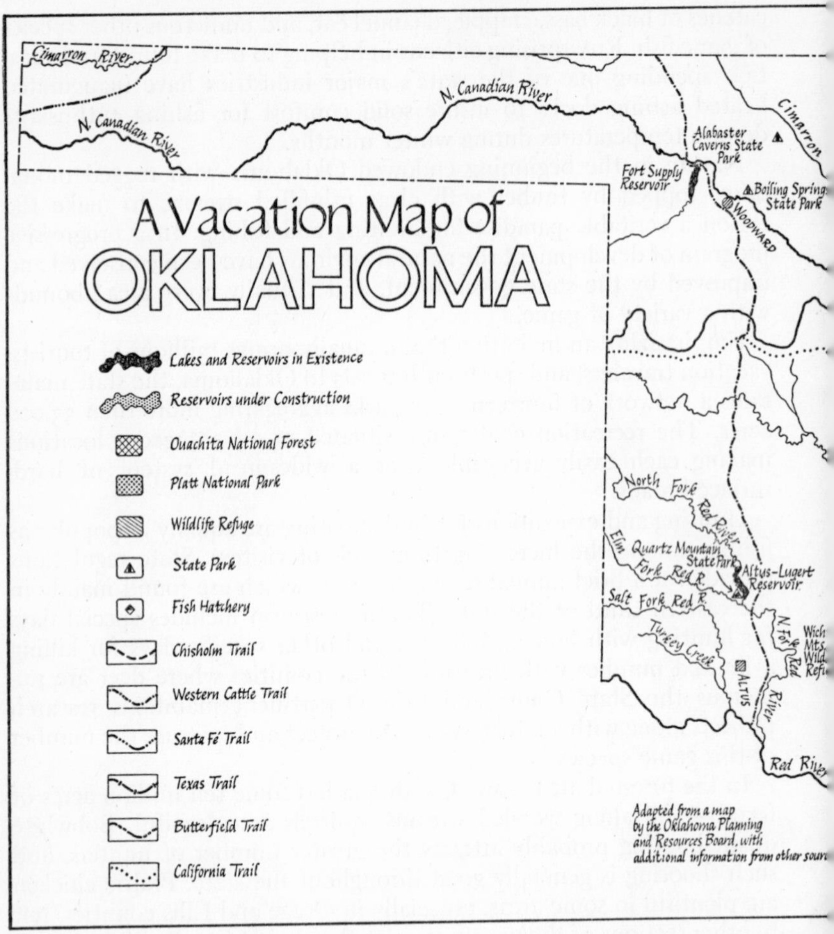

homa sportsmen attracted world-wide interest with terrapin races in the Ponca City area. In many parts of the state the trapping of small furbearers not only provides considerable winter sport for farm families but is also of substantial value economically.

The Oklahoma Game and Fish Department through restoration measures accentuates the program of wildlife conservation. Under this program of trapping, transplanting, establishing of refuges, public hunting areas and management, every effort is made to provide and perpetuate good hunting.

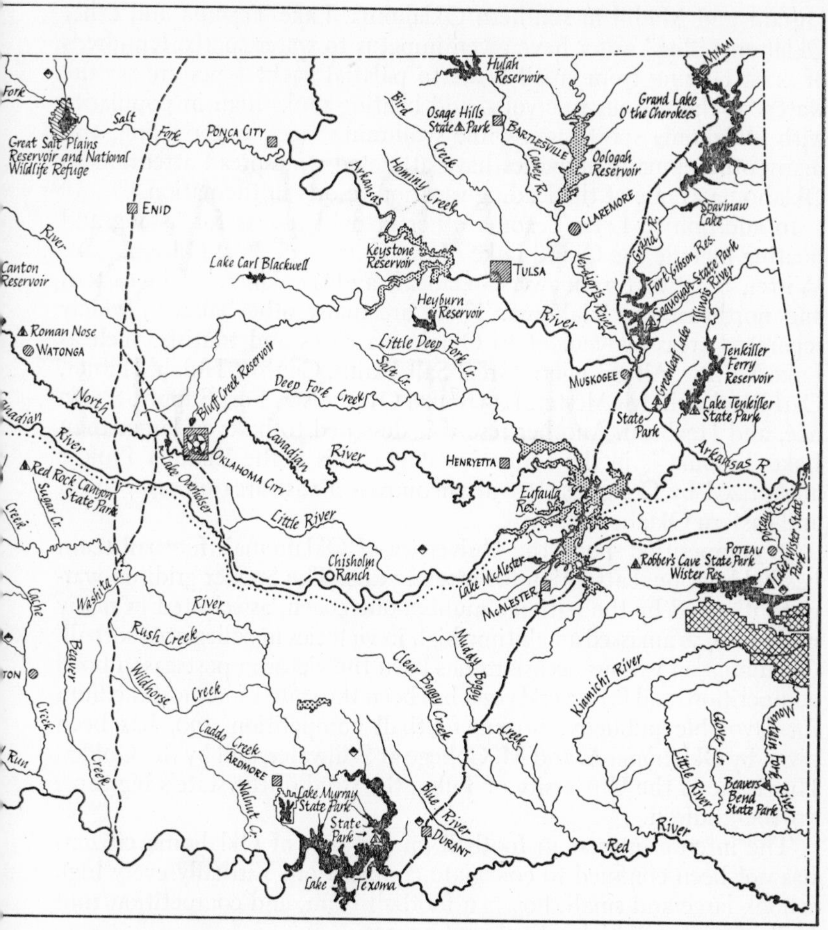

Four extensive scenic regions attract the sportsman and vacationist to Oklahoma—the mountains of the Ozark slope in northeastern Oklahoma, the Ouachita Mountains and National Forest, embracing most of southeastern Oklahoma, the Arbuckle Mountains in the south-central region, and the Wichita Mountains Wildlife Refuge in the southwest.

The largest impoundment of water is Lake Texoma, 93,000 acres in extent and one of the largest man-made lakes in the world. It lends enchantment to Lake Texoma State Park with its 2,600 acres near

Durant and Madill in southern Oklahoma. Lake Texoma and other Oklahoma "big" water have given impetus to water sports. Hundreds of craft ranging from small boats to palatial yacht types are on the waters at the various reservoirs, and boating ranks high in popularity with Oklahoma sportsmen, while swimming races, water skiing, and many other aquatic activities have attracted widespread attention to Oklahoma as one of the leading vacation resorts in the nation.

In addition to Lake Texoma other favored resorts for fishing and boating include the Grand Lake of the Cherokees, Fort Gibson, Lake Wister, the two Spavinaws, Greenleaf, and Tenkiller, all in eastern and northeastern Oklahoma. There are many other lakes in widely separated areas convenient to Oklahoma cities and tourists, such as Lake Murray, Altus-Lugert, Great Salt Plains, Canton, Hulah, Hefner, Carl Blackwell, McAlester, Lawtonka, Overholser, Fort Supply, Shawnee, and Heyburn. Another reservoir designed to be even larger than Lake Texoma is in the formative stage. This is the Eufaula Project authorized by Congress. It will encompass a vast area of east-central and eastern Oklahoma.

In competitive sports the University of Oklahoma's football team has held national attention for several years. The Sooner gridiron warriors, directed by the nation's number-one coach, as selected in many polls, in 1956 amassed an all-time high in victories in collegiate football. Oklahoma on various occasions has been the victor in postseason bowl competition, and for several years has been the state's foremost medium for favorable publicity. Strong football competition, too, has been given by Oklahoma A. and M. College at Stillwater, and by the Golden Hurricane of the University of Tulsa, the third of the state's big three on the gridiron.

The intense interest in football on the part of Oklahoma citizens has not been confined to collegiate competition. Virtually every high school, large and small, boasts a football team, and competition runs high in a score of high school conferences.

Basketball also is a popular fall and winter sport in Oklahoma schools, in both the smaller cities and the major institutions of learning. The "Aggies" of Oklahoma A. & M. College usually have basketball teams ranking high in conference competition. Strong teams also are the rule at Oklahoma City University, the University of Tulsa, and the University of Oklahoma. Basketball has scored signal success as a professional pastime, and for many years one of the nation's outstanding teams was known as "Phillips 66," sponsored by Phillips Petroleum Company of Bartlesville.

Both Oklahoma City and Tulsa maintain professional baseball clubs in the Texas League, and on numerous occasions one of the two Oklahoma clubs has been in the postseason Dixie Series—a competition between the Texas and Southern leagues. Another professional baseball circuit is the Sooner State League in which eight Oklahoma cities are represented in a full-scheduled season, most of them with major-league connections interested in the development of future major-league players.

There has been scarcely an era in which Oklahoma baseball players have failed to hold the spotlight in World Series play, and in the competition in both the American and National Leagues. In the current decade outstanding players have included Allie Reynolds and Tom Sturdivant, both of Oklahoma City, and each a stellar pitcher for the New York Yankees; Warren Spahn of Wilburton, outstanding pitcher of the Milwaukee Braves in the National League, and spectacular Mickey Mantle of Commerce, the fleet baserunner, outfielder, and home-run king of the New York Yankees. In earlier years Oklahoma provided such famous players as Carl Hubbell of the New York Giants, the Dean brothers, Jerome (Dizzy) and Paul, each gaining fame with the St. Louis Cardianals of the National League; John "Pepper" Martin of the St. Louis Cardinals, and a score of others who have gained recognition for their outstanding abilities with major-league clubs.

Wrestling teams of the Oklahoma A. & M. College on various occasions have been national champions in collegiate wrestling competition, and in recent years the University of Oklahoma has produced some of the outstanding teams and individual wrestlers in the nation. Professional wrestling is one of the featured sports activities in both Oklahoma City and Tulsa.

Golf long has been a favorite sport for both men and women in Oklahoma. Tulsa and Oklahoma City, in addition to many small cities of the state, have numerous country clubs and golf courses for public play. Outstanding golf tournaments are staged at regular intervals, and the state often has players rating high in national tournaments. Tennis is a widely popular sport and tennis courts are available in nearly every city and town. Oklahoma tennis players have attained national recognition in this sport.

Sports-minded Oklahoma citizens have participated in widely varied competitions—competitions ranging from horseshoe pitching, a favorite sport in many municipal parks, to the more grueling Golden Gloves boxing tournaments. Polo never has been recognized as a popular sport in Oklahoma, although polo teams have been active for many years in the larger military installations in the state, and polo games still are played at regular intervals in these localities.

Foremost in interest for thousands of Oklahoma citizens are rodeo performances. Hundreds of rodeos are held annually in cities and towns throughout the state. The larger ones, attracting national attention and world-famous performers include the Will Rogers Memorial Rodeo, held each year at Vinita; the rodeos at Elk City, Chickasha, Pawhuska, Woodward, Ada, Mangum, and especially the annual rodeos each year behind the walls of the Oklahoma Penitentiary at McAlester. The prison rodeo was inaugurated several years ago to bolster the morale of prisoners, and since has gained in popularity over wide areas of the Southwest.

EDUCATION

By Frank A. Balyeat

In 1907, when the state of Oklahoma was formed by joining Oklahoma Territory and Indian Territory, the organization of a school system presented difficult problems. Although the two territories were about equal in size and population, the nature and extent of schooling varied greatly.

Indian Territory had been settled much longer. In the decades preceding the Civil War, the Five Civilized Tribes (Cherokees, Chickasaws, Choctaws, Creeks, and Seminoles) had been removed from their homes in southeastern states. By 1861 they were well established in their Indian Territory homes and had resumed and improved the schools that they had enjoyed before removal. They established tribal schools, financed with funds from the sale of their lands and supervised by federal officials. Neighborhood schools for the many and boarding schools for the few were well under way when the Civil War began. The ravages of war prevented these schools from operating, but the missionaries of various denominations who had helped to staff the schools did all they could to keep alive the Indians' desire for education.

When the Civil War ended, the Indians resumed their former ways of living and in the regions that they had settled and improved. Treaties with the federal government included provisions for resumption of schools. Within a quarter of a century Indian Territory had fairly good educational opportunities for most Indian children, also for an increasing proportion of Negroes, and for a small minority of white children. Some Indians were sent to the schools of adjoining or more distant states at tribal expense.

Between 1889 and 1901 all of Oklahoma Territory had been opened to settlement, and the Indian tribes affected had been given individual allotments of land. The first territorial legislature met in the summer of 1890, too late to provide schools for the first year or to help much on the second year in the seven counties that comprised "Old Oklahoma." Congress had appropriated $50,000 to pay teachers until tax receipts and tuition could combine for the meager support of public schools. Parents furnished labor and materials for crude schoolhouses and built schoolroom benches. Three-month terms prevailed, with few teachers receiving more than $25.00 per month.

As the other areas opened, the territorial pattern was extended over the newly settled counties. Districts were nearly all three miles square. Each district elected three board members who chose the teachers. Little, and often poor, supervision was provided by the popularly elected county superintendents, who operated under a territorial superintendent and board appointed by the governor. Nearly all financial support came from an ad valorem tax on property in the district. The first schoolhouses were of material locally available, and varied from comfortable log buildings to cold frame buildings of native lumber, or even to sod houses in a few districts. Some schools were held in small residences that farmers had abandoned when they "proved up" on their farms and moved back to their homes in "the states." Home-built school furniture was meager and crude. Blackboards were homemade and usually poor.

At first there was a motley collection of textbooks brought by parents from their former homes, but soon the adopted texts gradually prevailed. These were McGuffey's Readers and Spellers, Barnes' History and Geography, Ray's Arithmetic, Harvey's Grammar, Steele's Physiology, and the Spencerian copybooks used in penmanship. Charts preceded the first readers, primers being almost unknown in the early years. Most schools were ungraded, with only "A," "B," and "C" classes, and sometimes a "D" class in numbers.

Most Oklahoma Territory pioneers, coming from nearly every state in the union, had formerly enjoyed good schools. Their determination to provide better and better schools in the new country did much to overcome the handicaps encountered. The local schoolhouse soon became the community center, providing a place for school programs open to the public, literary societies, box suppers, singing schools, Sunday Schools, and preaching. These contacts and experiences helped to entrench the small-district plan and to endear the schoolhouse to the patrons.

Oklahoma Territory had been developing a school system for eighteen years when the new state was formed. It had the federally assigned school lands and the revenue which helped to support public schools, including colleges. Such land could not be assigned in the Indian Territory, so Congress appropriated five million dollars to be added to the state school fund. The Indian Territory side was laid out in counties, similar to the western portion. Again, the district of nine square miles prevailed. Indian Territory towns were able to make effective transition to the pattern and program of the state of Oklahoma. At least a hundred towns were included in this reorganization into state schools.

In 1891, Oklahoma began to develop a system of higher education. The University of Oklahoma at Norman, the Agricultural and Mechanical College at Stillwater, and Central Normal at Edmond led the way for others. Two additional normal schools were established in a few years, Northwestern at Alva and Southwestern at Weatherford. The Agricultural and Normal College for Negroes was located at Langston and the University Preparatory School at Tonkawa. The Oklahoma College for Women, at Chickasha, was established in the early years of statehood.

The union of the two territories made it necessary to organize state schools in the Indian Territory. At Ada, Durant, and Tahlequah were established the East Central, Southeastern, and Northeastern Normal schools, to match those in Oklahoma Territory. These six schools now are a part of the teacher-preparation program, while also offering extensive work in arts and sciences. They are now senior colleges, having recently added a graduate program for teachers. Both the University of Oklahoma and the Agricultural and Mechanical College include varied programs of training for teachers, with work at the doctoral level in this and other areas.

On the Indian Territory side was soon established a preparatory school at Claremore to match the one at Tonkawa. It later became a military academy, while the Tonkawa school was made the Northern Junior College. Early under statehood six junior agricultural schools were established. The ones at Helena and Broken Bow were closed in a few years. Those at Lawton, Tishomingo, and Conners still exist as junior colleges with a vocational emphasis. There are two similar schools at Miami and Wilburton, established as schools of mines. The school at Goodwell became a senior college, the Panhandle School of Agriculture.

The University of Oklahoma now includes the most commonly found professional schools and colleges, with training in medicine and nursing at Oklahoma City. The Oklahoma Agricultural and Mechanical College, also with the varied fields common to such institutions, has established a School of Technical Training at Okmulgee, using the army hospital plant of World War II. The University of Tulsa, once a denominational school but now a privately endowed institution, grants advanced degrees, including the doctorate. A few other church senior colleges have survived, including Bethany-Nazarene at Bethany, Phillips University (Christian) at Enid, Benedictine Heights College

(Catholic) at Tulsa, Oklahoma City University (Methodist), and Oklahoma Baptist University at Shawnee.

Church junior colleges remaining in 1956 were: Bacone College at Muskogee, mainly for Indians; Central Christian College, now at Bartlesville but in the process of moving to Oklahoma City; and St. Gregory's College at Shawnee. Others that have been discontinued or have combined with other colleges include many tribal and church schools, especially in Indian Territory.

Since about 1920, Oklahoma has seen a good many "municipal" colleges established and later discontinued. They were really upper reaches of the local public school system and supported by tuition. In all, thirty-five cities have tried such experiments. In 1956 only six of these were in operation—at Altus, El Reno, Muskogee, Poteau, Sayre, and Seminole.

The State Regents of Higher Education, a nine-member lay board, aided by a chancellor and his staff, have co-ordinated the work of the colleges of the state since 1941. They approve policies and plans of state colleges and apportion the budget appropriated biennially by the legislature.

Much vocational education is provided by private institutions, some of them not at the college level. Some are accredited by the State Department of Education and others by their own professional boards of control. Among the former are about twenty business colleges, in almost that many cities. In the latter group are schools of theology, not connected with colleges; trade and industrial schools, in Oklahoma City and Tulsa; and several barber schools and schools of cosmetology. Also to be included among the vocational educational opportunities is the splendid program carried on by state and federal agencies in various lines of farming and homemaking. Most of this is not in credit courses but is very helpful to thousands of young people and adults.

Improved roads and better transportation make the small district of yesterday no longer needed nor economically practical. For several years there has been growing demand for fewer and larger districts. This makes for better schools and usually at less expense. But the strong attachment for local district schools under local control has delayed the inevitable change. When Oklahoma became a state, there were nearly six thousand districts; fifty years later there are fewer than two thousand. In an increasing number of counties the one-teacher school has entirely disappeared. Most of this change has occurred since World War II. Contributing to the change has been improved transportation for pupils. Now about 150,000 pupils, in grades one through twelve, ride in comfortable buses to better schools than can be provided in small districts. Safety in transportation is a major concern of the State Department of Education and the State Department of Public Safety, and they have accomplished much in this line.

One main advantage resulting from fewer and larger districts has been improved high schools. Of the larger number of districts at statehood, only 3.2 per cent could provide high schools, and many of them very inadequate. In 1956 more than 28 per cent offer improved high school work. Even so, many of the present high schools are too small to be either effective or economical. With little loss to academic work in most schools, there has been a steady addition of high school courses that enrich the lives of all and train the many who do not go to college. Much of the additional work is supported federally, especially the varied types of vocational training. Added to these are courses in business education, other homemaking and industrial arts courses, art, music, speech, journalism, and health and physical education, including safety education.

An inevitable difficulty arises with the enriched program, because some who enter college have had too little preparation for college success. To improve this situation, more and more high schools offer effective guidance in choosing courses that will prepare students for college as well as train those who will never attend college. This program of counseling and guidance is doing much to find and prepare young men and women needed for specialized work in our scientific age. Also, many are advised in health training, both physical and emotional.

Accreditation of schools, especially high schools, does much to upgrade the state's educational institutions. Oklahoma is a member of the North Central Association of Colleges and Secondary Schools. Working with the State Department of Education, this organization is able to strengthen the member schools while helping indirectly those not eligible for North Central membership.

To obtain the best textbooks available and at proper cost to those concerned has always been a problem. Oklahoma now has a system of multiple adoption. From approved texts local committees choose the books to be used in their schools. Today most of the textbooks in grades one through twelve are provided at state expense.

The depression of the thirties hastened the coming of the school lunch program, provided partially at public expense. This is now a federal program, with states operating through participating districts. Many pupils now have facilities for getting the right kind of lunches as well as receiving effective training in proper diet.

Securing and holding enough competent teachers and administrators has, from the beginning, been a matter of great concern. Indian Territory had made little progress in this line, and Oklahoma Territory needed more and better teachers. For several years under statehood, counties, and sometimes cities, issued most of the teaching certificates, the type depending upon the subjects in which an applicant was examined, the grades made on the examination, and teaching experience. Many of the teachers in rural schools were farmers who could teach the short term between crops. The county institute, or normal, prevailed through territorial days and through the first decade of statehood. Usually, in this four-week term the teacher reviewed for the examination which followed, studied further the subjects to be taught by him, and studied educational methods. Many attended summer after summer in an effort to obtain a more advanced certificate and the resultant increase in salary.

The handicapped child has too long been denied the type of schooling needed. Large numbers of slow learners, physically handicapped, partially blinded, with hearing defects, or with various kinds of speech defects are now getting more opportunity for education. The State Department of Education now contains a Division of Special Education to supervise this field. College courses now specifically prepare teachers for one or more of these areas. State money supplements that of the local district if the teacher has proper college credits. There is a state school for the blind at Fort Gibson and one for the deaf at Sulphur.

Gradually more and more college credits are required for teacher certification. The 1912 Biennial Report of the State Superintendent of Education states that at that time not more than 20 per cent of the town teachers had attended college, and not more than 5 per cent of the rural teachers. Summer sessions enabled some poorly prepared teachers to increase their college credits and make themselves better qualified to teach. In 1954 only 3.8 per cent of Oklahoma teachers had less than a bachelor's degree and 21.19 per cent had a master's degree. Not only have the required number of college credits been increased, but the teacher has also to acquire more college hours in his own particular field.

In recent years all certificates for teaching in grades one through twelve have been granted by the State Department of Education, with the seventeen colleges concerned assisting in recommending those whom they train. Since about 1950 there has been steady and marked progress in improvement of teacher education and certification, largely because of effective leadership of the Oklahoma Commission on Teacher Education and Certification.

The Oklahoma Education Association was formed in 1908 and has grown steadily in its influence on the raising of school standards and improvement of the teaching profession. Its official publication, *The Oklahoma Teacher*, serves to inform and stimulate the teaching personnel. The Parent Teacher Association and other organizations have worked effectively with the schools in programs of improvement.

Teachers' salaries remain a difficult problem in Oklahoma, as in most other states. Slowly, but steadily, the Oklahoma situation improves as the state legislature becomes increasingly respondent to providing more money for schools. The teacher retirement system and, in some schools, co-operation with social security have improved the prospects of teachers in both public and private schools.

Financing public education has become increasingly difficult. No longer is the local district in Oklahoma expected to bear the cost of its schools. State aid in various forms has increased steadily in recent years. In 1953–54 less than one half of the cost of building and maintenance was borne by the local district. State sources of school revenue include money from auto licenses, gross-production tax on minerals, school-land earnings, and appropriations for equalization of opportunity among the various districts to compensate for inequality of financial ability. There is federal aid for vocational education, Indian education, school lunches, and special needs of areas affected by federal projects. State and federal aid is usually dependent upon the local school's meeting specified standards of efficiency.

Since 1907 the various tribes of Indians have been relieved of the responsibility of educating their children. Only the Five Civilized Tribes ever had this responsibility to any great extent. Gradually, the tribal schools, government boarding schools, and the few denominational schools left have closed or have reduced their sphere of service. Increasingly the Indian children have been absorbed into the public schools, with a few still enrolled in denominational schools. Three government institutions, Jones Academy at Hartshorne, Eufaula Boarding School, and Carter Seminary at Ardmore, merely board the children, transporting them to the near-by town schools. Still operating as boarding schools are the Seneca Indian School at Wyandotte and the Sequoyah Vocational School near Tahlequah. On the Oklahoma Territory side of the state are the following Indian schools, under federal jurisdiction: Cheyenne-Arapaho Indian School at Concho; Ft. Sill Indian School at Lawton; Riverside Indian School near Anadarko; and Chilocco Indian Agricultural School in Kay County. These schools enroll a good many pupils from other states.

Gradually the national policy has been to absorb Indian children into the public schools of the community when possible. The first forty years under statehood were on the plan of federal reimbursement of the local school in proportion to the number of days attended. Since 1947 the U.S. Commissioner of Indian Affairs contracts with the public school system of the state. Oklahoma, with about one-eighth of the nation's Indians, is one of the states most concerned. Better plans of paying for "enrichment education" and home visitation have combined to improve both enrollment and attendance of Indians and their work in the public schools.

The 1955 report of the State Department of Education showed that in sixty-one of Oklahoma's seventy-seven counties, 562 schools enrolled Indian children, with federal payment and supervision. These schools then had enrolled 170,601 Indian boys and girls, and 349 of them finished high school that year.

NEWSPAPERS

By Roy P. Stewart

Oklahoma newspapers had their beginning in the *Cherokee Advocate*, which, with the Georgia stock, was brought in 1844 to Indian Territory by unwilling immigrants among the literate, pastoral Cherokees from their ancestral home in Georgia. But today's newspapers of the Sooner State bear no more resemblance to their prototypes than a modern tractor with pneumatic lift does to the obsolete walking plow.

The only reason for the survival of newspapers in Oklahoma as competitive news media is that they fill a community need, whether that community be the trade-area circulation of a small-town paper like the *Weatherford News*, or the state as a whole, regarded as just an enlarged community by the *Daily Oklahoman* in Oklahoma City. Not only have newspapers survived—they have flourished. On any given Thursday, the customary publication date of weeklies, 1,256,000 papers, representing the combined circulation of the state's 246 weeklies and that of its 55 dailies, go out to subscribers. This is 36,000 more than the number of adults the 1953 U.S. census showed Oklahoma to have in the 18 to 64 age group—from which come the majority of readers.

Technically, Oklahoma papers have kept pace with modernization of the state's basic agricultural and industrial enterprises. Only a few years ago as many as 174 papers still contained some boiler plate or patent insides, but by 1952 even the last, lingering handful of weeklies beset with man-power problems in the back shop had dropped that substitute for local news. Thirty of the state's papers have their own engraving plants to dress up their pages more easily and add stimulus to pictorial journalism. Some dry engraving plants, like the Fairchild systems, are owned jointly by several papers, which divide costs, while some wet plants do custom work for their neighbors. The result is the same—another significant development to keep papers abreast of the times.

This holds true also in the mechanical shops. No longer can a paper be operated with a case or two of hand-set type and a hand press. No longer do tramp printers wander in, as did Wesley Winans Stout, the former editor of the *Saturday Evening Post*, who joined the infant *Lawton Constitution*, reached for a stick, propped handwritten copy on a type case, and laboriously plucked letters out one by one. Even a small shop has its Linotype or Intertype. Most dailies and some weeklies now have teletypesetters. A large number of newspapers, even the smaller ones, have a Ludlow to cast headlines and display type.

The adoption of technical improvements in order to secure a better format, making the paper more pleasing to the eye typographically, more efficiently produced, has called for vastly greater plant investments than in the early days. Oklahoma newspapers are now big business, with the costs, troubles, and rewards of big business. In 1912, Fred Logan could buy the *Morrison Transcript* for $10.00 down and a pledge to pay the rest to Po Vandament. But Elsie D. Shoemaker had to pay quite a respectable price for the paper the last time it was sold, despite the fact that fast communication and a declining rural population have shrunk Morrison and its trade area appreciably in the intervening years.

A survey of actual sale prices for newspapers twenty years ago as compared with sale figures in 1956 bears out the general assertion that the average county-seat weekly in Oklahoma has increased in value five-fold in two decades, while other weeklies and some of the smaller dailies show an even greater rise in value. It takes more than a desire for self-expression, or a personality or political faction fight to start and support the smallest newspaper these days. The combination mastheads on many of our state papers attest to local conflicts long past, where, in effect, there were losers and winners.

With improved techniques and an awareness of public service, as contrasted to purely personal motives, Oklahoma's newspapers have proved their claim to, and have earned, homestead rights in the Fourth Estate. Granted that it is less nerve-racking to attack governmental or individual indiscretions at a distance than in one's own backyard, the personal journalism which once characterized frontier newspapering in Oklahoma—when a man in that business had to be ready to back his views with hand or gun—has not died out. As late as October, 1956, the editor of the *Yukon Sun* had to defend physically his right to "notice" the threat of crime and violence in his community.

The alertness of Oklahoma newspapers in detecting actual skulduggery on the part of public officials or others has caused many defense attorneys to charge that "trial by newspaper" has prejudiced the cases of their clients.

These comments are made only to illustrate that a spirit of vigilance and a sincerity of purpose are not characteristics confined only to our pioneer papers. There has been, and continues to be, newspaper support of every worthwhile project, from community funds to medical research. Dissemination of information on agricultural matters has been widespread; and a concerted publicizing effort has in three decades pushed 4-H Club and Future Farmers of America activities in Oklahoma to national prominence. On the basis of population percentages Oklahoma has had more national winners in both youth groups than any other state in the nation. These are examples of the acceptance of editorial responsibility by the newspapers of the state, and attest the community significance of their services.

But like all other institutions for good in America, newspapers must rely upon the ability of individuals. We are not now—nor shall we ever be so long as our historical heritage of freedom has any value—ready for lifeless uniformity of news matter or faceless anonymity for those who prepare it. But editors and writers today are less widely recognized than they might be, because the mores of a people have devalued the sort of hero worship which led Marquis James to follow Temple Houston down the streets of Woodward; because the weight of population in all except the smallest towns has made it impossible for the compact, pioneer neighborhood to continue its existence; and because the newsman today is not a creature living as an adjunct to society but as an assimilated member of the general business community.

Since the arrival of the Five Civilized Tribes a century and a quarter ago in eastern Oklahoma to enrich the life of the Indian Territory, newspapers have been integral with the cultural advance of this southwestern society. Even before Indian removal, our papers had a forerunner in the *Cherokee Phoenix* of 1828 in Georgia, edited by Elias Boudinot, a Cherokee, educated first by Moravian missionaries in Georgia and later in Connecticut. This young man took the name of the noted New Jersey philanthropist of the time, which accounts for its being different from that of his brother, the Confederate Brigadier General, Stand Watie. The Cherokees were ready for a newspaper, since George Guess, or Sequoyah, had invented the Cherokee syllabary perhaps five years before.

After the Cherokees moved to Oklahoma in the 1830's, their tribally supported newspaper, renamed the *Cherokee Advocate*, was published bilingually at Tahlequah, starting September 26, 1844. It had an influence beyond the lands of the Cherokee. It was at times staunchly promotional and suspicious of the white mans' designs. William P. Ross, a Cherokee of mixed blood, educated at Princeton, was the editor. Except for some days during the Civil War and when a disastrous fire destroyed the plant, the *Advocate* was published until the dissolution of tribal government in 1906, just before statehood.

The influence of the Cherokee publication led the Creeks in 1875 to urge in intertribal council the creation of a newspaper to represent all five of the Civilized Tribes. The council would not accept the idea, so the Creeks undertook it themselves, with a printing corporation listing the names of chiefs of the Five Civilized Tribes as officers. Called the *Indian Journal*, the paper first appeared at Muskogee in May, 1876. Ross was the editor and Myron P. Roberts, a northern white, was in charge of publication. The paper had columns in both Creek and English. Not content with fighting editorially for the betterment of his race in his own area, Ross undertook the active defense of all Indians in the United States. Subsidized for a time by the tribal government, the *Indian Journal* was never financially successful. From the tribe it passed into private hands and gradually lost its characteristics as spokesman for the Indians.

In 1883 the Choctaw council appropriated money for its own newspaper, the *Indian Champion*, employing two sons of Myron Roberts as editor and publisher. Allen Wright, a former chief of the Choctaws, well educated and brilliant, was editor of the Choctaw-language section of the paper. It was published at Atoka for a little more than a year.

Indian Territory journalism, like tribal life in general, was greatly influenced by missionary zeal and guidance. The *Cherokee Messenger*, preceding the *Cherokee Advocate* by a month, began publication at the Baptist Mission in 1844. It was the first periodical published in what is now Oklahoma. Its successor, a monthly also supported by the Baptists, was called the *Indian Missionary*. Very similar in text and appearance, *Our Brother In Red* was published by the Methodists in both the Cherokee and Creek languages. Started in 1882 as a monthly, it became a weekly in 1887.

Periodicals were issued from time to time by the faculties and students of boarding schools. They were influenced and often supported in part by missionary groups. One of these was a forerunner of the *Indian Journal*. Called *Our Monthly*, it was printed at Tullahassee from 1873 to 1876 by the Robertson family. With Creek assistants and supported by the Creek Council, it was distributed free. The female contingent of the Cherokees, from their tribal seminary at Park Hill, southeast of Tahlequah, in 1854 began publication of a lively, interesting magazine of prose and poetry called *Cherokee Rose Buds*. Equally ambitious, the young men of the Cherokee seminary near by had their publication, the *Sequoyah Memorial*, which, under the masthead motto of "Truth, Justice, Freedom of Speech and Cherokee Improve-

Land of the Indians

Will Rogers Memorial, Claremore.

Frank Bosin (age 93), Anadarko.

(*above*) Owen Tah (*left*), Apache Indian and oil refinery operator.

(*below*) Bacone College, Muskogee; exclusively for the American Indian.

Dancer, Indian City, Anadarko.

ment," printed academic viewpoints by fledgling writers as well as outside news. One of the editors was Joel B. Mayes, later principal chief of the Cherokees.

These accounts are given, not as part of the necrology of our state press, nor as an essay on Oklahoma publishing in general, but because they provide some of the essential background for an understanding of Oklahoma newspapers today. Our cultural past, so brief from the standpoint of historical time—as demonstrated by the late Roy Christian's slogan, "From teepees to towers in fifty years"—has been so thoroughly obscured by the immediate requirements of daily living during two generations that few among us have taken the time to look back.

Long before statehood in 1907 there were privately printed newspapers, too. Those appearing before the roll of drumbeats in the Civil War drowned the sound of hand- or foot-cranked presses lived but a short time. At least four such papers appeared before 1861—the *Choctaw Telegraph,* founded at Doaksville in 1848; the *Choctaw Intelligencer,* started in 1850 by a white man and a native preacher; the *Chickasaw Intelligencer;* and the *Chickasaw and Choctaw Herald,* published at Tishomingo in 1858 and 1859.

As restless souls and land-hungry families came into the Territory after 1880, presses and cases of often pied type were unloaded from beneath wagon bows too, and while some of the resultant newspapers later were gone with the wind, others remained through the troubled years into the statehood scramble in the early 1900's and grew with the state after that. The *Muskogee Phoenix* was one of those, founded in 1888 by Leo E. Bennett, a white man who married a Creek woman. He made a semiweekly of the paper in 1895, and a daily in 1901. It later became the property of Tams Bixby, then of his sons Joel and Tams, Jr., and now is in the third generation of Bixby ownership. The *Indian Chieftain,* started at Vinita in 1882, was edited at different times by the Cherokees, Robert L. Owen—later one of the first United States senators from Oklahoma—William P. Ross, and John L. Adair. By 1891 the *Chieftain* passed from Indian control and influence into the ownership of white men and became an exponent of the white man's point of view.

The first attempt at a daily newspaper in Indian Territory was the *Tahlequah Telephone* in 1889, but the first one to survive to adulthood was the *Daily Chieftain* at Ardmore in 1892. The *Daily Ardmoreite,* started in 1893, became one of the leading territorial newspapers under the management of Colonel Sidney Suggs, an early exponent of improved roads. It has continued to be one of the state's influential journals during the ownership of John F. Easley, who died in 1956.

The *Lawton Constitution*, born in a tent soon after the opening of the "Big Pasture" Kiowa-Comanche lands, was managed by John Shepler, who previously had started two weeklies at Pawnee. The *Constitution*, still under the management of the Shepler family, has continually progressed until it has become one of the state's better regional papers.

The first true daily on the East Side was the *Morning Times* of Muskogee, started in 1896 with white man's money but under the editorship of a clever, gifted writer of Creek blood named Alex Posey. In time it was merged with another paper, the *Muskogee Democrat*, and continues under the name *Times-Democrat*, which came under Bixby control as companion to the *Muskogee Phoenix*.

Even in that part of the state known as Oklahoma Territory, the first papers were subject to Indian influence because they were on restricted lands. In Indian Territory to the northeast, at Pawhuska, seat of the Osage Nation, the *Indian Herald* was published from 1875 to 1878 by William McKay Dugan, the agency physician. It reflected a Quaker viewpoint, which for a time dominated Osage tribal affairs through missions. At Darlington, northwest of El Reno, seat of the Cheyenne-Arapaho agency, the *Cheyenne Transporter* appeared in December, 1879, and survived for seven years. It, too, carried the voice of the missionary from the prairie eastward, supported educational and religious work among the Indians even after it passed from mission to private control, and helped the Indian in his losing battle against the opening of the country to white settlement.

The Boomers, those adventurers who looked at Oklahoma land with longing and whose desires were whetted by David L. Payne in speech and prose, had two different newspapers from 1883 to 1886, published along the Kansas border and eagerly purchased in the coveted land at ten cents a copy. For almost a two-month period in mid-1884 the *Oklahoma Chief* was published illegally in the Cherokee Outlet, northwest of present-day Ponca City, in the Boomer village of green cottonwood shacks and tents called Rock Falls. Then the United States army, guardian of the new lands, burned the printing plant and, almost from force of habit, escorted Payne and his men back to Kansas.

The hardy folk who replaced lawless elements in the Panhandle counties, which for a time were known only as "No Man's Land," had a stubbornness about them that not only conquered natural hazards of pioneer life, but backed newspapers that fought for recognition leading to union with the Territory of Oklahoma in 1890. The first paper of this region was the *Beaver City Pioneer*, which began a brief career in June, 1886, with the admirable literary slogan: "Westward the Star of Empire Takes Its Way." Then the *Territorial Advocate* was founded at Beaver City the next year, and the *Benton County Banner* at Benton in 1888. The *Hardesty Times*, soon renamed the *Hardesty Herald*, began publication in October, 1890, in a sod house typical of the region then. But editor Richard Briggs Quinn, who nursed the *Herald* through Hardesty's days as a wide spot on the cattle trail westward and through railroad booms and a townsite exploitation could not keep Hardesty from becoming a ghost town. Quinn then helped establish the town of Guymon at a railroad switch nineteen miles to the northwest, and his paper survives today as the *Guymon Herald*.

No account of Panhandle publishing would be complete without mention of Miss Maude O. Thomas, who came to the area as a child and later became editor of the *Beaver Herald* in 1902. For twenty-one years she fought for prohibition, pleaded for woman suffrage, begged support for good roads, and absorbed twelve competitors in what was then a masculine age.

Newspapers and newspaper people made rapid entrance into the Territory with the historic run of 1889, and Guthrie became the center of journalistic activity. The *Guthrie Getup* was probably the first paper published in the new territory, but like several others, it failed to last out the first year. Frank Hilton Greer's *State Capital*, first published at Winfield, Kansas, three weeks before the Opening, shifted to the territorial capital. The *Daily News* and the *Daily Leader* survived competition. The *News* was later absorbed, but the *Leader* is still flourishing.

Guthrie in those days was the mecca for newsmen. To it came Victor and Marcellus Murdock, eventually to become the fighting editors of the *Wichita Eagle;* Frank Shellenbarger, later the editor of the Paris edition of the *New York Herald;* Corb Sarchet, Fred Wenner, Jerry Pricer, and Buck Hayden, who later had the *San Antonio Light;* and A. B. McDonald, who became a Pulitzer prize winner on the *Kansas City Star*.

In Guthrie's rival settlement, Oklahoma City, destined to become the capital after a spirited election urged upon the people by the *Daily Oklahoman*, four dailies were launched in the first year after the Run. Even before that epic event the *Oklahoma City Times* was printed at Wichita from copy written and mailed from Oklahoma City, the first issue appearing December 29, 1888. That dateline, proclaiming a city that did not exist legally, attracted attention in all parts of the United States. Subscriptions came even from foreign countries. But the editor, like Payne, found himself accompanied northward by the military. From Wichita and from Purcell, south of the disputed land, he continued erratic publication, but on June 30, 1889, he was back in Oklahoma City.

On May 9, 1889, only a few days after the Run, the *Oklahoma Times* came out of its tent and from the hands of Winfield W. and Angelo C. Scott. Because of confusion in the names, the second issue of the *Oklahoma Times* became the *Oklahoma Journal*. By June 3, 1889, it was a daily. By the end of that year it bought its competition and the *Oklahoma City Times-Journal* started its course of ownership and growth which resulted in retention of the name, *Oklahoma City Times*, and its acquisition by the Oklahoma Publishing Company in 1916. It is now the state's largest afternoon daily.

The *Daily Oklahoman* and the *Evening Gazette* were started in 1889, but soon only the *Oklahoman* survived. Its staff in 1903 was augmented by the arrival of E. K. Gaylord, who became business manager and one of four owners, later acquiring the interests of the others except those of Ray Dickinson, and became principal owner, editor, and publisher of the *Daily Oklahoman*. In fifty-three years under his control, it has become one of the nation's most important papers, winner of national awards for typographical excellence, a "finishing school" for newspapermen and women, and builder of the largest Sunday circulation in the Southwest.

The *Enid Eagle* was established by Omer K. Benedict and Charles E. Hunter five days after the opening of the Cherokee Outlet. The *Eagle* and the *Enid News* today serve as outstanding examples of typical journalistic enterprise in mid-America.

Newspapers were started in Tulsa between 1900 and the advent of statehood. Tulsa boomed from a cowtown on the Frisco to a community trading site, and then paced the burgeoning oil industry to a "boom" era in which it could proudly proclaim itself "Oil Capital of the World." Its weeklies became dailies, the *Tulsa World* retaining its original title while the *Tulsa Tribune* became successor to the *Tulsa Democrat*. In civic and journalistic achievement these Tulsa newspapers are today on a comparable basis with metropolitan contemporaries in other parts of the country.

From Oklahoma papers in our era have gone out some of the nation's top newsmen and women—Jack Bell, head of the Associated Press senate staff in Washington; Paul Miller, manager of the Gannett chain in New York; Dick Pearce, novelist and editorial writer of the *San Francisco Examiner*; Walker Stone, editor in chief of the Scripps-

Howard Alliance; Ernie Hill, foreign correspondent for the *Chicago Daily News;* Inez Robb, Sigrid Arne, and many others.

That word "country" commonly applied to weeklies is a badge of pride. Like the nickname of "Cowboy" fastened on him in college, Gerald Curtin of the *Watonga Republican,* for example, can take pride in the historical past of his county-seat weekly. It was that paper which Thompson D. Ferguson, later to be appointed by Theodore Roosevelt as governor of Oklahoma Territory, started in 1892. Ferguson came to the bleak prairie from Sedan, Kansas, driving a covered wagon loaded with type and a press, while Mrs. Ferguson, in another wagon, brought household goods and her two small children. One of them, Walter, beginning his career on the *Guthrie Leader,* became widely known as a newspaperman himself, and his wife gained equal prominence in the profession. It was the elder Mrs. Ferguson's life and times, changed slightly and shifted in locale through literary license, that became the basis for Edna Ferber's great novel *Cimarron.*

Some enterprising novelist could make an equally good story of the *Marietta Monitor.* In late Indian Territory days Willis Choate was editor and publisher. Choate died and his widow, left with the paper as the principal estate, ran it while Willis, Jr. was growing up and going to school. Shortly before her death he took over the paper, but he too died before the usual allotment of time, and his wife, Wilma, now is operating the paper for the benefit of their son, Willis III.

For professional improvement, the Indian Territory Press Association was organized at Muskogee in 1888; in 1892 the Oklahoma Territory Press Association was formed at Kingfisher. In 1906 the two were merged into the Oklahoma Press Association. Its members today include all 55 of the state's dailies and 223 of the weeklies. This is all but two of those eligible to join under legal requirements. There are two yearly meetings of the Association, and in its office in the Biltmore hotel, Oklahoma City, it has available any type of statistical data on Oklahoma's newspapers.

LITERATURE

By Edith Copeland

Literature in Oklahoma, if the word be used in any but the most restricted sense, includes far too much for detailed discussion in limited space. This survey can mention only a few outstanding, representative names. When Mary Hays Marable and Elaine Boylan compiled *A Handbook of Oklahoma Writers* in 1939, the comprehensive mention alone of works and authors required more than three hundred printed pages. In eighteen years many new works have been added and many new writers have come on the scene.

Because the state has a unique history of which its writers are acutely conscious, the current of historical writing, including contemporary records, is most quickly apparent. Many writers have recorded the significant events they observed here since Thomas C. Batey, the Quaker missionary to the Kiowas and Comanches at Fort Sill, wrote *Life and Adventures of a Quaker Among the Indians* in 1875.

Contemporary observation of early Oklahoma in uncounted volumes received publication only in early-day newspapers. Frederick S. Barde of Guthrie, a newspaper correspondent during the state's formative years, left his valuable scrapbooks to the Oklahoma Historical Association. They hold columns of firsthand observations. Others are preserved in the unpublished memoirs collected as a federal writers' project, directed in Oklahoma by one of our foremost historians, Grant Foreman. Oklahoma newspapermen, conscious of the value of such records, organized in 1893 the State Historical Society for their preservation. *Chronicles of Oklahoma,* its quarterly magazine edited by Muriel H. Wright, herself a writer of Oklahoma history, is filled with such accounts.

Many memoirs record the beginnings of towns and cities—Stillwater, Lawton, Kingfisher, Oklahoma City, and others. They have been gathered by individuals and by groups and organizations. The origin of place names, Indian traditions and legends connected with streams and mountains, lakes and springs, and certain localities have greatly interested Oklahoma writers.

Treasured in collections of Americana concerning this area are recollections of roundup days and of early wolf hunts; of what it was like to travel without roads or maps or mechanized vehicles; to ford streams and herd cattle and brave the northers; to drive miles for a doctor that he might perform an emergency operation on a kitchen table. They recall the early political feuds, the bitter strife over political theories and practice, and the land quarrels that ended in death for some, prison for others. They tell how men and women managed to make a living while they broke the land and waited for crops through dry spells and late freezes, and at the same time built their institutions—their schools and churches and businesses.

Some few tell what it meant to be a woman in that time, with social standards and mores and traditions vital to maintain under such difficult conditions; how women lived in dugouts yet upheld standards of housekeeping and of family life; how more than one of them operated a salt mine or a farm or a newspaper or another business enterprise, while the men sought varied ways of making cash income, and looked after politics. Such records are constantly coming to light. Individuals who experienced those days are still writing the story; an account of life in Woodward, Oklahoma, in the century's beginning was published in 1956. Two lately written memoirs of much more recent times tell what it means to be an Oklahoman at war on foreign soil.

Three circumstances stand out clearly in early Oklahoma's foreground. They have been reiterated again and again, but no understanding of our literature is possible unless one keeps in mind those three events. They were the conquest of the Indian, the advancement of the frontier, and the coming of law and order. All three have plainly marked our poetry, our fiction, our nonfiction. A fourth, of recent date, is the state's progress and development, with increasing involvement in national and international affairs. During the third decade of the century our writers became suddenly articulate concerning this fourth factor.

A large body of Oklahoma writing centers around the Indian. The University of Oklahoma Press, which has justly been called "the hard core" of literature in Oklahoma, was founded in 1928 to extend regional expression. This was the ideal of William Bennett Bizzell, at that time president of the University of Oklahoma, who brought Joseph A. Brandt to establish the program which Savoie Lottinville has directed since 1938. In 1932, the Press began publication of *The Civilization of the American Indian Series,* now embracing forty-six volumes.

These volumes tell of many phases of Indian life and culture—the policies of Spanish governors, and of a later government which removed the Five Civilized Tribes from long-established homes where they had property and ties of many kinds; of the sad journey made by those tribes, forced out of an accustomed settled world into a wilderness where nothing was and all must be made anew. They tell of their governments and their leaders, their hunters and their chiefs. Here are the warlike Plains Indians, who caused the civilized tribes great fear; here are the hunters of the Labrador Peninsula, and the Oglala Sioux. Here are the Hopis and the Navajos, the Osages and the Cheyennes, the story of the Maya civilization, and of the Utes and the settlement of Colorado. They tell a far-flung saga.

Here are the stories of Indians with European contacts, with the white man's education and the red man's traditions. Here, too, are volumes concerned with white men who went among the Indians, as traders or missionaries or agents of the white man's government. The records talk of what they saw and experienced.

The authors of these books, and others, have helped revise a concept. Leaving the "noble savage" of the romantic view, and the extreme of hatred engendered by warfare, we have come to know the Indian as a human being, with problems which he attempts to solve in normal human ways. Through these books we know him as a man with a living to make, desperate when his chief source of sustenance vanished with the buffalo, who refused to believe a cruel fate and prayed to his gods for means of escape from unthinkable disaster. We know him as one who treasured the old ways, and took on change with difficulty and pain and conflict, repudiating what tradition told him was mean and small. We know him as a hunter, a fisherman, a potter, a silversmith. Or, we see in the Indian, not a savage, but a woman whose initiative and industry and skill brought better living for a whole tribe—María, whose story has been told by Alice Marriott in one of her best-loved books, *María, the Potter of San Ildefonso*.

A tremendous amount of factual information is offered in this series. An example is Muriel H. Wright's *A Guide to the Indian Tribes of Oklahoma*, dealing with the sixty-seven tribes associated with Oklahoma. Location, numbers, linguistic stock, origin of tribal names, ceremonials and dances, and much of their contemporary life and culture are recorded here.

In 1939 the University of Oklahoma Press inaugurated a second great series, *The American Exploration and Travel Series*, now containing twenty-three volumes of edited memoirs.

Prepared for publication in part by Oklahomans, these tell of the part the gold-seekers and the traders played in forcing the frontier to recede before the advance of civilization. Contrasts to the present encompassed here equal the fantasies of any fiction. Where today oil flows through pipelines and freight travels by air, less than one hundred years ago travelers experienced the intricacies of caravan travel and the difficulties of camp life on the plains in order to trade dry goods and hardware for silver and mules. In spots where now industrial smokestacks cloud and circle populous cities, travelers lost their way and lived on roots and bark for food.

Notes in the record carry a motif of universal, timeless human activity. Political pressures got roads across the plains and military protection for the gold-seekers. Encounters and conflicts with the Plains Indians, who regarded themselves as the legitimate owners of the prairie, protesting the presence of intruders, resulted sometimes in warfare, sometimes in palavers, conferences, treaties, and gifts made to obtain good will. We read of romances and marriages, births and deaths among the travelers on those western journeys. We see the tenacity of the men who struggled through the Cross Timbers, the discouragement of those who hunted work because lack of money forced them to delay their journey, the ebullience of those taking a last fling at the pleasures of civilization in Santa Fé before they headed for the wilderness.

Here is the army, represented by Captain Randolph B. Marcy and Captain G. B. McClellan, reporting on the exploration of the Red River's headwaters, and Lieutenant A. W. Whipple, exploring for a railway route from Fort Smith to Los Angeles, seven years before the Civil War. Adventure lies in the stories of Joseph Reddeford Walker in Arizona, and William Bollaert in early Texas, and the achievements of Zebulon Montgomery Pike in his explorations. These volumes tell of even earlier conditions on the northern frontier of New Spain, as experienced by Teodoro de Croix during the years 1776–83.

The two series mentioned form only part of the great body of historical writing by Oklahomans. There is also much work in political history; and there are biographies of men who helped make the history of the Southwest. Some of these are volumes in the *Civilization of the American Indian Series*. There are others. William E. Livezey's *Mahan on Sea Power* won the John H. Dunning Award from the American Historical Association for the outstanding book of 1947 on American history, and Fayette Copeland's *Kendall of the Picayune* was chosen by the Texas Institute of Letters as the best book about Texas in 1943.

There is the story of E. W. Marland, told by John Joseph Mathews. Marland's career, ranging from Pittsburgh to the University of Michigan, through West Virginia and on to the Cherokee Outlet, paralleled the transmutation of an area known chiefly for the Ponca Indian Reservation and the 101 Ranch into today's refinery center. It covered a unique period of Oklahoma's growth and cultural and political history.

Oklahoma's historians have concerned themselves with affairs far beyond the region. They have explored phases of the American Revolution, of the Lincoln story, of our relations with the Philippines. We have studies of Alaska, Russia, Turkey, Iran, Spain, and of international politics in Mexico. Closely related to the study of history is that of government. Oklahomans have written of national diplomacy, the national senate, congressional and presidential elections, and primary elections in the South. They have informed readers on national economic life in many of its aspects, and have given attention to matters of local government and finance as well.

Oklahoma, lying geographically almost in the center of the nation, is also a center for the development and exploration of ideas. There is nothing new about this. In the beginning, every Oklahoman came from some place else. He had twofold interests: he wanted news from home, and he wanted to tell what he found in his new surroundings. The result has been a population of eager, outgoing personality, zealous to know what the rest of the world thinks, equally zealous to communicate its own ideas. Within the state, as newcomers and the not-so-recently arrived, former citizens of almost every European country are contributing ideas, as they have done during the half century. This fact strikes forcefully on the mind when one notes the educational backgrounds of our authors, who have come not only from almost every noted school in our nation, but from those of many European nations as well.

Even before the University of Oklahoma Press was founded, Oklahoma took a most forward-looking step in the literary world when in 1927 Roy Temple House and several colleagues published a thirty-two page pamphlet devoted chiefly to French and German books. Coeditor Kenneth Kaufman, also the literary editor of the *Daily Oklahoman*, later became managing editor of *Books Abroad*. This quarterly has just completed thirty years of publication. Professor House, editor emeritus of *Books Abroad*, is one of the state's earliest cosmopolitan citizens. Born in Nebraska and educated in Ohio and Michigan, he came to Oklahoma in 1905. The author and editor of a number of books, he wrote for that early Oklahoma publication *Sturms' Magazine*, as well as for the *Virginia Quarterly Review* and more general magazines of national circulation; but he is best known for the founding of *Books Abroad*.

Ernst Eric Noth, now editor of the international quarterly, had a long literary career behind him in Europe when he came to Norman in 1949. Of his twelve books written in English, French, and German, four are novels. They deal with the serious issues that Germans faced during the Nazi regime—the divisions of families, the disintegration of the universities, the problem of exile for the politically dissenting.

Now, much more than formerly, Oklahoma's cosmopolitanism is a matter of exchange. Oklahoma-trained writers go constantly from every corner of the state to every corner of the globe. From cities all over the world they write political comment, report the news, send their novels back to the states for publication, and see them translated and published in many languages.

Oklahoma pioneers were a practical people. They had to be, in order to survive. Conditions were hard, and citizens had a common shared ideal: to improve everything fast, for themselves but especially for their children. They built schools even before they built homes, for the young must have a better preparation for life than their parents had. The concept of what that preparation must include has constantly enlarged. The pioneers welcomed every means to a faster, better, more profitable way to do everything. They expected their children to learn more than they themselves knew. They demanded for them a preparation which would produce competence above all, in their chosen fields.

From this attitude of expecting improvements to come about in every phase of daily living, Oklahomans have (especially since the thirties) produced a vast amount of communicated practical knowledge. They have specialists in soil erosion and flood control, in public health and the control of various diseases; and in political and economic problems of a practical nature. The state has writers who are experts in finance and business management and in farming. An Oklahoman has made a study of American pipelines, their industrial structure, economic status, and legal implications. Another has written of the fundamentals of reservoir engineering. Others write in such highly specialized fields as letter writing in its many applications, in public relations, and in sports—including football. Those at work in all these fields and more have communicated their knowledge and viewpoints, which have been eagerly received by the readers of their books.

In a state where oil has been the magic substance that has produced so much material progress, authors have written much about various phases of the oil industry, both practical and theoretical. Carl Coke Rister's *Oil! Titan of the Southwest,* with its maps, charts, and statistical tables, is a comprehensive history of the industry in the region. We have a petroleum dictionary, a study of petroleum production, and the record of a half century which W. L. Connelly spent as a trouble-shooter for the Sinclair Oil Company.

In agriculture, Oklahoma has had both remarkable development and acute problems; and that industry has consequently had much attention from our writers. The fundamental matter of co-operation with nature in the handling of soil and water and plant life has been considered from many points of view—those of the historian, the scientist, the conservationist, and the practical farmer. In giving such knowledge wide dissemination, the newspapers of the state serve a vital function. Such information makes up many of the columns that come daily and weekly from the presses of Oklahoma.

Our many specialists in the more abstract sciences also communicate their findings in a volume greatly increased since the 1930's. A larger part of this knowledge appears in monographs and printed reports and journals than in bound books, but it is preserved and available for use. Our scientists are publishing in every field—geography, geology, chemistry, physics, social psychology, medicine, and the rest. In genetics we have an outstanding authority whose work has been translated for publication in German, Spanish, Russian, and Chinese.

This is not to imply that all of Oklahoma's writing lies in the fields of history or of practical or applied science. We have philosophers, at least one of whom is published both in this country and in many languages in Europe, and writers in various fields of theory, educational, religious, and social, and in work exploring the relationship between education and society. Among our authors are recorders of folklore, including the folklore of the oil fields, of the pioneers, and of those who lived in rural areas during our earlier periods.

If we have less published poetry, and drama, which is so closely kin to poetry, than we had when Kenneth Kaufman surveyed literature in Oklahoma for this guidebook sixteen years ago, that seems to be the only field where publishing has declined. At mid-century we find ourselves in an age somewhat prosaic, very much in haste, not delicately tuned to the mysteries, the intricacies and allusions, and the timeless quality that poetry contains. This is perhaps the more true when we remember that Lynn Riggs, whose plays (notably *Green Grow the Lilacs,* upon which *Oklahoma!* was based) were almost pure poetry, wrote a decade and a half to two decades ago.

Another change has come about in these sixteen years. A large number of our writers are now busy anonymously, writing for movies and television. At least two of our early, most promising novelists deserted the printed page for these media, and many of our new writers are never known by name. Others, however, regard movie and television sales as pleasant and profitable by-products of their work, with the writing of books as their most important business.

Not for a good many years did Oklahomans write many important books for children. In 1935, Kenneth Kaufman complained bitterly of the scarcity of our native juvenile literature. Since then some of our finest writers have concentrated their work in that field. Some have interpreted the most meaningful and beautiful and strange among Indian customs and legends and traditions. Still others have presented with scientific accuracy the mysteries of bird, insect, and animal life in beautifully illustrated, well-written, well-printed texts. Some have written biographies; they have told the stories of Lucille Mulhall, Oklahoma's famous cowgirl, of our humorist Will Rogers, and Sequoyah, the great inventor of the Cherokee syllabary, and others.

The fields of music and of literary criticism were latecomers to our plains. We feel a faint glow of state pride in the great work *Main Currents in American Thought,* but Vernon Louis Parrington left the campus of the University of Oklahoma nineteen years before his first volume appeared. Not until the late 1930's did many of our writers concern themselves with literature and its analysis and interpretation, or with writing about music. Now, we have from Oklahoma writers books dealing with James Russell Lowell, Nathaniel Hawthorne, the Lambs, the Alcotts, Mark Twain, John Milton. A study has been made of imagism in modern poetry, and another of criticism in America. At least two writers have compiled critical bibliographies. Scholars have examined the influence and following of Edmund Spenser and Alexander Pope, and the work of William Hazlitt. One writer, whom it is true Oklahoma can claim only through brief residence here, has explored the modern novel in America, American writing in the postwar decade, and the "little magazines."

Translations have been made of Michel Barbi's *Life of Dante,* and the memoirs of the musician Alfredo Casella. The librettos of *Carmen, Lakmé,* and *Rigoletto* have been rendered into English. *Music, an Art and a Business* by Paul Carpenter is a keen analysis not only of music but of our cultural fabric. He saw clearly the present situation of music as a successful business, diminished as an art because of widespread factors. But he, who spent his life in improving the quality of Oklahoma's music, believed that cultural change must in the end submerge a frontier prejudice which saw the arts as time-wasting, effeminate, and expensive. The belief and the faith apply to more of the arts than to music alone.

Sixteen years ago, Kenneth Kaufman described Oklahoma's fiction as "sporadic and of very uneven quality." Today, he might offer it more praise. Few states of comparable population can boast of more short stories and novels published in books and magazines. Credit for this increase should go in part to the stimulus given professional writing in courses taught in the School of Journalism at the University of Oklahoma. They are climaxed annually by a summer short course directed by Walter S. Campbell (Stanley Vestal), who has written twenty-four books and edited four others. He has told the story of the fighting Sioux, Sitting Bull and Chief White Bull; of General Custer and Kit Carson, Buffalo Bill and the mountain men Joe Meek, Jim Bridger, and Bigfoot Wallace. Among his books are volumes about Dodge City, the short-grass country he knows so well, and the Missouri River and the people who have lived in its valley.

Working with him in the department and helping to direct the short course are Foster-Harris and Dwight V. Swain, each a prolific writer in more than one field. The speakers they bring here are Oklahomans who have gained reputation as writers. Since 1938 they have come annually, except during two war years, to a place where each has ties. From all over the nation, each year some of them come to share their vision, their technical knowledge, their enthusiasm for their chosen work. The conference is a place where writers meet editors, listen to those who have carved out places for themselves, and talk shop. Oklahoma's unique history holds the imagination of many of them. They feel the glamor of the Old West and the challenge of trying to re-create it. They wish to portray the sweep and power of pioneer days, the intense ambition of the newcomers, their land hunger, their driving will to accomplish quickly more and yet more tasks, their desire to achieve more and possess more and conquer the land and the elements. This story, writers for long will try to tell.

The dramatic, colorful days of the outlaws, the feuds between the cattlemen and the settlers, the land openings, all these have inspired Oklahoma novelists as well as many from outside the state. More than one has tried to picture the wild fantastic days of the boom towns and the coming of oil. At least two have written of the searing effects of poverty. John Joseph Mathews explored in serious fiction the impact of new money upon an unformed society. We have had novels of adventure, and of the conquest of the air. William Brinkley's satiric war novel, *Don't Go Near the Water,* went to the top of the list of national best sellers almost at once after publication in 1956, and held a place there for months. John Hunt's recent novel of unusual excellence, *Generations of Men,* is concerned with a deeply moving problem, enriched with the meeting of traditions and ways of life strange to each other.

But we have had few serious novels which explore our present, not our past. Yet to be written is the great novel which will show the impact upon individuals in a society recently and completely rural of the change to an industrial, urban world. No Oklahoman's novel has yet traced the penetrating fingers of politics through the layers of state organization, nor has one explored the distribution of wealth and its effect upon our contemporary society. None shows the striking contrasts between the fluid and the rooted elements of our culture, and the impact of those contrasts upon individuals. The great novel of oil has yet to be written.

Nineteenth-century fiction, as written by women, reflected the war between the sexes, with woman the loser, deeply dissatisfied with her situation. In that perennial conflict some contemporary fiction indicates that men today are as much displeased as women were a century ago. But no novel, so far, from Oklahoma indicates deep dissatisfaction with this or any other phase of contemporary social structure. Our best writers have not seriously concerned themselves with the inadequate or underprivileged groups or individuals of our society; we have no powerful novel questioning the commonly accepted values in any field. None has seriously explored grave social problems. We have had no significant novel of manners.

Some critics hold the theory that such work can come only from an old and well-established society, where the mold is set, the layers are distinct, the social classes plainly marked. If this theory has merit, the fluid condition of our society, which has produced so much valuable work in nonfiction, works against us in the field of fiction. Whatever the cause, the novel, as the work of Oklahomans, until now lies chiefly in the field of entertainment. In a sense, so far as our fiction writers are concerned, we remain an island, unique in our traditions and constant in upholding them, satisfied with the status quo. The formerly accepted purpose of the novel—to warn, to question, to stir the field of controversy, to point abuses and perhaps suggest their remedy—is left to our economists and educators, our writers of editorials, and our political commentators.

Some of the most valuable contributions Oklahomans have made to the world of books fit into none of the mentioned categories. *The Look of the Old West*, by Foster-Harris, describes and pictures all the minutiae of romantic days in the region. We have *Western Vacations* by Kent Ruth, a comprehensive travel book concerned with the contemporary West. Art and science combine in *Mexican Birds*, a handsome volume by George Miksch Sutton. Three outstanding volumes by Oscar Brousse Jacobson reproduce the art of Oklahoma Indians and trace Indian costume in North America from 1564–1950. The latter two have introductions and notes by Professor Jacobson and Jeanne D'Ucel, whose *Berber Art* reproduces selected objects decorated and used by the Berbers, and tells much about those strange and fascinating people.

Taken as a whole, literature in Oklahoma has made rather amazing progress during half a century, and the rich mine offered by our contemporary culture may well yield a comparable growth in the fifty years to come. It stands now on a firm, broad, comprehensive base from which more pinnacles can grow.

ARCHITECTURE AND ART

By John O'Neil

The first buildings in Oklahoma were temporary—hastily erected and short lived. Towns which grew up, seemingly overnight, along the pathways set down by wagon trails and the railroad had the usual false fronts, frame construction, and boxlike shape characteristic of most frontier structures in the West. No native style developed which tended to moderate climatic extremes, the hot wind and sun of summer, and the severe, if usually brief, winter storms. The split-log house was common, the timbers nailed together and the often wide crevices filled in with clay. Cheap construction made possible by the sawmill led to board shacks of one room divided by a partition. However, in the timberless western part of the state, the dugout, consisting of low earthen walls enclosing a cellar, was the usual habitation. As the cities grew in size and wealth, buildings were erected for more permanency, but forms were still borrowed mixtures, except in the South and Southwest where a few Indian leaders of means built more solidly and generously; these were frequently homes with high ceilings and broad porches, the size varying from eight to fifteen rooms. There were few great estates or outright pretentious buildings. In the early 1920's many large farms were in existence in north-central Oklahoma. These often had big houses and barns, undistinguished architecturally, and severe and stern in appearance.

There was no conformity in domestic building in the period between the two world wars, and very little awareness of international changes in architectural concepts. The Richard Lloyd Jones home in Tulsa, designed by Frank Lloyd Wright in 1929, was the first significant domestic structure in the state. Originally observed with somewhat puzzled interest by the Tulsa public, it has, in more enlightened days, come to be a landmark and a turning point in regional architectural thought. A more recent Wright house (1956) in Bartlesville, with warm red brick walls surmounted by a copper roof, is built for protection from dust, wind, sun, and snow while yet remaining charming and spacious in plan. With four separate living elements clustered about the entrance loggia, the building is masterfully laid out, providing both freedom and privacy. In spite of the growth of builders "additions" and "developments" in the larger cities, there have been a number of thoughtfully planned, well-designed homes constructed, particularly in the period after World War II.

The Kamphoefner House (1940) in Norman was one of the first homes in the area designed with an open scheme, including indoor-outdoor living accommodations and sun control in the roof overhangs. The architect, Henry Kamphoefner, then a faculty member at the University of Oklahoma, conceived a simple and direct plan that was to become influential in later structures. The Vahlberg House (Vahlberg-Palmer-Vahlberg, architects), built in 1951 in Oklahoma City, is similar in its trend toward large, uncluttered areas, and its sensitivity to setting, in this case a wooded acre. The Harris House in Yukon, designed by Richard Kuhlman, is remarkable for its comfort in the tropical heat of an Oklahoma summer without the employment of artificial air conditioning. By using the principle of warm air rising, and providing an air escape through the roof opening, a breeze is created in hot weather even when none exists outside. This pleasant house encloses garden oases of caladium and fern.

One of the first post–World War II houses of merit was the Ledbetter (now the Taylor) house in Norman, designed in long, extended horizontals by Bruce Goff. The structure employs large areas of glass, an inclined roof resting on a serpentine rock wall, and corrugated metal storage areas in striking visual patterns.

The Bavinger House, five miles east of Norman, begun in 1950 and completed in 1955, was also designed by Goff. With supporting walls of red rock accented with green glass, it rises from the earth in a spiral without interior walls around a center mast that is also a hub for stainless steel cables that help to carry the weight of the roof. Living and sleeping areas are upholstered bowls projected at varying heights from the center core. Tropical plants follow the first segment of the spiral wall, moving about an open pool on the ground level.

The Boston Avenue Methodist Church in Tulsa (1926), an early Goff design, was one of the first ecclesiastical structures in the region to win national attention for its originality and freshness of approach. The Catholic Church of Christ the King (1929), designed by Barry Byrne, and the Jewish Reformed Temple Israel are other meritorious Tulsa churches. One of Goff's most recent and effective ecclesiastical designs is for the Hopewell Baptist Church in Edmond. Its form, close to the tepee, was built by the parishioners, many of them oil-field workers—welders and riggers who used drill stem and line pipe that they were already accustomed to in oil-derrick structures. Seating four hundred people, it has outside trusses supporting a circular nave.

The impressive new (1956) addition to St. Luke's Methodist Church in Oklahoma City (Coston, Frankfurt, and Short, architects) has a 180-foot carillon tower and a circular sanctuary seating eighteen hundred people. The sanctuary contains eight stained glass windows designed by Emil Frei of Saint Louis. A more audacious design, in the same city, is the recently completed First Christian Church (R. Duane Conner, architect), a group of structures which includes a soaring and slender campanile, a separate main building constructed of reinforced concrete poured in the shape of a large dome, and a circular, metal-shuttered auditorium.

Some of the best architecture in the state has developed with the need for new schools and expansion of existing buildings. The architectural group of Caudill, Rowlett, Scott and Associates has been responsible for many of the better designs. Their new (1955) addition to the Bartlesville elementary school is a four-classroom structure which is spacious, airy, and light. The plan for the Senior High School, which includes a meeting place for students, exhibition area, and lounge, is economical and uncluttered. It contains an auditorium of 1,100 seats which is also used as a town meeting hall. The same firm designed the Roosevelt and Wilson schools (1954) at Miami. Built at the same time, using the same materials and the same type of structure, with dining, assembly and recreational areas, and with wide central halls, these are examples of highly efficient planning. With careful attention to details, such as the luminous ceiling and continuous skylight at Wilson, they sometimes achieve a classic and austere beauty. Both buildings use evenly distributed natural light and large overhanging roofs that provide protection from sun glare without the necessity of blinds or shades at the windows. The most impressive achievement of the firm, however, is the high school at Norman, which has received widespread and favorable national publicity.

The Price Tower (1955) in Bartlesville, a combined office and apartment building, was designed by Frank Lloyd Wright and is a development of ideas originally conceived in 1929 for a project for St. Mark's Tower in New York City. Rising nineteen floors above the surrounding prairie, it covers a quarter of a block in a city without other tall buildings. The construction is reinforced concrete with four central concrete shafts from which spring the cantilevered floors; all exposed surfaces except the supporting structure itself are copper, stamped with a design planned by the architect. Each of the eight luxurious apartments contained within the building has a balcony and most of the furniture throughout is built in. The richness and variety of patterns of the tower, changing subtly from each view, are a direct expression of the interior space.

The Main Library building in Oklahoma City, completed in 1953, is a reinforced-concrete structure entirely without interior supporting walls. Unusual features of the building include a 280-seat auditorium, one which is used for programs devoted to art, music, and drama, and an "Auto-Library" drive-up service window and book return.

Luxury resort lodges have been built in state parks since 1949; these buildings, although not brilliant architectural achievements, are nevertheless well planned, spacious, and elegant. Most have swimming pools, auditoriums, and restaurants in an informal, holiday atmosphere. The lodges at Texoma and Sequoyah state parks are particularly noteworthy; the former was designed by Don Gumerson and the latter by Black and West. Other new lodges have been built in the Quartz Mountain, Roman Nose and Lake Murray state parks; a 47-room structure is the next to be constructed at Lake Tenkiller.

Architectural instruction in the state is given by the two largest collegiate institutions. The School of Architecture at the University of Oklahoma offers two courses of study leading toward professional degrees. The school is accredited by the National Architectural Accrediting Board and by the Engineering Council for Professional Development. Opportunities are offered for specialized training in city and regional planning, the nature of materials, presentation techniques, and other fields. Students are encouraged to understand great buildings of the past or present without becoming imitative designers. With a teaching staff of eleven, three hundred major students, and lectures and exhibitions by visiting architects, the school has long been the most influential one in the region.

At Oklahoma Agricultural and Mechanical College at Stillwater, the School of Architecture and Applied Art is composed of the departments of architecture, architectural engineering, interior design, and art. The department has well-equipped studios, lecture, and drafting rooms. The problem method of instruction is followed, with school problems given to supplement those issued by the Beaux-Arts Institute of Design. Student work is judged in competition with other schools of architecture.

Although architecture in Oklahoma has little tradition to overcome, the growth of cities and towns has been dramatically swift, and therefore not always planned. The inept, the awkward, the transplanted copy, all are giving way, under the influence of a few architects of vision and courage, to new forms which are more expressive of time and place in a dynamic society.

ART

Art in Oklahoma has changed rapidly from its early beginnings in artist-reporters such as George Catlin (1794–1872) and John Stanley (1814–72), who illustrated the manners and customs of the Indian tribes at mid-nineteenth century, to the present condition of painters and sculptors, residents of the larger cities or members of college faculties, who are working in styles influenced by international leaders in the arts; the works of these artists have little or no identification of the region in which they were produced.

Perhaps the best known of the artist-reporters was Frederick Remington (1861–1918), who stayed at Fort Reno in the 1880's and managed to paint, sculpt, and write his interpretations of frontier life. His work is more interesting historically than it is valuable artistically, making as it did unique recordings of an era otherwise visually lost. Little was done other than amateur painting until after World War I, when the art departments both at the University of Oklahoma and at the Oklahoma Agricultural and Mechanical College became prominent centers for professional artists, who, through their own creative work and teaching, helped to set higher artistic standards throughout the state.

Although some art instruction was given in the mission schools as early as 1889, there was no supervisor of art in the public schools until 1905. Father Gregory Gerrer came to the state in 1908 and became the director of the art department at St. Gregory's College in Shawnee. A painter in his own right, he established the first state museum with a collection of items of historical and artistic interest. The first art instructor at the University of Oklahoma began teaching in 1910. At this time Nellie Shepherd, the first state artist who did original work of any merit, was painting and exhibiting her gentle impressionist landscapes.

Nan Sheets of Oklahoma City at this time became known as a generous sponsor of the arts who gave private instruction and opened her studio to loan exhibitions. This was the nucleus of activity which eventually, with Mrs. Sheets as director, grew into the Oklahoma Art Center in downtown Oklahoma City. Still inadequately housed, the Center is planning a new building which will meet the requirements of a large and growing city.

The influence of art schools in the state has been profound. Through instruction by professional artists, they have set critical standards that have had an effect on the reception of art by the public, in the training of teachers for public schools and colleges, and in the planting of a cultural awareness in graduates who have become established creative artists and others who have, in their turn, encouraged artists of collected art.

The School of Art at the University of Oklahoma, established in 1911, has ten full-time teachers. Both bachelor's and master's degrees are offered. Professional training is given in painting, sculpture and design, together with a program in the preparation of teachers for the public schools. Exhibitions by senior students are held throughout the school year; many graduates and former students, such as Stanley Hess, John Freed, Dana Gibson, and Lee Mullican, have become artists of importance or influential teachers; others are designers for commerce and industry. The art department of the Oklahoma Agricultural and Mechanical College was established in 1891. Its large staff gives training in a variety of fields. The University of Tulsa, founded in 1898, supports an active department working in all phases of the pictorial arts. Other collegiate institutions in the state offering courses or degrees in art are: East Central State College at Ada; Oklahoma College for Women at Chickasha; Southeastern State College at Durant; Northeastern State College at Tahlequah; Phillips University at Enid; Oklahoma City University; Oklahoma Baptist University at Shawnee; and Northeastern Oklahoma Agricultural and Mechanical College at Miami.

Museums of art or private collections of painting and sculpture, as would be expected in a young state, are neither numerous in Oklahoma nor wealthy in important works of the past or present. Most museums in the area have emphasized collections that are primarily historical and regional; few have yet been able to build up permanent collections that embrace significant world art. The Museum of Art at the University of Oklahoma, established in 1921, has galleries for traveling and permanent exhibitions. Creative work by local and regional artists, as well as circulating exhibitions brought from national sources, are included in the program. The Museum owns a collection of contemporary American paintings, among them Ben Shahn's *Renascence*, Jack Levine's *The Horse*, Abraham Rattner's *Yellow Table*, Georgia O'Keefe's *Cos Cob*, and Stuart Davis' *Waterfront*, also several hundred prints, American Indian paintings, a collection of Oriental art, and a group of Greco-Buddhist sculpture from Gandhara. (Open daily 8 to 12; 1 to 5; Saturdays 9 to 12; Sundays 2 to 5.)

Philbrook Art Center, 2727 South Rockford Road in Tulsa, was established in 1939 as a center for exhibiting art of all periods. Collections cover European and American paintings and graphics, as well as Indian paintings and crafts. Unique in the state is their important Kress collection of Italian Renaissance paintings, in which may be found the excellent Giovanni Bellini *Portrait of a Bearded Man*, an Andrea Mantegna *Mother and Child*, a Canaletto *View of Dresden from the Right Side of the Elbe* and a typical Luca della Robbia polychrome glaze terracotta. Each spring the center sponsors a competitive exhibition of work by Oklahoma artists. There is a regular program of adult's and children's classes, as well as lectures, gallery talks, and films. (Open 10 to 5, Sunday 1 to 5, Tuesday evening 7:30 to 9:30. Closed Monday.)

The Oklahoma Art Center in the Municipal Auditorium in Oklahoma City began in 1936 as a WPA project and was incorporated in 1945. The emphasis is placed on regional art activities rather than acquisitions. The Center is host to the Association of Oklahoma Artists' Annual Exhibition in the fall. Circulating exhibits are held September through June, with a full calendar of lectures, films, and gallery tours. (Open 10 to 5 daily, Sunday 2 to 5. Closed Monday.)

The Thomas Gilcrease Foundation in Tulsa has a large collection of frontier and Indian art, including some of the best work of Catlin, Russell, and Remington. Established in 1942, the galleries are free to the public daily. Outstanding paintings are Joseph Becker's *First Train of the Central Pacific* and Edward Hicks' *William Penn's Treaty with the Delaware Indians.*

The art gallery in connection with St. Gregory's College in Shawnee has a collection of over two hundred paintings, among which are found a *Madonna* by Estaban Murillo, *Archimedes* by José de Ribera, *Penitent Peter* by Guido Reni, and a Thomas Sully portrait.

There are many individual artists who have been trained in Oklahoma, and live and work in the state; others have become residents, usually in collegiate towns, after having received art instruction elsewhere. Several long-established state artists have built substantial national reputations; they exhibit widely, and are represented in important public and private collections. No style, either unique in the region or an outgrowth of group philosophy, is predominant.

Artists maintaining studios at Stillwater are Dale McKinney, a consistent award winner who works in oil, water color, and serigraphy; Elinor Evans, whose very lyrical paintings are dependent upon a fine color sense; Doel Reed, nationally known for his handsome aquatints, and with a distinguished history as a painter whose work has been acquired for important museum collections; J. Jay McVicker, painter, etcher, serigrapher, and sculptor, an artist who has received numerous awards and purchase prizes in these mediums; Sam Olkinetsky, painter and graphic artist; Idress Cash, ceramist; and Ella Jack, water-color painter.

Norman artists are active in a number of fields. Emilio Amero, originally affiliated with the Mexican school, is a leading color lithographer, painter, and muralist; William Harold Smith works in oil and tempera in a semiabstract vein. Oscar Jacobson for many years has been known as a painter of mountains and desert in stylized, formal color patterns; James Henkle paints well-composed, strongly patterned works in tempera, constructs welded metal sculpture, and is also a designer. R. W. Tomberlin is a leading metal craftsman who has maintained a high standard in jewelry design, silversmithing and enameled objects; the paintings of John O'Neil are in several museum collections as well as private ones; Eugene Bavinger is an abstract painter who has also found exciting forms in light patterns through the photogram; Donald Matheson is a water-colorist and print maker of distinction. Joseph Taylor has executed commissioned sculpture for public buildings and parks and has shown his work frequently in state exhibitions. Roger and Wilma Corsaw are fine ceramists, both of whom have won numerous awards for their work.

Alexandre Hogue, a painter who became known in the 1930's for his paintings of the Southwest, lives and works in Tulsa as does Duayne Hatchett, sculptor, painter, and graphic artist; in the same city are also Woody Cochran, painter, Layman Jones, Paul England, and Jay O'Meilia. Bernard Frazier, former director of the Philbrook Art Center, has long been respected as a sculptor and teacher. Other former Tulsans, now living elsewhere but who have exerted influence on art in the state, are Charles Okerbloom, Louis Weinberg, and Howard Whitlatch. Oklahoma City artists Loraine Moore, Edna Stevenson, Grace Chadwick, Edwin Walter, Richard Trickey, and Leonard McMurray have all contributed to art in the state, either through their own work or as teachers and administrators.

George Calvert, painter, works in Tahlequah and is best known for his canvases of somber street and city patterns, semiabstract in style. The Reverend John L. Walch of Newkirk is a painter and sculptor who has done much in the area to raise the level of ecclesiastical art. At present (1956) he is designing a bas relief, crucifix, and stations of the cross, as well as windows, for the St. Francis de Sales Preparatory Seminary. Richard West of Muskogee has executed numerous murals in the state, including one for Bacone College, and is an award winner at the National Exhibition of Indian Painting at Philbrook. Jack Jordan and Eugene Jesse Brown, of Langston, sculptor and painter respectively, have both been very active in state and national exhibitions. Charles Banks Wilson of Miami is a painter, lithographer, and illustrator; Derald Swineford and Paul Emerson both work and teach in Chickasha. Aline Jean Treanor in Oklahoma City and Maurice da Vinna in Tulsa are art critics who have had both energy and vision in publicizing and evaluating work by state artists.

The Association of Oklahoma Artists, founded in 1916, was one of the first groups dedicated to exhibition of work produced in the state. Originally showing annually at the Oklahoma Historical Society Museum, they have, in recent years, held their exhibits at the Oklahoma Art Center in Oklahoma City. A considerable advance in professional quality was made with the inauguration of a jury system and the awarding of prizes in each medium.

The Oklahoma State Fair in 1956 originated an invitational exhibition of Oklahoma artists' work from which purchases were made to form the nucleus of a permanent collection. Also established the same year was the Auchincloss Foundation, devoted to the enjoyment of the arts through the sponsorship of films, exhibitions, and concerts.

Perhaps the most important mural commission executed in the state is *The Birth of Oklahoma* by Fred Conway, a member of the art faculty at Washington University. Installed in the First National Bank and Trust Company building in Tulsa, the painting is a blazing kaleidoscope of brilliant warm colors, moving in an exciting progression from left to right. Planned to be seen at a distance in a spacious and restrained room, it can also be viewed at close range as a study of groups of people, animals, and wagons, all skillfully placed and magnificently drawn. A recently completed mural (1956), with Abraham Lincoln as the central figure, was painted by Emilio Amero, art faculty member, in Kaufman Hall on the University of Oklahoma campus. Vivid in color and sculptural in form, it is a thoughtful statement of Lincoln as a great humanitarian influence.

Oscar B. Jacobson, artist and director of the School of Art at the University of Oklahoma from 1915 to 1945, was most influential in the development of Indian painting in the state. He encouraged Indian students to use themes from their memory of tribal customs and ceremonies and set them down in tempera on paper. Through the publication of portfolios of color reproductions of their work, they came to the attention of a large audience, both in the United States and in Europe. Five Kiowa artists, Stephen Mopope, Monroe Tsa-to-ke, James Auchiah, Jack Hokeah, and Spenser Asah were particularly outstanding in this idiom.

The public awareness of art in Oklahoma as a cultural force is still not as vigorous as the work of individual artists. But there is clear indication that with the ending of the pioneering phase in the state new art centers and museums, public works of art, and the support and encouragement of artists will become a concomitant part of Oklahoma's cultural progress.

MUSIC, DRAMA, AND DANCE

By Spencer Norton

The three arts mentioned in the title of this chapter have made significant progress in Oklahoma, and the state has contributed significantly to national achievement in these fields. There are many points of contact between them, but for reasons of clarity it seems desirable to consider them separately, in the order named.

Oklahoma's background of folk music is typical of its position in the center of the United states. The state is a connecting link between Middle West and Southwest. Its pattern of settlement brought in people from all directions, and they carried their music with them.

Very little of the Indian music found in Oklahoma is indigenous to the state, as most Indian groups now resident here settled in their present locations during the nineteenth century. The Five Civilized Tribes (Cherokee, Creek, Seminole, Choctaw, and Chickasaw), who came from the Deep South, had already undergone considerable influence from the white civilization of America, and their culture had been modified accordingly. The Plains tribes who were settled on reservations after the Civil War had preserved more of their original pattern of life. Even today, their music retains its native character. It does not differ in any significant way from the Indian music which has been studied (principally by anthropologists and ethnologists) in other parts of the United States. Oklahoma has a relatively large Indian population, as compared to other states, and this fact gives especial interest to such gatherings as the American Indian Exposition at Anadarko. The visitor has ample opportunity to experience Indian music and dance at first hand.

Negro spirituals, work songs, and blues; the ballads and fiddle tunes of Appalachia; the cowboy songs of the Southwest—all came to Oklahoma with various elements of its heterogeneous population, and all are completely at home here. They are the familiar types of such material known in other parts of America, and Oklahoma has them in abundance. Its folk music is extremely varied, but there appears to be no local type which is completely unknown elsewhere.

After the period of settlement, there began the long process of evolution toward a more sophisticated musical culture which still continues today. Touring artists of fame began to be heard at a comparatively early date. In his memoirs the late Walter Damrosch describes a concert which he gave in Oklahoma City with a touring orchestra; the program included excerpts from Wagner's *Parsifal*, not too many years after this music was first heard in America. For over sixty years, artists of established rank have performed in the state. They had a great deal to do with the development of a musical public, especially during the earlier period before the rise of radio, television, and modern techniques of recording.

A noteworthy contribution to the creation of a taste for music has been made by the various women's club groups. The Oklahoma Federation of Music Clubs and its constituent member clubs have sponsored many types of musical projects over the years. One of their most important enterprises has been the regularly scheduled contests for student and young artist-performers. The MacDowell Clubs, with their special interest in the MacDowell Colony at Peterborough, New Hampshire, have stimulated progress in all of the arts by sending representative Oklahoma composers, painters, sculptors, and writers to the Colony.

Proper recognition should be given to the many private music teachers who worked zealously, from the earliest beginnings of cultural interest in the state, to raise the level of musical performance and to develop an understanding of music in their pupils. The Oklahoma Music Teachers' Association, affiliated with the Music Teachers' National Association, is their professional organization. It has adopted a system of accreditation which has done much to improve standards of teaching and to enhance the professional status of the teacher. Its membership now includes many college and university instructors.

Music in the schools of Oklahoma has made astounding progress, and has had a great deal to do with the growth of a musical public in the state. The Oklahoma Music Educators' Association, affiliated with the Music Educators' National Conference, is the professional organization of public school music teachers. Outstanding work is being done in the improvement of school bands and choral organizations.

Professional instruction in various branches of music at more advanced levels is offered in a number of the state's universities and colleges. The University of Oklahoma, Oklahoma City University, and the University of Tulsa maintain schools of music which offer curricula leading to professional degrees. Oklahoma Agricultural and Mechanical College, Phillips University, Oklahoma Baptist University, and Oklahoma College for Women, all have well-organized departments of music. Most of the smaller state colleges at least train music educators for the public schools. Such nationally and internationally known personalities as Eva Turner and Sylvia Zaremba (University of Oklahoma), Jacques Abram (Oklahoma College for Women), and Jerome Rappoport (University of Tulsa) are teaching the next generation of Oklahoma performers.

With this background, let us examine the present state of music in Oklahoma, giving special attention to those features which might be of most interest to the visitor. The state now contains two professional symphony orchestras: the Oklahoma City Symphony Orchestra (Guy Fraser Harrison, conductor), and the Tulsa Philharmonic Society. Both organizations give regular series of subscription concerts during the normal winter season, with the participation of distinguished soloists. The Oklahoma City Symphony Orchestra has had for several years a series of weekly broadcast concerts over the Mutual network, and these have had virtually world-wide distribution through their repetition by co-operating networks and stations in other countries.

Church music has made great progress because of the increasing tendency to employ professionally trained ministers of music in the larger churches. The resulting improvement in the quality of choir singing has been closely paralleled by a similar improvement in the quality of organ playing and in the number of competent organists.

The development of choral music in the public schools has already been mentioned. Important choral groups have grown up in the colleges and universities, and various of them often join in the performance of major choral works with the symphony orchestras. Such examples as the Beethoven Ninth Symphony and the Requiems of Brahms, Berlioz, Mozart, and Verdi are not strange to the Oklahoma public. The state possesses no strictly professional choral group, but inasmuch as choral music has been traditionally an amateur, rather than a professional, activity, Oklahoma is no worse off than most other sections of America in this regard.

No completely professional operatic organization exists in the state, but the public is not without opportunity to enjoy the traditional combination of music and drama. The Metropolitan Opera Company appears annually in Oklahoma City, and over a period of years has offered a representative selection of the standard operatic repertoire. Tulsa Opera, Inc., has developed an interesting system of production which combines local musical forces with imported soloists, and its performances have been generously praised. Several of the universities and colleges present operatic productions with some regularity, and tend to select a little less hackneyed repertoire: *The Magic Flute, Der Freischütz, The Pearl-Fishers* (University of Oklahoma), *The Prodigal Son* (Oklahoma City University), or *The Consul* (Oklahoma College for Women).

Most cities of any size maintain some sort of concert course which brings professional artists from outside the state to appear before local audiences. In centers such as Oklahoma City or Tulsa, or in some of the larger universities and colleges, the outstanding international performers of the present day are heard. Almost every college has its own local concert series presented by members of its own faculty, and some of these performances are of exceptional quality.

Oklahoma has produced several performing artists who made distinguished names for themselves elsewhere. Probably the outstanding such career was that of Joseph Benton (Bentonelli), who became a leading tenor of both the Chicago Civic Opera Company and the Metropolitan Opera Company. He is active in the music of the state today as a voice teacher at the University of Oklahoma. In the last few years, the Fulbright awards have called attention to a group of brilliant young artists who will undoubtedly be heard from in the future. Typical of this new generation is the pianist Karen Keys, already established as a rising star.

Native-born composers whose fame has been acquired largely outside the state include Roy Harris (born near Chandler), one of America's leading composers of the present day, and Gail Kubik (born in South Coffeyville), who has won various awards and has become known to a wider public in recent years through his film music. Those who have left the state after beginning musical careers here include Jack Kilpatrick (one of the few to make successful use of Cherokee musical motives), Wynn York, Frank Hughes, and Albert Kirkpatrick.

Composers now resident in the state include Harrison Kerr, Violet Archer (a distinguished Canadian) and Spencer Norton (native-born) at the University of Oklahoma; Bela Rozsa (Hungarian-born) at the University of Tulsa; Lemuel Childers (native-born) in Tulsa; Robert Dillon (native-born) in Bethany; Dan Hayes at the Panhandle Agricultural and Mechanical College in Goodwell. The growing interest in composition manifested by our younger musicians makes it certain that this list of names will require considerable expansion in the future.

The history of drama in Oklahoma has been somewhat analogous to that of music. Performances by touring companies in the early days were followed by attempts at local production and by the growth of dramatic projects in the public schools, often in connection with speech instruction.

The state now contains two prominent community theaters which have achieved notable stability and whose programs are quite ambitious. The Tulsa Little Theatre, Inc., has been in existence more than a generation and employs both a full-time director and an assistant director; it has its own air-conditioned establishment. The Mayde Mack Mummers of Oklahoma City are a more recent group who have specialized in the technique of theater-in-the-round. Both groups are active during the winter season.

The only professional school of drama in the state is at the University of Oklahoma. Dramatic instruction is offered, usually in connection with speech, at other institutions, notably the University of Tulsa and Phillips University.

A number of people who have made their mark professionally in dramatic activities are natives of Oklahoma or received their basic dramatic training in this state. The outstanding example is Van Heflin, the distinguished stage and screen star. Others who have appeared on Broadway, on the screen, in professional television, or in a combination of these activities include Erik Rhodes, Alice Ghostley, Lonnie Chapman, Dennis Weaver, and Amzie Strickland. The latest recruit to Broadway from Oklahoma is Glen Kezer, in the cast of the successful musical "My Fair Lady." The state has provided a number of luminaries to Hollywood, from the days of Tom Mix and the beloved Will Rogers to the present-day Jennifer Jones and Dale Robertson.

Various forms of the dance have been known in Oklahoma from earliest times. Many of the Indian dances, especially those of the Plains Indians, have been well preserved. Some have undergone revival in recent times as younger members of the tribes become conscious of their ancestral heritage and take pride in restoring it. As mentioned above, the visitor can best see these performances at such places as the Anadarko Indian Exposition. The square dances typical of Anglo-America have become the object of cultivation by recreational dance groups, and enjoy considerable popularity. Folk dances characteristic of European immigrant groups may be seen at such places as Prague, originally a Czech settlement.

The ethnic forms of dance should not be left without mentioning the work of Gladys and Reginald Laubin, who have made a devoted study of the earlier Indian dances and who have re-created a number of these on film for permanent preservation.

The dance as an educational offering is usually found in connection with physical education programs for women. The Tulsa schools have pioneered in introducing this work into the public school curriculum. Several of the state colleges and universities offer instruction in dance, both as a form of physical education utilizing both modern and folk-dance styles, and as a part of the teacher-training program for physical education majors.

The professional dance studios of Robert Bell in Oklahoma City and June Runyon in Tulsa have contributed greatly to the preparation of promising young dancers. Such dance groups as the Oklahoma City Dance Workshop (Fronie Asher, director) and the Oklahoma City Dance Theater (affiliated with Ballet Theater) are active in producing programs which give the young dancer the opportunity to gain experience in public performance. Helen Gregory at the University of Oklahoma is the leading exponent of modern dance techniques. Flourishing student dance groups are found at the University, at Oklahoma Agricultural and Mechanical College, at Central State College (Edmond), and at Oklahoma College for Women. These groups frequently participate in dramatic, operatic, or television productions.

Some of the outstanding dancers of the world in recent years have been natives of Oklahoma. Anyone acquainted at all with the contemporary history of ballet will note the names of Maria Tallchief, Marjorie Tallchief, Rosella Hightower, Yvonne Chouteau, and Milada Mladova on the roster of stellar eminence.

OKLAHOMA FOLKWAYS

By J. Stanley Clark

Fifty years ago, 112 delegates were assembled in Guthrie to frame a constitution for the proposed state of Oklahoma. Seven of the representatives were native-born citizens of the Indian Territory and the others had recently established residence in one of the Twin Territories. Two were foreign born and the remainder were from twenty-six states of the union. Each of the states of Kentucky, Tennessee, Alabama, Mississippi, Arkansas, and Texas was the birthplace of five or more delegates; these, with those born in Indian Territory, exerted a strong southern influence upon the convention and typified the southern background of the people. Because of the diversity of the population, however, there was transplanted into the new state folklore, the folkways, legends, and traditions from older settlements of the Middle West, East, and South, which, commingled with Indian lore and western tradition, have left their mark upon the people.

Call him what you will—a "Sooner" or an "Okie"—an Oklahoman is a tolerant being. His is a racial background of diverse sources, predominantly Indian, and he reflects this in a genial tolerance toward the man on the next ranch or down the street. More often than not, an Oklahoman in the 1950's is a city or small town dweller. Oftentimes he wears boots—because his father wore them; he square-dances because his parents and their parents square-danced. He knows cattle; he rides horses. He suggests that visitors make a trip through the Historical Society Museum, but he never goes. He or his people own land or grew up with the land; he enthusiastically contributes to the greatest legend of the West by supporting the movement for a National Cowboy Shrine. He likes to fish and he likes to hunt—he likes the outdoors.

Living in a state that points toward the West, he loves the exaggeration of frontier humor. He may truthfully recount outlaw exploits of Scarface Bill, Cherokee Bill, the Daltons and the Doolins, and the utter fearlessness of Bill Tilghman, Chris Madsden, Heck Thomas, J. P. Jones, and other United States marshals of territorial days. Then he may solemnly relate how he and a rival marksman one time decided to test their skill by shooting the barbs from a wire fence over a mile stretch. As each was equally successful in the contest, a further test was necessary. So, loading their guns with charges of glue, barbs, and powder, they galloped back over the course, shooting the barbs back onto the fence.

"An' if you don't believe that," he says, "I'll take you out and show you the fence where it happened!"

Because he lives so close to nature, there is heavily imprinted on the Oklahoman's mind the deep, red soil of the state, the scourging drought, the searing winds, the lean and the productive years. Toward the vagaries of weather he reflects a tolerance similar to that which his grandparents had as settlers on the dugout frontier or as transplanted Indians in a new, unimproved land. Like them, he talks a great deal about the weather—his most popular TV program is on this subject. He may study the sky for cyclone, windstorm, snow, or rain, as did an Indian predecessor, or like his dugout-dwelling grandfather, he may read the almanac. And like him, he may refer to houses on the plains equipped with a "crowbar hole." Upon being asked the purpose of the opening, he will say it is used to test wind velocity. If the crowbar merely bends when thrust through the hole, it is safe to go out. However, if the bar is broken off, it is better to stay in the house.

The listener may learn that it was on the Western Plains that a teamster had one mule die of heat prostration and while he was busy skinning it a "Norther" blew in and froze the other to death. Will Rogers used to say that no one should mind Oklahoma weather—just stay around a few moments and it will change.

Humor as well as staunch courage was needed to establish roots on the dugout frontier—like those qualities of the local undertaker in a new western settlement, a tall, rawboned, transplanted Arkansan, who went barefoot all summer. He set up business in an unpainted board shanty about ten feet square, with a sign painted over the door, 'Cold Drinks and Coffins,' telling the world he could refresh the weary wayfarer on his journey, and help put him away at its end!

A combination of tolerance and humor makes an Oklahoman appreciate the plight of the visitor from the fertile farmlands of Iowa in the hands of a land promoter. Driving in a buggy across miles of virgin land one hot August day, occasionally along eroded places they could see the thinness of topsoil, the layers of gypsum and alkali formations, but the promoter extolled the fertility of the region. Soon the buggy approached a California road runner or chaparral which quickly outran the team. "What bird is that?" asked the Iowan. "Oh, that? Why, that's a bird of paradise!"

The travelers rode a few paces, when the promoter inquired, "Well, what do you think of our bird of paradise?"

"All I can say is," was the reply, "it appears to me he's a hell of a long ways from home!"

The saga of the West is the story of the cowboy, and folklore has been enriched by his speech, mannerisms, and songs, which are still a part of present-day Oklahoma. His sense of humor and his attitude toward hard work may be illustrated by the following story recently related by a ranchman downstate. Among chores assigned to a young cowhand was the feeding of a litter of pigs. About six months later the owner inquired how the shoats were coming along. "To tell you the truth, I don't know," was the reply. "How is that?" "Well, it's like this. You get me up so early in the morning, its dark when I feed them hogs, and I'm out on the range 'til so late it's after dark when I feed 'em again, so I just naturally ain't never seen them critters!"

Several weeks later the cowboy was in town and an acquaintance who knew of his experience asked how the hog crop was coming along. "You know when Big Blue was on that rampage?" he said, "Well, overflow waters cut across the pigpen and that black gumbo balled up on the tails of them hogs and stretched their hides so tight they couldn't close their eyes, and they all died of insomnia!"

Home, to an Oklahoman, is a geographical pie. Cut the state from north to south near the center and you divide the pie into regions so divergent that before statehood leaders wanted two separate states made of the area. Cut the pie from east to west along the course of the Canadian River and you have northern "settlers" in the upper half, with Tulsa as their Republican stronghold. Southern influence with strong Democratic flavor blankets the area south of the river. Professor E. E. Dale, at the University of Oklahoma, used to illustrate this difference to a class in regional history by the following anecdote: A tobacco-chewing cowboy was sitting in the caboose of a cattle train bound for a Kansas market. As the train rumbled northward on a cold, blustery day, he used the hot, coal-burning, potbellied stove as his principal target of expectoration. A brakeman entered the caboose, saw what was happening, and pointed to a cuspidor. After he left, the cowboy turned to a companion, and complained, "That's the way with these northerners. The further up toward Kansas you get, the more particular they are!"

Oklahoma is a compound of regionalism. Ask the average native where he is from, and instead of naming town or county he will likely reply: "From the Panhandle," "From the Osage Reservation," "From the Chickasaw Nation," "From the Short-Grass Country," etc. Each treasures its legends and individuality. Think of the Panhandle, and there comes to mind grandsires against whom the federal government was willing to bet 160 acres or a town lot they wouldn't stay long enough to prove their claims. Many didn't. Some survived by

"Picking up bones to keep from starving,
"Picking up chips to keep from freezing,
"Picking up courage to keep leaving,
"Way out West, in No Man's Land."

As distant as possible from the Panhandle lies Little Dixie, southeastern Oklahoma, wooded, hilly, with clear running streams and free-speaking people, zealous in exercising their political rights, fiercely Democratic in their loyalties, proud of their Southern lineage. Here many cultures mixed: intermarried citizens of the Choctaw Nation, wealthy slave-holding members of the Choctaw tribe, full-bloods in isolated settlements, and, beginning in the 1870's, enclaves of European immigrants, who cut slopes and shafts into the green hills to tap the rich veins of coal.

Legend has it that "Uncle" Wallace Willis, a Choctaw slave, composed in the 1840's the spirituals "Swing Low, Sweet Chariot," "Steal Away to Jesus," and "I'm a Rollin'." In rare instances, too, the Choctaw funeral cry, a rich tribal heritage, is held by friends and relatives of the deceased. And with strong allegiance to their native lands, immigrants introduced societies and fraternal orders into the Choctaw communities. Slovaks belonged to the First Catholic Union and the National Slovak Association; Mexicans to the National Beneficial Society; Italians to La Minature, Vittorio Emmanuel II, and Cristoforo Colombo; Poles to the National Polish Society.

The European tradition that wine and beer are excellent refreshment substitutes for water was not abandoned by the immigrants. Indian agents, charged with enforcement of the Choctaw prohibition law, often made this a subject of comment in reports to their superiors. One wrote, "It is somewhat remarkable as a fact in the scientific world that the water is always bad in the immediate mining centers, but good in the adjacent neighborhoods."

In Little Dixie the popular fall and winter sport is a 'coon or 'possum hunt. Essentials, other than a party of men and boys, are good hunting hounds and a supply of "drinkin'" liquor. The dogs tree the quarry and stand guard until the hunters arrive. The liquor helps to kill the poison in the night air.

The situation concerning liquor and prohibition presents the anomaly of a state prohibition law in contrast to the reaction of a goodly number of Oklahomans toward its observance. Recent arrivals in the state are intrigued by this dualism, which has survived every assault upon it. Five times since statehood the provision has been successfully sustained by the voters, many of whom, according to Will Rogers, staggered to the polls to register a "dry" vote. Despite a general tolerance of "social drinking," Oklahoma remained dry at law half a century after statehood.

Oklahoma's constitutional prohibition is surrounded with folklore. . . . But the historical origins of prohibition in Oklahoma, as William H. (Alfalfa Bill) Murray, president of the Constitutional Convention and later governor of the state, related them some years ago in a conversation, offer one more confirmation of the power of an incident to change the course of history.

"Somehow," said Murray, "a helper of mine in the campaign to have Oklahoma admitted to the Union, got the impression that I was a dry. Actually, I didn't have any strong feeling, one way or the other, on the subject of prohibition. But he was a saloon keeper at Purcell, and that led to an interesting result.

"In the thick of the statehood campaign, this man made a series of speaking engagements for me in the northern part of the Territory. He routed me by train up to a small Kansas town, and there, he told me, I would be met by Territorial folks who would carry me down by horse and buggy to talk in one small Territorial community after another. Well, I arrived on time and went to a little hotel to meet the people who were to look after me. But I waited all afternoon and most of the evening and nobody came. Finally, I wired Oklahoma for instructions and was told by some of my other helpers to take a horse and buggy and go down to the first town in Oklahoma where I was to speak.

"As I drove along behind that horse next day, I thought a good deal about the effort that had been made to sidetrack me—probably on the theory that I would say something against liquor. And it occurred to me that I might just be able to kill two birds with one stone. Teddy Roosevelt was President at the time, you remember. He didn't want us to have statehood right then—that would do away with his Territorial patronage. If I could send out maybe a couple of hundred thousand duplicated letters to churches, temperance societies, and others, asking them to wire or write Roosevelt to admit us 'under the white banner of constitutional prohibition,' I'd have Roosevelt on the ropes. Also I'd be able to pay back the man who had let me sit in a Kansas hotel for nothing.

"Well, we did it. And it wasn't long before Roosevelt sent a wire to a political friend of his asking him to tell me to call off my dogs. He was ready to admit us. We put a prohibition clause in the constitution, and that's the story of prohibition in Oklahoma."[1]

Any native son of Oklahoma loves politics and is well schooled in the "up and at 'em brand." An observer of a recent political campaign commented that in most places people clean a carpet with a vacuum cleaner; in Oklahoma, they hang it on a line and beat it with a rock. This is particularly true in the eastern and southern parts of the state, formerly Indian Territory, where officials are usually elected in the Democratic primary and where people have a greater love for a good party fight than a hound has for potlicker. All of the chief executives of Oklahoma have been elected from towns or cities east of the Rock Island tracks, which split the state into eastern and western halves.

Legislators are responsive to demands made by the people in sparsely populated counties of the region; rarely do they misjudge the legislative needs of their constituents. Once, a few years back, during the closing days of a legislative session, a bill establishing a license fee for fishermen who used live bait or artificial lures was amended to include "other bait." The measure passed during the closing hours of the session. Soon a cataclysmic furor arose in Little Dixie—the heartland of scenic Oklahoma—when game wardens appeared along its creeks and rivers to exact a license from pole fishermen. The "earthworm bill" retired most of the members of the House of Representatives from the region to private life, and hold-over senators effectively marked the measure for repeal early in the next session. Oklahoma has not forgotten this lesson learned from its land of clear drinking water, hound dogs, ham meat, and little cash money.

Although the attitude of the people toward politics and prohibition may be unique in many respects, far more significant has been the influence of Indian traditions and lore. Their love of earth and sky, their reverence for Nature and growing things, their legends more numerous than the tribes—all have left a deep impress. Their legends

1 Related in a conversation with Savoie Lottinville during a street-car ride from the State Capitol to downtown Oklahoma City, 1944. Actually, the Enabling Act, passed June 16, 1906, provided that the Indian Territory and the Osage Nation should be dry for twenty-one years. Prohibition for the state as a whole was submitted to a vote of the people at the same time the Constitution was submitted to them for ratification on September 17, 1907.

portray the gropings for truth—such as the story of the old woman who lived on a high mountain, and who took the moon, after it had reached its fullness, and cut it into little stars and strewed them across the heavens; and the story of the milky way as a long pathway to the Spirit Land.

In the eastern half of the state, where the Five Civilized Tribes were settled more than a hundred years ago, the flowers called "Jack-in-the-pulpit" grow in profusion. They were brought from the South and transplanted by a hermit medicine man to show the Indians a way back to their southern homes in case they chose to return.

A legend current in the Arbuckle Mountains in the southern part of the state is a curious admixture of Indian-White cultures. It is the story of a giant rattlesnake "as broad as the back of a dog and as long as two ponies." He is the king of all rattlesnakes. In his head is a great diamond, and studding his long sides are other diamonds so dazzling they would strike blind any man who might see them in the light of the sun. Long ago a tribe of Indians, so goes the legend, brought this King of the Rattlers into the mountains, where regularly they came to observe their religious rites. To them the snake was sacred. Amidst their ceremonies they were attacked by hostile forces, and in their confused retreat they lost their sacred snake. But the story of the snake remained, along with the snake, and even today certain ingenuous whites of the mountains are hunting him. Once a hunter saw his awe-inspiring tail disappearing into a wild crevice called Rattlesnake Cave; at other times his discarded skin has been found, and the breaks and indentations in it show that he wears the great jewels in his body.

Until recently it was not at all unusual, on a visit to Anadarko, Hammond, Concho, or other places where older Indians of the Plains tribes gathered, to see an elderly Indian, his two beribboned braids hanging down his back, "talking" with others of his generation in the universal sign language of the Plains. These old men have disappeared; their children's children wear their hair, and dress and speak as others; few know their own tribal tongue.

But from these, the younger ones, have come our better artists; murals and other paintings in public buildings of the state and nation attest to this. And more than the small cells of foreign settlements in the state, more than any other racial group or nationality, Indians have kept and guarded their tribal traditions, myths, and ceremonial dances. This is peculiarly Oklahoma. A young man or woman who may be one-eighth, one-sixteenth, or one thirty-second Indian—perhaps even blond and blue eyed—will invariably and proudly declare that Indian blood. They may work in offices, factories, in any normal American profession, but just as normally, they still put on their priceless tribal finery for these tribal ceremonials that keep alive the inner spirit, the racial quality that is Indian—and American.

A new tradition, one that incorporates that blend of race that is Oklahoma, has begun a sturdy growth throughout the state—the tradition of the Big Red. The University of Oklahoma football team, nationally recognized as a power in the sports world, has, more than any other factor, instilled a pride of accomplishment throughout the state. Oklahomans who never sat in a college classroom, most of whom could not name the university president or faculty members other than coaches, can play back game after game and call by position and name those players who make the varsity squad. And when the Big Red makes a home appearance, whether against a lesser or more worthy opponent, the Highway Patrol masses itself as traffic snarls converge on the stadium to deposit the 60,000 spectators assembling to watch the nation's best in the nation's favorite college sport. Untold thousands with equally frenetic enthusiasm dedicate themselves to the broadcast of the game. Perhaps here, the average Oklahoman, unsure of himself when among others of more cultured or settled background, has found that in the rock'em and sock'em game of football, Sooners are among the nation's best, and he takes justifiable pride in vicarious achievement.

Few native sons remain from the era of the sod house, the dugout, or the log cabin, but the frontier is still vividly enough in mind for the preachment to exist that their sons and daughters must have better educational advantages than they had.

Perhaps it is true that educational systems were meager in territorial days, but the urge toward education, has been one of the strongest influences in the organization of the state. Junior colleges, senior colleges, universities, and church schools sprang up in all parts of Oklahoma, until now these institutions of higher learning encompass every regional area throughout the state. This overweening, this ruthless pursuit of education has helped undermine or overthrow folklore and traditions of an older generation which found mystic meanings in simple things, carried a rabbit's foot or a buckeye for luck, and adopted the cryptic mistletoe as its state flower.

The educated world of TV, radio, home encyclopedias, and biology teachers has shattered many well-founded beliefs of the older generation. Take Junior on a camping trip and receive a rude awakening. Explain how the rattlesnake, the prairie dog, and the owl shared common habitations, then be prepared for a learned dissertation on your fallacious belief. Express your fear of snakes, see one pop from his pocket. Or relate your favorite stories on hoop snakes, jointed snakes, or how snakes travel in pairs and how horsehairs turn into snakes, and receive a lecture on things reptilian. Try to induce him to eat fish by stating that it is a food for the brain, and he will lay bare your alimentary canal and your digestive processes, and inform you of vitamins and balanced diets. Accuse him of having a birdlike appetite and you will learn that birds never miss a chance to pick up a meal. Placate him by letting him know you think what he has said makes horse sense and, if he is a member of the 4-H Club or Future Farmers of America, or a collector of encyclopedic knowledge, listen patiently to a scientific explanation as to the relative merits of the intelligence of the horse, the pig, the cow.

Before bedding down, don't let him know that at other times, in earlier years, you always spread a rope around your pallet and wore asafetida around your neck, and chanted such oddities as "Ladybug, ladybug, to your home you must turn, your house is on fire and your children may burn," or "Sty, sty, leave my eye, catch the next person passing by."

But don't give up! You were too near a disappearing frontier, and generations of western tradition are so firmly a part of your speech that, despite Junior's "booklearning" and observations, you will hear him parroting such misstatements as "a barking dog never bites," "as blind as a bat," "eat like a pig," "as nervous as a cat," "like waving a red flag before a bull," "as silly as a goose," "as straight as a crow flies," "as wise as an owl," "playing 'possum," etc.—the folklore of yesteryear.

This, then, is your average Oklahoman—friendly, hospitable, a product of America's last frontier, closer akin to his neighbors to the south than those to the north. He has been conditioned to poverty and plenty. An abundance of mineral wealth—oil or gas production in 65 of the 77 counties, which, in many instances, has brought great prosperity to a neighbor and passed him by, or has placed him on a friendly footing with more fortunate men. Familiarity in speech typifies him. His governors are always "Raymond" or "Phatz" or "Roy" or "Red," seldom distinguished by proper surnames. He loves politics, and the caterwaulings of a one-party system; he votes Democratic, and subscribes to metropolitan papers with a strong opposition slant.

He is religious; his towns are filled with churches; he attends and supports the church of his choice, sometimes, perhaps, like the well-to-do Choctaw of territorial days who was asked by a preacher why his weekly contribution was only twenty-five cents. "Huh," replied the Choctaw, "Damn poor preach, damn poor pay!"

His favorite people are Texans. Their brashness pleases him and intrigues him, and leaves him a little bit envious. They like to tell the story of the grandsire seated in the Union Depot in Dallas, who called his grandson to him after he saw the boy engaged in conversation with strangers coming up the ramp. Upon learning that the boy was asking the travelers where they were from, he said: "Don't bother them people, boy. If they're from Texas, you'll know it. And, if they ain't, it don't make no difference no ways!" Perhaps the prolonged exposure to the attitude of Texans has weathered away the Oklahoman's feeling of unsureness; at any rate, more and more Oklahomans are taking greater and greater pride in their state and in its people. They feel, as it is expressed in the language of the oil fields, that the makers of the state, "got a good scald."

PART II: *Principal Cities*

ARDMORE

Railroad Stations: 217 E. Main St. for Atchison, Topeka & Santa Fe Ry.; Broadway and A St. for St. Louis–San Francisco Ry.
Bus Station: 28 S. Washington.
Airport: Ardmore Municipal Airport, 9.6 m. N. on US 77; Ardmore Air Force Base, 6 m. E. of Municipal Airport.
City Buses: Terminal, 201 S. Washington St., fare 10c.
Taxis: Fare 35c.

Accommodations: 21 first-class hotels and motels (537 units); trailer courts, $16–20 per month.

Information Service: Chamber of Commerce, 6 E. Main St.

Newspaper: (Morning) *Daily Ardmoreite.*
Radio Station: KVSO (1240 kc.).
Television Station: KVSO–TV (Ch. 12).
Motion Picture Theaters: 9, including 3 drive-ins.
Athletics: Walker Stadium, S St. and McLish Ave., S. W.; Baseball Field, Community Youth Foundation Park, 600 E. Main St.
Golf: Dornick Hills, 2 m. N. on US 77, greens fee $2 weekdays, $3.50 Saturdays, Sundays, and holidays; Municipal Golf Club, 2.5 m. N. on US 77, greens fee 50c weekdays, 75c Sundays and holidays.
Swimming: Walker Park, F St. and 5th Ave., N. E.; Community Youth Foundation Park (two pools), 600 E. Main St.; Lake Murray State Park, 9 m. S. on Washington St.
Boating: Lake Murray, 9 m. S. on Washington St.
Tennis: City courts, B and 9th Sts., N. W. and F St. and 3rd Ave., N. E., free.

Annual Events: Southern Oklahoma Free Fair and Exposition, Ardmore Coliseum, September; City Birthday Party, July 28; Southern Oklahoma Junior Livestock Show, March; Ardmore Rodeo, April; Amateur Field Trials, March.

ARDMORE (896 alt., 17,890 pop.; 1955 est. 27,542), seat of Carter County, was in 1887 but a naked station on the newly constructed Santa Fe Railroad. The name itself was selected, perhaps wistfully, by an official of the road in honor of the tree-shaded Philadelphia suburb that was his home town. The only building on the site, before the coming of the railroad, was the old "700 Ranch" operated by the Roff brothers.

The area was then Pickens County of the Chickasaw Indian Nation. The rolling, partially wooded countryside was fast filling with ranches and small farms, all desperately in need of markets. The Santa Fe, and Ardmore, provided the market, and from nothing in 1887, the town's population grew to 2,500 in 1890. Stores and wagon yards sprang up. The first newspaper, the weekly *Alliance Courier*, was established in 1888; the present paper, the *Daily Ardmoreite*, began printing in 1893. (In the early 1900's Ardmore also had two Negro weekly papers.)

But there was no municipal government at first. The city's fire department was a volunteer bucket brigade and its water supply came from cisterns dug by the Main Street merchants beside their stores. The only police force was a federal deputy marshal. Two years after Ardmore had become a station on the Santa Fe, a pioneer settler from Texas pictured it in these words:

"Father met us at the depot, and on the way to our new home we saw the public well and watering trough in the middle of Main Street. . . . I remember how my sister and I gazed at the cowboys standing at the well with their ten-gallon white hats, black-and-white checkered shirts, and slant-heeled boots. The spot seemed to be attractive to the town's hogs, also, as they had made a wallowing ground around the trough. Before reaching home we saw our first rattlesnake and prairie chickens.

"The first winter we were visited by a fierce, mangy herd of wild horses that stayed near our house for quite a while, snorting and pitching and making it unsafe for us children to venture outside."

But the land was quickly subdued. Native grasses grew tall and the soil was fertile for crops. Old-timers tell of corn ricked higher than a man's head along miles of fence rows. And five years after the coming of the railroad it is claimed that more than fifty thousand bales of cotton were sold on Ardmore's streets in a single season.

In 1896 a fire wiped out most of the downtown buildings, all of them of wood. The owners built back with brick and stone. Today, as a result, many buildings with cornerstones dated between 1897 and 1905 still stand along Caddo Street and East Main Street in the old section of town.

Oil was first discovered in 1905 when a well was completed near some asphalt outcrops in the western part of present Carter County. There was no market for the oil, however, and the discovery had little effect on the town's growth. The search for oil actually began as early as 1901. In that year a group of Ardmore citizens, excited by oil development in the Tulsa–Red Fork region (*see Tulsa*), formed a company to explore the near-by Red Beds. They had seen crude oil on the surface of water flowing from springs in the area, and despite the expert judgment of such men as Standard Oil Company's John D. Archbold—who rashly declared he would drink all the oil found in the Red Beds—they persisted in their explorations and found oil at four hundred feet.

In the meantime Oklahoma became a state (1907) and Pickens County was divided into several smaller counties. The area immediately surrounding Ardmore became Carter County. To the west was Jefferson County with Waurika as its seat. A strip to the south along Red River was made into Love County with Marietta as county seat. But the development favored Ardmore, and the growing town became the trading center for the entire area while the other county seats remained small towns. Agriculture flourished and, by 1910, Ardmore had a population of almost 9,000. Oklahoma's second governor, Lee Cruce (1913–17), came from Ardmore. In 1920, Ardmoreite John W. Harreld became the first Republican (of but two up to 1956) to be elected to the United States Senate from Oklahoma.

But oil was not forgotten. In 1907, Roy Johnson came to Ardmore to start a newspaper. The city's streets were being paved with rock asphalt at the time. And Johnson, after examining it, believed that this material had once been saturated with oil, that the asphaltum was merely the residue left after the light oil had drained away. With maps showing extensive beds of this asphalt residue near Ardmore, Johnson became convinced that he was on the right track. With a young partner he carried on persistent shoestring operations until he and his group brought in the first well in 1913. (Ten years later, looking back over a decade of feverish development in the region, he suggested that Archbold would have drunk a big mouthful of oil, had he made good on his promise. Up to that time the Red Beds had yielded some 167,000,000 barrels of oil.)

It was the discovery of the fabulous Healdton Field in western Carter County that was to change Ardmore from a town to a city, from the largest trade center in south-central Oklahoma to the most important metropolitan area between Oklahoma City on the north and Dallas, Texas, to the south. With local men and capital interested in the development of the fields—Ringling, Wirt, Fox, Hewitt, and others—Ardmore became the oil capital of Southern Oklahoma. By 1920 the population had grown to more than 14,000 in Ardmore itself, and to more than 40,000 in Carter County.

Proration—the rule of limiting output for maximum production over the years—saved Ardmore from the slump that hit many Oklahoma oil-boom towns after the initial gusher phase had passed. The oil industry continued to grow and assume ever greater importance in the city's economy. As it did, lower farm prices and increasing soil erosion and depletion began to take its toll. In the late 1920's and early 1930's many of the small farmers were wiped out and the land went largely into spreading cattle ranches.

The oil boom, however, was not without its tragic aspects. On September 27, 1915, a tank car of natural gasoline in the Santa Fe yards exploded, leveling much of the downtown area. Some fifty persons were killed and it is said that horses eight miles away were knocked to their knees. The railroad in the course of time paid out more than $1,000,000 in damages and the town was rebuilt better than before.

In general, Ardmore has a spaced, comfortable appearance with broad, tree-shaded streets. Particularly noticeable in the older residential sections are the many fine native hackberry trees arching over the sidewalks. As the city grew, parks were generously provided. In 1956 there were ten municipal parks, including the 60-acre recreational area now under development on the east side by the Community Youth Foundation. Organized and endowed by local citizens, the Foundation has already financed a new baseball field, and two new swimming pools, one of Olympic size at a cost of $132,000, and another at $72,000.

Ardmore's Negroes, who make up approximately 15 per cent of the population, live mainly on the east side around their East Main Street business district. Some hundreds of fullblood, and several thousand part-blood, Chickasaw Indians also live in and around Ardmore, some of the older ones among them still speaking only their native tongue.

Ardmore got its start as a tourist and recreation center during the depression of the 1930's. Federal-aid funds were used to build Lake Murray Dam (*see Tour 10*) on Andarche Creek southeast of the city, creating a 6,000-acre reservoir and a 22,000-acre state park. Besides Lake Murray there are in the area many smaller public, private, and club lakes, as well as a number of dependable fishing streams. Always popular, too, is the Arbuckle Mountains play area (*see Tour 10*) only a few minutes to the north.

From the first traditional one-room schoolhouse, Ardmore's educational plant has expanded to include modern high and junior high schools (1956 enrollment: 1,500), and seven elementary schools (2,500 pupils). Though the schools are officially desegregated, most of the more than five hundred Negro students still attend their own once-separate elementary and secondary schools. Indian children from Carter Seminary (*see Tour 10*) now attend classes in the public school.

Ardmore has also expanded economically. In 1956 some sixty industrial enterprises were located in the city, including two dairy-products processing plants, oil refineries, cotton-oil and flour mills, cotton gins and compresses, manufacture of leather goods, clothing, wood products, and pecan-cracking machinery. Oil production and marketing continue, however, to be the main economic support, with more than 140 district and main offices of oil companies located in the city.

Following World War II—which saw the establishment of the important Ardmore Air Force Base sixteen miles to the northeast—the oil industry went through a second and greater boom. Older shallow fields, which had been more or less abandoned in the 1930's and 1940's, are now producing once again from deeper oil and gas formations. Coupled with the discovery of new fields, they have continued to bring more industries and more people into the Ardmore area.

The Ardmore Sanitarium and Hospital, maintained by the Seventh Day Adventists, was supplemented in the early 1950's by the million-dollar Memorial Hospital of Southern Oklahoma. Construction costs were met by public subscription; oil pioneer Charlie B. Goddard contributed a $1,400,000-endowment for operation and maintenance. In 1945–46 the nationally known Samuel Roberts Noble Foundation was established east of Ardmore (*see Tour* 6) by Lloyd Noble, another pioneer oilman. He died in 1949.

POINTS OF INTEREST

The CARNEGIE LIBRARY, 502 Stanley Ave., a two-story gray stone building, is the successor to a reading room for young men provided by a citizens' committee in 1895. In 1956 it had more than 38,800 volumes. Mrs. Hosea Townsend started the movement for the present library in 1904 when she outlined Ardmore's need in a letter to Andrew Carnegie. He gave $15,000, and the building was opened in 1906. A MUSEUM (free) on the first floor has on display a small collection of documents and relics pertaining to southern Oklahoma history, as well as geological and biological specimens.

ST. PHILLIPS CHURCH (*open to visitors*), E St. and McLish Ave., built in 1927, is an interesting adaptation of the Gothic design of Merton College, Oxford University, England. A small church, seating only 250 worshipers, it is built of Missouri limestone. The stained-glass windows are particularly noteworthy.

In the belfry of the FIRST PRESBYTERIAN CHURCH, C St. and Broadway, is a chime of eleven bells, said to be the first to be installed in Oklahoma. The largest of the bells, weighing 2,500 pounds, can be rung independently.

The YWCA BUILDING, A St. and Broadway, is a small structure of cream brick, beautifully proportioned, modern in design and decoration. The interior is finished and equipped as a club. There are no rooms for rent. The building was dedicated in 1938.

The CARTER COUNTY COURTHOUSE, 1st Ave. between A and B Sts., S. W., is a solid, square building of gray limestone, adorned in front with tall, massive pillars. Its dome is one of the first objects to attract the eye as one approaches Ardmore.

The AMERICAN LEGION HUT, 3rd Ave. and Washington St., is the former station of the Ardmore-Ringling railroad, which was taken over by the Santa Fe. (Flamboyant circus man John Ringling was another colorful pioneer oilman. Annoyed by the poor roads between his wells and Ardmore, he built twenty miles of railway, extending the line later to the town bearing his name (*see Tour 6*) with a six-mile branch to Healdton.) The Legion leased the abandoned station in 1940 and turned it into a clubhouse.

The OLD 700 RANCH HOUSE, G St. and 2nd Ave., S. E., the first building on the site of Ardmore, and the first in the county, has been altered so extensively over the years that only a small part of it remains in its original state. As built, it was a double log house, the two sections divided by the traditional "dog-trot" breezeway.

POINTS OF INTEREST IN ENVIRONS

Noble Foundation, *2.1 m.*; Oak Hill Farm, *9.6 m.*; Lake Texoma State Park, *38.7 m.* (*see Tour 6*); Lake Murray State Park, *3.9 m.*; Turner Falls, *14.1 m.*; Price's Falls, *22.2 m.* (*see Tour 10*).

BARTLESVILLE

Railroad Station: Union Depot, 200 W. 2nd St., for Atchison, Topeka & Santa Fe Ry. and Missouri-Kansas-Texas R. R.
Bus Station: Union Terminal, 126 W. 2nd St.
Airport: Municipal (Class 4), US 60, W. of city, for Central and Continental Airlines.
City Buses: Fare 15c.
Taxis: Zoned from 35c.

Accommodations: 3 air-conditioned hotels; rooming houses; 7 modern motels.

Information Service: Chamber of Commerce, 521 Johnstone.

Newspapers: Morning Examiner and (evening) *Bartlesville Enterprise.*
Radio Station: KWON (1400 kc.).
Motion Picture Houses: 5, including 2 drive-ins.
Athletics: Municipal Stadium (baseball, softball, football), 1st St. and Dewey Ave., seating capacity 2,000; Senior High School Stadium and Athletic Field, 18th St. on Hillcrest Drive, seating capacity 7,000.
Swimming: Sanipool, 120 N. Seneca St., children 15c, adults 25c.
Golf: Sunset Club, 3 m. N. W., greens fee $1.00; Hillcrest Country Club, 4 m. S. E., greens fee $2.50 weekdays, $5.00 Saturdays and Sundays.
Tennis: Municipal courts, 1st St. at Osage Ave., S. edge of city; free.

Annual Events: Gas and Electric Appliance Show, 3rd week in April; Fall Festival, 2nd week in Sept.; Washington County Fair, 3rd week in Sept.

BARTLESVILLE (694 alt., 19,228 pop.; 1956 est. 25,050), seat of wealthy Washington County, might well serve as the model for what the modern, oil-dominated small city should be. Nature has been good to the Bartlesville area. Beneath its productive farmlands lie vast reserves of crude oil and natural gas, the life blood of present-day industry. Above ground there is sufficient water to take care of all foreseeable commercial needs, as well as to nourish the many trees that line the wide streets and give the city an air of graciousness and prosperity. Yet these favorable factors alone are not enough to explain the true character of the town of Bartlesville. That character can only be explained in terms of people.

Bartlesville claims a greater percentage of college graduates among its inhabitants than any other city in Oklahoma. Though such an assertion is not easily proved (or, for that matter, disproved), it is true that university men and women have been drawn to the city by the very nature of its principal economic load-carriers: the U. S. Bureau of Mines' experimental station and laboratory, with 134 workers; the Phillips Petroleum Company's vast research laboratories, employing 500 persons; the head offices of four major oil companies; the office and factory of a company that makes oil-well pumping equipment.

The impact of payrolls of this nature, of course, extends well beyond the industries themselves. Health services alone, in 1956, required two modern hospitals (200 beds), the services of thirty-four doctors, twenty-two dentists, and sixty-two registered nurses. Bartlesville has thirty-three churches. Social and cultural activities have instituted such organizations as a Town Hall discussion club with a membership of five hundred, a Little Theater Guild, a Community Concert Association, a Musical Research Society, artists' and writers' groups, and more than one hundred other civic, social, and fraternal groups. The YWCA and the YMCA both own their buildings and sponsor year-round activities for all ages. It was in Bartlesville that Oklahoma's first Little League baseball program got under way. And as the home of the Phillips 66 basketball team, Bartlesville can claim as its own one of the world's most famous amateur teams. Made up of full-time employees of Phillips Petroleum Company, they have been perennial holders of both national AAU and Industrial Basketball League titles, as well as three-time winners in Olympics competition.

But Bartlesville has not always been a town of famous basketball squads and teams of research chemists, of startlingly modern office buildings and gracious homes. Its beginnings three-quarters of a century ago were far more primitive. Yet all the color and romance of frontier life among the Indians and of the brash early days of Oklahoma's oil industry are mirrored in its brief history.

The city's embryo enterprise was a gristmill for grinding corn. This mill was built in 1868 on the bank of the Caney River by Nelson Carr, the first white settler in the Coo-wee-scoo-wee District of the old Cherokee Indian Nation. In 1875, Carr's mill was bought by Jacob Bartles, an enterprising pioneer who had been operating an Indian trading post at Silver Lake (*see Tour* 9), six miles to the southeast. Bartles had the right to live and trade among the Cherokees by virtue of his marriage to the daughter of Charles Journeycake, a consecrated native preacher and chief of a remnant of the Delaware tribe which had been granted equal rights in the Cherokee Nation.

Bartles built a store and trading post at the millsite, hoping to trade with the Osages, who five years before had been moved from Kansas onto a reservation carved out of the Cherokee grant. His hopes were dulled somewhat when he discovered that his Caney River property was several miles east of the Osage reservation, but he stuck with his new venture. Within a year he had hauled in a dynamo and was producing Oklahoma's first electricity. When Jim French and his two stepsons drove from Kansas in 1880 with wagons and four-mule teams to establish the first freight line in this section of Indian Territory, Bartles had developed his store and camp into a town.

Competition for Bartles appeared in 1884 when George B. Keeler and William Johnstone, two of his former clerks, built a store across the river. These pioneers were also adopted Cherokees. Keeler, though young, had had experience with the old Chouteau trading dynasty (*see Tour* 8); he spoke Osage fluently and was an expert in Indian sign language. Johnstone, like Bartles, had married into the Journeycake family. Along with storekeeping, they owned cattle and several sawmills. Around these rival stores developed the new town which was incorporated in 1897 and named for Bartles. In the same year the region's first telephone line was set up, connecting the two stores with Caney, Kansas.

Cattle raising and farming spurred the area's early economy. But a new factor entered the picture on April 15, 1897. On this date, just across the river from the old mill, the first "commercial" oil well in Oklahoma (*see Chelsea, Tour 1*) was brought in at 1,320 feet in the now famous Bartlesville sand. The town of Bartlesville was on its way.

The first railroad—the Santa Fe—appeared in 1898, built on the grade surveyed and leveled from Caney, Kansas, twenty miles to the north, by Bartles' men. With the tracks down, the inveterate town-builder moved four miles north to establish the town of Dewey (*see Tour 9*). A second railroad, the Katy, came to Bartlesville in 1903. By this time the extensive shallow oil field stretched from the eastern Osage border to the Verdigris River and beyond. Here in 1901 H. V. Foster established the Indian Territory Illuminating Oil Company which, under the more familiar ITIO symbol, brought in the Oklahoma City discovery well twenty-seven years later and developed into one of the major companies (Cities Service) maintaining its chief offices at Bartlesville.

Bartlesville's growth has been steady and balanced. The abundance of natural gas drew a glass plant to the city in 1904 and a zinc smelter two years later. As the industrial area spread west toward the higher blackjack hills of the Osage country, the better residential areas grew south toward the wooded shelf within the looping Caney River. Four parks have been established to meet the recreation needs of the growing city, and in 1956 there were fifteen modern schools with a total enrollment of more than 6,000.

POINTS OF INTEREST

The CIVIC CENTER, Johnstone Ave. between 6th and 7th Sts., was built in 1922 as a memorial to the Bartlesville men who lost their lives in World War I. It houses the municipal offices, an auditorium seating 2,000 persons, and a public library containing 30,000 volumes.

PHILLIPS "66" RESEARCH CENTER (*no visitors*), S. W. of the intersection of US 60 and State 23 on the west edge of the city, is a sprawling complex of laboratories where some five hundred employees are engaged in industry's never-ending struggle to improve and promote its products.

WASHINGTON COUNTY MEMORIAL HOSPITAL, Cherokee Ave. and Frank Phillips Blvd., was erected in 1921 at a cost of $225,000, expanded in 1952 at a cost of $750,000. Its modern facilities are now complemented by the recently constructed JANE PHILLIPS MEMORIAL HOSPITAL, N. of Frank Phillips Blvd., two miles to the east.

CITIES SERVICE BUILDING, 4th St. and Dewey Ave., a part of Bartlesville's budding skyline, houses the main offices of this major integrated oil company.

ADAMS BUILDING, a modern block-square structure between 4th and 5th Sts. and Keeler and Jennings Aves., contains the main offices of the Phillips Petroleum Company, plus an elaborately complete EMPLOYEES CLUB (*tours 10:00, 1:30, 5:30 weekdays; 4:30 Saturdays, Sundays, and holidays*). Particularly striking are the murals inside the Keeler Avenue entrance lobby.

The 19-story PRICE TOWER, 6th St. and Dewey Ave., is the latest, and by far most striking, addition to the Bartlesville skyline. Designed by the famed Frank Lloyd Wright, it incorporates many unique concepts of engineering and design based simply on a concrete shaft and cantilevered floors. Wright himself has described the remarkable building as "the tree that escaped the crowded forest." Seen lighted at night, it is particularly effective. Outstanding visual features of the concrete-and-glass structure are the floors, cantilevered in all four directions, and the vertical and horizontal copper louvers—preoxidized to get the blue-green patina—which shade the golden glass of the windows. The tower was built by H. C. Price, internationally known builder of pipelines, to house his company's offices. It was dedicated in 1956.

SENIOR HIGH SCHOOL, 18th St. on Hillcrest Drive, is one of the most modern and complete small-city school plants in the state. The two buildings, erected in 1940 at a cost of $500,000 ($50,000 of it given by Frank Phillips), are strikingly modern in plan and fenestration. Enrollment in 1955 was 1,009.

The MUNICIPAL STADIUM, Dewey Ave. and 1st St., is a complete athletic plant with fields for basketball, softball, and football. Constructed in 1930, its concrete stands have a seating capacity of 2,000.

JOHNSTONE PARK, through which the Caney River makes an almost perfect horseshoe loop, is Bartlesville's largest and most accessible picnic area and playground. It covers eighty acres at the north edge of the city. Aside from the fine old native trees, the main feature of the park is the DISCOVERY WELL. Here in 1897, at 1,320 feet, the Bartlesville sands were shot with nitroglycerin to create an initial flow of more than thirty barrels a day.

The well was drilled as the result of talk that had persisted in the area since George Keeler had discovered an oil seepage there in 1875.

The drilling rig was hauled from the Tulsa–Red Fork field over seventy miles of muddy winter roads—"fourteen days with fourteen teams," as oil historians have put it. As late as 1941, the well still produced a diminishing amount of oil. By 1956 it was no longer a commercial producer, but the derrick and drilling equipment had been restored to duplicate the original well.

The PETROLEUM EXPERIMENT STATION (*not open to visitors*), Virginia and Cudahy Aves., was opened in 1918 as a joint undertaking of the U.S. Bureau of Mines and the State of Oklahoma. In 1956 it employed 134 people and was one of the world's largest and best-equipped institutions devoted exclusively to the problems of the petroleum industry.

POINTS OF INTEREST IN ENVIRONS

Round Mountain, *1.8 m.*; Osage Hills State Park, *11.4 m.*; Woolaroc Museum, *14 m.* (*see Tour 4*); Hulah Reservoir, *81 m.*; Bar Dew Lake, *5 m.*; Silver Lake Agency, *5.1 m.* (*see Tour 9*).

ENID

Railroad Stations: 728 N. Independence Ave. for St. Louis–San Francisco Ry.; 722 N. Independence Ave. for Atchison, Topeka & Santa Fe Ry.; 129 E. Market Ave. for Chicago, Rock Island & Pacific Ry.
Bus Station: Union Terminal, 319 N. Independence Ave. for Missouri, Kansas, and Oklahoma Lines and Mid-Continent Coaches.
Airport: Woodring Airport, 5 m. E. on US 64, for Central Airlines (four flights daily).
City Buses: Public Square, junction for all routes; fare 15c.
Taxis: Fare from 30c.

Accommodations: 8 hotels; 15 motels on highway approaches to city.

Information Service: Hotel Youngblood, 302 N. Independence Ave.

Newspapers: Morning News and (evening) *Eagle.*
Radio Stations: KCRC (1390 kc.) and KGWA (960 kc.).
Television Station: KGEO–TV (Ch. 5).
Motion Picture Theatres: 6, including 2 drive-ins.
Baseball: Phillips-Failing Field, E. edge of city on US 64; softball.
Swimming: Government Springs Park, 501 E. Oklahoma; Lake Hellums, 6 m. N. on US 81 and 1 m. W.; Phillips University, E. edge of city; Champlin Company (AAU specifications), 400 W. Cherokee Ave.
Golf: University Lake, 400 S. 22nd St., 9 holes, greens fee 50c, 75c for two rounds; Meadowlake, S. of city, 18 holes, greens fee $1.00 weekdays, $1.50 weekends and holidays (50c and 75c for 9 holes). Oakwood Country Club (for members only).
Tennis: Free courts at all city parks; one free court at Phillips University.

Annual Events: Garfield County Fair, fall; Northwestern Oklahoma Junior Livestock Show, spring; Tri-State Music Festival, May; Sooner State Dairy Show, August; celebration of Cherokee Strip Opening, Sept. 16.

ENID (1,246 alt., 36,017 pop.; 1956 est. 40,489), the largest city of north-central Oklahoma, lies in the old Cherokee Outlet. Surrounded by flat and fertile fields, it is the state's most important center for the growing, storing, processing, and marketing of wheat. With three minor oil fields near by, it also boasts refineries with a daily capacity of more than twenty-one thousand barrels of crude oil and a number of oil-well supply and equipment companies. Contributing, too, to the town's well-being are two widely divergent institutions, Phillips University and Vance Air Force Base. Completed in 1941 at a cost of nearly $3,000,000, the latter has been expanded until it now provides for a personnel of approximately four thousand.

Enid has grown over the years from a tent city which sprang out of the prairie dust on the day of the Cherokee Outlet opening—September 16, 1893—to a typically prosperous, substantial, self-contained municipality. Its business section lies on a gently shelving hill, from which clean and spacious residential streets fan out. A fourteen-story hotel and two modern office buildings, eleven and fifteen stories high, combine to make an impressive bid for a large-city appearance. Staid and stolid old business structures placidly line the public square, while the newer buildings branch out into increasing lines of progress. It all adds up to a pleasant and attractive town, with all the markings of modern progress and Midwestern ease of living.

The seat of Garfield County, Enid actually began life some time before the historic opening as a watering place for nomadic Indians and stagecoach teams. It successfully avoided having the name of Skeleton thrust upon it (from its proximity to the head of Skeleton Creek) and owes its real name to a literature-loving Rock Island railroad official. Fond of Tennyson's "Idylls of the King," he felt that Geraint's wife ought to be honored by having a city named for her. (Unwittingly, he gave her a second claim to fame: with her four viable letters, Enid is the "Town in Oklahoma" most loved by the busy fabricators of crossword puzzles.)

Enid was chosen the site of a government land office in the Cherokee Outlet well in advance of the opening. Government surveyors and troops moved in about a year before to run section lines and plat townsites. On opening day in 1893, however, it was discovered that certain enterprising—and shrewdly profit-minded—Cherokee Indians had chosen allotments within the area planned for the town. When Secretary of the Interior Hoke Smith learned of the scheme, he ordered the townsite located three miles south of the original settlement around the railroad station. Consequently, with the government land office, the county courthouse, and the post office separated from the depot, rivalry between the north and south sections promptly developed into a feud. Each claimed the name of Enid, and the other (depending upon which faction one belonged to) was tagged a suburb, North or South Enid. The Rock Island had refused to recognize the government's ruling, continued to run its trains through South Enid without stopping. Then on July 13, 1894, a freight train went off the tracks into a ditch near South Enid, and investigation brought about the discovery that the bridge supports had been weakened by sawing. Rock Island officials announced that, while the company would respect any law the government might enact, it would not surrender to mob action. Secretary Smith's decision was upheld, however, by a presidential proclamation, and on September 16, 1894, a freight and ticket office was established in South Enid, which became the present city. A six-foot hatchet, symbol of strife, was later buried with due and proper ceremony by members of both factions. (All of these events were properly reported in the *Eagle*, Enid's present evening paper, which was founded by pioneer newspapermen Omer K. Benedict and Charles E. Hunter exactly five days after the opening of the Cherokee Outlet.)

One of the many escapades told of the rivalry between the towns concerned a massive, three-hundred pound bell which citizens of South Enid bought and installed to warn the bucket brigade of fires endangering the town's wooden buildings. The arrival one afternoon of a finely dressed liveryman who extolled the virtues of North Enid caused a loud clanging of the bell. This time the men who responded were also secretly organized into an "egg committee," supplied with amply over-ripe ammunition. The North Enidian was promptly turned back by a well-aimed barrage.

Enid's first celebration of the founding of the town and the opening of the Cherokee Outlet was staged just one year after the actual event. Fifteen thousand came to watch an authentic re-enactment of the race, and 150 Cheyenne Indians entertained with tribal dances and ceremonies. This same year, however, proved unfortunate for crops, little grain being raised because of drought. Free seed wheat was supplied by the Rock Island in 1894, but this crop too was a failure—as were those of 1895 and 1896—and many of the settlers began to move on. Then in 1897 the rains came. The harvest was good, and wheat prices shot up to $1.00 a bushel. And to furnish entertainment for a general celebration of this happy turn in the community's fortunes, the Ringling Brothers' circus was brought to town. On that occasion, September 25, the largest crowd that had ever assembled under the Ringling "big tent" overflowed its twenty thousand capacity to set a paid-admissions record of thirty thousand.

Another lusty incident in Enid's early days occurred in 1899 when a cakewalk contest was staged between Negroes from Enid and near-by Kingfisher. Bad feeling, fanned by previous rivalry and high-stakes betting, broke into the open when Kingfisher was awarded the prize. Gunfire and general confusion followed, but civic progress was the net gainer in the end. For general criticism of this and other "Wild West" tomfoolery prompted a determined campaign against lawlessness. Enid was shortly converted into the quiet, model town it remains, essentially, to this day.

Between 1897 and 1903, the Santa Fe and Frisco railroads laid track into Enid to challenge the Rock Island. Converging on the city from all directions, these three lines laid the foundation for Enid's becoming, and remaining, the terminal storage point for Oklahoma and one of its most important flour-milling centers. The town's population rose from 3,444 in 1900 to 13,799 in 1910, a tremendous gain for what was still a sparsely settled section of a new state.

Until the 1920's Enid depended commercially on agriculture, trade, and shipping. Then, with the discovery of the famous Tonkawa district in 1921 and the Crescent pool in 1926, both underlying the previously exploited shallow Garber pool, oil began to play an important part in the city's industrial life. Two refineries were erected, followed by the usual influx of oil-supply houses, foundries, and machine shops. In 1928, the Pillsbury Mill—the state's largest—was built. That same year Enid could boast storage facilities for fifteen million bushels of wheat. Today (1956) Enid's terminal facilities are the third largest in the nation, with a storage capacity of 64,731,500 bushels, exceeded only by Minneapolis and Kansas City.

In addition to grain and oil, poultry feed and eggs are important to Enid, representing an annual turnover of more than $8,000,000. Three packing plants in the industrial section turn out such varied products as meat, butter, canned eggs, dried buttermilk, and cheese. Enid stockyards do an annual business of $1,000,000, to provide the state with one of its best markets for cattle, sheep, and hogs. As a division point, the Frisco Railroad maintains at Enid large machine and car repair shops.

Spiritually, the city is served by fifty-eight churches representing thirty-two denominations. The kindergarten-to-graduate school scene shows some seven thousand students in the public schools, 477 in parochial schools, and 1,281 college students. Highlights on the cultural front are the semiannual exhibits in the Phillips University Music Hall by members of the Enid Artists' League. The group not only displays, and sells, its own work; it also brings in exhibits of worth-while art from the outside.

POINTS OF INTEREST

The new GARFIELD COUNTY COURTHOUSE, dominating the Public Square, is a three-story white Texas sandstone building with an additional story in the central section. Modern and functional in design, it is striking in its utter simplicity.

The half-million-dollar FEDERAL BUILDING AND POST OFFICE, south of the courthouse in the Public Square, is of white marble. It was dedicated in 1941.

The CARNEGIE LIBRARY, Independence and Pine Aves., represents an interesting victory for pioneer brashness over Scotch frugality. Andrew Carnegie's first offer of help—$10,000—was rejected as too small. It was not until he had raised his offer to $25,000 that the present site was purchased. The building, dedicated in 1910, now (1956) bulges with 51,000 volumes and plans are under way to provide a new one. The library had its origin in 1899 when the Enid Study Club established a reading room over a drugstore. Money raised from a "book social" provided the first 150 books. Curiously, the founders had the same difficulty giving away their embryo library that Mr. Carnegie had with his money a few years later. Their first offer was rejected by Enid city fathers on the grounds that the Study Club was a "silk stockinged" group.

Among the library's special collections are the Southard shelves of rare books, a D.A.R. historical and genealogical niche, and a large amount of Oklahoma material. This latter includes more than 700 volumes by Oklahoma authors, and thousands of clippings from newspapers and other sources.

PILLSBURY FLOUR MILL (*guided tours 8 to 5 daily*), 515 E. Spruce St., has a capacity of 8,000 hundredweights per day of flour. Built in 1928, it has operated almost continuously since that date on a 24-hour schedule. Visitors, taken to the top by elevator, walk down through the various departments and levels to the ground floor.

GOVERNMENT SPRINGS PARK, 5th St. and Oklahoma Ave., was perhaps the most noted stopping place on the Chisholm Trail. The springs did not furnish enough water for stock, but there was usually an ample supply in Skeleton Creek, two miles to the east. Trail drivers usually grazed their herds near the creek while they themselves rested at the springs. The park received its name when government men camped there while surveying the townsite and section lines.

The old drinking hole has been cleaned out and walled in. Today the spring supplies water to a pretty, tree-lined lake (*picnic facilities*). Across the street to the north are the SUNKEN GARDENS, planted with many varieties of native flowers. The park also contains a modest zoo and a municipal swimming pool and bathhouse. A block north, at 5th St. and Maine Ave., an old Frisco steam locomotive, No. 1519, is on display in a small park.

Coeducational PHILLIPS UNIVERSITY, on Broadway at the east edge of the city, was chartered October 11, 1906, as Oklahoma Christian University. Seven years later, after the death of T. W. Phillips of Butler, Pennsylvania, whose generosity made possible the founding of the school, its name was changed to honor him. Though nonsectarian, it is controlled by the Christian Church (Disciples of Christ) and dedicated to Christian education. Its faculty numbers sixty-six, and nearly a third of its more than one thousand students (1956) are enrolled in the Bible College.

The 36-acre landscaped campus contains eleven buildings, including a recently erected men's dormitory and a stadium seating 2,000. A museum (*free*) in the Science Building offers a zoological collection of insects, snakes, mounted birds, and shells; a large number of geological specimens; and botanical items from Oklahoma, New Mexico, Arizona, Nevada, and California. The University swimming pool is heated for winter aquatic activities.

Music is emphasized at Phillips, where musical organizations include a University Concert Band, Enid-Phillips Symphony, String Ensemble, University Chorus, Woodwind Quintet, Seminary Choir, and other groups. To promote educational activities beyond the regular day schedule, Phillips' New College offers evening classes and short courses for those outside the University who wish to continue their education, acquire trade and professional training, and pursue special interests in arts and crafts.

LAKE VIEW ASSEMBLY GROUNDS (*fishing, golf, picnicking*), lying just south of the Phillips University Stadium, is a 77-acre tract containing a spring-fed lake encircled by a golf course.

ENID STATE SCHOOL (*open weekdays 9–11, 1–3*), 2600 Willow Ave. at N. E. corner of the city, is one of two state-owned institutions in Oklahoma caring for feeble-minded children. Founded in 1909, it ranks today as one of the top schools of its kind in the nation. The 693-acre tract contains seventeen buildings, which house about 1,400 pupils. Regular school instruction and training in the crafts are provided by the institution's staff of 280.

POINTS OF INTEREST IN ENVIRONS

Wild Fowl Hunting Grounds, *14.8 m.*; Meno, largest Mennonite community in Oklahoma, *18.2 m.* (*see Tour 4*).

LAWTON

Railroad Stations: Railroad St. and C Ave. for Chicago, Rock Island & Pacific Ry.; 5th St. and F Ave. for St. Louis–San Francisco Ry.
Bus Stations: Union Bus Station, 421 C Ave.; Lawton–Fort Sill Bus Co., 202 C Ave.
Airport: Municipal, S. of city.
Taxis: Zone rates from 25c.

Accommodations: 5 hotels, numerous fine motels (total capacity: 500 rooms).

Information Service: Chamber of Commerce, 607 C Ave.

Newspapers: (Morning) *Press,* (evening) *Lawton Constitution,* (combined Sunday) *Constitution-Press.*
Radio Stations: KSWO (1380 kc.) and KCCO (1050 kc.).
Television Station: KSWO–TV (Ch. 7).
Motion Picture Theaters: 8, including 3 drive-ins.
Athletics: High School (Roosevelt) Stadium, 14th St. and Bell Ave., football; High School Field House, 11th St. and Ferris Ave., basketball.
Swimming: Doe Doe Park, 2300 D Ave., Lawton Country Club; wading pools in city parks.
Golf: Municipal Golf Course, Municipal Airport, S. of city, 18 holes, greens fee $1.00 weekdays, $1.50 Saturdays, Sundays, and holidays; Lawton Country Club, west of city, 9 holes, greens fee for out-of-town golfers $3.00 Saturdays, Sundays, and holidays.
Tennis: Lawton High School, 11th St. and Ferris Ave.; city parks.

Annual Events: Pioneer Day, Aug. 6; Lawton Rangers Rodeo, Aug.; Wichita Mountains Easter Pageant (*see Tour 3B*).

LAWTON (1,116 alt., 34,757 pop.; 1956 est. 54,000), the seat of Comanche County, is a pioneer-built town that owes its "city" status largely to its proximity to burgeoning Fort Sill (*see Tour 3A*). It was named in honor of Major General Henry W. Lawton, who was killed in the Philippines in 1899.

Lawton came into being August 6, 1901, just six days after the opening by lottery of the three-million-acre Kiowa-Comanche Indian reservation to white settlers. The site had been designated by the United States Land Office as one of the three county seats to be established; Hobart (*see Tour 12*) in Kiowa County and Anadarko (*see Tour 3*) in Caddo County were the others. Almost overnight Lawton had a population of ten thousand, made up for the most part of men, with their families, who had failed to get 160-acre homesteads in the August 1 lottery and moved on to the townsite in the hope of bidding successfully at the sale of lots. By August 3—still three days before the sale and with only three officially laid out streets—the town had some four hundred business structures, nearly all of them tents, and a newspaper, the *Lawton State Democrat*.

The sale of the lots platted on the 320-acre townsite raised $414,845, of which some $125,000 was turned over by the government to meet the expenses of the new town. By March 1, 1902, five banks were in operation, with deposits of $635,000, and a railroad was building in from the north. Although some of the 1,119 inhabitants were still sleeping out of doors, the town in general was adequately "housed, fed and watered."

In brief, Lawton telescoped into a period of months the pioneer phase of a western town which usually extended over years. Until 1930 its progress was steady, if not spectacular. Then, owing largely to the expansion of Fort Sill as the principal Artillery School of Fire for the U.S. Army, a rapid growth began. Between 1930 and 1940 the percentage of population increase was greater than that of any other city in Oklahoma, its numerical increase—5,934—exceeded only by that of Oklahoma City. Lawton's population in 1950 was 34,757, as compared to 18,055 in 1940. And a detailed survey made early in 1956 placed the city's population at 54,000. In the meantime, Lawton has begun to develop local industries and has further strengthened its position as the wholesale trade and medical center of southwestern Oklahoma. And Fort Sill, now the nation's Artillery and Guided Missile Center, has announced plans for further expansion of its facilities (*see Tour 3*).

The older part of Lawton is on the second bench of land that rises from the western bank of Cache Creek. In its growth, the city has pushed higher up the slope, toward the north and northwest. Its business section consists of blocks of brick buildings, most of them modernized inside and out during the past five years. As for the people on its downtown streets, they represent a true cross section of Oklahoma: whites, Indians, and Negroes (about 10 per cent of the population). The military uniform, of course, is more common here than in any other state city, though this, too, seems to fit all three racial groups

In the Cities

Tulsa.

(*above*) Thomas Gilcrease Museum.

(*below*) Utica Square Shopping Center.

LAWTON.

(*above*) NATIONAL GUARD ARMORY.

(*below*) MCMAHON MEMORIAL AUDITORIUM.

Evans Hall, University of Oklahoma, Norman.

(*above*) Price Tower, Bartlesville.

(*below*) Fort Gibson Stockade (*restored*), Muskogee.

Cement Kiln, Ada.

(*above*) Student Union Building, Oklahoma A. & M. College, Stillwater.

(*below*) Indian Sanatorium, Shawnee.

impartially. There is a variety of residences, ranging from the modest dwellings on the south to the expensive homes in the newer additions to the west. Lawton has an arid, clean-swept look. Trees are plentiful only in some of the older sections.

The city's initial and permanent growth was helped by the fact that it lay under the shadow of Fort Sill and became a sort of civic center for that important army post. But it is also the metropolis of an extensive farming area, and a large percentage of Comanche County's income stems from 2,200 farms with 500,000 acres of crop and pasture lands. Principal agricultural products, in the order of their importance, are beef cattle, wheat, dairy cattle, cotton, alfalfa, peanuts, and feed grains.

To serve its extensive trade territory—250,000 people within a radius of seventy-five miles—Lawton has nine hundred retail outlets (1956 sales: in excess of $51,000,000) and seventy-five wholesale companies. On the city's western edge is Cameron State Agricultural College (*see below*). Near-by deposits of asphalt and mountains of granite and other building stone (*see Tour* 3) have also contributed to Lawton's growth. And within an hour's drive lie a number of the state's finest scenic attractions.

Lawton, last of Oklahoma cities to be born overnight out of the dust and clamor of an Indian reservation opening, was fortunate in having among its first settlers many who were aware of the color and drama surrounding that event. In "Prairie Days," the well-known poet (and 1912 Lawton High School graduate) Don Blanding described it this way:

> Lawton, the new town, sprang from the prairie land,
> Grew as a mushroom grows . . .
> All night long the hammers sounded . . .
> Houses grew in the flare of kerosene torches.

As the men streamed in looking for shade, sweat-drenched pants pockets bulging with rolls of currency to pay for the auctioned lots, they saw the townsite's lone oak tree. They looked over F. M. English's bank—a one-room frame shack—poised on rollers, ready to be wheeled to the lot the banker intended to buy. They watched an enterprising citizen take $500 in dimes for registering would-be lot bidders at ten cents apiece. They heard over and over the cry of "Stop thief!" from men and women whose purses had been snatched—and the more ominous mutterings of men whose teams had been stolen. They choked in the dust raised by water haulers who brought tepid water from Cache Creek and retailed it at five cents a cup until competition forced the price down to fifty cents and then to twenty-five cents a barrel.

In *Neath August Sun,* a volume assembled by Lawton's business and professional women, the August 6 lot sale is re-created in the words of scores of persons who were there. The government auctioneer stood on a dry-goods box beside a big tent and hour after hour and day after day cried the lots, beginning at the northern limits of the platted townsite. When he shouted "Sold!" a soldier escorted the successful bidder between lines of other soldiers and into the tent. There, he was given title to his lot if he paid down the amount of its purchase price in cash. In case he did not have the whole amount with him, he could pay $25 to hold the property for thirty minutes.

That provision was to allow him time to withdraw the needed cash from one of the townsite's two banks—Mr. English had a competitor by this time. Often, however, waiting lines were too long to permit the buyer to make the thirty-minute deadline. When this happened, his $25 deposit was forfeited and the lot was resold. One story in the collection tells of the man who, seeing it was hopeless to wait in line, persuaded a friend inside the chicken-wire cage to toss over a package containing $1,000 in bills with which he could seal his purchase. The first lot sold for $420. The top price—paid for the lot opposite the land office—was $4,555. (These frenzied operations, of course, gave currency to the still common expression, "a land-office business.")

Told, too, is the story of a man named Woods, who had drawn number one in the reservation land lottery. Instead of taking the usual half-mile-square homestead, he chose a strip a mile long and a quarter of a mile wide alongside the Lawton townsite, thereby ungallantly shutting off from the town-to-be a young lady by the name of Mattie Beal, who was number two. The man promptly earned the nickname "Hog." As for the wronged—and presumably personable—Miss Beal, nationwide publicity earned her five hundred proposals of marriage from all parts of the United States.

Lawton, of course, had its "ragtown" section. Here was located the eating place called the Goo-Goo (after the street of the same name). That was the summer when young men learned from a woman singer with a wagon show the words of "When you make dem goo-goo eyes at me!" It was at the Goo-Goo that a client, if he dared to order a moderately priced steak, could expect the waiter to call back to the kitchen, "One for the dog!"

Described as a "rollicking, hilarious tent and shack city," Lawton had eighty-six saloons—one for every hundred inhabitants—in November, 1901. One of these, in honor of the famous temperance crusader of the day, displayed the sign: "All nations welcome here except CARRIE." And gambling joints grew so numerous that a volunteer committee of citizens finally had to rise up and sweep them out. The town's first serious fire that threatened to destroy the shanty town was checked by the traditional bucket brigade, reinforced by frantically galloping water haulers and hundreds of men and women wielding wetted quilts and blankets. And the first big official celebration—a slightly delayed first birthday celebration—featured a bull fight (complete with authentic Spanish toreador costumes) and a colorful Apache Indian dance staged by Fort Sill's most distinguished prisoner, old Chief Geronimo himself.

For a time the nearest railroad station was Marlow, on the Rock Island. Passengers had to hire a team and wagon for the rest of the trip to Lawton. The frontier experience of the Lawton-bound traveler could be gauged by the speed and dexterity with which he clambered through the train windows to beat his competitors to the best rigs. And many an ambitious Eastern businessman, camping out overnight on the prairie, trembled at the crazy barking of encircling coyotes and got his first spine-tingling initiation into life in the Wild West.

Among the town's first settlers were two men who became United States senators Thomas P. Gore and Elmer Thomas. Lawton's first attorney was Jake L. Hamon, who was later to become prominent in Oklahoma oil and Oklahoma politics (two fields that have consistently shown a strong affinity for one another in the Sooner State down to the present day). It has also been recorded that Heck Thomas, the town's first peace officer and a well-known outlaw-catcher, once chased Lon Chaney (then a Lawton photographer and later a famous movie actor) for speeding—on horseback.

POINTS OF INTEREST

(Numbers below refer to circled numbers on the Lawton city map in this section.)

1. The CARNEGIE LIBRARY, 5th St. and B Ave., is a small, neat building of buff brick erected in 1921 at a cost of $30,000. The first books were collected in 1903, the second year of the town's existence, by a library committee of the City Federation of Women's Clubs. In 1956 there were 40,843 volumes.

2. COMANCHE COUNTY COURTHOUSE, 5th St. and C Ave., was dedicated in 1939. It is a chaste, solid, three-story structure of buff sandstone, trimmed with chromium steel.

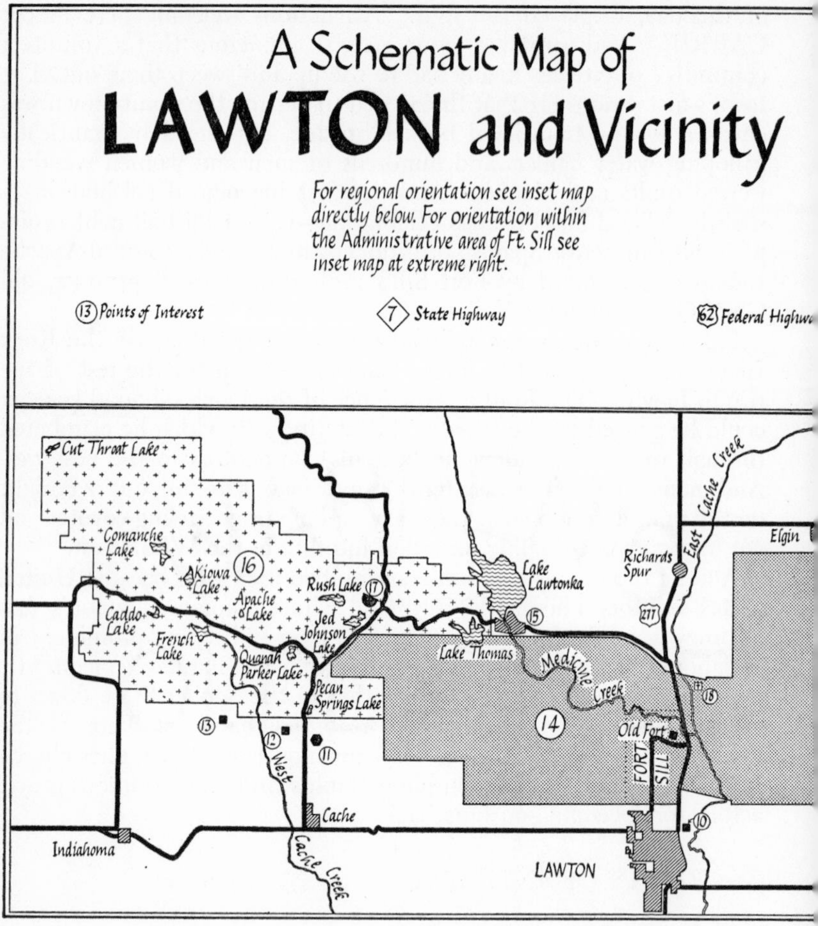

3. CAMERON STATE AGRICULTURAL COLLEGE, on the west edge of the city, south of Gore Boulevard, is Oklahoma's largest junior college (1956 enrollment 1,633). The 350-acre campus includes four classroom and laboratory buildings, a library, an auditorium, four dormitories, an infirmary, and many agricultural buildings.

Named in honor of the first State Superintendent of Schools, the college was founded in 1909 as one of six agricultural high schools in the state. It became a junior college in 1927. The Associate of Arts degree is conferred in agriculture, as well as in many fields of the arts,

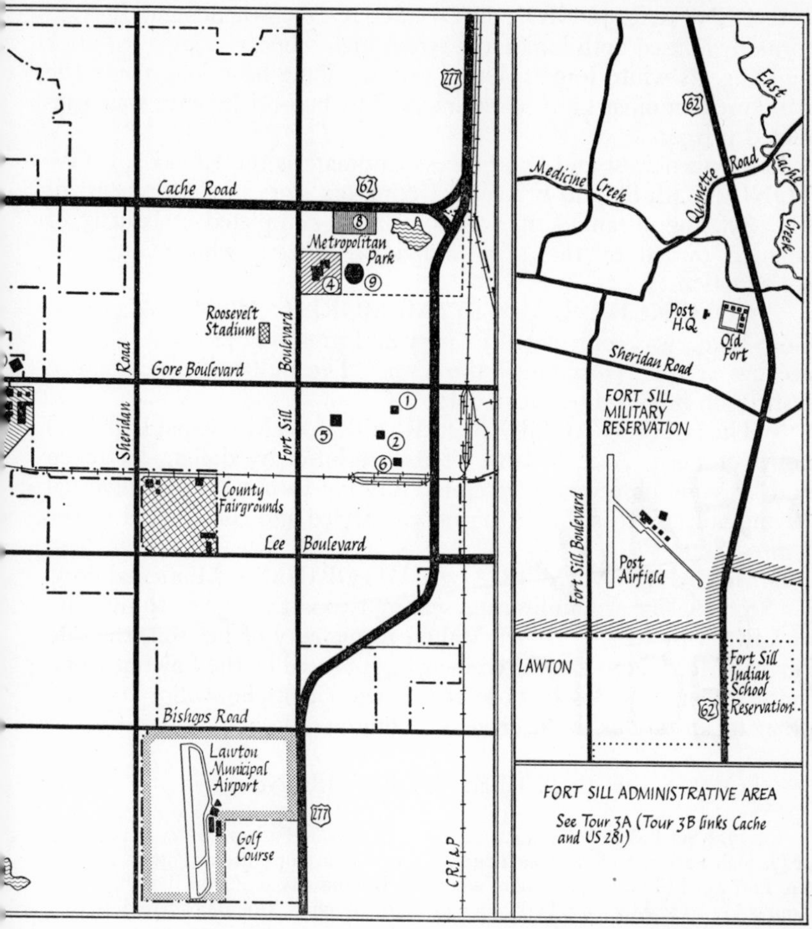

sciences, and preprofessional branches. Evening classes are offered to adults.

4. LAWTON HIGH SCHOOL, Ferris Ave. and Fort Sill Blvd., is one of the state's newest and most modern school plants. Constructed of buff brick the building is two blocks long, one block wide, and accommodates 1,200 students. Costing $2,761,000, the building was finished and dedicated in 1956. More than half of the cost was borne by the federal government because the large personnel of Fort Sill necessitates greatly expanded facilities.

5. CENTRAL JUNIOR HIGH SCHOOL, 8th St. and B Ave., formerly housed both junior and senior high schools. A large red-brick building, its white Ionic columns and its dome have long made the structure a familiar Lawton landmark. The buff-brick annex was completed in 1940.

Lawton's newest and handsomest landmark is the HOTEL LAWTONIAN, 4th St. and E Ave., towering ten stories over the heart of the city. The ultramodern, 153-room hotel, completed in January of 1955, is owned by the 1,671 individual citizens who financed its construction.

7. COMANCHE COUNTY MEMORIAL HOSPITAL, 3600 Gore Blvd., was constructed in 1951 and promptly received national acclaim as the "Hospital of the Year." The million-dollar, 100-bed institution is owned by the county.

8. The NATIONAL GUARD ARMORY, on Municipal Park land north of Ferris Ave., because of its revolutionary design, has been said by some observers to resemble nothing so much as an inverted "flying saucer." It is the first armory so styled and constructed in the United States.

9. McMAHON MEMORIAL AUDITORIUM, in Municipal Park, is a $500,000 fine arts auditorium seating 1,500. It was given to the City of Lawton by Mrs. E. P. McMahon in memory of her son, the late Eugene McMahon. Dedicated in 1955, it is used by the Lawton Community Concerts Association, the Lawton Symphony Society, and other organizations, both civic and commercial.

POINTS OF INTEREST IN ENVIRONS

10. Fort Sill Indian School, *0.8 m.* 11. Craterville Park, *19.6 m.* 12. Home of Quanah Parker, *20.6 m.* (*see Tour* 3). 13. Grave of Quanah Parker, *25.1 m.* 14. Fort Sill Military Reservation, adjoining Lawton city limits on the north (*see Tour* 3A). 15. Medicine Park, *13.1 m.* 16. Wichita Mountains Wildlife Refuge, *17.4 m.* (*see Tour 3B*). 17. Easter Pageant amphitheater, *22.4 m.* 18. Indian Cemetery (burial place of Geronimo).

MUSKOGEE

Railroad Stations: Intersection of Broadway and tracks for Missouri-Kansas-Texas R. R.; 2nd and Elgin Sts. for St. Louis–San Francisco Ry. and Midland Valley R. R.
Bus Station: 201 S. 5th St. for Continental Trailways.
Airports: Hatbox Field, 40th St. and Arline Rd., for private and chartered planes; Davis Field, 5.5 m. S. E. of city, for commercial airlines (six flights daily) and 713th Fighter-Bomber Squadron, U. S. Air Force Reserve.

City Buses: Fare 15c.
Taxis: Zoned fares from 35c.

Accommodations: 8 hotels, including 2 for Negroes; 21 motels with 273 units.

Information Service: Hotel Severs, 215 State St.

Newspapers: (Morning) *Phoenix* and (evening) *Times-Democrat.*
Radio Stations: KBIX (1490 kc.) and KMUS (1380 kc.).
Television Station: KTVX (Ch. 8).
Motion Picture Theaters: 9, including 3 drive-ins.
Baseball: Athletic Park, Boston Ave. and 5th St.
Softball: Memorial Stadium, Chestnut and Elmira Sts.
Swimming: Municipal Pool, Honor Heights Park, 40th St. and Park Blvd.; Spaulding Park, E. Okmulgee Ave. and Eastside Blvd.; Elliott Park, 400 Tower Hill Blvd.
Golf: Muskogee Town and Country Club, Club Blvd., 2.5 m. N. E. on US 62, 18 holes, greens fee $2.00; Meadowbrook Golf Club, 18 holes, 1.5 m. S.W. on US 62–64, 18 holes, greens fee 75c weekdays, $1.00 Sat. and Sun.
Tennis: Municipal courts at Spaulding, Rotary, and Airport parks, free.

Annual Events: Oklahoma Free State Fair, third week in Sept.; Flower Show, spring and fall; Kennel Show, first week in Nov.

MUSKOGEE (617 alt., 37,289 pop.; 1956 est. 45,000), was named for the Muskogee (Creek) Indians and lies just south of the confluence of the Verdigris, Grand, and Arkansas rivers. It is surrounded by low, gently sloping hills, blending into a rich, flat-to-rolling farming section. The tracks of the Missouri-Kansas-Texas Railroad pass squarely through the town from north to south, dividing it into almost equal parts. Streets are wide and bordered by trees, with old-fashioned houses two- and three stories high set far back in well-kept lawns. Many small parcels of land, ordinarily eyesores in most cities, are developed here into flower gardens and parks. The city maintains twenty-two of these garden areas, comprising a total of 540 acres.

Thomas Nuttall, widely traveled English naturalist and later curator of the botanical gardens of Harvard University, on a journey up the Arkansas in 1819, predicted that "if the confluence of the Verdigris, Arkansas, and Neosho [Grand] rivers shall ever become of importance as a settlement—which the great and irresistible tide of western emigration promises—a town will probably be founded here at the junction of these streams." Earlier (1805), Meriwether Lewis had recommended this site to President Jefferson for a trading point. And in 1806, James B. Wilkinson advised the government to establish a factory there, and also "a garrison of troops."

It was natural for Nuttall and others to assume that river traffic would determine the location of the town. But the importance of river transportation and river trading posts increased little after Nuttall's visit and became negligible as soon as railroads were built into the territory.

Before Nuttall wrote about the region, the "Three Forks" (*see Tour* 3) had become a center of trade and a rallying point for buyers and sellers of furs. There the traders Hugh Glenn, Nathaniel Pryor, French and Rutherford, Thompson and Drennan, Jesse B. Turley, the Creek Benjamin Hawkins, and—best known of all—Auguste P. Chouteau were all active. They traded both with the Osages, who came down the Grand River from the North, and with the nomadic tribes who brought their peltries down the Salt Fork, the Deep Fork, and the Arkansas rivers and across the comparatively short stretch of country between "Three Forks" and the Canadian.

By 1829, emigration of Creeks from Alabama—in response to United States government pressure—was well under way, and some twelve hundred were located near the mouth of the Verdigris on land which turned out to be part of the Cherokee Nation. The Creeks were then moved south of the Arkansas, and their agency was established in the vicinity of Fern Mountain, some three miles northwest of Muskogee.

It was at this agency that the first settlement in the Muskogee region started. But not until 1872, when the Missouri-Kansas-Texas Railroad crossed the Arkansas, did the town itself come into being. Its first white inhabitants were those hopeful and adventurous fortune seekers who had waited in camp on the north bank of the river for the completion of the bridge. They rode the first train over, got off at the station, and began to build stores and residences on both sides of the track.

Across the site of the new town ran the old Texas Road, over which thousands of settlers had traveled southward by wagon and over which many herds of Texas cattle had been driven northward. A few Creek Indians lived in the neighborhood, but the population was predominantly Negro—Creek freedmen who had chosen the area as especially suited to their agricultural needs and knowledge. And for a considerable time after the town was established, the Creeks refused to consider it as an official Indian settlement.

Old-timers in Muskogee are apt to point with pride to the city's steady and vigorous growth, its solid and law-abiding people, and then recall to memory the early days, when hogs rooted and wallowed in the streets and Bradley Collins, bootlegger and bad man, amused himself by shooting them. They will tell of the time one of Bradley's shots winged a United States marshal, and how he was acquitted of blame because "it was a private quarrel and both men had sworn to shoot on sight."

Another memory of Muskogee's early days centers on the old federal jail, the first to be erected in the Indian Territory. It stood at what is now the corner of Denison and Third Streets and consisted of a number of wooden buildings surrounded by a twelve-foot stockade. For walls, the jail had two-by-six boards covered with sheet iron. Sometimes, before a federal court was established at Muskogee in 1889, as many as 350 prisoners were held there at one time. And it is recorded that a number of women once remained behind the board walls for two years before being removed for trial in the nearest federal court, at Fort Smith, Arkansas.

When Muskogee was made a railroad division point the town's permanence was assured. Its importance as a business center was further enhanced by the establishment in 1874 of the Union Agency for the Five Civilized Tribes. Eufaula (*see Tour 8*) had also made a bid for the agency, and an inspector was sent from Washington to determine which of the two towns was better fitted to care for employees. A perhaps apochryphal story has it that the night before his arrival a resident of Muskogee emptied a barrel of salt into Eufaula's town well, with the result that the inspector, after one taste of the water, decided that Muskogee should be the administrative headquarters of Indian Territory.

In contrast to this phase of Muskogee's history was the organization in 1877—when the town was still hardly more than a huddle of shacks and tents—of the International Indian Fair for the encouragement of farming and stockgrowing, especially among the more backward Indians of the Five Tribes and of the western Plains tribes. The announcement of the eleventh fair said that those who came "must bring corn, wheat, cotton, potatoes, fruits and flowers, livestock, and works of art. In all the departments there will be lively contests for prizes, and especially in the musical department."

This annual gathering of Indians with the purpose of maintaining the Indian character, reached its peak of importance in the fall of 1879, when the threat of "Boomer" invasion of their unoccupied western lands had become serious. Secretary of the Interior Carl Schurz was a visitor to this fair. He inspected the exhibits, watched the sale of baskets and beadwork made by the Plains Indians, and sat with them in councils in the big barnlike pavilion in which their products were shown.

The amalgamation of Oklahoma's Indian and white populations and the Indians' more or less complete adoption of white methods lessened the need for such a fair and it was finally dropped. But the idea was adopted by the United States Indian Bureau for the more backward tribes living on reservations in other western states.

Climatic conditions in the Muskogee area were favorable to diversified agriculture and many farmers had drifted into the neighborhood. Tribal ownership of the land, however, retarded development, and the town did not make any rapid growth until 1894, when the Dawes Commission, set up the year before to allot land to individual Indians, established headquarters in Muskogee. The town was incorporated in 1898 under Arkansas statutes, and its first public school was attended by 235 pupils. The opening of near-by oil and gas fields in 1904 gave added impetus to Muskogee's growth. (Actually, traces of oil had been found as early as 1894, but there was little activity until the Dawes Commission made it possible for white promoters to get valid titles to Indian land.)

As soon as Indian land could be acquired, so many white men flocked into the area that the supremacy of the Indians was seriously threatened. Chiefs of the various tribes met at Muskogee in 1905 with the hope of forming a constitution and completing plans to make the territory an Indian state, which was to be called Sequoyah after the inventor of the Cherokee alphabet(*see Tour 15*). The vision of an Indian state vanished, however, when the Enabling Act of 1906 joined Indian Territory with Oklahoma Territory to form a single state (*see History*).

In the eleven years, 1889–1900, Muskogee's population increased from 2,500 to 4,254. Largely because of oil development between 1900 and 1907, the number of inhabitants more than tripled, and by 1910, when the city charter was granted, it stood at 25,278. In that year Muskogee was the state's second largest city, surpassing Tulsa by some six thousand persons. But as the oil interests gradually shifted from Muskogee to Tulsa over the next twenty years, census figures rose only to 32,025. And in the 1930–40 decade there was a population gain of only 306.

World War II pushed Muskogee forward again. It brought three military installations to the Muskogee area—Camp Gruber, an air base, and a flight training school—with the attending influx of civilian employees. By 1950, the city's official population had grown to 37,289, with an additional 6,500 in the fringe areas. And continued growth was virtually assured with the announcement in 1956 of the location east of Muskogee of two new industries: a $6,500,000 metals processing plant and a $38,000,000 Navy fuel plant.

Throughout Muskogee's history the Negro population has been

large. In 1956 it amounted to about 21 per cent of the total, and the Negro city-within-a-city, centered around South Second Street, largely provides its own business and service institutions, its schools and amusement places, its churches and clubs.

Oil development in the early 1900's brought Muskogee three new railroads: the Frisco, the Midland Valley, and the Kansas, Oklahoma & Gulf. Farming expanded, and on the rich Arkansas River bottom lands truck gardening has flourished to the extent that canning is now an important industry. The area is also noted for cotton, potatoes, corn, soybeans, and spinach.

"Hard goods" manufacturing has long been important in Muskogee. A small ironworks, established in 1917, now turns out derricks, transmission towers, transformer racks, road-building and oil-field equipment. Another company, founded the same year, manufactures winches, hoists, and other kinds of machinery. Newer manufacturing companies (nearly one hundred of them) now produce such varied items as glass and glass products, corrugated paper containers, ladies' garments, furniture, optical equipment, fertilizer, dried foods, and tire-patch materials. As the principal city between Tulsa and Fort Smith, Arkansas, Muskogee is also headquarters for twenty-five wholesale houses. And its continuing importance as the agricultural trade center of the Arkansas River valley is shown by its two large grain elevators, six produce houses, and two meat packing plants, and by its cottonseed-oil mill, cotton compress, and several gins.

Under a city manager form of government since 1920, Muskogee owns its own water system. Light and power come from a new $25,000,000 Oklahoma Gas & Electric Company power plant, dedicated in 1956, on the near-by Arkansas River.

Its closeness to Indians and Indian problems has given Muskogee a long and interesting history in the field of journalism (*see Newspapers*). First on the scene in 1876 was the *Indian Journal*, proposed originally as an instrument of the Intertribal Council, later edited privately by William P. Ross, a Princeton-educated Cherokee. Until it was moved to Eufaula (*see Tour 8*), the *Journal* was an ardent champion of all Indians and their threatened rights. Another instrument of justice for the Indians was *Our Brother in Red*, a Methodist missionary paper started in 1882. Like the *Indian Journal*, it had at first both English and Creek language sections.

The present *Phoenix* was founded in 1888 by Leo E. Bennett, a young white man who had married a Creek citizen. It became a daily in 1901. The first daily in Muskogee, however, was the *Morning Times*, started in 1896 and edited for a time by that talented mixed-blood

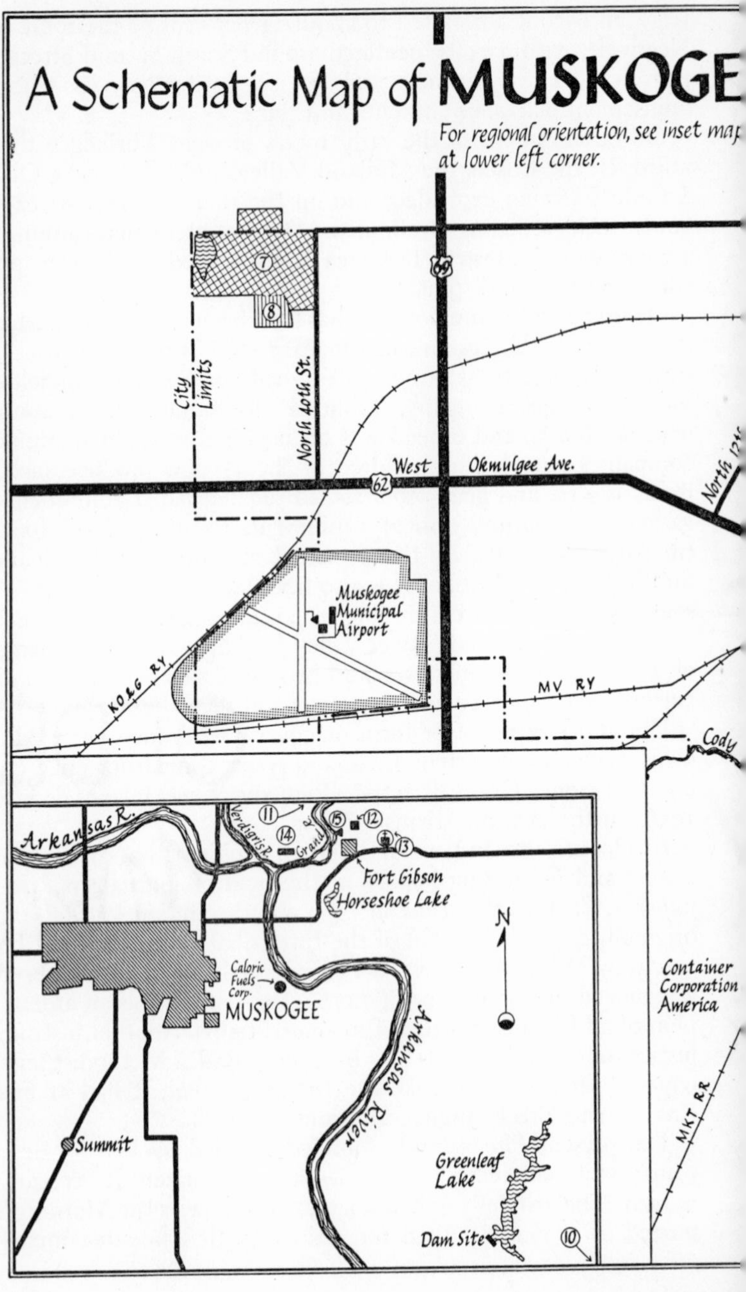
A Schematic Map of MUSKOGE
For regional orientation, see inset map at lower left corner.
City Limits
North 40th St.
West
Okmulgee Ave.
North 12t
Muskogee Municipal Airport
KO&G RY
MV RY
Cody
Arkansas R.
Verdigris R.
Grand R.
Fort Gibson
Horseshoe Lake
N
Caloric Fuels Corp.
MUSKOGEE
Arkansas River
Summit
Greenleaf Lake
Dam Site
Container Corporation America
MKT RR

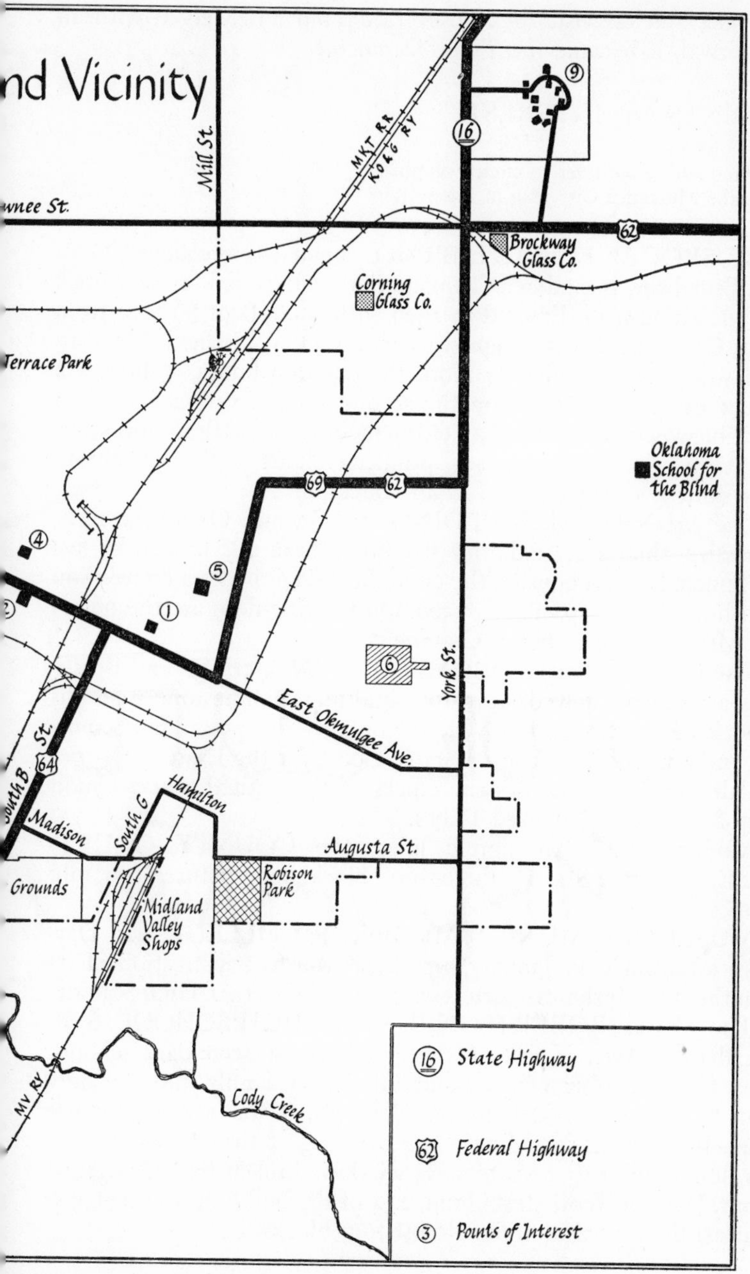
nd Vicinity
Mill St.
MKT RR
KO&G RY
16
9
wnee St.
62
Brockway Glass Co.
Corning Glass Co.
Terrace Park
69
62
Oklahoma School for the Blind
4
5
1
6
York St.
East Okmulgee Ave.
South B St.
64
Hamilton
Madison
South G
Augusta St.
Robison Park
Grounds
Midland Valley Shops
MV RY
Cody Creek
16 State Highway
62 Federal Highway
3 Points of Interest

Creek poet and essayist, Alex Posey (*see Tour* 8). Merged with an evening rival, it became the *Times-Democrat.*

POINTS OF INTEREST

(Numbers below refer to circled numbers on the Muskogee City map in this section.)

1. MUSKOGEE PUBLIC LIBRARY (*open 9–9 weekdays*), D St. and E. Broadway, is modified Georgian in design, of red tapestry brick and white stone trim. Erected in 1909 with the gift of $60,000 from Andrew Carnegie, it was designed by Henry D. Whitefield, Mr. Carnegie's son-in-law. Besides its more than 70,000 books, it houses a MUSEUM OF INDIAN RELICS on the second floor. Exhibits include a rare double-weave Cherokee basket, medicine-man rattles, moccasins, drums, clubs, knives, arrowheads, primitive chairs, and other curios. On the same floor there is also an art collection.

2. The MUNICIPAL BUILDING, 3rd St. and Okmulgee Ave., is a massive, three-story red-brick structure, its façade broken by five tall columns. Besides housing the city offices, it provides a convention hall with a seating capacity of 3,500. On the first floor are the offices of the Muskogee Chamber of Commerce.

3. The million-dollar FEDERAL BUILDING, 5th St. and Broadway, is a many-windowed, four-story building of limestone that fills the block of 5th Street frontage. It contains the post office, courtroom, and offices of the United States Court for the Eastern District of Oklahoma. It also houses the offices of the United States Union Agency for the Five Civilized Tribes.

4. Modern and with simple lines, the COUNTY COURTHOUSE, 216 State St., is a three-story, blocklike structure of granite and limestone.

5. MUSKOGEE MUNICIPAL JUNIOR COLLEGE, 420 Dayton St., established in January, 1920, was the first institution of its kind in the state. It shares quarters with the old CENTRAL HIGH SCHOOL.

6. The ALICE ROBERTSON JUNIOR HIGH SCHOOL, S St. and Callahan Ave., is one of the state's finest secondary schools. Named for a member of a famous missionary family and the only woman to represent Oklahoma in Congress, it was opened for use in 1940. It is a wide-spreading white building of two stories, square-cut in design, with its rows of wide windows broken by flat engaged columns. With its football stadium, east of the building, seating 6,500 spectators, the school occupies almost four blocks.

7. HONOR HEIGHTS PARK (old Agency Hill Park), 40th St. and Park Blvd., has been developed as a memorial to veterans of World War I. Covering 30 acres of the 100 which constitute the grounds known as Agency Hill, this beautiful landscaped and watered park tumbles down the hillside in terraces, cascades, pools, flowered borders, and grassy plots to the large lake and public swimming pool at the foot of the hill. Here can be found nearly every flower and shrub native to Oklahoma. And in addition to evergreens in profusion, there are oaks, maples, redbud, dogwood, hackberry, native and Chinese elms, and plum, peach, and cherry trees, which succeed the redbud and dogwood as splashes of bloom in the spring. In 1935 this park was awarded a $1,000 prize as the most beautiful rock garden in a *Better Homes and Gardens* contest. UNION AGENCY BUILDING, in the park, is a dignified and beautiful stone structure that was used for a time as headquarters for the government's business with the Five Tribes, and then for a school for freedmen by the Creeks. In 1956 it was converted into the Five Civilized Tribes Museum. Near by is the site of the Alice Robertson home, "Sawokla."

8. UNITED STATES VETERANS' FACILITY (open 2–4 daily), established as a veterans' hospital in 1923 and as a combined facility of the United States Veterans' administration in 1938, lies just south of Honor Heights Park. Its 20 buildings are set in an attractively landscaped area of 16 acres that overlook the city and the hills that rise toward the western edge of the Ozarks. The main building, modified U-shape in plan and classical in design, rises four stories above a basement. Like the other principal structures, it is built of brick, terra cotta, and artificial stone.

POINTS OF INTEREST IN ENVIRONS

9. Bacone Indian College, 2.3 *m.* 10. Lake Tenkiller Dam, 32 *m.* (*see Tour* 2). 11. Fort Gibson Dam, 13 *m.* (*see Tour* 3). 12. Fort Gibson Stockade, 9 *m.* 13. Fort Gibson National Cemetery, 31.1 *m.* 14. Three Forks Marker, 7.2 *m.* 15. Site of old Steamboat Landing, 9.4 *m.*

NORMAN

Railroad Station: Intersection of Comanche St. and tracks for Atchison, Topeka & Santa Fe Ry.
Bus Station: 105 W. Main St. for Oklahoma Transportation Co., Continental Trailways, and Greyhound Lines.
City Buses: Fare 15c.
Taxis: 35c.

Airport: Max Westheimer Field (owned by the University of Oklahoma), 1.5 m. N. W. on State 74.

Accommodations: 3 hotels; 4 tourist courts.

Information Service: Chamber of Commerce, 115 E. Gray St.

Newspapers: Norman Transcript (daily except Sat.); *Oklahoma Daily* (published by the University of Oklahoma School of Journalism).
Radio Stations: KNOR (1400 kc.); WNAD (640 kc.).
Motion Picture Theaters: 6, including 2 drive-ins.
Golf: University Golf Course, S. of University, 18 holes, greens fee 75c and $1.25 weekdays, $1.00 and $1.75 Saturdays, Sundays, and holidays; Twin Lakes Golf and Country Club, 5 m. E. of city, 9 holes, greens fee $1 weekdays, $1.50 Saturdays, Sundays, and holidays.
Swimming: North Campus, 1 m. N. of Norman (operated by the University of Oklahoma).
Tennis: University of Oklahoma main campus.

Annual Events: (fall) Homecoming Week, Dad's Day, Religious Emphasis Week, Varsity Show, Band Day, (spring) Brotherhood Week, Mother's Day, Engineers' Week, All-Sports Day, Class Reunions, Sooner Scandals, Frontier Days, Commencement.

NORMAN (1,160 alt., 27,006 pop.; 1956 est. 35,000) is a pleasant, tree-shaded college town situated on a plateau overlooking the valley of the South Canadian River. The city is divided in a northwest-southeast direction by the Santa Fe Railway, and the streets of the central part of town run in the same general direction, forming an approximate square. Outlying streets are laid out straight with the compass. Norman's economic growth in the past has been largely dependent upon the surrounding country-trade area and the establishment there of the state university in 1892. The Central State Hospital, started in 1893 as a privately owned sanitarium, became a state institution in 1915. It has been a second important economic factor in the town's development.

The *Norman Transcript*, in 1893, accurately expressed the character of Norman's development. "It is not claimed for this city that she will ever be a great metropolis, but it is a city of homes, and one of the most desirable places of residence of which the mind can conceive." Lacking industries in its early existence, the town has attracted residents over the years through civic improvements and the educational and cultural advantages that go with a college town. Growth, if not spectacular, has been steady since its establishment in 1889. The population increased from 2,225 in 1900 to 3,724 in 1910. It was 5,005 in 1920, and 9,603 in 1930. World War II and the presence of two military bases brought the biggest spurt in population—from 11,433 in 1940 to 27,006 in 1950.

Norman was named for a government engineer who pitched camp about eighteen miles south of the present site of Oklahoma City in 1872. Little is known of the engineer beyond the fact that when the Santa Fe Railroad laid tracks through the Territory several years later, a boxcar, placed near the spot where he had camped, designated it as "Norman Switch." The present city of Norman did not evolve until the Territory was opened for settlement on April 22, 1889.

By nightfall on opening day the population of Norman Switch had jumped to five hundred and the town was on its way. On January 25, 1890, the *Norman Transcript* boasted that the community already had "two newspapers, four churches, and twenty-nine business houses of importance." In April of that same year the Southern Methodist church began negotiations for the establishment of a college within the new Oklahoma Territory. Norman was selected as the site, and on September 18, 1890, High Gate Female College opened its doors with an enrollment of 130. Students were not allowed to attend places of amusement and male faculty members, when appearing on the streets, were required to wear a silk tie and a Prince Albert coat. When the state university opened in 1892, enrollment at High Gate decreased rapidly, and the next year its buildings were sold to the Oklahoma Sanitarium Company, to become in 1915 the state-owned Central State Hospital.

Differing little from any other small city, the greater part of the modern business district has spread along the increasing length of Main Street. Near the University, however, the traditional college atmosphere prevails. Here the shops, restaurants, and other business establishments cater almost entirely to the faculty and students. Norman has some five hundred modern stores and shops, with an annual sales volume of more than $26,000,000. There are two dairy processing plants and a number of light industries. The maintenance shops of the Oklahoma National Guard are located just north of town on US 77. East of Norman, on State Highway 9, is the recently constructed Cerebral Palsy Institute, a pioneering project erected and equipped at a cost of $375,000.

THE UNIVERSITY OF OKLAHOMA

THE UNIVERSITY OF OKLAHOMA, encompassing in general the areas between Elm and Jenkins Avenues south of Boyd Street, is the state's largest institution of higher learning. The main campus occupies 285 acres and contains more than 30 major buildings, ranging architecturally from the predominant Collegiate Gothic to the more functional contemporary style of recent years. In addition to the main campus, the university owns more than 2,000 acres of land elsewhere, including the Medical Center in Oklahoma City (*see Oklahoma City*), with its schools of medicine and nursing, the University Hospital, Crippled Children's Hospital, and the Speech and Hearing Clinic; the Biological Station near Willis, Oklahoma, on Lake Texoma; and the North Campus at the north edge of Norman, containing laboratories of the School of Aeronautical Engineering, the University School (grades 1–12), the Extension Division, and Max Westheimer Field, the world's largest college-owned airport.

The university is supported principally by funds appropriated biennially by the state legislature. Immediate supervision of the University is in charge of the University of Oklahoma Board of Regents, consisting of seven members appointed by the governor. In the fall of 1956 the faculty numbered 540 and the student enrollment was 11,500. Some three thousand usually attend the summer school, while another seven to eight thousand students enroll in extension and correspondence courses.

One of the nation's youngest state universities, the school first began in September, 1892, in a rented store building located in what is now the Norman business district. David Ross Boyd, its first president, and three other teachers made up the first faculty. The curriculum provided for preparatory courses and two years of college work. In addition to his aggressive ideas on education, which laid a solid foundation for the University's tremendous growth that was to come, President Boyd actively encouraged the planting of trees. Today the university grounds contain some seventy-five varieties of trees, which contribute greatly to the beauty of campus design, and constitute an area of botanical interest as well.

The university is now composed of the University College; Colleges of Arts and Science, Engineering, Law, Business Administration, Pharmacy, Education, and Fine Arts; the Graduate College; and the Schools of Medicine and Nursing. It is Oklahoma's only institution of higher learning to offer ROTC training for all branches of the service: Army, Navy, Air Force, and Marines. The university is also extremely active in the field of institutes, special conferences, and short courses. Attendance at some 176 of these during the 1955–56 school year totaled more than 32,000.

The name "Sooners," applied to Oklahomans generally, is given to athletic teams of the university. Among the many colorful events staged throughout the school year are Homecoming, in the fall; Frontier Days, in the spring; the Sooner Scandals, an all-student variety show; and Engineers' Week, in March.

CAMPUS TOUR

The buildings are listed below in roughly the order of their location from the main entrance, University Blvd. and Boyd St. The list is not exhaustive, but attempts to include those of special architectural or historical interest, as well as those which have displays and exhibits of general interest. All are open during school hours.

The PRESIDENT'S HOME, just north of the main entrance, is a two-story frame house of classic revival design.

HOLMBERG HALL (Fine Arts), a three-story structure of concrete, brick, and stone, houses the university auditorium. Originally completed in 1918 (additions have been made in recent years), it was named for the late Fredrik Holmberg, professor of music and dean of the College of Fine Arts.

EVANS HALL (administration) at the head of Vernon Parrington Oval, is a fine example of Collegiate Gothic. History, not architecture, distinguishes the old EDUCATION BUILDING, next in position around the oval. Erected in 1904 as the Carnegie Library, it has perhaps provided for more functions and services over the years than any other building on the campus. Tradition and reinforcing rods support it in apparently equal proportions.

MONNET HALL, known as the "Law Barn," is a three-story structure of white Bedford stone. It contains the offices, lecture rooms, courtroom, and library of the School of Law.

JACOBSON HALL (University Art Museum) and CARPENTER HALL (School of Art) face Boyd Street between the University Boulevard and Asp Avenue entrance to the campus. Jacobson Hall, a concrete, brick, and Algonite stone structure erected in 1920 as the library, housed the art school from 1930 until recent years. In its exhibition rooms are displays of paintings, etchings, sculpture, and items of industrial art. Most of the exhibits, changed periodically, are representative student work or loans. Among the university's art holdings are the Woodruff Collection of paintings, and the Wentz-Matzene Collection of Oriental Art. Valued at more than $100,000, this latter collection includes Chinese, Manchurian, Japanese, East Indian, and Persian works. American Indian graduates of the School of Art have attracted national recognition for their authentic paintings of Indian life.

FELGAR HALL, at the Asp Avenue entrance (L), is the home of

the College of Engineering. Much of its valuable equipment has been given to the university by private industry for use in training tomorrow's engineers. The importance of oil to Oklahoma's economy is shown by the engines, pumps, drilling equipment, and other oil-industry machinery in a large laboratory on the south side. Across the street a black oil derrick pokes its steel head above other engineering structures and laboratories. Near by is a low velocity WIND TUNNEL. (A supersonic wind tunnel is one of the features of the Aeronautical Engineering Building on the North Campus.)

The low, modernistic building housing the UNIVERSITY OF OKLAHOMA PRESS lies to the south, toward the stadium. The Press, one of the country's top university publishing houses, in 1956 was issuing more than twenty-five new books a year and nearly as many reprint editions. Included in the nearly 400 books now under its imprint (two Indians smoking a peace pipe) are several notable series: the "Western Frontier Library," the "Civilization of the American Indian" series, and the "American Exploration and Travel" series. The Press also publishes *Books Abroad*, a quarterly review magazine (for publications in all languages other than English) that was founded in 1927 and now enjoys an international reputation and a world-wide subscription list. It is also the publisher of the *Oklahoma Law Review*.

Perhaps the most prominent building on the campus is the MEMORIAL (Student) UNION, with its high, clock-faced tower. The center of campus student life, it was built in 1928. The tower was added in 1936; further extensive additions were completed in 1951. Facilities include a ballroom, the Will Rogers cafeteria (seven-part mural on the life of Oklahoma's famed humorist), the Ming Room (modern Chinese decor), and the studios of WNAD, the University's radio station.

OWEN FIELD, with its 55,000-seat MEMORIAL STADIUM, is a horseshoe-shaped monument to the prowess of Sooner football teams and to the enthusiasm with which the state as a whole supports them. Beneath the north wing is the undergraduate library and School of Architecture student displays.

West of the stadium is GOULD HALL, which houses one of the largest schools of geology in the nation. A handsome, modernistic building, its hallways are lined with cases displaying fine examples of fossils and other geological specimens. One wing of the building is occupied by the Oklahoma Geological Survey.

The WOMEN'S QUADRANGLE, at the south end of the South Oval, is a good example of modern design in student living. Each of the four dormitories is divided into four houses, all sixteen of which are named for former women members of the university faculty. A nearly identical unit, CROSS CENTER (for men), named for President George L. Cross, is two blocks to the southeast.

The STOVALL MUSEUM, east of the Women's Quadrangle, is a general museum that includes exhibits in botany, classical art and archeology, history, anthropology, geology, paleontology, and zoology. Among the more interesting displays are Indian relics (representing tribes from North, Central, and South America); unusual jades; and remains of prehistoric animals of the Southwest. Adjacent to the Museum is the UNIVERSITY BIRD RANGE, representing several thousand bird specimens from all parts of the world.

New, and for the most part functional, classroom buildings line the west side of the South Oval. From north to south they are the GITTINGER and KAUFMAN HALLS and the GRADUATE EDUCATION BUILDING. Next is the site for the location of the new Journalism Building, which is to be erected in the near future.

To the north of these facing on Brooks Street, is the RESEARCH INSTITUTE AND PHYSICS BUILDING, containing the university's electron microscope, spectrographs, and other research apparatus. (In late 1956 preliminary negotiations with the government were under way for an atomic reactor.)

Another fine example of Collegiate Gothic, and a companion building to the Administration Building, with which it is to be joined, is the BIZZELL MEMORIAL LIBRARY. Additions were under construction in 1956 to afford facilities for over one million books. Notable special collections include the PHILLIPS (western and southwestern history); DEGOLYER (history of science and technology); BASS (business history); and the BIZZELL, some 665 Bibles from the library of the late William Bennett Bizzell, president of the University from 1925 to 1941. A statute of President Bizzell—done by Joseph R. Taylor of the art faculty and dedicated in 1949—faces the library from the head of the South Oval.

ADAMS HALL, to the east, housing the College of Business Administration, is another of the Collegiate Gothic structures on the campus. Topping the pylons at each side of the main (south) entrance are statues representing Industry and Commerce. A horizontal frieze of famous coins of history surmounts the octagonal bay. The stone gable is ornamented with conventionalized carvings of Oklahoma agricultural products: cotton, corn, and kaffir. Panels on the first floor represent the state's four major sources of income: oil, mining, agriculture, and commerce; and in recessed niches are other murals depicting all phases of Oklahoma industries. Grotesque corbel-heads, symbolic of the inhabitants of the Oklahoma plains and their relation to history, adorn the second-floor auditorium.

RICHARDS HALL, southeast of Adams Hall, is decorated with a series of conventionalized carvings of animal types done in stone by Joseph R. Taylor. Inside are hallway displays of the zoology department and a herbarium of Oklahoma plants.

The HOME ECONOMICS BUILDING, at Elm and Cruce Sts., is a contemporary structure of pink brick and blue-tinted glass. It is one of the outstanding modern structures on the campus.

OTHER POINTS OF INTEREST

McFARLIN MEMORIAL CHURCH (Methodist), University Blvd. and Apache St., was built at a cost of more than $1,000,000 by Robert M. McFarlin as a memorial to his son. Neo-Gothic in design and impressively simple, the interior of the white stone structure is richly ornamented with hand-carved walnut woodwork and other decorative features.

CITY PARK, a 16-acre development of the mid-1930's, features an amphitheater seating 2,200. Norman also maintains some sixty additional acres within the city limits devoted to parks and playgrounds.

NORMAN HIGH SCHOOL, occupying a 40-acre tract on W. Main St., was completed in 1953 at a cost of approximately one million dollars. Promptly called "America's best secondary school" by *School Executive* magazine, it also won a top honor award given by the American Institute of Architects. Classrooms are served by glass-walled hallways that look out onto a large outdoor terrace. Plastic skylight bubbles provide even light.

CENTRAL STATE HOSPITAL (*visitors by appointment*), at the east end of Main St., is the state's largest institution for the treatment of mental disorders. Representing an investment of more than $10,000,000, it has 1,000 acres of land and 111 buildings for 955 employees and 3,200 patients. The institution operates its own farm, dairy, bakery, laundry, and mattress and furniture factories.

The UNITED STATES NAVAL AIR TECHNICAL TRAINING CENTER, 1 m. S. of the University on Jenkins Ave., provides training for various branches of naval aviation technical work. At any one time approximately 3,800 persons are stationed or employed at the base. More than 2,800 of these are students receiving an eight-week course in the fundamentals of naval aviation. Another 750 form the permanent military staff.

OKLAHOMA CITY

Railroad Stations: Union Station, 300 W. Choctaw St. for St. Louis–San Francisco Ry. and Chicago, Rock Island & Pacific Ry.; Santa Fe Station, Santa Fe Ave. and California St. for Atchison, Topeka & Santa Fe Ry.; Katy Station, 200 E. Reno St. for Missouri-Kansas-Texas R. R. and Oklahoma City-Ada-Atoka Ry.
Bus Stations: Union Bus Station, 427 W. Grand for Oklahoma Transportation Co., Greyhound Lines, Continental Trailways, Mid-Continent Coaches, Missouri-Kansas-Oklahoma Coach Lines. 316 W. Grand for Nichols Hills Transportation Co. (298 schedules daily.)
Airports: Will Rogers Field (Municipal Airport), 10 m. S. W. on US 62, for Braniff International Airways, Continental Air Lines, American Airlines, Central Airlines, Trans World Airlines, and Slick Airways (cargo); Downtown Airport, 1701 S. Western, for private planes; Tinker Air Force Base, S. E. of Oklahoma City (headquarters of Oklahoma City Air Materiel Command).
Taxis: Metered fares from 35c.
City Buses: Fare from 10c.
Traffic Regulations: Parking meters on downtown streets, 5c to 10c. No charge between 6 p. m. and 7 a. m. Many one-way streets in business sections. No right turn on red light permitted within city limits.

Accommodations: 128 hotels (5,756 rooms); 28 first class motels; many tourist courts and trailer parks.

Information Service: Oklahoma City Chamber of Commerce, Skirvin Tower Hotel, Broadway and Park Ave.

Newspapers: (Morning) *Daily Oklahoman* and (evening) *Oklahoma City Times*.
Radio Stations: KOMA (CBS, 1520 kc.), WKY (NBC, 930 kc.), KTOK (ABC, 1000 kc.), KOCY (Mutual, 1340 kc.), KBYE (890 kc.), KTOW (800 kc.), KLPR (1140 kc.).
Television Stations: KWTV (CBS, Ch. 9) and WKY-TV (NBC, Ch. 4).
Theaters: Municipal Auditorium, Walker Ave. between Park Ave. and 2nd St., for local and touring state productions, opera, etc.
Motion Picture Theaters: 34, including 8 drive-ins.
Swimming: Springlake, 1800 Springlake Dr.; Black Hawk, 23rd St. and Grand Blvd.; Northeast, N. E. 33rd St. and Everest Ave.; Village, Huntleigh and Pennsylvania Aves.; Will Rogers Aquatic Center, 30th St. and N. Portland Ave.; Rotary, S. W. 15th St. and Westwood Ave.; Elmwood, 49th St. and S. Shields Blvd.; Jamboree, 3010 N. Paseo; Twilight Beech, N. W. 54th St. and May Ave.; Washington, N. E. 4th St. and High Ave.
Golf: Lincoln Park, N. E. 36th St. and Eastern Ave.; Trosper Park, S. E. 29th St. and Eastern Ave.; Woodson Park, 3000 S. W. 29th St.; Green Hills, 2701 N. E. 50th St.; Lake Hefner, N. W. of city; Meridian, N. W. 23rd St. and Meridian Ave. First three are municipal; greens fee on majority of courses $1.00 weekdays, $1.50 weekends.
Tennis: Municipal courts at Carverdale Ave. and N. E. 10th St.; N. E. 33rd St. and Everest Ave.; N. W. 36th St. and Western Ave.; S. W. 15th St. and Rotary Dr.; N. E. 19th St. and Miramar Ave.; N. E. 23rd and Glen Ellyn; N. W. 25th St. and Robinson Ave.; N. W. 12th St. and McKinley Ave.; S. W. 29th St. and Broadway; Reno and Blackwelder Aves.

Baseball: Texas League Park, 1837 N. W. 4th St., Texas League (Class A).
Wrestling: Stockyards Coliseum (Wednesday nights during the winter).
Boating and Fishing: Lake Overholser, west of city on 39th St.; Lake Hefner, northwest of city on May Avenue. (No swimming is allowed in these municipal lakes.)
Parks and Playgrounds: Oklahoma City has 67 developed park areas scattered throughout the city.

Annual Events: Parade of Homes, Sept.; Oklahoma State Fair, last week in Sept.; Oil Progress Week, Oct.; Oklahoma City Symphony season, Oct. to May; Oklahoma 4-H Club Congress, Thanksgiving weekend; Greater Oklahoma Home Show, March; Oklahoma City Livestock Show, March; State All-Star Games (high school football, basketball, baseball), mid-March; Spring and Fall Fashion Shows; Southwest Horse Cavalcade, May; National Cowboy Hall of Fame Rodeo, May; National Land Judging Contest, May; Trans-Mississippi Golf Tournament, June.

OKLAHOMA CITY (1,243 alt., 243,504 pop.; 1956 est., 317,500) is Oklahoma's capital and largest city. It is also the most representative of all phases of Oklahoma life—with one important exception: it began as a pioneer town, mushrooming from the run of 1889, without the Indian history which still gives color to the major part of the state. Sprawling over the onetime prairie along the banks of the sand-dry North Canadian River, the city takes in gleaming skyscrapers, a fabulously rich oil field with oil rigs looming up out of the back yards of many homes, scores of parks and playgrounds, an excellent medical school and a fine college, a splendid Civic Center, a rapidly expanding system of super-highways to take care of an ever mounting flood of automobiles, a bustling industrial district, and a growing fringe of shiny new residential areas. All are as typically Oklahoman as the rows of native elms along the streets of the city's older sections.

Downtown, on the streets and in the stores, fur coats and overalls, oil-field workers, clerks, military personnel, unfortunates and sophisticates—all mingle to make Oklahoma City a representative American metropolis.

At the edge of the prairie plains country that rises gradually to the Rockies, the city gives an impression of altitude not justified by the figures. Viewed from a distance, it strengthens that impression by a skyline broken by tall buildings. In climate and clarity of air, too, Oklahoma City suggests a mountain-slope city rather than one in the Mississippi Valley.

Bisected from east to west by Grand Avenue and from north to south by Broadway, the city falls roughly into four fairly equal sections. And nowhere can the visitor get a better over-all view than from the observation tower atop the 32-story First National Building in the heart of the business district. To the north and east is the domeless capitol and the governor's mansion, on 23rd Street, overtopped by the clean-cut, spidery steel towers of oil wells that tap rich oil-bearing strata some six thousand feet below. Angling shafts permit some of them to produce from directly beneath the capitol itself. Eastward from there, are wide sections of new homes. And then, below 13th Street, there are the older homes, tree-shaded and reflecting the architectural styles of the 1890's and early 1900's.

Directly to the east, beyond the webbing of railroad tracks almost immediately beneath the tower observation point, is the large Negro section. Here, over rolling ridges once covered by blackjack oaks, are the homes, business houses, churches, and schools of most of the city's large Negro population.

A survey of the southeastern quarter of the city makes apparent what is meant by the familiar oil-field expression, "forest of derricks." They literally crowd, row on close-set row, across virtually the entire quadrant of the city, almost blotting out the few residences that remain. Lost, too, in this maze of derricks is the discovery well, some six miles to the south, which brought in the field on December 4, 1928. In the distance is Midwest City and the great Tinker Air Force Base.

Southward along the Santa Fe tracks and slightly to the west is Capitol Hill, a section of modest homes set close together facing wide streets. Beyond lie productive farms, rapidly being encroached upon by suburban developments which began after World War II. And still farther in the distance is the line of timber marking the South Canadian River (five times as wide and sandy, and just as waterless as Oklahoma City's own North Canadian). To the right, almost directly southwest, lies Will Rogers Field—the municipal airport—and the expanding Civil Aeronautics Center.

To the west is Packingtown, a sixty-acre area of stockyards and meat-processing plants which make up the state's principal livestock market. (With receipts in 1954 running to 1,801,355 head Oklahoma City was the eighth largest cattle market in the nation.) Capacity of the yards here is 33,000 head of livestock and approximately three hundred truckloads, in addition to rail shipments, are handled every twenty-four hours. In this general area, too, are located many of the six hundred manufacturing concerns, large and small, which pump millions of dollars a year into the city's healthy economic system.

The northwestern quadrant, finally, is Oklahoma City's housekeeping section. Fanwise, the streets stretch out mile after mile, new development after new development, the diminishing density of shade trees providing a dependable scale for measuring the city's year-by-year growth. Here in democratic proximity live the wage-earner, paying installments on a tract house, and the millionaire, enjoying the paid-in-full comforts of his elaborate Nichols Hills mansion. Imbedded here and there among the houses and trees are apartment houses, school buildings, the library tower of Oklahoma City University, a handful of hospitals, and asphalt shopping centers.

A common description of western towns is that they "sprang up overnight." In the case of Oklahoma City, the literal truth is that it came into being between noon and sunset of April 22, 1889. Certain cynical historians insist that a considerable part of the population had appeared on the site within fifteen minutes after the noon signal for the "run" was given—although the starting line was more than thirty miles away! Three years later, Richard Harding Davis (in his *The West from a Car-Window*) said that "men of the Seminole Land and Town Company were dragging steel chains up the street on a run" at 12:15 P.M. that day. In any case, ten thousand settlers had camped by nightfall over the wide expanse east and west of the Santa Fe's single-track boxcar station, where land had been set aside for a townsite.

A month after the run—on May 23, 1889—the settlers formed a provisional city government, choosing first a committee of fourteen, then a mayor and council. But only with the setting up of Oklahoma Territory on May 2, 1890, did the community enjoy "legal" municipal existence. The first provisional mayor was William L. Couch, who had succeeded David L. Payne as leader of the "Boomers" *(see History)*. He and the makeshift council were chosen at a mass meeting "on their looks," for when a man was named for a place he stood up on a dry-goods box to be appraised by the crowd. (One candidate who failed of election because he did not please the people was James B. Weaver, once a candidate for President of the United States on the Populist ticket.) Mayor Couch held office only briefly—he died in an "argument" over title to land which is now the center of the city.

Another "argument," which fortunately did not reach the gun-arbitration stage, arose between two townsite companies. One, working north of Grand Avenue, made its survey west from the Santa Fe tracks. The other, platting south of Grand Avenue, took as its eastern base a true north and south line. When the surveys met, the streets failed to jibe. And since neither company would yield to the other, today's north-south streets still jog without apparent reason.

At times during the months of provisional city government, United States deputy marshals were called in to enforce federal law. And on at least one occasion—when an enterprising citizen took possession of the only pump in town and began to sell water—troops were required to prevent bloodshed. On the whole, however, Oklahoma City's first settlers succeeded surprisingly well in governing themselves.

The second phase of the city's history—from its formal organization as a municipality on May 23, 1890, to 1910, when the capital was won, by vote, from Guthrie—was one of vigorous growth as the trade center of an expanding new territory. In those twenty years, the population grew from 10,037 to 66,408, and it had become by far the state's largest city. Four other railroads had reached in to help the wholesale merchants extend their trade areas. To serve the farmers flour and cottonseed-oil mills grew in size and numbers; and in 1910–11, two meat-packing plants were established. As the state capital, Oklahoma City attracted thousands of state employees, many of whom remained after their political employment ceased. And with the development of the state's natural resources of oil, coal, and metals, the city became a financial and manufacturing center as well. Stimulated by the World War I boom, Oklahoma City's population in 1920 was 91,295. It has steadily increased from that time to the 1940 figure of 204,424, to 243,504 in 1950. In 1956, the population of "metropolitan" Oklahoma City was estimated at 400,000.

After World War I, wholesalers intensified their activities. Manufacturing became less bound up with agriculture and expanded into new fields, and in the late 1920's, a gusher oil field was developed on the east side, within the city limits. As Oklahoma City grew industrially, it added new iron and steel plants, factories for making furniture, clothing, and electrical equipment. Various large utility companies, brokerage houses, and commission concerns also established their headquarters downtown.

Generally speaking, the growth and development of the Negro community has kept pace with that of Oklahoma City as a whole. Like the white sections, it has its occasional near-slum areas, its preponderance of modest, middle-class homes and apartment houses, and its scattered sections of more pretentious dwellings. It has had, too, its public-spirited leaders. One of these, W. J. Edwards, has put much of his wealth (from wholesale scrap metal) into the building of FHA-approved homes for Negroes, and a modern hospital. The weekly *Black Dispatch*, established in 1916, has had a strong and responsible influence for many years, while Negroes, as individuals and in groups, have figured in the cultural and entertainment fields. Since the desegregation of the schools in 1955, Negroes are participating in more and more activities, particularly in the sports field.

Oklahoma City's education picture as a whole shows ninety-three public schools, including three senior high, seven junior-senior high, and six junior high schools. In 1956 some 1,602 teachers took care of an enrollment of 52,965. Inside the city, too, are fourteen parochial schools, ten trade and vocational schools, and five business colleges. Along with the growing Oklahoma City University and the University of Oklahoma School of Medicine, there are also a number of small denominational colleges. The new Oklahoma City Library, at N. W. 3rd Street and Robinson Avenue, is one of the finest in the Southwest.

The city's growing interest in the arts is perhaps best symbolized by the Oklahoma City Symphony orchestra. Since its founding in the 1930's, it has grown rapidly in stature. For the past ten years its winter concert series has enjoyed a world-wide audience through the Mutual Broadcasting System, the Canadian Broadcasting Corporation, the Voice of America, and the Armed Forces Radio Service. Recently it has reached new listeners over Radio Free Europe. Also prominent on the city's cultural scene is the Oklahoma Art Center (*open weekdays 10–5 except Mondays, 2–4 Sundays*), 5th floor of the Municipal Auditorium. Its galleries display both permanent and traveling exhibitions.

Four daily newspapers were started during the first year of Oklahoma City's existence. One of them—the present *Oklahoma City Times*—actually began before the land was opened to settlement. Prior to his ejection as a trespasser, its editor wrote his copy on the site of the future capital, then sent it to Wichita, Kansas, where the paper was printed. The first newspaper printed in Oklahoma City, the *Oklahoma Times,* was first issued from a tent. The *Daily Oklahoman,* the city's only other daily today, was also established in 1889.

The opening of the fabulous Oklahoma City oil field in 1928 was one of the highlights in the dramatic story of the oil industry in the Middle West. It attracted national attention because of its amazing productivity, (as much as 60,000 barrels a day from a single well), its enormous gas pressures (resulting in spectacular mid-city fires such as the industry had never known before), and the then unprecedented depth (four thousand to seven thousand feet) to which the drill bits were plunged into the earth. This pool remains today one of the richest ever to be developed.

For several years before the discovery well came in on December 4, 1928, geologists suspected that oil might be found under this area. But they believed it lay at such depths as to make exploration impracticable. Exploitation had to await improved drilling equipment.

After drilling started, it was learned that the main part of the pool lay under the southeastern sector of the city, and an army of derricks marched toward the city limits. Then in March, 1930, the Mary Sudik blew in and got out of control. For eleven days it ran wild, spouting ten thousand barrels of oil a day—with some twenty thousand cubic feet of gas—in a roaring brown-black geyser that deluged the surrounding areas, with air-borne spray reaching as far as the town of Norman, fifteen miles to the south. The fire hazard was so great that the other wells were closed down and the area was put under police control. Before being abandoned, the Mary Sudik produced a total of one million barrels of oil.

As development pushed the field farther north and west, a controversy arose over the question of drilling within the city limits. One group argued that the wells outside were drawing oil from under the city. They demanded the right to share in the profits by sinking wells, if necessary, in their back yards. Others, remembering the threat of a disastrous fire posed by the Mary Sudik, demanded that the derricks stay out of town.

In July, 1930, the city council, in an effort to please both sides, enacted two ordinances. One established new safety regulations. The other allowed drilling in the southeast corner of town, and shortly derricks were towering above the homes in that residential district. Additional ordinances were enacted setting stricter rules for safety and providing a system of permits and rigid inspection.

Demands for extending the drilling zone forced the city council to call a special election in the spring of 1935. The result was that derricks moved north along the east side of town. Another election in the spring of 1936 again enlarged the drilling zone to include the vicinity of the state capitol. Governor E. W. Marland (*see Ponca City*) had demanded that the state-owned land around the capitol also be included in that area so the state might share in the revenue. When the city council refused, he put the lands under martial law and issued drilling permits in defiance of the city government. Twenty-four wells went down immediately, some within a few yards of the capitol and of the governor's mansion. Many of these, still producing, can be seen on the capitol grounds. (A model display in the first-floor rotunda of the Capitol shows the "whipstock" or directional drilling method of recovering oil from beneath the building.)

Whether or not oil also underlies the downtown business district may never be known. But the Oklahoma City field now has 14,320 proved acres. Total production has been approximately 690,000,000 barrels of oil. In 1956 there were 570 wells still producing 10,000 barrels of oil daily.

Oklahoma City is recreation- and sports-minded. Among its sixty-seven parks are four of considerable size, located at what were once the four "corners of the city" and connected by an outer drive known as

Grand Boulevard. Since World War II, these corners have been turned by spreading residential areas. But Grand Boulevard itself, laid out years ago by farsighted city fathers, is now becoming a looping expressway around the city. And Lincoln Park, the northeast corner, remains Oklahoma City's principal playground, with its zoo (*see Tour 3*) and extensive picnic areas.

All these and many more "little" items go to make up present-day Oklahoma City. It has 330 churches representing forty-five denominations. With an annual rainfall of 30.22 inches, it is one of the few spots in the country where the wheat and cotton belts overlap. Its ten hospitals provide approximately 1,750 beds, and the city also has a new 500-bed Veterans Administration hospital. Each year some 200,000 to 250,000 visitors are drawn to the city by seven hundred or more conventions. In the words of a popular musical, Oklahoma City—like Oklahoma—seems to be doing fine.

POINTS OF INTEREST

1. The STATE CAPITOL, Lincoln Blvd., between 21st and 23rd Sts., an example of neoclassic architecture, was designed by S. A. Layton, of Oklahoma City. Erection of the building was started in 1914 and finished in 1917. The original design called for a dome on the central tower, but it was not built for reasons of economy. The matter is no longer the lively political issue it once was.

The massive five-story edifice is in the form of a cross with projecting central pedimented pavilions at the front and rear. A low central tower, over the crossing, is the base of the proposed dome. The east and west section is 434 feet in length and 136 feet in width; the north and south division is 304 feet long and 88 feet wide. The exterior of the building is of granite to the second-floor level, and the superstructure is of Indiana limestone. Entrances are provided on all four sides of the building, with the main entrance on the south, but the need for space has long since closed the west entrance to permit the use of the west corridor for offices. Before the south entrance stands a STATUE OF A COWBOY on a wild pony, done by Constance Whitney Warren. (Old-timers have consistently maintained that "it don't look much like the real thing.") There are replicas in Texas and Colorado. The north and south façades have Corinthian porticoes, and the east and west have Corinthian pilasters.

The interior is decorated with classic features in harmony with the exterior—lobby floors, stairs, and balustrades are of light-colored marble. Columns, pilasters, painted beams, lunettes, and Italian elliptical vaulted ceilings adorn the various offices. The second and the fourth floors are the most elaborate in the building.

The governor's office and reception room are on the second floor, as are the courtrooms and offices of the two appellate courts, the state supreme court, and the criminal court of appeals. On the fourth floor are the two chambers of the state legislature. Over the grand stairway, on the south wall of the corridor of the fourth floor, are three World War I memorial murals, painted by Gilbert White and presented to the state by oil man Frank Phillips (*see Bartlesville*). The artist, a painter in the conservative French tradition, combined classic allegory with realistic portraiture to memorialize Oklahoma's part in the war.

2. The CAPITOL OFFICE BUILDING (ANNEX) (*open during office hours*), S.W. of the Capitol, on Lincoln Blvd., is a severely plain neoclassic six-story white limestone structure built to relieve congestion in the capitol. Chromium steel is used for the light standards at the north and east entrances and for the decorations under the wide windows between the first and fourth floors. There are low-relief sculptures over the east entrance and on the walls of the first-floor lobby. The architect was J. Duncan Forsyth, of Tulsa.

3. The STATE HISTORICAL SOCIETY BUILDING (*open 8:30–4:15 weekdays, 8:30–12 Sat., 2–5 Sun.*), S. E. of the Capitol, on Lincoln Blvd., is a three-story neoclassic structure completed in 1930 at a cost of $500,000. With a Georgia granite base and an Indiana limestone superstructure, it houses the society's museum and library. Interior arrangement is simple and utilitarian; the corridor walls are decorated with life-size figure paintings of Indian dances by Stephen Mopope and Monroe Tsa-to-ke, Kiowa Indian artists.

The Oklahoma Historical Society was founded at Kingfisher on May 26, 1893, by the Oklahoma Territorial Press Association. It became a Territorial institution under Governor W. C. Renfrow on February 21, 1895. The early history collections and library remained in a tiny room of the courthouse at Kingfisher until the first day of January, 1902, when they were moved to the Carnegie Library in Oklahoma City. When the State Capitol was completed in 1917, the Society found its third home, its last before moving to its present building in 1930.

The archives, in the basement, contain many of the most historic documents in existence concerning the history of Oklahoma. In this department are more than three million papers and letters of the Five Civilized Tribes. The 26,000-volume Library is located on the second floor. Ranking with that of any other historical society is the news-

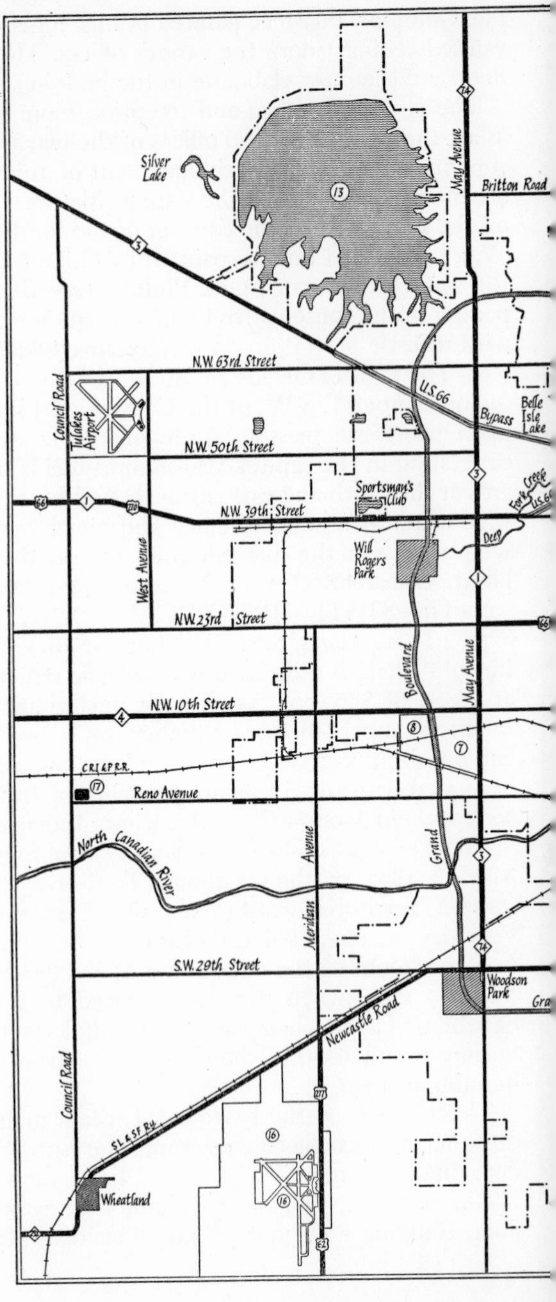
Silver Lake
13
May Avenue
Britton Road
N.W. 63rd Street
Council Road
Tulakes Airport
U.S. 66
Bypass
Belle Isle Lake
N.W. 50th Street
Sportsman's Club
Fork Creek
N.W. 39th Street
Deep
Will Rogers Park
West Avenue
N.W. 23rd Street
Boulevard
May Avenue
N.W. 10th Street
8
7
C.R.I.&P.R.R.
17
Reno Avenue
North Canadian River
Meridian Avenue
Grand
S.W. 29th Street
Woodson Park
Newcastle Road
Council Road
S.L.&S.F. Ry.
16
Wheatland

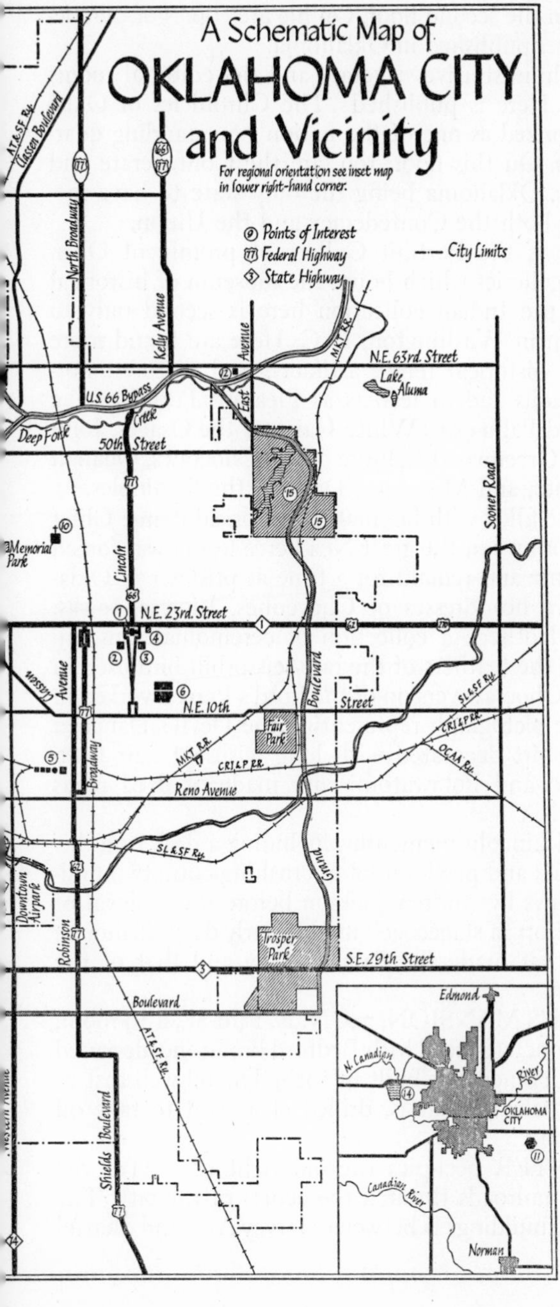
A Schematic Map of
OKLAHOMA CITY
and Vicinity
For regional orientation see inset map in lower right-hand corner.
Points of Interest
Federal Highway
State Highway
City Limits
AT&SF Ry.
Classen Boulevard
North Broadway
Kelly Avenue
East Avenue
MKT R.R.
N.E. 63rd. Street
Lake Aluma
U.S. 66 Bypass
Deep Fork Creek
50th Street
Sooner Road
Memorial Park
Lincoln
N.E. 23rd. Street
Classen Avenue
Boulevard
Street
N.E. 10th
SL&SF Ry.
CRI&P R.R.
Fair Park
MKT R.R.
OCA&A Ry.
Broadway
Reno Avenue
SL&SF Ry.
Downtown Airpark
Grand
Robinson
Trosper Park
S.E. 29th. Street
Boulevard
AT&SF Ry.
Shields Boulevard
Edmond
N. Canadian
River
OKLAHOMA CITY
Canadian River
Norman

paper collection, also on the second floor. On file are copies of practically every newspaper ever published in Oklahoma.

The offices of the administrative secretary and the editorial rooms are on the third floor. Here is published "The Chronicles of Oklahoma," generally recognized as one of the nation's outstanding quarterly history magazines. On this floor, too, are the Confederate and Union Memorial Halls, Oklahoma being the only state to have memorial rooms honoring both the Confederacy and the Union.

On the fourth floor is the Portrait Gallery of prominent Oklahomans, and the large galleries which house the museum of historical facts. Critics say that the Indian collection here is second only to that of the Smithsonian in Washington, D.C. Here are found more than sixteen thousand historical relics, artifacts, and pictures. Portraits include such famous Indian leaders as Pleasant Porter of the Creeks, Bacon Rind and Pahu-çka (White Hair) of the Osages, John Ross of the Cherokees, Greenwood LeFlore of the Choctaws, Quanah Parker of the Comanches, and Mrs. Alice Davis of the Seminoles.

The museum cases are filled with fascinating historical items: Chief Joseph's war bonnet, worn when the great Nez Percé leader was forced to leave his Oregon home and remain for a time as prisoner in Oklahoma; highly decorative headdresses of Cheyennes, Kiowas, Iowas, Osages, Delawares, and others; a collection of ceremonial fans, including one made from the feathers of the rare scissorbill bird used in the peyote ceremony; a Choctaw version of the Lord's Prayer worked in needlepoint; an Apache pictograph representing the Devil's Dance; a Cheyenne ceremonial shirt decorated with long wisps of hair from enemy scalps; Kickapoo and Potawatomi rugs made of dyed reeds and cattails.

There are also several Lincoln mementos, including a desk from his Illinois law office; mortars and pestles used in crushing corn; two millstones given the Choctaws by Andrew Jackson before the removal of the tribe to Indian Territory; a stagecoach used in early-day Oklahoma; and a covered wagon that made the Run of 1889 and that of the Cherokee Outlet in 1893.

4. The GOVERNOR'S MANSION, 700 N. E. 23rd St., a 19-room, three-story building of concrete faced with Bedford limestone, designed in the Dutch Colonial manner, was built in 1928. The oil well east of the mansion is "whipstocked," that is, drilled at a slant to take oil from beneath the building.

5. The CIVIC CENTER occupies the old right of way of the Frisco and Rock Island railroads through the center of the city. The group of city and county buildings is between Harvey Ave. and Shartel

Ave. on the east and west, and between Park Ave. and 2nd St. on the north and south. Construction of the Center began in 1935, was completed in 1936–37 at a cost of more than $10,000,000.

The COUNTY BUILDING, between Harvey and Hudson Aves., is a successful adaptation in Bedford limestone of the classic style. Over the broad main entrance on Park Ave. is a sculptured group in deep bas-relief representing Indians, cowboys, early settlers and, at either extremity, Lincoln and Washington.

In the lobby, with its terrazzo floor and walls of rose-colored marble broken by flat fluted columns of black marble, is a frieze of separate squares depicting such appropriate symbols as the lamp of truth, the scales of justice, the book of knowledge, and the Roman fasces. Doors, window frames, and ornaments are of aluminum. The first six floors provide for five district courtrooms, two common pleas courts, and the county court, as well as the necessary jury rooms and other offices. On the seventh and eighth floors is a modern jail.

The MUNICIPAL BUILDING, between Walker and Hudson Aves., was designed to harmonize with the courthouse and the auditorium both in the use of Bedford limestone for exterior facing and in its modified Romanesque architectural motif. Set in the center of a smoothly landscaped square, like the other buildings of the group, this three-story-and-basement structure consists of a main section, with six flat fluted columns that rise from the broad steps leading to the first-floor lobby to the capitals under the roof, and two perfectly plain attached office sections. In front of the main entrance on the east, facing Hudson Ave., is a fountain dedicated to the 89'ers, the city's first settlers.

The MUNICIPAL AUDITORIUM, between Lee and Dewey Aves., is an all-purpose, completely air-conditioned community meeting house that fills almost the entire block. Its main hall has seats for 6,000, and a convention hall seats 900. There are galleries for art exhibits, twenty-two committee rooms, and an exhibition hall with 38,000 square feet of floor space. Within the auditorium are staged conventions and trade shows, the programs of touring musical and theatrical groups (including the Metropolitan Opera Company), concerts of the city's own symphony, basketball and ice hockey games, indoor tennis and track events. Described as modern classic, with the accent on the practical, the exterior is faced with Bedford limestone. The main entrance is to the east.

6. The MEDICAL CENTER, 800 N. E. 13th St., is the primary medical education center of the state and an impressive monument to medical progress in the Southwest. The complex of buildings that line the street combines the objectives of medical education, commu-

nity medical service, and medical research. Included are the University of Oklahoma School of Medicine, the University Hospital, the University's School of Nursing, the Crippled Children's Hospital, and a Speech and Hearing Clinic. Also on the grounds are the new 500-bed Veterans Administration Hospital (completed in 1953 at a cost of $8,000,000) and the unique Oklahoma Medical Research Institute (privately owned and operated), with its adjacent research hospital.

7. The STATE FAIR GROUNDS, N. W. 10th St. and May Ave., was opened in 1954 as one of the most modern of such facilities in the nation. It covers 480 acres. Annual attendance at the week-long State Fair (late September) averages 350,000.

8. The DEMONSTRATION FARM, N. W. 10th St. and Portland Ave., is operated by Oklahoma A. & M. College. This once worn-out, 160-acre farm was rebuilt in a day—October 7, 1948—an event which attracted nationwide attention. It now serves as a demonstration of modern soil conservation and crop production methods. The farm, along with the model farm home, guest houses, and farm buildings, is always open for inspection.

9. OKLAHOMA CITY UNIVERSITY, N. Blackwelder Ave. and 24th St., a nonsectarian Methodist institution, includes a College of Liberal Arts, a College of Fine Arts, and an Industrial School. In 1956 it had an enrollment of 4,493, and a faculty of 137. Founded in Oklahoma City in 1904 as Epworth University, the school moved to Guthrie in 1911 to become the Methodist University of Oklahoma. It was established at its present site, and under its present name, in 1919.

The ADMINISTRATION HALL is a large brick and stone structure of collegiate Gothic design. Directly to the north is the FINE ARTS BUILDING, erected in 1928. Recently completed to honor the school's war dead, the striking GOLD STAR MEMORIAL BUILDING houses the School of Religion and the library. Its tower not only dominates the campus but provides Oklahoma City's west side with its most prominent landmark. The school's basketball team, the Chiefs, and its music organizations have helped most to make Oklahoma City University known and respected throughout the state and the nation.

10. The CHURCH OF TOMORROW (Christian), N. W. 36th St. and Walker Ave., is one of Oklahoma City's newest (1956), costliest ($1,124,000), and certainly most striking religious structures. The three-building complex includes a sanctuary which seats 2,000, a four-story educational building, and a theater-in-the-round. It is an extremely modernistic, yet strictly functional group. The church itself has been described as "a monstrous egg half buried in the ground, pierced by a twisted steel tower." The separate, 150-foot concrete bell

tower, housing an electronic carillon system, is topped with a natural-gas flare that symbolizes "The Flame of Religious Freedom."

11. TINKER AIR FORCE BASE, S. E. 29th St., 8 m. from the city, is the world's largest air depot. The $215,000,000 installation employs more than 20,000 civilians and 6,000 military personnel, and acts as chief modification center for heavy bombers and jet engines. The base also serves as an important nerve center for the nation's air defense setup.

12. The SITE OF THE NATIONAL COWBOY HALL OF FAME AND MUSEUM, US 66–77 at Eastern Ave., will shortly be occupied by an impressive memorial to the West's most familiar figure. In the spring of 1956 the Oklahoma City site for the $5,000,000 structure was selected in a competition that involved four hundred other cities in seventeen states. In 1957 contests were under way among architects for the best plan for the Hall of Fame. Oklahoma has already raised its one-million-dollar share of the project's total cost.

POINTS OF INTEREST IN ENVIRONS

13. Lake Hefner, 7.9 *m.* 14. Lake Overholser, 9.1 *m.* (*see Tour* 1). 15. Lincoln Park, 4.5 *m.* (*see Tour* 3). 16. Will Rogers Airfield, 7.2 *m.* 17. Site of the new Western Electric plant, 8.6 *m.*

OKMULGEE

Railroad Stations: E. 5th St. and tracks for St. Louis–San Francisco Ry.; 723 W. 6th St. for Okmulgee Northern Ry. (no passenger service).
Bus Station: Union Terminal, 220 W. 7th St. for Greyhound Lines, Santa Fe Trailways, and Union Transportation Co.
Airport: Municipal Airport, 2 m. N. on US 75.
City Buses: Fare 10c.
Taxis: Fares from 35c.

Accommodations: 4 hotels, 1 for Negroes; rooming houses; 4 tourist courts.

Information Service: Chamber of Commerce, Creek Indian Council House, 6th and Morton Sts.

Newspaper: (Morning) *Daily Times.*
Radio Station: KHBG (1240 kc.).
Motion Picture Theaters: 3, including 1 drive-in.
Athletics: Harmon Stadium, 12th St. and Creek Ave.; Hospital Park, N. Okmulgee Ave., Melrose to Belmont Aves., for baseball and softball; Rodeo Grounds, US 75; several softball parks.
Wrestling: Armory, 2nd St. and Alabama Ave.
Boating: Lake Okmulgee (*see Tour* 3), 7 m. W. on State 56.

Swimming: 2 municipal pools, Greenwood Lake, adjoining city on S. E.; Okmulgee Country Club, on Mission Rd., adjoining city on S. E.
Golf: Okmulgee Country Club, greens fee $1.50 weekdays, $2.50 Sundays and holidays.
Tennis: Hospital Park (6 city-owned courts).

Annual Events: Creek Indian Stomp Dance, mid-July, at near-by Henryetta (*see Tour* 3); Pioneer Powwow and Rodeo, mid-June.

OKMULGEE (752 alt., 18,317 pop.; 1956 est., 20,000), seat of Okmulgee County, and capital of the Creek Nation from 1868 until the tribal government was extinguished by the coming of statehood in 1907, emphasizes both its Indian past and its industrial present. It retains its annual Indian powwow and also uses as its slogan, "Where oil flows, gas blows, and glass glows," to point up its varied modern qualities.

The city is set in a wide valley between low, timber-covered hills. Its business section has spread over the lowland, and its residences, parks, and playgrounds are spotted on the view-giving slopes on the northwest, west, and south. To the north and east, the city fades into fertile, level farms.

It is said that in choosing Okmulgee as the site of their capital, the Creek Indians assured themselves immunity from tornadoes. In justification of their choice, the people who live in the two or three square miles of comfortable homes with porches and shade trees have never yet, at least by 1956, been visited by a tornado, though "twisters" have skirted the region.

Oil was discovered within a half mile of the old Creek Council House in 1904, and three years later had become a leading factor in the town's growth. Five glassmaking plants have been built during Okmulgee's history. It also depends today on its packing plants, cotton-processing industries, oil refineries, and markets for peanuts and pecans.

The city's period of swiftest growth—what it calls its "golden decade"—was from 1907 to 1918, when oil development reached its peak. By 1930 the population had reached 17,097. The decrease of more than six per cent between that date and 1940 reflects the waning importance of oil and allied industries. But in the decade from 1940 to 1950 the population swelled again, to 18,317, and it continues to grow moderately. Old oil fields are again producing through modern methods of secondary recovery, and there has been some expansion in the city's refining and glass-producing industries. This latter now includes three glass-manufacturing and two glass-processing plants. Okmulgee has a city manager form of government. Its water supply is municipally owned and the county provides abundant supplies of fuel oil, natural gas, and coal.

The story of Okmulgee goes far back in the history of the Creek Indians, beginning actually long before their removal to what is now Oklahoma. According to tribal tradition, these Indians originated somewhere in the western part of America, migrating in the course of time to the Alabama-Georgia region, where the white men first found them. Arriving there, the Indians sought as a site for their principal (capital) town a never-failing spring. Having found it, they called it Okmulgee, which means "bubbling water." It was there, they say, that the powerful confederation of the tribes of Muskhogean stock was formed to resist the encroachment of whites on Indian lands. In course of time, the white name for one of the tribes—the Creeks—became fixed upon it, although it is still sometimes called Muskogee.

From the time of their enforced exile from the East, 1829–36, when twenty thousand were settled in the new Indian Territory, to the building of their Council House at Okmulgee in 1868, the tribal meeting place was at High Springs, near Council Hill, some twenty miles southeast. Factional strife and the almost complete destruction of property in the Civil War led to the selection of this new site, and the name Okmulgee which was sacred to all.

Their first capitol was a two-story log structure, with a roofed-over breezeway separating the meeting places of the two branches of the Council: the House of Kings, anciently concerned with civil administration, and the House of Warriors. There, encouraged at first by the United States government, met not only the Creek lawmakers but also the important Intertribal Council composed of the head men of the Five Tribes and, in the later years, delegates from the so-called wild western tribes, Comanches, Kiowas, Caddoes, Cheyennes, and Arapahoes. Others that came in the years from 1870 to 1875 included the Sacs and Foxes, Osages, Shawnees, Ottawas, Wyandottes, Quapaws, and Peorias—mainly remnants of once powerful tribes east of the Mississippi and north of the Ohio River. At the last meeting, in 1875, twenty-nine tribes were represented.

The Council was finally discontinued because of a basic clash between the views of the United States government and the Indians. The delegates had reached the point of proposing to form an Indian Territory according to their own conception and to write out a constitution for its government. But when they realized that Washington would insist upon retaining the veto power over any action taken by the Territory's legislature, they felt that no reason still existed for the Council. It never met again.

Silas Smith, a blacksmith, was the first white resident of Okmulgee. He was sent there by the federal government to help the Creeks secure and keep in order the tools necessary for their farming operations. By 1878, Okmulgee had become an active Indian trade center. The Creeks had recovered from the ravages of war, their farmers and ranchers were prosperous, and their tribal schools were flourishing. It was thus decided that the old log Council House must go. It was torn down, and on the site a square two-story-and-cupola stone structure was erected. Set in the town square with a fringe of stores around it, the new capitol served also as a community meeting place and schoolhouse.

In 1894, there arose the question of allotting Creek lands and coming under a territorial government which all realized would quickly be dominated by the whites. After the issue had been hotly debated between Indian leaders and the representatives of the federal government, Chief Legus C. Perryman called for a vote. He asked all who opposed allotment to move to the west side of the Council House grounds, and all those who favored it, to the east. All but one moved west. Only Moty Tiger alone stepped east and turned to face the three thousand who opposed allotment. When called upon to explain his stand, he said that whatever the Indians did the whites would overwhelm them, that it would be best to accede to the federal government's desires and obtain whatever favors they could from the white man's government. Five years later, allotment was accepted and Moty Tiger's stand was fully vindicated.

As a modern city, Okmulgee's history began after the Creek tribal lands, in 1899, ceased to be held in communal ownership and were allotted to individuals. That change meant the coming of whites and a great stimulus of trade and commerce. The first bank was opened in 1900, and in the same year train service was begun.

Okmulgee's growth from a trading point with a population of some two hundred to an incorporated municipality, with a mayor and four aldermen, with telephone service to Muskogee, and a determination to dominate the region, was swift after allotment. By the end of 1905, thanks to oil discoveries near by, the city's population had risen to four thousand.

Okmulgee citizens call 1907 their year of years. It brought statehood and the first of the gusher oil fields to be opened in its territory. In April a well was brought in that produced five hundred barrels a day. In June a thousand-barrel well blew in, and the rush of drillers, lease hounds, speculators, and the platoons of oil camp followers soon boosted the population to six thousand. By 1910, the surrounding oil region was so well established that a refinery was built.

Until 1916, the old Creek Council House served more or less adequately as the Okmulgee County Courthouse. Then the need for more space became pressing, and a $125,000 bond issue was voted for the construction of a new one. When these bonds were offered for sale, the white guardian of an illiterate Creek woman, Katie Fixico, who had been ruled an incompetent by the County Court, used $133,379 of her money to buy them. Her wealth had, of course, come out of oil wells drilled on her allotment.

Much of Okmulgee's history revolves about the lives of its better known sons and daughters: General Hugh Johnson; Katie Fixico; wealthy oilman W. B. Pine, rancher and Republican U. S. Senator (1924–30); Dr. L. S. Skelton, who established the first glass-manufacturing plant at Okmulgee and contributed to many other enterprises; Captain F. B. Severs, an early-day trader and the city's first dealer in nuts from Okmulgee County's 125,000 pecan trees; Enos Wilson, said to be the richest Indian since the death of Jackson Barnett; E. H. Moore, another pioneer oilman; and Dr. R. M. Isham, an oil chemist and researcher of national reputation.

With Muskogee, to the northeast, and McAlester, to the southeast (*see Tour 5*), Okmulgee shares the trade of the eastern section of the state. It is also the trade center of Okmulgee County, which contains some 160,000 acres of cultivated land. Cotton is a million-dollar-a-year crop, and nearly five million pounds of pecans are harvested from Okmulgee County's groves—mostly of wild trees, but some in which the big papershell species have been grafted on native trees. Truck farming, poultry breeding, and dairying also contribute largely to its business. Negroes make up approximately 20 per cent of the population.

Newspaper history in Okmulgee began when E. P. Gupton started the *Record*, printed at Muskogee, on April 3, 1900. It lasted only a few weeks. On August 23, 1900, Valdo Smith established the weekly *Democrat*, which, after various changes of ownership, has continued. And on September 3, 1901, George Wood put out the first issue of his *Creek Chieftain*. This paper became the *Times* in 1918, began publication as a daily, and remains the city's only daily today.

POINTS OF INTEREST

The CREEK INDIAN NATIONAL COUNCIL HOUSE (*open 9–4:30 free*), 6th and Morton Sts., downtown, is set in a square shaded by enormous maple trees. And although a past mayor once made every effort to have it removed as a crumbling eyesore—he hoped to locate a new Federal Building on the site—it stands sedate and serene, still a source of pride to the city.

A plain, four-square, two-story structure of brown stone, topped by a cupola, it suggests in its simplicity and excellent proportions the best of New England Colonial architecture. It was acquired by Okmulgee from the Creeks when their tribal government ceased, and the building is now under the care of the city and the Creek Indian Memorial Association. The purpose of this latter group is to preserve the Council House and to gather and exhibit in it "all data relating to the history, traditions, folklore, relics, handicraft, art, music, and all that is finest and best in the life of the Creek tribe. . . ." The growing Museum of Creek History, occupying the four spacious first-floor rooms, already contains one of the state's most interesting tribal collections. The upstairs rooms, where the House of Kings and the House of Warriors met when the Council was in session, now provide a community center.

The OKMULGEE PUBLIC LIBRARY, 218 S. Okmulgee Ave., is a one-story brick building trimmed with white stone. The library itself developed from a tiny reading room stocked with a secondhand Bible and eight other books contributed at a "pink tea and book shower" given by the Civic Club in May of 1907. In 1910, it moved into two rooms of the old Council House.

When these rooms became overcrowded, Okmulgee asked the Carnegie Corporation for funds with which to build a library. The offer of $15,000 was deemed inadequate, so the city voted $75,000 in bonds, later adding $25,000 for furniture and equipment. In 1956 the library contained more than 32,000 volumes. It also serves as a community center, housing the Okmulgee Law School and the Okmulgee Little Theater. In 1923 the library acquired a considerable collection of books belonging to William H. ("Alfalfa Bill") Murray, who later became governor (*see History*).

The FEDERAL BUILDING, 4th St. and Grand Ave., is a modern three-story, blocklike structure of granite and limestone. Its tall, square-pillared façade is of striking appearance.

OKLAHOMA A. & M. TECH, at the east edge of the city, represents a uniquely effective way of "pulling the state's industrial and agricultural picture into an economic balance." A trade school with no strict academic requirements, it stresses the "learn by doing" method of instruction to some 1,500 students in thirty-five different fields. The 164-acre campus contains ninety permanent buildings, and equipment in the automotive department alone is valued at over a quarter of a million dollars. Under the supervision of Oklahoma A. & M. College (*see Stillwater*), the school is one of but two of its kind in the nation, the only one west of the Mississippi River.

HARMON STADIUM, 600 E. 12th St., is a modern concrete amphitheater, enclosing a football field, capable of seating 5,000 spectators. It is also used for track meets and many other outdoor community activities.

HOSPITAL PARK, Okmulgee Ave. and Belmont St., a landscaped six-block area, is the city's principal playground. Adjoining the park are the Okmulgee County fair grounds. Among the facilities are picnic grounds, baseball and softball diamonds, wading pools, and six concrete-surface tennis courts, where the annual summer tennis carnival is held. Four smaller parks are included in Okmulgee's park system.

BALL BROTHERS GLASS PLANT, S. Madison St., the SOUTHWESTERN SHEET GLASS COMPANY, W. 20th St., and the AMERICAN WINDOW GLASS COMPANY (*all open to visitors during working hours*) illustrate one important phase of the city's industrial activity.

POINTS OF INTEREST IN ENVIRONS

Lake Okmulgee, 7 *m.*; Nuyaka, 16 *m.* (*see tour* 3).

PONCA CITY

Railroad Stations: 1st St. and W. Oklahoma Ave. for Atchison, Topeka & Santa Fe Ry.; 700 S. 3rd St. for Chicago, Rock Island & Pacific Ry.
Bus Station: 201 N. 2nd St. for Santa Fe Trailways and Missouri-Kansas-Oklahoma Lines.
Airport: Municipal Airport, 1.5 m. N. W., for Central Airlines.
Taxis: Fare from 40c.

Accommodations: 14 hotels; rooming houses; 10 motels.

Information Service: Chamber of Commerce, Community, Bldg., N. 3rd St.

Newspaper: (evening) *Ponca City News.*
Radio Station: WBBZ (1230 kc.).
Motion Picture Theaters: 5, including 2 drive-ins.
Athletics: Blaine Park Stadium, Brookfield Ave. and 6th St.; Conoco Ball Park, S. W. edge of city.
Golf: Wentz Golf Course (municipal), 18 holes, greens fee 50c weekdays, $1.00 weekends and holidays; Ponca City Country Club, 18 holes, greens fee $1.00 weekdays, $2.00 weekends and holidays.
Swimming: Wentz Pool (*children 20c, adults 35c*), 5.5 m. N.E. of city; Municipal Pools (*free*) at Ponca Ave. and S. 6th St., W. Chestnut and Palm Sts., and Attucks School, S. 12th St.
Boating: Lake Ponca, 4 m. N. E. of city on Cann Blvd.
Tennis: Municipal Courts (*free*) at N. 7th St. between Highland and Overbrook Aves.; N. 7th St. between Grand and Cleveland Aves.; W. Otoe Ave. and S. Oak St.; between S. 12th and 14th Sts. and Madison and Scott Aves.

Annual Events: Ponca Indian Powwow, 3rd week in Aug.; Cherokee Outlet Opening, Sept. 16, 1957, and every 3 years thereafter.

PONCA CITY (1,003 alt., 20,180 pop.; 1956 est., 25,730), "built on oil, soil, and toil," as its people say, lies nearly in the center of a triangle at the points of which, roughly one hundred miles away, are the cities of Tulsa, Oklahoma City, and Wichita, Kansas. It is the chief city in Kay County, which borders on Kansas. Taxes are low, since the municipality, under the city manager form of government, is supported largely from the earnings of its municipal light plant and waterworks.

Ponca City impresses one as a clean, modern city set in a prairie landscape. It is built on a tableland, rolling slightly toward the east where its outskirts approach a belt of scrub oak. The streets with their widely spaced homes suggest comfort and well-being, rarely luxury or ostentation. Most of the city's growth was in the two and one-half decades from 1915 to 1940, an era of prosperity—largely due to oil—that saw buildings, paving, parks, and other public conveniences planned and provided generously. During this period, too, came the inspiration to depart from the usual semiclassic Greek type of public buildings in favor of warmer Spanish models, virtually unique in Oklahoma.

Oil was responsible for Ponca City's 129 per cent increase in population from 1920 to 1930, as compared with a growth of only 4 per cent in the following decade, when oil production in the region had become stabilized. However, in the fifteen years between 1940 and 1955 the city experienced another remarkable boom, its population spurting from 16,794 to an estimated 25,730. This growth can be credited to the expansion of the farming and trading area and to increased industrialization. The city's oil refineries were expanded and there was an influx of new companies, not all of them based on oil. Industrial employment in 1955 had reached 4,100, with a payroll of $23,000,000 annually. Total consumer income reached $39,000,000, consumer sales, $33,000,000. Total employment in all categories was 9,000 persons.

Ponca City—like a number of northern Oklahoma cities (*see Enid*) —came into existence in an afternoon. At noon of September 16, 1893, its site was raw prairie, a part of the six million and more acres of the Cherokee Outlet that the United States was opening to white settlement. By nightfall, thousands of homeseekers had covered the twenty miles from the Kansas border by wagon and buggy, on horseback, and by train—some of the overflow clinging to the steps or riding the Santa Fe engine cowcatcher—and three thousand were camped on the spot, three miles north of present-day Ponca City, where government maps indicated the town of Cross was to be laid out. But a group of men headed by B. S. Barnes decided that a more logical location would be to the south, near the border of the Ponca Indian reservation. Inside the reservation was a Santa Fe station called White Eagle by the government, and Ponca by the railroad. Barnes and his associates promptly dubbed their location New Ponca, and in the spirit of pioneer townbuilders undertook to "wipe Cross off the map."

The railroad, of course, did not recognize New Ponca at first and refused to stop its trains there. But the town's hopeful citizens persisted, and here and there an old-timer remains who remembers the crowd of elated citizens that rode down from Cross on the first train to stop at New Ponca. They distributed cigars to the male passengers, flowers to the women, and passed out cards reading, "The train stops at New Ponca the same as Chicago." Ponca City grew far enough in time to absorb Cross and make its victory complete.

Ponca City's first one-room school building, erected by public subscription, was completed just sixty days after the run. The event obviously called for a holiday, and excursion trains brought celebrators from Guthrie, Perry, Orlando, and Arkansas City, Kansas. Thousands were on hand, and to feed them, beeves were slaughtered and barbecued over huge firepits by Ponca Indians from the reservation a few miles to the south. (Since that time nearly $6,000,000 has been spent in Ponca City on public school buildings.)

Oil production, in fields developed in the Ponca Indian reservation south of the city, and in the Osage holdings to the east, began before 1909, when wildcatting brought showings on the big Miller 101 Ranch (*see Tour 10*), leased from the Ponca Indians. But the fields were small until E. W. Marland, an operator from Pennsylvania, with a "nose for oil and the luck of the devil"—plus solid financial backing in New York—arrived on the scene. With his arrival the picture changed dramatically.

In the choice of drilling locations it was said that Marland couldn't go wrong. Certainly, under his leadership the Ponca Pool was extended year after year. Wildcatters soon learned that the trend was eastward into the Osage country, and the opening of the Burbank and Shidler fields (*see Tour 4*) drew national attention. With an apparently limitless supply of crude oil thus available, Marland began to build what is known as an integrated company, one which handles the oil all the way from the well to the service station pump. Ponca City became the site of the largest refinery in the Midwest field. The name Marland went up over filling stations in an ever expanding area, and Marland pipe lines reached out into widening fields to gather the crude from Marland wells.

Wealthy, generous, and with a genuine liking for his fellow men, Marland undertook to make his adopted town a model community, to make his company something of a country club. Oil, however, is a slippery thing, and a man's luck in the oil game seldom lasts beyond a brief decade. When Marland's luck ran out, and when his extravagant organization could no longer support itself and eastern financial support was withdrawn, outside interests took over. The Marland Company polo team was disbanded and Marland retired from his baronial mansion on the outskirts of Ponca City to live in the estate's gate lodge. The end has apparently been written to another epic of oil titled "From Riches to Rags."

But after a period of eclipse he entered the oil business again, in a small way. He became interested in politics, and was elected to Congress. After one term in the House of Representatives, he came back to seek, and capture, the Democratic nomination for governor. He was elected in 1934 (*see History*).

In a sense, Marland's successor as the dominant figure in the oil business of the Ponca area—and as the generous, public-spirited first citizen of the growing city—was Lew (Lewis Haines) Wentz, another Pennsylvania-trained oilman. The best evidence of his interest in people is the big Wentz Educational Camp (*see Tour 10*) northeast of the city. No one has ever said anything about the "Wentz luck," but it seems to have been the sort that, though unspectacular, held firm. And following the Marland transition from oil to politics, Wentz was long prominent as a state Republican leader.

Four grain elevators (storage capacity: 1,095,000 bushels), a packing plant, and a creamery stimulate the area's farming and stock-raising activities. In addition to two big refineries (*see below*), the Ponca City industrial scene includes a $3,000,000 Continental Blacks plant, the Hans Gruner Company (manufacturer of drilling bits), the Great Lakes Carbon Corporation, and a number of oil-drilling and well-servicing companies.

Recreation facilities in Ponca City include thirteen parks (some 1,335 acres), fishing and boating on an 800-acre suburban lake, three supervised playgrounds, ten gymnasiums, and ten auditoriums. Enjoyed, too, by the people of the city are Continental Oil Company's baseball grounds, swimming pool, tennis courts, and a large recreation building.

POINTS OF INTEREST

PONCA CITY LIBRARY, Grand Ave. at 5th St., is a substantial two-story building of yellow brick of modified Spanish design, occupied in 1935. With its auditorium, kitchen, and other facilities for club meetings, the library serves as a community center. In its stackrooms, which hold more than 31,340 volumes, is a section devoted to the works of Oklahoma writers, with practically every book autographed by its author. There is also an exceptional exhibit of beautiful and authentic Indian and other historical relics.

The MUNICIPAL BUILDING, Grand Ave. opposite the library, an example of Spanish-Moorish architecture, is said to be one of the most beautiful buildings in the state. Set in landscaped grounds, its southwestern mission type tower stands out as a distinctive feature. On the lawn is a statue of E. W. Marland.

In BLAINE PARK, a 10-acre playground between 5th and 7th Sts. on Brookfield Ave., is the modern flood-lighted PONCA CITY STADIUM, built of native stone, with seats for 4,000. It has a well-sodded and drained football field, a quarter-mile cinder track around the field, and baseball and softball diamonds.

The city's SENIOR HIGH SCHOOL, 7th St. and Overbrook Ave., built in 1926, has been expanded several times. There is now a field house, a shop building, a $700,000 classroom addition, and a girls' gymnasium. A feature of its attractive campus is a World War II memorial constructed by the students themselves and financed entirely from money earned in business enterprises.

CONOCO REFINERY and CLUB (*club and cafeteria open to public*), at the S.W. corner of the city, together with the extensive TANK FARM where 10,000,000 barrels of crude oil can be stored, dramatically symbolize Oklahoma's most important industry. This refinery—capable of converting 55,000 barrels of crude oil daily into gasoline and other products—is one of the largest in the state and one of the most modern in the world. Taken over in 1929 by the Continental Oil Company, with all other properties of the old Marland Refining Company, it has been constantly enlarged and improved. In 1956 it employed some 3,000 workers, the majority of them Ponca City homeowners. Continental's research facilities, built at a cost of three and one-half million dollars, employ 350 people.

The Conoco Club developed out of the company's need for more office room and its wish to provide its workers, their families and their friends, with additional recreation space. One wing of the building is for work, the other for play (gymnasium, cafeteria, game room). Between the two wings is a year-round swimming pool for the children of Conoco employees (*others by special arrangement*).

CITIES SERVICE REFINERY, S. edge of Ponca City, has been modernized and expanded at a cost of $14,000,000 in recent years. The company employs some five hundred people.

POINTS OF INTEREST IN ENVIRONS

Pioneer Woman Statue, *1.5 m.*; Ponca Indian Reservation, *5 m.*; 101 Ranch, *10.2 m.*; White Eagle Monument, *12.2 m.*; Ponca Military Academy, *3 m.*; American Legion Home School, *3 m.*; Lake Ponca and Lake Ponca Park, *4 m.*; Assumption Villa (former Marland mansion), now occupied by Felician Sisters, *1.4 m.* (*see Tour* 10).

SHAWNEE

Railroad Stations: Main St. and Minnesota Ave. for Atchison, Topeka & Santa Fe Ry.; S. Union and tracks for Rock Island Ry.; 225 S. Broadway for Oklahoma City-Ada-Atoka Ry.
Bus Station: Union Station, 200 W. Main St. for Oklahoma Transportation Co. and Turner Transportation Co.
Airport: 1 m. W. of city limit on US 270.
City Buses: Fare 15c.
Taxis: Fare from 35c.

Accommodations: 9 hotels, 6 tourist courts.

Information Service: Chamber of Commerce, Aldridge Hotel, 9th St. and Bell Ave.

Newspaper: (Morning) *Shawnee Daily News-Star.*
Radio Station: KGFF (1450 kc.).
Motion Picture Theaters: 6, including 2 drive-ins.
Athletics: Athletic Park, Burns and Pottenger Aves., for baseball, track, and football.
Swimming: Municipal pool, Woodland Park, 401 N. Broadway; fee 50c.
Tennis: 12 free municipal courts at 401 N. Broadway; 301 W. Hays St.; 800 N. Louisa St.
Bowling: Shawnee Bowling Alley, 219 N. Bell St.
Boating: Shawnee Lake, 8 m. W. via W. Highland Ave. and unnumbered graveled highway.
Golf: Shawnee Country Club, 2 m. E. on US 270, 9 holes, greens fee $1.00; Elks Country Club, 5 m. N.W., 18 holes, greens fee 50c.

Annual Events: Livestock Show, in March; Pottawatomie County Fair, in the fall.

SHAWNEE (1,008 alt., 22,948 pop.; 1956 est., 30,000), seat of Pottawatomie County and not too far from the geographic center of Oklahoma, might very well stand as a Sooner State miniature, so far as racial background, early-day history, preliminary accomplishments, shattering vicissitudes, and heroic mid-twentieth-century strivings are concerned. In each of these categories the Shawnee story reflects to a varying degree that of Oklahoma as a whole. To know and appreciate the experience of the city is to know and appreciate the state's struggles to adapt its long-time dependence on soil and oil to the complex industrial technology of a new age. That Shawnee in 1956 gave every indication of coming back strong is perhaps the best indication that Oklahoma herself is winning her fight to keep pace with the nation, and gain a pace or two on the turn.

Shawnee lies on land that has been claimed at different times by Spain, France, England, the Creek and Seminole Indian nations, and the Sac and Fox tribe. The first settlement was called Shawnee Town, because it was a trading place for the Shawnee Indians, whose reservation lay near by. The area—including the reservations of the Sac and Fox, Iowa, and Shawnee-Potawatomi Indians—was opened to white settlement on September 22, 1891. From pioneer memories is told the story that Etta Ray and her sister, young women from still young Oklahoma City, stood on Kickapoo land with their toes touching the western border of the territory to be opened. When the gun was fired, they stepped across the line and drove their claim stakes. On this 160-acre claim the new town began to grow. Later, when the first railroad sought right of way eastward from Oklahoma City, Etta Ray, then Mrs. Henry G. Beard, gave one half of her farm on the condition that the railroad station should be built there.

All of this is more or less routine Oklahoma history—as is the fight Etta Ray had (and won) with the man who contested her claim, and the fight Shawnee had (and won) with Tecumseh for the county seat. Shawnee's early development, too, followed a familiar pattern. In the spring of 1892 a town-building company was formed. Trees were cut to open a street and a sawmill was brought in to save the long hauling of lumber by ox team from Oklahoma City, forty-five miles to the northwest. Because of the nationwide depression of 1893, the coming of the first railroad was delayed until the summer of 1895. But the eventual arrival of a train of the Choctaw, Oklahoma and Gulf (now the Rock Island) was the outstanding feature of that year's Fourth of July celebration, so far as the town's three hundred inhabitants were concerned. The Santa Fe reached Shawnee in March, 1902, and two years later the Oklahoma City-Ada-Atoka line was laid.

About 1910, when it became evident that the state capital was to be moved from Guthrie (*see Tour 10*), the citizens of Shawnee made an attempt to get it. The struggle with much larger Oklahoma City was no serious contest. The setback, however, was only one of many to befall the city. Location in Shawnee of the big Rock Island shops, as well as shops of the Santa Fe—together employing some nine hundred workers—made the city acutely aware of the countrywide strike of railroad shopmen in 1922. The dispute against a wage cut began July 1 and was drawn out to October 1. And despite the heavy guard thrown around the railroads' property, a volley of shots was fired into the Rock Island's yards on the morning of August 18. News reports went out that conditions at Shawnee were the worst in the United States, and that radical agitators were in control. This, however, was promptly denied by Shawnee peace officers. And it is said that during the entire period of the strike mail trains were never delayed and regular service was little affected. Certainly, the loss of the Rock Island shops to El Reno in more recent times was a far more serious economic blow.

Misfortune of a different kind struck Shawnee on March 28, 1924. A devastating tornado leveled a twenty-eight-block section of the city's northwestern residential area, killing eight persons and causing property damage in excess of one-half million dollars. Four years later, twice that amount of damage was left in the wake of a flood on April 4, 1928. A torrential seven-inch rainfall sent the near-by North Canadian River out of its banks, choked the deep and narrow channel of Shawnee Creek, which runs through the city. Hundreds of houses were swept off their foundations by the rushing waters and at least a half dozen people were drowned.

By this time, however, Shawnee was able to take tragedy in stride. The principal city of the Greater Seminole Field boom (*see Tour 5*), it had become the supply point for what was up to that time one of the largest and most productive oil fields in the world. A map issued by Shawnee businessmen at the crest of the oil boom in the 1920's listed six rich fields within the city's trade area. Thousands of highly paid workers and much of the wealth from the ten thousand and more producing wells in the region gravitated largely to Shawnee. And like many another Oklahoma town before and since, it was hard pressed to care for the flood of newcomers. These were days when the hungry visitor paid a dollar for a sandwich, when he was lucky enough to get it. These were nights when the same visitor paid five dollars for a cot, and did not dare to complain because he had to share it with several strangers. Earlsboro, Seminole, Cromwell, and many other fields were bursting into prominence, and for a while Shawnee was said to have a population—even if a highly unstable one—of nearly thirty-five thousand. But in 1930, when the rush was beginning to subside, the official census count was 23,283, still good enough to earn Shawnee the rank of fifth city in size in the state.

Shawnee's population remained fairly stable during the 1930's and 1940's, and began to climb once again only in the early 1950's. Throughout this twenty-year period, however, agriculture was, and continues to be, a strong stabilizing factor. Of the county's half million acres, some 160,000 are devoted to farming, with cotton, alfalfa, and peanuts being the principal cash crops. Livestock and poultry have become increasingly important, while vegetables, berries, and fruits are also marketed in Shawnee.

Two of the state's principal denominational colleges combine to give Shawnee an importance in the Oklahoma religious picture out of all proportion to its size. Many of the state's Baptist preachers have received all or at least part of their training at Oklahoma Baptist University (*see below*). And in a similar way the city contributes to Catholic training and education through the work of St. Gregory's College (*see Tour 5*), many of whose students are preparing for the priesthood.

In recent years Shawnee has joined Oklahoma in an all-out drive for new industries. Though the near-by oil fields are still active, and servicing them, as well as marketing their production, remains economically important, the city's three largest industrial establishments are Sylvania Electric Products, Fairchild Aircraft, and Shawnee Milling Company. In addition, processing plants here handle the area's peanuts, fruits and vegetables, poultry, and dairy products. And Shawnee manufacturers turn out such varied products as women's clothing and crankshafts, hair driers and church furniture, fireworks and truck bodies.

Two onetime citizens of whom Shawnee is increasingly proud are the late Jim Thorpe, one of the greatest Indian athletes of all time, and Brewster Higley. An obscure physician in Shawnee, Higley died some thirty-eight years ago. Although his name is not so widely known as that of the colorful Thorpe, he is the author of one of the country's most familiar songs, "Home on the Range," which comes close to symbolizing for the rest of the nation the West that was. Thorpe is buried in Pennsylvania, but Higley's grave is in Shawnee—in Fairview Cemetery at 1400 N. Harrison—and consideration is being given to the erection of suitable memorials to both men.

POINTS OF INTEREST

The MUNICIPAL AUDITORIUM, 400 N. Bell Ave., in the center of downtown Shawnee, is also the center of the city's sports, entertainment, and convention activities. It is a red-brick structure seating 2,700, with a modern stage and two gymnasiums.

WOODLAND PARK, four blocks in area, is directly north of the auditorium and is dominated by its large swimming pool. Concrete tennis courts and picnic facilities are scattered about under its tall ash and elm trees. At its center is the BEARD LOG CABIN (*private*), the first residence in Shawnee.

The POTTAWATOMIE COUNTY COURTHOUSE, in the 300

block on N. Broadway, is a three-story structure, simple and modern in design, built in 1934. Its base of black Missouri limestone supports walls of Indiana limestone, trimmed at the corners in terra cotta. Its façade is ornamented with aluminum spandrels, and plaques above the granite steps picture the Indian, the Pioneer, and Justice. Inside, a wide, branching stairway of warm-tinted marble leads to an elaborate mezzanine and the modernistic courtroom.

OKLAHOMA BAPTIST UNIVERSITY, at the northwest corner of the city, in 1955 had an enrollment of 1,560 students and a faculty of 86. Plans for its founding were made in 1906, and its first classes met in September, 1911, in the basement of the First Baptist Church and in Convention Hall. It is coeducational.

The original campus of sixty acres was donated by the city. By 1915, the first building—Shawnee Hall—was ready for use, and by 1956 the campus had grown to 122 acres, with eighteen permanent buildings. Noteworthy is Brittain Library, completed in 1946, which contains more than 52,000 volumes. Its principal collections are the W. B. Bizzell (*see Norman*) personal library, the Gillon collection of religious books and denominational records, and the E. C. Routh library of missions.

The College of Fine Arts is widely recognized for its musical organizations. These include the Bison Glee Club and the 200-member Shawnee Choral Society.

ATHLETIC PARK, at the western edge of the city, contains both a baseball and a football field. Both are lighted for night contests. The baseball plant has seats for 3,000, while 4,500 can be seated in the football stadium.

SYLVANIA ELECTRIC PRODUCTS, 1200 W. Benedict St., manufactures tubes for radio and television, and other electronic equipment. Established in 1950, the plant carries Shawnee's largest payroll. Special guide tours can be arranged by student and civic groups.

POINTS OF INTEREST IN ENVIRONS

Shawnee Quaker Mission and Shawnee Indian Sanatorium, *2.5 m.*; St. Gregory's College, *3.3 m.* (*see Tour 5*). Girls Town (State Industrial School) at Tecumseh, *5 m.* S. on State 18.

STILLWATER

Railroad Station: E. 9th St. and tracks for Atchison, Topeka & Santa Fe Ry.
Bus Station: 222 E. 6th St. for Missouri-Kansas-Oklahoma Lines.

Airport: Municipal, 2 m. N. on State 40 and 0.5 m. W. for Central Airlines.
Taxis: Zoned from 25c.

Accommodations: 4 hotels; 5 motels; Oklahoma A. & M. College Student Union.

Information Service: Chamber of Commerce, Municipal Bldg., 8th and Lewis Sts.

Newspapers: (Evening) *News-Press* (daily) *O'Collegian,* A. & M. student paper.
Radio Station: KSPI (780 kc.).
Motion Picture Theaters: 4, including 1 drive-in.
Golf: Lakeside Memorial, 3 m. N. on State 40, 18 holes, greens fee 75c on weekdays, $1.00 weekends; college-owned Hillcrest, 1.5 m. N. on State 40 and 0.5 m. W., 18 holes, no greens fee; Yost Lake (4 holes), 4 m. N. and 3 m. E. on State 40, greens fee 50c.
Swimming: Crystal Plunge, 500 E. 6th St.
Boating, Swimming, Water Sports: Lake Carl Blackwell, 9 m. W. on State 51C (*see Tour 2A*); Boomer Lake, 1.5 m. N. on State 40; Yost Lake, 4 m. N. and 3 m. E. on State 40.

Annual Events: Junior Livestock Show, March; 4-H Club Roundup, June; Farm Home Women's Conference, Aug.; Aggie Sports Car Races, Labor Day; Payne County Fair, 3rd week in Sept.; Aggie Homecoming, Oct.; Stillwater Yulebilee, Dec.

STILLWATER (985 alt., 20,238 pop.), seat of Payne County and home of Oklahoma Agricultural and Mechanical College, was laid out, legally, immediately after the opening of the original Oklahoma Territory in 1889. The site, however, had long been familiar ground to the "Boomers," those persistent men who contended that this unoccupied Indian land could and should be homesteaded. William L. Couch (*see Oklahoma City*), "President of Payne's Oklahoma Colony," led the first organized attempt to establish a town in 1884. On December 12, he settled some two hundred Boomers just southeast of what is now Stillwater. Federal troops commanded by Colonel Edward Hatch forced these would-be homesteaders back to Kansas, not by firing on the entrenched intruders, but by cutting their supply lines and starving them out.

The present city was located on Stillwater Creek by a group of men who made the Run together. A 240-acre tract (later increased by 80 acres) was assembled from their 160-acre claims by five men, in honor of whom Lewis, Duck, Husband, Lowery, and Duncan streets are named. Dr. J. G. Evans was elected the community's first mayor on June 11, 1889. The first building was erected the same day, the first business established the next. In the beginning, $5.00 would buy one business or two residential lots. Money from the sale was spent for bridges, a well, and street improvements. But until passage of the Organic Act of 1890 the government of the town was wholly voluntary and without formal authority.

On April 7, 1891, Stillwater citizens voted unanimously to incorporate their city. The second recorded action taken by the newly elected officials was to provide for a vote on whether the town should issue $10,000 in bonds to aid in "the construction of the Agricultural and Mechanical College" which the Territory's first legislature had just authorized. The vote in favor of the proposition was unanimous, and since that time Stillwater and the college have grown up together.

The town's first boost, after the location of the college, was its designation as a registration point for the opening of the Cherokee Outlet in 1893. The next big help was the arrival of the Eastern Oklahoma Railway in March, 1900. Before that time, the outside world was reached at Wharton (now Perry), twenty-five miles away by hack.

On a slight slope north of Stillwater Creek, the city spreads northwest to, and beyond, the A. and M. campus. An overgrown small town in appearance, Stillwater's business buildings are low, trim, and solid. Set in big yards and half-hidden by trees, its houses—particularly in the older sections—are large and comfortable. Principal small industries include a flour mill, creameries, hatcheries, oil-field service firms, and an electronics laboratory.

Stillwater describes itself as "friendly Aggieland," a center for business, education, conventions, sports, and research. Four-fifths of all Oklahomans live within seventy-five miles of Stillwater. And in addition to its 10,000 on-campus students in 1956, it draws each year some 60,000 persons to a wide variety of conventions, short courses, and conferences, another 100,000 to its many college sporting events. If Stillwater is neat and friendly, it is also one of the country's most traffic-safe cities of its size, with numerous National Safety Council awards to prove it. And if the city is aware of present-day problems, it also remembers its dramatic past. In 1956, the name of Fair Park, the site of Couch's premature attempt to found the city, was changed to Couch Memorial Park. A museum is currently being planned.

OKLAHOMA AGRICULTURAL AND MECHANICAL COLLEGE

Under the Morrill Act of 1862, signed into law by President Abraham Lincoln, Oklahoma A. and M. has a three-fold responsibility for service to the people of Oklahoma: to provide resident instruction, to carry on research, and to give off-campus help through extension activities.

In fulfilling these responsibilities, A. and M. today provides campus instruction to some 10,000 students a year under eight main divisions.

These are the Schools of Agriculture, Arts and Sciences, Business, Education, Engineering, Home Economics, Veterinary Medicine; and the Graduate School. It is responsible for teaching thirty-five trades to an additional 1,500 students in its branch at Okmulgee *(see Okmulgee)*. On the main campus, students may work for bachelor's degrees in seventy-three major fields, for a master's degree in fifty-one fields, and for doctor's degrees in nineteen areas of study.

A. and M. research activities spring from three separate agencies of the college: the Agricultural Experiment Station, the Engineering Research Division, and the A. and M. Research Foundation. At Experiment Station headquarters more than one hundred scientists and some sixty graduate students are engaged annually in three hundred active experimental projects. Completing the organization are nineteen special stations in various parts of Oklahoma, six of these operated in connection with the U. S. Department of Agriculture. Two of the most important are the 6,500-acre animal research station at Fort Reno (*see Tour 1*) and the 920-acre veterinary research station at Pawhuska. Outstanding contributions to the agricultural well-being of the state during these sixty-five years of research include the discovery that cottonseed meal is not poisonous to livestock and can be fed in unlimited quantities; new methods of using Oklahoma-grown feeds to produce high-quality meat animals; and the invention of a brush-type cotton plant stripper.

The Engineering Research Division conducts investigations of basic engineering problems, as well as sponsored projects for the state and federal governments, and for private industry. Perhaps the top achievements here have been the discovery of a dependable method of tracking tornadoes and severe thunderstorms; the compounding of a formula used in asphaltic concrete; and—though this may be disputed by many motorists—the invention of the ubiquitous parking meter.

The A. and M. Research Foundation fosters studies in areas not covered by the other two research groups. About fifty faculty members and a similar number of graduate students are employed annually on some twenty-five different projects supported by approximately one-half million dollars in contracts and grants. The foundation maintains a radio-isotopes and radiations laboratory, and a computing center. A tribute to the college's efficiency in the field of research is its recent selection, by the National Science Foundation, to originate and sponsor a national training program to improve the competence of high school teachers in science and mathematics.

Best known perhaps of all A. and M. activities—because it takes its program for better farm and homemaking practices into each of the state's seventy-seven counties—is the work of the Extension Service. It looks after Oklahoma's 75,000 4–H Club members and provides guidance for more than 30,000 local leaders, volunteers who in turn carry educational programs in agriculture and home economics to 150,000 Oklahoma farms and ranches. In recent years, through the federal government's Point IV program, Oklahoma A. and M. has also reached out to extend technical assistance overseas, particularly in Ethiopia and Pakistan.

The first Territorial legislature of Oklahoma established the college at Stillwater (*see above*) on Christmas Day, 1890. The first two hundred acres of land, says an early college catalogue, were "untouched by plow or other implements, with the exception of about sixteen acres." But most of "the good people of Stillwater" helped the first Experiment Station director burn off the tall grass that hid the corner markers of the property. They assisted again when the first furrows were turned in December, 1891.

"A pair of mules," once wrote the station's head, "was probably the first property acquired. . . . Tradition has it that one evening Professor Magruder, overseer of the farm, caught a pair of runaway mules and held them until the owner came up in a furious mood and offered to sell them to any man who would offer a price. Magruder got the mules." Presumably, he also tamed them.

First classes were begun on December 14, 1891, in Stillwater's Congregational Church (Duncan and 6th Streets). Along with the Experiment Station director, and the president, the fledgling college could boast four professors. By the end of this first term, enrollment was up to forty males and thirty-six females.

Because of a misinterpretation of federal legislation relating to land-grant colleges, it was assumed that these women, as well as the men, were subject to military training. And so the A. and M. memory file includes the mental picture of thirty-six coeds, dressed in the fashion of 1891, doing squads left and right. One of the first student regulations of the college, incidentally, stated succinctly that "firearms are not permitted in the classrooms."

Six men received diplomas at the first commencement ceremony in 1896, eleven years before Oklahoma was admitted to the Union. (All graduates up to 1915 had to return for additional work in order to have their degrees recognized.) Commencement exercises, actually, were held at the end of each college year before 1896, but as a Stillwater newspaper summed up the 1893 affair: "This was a commencement without a graduate, although the sweet girls were there just the same."

CAMPUS TOUR

The main campus consists of 146 acres, on which are scattered forty-one buildings. Adjoining it are 1,420 acres of college farms. And one of the first visual impressions the visitor is likely to get is that of uniformity in architecture, a tribute to the late Dr. Henry G. Bennett, president of the College from 1928 to 1951. He conceived the plan in the early 1930's and virtually every new structure since that time is of modified Georgian design, usually three or four stories in height, of red brick, and slate roofed. Perhaps the second impression—a surprising one, since the school is primarily concerned with agriculture—is the general absence of traditional college landscaping and wide-spreading shade trees. Below is a partial list of some of the more important buildings (*all open ordinarily during school hours*), fanning north and west from the corner of Knoblock St. and College Ave.

"OLD CENTRAL," set back from Knoblock St. (L), was the first building erected on the campus for classroom use. A quaint, pink-brick period piece, it was described at its dedication in 1894 as "a handsome structure . . . 67 by 67 feet in size, consisting of two stories, and contains 16 rooms." Its offices and classrooms still in use, it remains, if not a model of academic efficiency, at least a structure of sentimental beauty to loyal Aggie students and alumni.

The COLLEGE AUDITORIUM, Knoblock St. and Morrill Ave., is a brick and reinforced-concrete structure erected in 1920. MORRILL HALL and GARDINER HALL, facing Morrill St. north of the Auditorium, are also brick-and-stone reminders of the school's early days. Both replaced still earlier structures of the same name that were destroyed by fire in 1914. With the first Morrill Hall went all the student records kept in the registrar's office.

GALLAGHER HALL (basketball, wrestling), the 7,000-seat field house named for the Aggies' long-famed wrestling coach, and LEWIS FIELD (football stadium) are at the north end of Knoblock St. To the northeast is the huge HENRY G. BENNETT HALL, said to be one of the finest college residence halls in the nation. It is a four-story, multiwinged building, containing four dining halls and living quarters for 1,100 boys. The number and size of resident halls is an impressive characteristic of the A. and M. campus. Besides Bennett Hall, men can also choose between CORDELL, HANNER, and THATCHER HALLS, all to the north and east of the campus. On the west are handsome MURRAY, WILLARD, and STOUR HALLS for women. A total of 3,300 students can be housed in these seven dormitories.

West on College Ave. is the HENRY G. BENNETT MEMORIAL CHAPEL (R), nondenominational religious shrine located on the site of the former president's home. It was erected in memory of the A. and M. war dead and the late Mr. and Mrs. Bennett, both of whom were killed in a plane crash near Teheran, Iran, on December 22, 1951, while on a Point IV inspection tour of the Middle East.

The STUDENT UNION, N.W. of the Chapel, is one of the finest buildings of its type in the nation. Completed in the summer of 1950 at a cost of $3,500,000, it is a block-long, six-story, air-conditioned structure that contains 500,000 square feet of floor space. It provides hotel accommodations for 160 persons; two snack bars, a cafeteria, a coffee shop, and fifteen private dining rooms; twenty-two meeting rooms for up to 1,300 people; a complete shopping center; recreational facilities that include eight bowling lanes, two outdoor terraces for dancing, four ballrooms, and three lounges.

Just as impressive and even newer, built in 1953, is the LIBRARY, N. of the Student Union. A six-story structure, topped by a 110-foot tower and spire, it can accommodate one million books and 2,500 students, most of whom appreciate the air conditioning, the casual furniture, the open shelves that encourage browsing, and the general home-library atmosphere.

The agricultural facilities of the college spread out from the northwest corner of the campus. Even the most urban-minded visitor will be struck by the fact that at Oklahoma A. and M. the livestock, too, go strictly first class. The impressive ANIMAL HUSBANDRY BUILDING has a rounded roof and tall Ionic columns supporting a lofty porch. Within is a 2,000-seat arena. Farther west is the huge H-shaped BEEF CATTLE BARN, flanked by enormous brick silos. Equally commodious, and comfortable quarters are provided for the hogs, the sheep, the poultry, and the rest of the school's animals.

POINTS OF INTEREST IN ENVIRONS

Lake Carl Blackwell, 13 *m.;* Ingalls, 12.8 *m.;* Round Mountain Battlefield, 17 *m.* (*see Tour* 2A).

TULSA

Railroad Stations: Union Depot, 3 S. Boston Ave., for Atchison, Topeka & Santa Fe Ry., St. Louis–San Francisco Ry., and Missouri-Kansas-Texas R. R.; Frankfort Ave. and 6th St. for Midland Valley R. R. (no passenger service).
Bus Stations: Bus Terminal, 319 S. Cincinnati Ave. for Arkoma Coach Lines,

Continental Trailways, Greyhound Lines, M. K. & O. Lines, Union Transportation Co.; Bus Depot, 215 E. 4th St. for Kansas Trails, American Trailways.
Airport: Municipal, E. Apache Ave. and Sheridan Rd. for American Airlines, Braniff International Airways, Central Airlines, Continental Air Lines, and Trans World Airlines; limousine service (fare $1.25) from all hotels and downtown ticket offices 50 min. before flights; taxi service (metered fares).
City Bus Lines: Tulsa City Lines, fare 15c; Tulsa Transit Co., fare 15c within city, graduated rates outside city limits.
Taxis: Metered fares from 35c, each extra passenger 10c.
Traffic Regulations: One-way traffic on many downtown streets, where left turns are generally prohibited, except onto one-way streets. Many pedestrian lights and special left-turn lights throughout the city. Parking meters generally 10c. Speed zones (varying, but well marked) are radar patrolled.

Accommodations: 37 hotels, 8 for Negroes; many luxury motels; tourist courts; trailer parks.

Information Service: Chamber of Commerce, 616 S. Boston Ave.; Auto Club of Oklahoma (members only), 1316 S. Peoria Ave.

Newspapers: (Morning) *World* and (evening) *Tribune*.
Radio Stations: KAKC (970 kc.); KFMJ (1050 kc.); KOME (1300 kc.); KRMG (740 kc.); KTUL (1430 kc.); KVOO (1170 kc.); KWGS (FM, 90.5 mc.).
Television Stations: KOTV (Ch. 6); KTVX (Ch. 8); KVOO–TV (Ch. 2).
Theaters: Tulsa Little Theater, 1511 S. Delaware Ave., local productions during fall, winter, and spring (Junior Theater during summer); Municipal Theater, 101 W. Brady St., local opera productions, concerts, occasional road shows.
Motion Picture Theaters: 24, including 8 drive-ins.
Athletics: Texas League Baseball Park (Class A), 4300 E. 15th St.; Skelly Field (public high schools, University of Tulsa), 2900 E. 11th St.; Tulsa State Fair Grounds (wrestling, auto races, ice skating), 15th to 21st Sts. between Louisville and Yale Aves.
Boating: Yahola Reservoir in Mohawk Park (*see Tour* 9A).
Swimming: Newblock Pool (municipal), 20 blocks W. of Main St. on US 64, 20c and 40c; East Side Pool (McClure Park, municipal), 73rd E. Ave. and 8th St., 20c and 40c; YMCA, 515 S. Denver Ave., open to members, free; YWCA, 116 W. 5th St., open at certain times to women nonmembers, 35c.
Golf: Mohawk Municipal Course, Mohawk Park, 5 m. N. (*see Tour* 9A), 36 holes, greens fee 75c weekdays, $1.50 weekends and holidays; Western Village, 8 m. E. on State 33, 18 holes, greens fee $1.00 weekdays, $2.00 weekends and holidays; Admiral Heights, 10 m. E. on State 33, 18 holes, greens fee 50c weekdays, $1.00 weekends and holidays.
Tennis: Free municipal courts at Admiral Blvd. and Victor Ave.; Archer St. and Delaware Ave.; 9th St. and Alleghany Ave.; 48th St. and 29th W. Ave.; Cheyenne Ave. and Queen St.; 21st. and Gary Pl.; 25th St. and Quanah Ave.; Virgin St. and Madison Ave. (Negro); 13th Pl. and Cincinnati Ave.; Edison St. and Quanah Ave.; 41st St. and Union Ave.; 8th St. and Delaware Ave.; Pine St. and Zunis Ave.; 11th St. and Peoria Ave. (lighted); 4th St. and Jamestown Ave. All courts concrete and enclosed.

Annual Events: Northeast Oklahoma Square Dance Festival, March; Johnny Lee

Wills Stampede (rodeo), April; Mid-Continent Kennel Club Dog Show, April; Tulsa Charity Horse Show, May (all at Fair Grounds Pavilion); Indian Powwow, Mohawk Park, June; Tulsa State Fair and Exposition, Fair Grounds, Sept. and/or Oct.

Quadrennial Event: The International Petroleum Exposition, 21st St. and Pittsburg Ave., May. The event, previously held every four years, was set for 1950 to coincide with the 100th Anniversary of the Drake Discovery Well in Pennsylvania.

TULSA (744 alt., 182,740 pop.; 1956 est., 254,100) is built chiefly on low, rolling hills and on the flat between those hills and the east bank of the Arkansas River. The city has reached out across the river, however, and includes West Tulsa, Garden City, Red Fork, and Carbondale. Stretching away to the south is one of Oklahoma's most fertile farming and fruit-growing sections; toward the north and east is broken grazing land; and to the northwest lie the lower ranges of the Osage Hills, a part of the Osage Indian oil lands.

Tulsa, the second largest city in Oklahoma, is the oil center of the great Mid-Continent area and the state's largest oil refining center, yet it is neither typically Oklahoman nor a typical oil-boom town. It is a city of contrasts, resulting from the transplanting of a metropolitan population to a small settlement of Indians and white pioneers. In certain sections—north of 3rd Street, for example—old Tulsa still exists with the squat one- and two-story frame, stone, and brick buildings of its earlier days. Generally, however, the city is eastern in the character of its people, in its office buildings now spread out over a large downtown area, and in its southern sections, where elaborate homes suggest New York or Philadelphia suburbs rather than Oklahoma. The sections flanking the railroad tracks between 1st Street and Archer Avenue and West Tulsa, across the river, are industrial in character. Beyond Archer to the northeast lies the extensive Negro district.

A dramatic view of Tulsa from the southwest, across the vast refinery plant dominating West Tulsa and the wide sand-carpeted bed of the river, shows tall, smoke-stained stacks giving way, on the skyline, to the taller modern-city group of skyscrapers that serve the office and hotel needs of its hundreds of oil companies. It is a visual summary of the city's description of itself as the oil capital of the world.

Although Tulsa's population is more than 98 per cent American born, it is composed of many elements. The first organized settlement was made by civilized Indians, and the first whites were a mixture of workmen, small-scale merchants, missionaries, and adventurers. After statehood brought the right to buy land, many farmers and ranchmen came from the South and the West to settle in the vicinity, and their children built homes in the city. To this already conglomerate citizenry, the oil industry added thousands of administrative, technical, and clerical workers from the North and East.

Tulsa has wealthy citizens whose fortunes are generations old and others whose wealth is new. Many of the poor became rich and many of the rich lost their money in the fluctuating "boom-bust" cycles of Mid-Continent oil development. Indians and whites intermarried extensively; factory workers drifted in; leisure classes developed; businessmen retired and took up the hobbies of leisure. And the city's great middle class—junior oil executives, merchants and clerks, mechanics and office workers—has increased steadily.

Tulsa has citizens of all degrees of Indian mixture, but even those of less than one-eighth proudly call themselves Indians. They boast, as did the late Will Rogers—a Cherokee member of Tulsa's Akdar Shrine—that their ancestors were not Mayflower passengers, but were on the "reception committee." Tulsa's Indians, however, are not easily identified unless they are of more than one-quarter blood. In dress, pursuits, and attainments they are much the same as their white counterparts.

Slightly more than 9 per cent of Tulsa's population are Negroes, most of whom live in an area of which Greenwood Avenue is the principal business street. This district lies to the northeast of the Union Depot, running in a fan shape from a line almost due north to a line approximately northeast, and extending indefinitely to the city's edge. The section is generally poorer, reflecting the income of a people still dependent for the most part on work as servants or casual laborers. There are fine residences, however, the homes of successful business and professional men. And new housing developments constructed especially for Negroes reflect the same modern trend as the city's other moderately priced developments. The Greenwood district has its own hotels, churches, park, places of business and amusement, and municipal hospital. Though Tulsa public schools have been integrated, the Greenwood schools are still attended almost exclusively by Negro children.

Tulsa existed as early as 1879 as a post office on the pony mail route through Indian Territory. The office was in the home of a Creek rancher, George Perryman—near present 41st Street—and the rancher's brother was the first postmaster. Into this primitive section, unknown to any whites except a few cattlemen and those who had married into the tribe, the old Atlantic & Pacific Railroad built in 1882. Originally the builders planned to stop in the Cherokee Nation, about a mile from the river bank. But since the Cherokee laws prohibited trading except by native, intermarried, or adopted Cherokee citizens, the rails were extended into the Creek Nation, where whites were permitted to trade by posting a bond. There, on the site of the present Tulsa business section, the railroad established a terminal with a roundhouse and a large loading pen. The vast herds of cattle from the locality, formerly driven overland to Vinita (*see Tour 1*), were now loaded in Tulsa for shipment to the stockyards of St. Louis and Chicago. Trains began making daily trips between the terminus and Vinita, stopping at intervals to let the passengers shoot prairie chickens along the way. When traders and an occasional professional man began finally to drift in, rancher Perryman moved his post office to the rail terminal, too.

The town was first called Tulsey Town, for the Creek Indians who belonged to the Tallassee or Tulsey community. The present Tallassee, Alabama, was the home of this group before the Creeks were removed to Oklahoma.

In 1882, guerrilla warfare was rampant throughout the Creek Nation. Isparhecher ('Spa-hich'-se), an insurgent Creek leader, organized a small army of full bloods with which he harassed tribesmen loyal to Chief Checote. The little stores of Tulsa, unable to replenish their stocks for fear of looting, did practically no business all fall and winter. But by August, 1883, the Creek trouble was settled and the town began to breathe normally. Floored tents were replaced by wooden shacks, plank-built stores were provided with covered porches, and Tulsa had all the earmarks of what its inhabitants called a "fair little city," complete with a community water well and a Negro barber.

But early town planners, unfortunately, felt that one hundred feet was "too far to wade the mud." Main street was thus made only eighty feet wide. And unfortunately, too, the street was surveyed by a railroad engineer who ran his line at right angles to the railroad. The result was what the old-timers called a "cattywampus" business district, while the rest of the city is straight with the compass. In writing of this Main Street a pioneer recalled that "whether it was dusty or muddy depended upon the weather. We had to dodge roaming hogs, goats, and cows when crossing, and sometimes wild animals would venture into the middle of town."

The town had still other, and more serious problems. Although alcoholic liquor was prohibited under Indian Territory law, thousands of gallons of it poured into the town anyway. And since there were no important trading points within a radius of sixty miles, Tulsa's isolation made it a convenient resort for gamblers and assorted bad men. The only law for a while was that enforced by the Creek light-horsemen, an occasional U.S. deputy marshal, and the "two volumes of common law" strapped to a man's thighs. In spite of this wild-west atmosphere, however, the first organization of any kind was a union Sunday school, formed in 1883 in the tent of a railroad carpenter.

In 1884 the Presbyterian Home Mission Board of New York City erected a small mission school on the summit of a wooded hill at what is now the southeast corner of 4th Street and Boston Avenue. Here Tulsa's first congregation was organized, one that included many Indians and an elder who used the Creek language when called upon to pray. It was near the old cattle trail, and herds of cattle were driven past it regularly until 1888. The site is now occupied by the Mid-Continent Building.

Many things combined to retard the development of Tulsa. There was the long fight with railroad officials who claimed a right of way three hundred feet wide south of the tracks that would have included a goodly number of the town's buildings. Then certain of the Indians, eyeing the site of the little settlement, shrewdly claimed most of it as their personal allotments when the Creek's land, formerly held in common, was divided. But perhaps the most serious problem was the lack of an adequate water supply, which caused the railroad to shift its terminal to Sapulpa. In 1900, as a result of all these difficulties, Tulsa had a population of only 1,390, and was merely another unimportant Indian Territory town.

Then on June 25, 1901, Tulsa rocketed into the national limelight. Across the river at Red Fork (now within the city limits) the state's first commercially important oil well was brought in. During the next two years Red Fork and Tulsa both grew rapidly. Since Tulsa was cut off from oil development by the Arkansas River, however, there was still a good chance that she might become a suburb of the other town. When a bond issue to build a wagon bridge failed, the time for drastic action had come. Three Tulsa citizens promptly rose to the occasion. With their own capital they built a toll bridge across the river. And Tulsa proceeded at once to invite the ever increasing horde of oilmen to "come and make your homes in a beautiful little city that is high and dry, peaceful and orderly. Where there are good churches, stores, schools, and banks, and where our ordinances prevent the desolation of our homes and property by oil wells."

The oilmen apparently took Tulsa at its word. By 1910 a building boom was in full swing and brick plants were working at capacity to meet the demand. Pipelines were opened to the Gulf of Mexico and oil prices began to climb. Hotel and office buildings were erected. Streets were paved. Banks were established. The total value of buildings under construction by late August reached $1,365,000. Down through the Creek country and up through the lands of the Osages went the drillers. But in Tulsa, significantly, the bosses lived, and it was here that the operating money was banked. The population leaped from 18,182 in 1910 to 72,075 in 1920, and to 141,258 in 1930. Growth lagged during the depression years, the 1940 census showing only 142,-157. But the spark was rekindled in the next decade and the city's population grew to 182,740 in 1950. It continues to grow steadily.

Immediately following World War I, however, there was increasing racial bitterness largely because of the influx of both white and Negro laborers seeking employment in the oil fields. After months of unrest and threats of vigilante activity, a minor incident on June 1, 1921, developed into a serious race riot. Armed conflict between whites and Negroes spread to several sections of the city. Vigilantes invaded the Greenwood (Negro) district and laid it waste by fire. It is estimated that more than thirty-six persons were killed in the various clashes. But after a night of terror and two days of martial law, the whites organized a systematic rehabilitation program for the devastated Negro section and gave generous aid to the Negroes left homeless by the fires. Nationwide publicity of the most lurid sort naturally followed the tragedy, and Tulsa's whites and Negroes joined in an effort to live down the incident by working diligently—and on the whole successfully—for mutual understanding.

Many of the early settlers were cultured people, and the city's many-sided interest in music has developed from their activities (*see Music*). One of the first ensembles of one hundred pianos heard in the United States played in Tulsa in 1934, and the program was broadcast by the Columbia Broadcasting System.

There was a time when seemingly everyone in Tulsa owned an oil company, worked for an oil company, or sold goods to the oil people. And although the city's expanding economy has created some competition from other industries, oil is still the most common topic of conversation on the streets and in the hotels and clubs. There are more than 850 oil companies or allied industries—including scores of the nation's best-known makers of drilling rigs, steel tanks, oil-field tools, and other equipment—with headquarters, offices, service establishments in Tulsa. It is estimated that oil companies in Tulsa purchase approximately $600,000,000 worth of supplies and equipment annually for their world-wide exploration, drilling, production, and marketing activities. And much of the financing is made possible by the city's banks, which specialize in oil-field enterprises and handle successfully oil promotions that other banks would not consider. As a center for financing such operations, Tulsa ranks among the foremost in the nation.

All phases of the complex petroleum industry are represented in Tulsa, including refining. The largest refinery in the state, with a daily capacity of 75,000 barrels of crude oil, is across the Arkansas River from the business district (*see below*). A second 35,000-barrel refinery is near by.

Central inland location, cheap fuel, abundant water, and a good labor supply account for the city's industrial importance in fields other than those associated with oil. Upwards of 15,000 persons are employed by the aircraft industry, which is dominated by the Douglas Aircraft Company's huge manufacturing plant and the central overhaul and supply depot for the entire American Airlines fleet. In the Sand Springs district (*see Tour 2*) are glass plants, the largest cotton textile mill west of the Mississippi, and a large steel plant. The Tulsa industrial scene also includes chemical works, a truck-body plant, tile and brick yards, the largest home-trailer plant in the United States, and a number of fishing-tackle manufacturers, capitalizing on the water sports boom that has followed completion of several large eastern Oklahoma lakes.

This development of water resources (*see Tour 15*) has been of prime importance in Tulsa's continuing growth. The city is surrounded by huge lakes constructed for flood control, conservation, and the generation of electric power. Two of them—Lake Spavinaw and Lake Eucha (*see Tour 15*)—are municipally owned reservoirs that furnish domestic water to the city. All of them together provide the recreation facilities that companies seek for their employees.

As Tulsa grew with the oil industry, so did its two struggling weekly newspapers, the *Democrat* and the *World*, which soon became dailies. In 1920, the name of the evening *Democrat* was changed to the *Tribune*. Also published in Tulsa today is the weekly *Oil and Gas Journal*, generally considered the country's most important and authoritative oil publication. Read by oilmen all over the world, it is reputed to carry more pages of advertising annually than any other magazine in the United States. Only memories now, *The Oklahoma Constitution*, the *New State Farm and Home*, and *Sturm's Statehood Magazine* were started in the 1904–06 period to further the movement for statehood.

POINTS OF INTEREST

(Numbers below refer to circled numbers on the Tulsa city map in this section.)

1. The BOSTON AVENUE METHODIST CHURCH, Boston

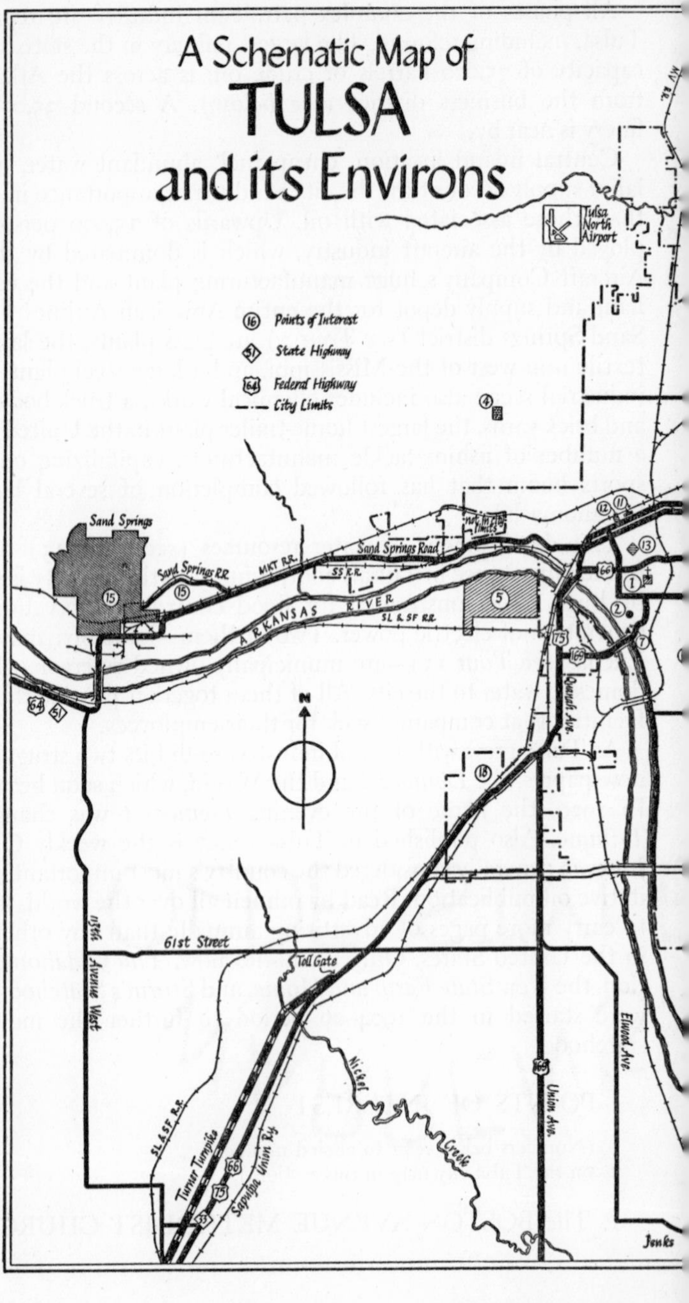
A Schematic Map of
TULSA
and its Environs
Points of Interest
State Highway
Federal Highway
City Limits
Tulsa North Airport
Sand Springs
Sand Springs Road
Sand Springs R.R.
MKT R.R.
SS R.R.
ARKANSAS RIVER
SL & SF R.R.
Quanah Ave.
61st Street
Toll Gate
Avenue West
Nickel Creek
Turner Turnpike
Sapulpa Union Ry.
Union Ave.
Elwood Ave.
Jenks

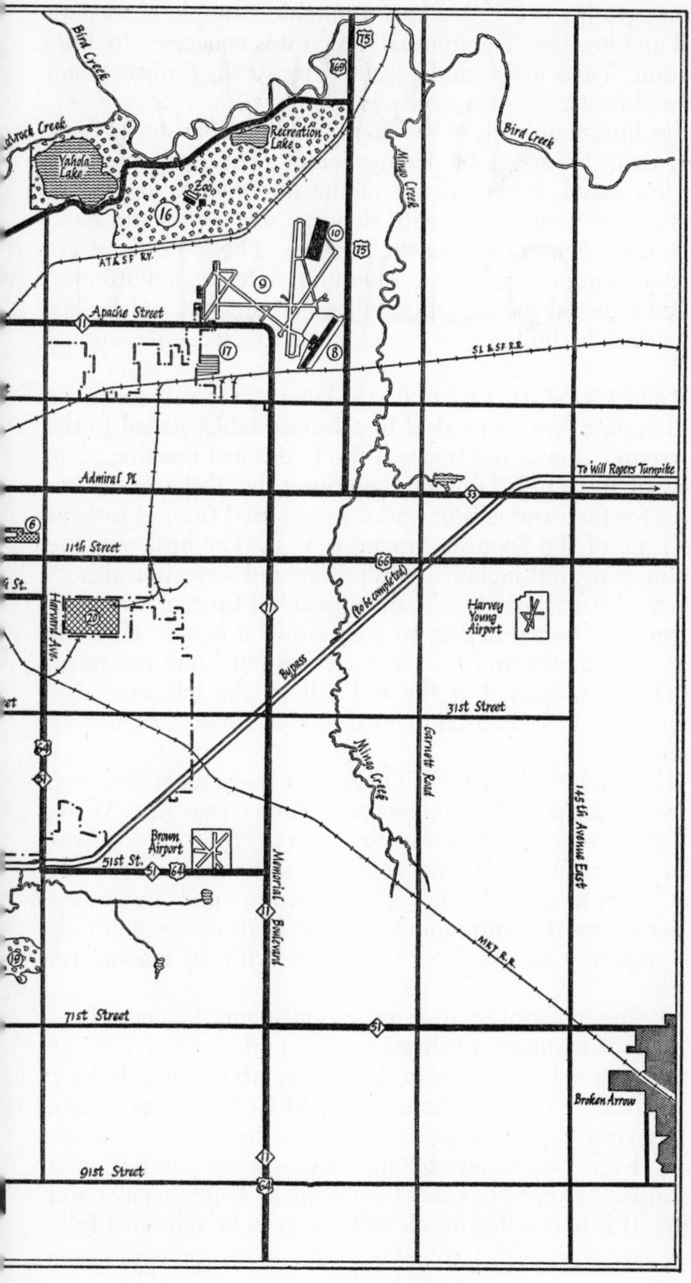
Bird Creek
Bird Creek
Mingo Creek
Recreation Lake
Yahola Lake
Zoo
16
10
9
8
17
6
20
19
75
169
75
AT&SF RY.
Apache Street
11
SL & SF R.R.
Admiral Pl.
To Will Rogers Turnpike
33
11th Street
66
(To be completed)
Bypass
Harvey Young Airport
Harvard Ave.
31st Street
Garnett Road
Mingo Creek
145th Avenue East
64
51
Brown Airport
51st St.
51
64
Memorial Boulevard
11
MKT R.R.
71st Street
51
Broken Arrow
11
91st Street
64

Ave. between 13th St. and 13th Pl., is a notable example of modern ecclesiastical architecture. The unusual design was conceived by Miss Adah Robinson, Tulsa artist, and executed by Rush, Endicott, and Goff, Tulsa architects. Construction was completed in 1929.

The massive limestone walls of the main building, four stories high, terminate in cubistic images of praying hands. The same symbolic imagery, in less detail, is carried out in the illuminated tower that rises 290 feet above the doorways with their pointed arches and terra-cotta and bas-relief figures of pioneer characters. The lower floors are occupied by a community hall, gymnasium, kitchen, auditorium, chapel, and educational rooms. Other offices, classrooms, and studios are in the tower. The building of the church attracted international attention.

2. The OLD COUNCIL TREE, on the lawn of a private residence at 1730 S. Cheyenne Ave., is marked by a bronze tablet nailed to the trunk. The ground around the tree was the traditional meeting place for the heads of the Creek families composing the Tallassee Lochapokas (town) for their councils or busks. It was used from as early as 1836 to the time of the Spanish American War. The busk was the official town meeting, but included purification and recreation rites as well as business. Several days before the appointed time, a messenger from the town chief would deliver to each family a bundle of sticks. One stick was withdrawn and broken each day until one remained. This last stick was presented at the roll call on the following day. Feasting, dancing, and Indian ball constituted an important part of the ceremonies.

3. The PHILBROOK ART CENTER (*open 10–5 except Sun. 1–5, 7:30–9:30* P.M. *Tues.; closed Mondays and holidays; free Sun., Wed., and Tues. nights, 25c for adults other times*), 2727 S. Rockford Ave., is the former residence of Mr. and Mrs. Waite Phillips, who made it into an art center in 1938. Along with the mansion and the twenty-three landscaped acres that surround it, the couple also gave additional commercial properties to provide the trustees with an income for maintenance.

Since its opening in October, 1939, various gifts and purchases have made the Philbrook permanent collections Oklahoma's finest. Particularly outstanding are the American Indian paintings, which have attracted nationwide attention; the Clark Field Collection of American Indian baskets and pottery, distinguished for its rarity and range; the Samuel H. Kress Collection of Italian Renaissance paintings and sculptures; and the George H. Taber Collection of Chinese jades and decorative arts. It is impossible for all collections to be exhibited fully at all times, but the Laura A. Clubb Collection of oil paintings of the eighteenth and nineteenth centuries (*see Tour 10*) is always on view. Various collections, including paintings of the oil industry from the Standard Oil Company of New Jersey Collection, are rotated frequently, and about sixty special exhibitions are planned each year. Permanently installed are rooms illustrating colonial source cultures, Spanish, English, and French. To further the appreciation and understanding of all the arts, Philbrook conducts art classes for children and adults, and presents special programs throughout the year.

4. The THOMAS GILCREASE INSTITUTE OF AMERICAN HISTORY AND ART (*open 9–5 daily except Sun. 1–5, free; guided tours for groups by appointment*), Newton St. and 25th Ave. W., is generally acknowledged to be the world's outstanding collection of its kind. The museum was founded in 1942 by Tulsa oilman Thomas Gilcrease, himself of Creek descent. The $12,000,000 collection of Americana represents a sizable share of the Gilcrease oil fortune. Having assembled most of the items himself, Gilcrease transferred title to the entire collection to the City of Tulsa in 1955.

The main museum building is composed of fourteen galleries, a two-level library, and storage rooms. Other smaller buildings contain additional exhibits. Although the collection is devoted primarily to the history and art of the American Indian, in the museum's library of 85,000 items are the only original certified copies of the Articles of Confederation and the Declaration of Independence which exist outside the Library of Congress in Washington, D.C.; the original document —dated April 29, 1775—appointing Paul Revere to make the historic "midnight ride"; a letter signed by Diego Columbus, Christopher's son, which is the first letter sent from the New World (written in January, 1512); and other important American historical documents. In addition to its paintings, sculpture, and manuscripts, the museum contains 10,000 items that exemplify the handicraft of early Indian cultures of all the Americas. The Pre-Columbian items include extremely rare and valuable gold and jade work. Outstanding among the museum's many exhibits are the world's largest collection of western paintings and sculpture by Frederic Remington and Charles M. Russell. The museum's library is constantly used for historical research.

5. The D–X SUNRAY OIL COMPANY REFINERY (*tours weekdays at 10 A.M. and 2 P.M.*), 17th St. and Union Ave., West Tulsa, is one of the world's largest refineries operating exclusively on high gravity, paraffin-base crude oils. Within its 840 acres on the banks of the Arkansas River refining processes are carried on under conditions that vary from 40° F. below zero to 1,000° F. above zero.

Reactors and fractionating towers rise 120 feet or more in the air, and hundreds of miles of pipe are buried in the ground. The plant has a capacity of 3,150,000 gallons of crude oil daily. It operates on a 24-hour schedule, and employs 1,600 workers. Crude oil comes entirely from Oklahoma wells through the company's 2,900-mile pipeline system.

The refinery opened in October, 1913, with only one battery of stills and a few tanks. Now its storage tanks hold more than four million barrels and the refinery circulates more than 120,000,000 gallons of cooling water every day. Daily production from this refinery, the largest in Oklahoma, includes 1,700,000 gallons of high octane gasoline; 1,000,000 gallons of diesel, distillate fuels, and kerosene; 300,000 gallons of lubricating oils; 120,000 pounds of paraffin wax; and 300 tons of petroleum coke.

6. The UNIVERSITY OF TULSA, between 5th and 7th Sts. and Delaware Ave. and Gary Pl., is the largest privately endowed college in Oklahoma. It is also the largest educational institution in the nation organically related to the Presbyterian Church, U.S.A. With an enrollment in 1956 of 5,000 students and a faculty of 300, the university includes two pieces of property other than the 50-acre main campus. At 1136 N. Lewis Ave. is the former research laboratory of Stanolind Oil and Gas Company. A gift to the university by that company, it is now used by the College of Petroleum Sciences and Engineering. A third part of the campus is the five-story building at 512 S. Cincinnati Ave. that houses the university's School of Law. Many of the buildings and grounds were gifts of Tulsa philanthropists, oilmen, and oil companies. Some of the school's $6,252,000 endowment, however, has come from public subscription.

The university was founded in 1894 at Muskogee, Indian Territory, as an Indian Mission school called Henry Kendall College. It was moved to Tulsa in 1907, the year of statehood, and the name was changed to the University of Tulsa in 1920. The school continued as a synod college until 1928, when control was turned over to a self-perpetuating board of trustees made up of men from the community.

The central part of the main campus is grouped around a horseshoe drive with MCFARLIN LIBRARY (*open 8–9:30 weekdays, 8–12 Saturdays; closed during Aug.*) at the head of the "U." East of the library are KENDALL HALL (containing the historic bell which rang out the news of statehood to Tulsa citizens in 1907), the original red-brick building from which the campus grew, and the new STUDENT ACTIVITIES BUILDING, with modern styling in Tennessee limestone and monolithic concrete. Other buildings around the drive (mostly of modified and collegiate Gothic architecture) include the Waite Phillips Engineering Building and the Petroleum Sciences Hall.

7. The JAYCEE WAR MEMORIAL BUILDING (*tours 8–5 weekdays*), 21st St. and Boulder Ave., is national headquarters of the United States Junior Chamber of Commerce, the world's third largest (200,000 members) civic organization. The strikingly modern $100,000 structure was dedicated in August, 1951. Unique feature of the building is the series of memorial plaques—one for each state and territory—honoring America's war dead. Each is made of stone, wood, or other material typical of the area it represents. A 52-member staff here carries out the program adopted by the organization's 3,200 local chapters. The Jaycee White House, 4332 S. Atlanta Ave., is the lavish, $70,000 home of the Jaycee's president. It gets a new "first family" each year through the organization's policy of electing officers for only one term.

8. The DOUGLAS AIRCRAFT PLANT, 2000 N. Memorial Dr., the largest manufacturing plant in Oklahoma, employed 21,932 people during its peak production period in 1945. Dedicated in 1942, the huge operation was closed following World War II, but was reopened again in 1951. In 1956 it added its own engineering and design departments to become a wholly integrated aircraft plant.

The Assembly Building, 4,003 feet in length, is one of the country's largest windowless structures. Completely air conditioned, it is lighted by 32,000 fluorescent tubes. Its 1,284,000 square feet of space on the ground floor includes enclosed trackage for ten railroad freight cars. And the entire plant consisting of many buildings, large and small, is set in a sea of concrete—21,270,000 square feet, or more than three-fourths of a square mile. A total of thirty-five miles of high-voltage power lines serve the plant; underground storage tanks hold up to a quarter of a million gallons of fuel.

9. TULSA MUNICIPAL AIRPORT, Sheridan Rd. and Apache Ave., was, in 1930, the world's busiest airport, outranking in volume of traffic Le Bourget (Paris), Tempelhof (Berlin), and Croydon (London) fields. During the quadrennial staging of the mammoth International Petroleum Exposition, it can still lay claim to that rank, if only for a few days. Covering an area of 2,000 acres, it is one of seven municipal airports in the United States with the 10,000-foot runways needed to handle the largest commercial and military aircraft.

10. AMERICAN AIRLINES MODIFICATION CENTER *(tours arranged upon request)*, at Tulsa Municipal Airport, is home base for the nation's biggest air line. Built during World War II as a modifica-

tion center for military aircraft, the installation was leased by American Airlines in 1946. It handles an average of 130 planes a month. With 3,850 employees at the depot and an additional 760 in the city, American is Tulsa's second largest employer. (Douglas Aircraft is the largest.) Among the records claimed for American's depot crews is that of making a complete engine change in thirty-five minutes—while the plane's passengers were having lunch.

11. UNION DEPOT, 3 S. Boston Ave., in the heart of old Tulsa, was completed in 1931 as the first union depot in Oklahoma. Because the railroad tracks were on a level with the diked banks of the Arkansas River and could not be lowered, the streets in the neighborhood were raised to cross over them. Thus, while the main entrances and waiting room of the depot are at street level, they are thirty feet above the tracks. The outstanding feature of the building is the foyer extending from Cincinnati Avenue to Boston Avenue.

12. The FEDERAL BUILDING, Boulder Ave. between 2nd and 3rd Sts., is a three-story limestone structure of neoclassic design with a Corinthian colonnade across the front. The southern third of the building was erected in 1915, and it was enlarged to its present size in 1932, with the same basic design and structural materials.

13. The TULSA COUNTY COURTHOUSE, N.E. corner of 6th St. and Boulder Ave., was erected in 1910–11. It is a four-story limestone structure of modified Greek design. On this site in 1886, George Perryman, brother of Legus Perryman, who was a principal chief of the Creek Nation, built a sizable residence which, at the time, was considered "way out in the country."

14. The TULSA GARDEN CENTER (*library open 10–4 Mon. through Sat.*), 2415 S. Peoria Ave., and the TULSA ROSE GARDENS, immediately N. of the Center, qualified this section of Tulsa's southside residential area as one of the city's beauty spots. The Center began in December, 1950, as a combined project of several of the city's garden clubs. For four years, however, its activities revolved only around a branch city library, in one corner of which it maintained its own library. Then in 1954 the City of Tulsa purchased, and leased to the Center, the Snedden Estate, a mansion of classic design built on nine acres adjacent to the Tulsa Rose Gardens. The building (a 400-seat auditorium has since been added) houses the Center's 500-volume library on all phases of horticulture, and provides rooms for horticultural exhibits. The estate also contains three greenhouses. The staff work is supplemented throughout the year by the city's more than one thousand garden club members.

Rose-growing experts have called the TULSA ROSE GARDENS the

"finest municipal rose gardens in the nation." This scenic floral development, with more than 12,000 plants, is located in Woodward Park, 21st and Peoria Ave. It is a 40-acre tract of forested hill land in one of the highest points in the city. The six-acre rose garden was established in 1934 as a joint project of the Tulsa Federation of Garden Clubs and the City of Tulsa. In 1945 the Rose Garden was chosen as official test garden for the South by the All American Rose Selection Committee.

The TULSA TOUR, its prominent red-and-white arrows guiding the motorist to Tulsa's outstanding scenic landmarks, makes sightseeing comparatively easy, even for complete strangers. Starting downtown, the tour winds past many of the points of interest described above, and also provides a carefully marked route through Tulsa's south-side residential area, the city's finest. The tour eventually returns to its downtown starting place. There is also an alternative route that covers the industrial area west of the Arkansas River.

POINTS OF INTEREST IN THE ENVIRONS

15. Sand Springs Home Interests, 10.3 *m.* (*see Tour* 3). 16. Mohawk Park, 9.9 *m.* (*see Tour* 9A.) 17. Spartan Aircraft Company, 2.3 *m.* 18. Red Fork industrial suburb, 6.9 *m.* 19. Southern Hills Country Club, 8.3 *m.* 20. Tulsa State Fairgrounds, 1 *m.*

PART III: *Tours*

TOUR 1

(Baxter Springs, Kan.)—Tulsa—Oklahoma City—El Reno—Clinton—Sayre—(Shamrock, Tex.); US 66, Kansas Line to Texas Line, 376.4 m.

Frisco Ry. parallels route between the Kansas Line and Oklahoma City; Rock Island Ry. between Oklahoma City and the Texas Line.
Roadbed paved throughout; rapidly being four-laned from Kansas to Texas.
Full range of accommodations from one end to the other.

The so-called "Main Street of America," US 66 has indeed grown up with Oklahoma and the nation. In 1916 its western half was improved as a postal highway. In the 1930's it carried its share of Grapes of Wrath families and, for comic relief, the hungry contestants in "Cash and Carry" Pyle's Bunion Derby. In 1953 a sizable section of it was paralleled by the 88-mile Turner Turnpike, the nation's first toll road west of the Mississippi River. The Will Rogers Turnpike opened in 1957, and eventual four-laning of all of US 66 is scheduled under the new federal interstate road building program.

From trails worn deep in virgin prairies and blazed through blackjack tangles, US 66 has evolved to high-speed superhighways that serve a representative cross section of the Sooner State. Connecting Oklahoma's two dominant cities—Oklahoma City and Tulsa—it ranges topographically from forested hills to virtually treeless plains, tracing an economic course from mining districts, through oil and gas fields, to farm and ranch country. Southwestward from Kansas to the center of the state it traverses much of the heavily wooded area visited by Washington Irving (*see Tour 2A*) in 1832. As it nears the Texas Panhandle to the west, it climbs gradually to higher elevations, into the aptly named "short grass country" of clean, mirage-like towns looming at great distances above the level, almost treeless land. Varied in scenery and rich in history, US 66 provides the motorist with an interesting 375-mile Cinerama picture of the nation's forty-sixth state.

Section a. KANSAS LINE *to* TULSA, *107.6 m. US 66*

Crossing the KANSAS LINE, 0 *m.*, three miles south of Baxter Springs, Kansas (*see Kansas Guide*), US 66 passes through the rich Tri-State Mining District, in which are located some of the world's greatest lead and zinc mines. For about fourteen miles huge man-made mountains of chat (waste rock) border the highway. The lead and zinc deposits were discovered shortly after the Civil War by adventurers searching for gold.

At 0.8 *m.* is an abandoned mine (L) that admits visitors (*adults, $1.25; children, $0.65*) to the 100-foot level. The mine, parts of which extend under the highway, yielded $10,000,000 worth of ore to its first owners.

QUAPAW, 4.1 *m.* (840 alt., 938 pop.), was built on land once owned by the Quapaw Indians. The tall prairie grass, abundant in the surrounding country, made the town a logical center for hay shipping at the turn of the century. Cattle grazing later became important.

Zinc mining, however, which makes this section an industrial hub, is still a commercial mainstay of the town. Mining began in this region as early as 1897. By 1907, ores from the Dark Horse Mine, opened in 1904, were being taken out in paying quantities. After World War I, when the demand for the two metals had lessened, the fast growth of Quapaw was arrested. The modern tree-shaded residential section, however, indicates the prosperity which mining leases have brought to the citizens. A large number of Quapaw Indians live in the town, many of whom received immense royalties from their allotments during the boom years of 1917–18.

The Seneca-Cayuga Green Corn Feast and Dances (*visitors welcome*) are held each year near Quapaw during the second week of August. The Quapaw Indian Powwow, traditionally held July 4 at the Devil's Promenade east of Quapaw on Spring River, is one of Ottawa County's oldest celebrations. It was instituted soon after the tribe was moved to Oklahoma in 1833, but in 1956 it was moved to the county fairgrounds in near-by Miami. The Promenade itself is still interesting scenically.

COMMERCE, 9.4 *m.* (805 alt., 2,442 pop.), is a mining town surrounded by sprawling mounds of chat. Inside the city limits is the Turkey Fat Mine, the first in the area.

Commerce is at the junction with US 69, which unites southward with US 66 for thirty-eight miles (*see Tour* 8).

MIAMI, 13.6 *m.* (800 alt., 11,801 pop.), long the financial center of the Tri-State mining area, has recently developed as an important industrial center as well. The town was originally a trading post called Jimtown in the sparsely settled region set aside for a number of small

Indian tribes. This post, in the vicinity of the present North Miami, was the home of four farmers named Jim. In 1890, mail for the near-by Quapaw Agency had to be brought from Baxter Springs, Kansas. To facilitate delivery of the agency mail, arrangements were made with Jim Palmer (one of the four Jims) to establish a post office. The name chosen was Miami, in honor of Palmer's wife, who was of Miami Indian blood. A year later the townsite was platted and the first lots sold.

Miami might have followed the usual development from a trading post in Indian Territory to a small town in a farming community had it not been for the discovery of lead and zinc in 1905. Boom excitement caused the population to increase 141 per cent in a brief period. However, cattle raising and dairy production from purebred Angus and Hereford cattle remain economically important in the area.

Eight blocks east of US 66 on Third Avenue, at the eastern edge of the city, is the NORTHEASTERN OKLAHOMA A. & M. COLLEGE. Established by the state legislature as the Miami School of Mines in 1919, when the lead and zinc mines were booming, it became a junior college when mine production began to sag, and was later changed into a district agricultural college. With a coeducational enrollment of around one thousand, it also offers work in fine arts, liberal arts, and industrial arts, as well as in agriculture. The school's modern buildings are scattered over a tree-shaded forty-acre campus.

West of US 66, on Goodrich Boulevard, at the northern edge of Miami, is the B. F. GOODRICH PLANT, manufacturer of rubber products (*conducted tours 1:00 P.M. Thursdays*). With 1,500 employees, it is the city's biggest industry. Furnaces, air conditioners, aluminum boats, and pottery (Winart) are also manufactured in Miami. For recreation the city offers year-round fishing in beautiful Riverview Park on the Neosho River, a municipal swimming pool, tennis, and golf. Access to the Will Rogers Turnpike is gained via State 10 one-quarter of a mile east of Miami.

At 14.3 *m.* US 66 crosses the Neosho River, and at 15.8 *m.* it joins with US 59 (*see Tour 15*) from the right. Combined US 59–66–69 go under the Will Rogers Turnpike, and at 23.8 *m.* join with US 60, from the left, at a cloverleaf intersection. (For access to the turnpike, veer right, following the signs.)

The WILL ROGERS TURNPIKE, started in 1955 and completed in 1957, at a cost of $68,000,000, will extend 88.5 miles from the Missouri Line southwest of Joplin to a point just east of Tulsa. Roughly paralleling US 66, it is a four-lane, limited-access road (*dining and car servicing facilities at convenient intervals*). In addition to the Joplin and Tulsa

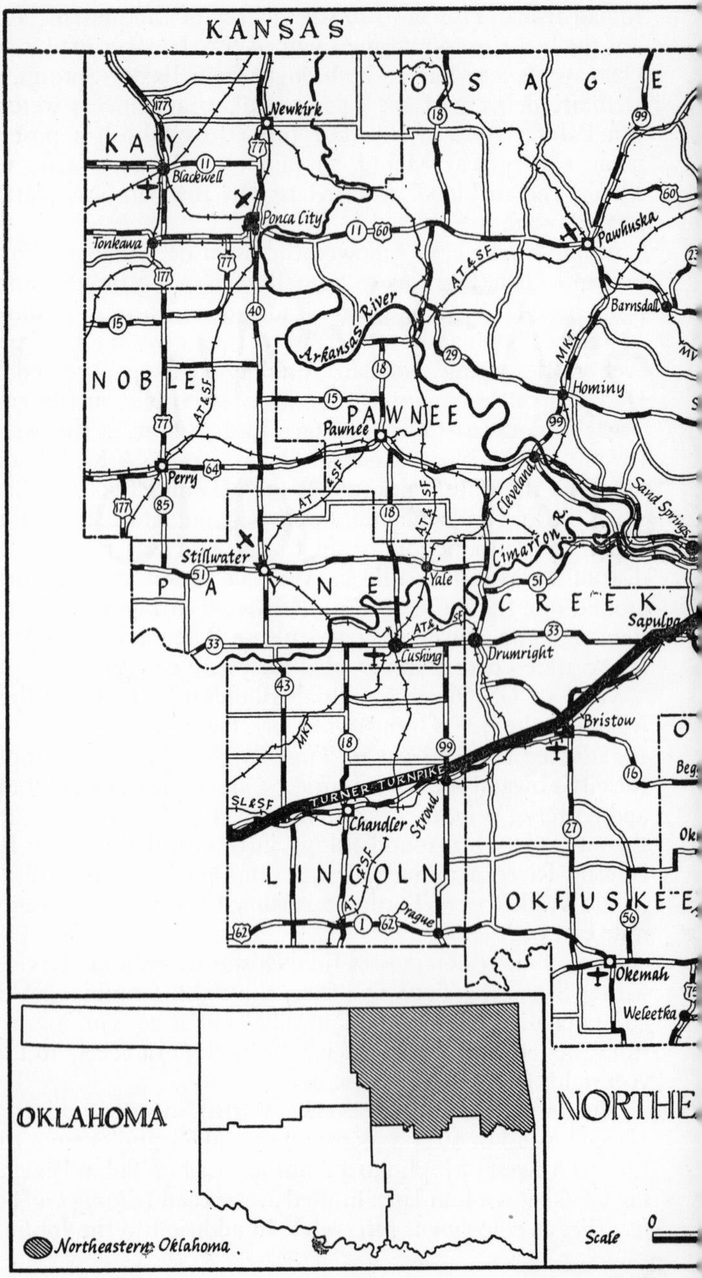
KANSAS
OSAGE
KAY
Newkirk
Blackwell
Ponca City
Tonkawa
Pawhuska
Barnsdall
Arkansas River
AT&SF
MKT
NOBLE
PAWNEE
Pawnee
Hominy
Perry
Cleveland
Sand Springs
Cimarron R.
Stillwater
Yale
PAYNE
CREEK
Sapulpa
Cushing
Drumright
Bristow
TURNER TURNPIKE
SL&SF
Chandler
Stroud
LINCOLN
Prague
OKFUSKEE
Okemah
Weleetka
OKLAHOMA
Northeastern Oklahoma
NORTHE
Scale
0

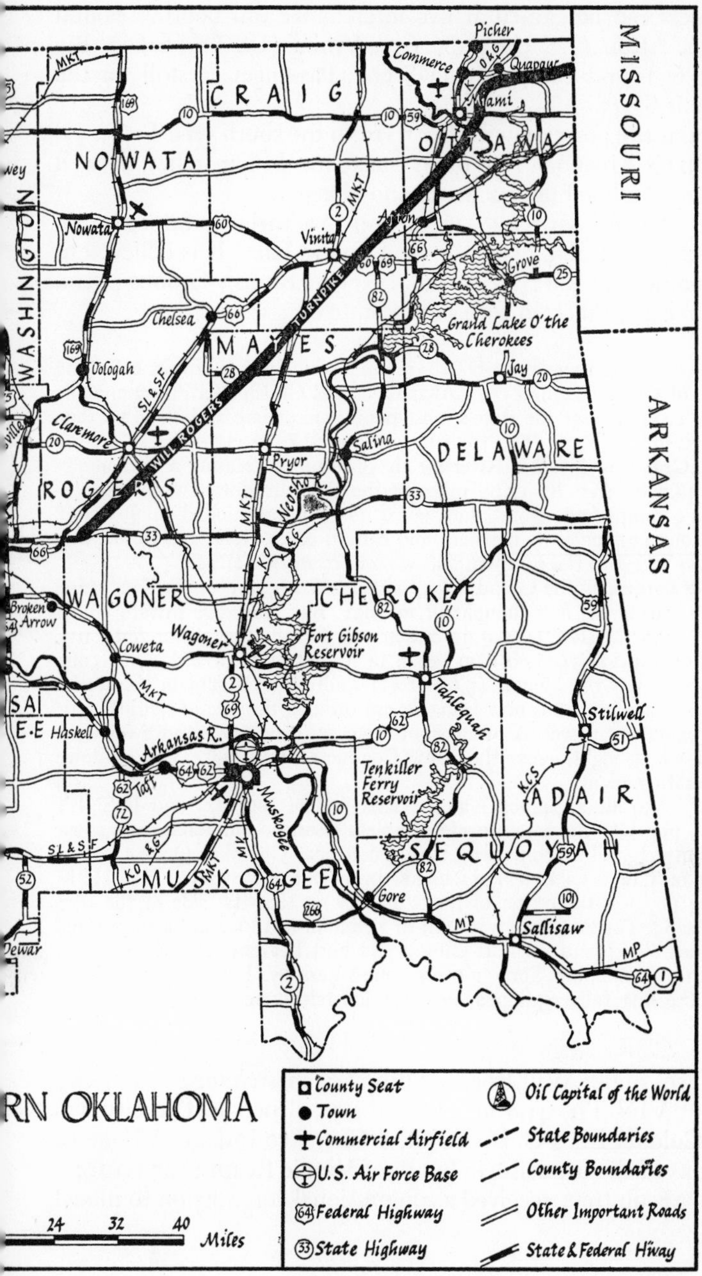
MISSOURI
ARKANSAS
CRAIG
NOWATA
OTTAWA
WASHINGTON
MAYES
DELAWARE
ROGERS
WAGONER
CHEROKEE
ADAIR
SEQUOYAH
MUSKOGEE
Picher
Commerce
Quapaw
Miami
Afton
Vinita
Nowata
Grove
Chelsea
Grand Lake O'the Cherokees
Oologah
Jay
Claremore
Salina
Pryor
Neosho R.
WILL ROGERS TURNPIKE
Broken Arrow
Coweta
Wagoner
Fort Gibson Reservoir
Tahlequah
Stilwell
Haskell
Arkansas R.
Taft
Muskogee
Tenkiller Ferry Reservoir
Gore
Sallisaw
Dewar
MKT
SL&SF
KO&G
MP
KCS
RN OKLAHOMA
24
32
40
Miles
County Seat
Town
Commercial Airfield
U.S. Air Force Base
Federal Highway
State Highway
Oil Capital of the World
State Boundaries
County Boundaries
Other Important Roads
State & Federal H'iway

termini, access can be gained at five interchange toll booths: Miami (US 66–69), Afton (US 59–60–66–69), Vinita (US 60–66–69), Big Cabin (US 69), and Claremore (US 66). Passenger car toll for the entire route is $1.45.

At 25.8 *m.* is the junction with US 59 from the south (*see Tour 15*). BUFFALO BILL'S MUSEUM (L) offers authentic Indian relics, as well as buffalo and buffalo-brahma herds (*no charge*).

AFTON, 26.2 *m.* (792 alt., 1,252 pop.), a thriving farm center, lies in a level area of rich, black soil near Grand Lake. It is believed to have been named for the river Afton of Robert Burns's famous poem.

At 35.5 *m.* is the junction with paved State 82.

Left on this road to the PENSACOLA DAM, 15.5 *m.*, a large power project belonging to the people of Oklahoma, and the LAKE OF THE CHEROKEES, commonly called GRAND LAKE, one of the state's most popular resort areas, with more than two million visitors in 1955. The sprawling, octopus-like reservoir backs up the waters of the Grand, or Neosho, River for sixty-five miles, creating a normal surface area of 46,500 acres. Its 1,300 miles of shoreline are dotted with nearly a hundred fishing camps and resorts, and half a dozen resort-minded small towns. US 59 (*see Tour 15*) serves its northern and eastern edges. State 20, 28, 82, and 85 provide easy access to the southern and western recreation areas.

The idea of harnessing the Grand River, which is fed by streams in Kansas and the Missouri Ozarks, was first thought of in 1891. But successive private efforts failed, and in 1935 the state legislature created the Grand River Dam Authority. Construction on the $22,750,000 dam began in August of 1938 and, when completed in 1941, it was the longest (5,680 feet) multiple-arch dam in the world. The cost of the huge project is now being repaid through the sale of hydroelectric (and steam generated) power. A twenty-foot driveway (State 28) and a four-foot walkway, lighted at night, cross the dam. Conducted tours take visitors down into the generating plant.

LANGLEY (859 alt., 204 pop.) at the west end of the dam and DISNEY (690 alt., 189 pop.) to the east provide complete resort accommodations for the immediate dam area. The 200-passenger excursion boat Cherokee Queen, one of two operating on Grand Lake, makes scheduled runs out of Langley. KETCHUM (760 alt., 254 pop.) is the center of resort activity on the west side of the lake, served by State 85. The first store was built in Ketchum in 1860, and a stage stand (on the Military Road between Fort Gibson and Fort Leavenworth, Kansas) was installed at the old Sulphur Springs campground near by. Ketchum also claims to have had the first fully equipped, nonattended telephone switchboard in the nation.

US 66 passes under Will Rogers Turnpike (*interchange to R.*) two miles east of VINITA, 41.8 *m.* (702 alt., 5,518 pop.). The city was named by Colonel Elias C. Boudinot, a Cherokee Indian and one of the promoters of the townsite, in honor of Vinnie Ream (1850–1914). Miss Ream, a sculptress, received a congressional commission to model the life-size statue of Abraham Lincoln which stands in the capitol at Washington, D.C.

Although there was a small settlement, known as Downingville, here in 1870, Vinita was not founded until 1871 when two railroads were extended into the region. Vinita's early history, like that of many frontier villages, was linked with railroad controversies. The Missouri-Kansas-Texas Railroad had planned to make a junction with the Atlantic & Pacific Railroad (now the Frisco) at a point north of Big Cabin (*see Tour 8*) and so refused to stop its trains at Vinita. The Atlantic & Pacific, however, stopped at a crossing near Vinita whenever a Katy train was due to pass. Eventually, the Katy capitulated and a station was built at Vinita.

The Will Rogers Memorial Rodeo is held here annually each fall. Rogers had planned to be present at the first event in 1935, but was killed on August 15 of that year. He attended a secondary school here, and in his writing facetiously referred to Vinita as his "college town."

On a tree-shaded hill just northeast of Vinita, EASTERN STATE HOSPITAL treats some 2,250 of Oklahoma's mentally ill. It was here that a patient, under the pseudonym, "Inmate Ward 8," wrote (1932) the book, *Behind the Door of Delusion.*

At 45.8 *m.* is the southern junction with US 69 (*see Tour 8*).

At 47.0 *m.* is the southern junction with US 60 (*see Tour 4*).

CHELSEA, 60.1 *m.* (723 alt., 1,437 pop.), was frequented by Will Rogers in his boyhood. A Boy Scout cabin, for which Rogers contributed the money, is located in a near-by park.

One of the earliest oil wells in the Indian Territory was discovered west of Chelsea about 1889 by Edward Byrd, who had secured a lease from the Cherokee Nation. The well was thirty-nine feet deep and yielded several barrels of oil per day. Prior to the passing of legislation regarding the leasing of Indian land for drilling, development of the known fields was difficult. But after paying quantities of oil were found in the Tulsa and Red Fork districts in 1901, the United States government assumed complete control over the mineral leasing of Indian-owned land. Near-by shallow fields were quickly developed. Oil continues to be economically important to the town.

BUSHYHEAD, 65.9 *m.* (700 alt., 50 pop.), is a small farming community named for Dennis W. Bushyhead, at one time (1879–87) chief of the Cherokee Nation.

At 67.2 *m.*, the highway passes between waste piles from strip coal mines.

CLAREMORE, 79.5 *m.* (602 alt., 5,494 pop.), is the seat of Rogers

County, named in honor of Clem Rogers, father of Will Rogers. Beginning as a Cherokee trading point, the town took its name from that of an Osage chief whose band lived some twenty miles away. The name is a variation of the French spelling, *Clermont* or *Clermos*. A famous battle between this settlement of Osages and a party of Cherokees took place in 1817 on Claremore Mound, northwest of the city.

The water at Claremore, which still attracts people seeking its healing power, was discovered in 1903, when a test oil well was drilled. Instead of oil, the drill struck a large flow of artesian mineral water at a depth of eleven hundred feet. The UNITED STATES INDIAN HOSPITAL, erected in 1928, is supervised by the Department of the Interior. The Mason Hotel houses what is said to be the largest individual COLLECTION OF GUNS (22,000) in the United States, owned by J. M. Davis. Some 61,000 items in all are displayed, and there is no charge.

Extensive publicity has been given to Claremore by many who erroneously believe it to be the birthplace of Will Rogers. Rogers himself was mainly responsible for the error, since, in his own words, he was born "half-way between Claremore and Oologah (*see Tour 9A*) before there was a town at either place." He referred more to Claremore than Oologah because "nobody but an Indian could pronounce Oologah."

Oklahoma honored its famous and beloved citizen by the erection of the WILL ROGERS MEMORIAL (*open 8–5, free*), approximately ten blocks west (R) of US 66. Rogers had owned the original twenty-acre site on the side of the hill for more than twenty-five years, and after his death it was given to the state by his widow. In 1937, the Oklahoma legislature appropriated $200,000 to construct the memorial. The building resembles a low, rambling ranch house of brown stone. The exterior is finished with stone quarried at Catoosa, the interior with Silverdale limestone from Kansas, and the floor of the foyer is of split rock from Maine. The Memorial houses four principal galleries—Indian, Pioneer, Historical, and Educational—with a fifth gallery reserved exclusively for the display of keepsakes and mementos of the famous humorist. The statue of Rogers, in the main entrance, is a duplicate of the one by the sculptor Jo Davidson, which stands in the national capitol. The memorial building was dedicated on November 4, 1938, which would have been Will's fifty-ninth birthday.

Claremore was also the home of Lynn Riggs, the author of *Green Grow the Lilacs*, from which the Rodgers and Hammerstein musical, *Oklahoma!* was developed, and of many other notable plays and works of verse.

Adjoining the memorial grounds on the south is the OKLAHOMA MILITARY ACADEMY, established in 1920 by the state. OMA offers four years of high school and two years of college work. Enrollment is limited to approximately 300 boarding students.

CATOOSA, 90.7 *m.* (618 alt., 438 pop.), was named for "Old Catoos," the rounded hill just west of the town. The name is said to be a derivation of the Cherokee expression, "Gi-tu-zi," meaning "Here live the People of the Light." The story is that the "People of the Light" clan formerly met on the summit of the hill.

As a result of treaties made with the Indians after the close of the Civil War, the railroads made slow but inevitable advances west through Indian Territory, each step tapping a new reservoir of wealth in cattle. For a short time in 1882, Catoosa was the terminus of the St. Louis–San Francisco Railway before that line was extended to Tulsa. During this period, the town was typically frontier—the Saturday-night gathering place of roistering cowboys who had driven cattle here to the stockyards.

On the summit (R) of LOOKOUT MOUNTAIN, 91.9 *m.* (914 alt.), the Indians built a cairn, presumably as a trail-marker.

At 93.7 *m.* is the junction with paved State 33. To the left is the western terminus of the Will Rogers Turnpike.

In TULSA, 107.6 *m.* (750 alt., 182,740 pop.) (*see Tulsa*), are junctions with US 64 (*see Tour 2*), US 169 (*see Tour* 9A), and US 75 (*see Tour* 9), which unites southward with US 66 for fifteen miles.

Section b. TULSA *to* OKLAHOMA CITY, *114.0 m.* US 66

The country southwest of TULSA, 0 *m.*, is mostly rolling prairie, dotted with clumps of scrubby post oak and blackjack trees. Mistletoe, the official state flower, clings in scattered clusters to the trees. In spring, the creek banks and small ravines are bright with redbud blooms.

At 3.0 *m.* the ARKANSAS RIVER is crossed. Beyond, US 66 passes between the sprawling tanks and towers of two huge refineries (*see Tulsa*), SUNRAY-DX (R) and TEXACO (L), then enters RED FORK, 6.9 *m.*, an important industrial suburb of Tulsa.

At 9.0 *m.* is the entrance (R) to the TURNER TURNPIKE, an 88-mile, four-lane, limited-access road (*eating and car servicing facilities at convenient intervals*) that parallels US 66 between Tulsa and Oklahoma City. It was opened to traffic in May, 1953. In addition to the two termini, there are four interchange toll booths: Sapulpa (US 64–66–75), Bristow (US 66), Stroud (US 66, State 99), and Chandler (US 66). Passenger car fare for the full route is $1.40.

SAPULPA, 15.5 *m.* (712 alt., 13,031 pop.), an industrial city, is also in the center of productive oil and gas fields. Sapulpa's largest field

(L) was a part of the rich Glenn Pool (*see Tour* 9), which extended to within four miles of the town.

About 1850, Jim Sapulpa, a Creek Indian, came to this point from Alabama and began farming on near-by Rock Creek. Later he started a store in his home, hauling his goods by team and pack horse from Fort Smith.

In 1886 the Frisco Railway built to this point, and for a few years Sapulpa was the rail terminus. This laid the foundation upon which the city later became an important cattle-shipping center. The EUCHEE BOARDING SCHOOL, one of many established by the Creek Indians as a part of their well-knit educational system was opened here in 1896. The institution was founded for the Euchees, an alien people who had united with the Creeks in their former eastern home and had consequently been moved here with them. The language of the Euchees was so foreign and unintelligible (even to the Creeks) that all communication between the tribes had to be carried on through interpreters. Cut off as they were from their neighbors by this linguistic wall, the Euchees were particularly observant of customs and traditions (*see below*). The school was finally closed in 1947.

The FRANKHOMA POTTERY PLANT (*guided tours, weekdays*), on Old Kiln Road in north Sapulpa, is one of the city's largest employers (75 men and women turn out some 3,500 pieces a day) and one of the state's better known attractions. Creator of the native clayware is John N. Frank, a former faculty member of the University of Oklahoma (*see Norman*). Sapulpa's diversified industries also include two glass plants and a brick and tile plant, as well as several oil-field equipment and steel-tank manufacturing concerns.

At Sapulpa is the southwest junction with US 75 (*see Tour* 9).

At 19.9 *m.* is the junction (R) with State 33 (*see Tour* 1A).

KELLYVILLE, 23.7 *m.* (764 alt., 528 pop.), is surrounded by several shallow oil fields that are still productive.

Just southwest of Kellyville are the DANCE GROUNDS of the Creek and Euchee Indians. Celebrations known as "busks" are usually held here in June and July (*small admission, cameras by permission*). They last four days, the number "4" being sacred to the Creeks. On the eve of the first day the celebrants purify their bodies with *Micco-Hon-e-ja* (King of Purgers), the root of the red willow, which produces vomiting. After this they usually perform the *Yun-nus-sa Punga* (Buffalo Dance). The next day is devoted to Indian ball. An ox or deer skull is nailed to a tall post, a ball of hide is thrown into the air and the players catch it in the cup-shaped ends of their two-foot-long ball sticks, then fling it at the skull. The women frequently play against the men;

they are permitted to throw the ball with their hands while the men must use the sticks. The *Punga-Harjo* (Crazy Dance) climaxes the busk. The dancers literally "go crazy," no restrictions being placed on their enthusiasm.

At 26.8 *m.* US 66 goes over the Turner Turnpike. At 30.0 *m.* is the junction with a gravel road.

Right on this road to HEYBURN LAKE 2.4 *m.* A federal flood control reservoir, it has a normal surface area of 1,070 acres. Accommodations are limited, but the waters are well stocked with crappie, catfish, and black bass.

US 66 goes under the Turner Turnpike (access to left) at 37.6 *m.* and enters BRISTOW, 38.9 *m.* (818 alt., 5,400 pop.). Following the pattern of many eastern Oklahoma towns, Bristow began in 1897 as a Creek trading post. The town was founded December 23, 1901. The arrival of the Frisco Railway from Sapulpa added to its growth. Discovery of near-by oil fields in 1916 and 1922—there were 259 of these wells still producing in 1956—finally established the city and set the tone of business and social life down to the present. In or near the city are the plants and offices of a number of large oil companies. Bristow's recreational facilities include a 320-acre city park with its swimming pool, a nine-hole golf course, and a forty-acre lake for boating and fishing.

Between Bristow and Stroud is the largest of the state's four underground gas storage reservoirs. Operated by the Oklahoma Natural Gas Company, which took over the old Stroud gas field when it was originally depleted, it holds gas injected into it from other fields during periods of low consumption. This natural "tank farm" deep underground has a peak storage capacity of seventy-five billion cubic feet of gas.

STROUD, 66.2 *m.* (905 alt., 2,450 pop.), was founded in 1896, a few years after this part of Oklahoma Territory was opened to white homesteaders. Only two miles from Indian Territory, it became a large shipping point for cattle from near-by Creek land and, because of this, attracted much illicit liquor trade. Whisky, denied to the Indian by the government, was often hidden in supply wagons of groceries and commodities headed for the Territory. For a while the consumption of liquor by celebrating cowhands was no small part of the town's business. Statehood, of course, meant the closing of Stroud's nine flourishing saloons, but discovery of the Stroud Field in 1923 (388 producing wells in 1956) gave the town a much more dependable industry. An asphalt and several gasoline refineries, plus a brick and a roofing plant, are now Stroud's principal industries.

Stroud is at the junction with State 99 (*see Tour 14*), access road to the Turner Turnpike (R).

DAVENPORT, 63.6 *m.* (840 alt., 841 pop.), was founded in 1903, when a group of Southern Methodists, wishing to establish a community, purchased a farm and laid out a townsite. In 1924, oil was discovered near by, creating the boom sale of eighty additional acres which were platted as town lots. Shortly after this hasty expansion, however, the big Seminole Field came in (*see Tour 5*) about thirty-five miles to the south, and several thousand Davenport newcomers promptly migrated to Seminole. Oil is still important in the Davenport area, but the principal activity has moved westward in recent years toward Chandler.

CHANDLER, 70.5 *m.* (865 alt., 2,724 pop.), seat of Lincoln County, was founded in September, 1891. The town was platted on a series of low hills and named for George Chandler of Kansas, assistant secretary of the interior under President Harrison (1889–93).

Every building in Chandler (except the Presbyterian Church) was razed and fourteen persons were killed in the 1897 cyclone. When the small group of citizens who had taken shelter in the church emerged, they found that tall trees had been hurled through the air, and houses, barns, and animals had been blown across the town. Rebuilt and prosperous, Chandler today is recognized as one of the nation's largest pecan-shipping points. Near by is a large state-owned pecan orchard and an experimental station.

At 92.7 *m.* is the historical marker for the EAST BOUNDARY OF THE RUN OF '89. At the opening of "Old Oklahoma," April 22, 1889, this was the east line for the Run, starting at twelve o'clock noon. Before nightfall prairies and hills in the 2,000,000-acre tract held tens of thousands of people, and a number of tent cities had sprung up.

A marker designating WASHINGTON IRVING CAMP (L) at 96.9 *m.*, on the east edge of ARCADIA, notes that near here the Irving party hunted wild horses in 1832 (*see Tour 2A*).

From 97.7 *m.* just west of Arcadia, one can turn left and drive along country roads to the North Canadian River, three miles to the south. Here, on the north bank of the river, is the site of the famous CAMP ALICE, established February 8, 1883, by David L. Payne and his group of land-hungry Boomers. From here—as from other locations which they had attempted to settle both before and after this date—the Boomers were driven back to Kansas by United States troops.

At 103.1 *m.* is the junction with US 77 (*see Tour 10*), which unites southward with US 66 for 10.9 miles. Here, too, is the junction with State 66.

Right (west) on State 66 is EDMOND, 3.4 *m.* (1,200 alt., 6,066 pop.), a pleasant college town that claims Oklahoma Territory's first church, first newspaper (the *Edmond Sun*), first public school, and first public library. Established as a watering and coaling station when the Santa Fe built into the Territory in 1887, it was named for one of the railway officials. Edmond served as a shipping point for cattle and a receiving point for supplies destined for the Kickapoo and Iowa reservations. Following the Run of '89 the townsite was homesteaded. Until 1943, when oil discoveries opened the West Edmond Field (cumulative production to mid-1955: more than 103,000,000 barrels), Edmond was an agricultural trade center with a flour mill and several small factories. Since then, and following the development of the East Edmond Field, in 1947, oil has played an increasingly large role in the town's steady growth.

On the east edge of Edmond is CENTRAL STATE COLLEGE, a coeducational institution with a 1956 enrollment of 2,222 students. As a Normal School, it registered twenty-three students on November 9, 1891, to become the first institution of higher learning in Oklahoma Territory. Influential in the early development of both the college and Edmond was Milton W. Reynolds, founder of the *Sun*. In pre-Territorial days, as a correspondent for eastern newspapers, he had glowingly described the town as the "Boston" of Oklahoma, and personally persuaded many of his educated friends to enter the new territory with him. The presence of leaders of this type perhaps explains the effort of the Normal School in 1895 to admit Negro students, six full decades before the United States Supreme Court made the step mandatory.

NORTH TOWER, the oldest of thirteen buildings on the campus, although enlarged and modernized since it was first occupied in 1893, still displays the word "Normal" above the doorway. MAX CHAMBERS LIBRARY, the newest building, which was to be completed in 1957, will have shelf space for more than 100,000 volumes.

MEMORIAL PARK, three miles south of Edmond on State 77, is an unusually beautiful cemetery dominated by the Tower of Memories, a dressed limestone structure seventy-two feet high and containing a set of chimes. Here is buried Wiley Post, well-known aviator of the 1930's, who made a record round-the-world flight and a nonstop flight from Brooklyn to Berlin. Post died, with Will Rogers, in a plane crash near Point Barrow, Alaska, August 15, 1934.

South from here combined US 66–77 are four-laned. At 106.9 *m.* is the junction with the western terminus (L) of the Turner Turnpike. At Britton Road overpass, 109.4 *m.*, the two soaring steel towers to the right belong to Oklahoma City's two television stations, WKY–TV and KWTV, the latter's 1,572-foot height making it the world's tallest man-made structure.

At 111.6 *m.*, is Oklahoma City's urban by-pass to the east (U. C.), which will eventually carry US 77 around the state's capital. Both highways continue on the northern by-pass to an interchange at 114.0 *m.*, where US 77 turns left approximately 2.5 miles north of the Oklahoma State Capitol.

OKLAHOMA CITY, 114.0 *m.* (1,194 alt., 243,504 pop.) (*see Oklahoma City*), is at the southern junction with US 77 (*see Tour 10*), US 62 (*see Tour 3*), and the eastern junction with US 270 (*see Tour 5*).

Section c. OKLAHOMA CITY *to* TEXAS LINE, *154.8 m. US 66*

From Oklahoma City to the Texas Line US 66 climbs gradually through a region of farms and small ranches. Although roughly the western half of it lies within the much publicized "dust bowl," consolidated farm holdings, improved farming methods, and an increasing use of well-water irrigation make it generally productive. Wheat, feed grains, alfalfa, and cotton are the principle crops in Oklahoma's "short grass country."

Looping west through residential and small-industry sections of OKLAHOMA CITY, 0 *m.*, US 66 joins with US 270 (*see Tour 5*) at May Avenue, 4.2 *m.* The two highways unite for the next 32.7 miles.

At 7.2 *m.* is the junction with MacArthur Boulevard.

Right on this street to LAKE HEFNER (R), 2.5 *m.*, part of the Oklahoma City municipal water supply. A gravel road cups the north end of the reservoir atop the earth-fill dam. No swimming is permitted in the lake, but it offers dependable fishing.

BETHANY, 7.8 *m.* (1,212 alt., 5,705 pop.), despite much suburban-area growth in recent years, is primarily the home of the Nazarene religious sect. The church's strict principles of daily living are reflected in city ordinances that forbid theaters, pool rooms, and dance halls, as well as the sale of beer. According to the county attorney's office, there is less crime and vice in the Bethany area than in any other section of Oklahoma County.

BETHANY NAZARENE COLLEGE is an accredited four-year liberal arts institution occupying fourteen buildings on a twenty-acre campus in the center of town. Founded in Oklahoma City in 1906, it moved to Bethany in 1908, and now has an enrollment of close to one thousand students.

US 66–270 cross the NORTH CANADIAN RIVER, 9.9 *m.*, and skirt the northern end (L) of LAKE OVERHOLSER (*fishing, hunting, boating, picnicking*). This 1,700-acre lake with its ten-mile shoreline was created by the damming of the North Canadian in 1916 to provide a water supply for Oklahoma City. It was named for Ed Overholser, mayor of the city (1915–18).

About six miles southeast of the lake, on the east side of the Canadian River, is the site of a camp established in 1884 by one of David L. Payne's men. Twice Payne and his land-hungry band of Boomers had attempted to settle in the territory that is now the state of Oklahoma (*see above*), and twice United States troops had halted the invasions. But in October, 1884, a large caravan of wagons with men, women, and children, reached this spot, where they set up camp. Here the group surveyed and platted a townsite and laid out the site of a capitol for the new state they hoped to create. The colonists also staked out farms and began plowing in order to put in crops. In the following month, however, a company of United States infantry destroyed the camp and forced the colonists to return to Kansas. In June of 1884, Payne had led another group to a site near the present city of Blackwell. These would-be colonists were also taken back into Kansas. Payne died in Wellington, Kansas, on November 28, 1884.

YUKON, 14.9 *m.* (1,298 alt., 1, 990 pop.), an agricultural and milling center, was laid out in 1891 by the Spencer brothers, who owned the 160-acre site. Frisco, a small town of one thousand population, had been established near by, but when the railroad was built through Yukon, most of Frisco's people moved there. The large flour mill (L) and feed mill (R) on the east edge of Yukon dominate the town's economy as well as its skyline. Both were built by Czechoslovakian families, and Czech influence in Yukon, as in Prague (*see Tour 3*), is reflected in the general neatness of the town's homes and yards.

Combined US 66–270 cut across rolling, fertile farmlands to 25.5 *m.*, where they are joined for 2.2 miles by US 81 (*see Tour 11*).

EL RENO, 27.7 *m.* (1,363 alt., 10,991 pop.), the seat of Canadian County, located near the south bank of the North Canadian River, was founded when the Rock Island railroad was routed to the site two months after the Run of April 22, 1889. The town took its name from near-by Fort Reno (*see below*) but continues to derive much of its economic strength from the Rock Island.

Reno City was located on the north bank of the North Canadian immediately after the Run. With a population of fifteen hundred, it confidently expected to have the rail connection. The Rock Island, however, changed its plans when the Reno Cityans refused to pay the

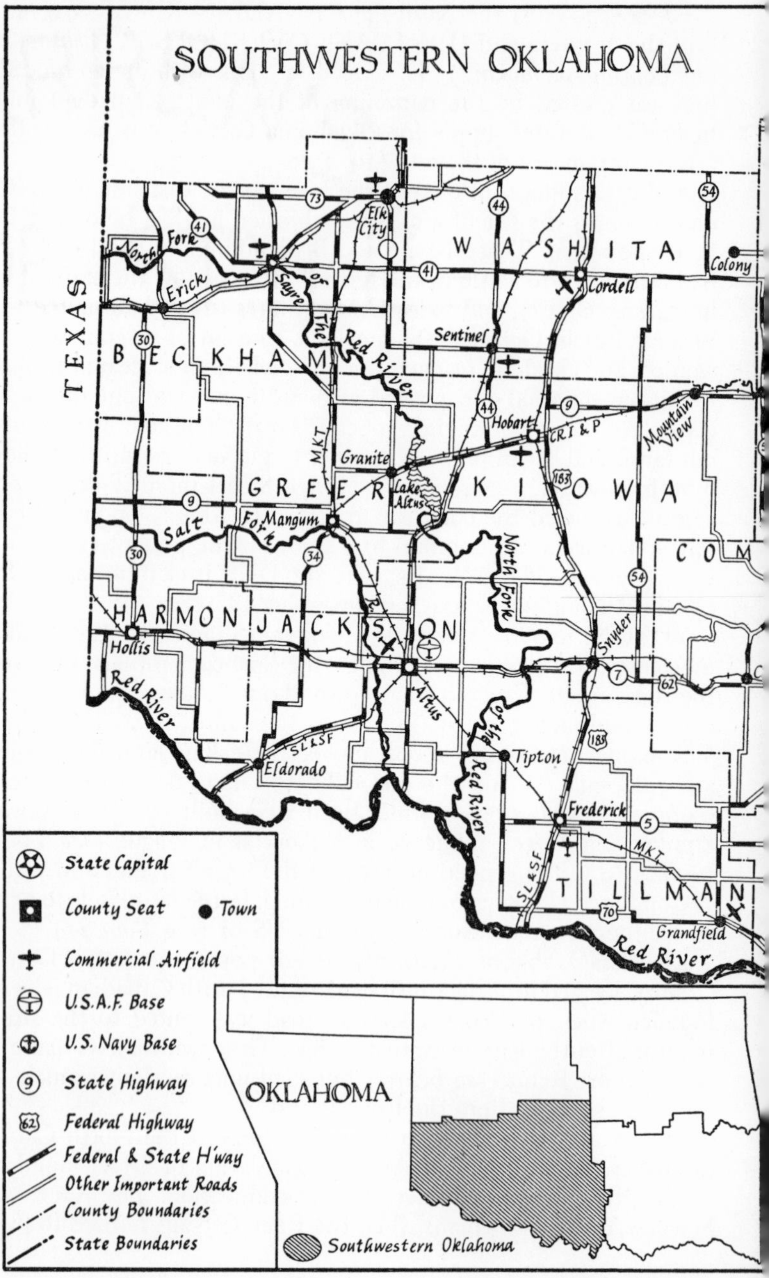
SOUTHWESTERN OKLAHOMA
TEXAS
BECKHAM
GREER
HARMON
JACKSON
KIOWA
WASHITA
TILLMAN
COM
Elk City
Erick
Sayre
Sentinel
Cordell
Colony
Hobart
Mountain View
Granite
Lake Altus
Mangum
Hollis
Altus
Snyder
Tipton
Frederick
Eldorado
Grandfield
North Fork of the Red River
Salt Fork
North Fork
Red River
CRI & P
MKT
SL&SF
State Capital
County Seat
Town
Commercial Airfield
U.S.A.F. Base
U.S. Navy Base
State Highway
Federal Highway
Federal & State H'way
Other Important Roads
County Boundaries
State Boundaries
OKLAHOMA
Southwestern Oklahoma

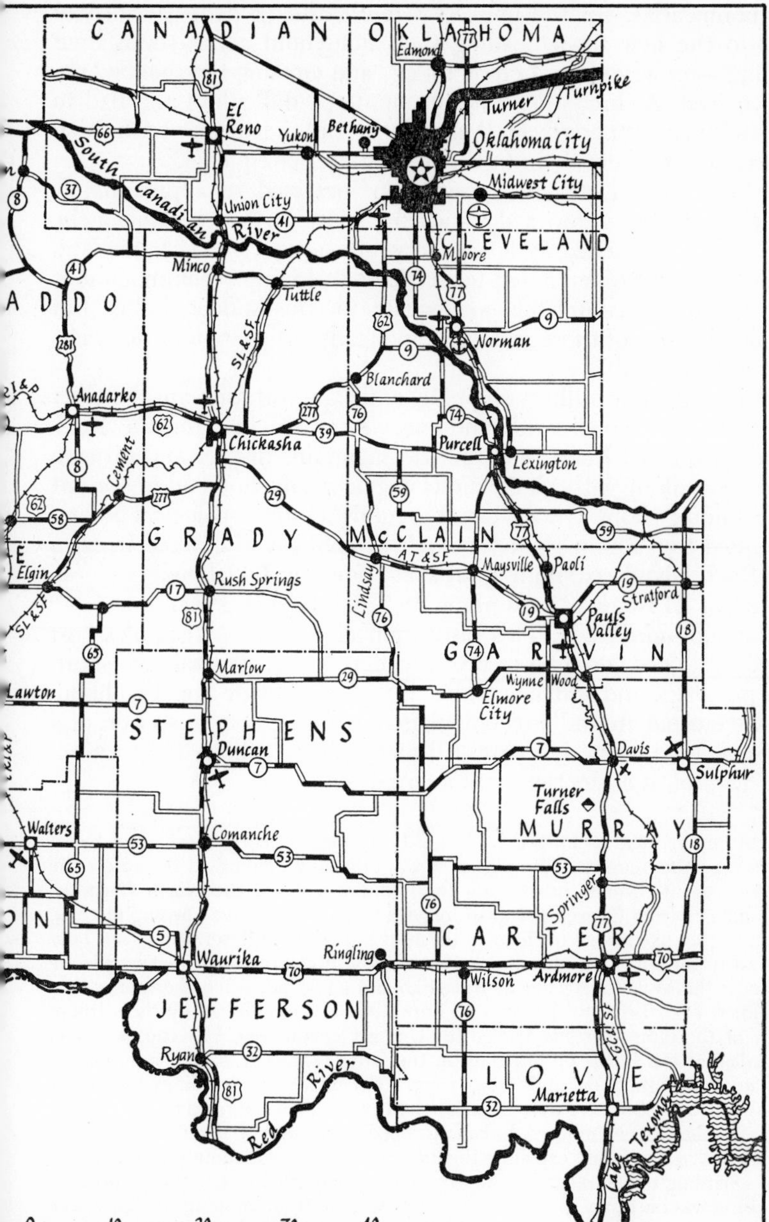
CANADIAN
OKLAHOMA
Edmond
Turner Turnpike
El Reno
Yukon
Bethany
Oklahoma City
Midwest City
South Canadian River
Union City
CLEVELAND
Moore
Minco
Tuttle
ADDO
SL&SF
Norman
Blanchard
Anadarko
Chickasha
Purcell
Lexington
Cement
GRADY
McCLAIN
AT&SF
Maysville
Paoli
Elgin
Rush Springs
Lindsay
Stratford
Pauls Valley
GARVIN
Marlow
Wynne Wood
Elmore City
Lawton
STEPHENS
Duncan
Davis
Sulphur
Turner Falls
MURRAY
Walters
Comanche
Springer
CARTER
Waurika
Ringling
Wilson
Ardmore
JEFFERSON
Ryan
Red River
LOVE
Marietta
Lake Texoma
0 10 20 30 40 Miles

high bonus asked for the line. As a result, the residents decided to move to the new town, loading their household goods—even their buildings—on wagons and crude rollers, and crossing the shallow, unbridged river. A three-story hotel encountered difficulties and had to be abandoned temporarily on the river bed. But in true pioneer fashion it operated continuously until the removal was completed.

In July, 1901, El Reno's population increased to approximately 145,000—literally within a day—when the Kiowa-Apache-Comanche reservation was opened by lottery to white settlers, the last free land in the Territory to be offered for settlement. Living accommodations were, of course, completely inadequate for this sudden influx, but fortunately most of those seeking homesteads left as soon as the drawing was completed.

Marketing, flour milling, shipping, and transportation are the chief industries. The north-south and east-west main lines of the Rock Island cross at El Reno. The railroad maintains district and division offices here, along with a large diesel engine repair shop and important car rebuilding shops. On the depot grounds stands a geological oddity, a petrified tree stump eight feet high, which was discovered in 1914 by a Rock Island coal-mining crew at Alderson, Oklahoma.

West of El Reno, at 30.6 *m.*, is the UNITED STATES REFORMATORY (*visitors not admitted*). This institution (L), built in 1934 at a cost exceeding $1,000,000, houses first offenders against federal law, short-term prisoners, and convicts under thirty-five years of age. The buildings are erected around a rectangular court in the eastern section of a 2,500-acre tract formerly a part of the Fort Reno Military Reservation.

At 32.5 *m.*, is a junction with a paved road.

Right on this road to FORT RENO, 1.8 *m.*, until recently the United States Army's largest remount station. The post was originally established to protect the old DARLINGTON INDIAN AGENCY on the opposite bank of the North Canadian (*see Tour* 11) from Cheyenne Indian forays. During a Cheyenne uprising in 1874, the Darlington agent sent for help to the Fort Sill Military Reservation (*see Tour* 3A) and to the fort at Leavenworth, Kansas. The Fort Sill troops met hostile Indians near the Wichita Agency at Anadarko and could not reach the agency, but the soldiers from Leavenworth arrived. Fort Reno was established by these troops in July of the same year and named for Union General Jesse L. Reno, who had been killed at the Battle of Antietam in the Civil War. The Indian insurrectionists were finally subdued in March, 1875. Permanent fort buildings were then erected, and by 1880 there were three hundred cavalrymen stationed at the garrison to oversee the fifteen hundred Indians camped near by. For the next five years, the troops were kept busy expelling Boomers from the surrounding region and—in 1889—guarding the boundary of the new land to be opened to settlement. Military supervision was necessary in order to keep the Sooners from jumping the line ahead of the starting gun. With the coming of the white settlers and the allotment of In-

Industries

Oil Well, in the East Lindsay Pool.

(*above*) Gasoline Plant, processing gas from the Golden Trend Area.

(*below*) Oil Pumping Unit, on the Osage prairie.

Pressure Maintenance in Oil Sands, to increase normal production.

(*above*) Oil Refinery, Ponca City.

(*below*) Oil Well Cementing Shops, Duncan.

(*above*) SPHERES FOR BUTANE STORAGE, Tulsa.

(*below*) WEST TULSA REFINERY, by night.

(*above*) World's Largest Lead and Zinc Concentrate Mill, Miami.

(*below*) Textile Mill, Sand Springs.

(*above*) Hauling Saw Logs, McCurtain County.

(*below*) Lumber Stacked for Air-drying, Broken Bow.

(*above*) The Aero Commander, designed and manufactured in Oklahoma City.

(*below*) Jet Assembly Line, Tulsa.

dian lands, need for troops at this point decreased and the fort was abandoned in February, 1908. But in April of the same year, it was re-established as a remount station, where horses were broken and trained for other military camps.

This remount station was used extensively through World War I and II, and through the Korean conflict. Many thousands of horses and mules went through "basic training" at Fort Reno and were then shipped out, a good percentage of them to foreign countries. The old fort today, though no longer in existence as such, has many reminders of the early days. A headquarters building, constructed for the commanding officer in 1874, still stands, an interesting historic landmark. It was first occupied by General Phil Sheridan, later by General Nelson A. Miles, both of Civil War fame. Still later it served General George W. Goethals and General George C. Marshall, chief of staff during World War II. On a knoll just west of the headquarters buildings, a small cemetery contains the graves of many early day Indian fighters and scouts. It is also the burial ground of 105 World War II German prisoners of war who died while stationed at POW camps here (to the east) and at Alva (*see Tour 4*).

In 1949, the Department of Agriculture, in co-operation with Oklahoma A. & M. College (*see Stillwater*), established the FORT RENO LIVESTOCK RESEARCH STATION on the old reservation. The line of trees to the north of the fort marks the course of the North Canadian River. The water towers beyond belong to Darlington and to the Cheyenne and Arapaho Indian School at Concho (*see Tour 11*).

At 36.9 *m.* is the junction with US 270 (*see Tour 5*), which turns here (R) for northwest Oklahoma. Beyond, the terrain becomes rougher as US 66 cuts across red-rocked, tree-filled canyons. Joining US 281 briefly at 47.4 *m.*, the highway then crosses the broad SOUTH CANADIAN RIVER, 48.3 *m.* The graceful steel-and-concrete bridge, the state's third longest structure (3,940 ft.), passes over a wide, sandy bed that is often virtually dry and covered in many places with young growth of tamarisk and cottonwood trees.

At 50.3 *m.* is the second junction with US 281.

Left on this road is HINTON, 4.8 *m.* (1,650 alt., 1,025 pop.), home of one of Oklahoma's oldest and best known rodeos (early July). South of town, on US 281, is the junction (L), 5.8 *m.*, with an asphalt road. Left from this point the road becomes a narrow ledge blasted from the sheer sandstone wall of a canyon one hundred feet deep. The road drops down sharply into KIWANIS PARK (*swimming, picnic facilities*), 6.8 *m.* The 150-acre tract, first developed by Hinton, is now owned by the state, which hopes to bring it up to state-park standards within the next few years.

This entire area southeast of Hinton is gashed by a number of similar canyons, difficult to enter because of their steep walls. Usually fifty to one hundred feet wide and several miles long, all are studded with trees. Springs gush from crevices in the rocks. KICKAPOO CANYON and WATER CANYON lie near by, while five miles to the southeast is DEVIL'S CANYON, the site of a Methodist church camp.

At 58.4 *m.* is the "Rock Mary" historical marker (L), calling attention to the flat-topped promontory three and one-half miles to the southwest. The most prominent landmark seen on the California Trail by Captain R. B. Marcy, it was first visited May 23, 1849, at which time the United States flag was raised. The peak was named in honor of Mary Conway, cousin of President James Madison.

At 62.9 *m.* is the junction with paved State 58.

Left here to junction with improved dirt road, 13.5 *m.;* R. here to junction with graveled road, 19.4 *m.;* then L. to the site of SEGER COLONY, 19.7 *m.* The settlement was begun by the Cheyennes and Arapahoes in 1886 under United States supervisor, John H. Seger, long-time friend of the Indians. SEGER INDIAN INDUSTRIAL SCHOOL was opened in 1893. (It closed in 1941.) The mission was founded in 1895 by Rev. Frank H. Wright, under the auspices of the Dutch Reformed church. Two of its buildings are used at present by the public school system of near-by COLONY. Another has been converted into a summer camp for underprivileged children. The rest, abandoned, are falling into ruins under a magnificent grove of ancient oaks, cottonwoods, and native elms. Seger Colony stands, nevertheless, as one of the state's brighter examples of enlightened Indian–white man co-operation.

WEATHERFORD, 71.1 *m.* (1,644 alt., 3,529 pop.), is a neat college town in the center of a fertile farming area. Founded in 1893, it was named for William J. Weatherford, a United States marshal stationed here in Territorial days. On a hill (R) at the northern edge of town is SOUTHWESTERN STATE COLLEGE, established in 1901. Enrollment is approximately 1,400. The 65-acre campus has twenty-two buildings (including the recently completed, $550,000 MEMORIAL STUDENT CENTER), an amphitheater, and a football stadium. Here also is located the SOUTHWEST OKLAHOMA MUSEUM.

At 85.2 *m.* is the CLINTON INDIAN HOSPITAL (R), an institution opened by the federal government in 1933 to care for the sick among the Indian population. The three one-story red-brick buildings stand on an eight-acre tract. The Indians were at first hesitant to accept the benefits of medical care, but now generally welcome the aid offered here.

Just beyond (L) is MOHONK LODGE, where a practical and successful experiment in preserving the distinctive Indian arts and crafts of the Cheyennes and Arapahoes is being carried on. Now privately owned, the experiment was established in 1898 at Seger Colony (*see above*) with funds obtained by Mr. and Mrs. Walter C. Roe, missionaries working on the Cheyenne and Arapaho reservation. It was named for Lake Mohonk in New York, where, at a Dutch Reformed church conference, the idea was originated. The lodge was moved to Clinton in 1941. It continues to provide a workshop for the Indians and a market for their buckskin work, beadwork, blankets, and basketry. These authentic Indian articles are produced not only by the local Cheyennes and Arapahoes, but also by the Apaches of the Fort Sill and Mescalero, New Mexico, bands; the Northern Cheyennes and Rocky Boy band of Crees from Montana; and the Navajos of Arizona.

US 66 crosses the Washita River, 85.7 *m.*, and enters CLINTON, 86.1 *m.* (1,564 alt., 7,555 pop.), situated on a level plain within a bend of the river. Upon the opening of the Cheyenne and Arapaho reservation in 1892, the land where Clinton now stands was a cattle range. The town was founded in 1903, when the Frisco Railway built to the site. It was named for Federal Judge Clinton F. Irwin.

Clinton has grown to be an important shipping center for the surrounding cattle lands and fertile farms. It also has twenty-six small industries. Because of its high elevation and the dryness of the atmosphere, the city also has two large state hospitals. McLain Rogers Park, on US 66 at the west edge of town, is the largest of five city parks. It has a large swimming pool, as well as picnic and play facilities. Visitors are also welcome to play golf (*greens fee*) at the Riverside Golf and Country Club, north of US 66 on the east edge of town. Besides the Custer County Free Fair (in September), most popular special event is the annual Indian Powwow (in July), staged and managed by the Cheyenne and Arapaho Indians.

Clinton is at the junction with US 183 (*see Tour 12*).

The WESTERN OKLAHOMA TUBERCULOSIS SANATORIUM (*visitors by appointment*), 86.6 *m.*, was first established at Supply in 1917, but was moved to Clinton in 1919. The large state-owned hospital (L) consists of fifty-five buildings on a 320-acre tract of ground.

At 100.9 *m.* a paved road (L) leads south seven miles to the Clinton-Sherman Air Force Base, being readied in 1956 for intercontinental bomber units of the Strategic Air Command.

At 104.8 *m.* is the junction with a graded dirt road.

Right on this road is the LAKE CLINTON DAM AND WATERWORKS, 0.5 *m.*, which forms a 335-acre body of clear water noted for its fine game fishing (*permit: 30c per day*). Clinton maintains a landscaped public park (*picnicking*) around the lake, an improved campground below the dam.

Westward, US 66 crosses a number of tree-bordered creeks into a section where barren red hills rise suddenly above almost level prairies.

On the eastern edge of CANUTE, 107.7 *m.* (1,910 alt., 355 pop.), is the ROMAN CATHOLIC CEMETERY (R), in which is a replica of the Crucifixion Scene. Surmounting a low hill is a bronze figure of Christ on the cross, with the two Marys kneeling below. In the side of the hill, a glass-enclosed sepulcher holds the waxen image of Christ. The scene was planned by Father Peter Paul Schaeffer, of the Holy Parish.

West of Canute, the land is rolling and hilly, the soil deep red.

At 112.9 *m.* is a Y-junction with State 34. A granite marker in the center of the Y designates State 34 as the Chisholm Trail (*see Tour 11*). Actually, however, it marks the old Western or Texas Cattle Trail (*see Tour 12*), a later route.

ELK CITY, 116.0 *m.* (1,926 alt., 7,926 pop.), was originally named Busch, in honor of Adolphus Busch of St. Louis. Because of the similarity of the name to that of another post office, it was renamed Elk City. Elk Creek skirts the city limits. COMMUNITY HOSPITAL, established by Syrian-born Dr. M. Shadid, is one of Oklahoma's first co-operative medical ventures.

Discovery of the Elk City Pool in December, 1947, has brought considerable growth to the city. Nearly twenty-seven million barrels of oil were produced during the field's first six years. The 301 producing wells are now unitized for maximum recovery, and the Elk City Processing and Gas Cycling Plant, three miles south of the city, returns the gas to the producing zone after the liquids have been extracted.

North and west of Elk City is the SANDSTONE CREEK PROJECT (*see Tour 13*), the nation's first and largest attempt at scientific upstream flood control. The project has received nationwide acclaim as the most effective way, not only to halt flooding, but also to conserve irreplaceable soil.

Newly developed ELK CITY PARK offers a swimming pool, complete sport and recreational facilities, plus an elaborate playground for children. An outstanding local event is the three-day Elk City Rodeo (early September), staged by the famed Beutler Brothers of Elk City, producers of some of the nation's top rodeo shows.

SAYRE, 131.9 *m.* (1,810 alt., 3,362 pop.), seat of Beckham County, was named for Robert H. Sayre, a stockholder in the railroad extended to the city at its founding, September 14, 1901. A division point on the Rock Island, it profits from a sizable railroad payroll, as well as from its surrounding farms and ranches. Jess Willard, former world's champion prize fighter, once ran a rooming house in Sayre. Another famous son Giuseppe Bentonelli (Joseph Benton), onetime Metropolitan Opera tenor, and now an instructor at the University of Oklahoma, was brought here as an infant in 1900.

Sayre is at the junction with US 283 (*see Tour 13*).

Westward for a few miles, there are weed-covered sand dunes and patches of gnarled dwarf trees. Then the highway descends into a valley where there is more vegetation, although most of the land is uncultivated.

Prior to 1896, Texas claimed the land south of the North Fork of the Red River, crossed at 134.1 *m.* In that year the United States Supreme Court ruled that the southern fork of the Red River was the northern boundary line of Texas, and the area between the forks was added to Oklahoma Territory.

ERICK, 147.6 *m.* (2,080 alt., 1,579 pop.), was incorporated in 1902 and named for Beech Erick, a member of the townsite company. US 66 passes between two long rows of widely spaced houses and bisects the eight-block business section. The town is surrounded by rich farming lands, cattle ranches, and a small natural-gas field.

Southwest of Erick is an old SALT SPRINGS, nature's gift to early-day cattlemen. As the herds were driven north from Texas ranches each spring, many herders made this a stopping place so that the cattle might lick the salt. The fresh-water springs, which flow through COX'S CAVE near by made the spot an ideal camping spot in that early period. The springs have been operated commercially for more than sixty years and they still produce more than 250 tons of coarse salt a year.

Between Erick and the Texas Line, the prairie stretches away in shelving levels to the west. Most of the land is under cultivation.

TEXOLA, 154.4 *m.* (2,150 alt., 265 pop.), on the Texas-Oklahoma border, combines syllables from the two state names to form its own. On the west edge of town, a historical marker (R) calls attention to the fact that this region, "The Land of Greer," was in land claims of fourteen different governments from 1629 down to the present. It was granted to the Choctaw Indians in 1820 at a meeting of Chief Pushmataha and General Andrew Jackson. Organized as Greer County, Texas, in 1860, it was opened to white settlement in the 1880's and, after the Supreme Court decision of 1896, it became a part of Oklahoma.

At 154.8 *m.* US 66 crosses the Texas Line, fifteen miles east of Shamrock, Texas (*see Texas Guide*).

TOUR 1A

Sapulpa—Cushing—Langston—Guthrie; State 33, 75.5 m.

Roadbed paved.
The Santa Fe Ry. parallels the route between Drumright and Guthrie.
Accommodations at Drumright, Cushing, and Guthrie.

State 33 crosses the northwestern corner of the former Creek Nation, traverses for some fifteen miles the old Cushing-Drumright oil field, passes some of the hundreds of huge steel oil storage tanks that long made this the largest tank-farm area in Oklahoma. The route rolls over low wooded hills for some thirty miles, then climbs to the prairie upland north of the Cimarron River. After crossing that river it rises again to wind through red highland farms.

State 33 branches west from its junction with US 66, 0 *m.*, five miles west of Sapulpa (*see Tour 1*), crosses the Turner Turnpike, 0.3 *m.*, then plunges up and down over blackjack-covered hills for approximately twenty miles.

At 4.7 *m.* is the entrance (L) to HEYBURN LAKE and DAM (*see Tour 1*). Another access to the Heyburn Lake recreation area is at 8.8 *m.*

At DRUMRIGHT, 24.4 *m.* (866 alt., 5,028 pop.) (*see Tour 14*), State 33 joins with State 99 from the north. The two routes are one to 27.7 *m.*, where State 99 turns south to Stroud (*see Tour 1*).

CUSHING, 35.6 *m.* (940 alt., 8,414 pop.), was a brawling, boisterous boom town that oil built. Sophisticated Tulsa, some fifty miles to the east, justifies its claim to being the Oil Capital of the World on the basis of corporate greatness. Tin-hatted Cushing, on the other hand, draws its life blood from the forest of derricks that surround it, from the maze of tank farms, refineries, and pipelines that store, process, and ship out this underground wealth. To carry the parallel to the legendary gold and silver days of the American West, Tulsa is the staid Denver or San Francisco, while Cushing is the heel-kicking Tombstone, Cripple Creek, Virginia City, or Deadwood. More so than Tulsa, then—more so perhaps than any other city in the state—Cushing is the symbol of Oklahoma Oil.

The settlement began in 1892 on the old Turkey Track Ranch in the northern part of the Sac and Fox territory. It was named for Marshall Cushing, private secretary to John Wanamaker, then Postmaster General of the United States. In 1894 it was incorporated as a town. Then on April 11, 1912, the Wheeler No. 1 blew in twelve miles to the northeast, and overnight Cushing became a city. Frenzied development of the field followed, and by the end of 1915 there were 710 wells gushing out a fantastic seventy-two million barrels of oil annually. (Cumulative production by mid-1955 topped the four-hundred-million-barrel mark.)

To care for this enormous output, twelve refineries were built in the Cushing area. Seven hundred huge steel tanks, capable of storing nearly thirty-nine million barrels of oil, were soon dotting the near-by prairies. And to connect these giant tank farms, with the wells that produced the black gold on the one hand, and with distant markets on the other (some of these as far away as the Atlantic seaboard), a giant cobweb of pipelines developed. Cushing's present-day title—the "Pipe Line Crossroads of the World"—springs from this intricate underground transportation system.

But while Cushing oil was allegedly creating its hundred millionaires—picturesque characters like Tom Slick, John Markham, Josh Cosden, and Charlie Wrightsman—it was also creating its problems. Cushing gushers were so bountiful that, like those of the Seminole Field (*see Tour 5*) in 1927, they almost ruined the industry. They pushed the price down to nineteen cents a barrel and forced eastern oil companies to step in to limit production.

And Cushing oil was also creating legend and folklore. Tales like that of the drunken tool pusher who looked the town over and told the crowd who gathered around him, "You got new buildin's here; you got new stores an' new churches: an' I'm goin' to start a new graveyard!" When he attempted to carry out his promise, the hammer of his six-gun caught on his belt and he shot himself in the leg. Cushing oil even added words to the dictionary. Words like "hijacker," the highwayman who waited in the blackjacks between Cushing and Tulsa to waylay incoming bootleggers.

But Cushing has slowed down somewhat with advancing age. Prorated oil production is down to only a trickle of the 305,000-barrel-a-day peak it hit in May of 1915. And social life has also matured. Approximately one hundred new homes have been built annually for the past few years. Cushing has twenty-eight churches, an eighteen-hole golf course, a public library, parks, and a modernistic above-ground swimming pool. The town has become an agricultural as well as an oil center.

Yet it was the Cushing Field—one of the Southwest's most colorful—that forty-odd years ago established Oklahoma as a top crude-oil producer. And Cushing remains today an interesting and peculiarly characteristic symbol of Oklahoma.

State 33 crosses the CIMARRON RIVER at 43.5 *m.* At 49.3 *m.* is the junction with paved State 40.

Left on this road to PERKINS, *1 m.* (829 alt., 706 pop.), established at the time of the opening of Old Oklahoma to settlement in the Run of April 22, 1889. Perkins is the home of Frank "Pistol Pete" Eaton, 95-year-old Oklahoma pioneer, who at fifteen packed "the fastest guns" in Indian Territory and later became a well-known United States Marshal.

Continuing south, State 40 crosses the Cimarron River, 2 *m.*, and enters the former Iowa Indian Reservation. Here in 1952 was started the I-O-A RANCH—for *Individual, Opportunity, Achievement*—a public-supported "School in Family Living" for boys and girls. In 1956 the institution included five separate farms totaling 650 acres.

South and east of the I-O-A Ranch the Iowa Indians still hold their spring and fall green corn dances and other traditional festivals.

At 50.3 *m.* State 40 leaves State 33 (R) for Stillwater (*see Stillwater*).

On the grounds of the IXL COMMUNITY CENTER, 53.4 *m.*, is a WASHINGTON IRVING MARKER (L) placed by citizens of Payne County to commemorate Irving's passage in 1832 (*see Tour 2A*). An actual camp site (October 21) of the Irving party, unmarked, is about 1.5 miles northwest of the marker, near the north bank of Wild Horse Creek. The grove of trees (now gone) described by Irving is remembered by old settlers in the area. It was here, Irving readers will recall, that the party had its first exciting experience in capturing wild horses.

State 33 crosses the Cimarron River at 61.0 *m.*

Once named Iowa City, COYLE, 62.1 *m.* (866 alt., 360 pop.), first located two miles to the northwest, was moved to its present site when the Santa Fe built through in 1900. Fine old elms overarch the highway and principal street.

LANGSTON, 64.1 *m.* (962 alt., 685 pop.), is the all-Negro town founded in 1890 by E. P. McCabe, and named for the Negro educator and member of Congress (1890–91), John M. Langston, of Virginia.

As early as 1885, the movement to establish an all-Negro community—possibly a state—was started by S. H. Scott, a Negro lawyer of Fort Smith, Arkansas. After the Opening of 1889, McCabe, who had been State Auditor of Kansas, promoted the town at the present site, and it is said that at one time its population exceeded two thousand. But it shrank radically when the Negroes who had been attracted to the town by McCabe's enthusiastic words had exhausted their savings and found it impossible to earn a living. Many—including McCabe, who became deputy auditor of Oklahoma (1907–1908)—moved on to Guthrie, the Territorial capital.

LANGSTON UNIVERSITY was authorized for Negroes by the Territorial legislature in March of 1897. State and federal funds, plus grants from the General Education Board and the Rosenwald Fund, have built it up over the years until it compares favorably with most of Oklahoma's other state-supported colleges of similar size. A four-year, coeducational institution, it offers degrees in five major divisions, fairly extensive preprofessional courses, and a recognized ROTC program. Its 1,250 students have always competed actively in intercollegiate sports. The college's Dust Bowl Players is a well-known dramatic group. In recent years a library, an auditorium, a gymnasium, and other buildings have been added to the 400-acre campus, and trees, lacking for a long time, have begun to relieve the impression of barrenness suggested by the essentially plain red-brick buildings.

Dr. G. L. Harrison, long-time president of the college, is the successor to other able Negro educators who have helped to make the school one of the better Negro institutions in the country. The program suggested in the act creating the school was to train teachers, to give instruction in industrial arts, and to teach the boys to be good farmers. Langston has consistently carried out this program, while expanding it in recent years to put more stress on music and the liberal arts. Along with sports, most of the usual extracurricular activities are carried on by the Y's, the eight Greek letter fraternities and sororities, and various clubs. Langston's progress has been steady and impressive.

Desegregation of the state's schools, ordered by the United States Supreme Court in 1954 and rapidly being implemented throughout Oklahoma on all levels, casts some doubts over the future of Langston. Even before the Supreme Court decision Negro graduate students had been admitted to the University of Oklahoma and Oklahoma A. & M. Since 1954, the number of Negro students in previously all-white colleges and universities has steadily increased. Langston, however, with its greatly improved facilities and professional standing—and the advantage it has of being able to offer what is perhaps the most economical educational program of the state's four-year colleges—seems assured of holding on to its hard-won position as a respected member of Oklahoma's institutions of higher learning.

GUTHRIE, 75.5 *m.* (1,021 alt., 10,113 pop.) (*see Tour 10*), is at the junction with US 77 (*see Tour 10*).

TOUR 2

(Fort Smith, Ark.)—Gore—Muskogee—Tulsa—Enid—Alva—Guymon—Boise City—(Clayton, N. M.); US 64, Arkansas Line to New Mexico Line, 596.6 m.

Roadbed paved through.
Missouri Pacific R. R. roughly parallels route between the Arkansas Line and Muskogee; the Katy between Muskogee and Cleveland; the Frisco between Pawnee and Alva; the Santa Fe between Alva and Buffalo; and the Katy between Gate and Boise City.
Good accommodations available throughout, but at greater intervals across the Panhandle.

The longest federal highway in the state, US 64 crosses Oklahoma from the mid-east to the far northwest, and is marked by a wide variety of landscape, climate, and population. Leaving the Arkansas border and the verdant Cookson Hills, it cuts through the timber of the beautiful Illinois River valley, then crosses the Arkansas and the Cimarron, rivers that alternate between occasional flood stages and prolonged periods when they are little more than wide ribbons of blowing sand.

As it pushes westward, the route climbs steadily to higher, more arid country, where trees are scarce and burning summer winds are a constant threat to maturing crops. Skirting the Great Salt Plains, an important wildlife refuge, it plunges at last across the length of the Panhandle, impressive in a barrenness never quite broken by the occasional modern town, irrigated field, and natural-gas pumping station.

Varied, too, are the personalities and history of the towns through which the route passes, for they range from the earliest Indian settlements to frontier towns that mushroomed into existence within the memory of many still living today. But the great drama of US 64—a tragedy of heroic proportions—is outlined by its first forty miles. For here, roughly from the Arkansas Line to Gore, it follows the Cherokee "Trail of Tears," broken by the exiles from Georgia and Tennessee during the two decades from 1819 to 1839.

Among those who have given character to the region through which the route passes are such diverse figures of history as Washington Irving, the effete traveler who found that he could also rough it; Robert M. Loughridge, hardy missionary to the Creeks; Sam Houston, pausing off stage three years between his Tennessee and Texas careers; Kit Carson, who by mistake established a frontier fort within the boundaries of Oklahoma; Dull Knife, the Cheyenne, and Bacon Rind, the Osage, heroic figures out of an almost legendary Indian past; the notorious Dalton Boys, brothers who made outlawry a life work, with the robbing of trains and banks as their skilled trade; and the ubiquitous Coronado.

Section a. ARKANSAS LINE *to* TULSA, *133.2 m. US 64*

Crossing the ARKANSAS LINE, 0 *m.*, at the Arkansas River immediately west of Fort Smith, Arkansas (*see Arkansas Guide*), US 64 approaches the rough Cookson Hills of the Ozark region. Though accommodations are in the main limited to the larger towns and the state parks, the area is a paradise to the sportsman and the general vacationer. Water resources range from small clear streams to huge man-made lakes. The rolling hills are covered with oak, an occasional stand of pine and, in the spring, splashed with color from the redbud, dogwood, and many wild flowers. To the north (R) is the HOME OF SEQUOYAH (*see Tour 15*).

SALLISAW, 23.7 *m.* (531 alt., 2,885 pop.), once a trading post and a camping site, is now an agricultural center. But industry (strip coal mining east and south of town, and a lime plant to the west) and tourist services are becoming increasingly important factors in the town's progressive and prosperous appearance. The Cherokee–Cookson Hills to the north and the Arkansas River bottom to the south afford excellent fishing and hunting. French trappers named the place *Salaison,* meaning salt provision or salt meat, because of the large salt deposits near by.

In Sallisaw is the junction with US 59 (*see Tour 15*).

At 28.9 *m.* is the official DWIGHT MISSION historical marker. This famous Oklahoma institution, about seven miles to the northeast, was established by the Presbyterian Mission Board in 1829 and maintained as a coeducational Indian school for over a hundred years. It is now a youth conference retreat for the Oklahoma synod of the church.

At VIAN, 34.7 *m.* (545 alt., 927 pop.), a small community nestled in the foothills of the Cookson Hills area, is the junction with State 82.

The thirty-two-mile stretch of this road between US 64 and US 62 (*see Tour 3*) —most of it paved, the rest graveled—serves one of the state's newest and finest recreation areas. Twisting through the wooded, creek-filled Cookson Hills, it provides easy access to LAKE TENKILLER STATE PARK (*see below*) and to the fishing camps and resorts that line the eastern shore and upper reaches of TENKILLER FERRY RESERVOIR. The lake is thirty-four miles long, covers some 12,500 acres, and boasts a normal shore line of 130 miles. Blackgum Landing, Snake Creek Cove, Chicken Creek Point, Cookson Bend, Standing Rock, Cherokee Landing, and Horseshoe Bend are but a few of the resort areas within a few miles of the road. State 82 joins US 62 at Park Hill just below Tahlequah (*see Tour 3*).

Near the tiny community of BOX, 6.2 *m.*, are the meeting places of at least two clans of the Kee-Too-Wah Society of the Cherokee Indians. Here (*make local inquiry*) they hold their annual Sacred Fire Ceremony on July 19 (*visitors welcome*). The ceremony expresses what is generally accepted as the original Cherokee myth. The Great Spirit gave the sacred fire to the Cherokees, who were to keep it perpetually burning. The priests or *ku-ta-ni* were to tend the flames, but designing ones among them stole it. For this crime, all priests were executed; and thus all primal religious practices were closed to the Cherokees, since the tenets had been kept alive only verbally as priest succeeded priest. Some authorities hold the derivation of the name Cherokee is *a-che-la* (fire) and *ah-gi* (he takes).

The Kee-Too-Wahs, whose organization is both ancient and secret, brought the sacred fire from Georgia, according to members of their fullblood clans, and have kept it burning ever since. Their aim is to perpetuate tribal tradition and history. The ceremonial begins normally at the noon hour and lasts until approximately sunrise the following morning.

At 38.5 *m.* on US 64 is the junction with a dirt road.

Right on this road, up a steep slope, is an old SALT SPRING, 3.2 *m.*, once the source of supply for a large salt factory near by.

The ILLINOIS RIVER is bridged at 41.3 *m.* From near here, according to John Steinbeck's famed depression-days novel, *Grapes of Wrath*, the Joads started their long trek to California. Motorists may be a bit surprised (as were no few Oklahomans) that this area through which they have just passed—an area of well-wooded hills, abundant water, and little agriculture—was represented in the book as a land of dust storms and tenant farms.

Near the east bank is the site of the Cherokee town, TAHLONTEESKEE (R), which served as a meeting place for national councils and lawmaking bodies from 1828 to 1838.

At 43.6 *m.* is the junction with State 10.

From this intersection interesting side tours can be made.

Right on paved State 10 to GORE, 0.6 *m.* (480 alt., 387 pop.), is the southern gateway to two of Oklahoma's newest lake-centered state parks. On the east bank of the Arkansas River, Gore first appeared on a map by Guillaume de Lille, a French explorer, as Mentos or Les Mentous in 1718. The town was called Campbell when it was a stop on the Fort Smith–Fort Gibson stage line. When the railroad came through in 1888, the name was changed to Illinois. After statehood, it was finally called Gore to honor United States Senator Thomas P. Gore.

It was to this Cherokee settlement that Sam Houston came in 1829, after his designation as governor of Tennessee. By a special act of the Cherokee Council in 1829 at Tahlonteeskee, Houston was formally adopted by the tribe. He took an Indian wife and lived in the vicinity of Fort Gibson (*see Tour* 3) for several years.

State 10 passes through a section dotted with the cabins of an isolated group of Indians. The majority of these people are fullblood Creeks who became members of the Cherokee tribe. While yet in their eastern homes, they opposed removal to the new Indian Territory and fled to the Cherokee Nation. Later, when the Cherokees were also forced to move, these adopted sons and daughters continued to live with them. Scattered among them are a few Natchez, members of a tribe which is usually regarded by ethnologists as extinct.

At 1.0 *m.* is the junction (R) with another asphalt road.

Leaving State 10, this road passes near the ruins (L) of an old SALT WORKS on Saline Creek that operated in 1820. From the one hundred huge kettles of salt water kept boiling most of the time, the refined salt was taken to a warehouse just above the near-by falls (*see below*), where it was stored until keel boats could carry it down the river to Arkansas and Louisiana. A few years later, after the Cherokees were removed to this part of Indian Territory, the works were taken over by Walter Webber, a wealthy mixed-blood Cherokee for whom the town of Webbers Falls was named.

At 8.7 *m.* is the $23,000,000 TENKILLER FERRY DAM, completed in 1953. The road continues across the dam itself (power plant to the right and below), a section of mainland, and then a long earthen fill to LAKE TENKILLER STATE PARK (*cabins, camping, boating, swimming, fishing, picnicking*). The park includes three developed areas and five islands, occupying a wooded bluff on the east side of the huge reservoir. Private accommodations and recreational facilities are available at many coves and inlets around the lake (*see above*).

North on State 10 at 9.7 *m.* is the junction with another asphalt road. Right on this road to the 1,475-acre GREENLEAF LAKE STATE PARK, 1.4 *m.* Accommodations are still somewhat more limited than at Lake Tenkiller, but facilities include cabins and picnic areas, boat docks, swimming beaches, and excellent fishing on the lake's 920 surface acres. The park is also a game refuge.

Near-by GREENLEAF MOUNTAIN has been a favorite ball field for the Cherokees and Creeks for more than a century. The Indian game—which combines features of baseball, basketball, and football—is played with two sticks, with oval netting at one end. The player must catch the ball in the net and pitch it to hit the goal at the top of a forty-foot pole. Among the hundreds of Indian paintings by George Catlin, nineteenth-century artist, there are several of this strenuous game. It is also played by the Euchees (*see Tour 1*). This concludes the State 10 side tour, returning to US 64 for the main tour.

WEBBERS FALLS, 44.9 *m.* (479 alt., 489 pop.), was named for Walter Webber (*see above*) and for the falls in the Arkansas River. These are now hardly more than a riffle across the channel, though they were once several feet high at a normal stage of the river.

In WARNER, 55.6 *m.* (570 alt., 382 pop.), a farming community, is the CONNORS STATE AGRICULTURAL COLLEGE. Established in 1908 as a preparatory school, the curriculum was extended in 1927 to include junior college courses. Coeducational, the college has an enrollment of 350 to 400.

Left from Warner on paved State 2 is PORUM, 11 *m.* (583 alt., 616 pop.), once the home of Tom Starr, ardent supporter of the treaty faction during the turbulent days of the establishment of the Cherokee Nation. A half-blood—Irish and Cherokee—he had five sons, one of whom became the husband of Belle Starr. Dissension between the "Old Settlers" and "Newcomer" Cherokees, arising from the fact that one party had signed the Removal Treaty with the United States, broke into open warfare with a series of brutal assassinations. Among those of the treaty party who were killed was Tom's father, James Starr. To avenge the family, Tom set himself to the task of killing as many of the antitreaty faction as possible, and the war became so intense that the Cherokee government, not able to capture or kill him, finally made a treaty with him. Provisions of the act—said to be the only treaty with an individual in the history of the Cherokee Nation—gave Tom Starr complete amnesty and $100,000 on condition that he end his bloody fight. To avoid further trouble, he moved to the Canadian River near Briartown, fulfilled his part of the agreement by becoming a leader in the community.

Right from Porum on a dirt road to a junction with a second dirt road, 4.5 *m.*; left here to a junction with a third road, 8.7 *m.*; right here to BELLE STARR'S GRAVE, 9.7 *m.* The crypt—at present weed choked and neglected—is a small stone mausoleum on the north bank of the broad Canadian River. The headstone is of granite, engraved with her name, a verse, and her horse's picture. Though her Missouri parents were respectable and wealthy, Belle was a notorious woman outlaw. In the Civil War she became a Confederate spy, during which time she made the acquaintance of the James and Younger boys. Her first marriage was to Jim Reed, one of Quantrill's men. After he was killed by officers of the law she married Sam Starr, son of Tom Starr. They settled on a farm on the Canadian River near Eufaula, and their home soon became a rendezvous for outlaw friends. Both met violent deaths. Eufaula Dam, now under construction (*see Tour* 8), will back water to within a half mile of the grave.

At Warner, US 64 turns sharply north (R).

In MUSKOGEE, 74.5 *m.* (617 alt., 37,289 pop.) (*see Muskogee*), are junctions with US 69 (*see Tour* 8) and US 62 (*see Tour* 3), with which US 64 unites westward for 15.8 miles.

Right on a graveled road from the junction of 40th Street and the Kansas-Oklahoma-Gulf tracks to a V junction with two improved roads, 2 *m.* Right from this junction to the SITE OF THE TULLAHASSEE SCHOOL, 6 *m.* This, the largest of the early Creek Nation mission schools (other missions were at Eufaula and Coweta), was established in 1850 by the Rev. R. M. Loughridge, a Presbyterian minister under contract with the tribal government. The list of graduates from the school in its prime reads like a roll call of subsequent Creek tribal leaders. The school was damaged during the Civil War when much of the surrounding country was laid waste. The Creeks repaired the plant, however, and operated it until it was destroyed by fire in 1880. Rebuilt once again, it was used by the Creeks through the rest of the tribal period for the education of their Negro freedmen.

TAFT, 85.3 *m.* (605 alt., 541 pop.), is an all-Negro community which grew up because of the large number of Negro freedmen who settled near the confluence of the Arkansas and Verdigris rivers shortly after the Civil War. The United States required the Creeks to adopt their former slaves as citizens, and many allotments in this district were given to Negroes, who were thus listed on the rolls of the Creek Nation. The original townsite was platted on sixteen acres, purchased from a freedman, and named in honor of a prominent Negro, W. H. Twine. Later the town was renamed for President William Howard Taft.

In Taft (R) is the STATE DEAF, BLIND, AND ORPHANS INSTITUTE, founded in 1909. This school affords a home for approximately two hundred orphans and twenty handicapped children. Here also is the STATE TRAINING SCHOOL FOR NEGRO GIRLS, supervising some forty inmates. Six hundred of its 1,242 acres are under cultivation, with dairy, swine, poultry, and garden-produce units, which help to make the institution self-supporting. At 85.8 m. is the TAFT STATE HOSPITAL (L), opened in 1933. The $500,000 hospital building has twelve wards accommodating fifty inmates each. Adjoining farm land also produces food and provides pasture for the institution's dairy herd.

At 90.3 *m.* is the western junction with US 62 (*see Tour 3*). US 64 turns northwest, paralleling the Arkansas River for some twenty-three miles.

At 94.5 *m.* is the LA HARPE'S COUNCIL historical marker (R) commemorating the first peace council and alliance in Oklahoma between a European nation and Indian tribes. The meeting was held near here at a Tawakoni village by Commandant Bernard de la Harpe on September 10, 1719. This date marks the beginning of French place names and trade activities in Oklahoma.

HASKELL, 95.5 *m.* (620 alt., 1,676 pop.), honors the first governor of Oklahoma, Charles N. Haskell (1907–11). To the southeast is the site of the old Blue Creek Mission of pre–Civil War days. Chief Pleasant Porter, elected head of the Creeks in 1899, was born in this vicinity. President McKinley once called Porter the greatest living Indian of his time. Porter continued to work for the betterment of his people until his death in 1907.

Right from Haskell graveled State 72 runs through a historic region of the former Creek Indian Nation. The highway crosses the ARKANSAS RIVER, 8 *m.*, and then follows the course of Coweta Creek—on whose banks the Coweta division of the tribe settled—to COWETA MISSION SITE (R). Here the Reverend Robert M. Loughridge established the first of three missions in 1843; he preached and his wife conducted a boarding school for the children of the near-by Creek families. The mission grew in size and holdings, but its buildings were burned during the Civil War and never replaced. Northeast of the site of the church, Loughridge, his young wife, and their baby, Olivia, are buried in an abandoned hillside cemetery. The headstones have long since fallen and been covered with debris.

The COWETA CEREMONIAL GROUNDS (L) was the scene of many solemn councils in the nineteenth century. Four brush arbors for the accommodation of spectators and participants surrounded a square where the ceremonial fire was kindled. Near by was a ball ground where men and women played the Indian ball game for recreation, and also (R) the ball ground reserved for formal, and always strenuous, games between towns.

COWETA, 10.2 *m.* (625 alt., 1,601 pop.), is on the site of the early settlement named by the Creeks for their famous town in Georgia before the removal to Indian Territory. At that time, the Creek Nation was a confederacy formed by the union of semiautonomous towns. Governmental functions were divided into "peace" and "war" activities, with the towns classified as "white" or "red" according to the function. Coweta was the leading "red," or "war," town and the scene of many important treaty councils. When the tribe migrated to the West, members of Coweta Town settled here in the valley of the Arkansas. The white settlement which gradually supplanted it has perpetuated the ancient name.

The tradition of the towns has never passed from the memory of the Creeks. When they adopted the white man's system of agriculture, they gradually moved out from these compact settlements to individual farms. But they continued to recognize the town organization as a social, ceremonial, and governmental unit. Even today, scattered throughout Oklahoma as they are, all Creeks remember their town affiliation.

These tribal traditions and institutions were almost completely wiped out by the domination of the white man and the adoption of the Indians into American citizenry. The Oklahoma Indian Welfare Act, however, passed by Congress in 1936, authorizes groups of Indians to incorporate for the purpose of acquiring land and carrying on collective acitvities. It is thus sympathetic to the traditional forms. The ancient Creek town organization formed the basis for the newly chartered associations.

Near Coweta (L) is the SITE OF THE COWETA DISTRICT COURT, where the Creeks dispensed justice, sentencing and punishing almost simultaneously. Whipping was the most common punishment for all offenses.

At 112.1 *m.* is the junction with an improved county road.

Right to the SITE OF WEALAKA MISSION, 5 *m.*, on the south bank of the Arkansas River. Founded by the Creeks in 1881, with Rev. R. M. Loughridge as superintendent, the mission was built on land once belonging to Chief Pleasant Porter. The chief is buried not far from the site. The mission served as a Creek tribal school during and after Territorial days.

BIXBY, 113.1 *m.* (649 alt., 1,517 pop.), established on the site of Old Town, emerged from a wild, outlaw past into a prosperous agricultural center. It was named for Tams Bixby, chairman of the Dawes Commission, which was created by Congress in 1893 to settle the affairs of the Five Civilized Tribes.

At 129.5 *m.* is the junction with 41st Street on the southern edge of Tulsa.

Left on 41st Street to TULSA'S FIRST POST OFFICE, 1.1 *m.*, marked by a red granite stone bearing an inscription and the date of establishment, March 25, 1879. The building (*private*) originally was the home of George Perryman and was the headquarters of the Figure-4 Ranch. Lumber and material for its construction were hauled in wagons from Coffeyville, Kansas. Though some changes have been made and some materials replaced, the moss-covered foundation blocks, the brick flues, sills, wainscoting, molding, and six-inch flooring still remain. The sills were hewn by hand, then mortised; the walls were covered with canvas and then papered.

It was in the spring of 1878 that the Post Office Department decided to extend service from Fort Smith westward to the Sac and Fox Agency. A post road was routed and a post rider delivered mail once a week to the Perryman house. Josiah C. Perryman, a brother of George and one of the most respected citizens of the Creek Nation, was appointed postmaster. When the Frisco Railway came to Tulsa in 1882, the post office was moved from the Perryman home to a store near the tracks.

TULSA, 133.2 *m.* (750 alt., 182,740 pop.) (*see Tulsa*), is at the junction with US 66 (*see Tour 1*), US 75 (*see Tour 9*), and US 169 (*see Tour 9A*).

Section b. TULSA *to* ENID, *126.3 m. US 64*

West of Tulsa, 0 *m.*, are many towns which grew from early Indian settlements. The highway follows the Arkansas River for about twenty miles, skirts the southern edge of the Osage reservation, and crosses the Pawnee reservation and the Cherokee Outlet.

SAND SPRINGS, 7.6 *m.* (700 alt., 6,994 pop.), is an industrial city that began as an unusual philanthropic venture. The business section of Sand Springs—where a Creek settlement was located in 1833 and named Adams Springs, in honor of a prominent Creek family—is to the right of the main highway. The sandy springs in the near-by Osage Hills gave the city its present name. Washington Irving tells in his *Tour on the Prairies* that he first saw the Cimarron River—the "Red Fork of the Arkansas River," as he called it—from a hill called Beattie's Knob, north of present Sand Springs.

In 1907, wealthy oilman Charles Page bought a 160-acre tract of land, on which he built a home for widows and orphans in 1908, and connected it with Tulsa by an electric railway. Industrial interests soon began locating here, and in 1911 the city of Sand Springs was platted. Some one hundred and fifty industries operate in the Sand Springs area, employing more than five thousand workers with an annual payroll in excess of $22,000,000.

PAGE MEMORIAL LIBRARY (*open Mon. and Thurs. 3–9; Tues., Wed., Sat., 3–5:30; closed Fri.*), 3rd and Main Sts., was built by Mrs. Page as a memorial to her husband, who died in 1926. The $100,000 structure, buff stucco with bronze trim, is modern in design and houses 13,500 volumes. Across the street from the library is TRIANGLE PARK, a small plot of ground in which stands a life-size bronze statue of Page, with smaller figures of orphans looking up to him. The group is the work of Lorado Taft.

Right from Sand Springs on Broadway to Sand Springs Home, 1 *m.*, founded by Page to provide for orphans and needy widows with children. The property includes more than sixteen thousand acres of farm land, with modern buildings, affording comfortable homes for the orphans and widows. Some of the city's industries lease land and warehouses owned by the Home, the income from such

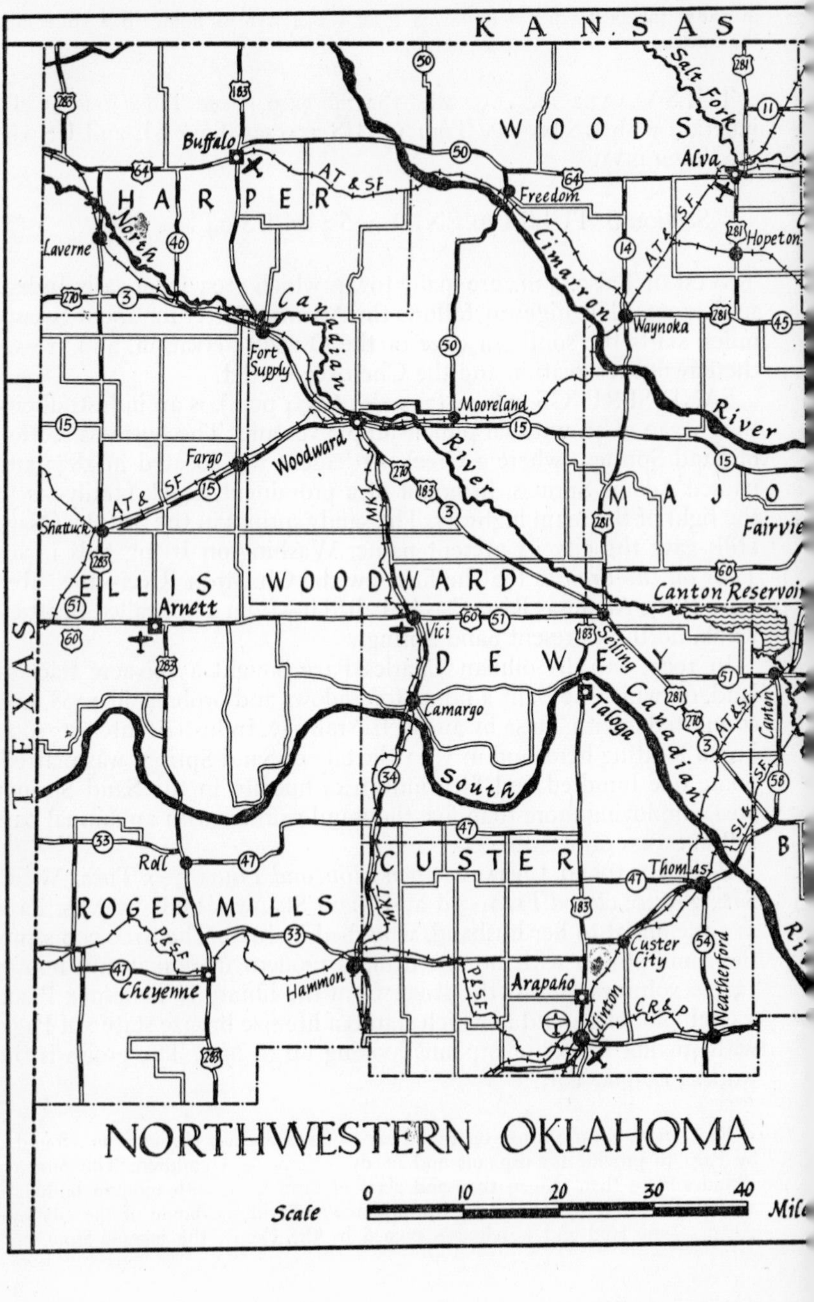
KANSAS
TEXAS
WOODS
HARPER
MAJO
ELLIS
WOODWARD
DEWEY
CUSTER
ROGER MILLS
B
Salt Fork
Cimarron River
North Canadian River
South Canadian
Canton Reservoir
Buffalo
Alva
Freedom
Hopeton
Laverne
Fort Supply
Waynoka
Mooreland
Woodward
Fargo
Shattuck
Fairvie
Arnett
Vici
Seiling
Camargo
Taloga
Canton
Roll
Thomas
Custer City
Cheyenne
Hammon
Arapaho
Clinton
Weatherford
AT & SF
MKT
P & SF
CR & P
SL & SF
NORTHWESTERN OKLAHOMA
Scale
0
10
20
30
40
Mile

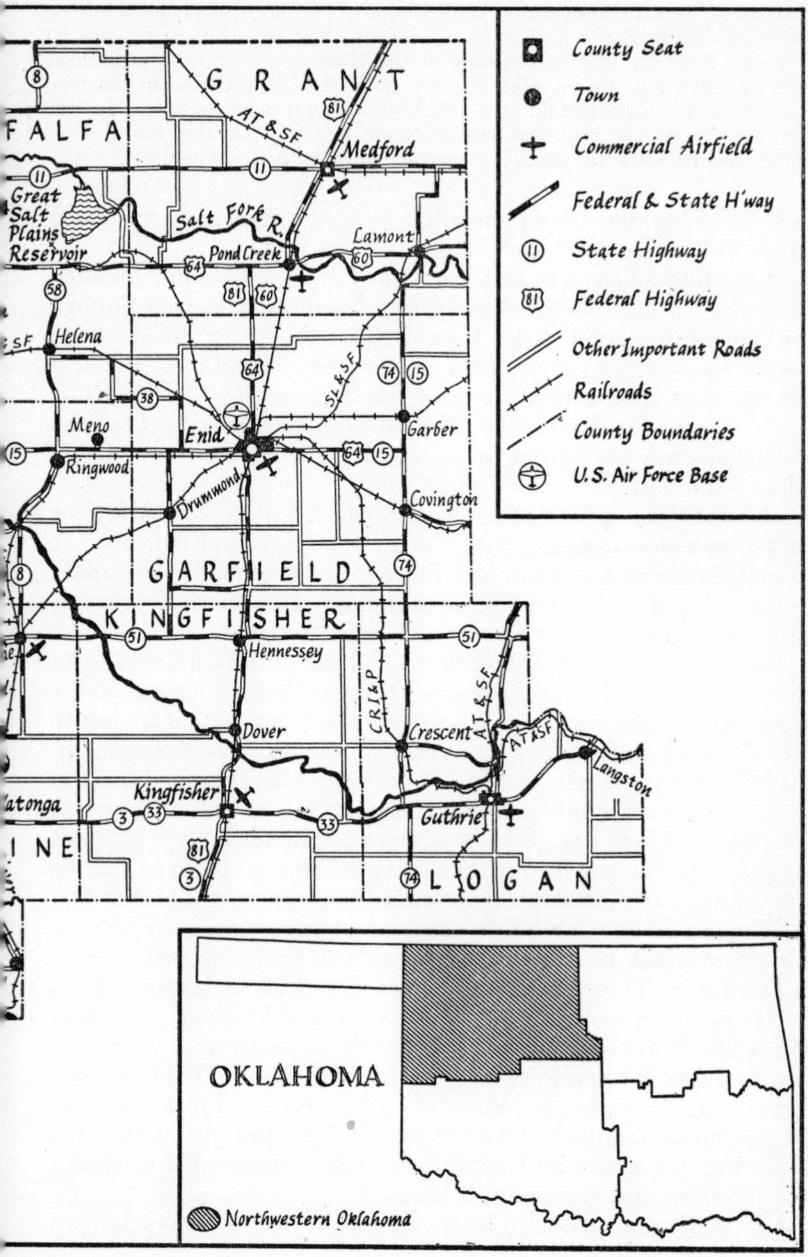
County Seat
Town
Commercial Airfield
Federal & State H'way
State Highway
Federal Highway
Other Important Roads
Railroads
County Boundaries
U.S. Air Force Base
GRANT
FALFA
GARFIELD
KINGFISHER
LOGAN
INE
Medford
AT & SF
Great Salt Plains Reservoir
Salt Fork R.
Lamont
Pond Creek
Helena
Meno
Ringwood
Enid
Garber
SL & SF
Drummond
Covington
Hennessey
Dover
Crescent
CRI & P
AT & SF
Langston
Kingfisher
Guthrie
atonga
OKLAHOMA
Northwestern Oklahoma

leases going toward the support of the institution. The farms supply much of the institution's foodstuff.

Right, from the western boundary of the Home, on an oiled asphalt road through a gateway, 0.9 *m.*, then left 3.3 *m.* is SHELL CREEK. In the four DALTON CAVES, which line the creek, the Dalton gang is supposed to have hidden after their spectacular bank and train robberies. It is said that they buried some of their loot in or near the caves, but treasure hunters have never found it.

At Sand Springs, US 64 turns left at right angles and crosses the Arkansas River bridge, 8.2 *m.*

At the turn a CREEK BURIAL GROUND (L), more than one hundred years old, has been enclosed by an iron fence and preserved through the philanthropy of Charles Page. Beyond the bridge the highway follows the winding course of the broad, sandy Arkansas for the next ten miles. At approximately 17.0 *m.* can be seen (R) the site of the new KEYSTONE DAM across the Arkansas River. The huge $153,000,000 installation was authorized in 1956 and preliminary construction is scheduled for 1957.

KEYSTONE, 19.6 *m.* (684 alt., 228 pop.), will be flooded by the backed-up waters from Keystone Dam, when it is completed. And the town is already making plans for a move to higher ground to the south. But today it is still a quiet farm community that shows few traces, either of its impermanent future or of its frontier past.

The town was first settled on the south bank of the Cimarron River at its confluence with the Arkansas. The Osage reservation was to the north, bordered by the Arkansas, and the Creek reservation lay just to the south. The white man's "firewater," abundant in Keystone, attracted cowboys, farmers, and outlaws, as well as the prohibited Indians.

About 1903, real estate promoters bought two cornfields on the north bank of the Cimarron, just across from Keystone. In typical boom fashion, they laid out the townsite of Appalachia, pictured in alluring colored maps as a busy river port reached by steamboat. The fact that the Cimarron rarely has much water except after heavy rains was apparently ignored, for the new town began to spring up with saloons in abundance. The enterprising promoters and saloon-keepers built a rickety swinging footbridge across the river, and hundreds of wagons and saddle horses were often waiting on the Keystone side while their owners visited the new town's more attractive saloons. Often, on their return trip, the revelers fell into the chilly waters, and many of them sobered up sufficiently to take the pledge. Appropriately enough, the footbridge was named for Carry Nation, whose temperance campaign was in full swing in Kansas at the time.

A U.S. marshal arrived to keep order at the height of Appalachia's prosperity; instead, he opened a saloon on the Keystone side. Others followed his example, and Appalachia was soon abandoned.

Keystone is at the junction with State 51 (*see Tour 2A*). US 64 crosses the Cimarron River at 20.1 *m.*, then veers northwest through heavily wooded hills for the next seventeen miles. Just beyond the Cimarron bridge, and off to the right near the Arkansas River, is BEARS GLEN, the October 15, 1832, camp site of the Washington Irving party (*see Tour 2A*). It, too, will be flooded eventually by the Keystone Dam. But today the rocky, wooded ravine appears much as it was described in *A Tour on the Prairies*.

CLEVELAND, 36.9 *m.* (740 alt., 2,464 pop.), named for President Cleveland, was established by a townsite company shortly after the opening of the Cherokee Outlet in 1893. The Osage reservation was near by, and "going to town" for the Osages meant going to Cleveland, whose muddy streets were usually lined with their ponies. For some time the bridge across the Arkansas River at Cleveland was the only crossing between the one at Tulsa to the east and the Kansas Line to the northwest. During this period Cleveland gained the title of "Gate City."

Oil fields in the vicinity have produced large quantities of crude oil for many years and two refineries are in operation here, although Cleveland has never had the typical boom town appearance. A 200-acre lake supplies water to the town, and provides fishing and other recreational facilities. There are also two parks and a municipal swimming pool.

In Cleveland is the junction with State 99 (*see Tour 14*), which unites westward with US 64 for six miles.

At 45.6 *m.* is a junction with a graveled road.

Right on this road is BLACKBURN, 6.1 *m.* (798 alt., 135 pop.), where the annual reunion of the Drought Survivors of 1901 is held on the second Sunday in June. In that year, hundreds of people abandoned their farms and homesteads here. Those who stayed banded together into an association, and the group—about two hundred still meets for a reminiscent get-together.

Left from Blackburn, 5 *m.*, on a dirt road, is SKEDEE (833 alt., 170 pop.), named for the Skidi division of the Pawnee tribe, and once known as the Crystal Creek Campgrounds. It was the home until he died of Colonel E. Waters, an auctioneer who participated in many of the fabulous oil deals during the days when million-dollar lease sales in Osage County (*see Tour 4*) were not uncommon. Much of his collection of Indian curios can now be seen at the Mason Hotel in Claremore (*see Tour 1*).

PAWNEE, 57.9 *m.* (822 alt., 2,861 pop.), originally a trading post, was made the site of the Pawnee Agency in 1876, when that tribe was removed from its home in Nebraska to new lands in Oklahoma. In

1893, when the Pawnees accepted allotments, the residue of their land was opened for settlement, and the present-day town began to develop. Scenes of pioneer and Indian life are carved on the limestone panel above the main entrance of the PAWNEE COUNTY COURTHOUSE.

The blanketed Indian, of course, is no longer a common sight anywhere in Oklahoma, but Pawnee still retains much of the flavor of its early days. This is especially true if one visits the PAWNEE AGENCY (school and hospital) on the east edge of town, with its massive stone buildings set in a grove of fine old trees. It was from this center that General George A. Custer recruited Indian scouts to aid him in his campaign against the wild Plains tribes (*see Tour 3A*), and gave rise to one of those curious tales so characteristic of Indian history. A group of these scouts was sent north to Wyoming by Captain Luther North on June 10, 1876. But a few of the men who had been on a hunting party were delayed and had to set out later. It was these who returned to the agency within a few days, explaining that smoke signals had told them Custer was dead. Ten days later the Pawnee agent received official word of Custer's death in the Battle of the Little Big Horn.

Though Pawnee is now a modern ranching center with its eye fixed firmly on the present, the town does turn the clock back officially each year during the second week in July. The occasion is one of the country's largest *free* Indian powwows. And at this time the visitor can see hundreds of Plains Indians from all over Oklahoma, many of them dressed in their tribal costumes and living in the tipis and grass huts of their ancestors.

Started in 1946, when some of the older Indians decided to honor and welcome home their sons and daughters who had served in World War II, the "Pawnee Pow Wow" has been continued and expanded. The celebration is unique in that it is planned, sponsored, and promoted by Indians, and for Indians. The white man is merely invited to come and look on. (Visitors from twenty-one foreign countries and thirty-five different states were registered recently for a single performance.) Stick ball and other traditional Indian games are played during the day. At night, on the lighted football field, there are tribal costume dances, along with performances of the buffalo, snake, and other special dances.

On BLUE HAWK PEAK, just southwest of Pawnee, stands the rambling brick home of Major Gordon W. Lillie—better known as Pawnee Bill—Indian interpreter, frontiersman, scout, and originator of Pawnee Bill's Wild West Circus, with which he toured widely for a number of years. Born in Illinois in 1860, Lillie came to Indian Territory in 1882 and joined a cattle outfit in the Cherokee Outlet. He was an instructor for a time in the government school at the Pawnee Agency. And he was also a leader among the Boomers, the group of whites who attempted to settle in Indian Territory before the area was officially opened. Pawnee Bill's circus ventures took him abroad to the World's Fair at Antwerp, Belgium, in 1894; on a successful tour of America; and once joined him in partnership with Buffalo Bill (W. F. Cody) in a show called "The Two Bills." The estate is now a fine cattle ranch operated by his sister, Mrs. Albert Judy. But many of the old showman's memorabilia—along with Indian relics and handicrafts—are on display in PAWNEE BILL'S TRADING POST near the southeast corner of the square.

Another colorful character of whom Pawnee can boast is Dick Tracy, whose creator, Chester Gould, was born and educated in Pawnee.

Right from Pawnee on paved State 18 to LAKE PAWNEE (*swimming, boating, water skiing*), 1 *m.*, which covers 305 acres. Five hundred acres around the lake have been developed by the town into a park and recreation center that offers picnic facilities, trap shooting, and a nine-hole golf course.

At 73.6 *m.* is the junction with State 40. Left here to Stillwater and Lake Carl Blackwell (*see Tour 2A*).

PERRY, 85.7 *m.* (1,005 alt., 5,137 pop.), seat of Noble County, is a center for both agriculture and extensive oil field development. Its most colorful event is the annual Cherokee Strip celebration. On the morning of September 16, 1893, the first of the Santa Fe special trains entered the Cherokee Strip, loaded with eager, shouting land-seekers. The first stop was at a station named Wharton, one mile south of the present Perry station. Clambering off, the passengers rushed into the already platted townsite, designated a land-office town by the Department of Interior and named for a member of the Federal Townsite Commission. They drove their stakes into the ground, and the mushroom town of tents and clapboards was born.

Sooner Land (1929), by George Washington Ogden, a native of Kansas, gives a colorful description of the early days of Perry. It tells of the large number of Sooners, the fourteen saloons, the many gamblers, and their hangers-on which caused the federal government to send in three marshals, including the famed Bill Tilghman, until a city government could be organized. Today a modern courthouse, post office, and CARNEGIE LIBRARY stand in the tree-shaded square, and the rip-roaring early days—except on September 16—are nearly forgotten.

Two well-known Perry enterprises welcome visitors. Along US 64 (L) at the southwestern edge of town is the home of TAMAC pottery. Farther southwest is the PERRY CARLILE PONY FARM, scene of an annual five-day Shetland pony sale (usually in late July), which sees buyers from all parts of the country pay close to a half million dollars for as many as 1,500 animals. Record price for a recently sold pony was $12,000. Perry is at the junction with US 77 (*see Tour 10*), which unites westward with US 64 for 5.6 miles.

COVINGTON, 103.9 *m.* (1,141 alt., 769 pop.), was named for John Covington, an early settler. Having no sons and wishing to perpetuate his name, he persuaded Arkansas Valley & Western Railroad officials to grant him this honor when they located their station here.

West of Covington, wheat fields line the highway and the towers of more than a half-dozen giant grain elevators in and around Enid shimmer in the distance. This section is one of the state's most productive wheat-raising regions. But oil development, which followed the drilling of the Hoy Well in 1916, is still extensive from Covington to Garber.

At 110.1 *m.* is the junction with paved State 15.

Straight ahead (north) on this road is GARBER, 3 *m.* (1,148 alt., 957 pop.). Like Perry, the town stages an annual Cherokee Outlet celebration on September 16, at which time whiskers and the "sunbonnet" fashions of the pioneers are likely to make their once-a-year appearance. In 1955 an annual pre-Easter Biblethon was started in one of the local churches. The cover-to-cover reading aloud of the complete Bible begins Wednesday evening and more than one hundred volunteer readers take turns in the pulpit.

ENID, 126.3 *m.* (1,246 alt., 36,017 pop.) (*see Enid*), is at the southern junction with US 60 (*see Tour 4*) and US 81 (*see Tour 11*).

Section c. ENID *to* NEW MEXICO LINE, *337.1 m.* US 64

Between Enid and the New Mexico Line, US 64 passes through an agricultural section in which the leading crops are small grains and forage. The land, especially in the far western Panhandle, is high and arid. Towns are far apart, comparatively small, and almost invariably marked by a towering concrete grain elevator.

North of Enid, 0 *m.*, US 60 and US 81 unite with US 64 to 18.7 *m.*, where the route turns sharply west.

At 33.7 *m.* is the junction with an improved dirt road.

Right at this point on a series of improved roads—R. at 1 *m.*; L. at 2 *m.*; and L again at 6 *m.*—to the GREAT SALT PLAINS DAM, 6.5 *m.*, a $2,000,000 structure completed in 1941. The dam is a 5,700-foot earth embankment with a concrete spillway 310 feet wide. The height of the dam is 72 feet above the bed of the stream. The reservoir, created for flood control and conservation, has a normal surface area of 9,300 acres. Completely filled, the lake would extend ten miles up the Salt Fork of the Arkansas River, with a maximum width of twelve miles. Most of the 19,453-acre area of the reservoir is included in the Great Salt Plains National Wildlife Refuge. It is the largest lake in the Western Plains region and the state's most famous hunting area for wild geese and ducks. During the summer months an average of 15,000 visitors a week come to picnic, camp (cabins are available), and fish (striped sea bass were recently dropped into the brackish waters by airplane). Boating facilities attract thousands, and there is a sandy beach for swimming and sunning enthusiasts.

Geologists hold conflicting theories as to the formation of the Great Salt Plains. One explanation, now judged implausible, is that the area was once covered by a great prehistoric sea which has evaporated, leaving the salt bed. Another, advanced by a University of Oklahoma geologist, is that the Plains were the result of consistent weathering of a soil that does not support enough vegetation to prevent erosion. The soluble salt, laid down in geologic formation fifty million years ago, "sweated up" out of the ground or crystallized about salt springs fed by water that flowed through salt beds not far from the surface. Around the edges of the reservoir the salt forms a thin, wafer-like crust on the flat surface. When it rains, this salt crust dissolves and the clay and sand beneath the surface become extremely unstable. Although quite barren, the plains support four forms of life—two birds (the least tern and the snowy plover) and two insects (the tiger beetle and the sea blite). Climatic conditions in the region are the most extreme outside a desert. Spring rains are followed by hot and dry months when 114° F. is not uncommon. Winter often brings blizzards that force the temperature well below zero. Salt springs, feeding the Salt Fork (which winds along the north and east edges of the Salt Plains area), flow thousands of gallons of brine daily.

According to available records, the first white men to see the Plains were those in the party of Major George C. Sibley, Indian agent from Fort Osage, Missouri. In 1811, Sans Oreille, an Osage Indian, with others of his tribe, guided them to the spot, which Sibley called the Grand Saline. The Salt Fork of the Arkansas River, flowing around the plain, was known to the Osages as *Nescatunga* (big salt water). Another early explorer to see the Great Salt Plains was Captain Nathan Boone, son of Daniel Boone, who headed a government expedition from Fort Gibson into what is now central Kansas in 1843. Boone described the phenomenon as a "lake of white water."

In drafting the treaty which made the territory the so-called permanent home of the Cherokees in 1828, the United States government withheld the Salt Plains area with the provision that, "The right is reserved to the United States to allow other tribes of red men to get salt on the Great Salt Plains in common with the Cherokee Tribe." Possession of the Plains had probably been the cause of many Indian battles, since its value lay not in its salt alone but in the rich hunting afforded by the animals migrating here for the salt supply. The Great Salt Plains have thus been the scene of many Indian councils both of war and peace. A war council of Plains Indians was called to meet here in 1845 to plan concerted opposition to immigrant Creek Indians, whose reservation lay farther to the east. Creek diplomacy and emotional appeal resulted in peace and, thereafter, the councils held on this spot were usually of a peaceful nature. In the early 1940's the barren plains provided an ideal target for practicing bomber crews in World War II.

The commercial value of the salt was highest during the earliest days of the settlement of the Indian Territory, when transportation to this wild country was difficult. Western Kansas and Texas cattlemen often sent wagons here to haul away great loads, and near-by farmers used the salt for livestock.

CHEROKEE, 51.8 *m.* (1,181 alt., 2,635 pop.), thrives on the fertile farm lands that surround it. Wheat, alfalfa, poultry, and livestock are the leading farm income sources, and milling is an important industry. Cherokee is also the seat of Alfalfa County, which ranks twentieth among all counties in the United States in wheat production.

Mrs. Walter (Lucia Loomis) Ferguson, whose daily syndicated column, "A Woman's Viewpoint," appears in many newspapers, formerly lived here. With her husband, Walter Ferguson (d. 1937), former state legislator and son of the sixth Territorial governor, Thompson B. Ferguson, she published the *Cherokee Republican.*

Right on Fifth Street in Cherokee four miles to the west edge of the Great Salt Plains. An Observation Tower affords an excellent view of the desolate flats.

At 54.9 *m.* is the junction with State 58 and State 11.

Straight ahead (north) on State 58 to a junction with graded County Highway 15, at 4.5 *m.*; R. here to the DRUMM MONUMENT, 7.7 *m.*, marking the site of the old 150,000-acre U Ranch, which Major Andrew Drumm (1828–1919) established in 1874. One of the first cattlemen to turn his herds to graze on the rich native grass of the Cherokee Outlet, he was also the first president of the Cherokee Strip Livestock Association. The U Ranch, along with the 6,000,000-acre Cherokee Outlet, was opened to settlement in 1893.

Right (east) from this same junction on State 11 to the Byron STATE FISH HATCHERY, 12.2 *m.* The plant was established in 1929 on an eighty-acre tract (L). Artesian wells provide water for the twenty-five culture ponds at an average temperature of 60° F.

At 71.8 *m.* is NORTHWESTERN STATE COLLEGE (L), founded in 1897, the state's second oldest normal school. The first building, constructed in 1898 at a cost of $110,000, was underwritten by the citizens of Alva, then a town only a few years old. Called "The Castle on the Hill," the building was destroyed by fire in 1935, along with its 60,000-volume library. Since then the Carter, Jesse Dunn, and Herod Halls have been built, as well as fine arts and industrial arts buildings, and a student center. Both a scientific and a historical museum are open to visitors.

In the rare books collection of the library is a small brown leather book of forty pages containing signs and symbols indicating cattle identification brands registered with the Cherokee Strip Livestock Association for the roundup of 1886. The book shows approximately six hundred listings for three hundred ranches. Two methods of branding were used: one, a running brand of letters, figures, or symbols applied with a red-hot, poker-like iron; the other, a set brand burned in with an iron shaped in the trade mark of the rancher. Among the better known brands are the Bar-M, Lazy-B, Turkey Track, Ox-Yoke, and Mule-Shoe.

Right from Northwestern State College, on College Avenue, is the business district of ALVA, (1,351 alt., 6,505 pop.), the seat of Woods County. Alva was designated as one of the four land-office towns at the time of the opening of the Cherokee Outlet (1893). Originally a Santa Fe Railway stop, it was named for Alva B. Adams, attorney for the railroad and later governor of Colorado. The clean, progressive town, built around the courthouse square, is a business and cultural center for a large farming and ranching area.

Left from the college on US 281 to HOPETON, 7 *m.*, a village with a population of 75, and a bank with deposits totaling almost $1,000,000. US 281 continues to WAYNOKA, 25.8 *m.* (1,475 alt., 2,018 pop.), a main division point on the Santa Fe, which operates extensive railway maintenance and repair shops here, as well as the state's largest ice plant. (Two mechanical rail-car icers can handle sixty-six refrigerator cars on each of two tracks at the same time.) Twenty-seven-acre Santa Fe Park has a swimming pool, playground, and picnic and sports facilities.

Waynoka has grown from a rail siding known as Keystone, which was established in 1886. Platted in 1893, the present town was named Waynoka by a sub-chief of the Cheyennes, Man-on-Cloud. The Indian word, *Winneoka,* means good water. Like Okeene (*see Tour 5*), Waynoka has capitalized on a "surplus commodity" most communities would ignore. This abundant local product is the dangerous diamondback rattler, and the annual Waynoka Snake Hunt (*early April*) brings in crowds of up to ten thousand hunters who often capture or kill as many as one thousand rattlesnakes.

South and west of Waynoka erosion has taken its toll. Sand dunes, evidence of centuries of shifting of the course of the Cimarron River, extend to the river bed, some six miles south of Waynoka. Some of the dunes are more than one hundred yards wide, with steep slopes of from twenty to fifty feet. In its slow movement, the sand covers all vegetation, even large trees. Near the river, where the sediment has been washed or blown away, roots of trees that sprouted from trunks while they were imbedded in sand are often seen a yard or more above ground. The tops of telephone poles, showing from two to fifteen feet above the dunes, indicate an old line built along a road running here before the present US 281 was surveyed.

Dull Knife, Northern Cheyenne chieftain, camped south of the Cimarron River in 1878 with a small band of followers while fleeing Oklahoma to their former home on the northern plains. After the Custer massacre (*see Tour 13*), when the resistance of the northern Indians had been broken, Dull Knife and his band were brought to the Cheyenne reservation near El Reno, where they were promised subsistence. Later, suffering from homesickness and illness, the group pleaded to be allowed to return to Dakota. When their request was denied, the band of 89 warriors and 246 women and children, led by Dull Knife, set out in flight for the north. A skirmish with federal troops sixty miles from the reservation resulted in the death of three soldiers. Along the way, several settlers and cowboys were killed, houses were burned, and supplies were confiscated by the desperate Indians. News of the march spread to military outposts and, at one time, some twenty-four companies of cavalry and infantry were pursuing the fleeing Indians. Another engagement with troops near Fort Dodge, Kansas, turned into a rout for the soldiers.

Finally, near Fort Robinson, Nebraska, Dull Knife and his group were captured and held during the winter. Once again they broke away and started northward, with the military in pursuit. Dull Knife met defeat finally in Dakota when, surrounded in a snowbound canyon, he and his remaining followers were forced to surrender. But his epic march has been described as a masterly feat of military strategy.

At 97.5 *m.*, on US 64 again, is a junction with State 50, a partially paved road.

Left on State 50 to FREEDOM, 3.1 *m.* (1,521 alt., 232 pop.), center of a broad wheat and cattle raising area. Here on the school grounds stands an impressive tribute to "The Cimarron Cowboy," a 9,000-pound granite monument commemorating the colorful and exciting early-day history of northwest Oklahoma. A huge two-side affair—ten feet long, four feet high, and fourteen inches thick—the monument was dedicated April 14, 1950, by the Cimarron Cowboys Association. One side is devoted to the period from 1883 to 1890, and the big ranch spreads operating in the area are located on a large center map. The mural around the base shows the first herds coming, the arrival of the Santa Fe Railway in 1886, and the terrible blizzard of the same year. The other side of the monument brings the history up to date from the opening of the Cherokee Outlet in 1893. A chuck wagon in the center is flanked by names of cowhands and brands of the old spreads. The base mural shows a present-day rodeo, the only sport which had its beginning in an industry.

Northwest of Freedom lies the LITTLE SALT PLAIN, also called the Edith Salt Plain, after the settlement lying between the Plain and the Cimarron River. This Plain, three miles wide and extending for twelve miles along the river, is smaller than the saline deposit at Cherokee, but still more barren. Only in a faintly salt tributary to the east have two microscopic forms of ocean life been discovered. Ninety-seven per cent pure, it is widely sold to ranchers in the area as a stock salt.

State 50 crosses the Cimarron River to a junction with a gravel road, 6.2 *m.*; L. here to the main entrance of rugged CEDAR CANYON PARK. The approach is through prairie country, but the park lies in a deep valley between the rough, red-clay walls of a canyon. A spring-fed stream tumbles through the wooded gorge. Knives, arrowheads, and primitive tools of volcanic rock have been found in the region, indicating that it was one of the early-day camping grounds of the Indians.

Just outside the entrance to the park stands a CLUBHOUSE. Near by is the (so-called) EXTINCT GEYSER FIELD, where great holes, lined with solid rock, are pitted with pockets probably formed by water percolating to, and dissolving, the gypsum. Geologists believe, however, that these were formed by movement of the deposits of salt and gypsum in the underlying beds. Across a small canyon is a Natural Bridge, perched at an elevation of nearly nineteen hundred feet above sea level and 150 feet above the canyon floor. The perfect arch, forty feet wide and thirty feet high, carved by ancient rushing waters through a barrier of solid gypsum, gives a splendid view of Cedar Canyon's wonders.

About one hundred yards northeast of the clubhouse is the entrance to the ALABASTER CAVERNS STATE PARK (*adm.* $1.25). Inside the entrance, a vestibule, lined with great slabs and masses of stone blasted from the ceiling, is the starting point for a fascinating hour-long trip through the caverns. Often the roar of subterranean waters is heard. The visitor ascends gradually to the upper reaches and emerges at last on a plateau, where there is a panoramic view of the park and the Cimarron River country.

Millions of bats live in the caves, and between sunset and dusk in summer they pour out in a great funnel-shaped black cloud. From the first frost, usually in October, until the warm days of March the bats remain hanging to the walls of the caverns without sustenance, waking to squeak in protest only if plucked from their perch. The brown-coated, flat-headed mammal is of the *Tadaria vulgaris* or common Guano variety.

Large translucent crystals sparkle from the roof of the Milling Chamber, their beauty enhanced by colored electric lights. A corridor (R) leads to the crystal-decked Aladdin Chamber, in which is a tiny lake of clear spring water. In the Encampment Room, once used by Indians as a meeting place, have been found many arrowheads, lance points, ornaments, and pieces of pottery.

Other features of the caverns are Gun Barrel Tunnel, a round passageway hollowed out by a stream of water through the rock; Pulpit Hall, a room decorated with tiny stalactites; the Bathtub, a concavity in a ledge of solid rock into which a thin stream of water falls from a hole in the ceiling; and the White Way, a section of the passage lined with fantastic formations of alabaster, carved by water action. Cavities resembling geyser vents are lighted by electricity, bringing out the delicate tracings and scroll work. Blind Fish Cavern is so called because crayfish, washed into the water through the vents and fissures above, become transparent after many generations, and many have a growth of skin covering their eye sockets.

Back on US 64, the state historical marker (L) at 98.3 *m.* notes the camp site of Captain Nathan Boone. In the summer of 1843 this son of Daniel Boone led an army exploratory expedition onto the western prairies. On its way from Fort Gibson to Kansas the party camped just south of the Cimarron River on Trader Creek (3.4 miles southwest) on July 2, 1843.

From here on west to the Cimarron River Bridge, 110.4 *m.*, the motorist will be struck by the beauty of the scene to his left, the deep magenta of the bluffs on the river's south bank contrasting sharply with the white salt flats at their base. From a distance the effect is that of a great flood of water lapping at a giant retaining wall. The Cimarron itself is almost a mile wide in places and bordered by extensive sand dunes.

At 127.4 *m.* is a junction with US 183 (*see Tour 12*), which unites southward 1.9 miles with US 64.

West of BUFFALO, 129.0 *m.* (1,791 alt., 1,544 pop.) (*see Tour 12*), the rolling plains are dotted with clumps of sagebrush and cactus. Small gullies and ravines break the smooth fields, exposing the red clay, which contrasts sharply with the green and gray of the grass.

At 137.5 *m.* is a junction with an improved dirt road.

Right on this road to intersection, 1.2 *m.*; L. to 1.7 *m.*; then L. again to DOBY SPRINGS, 2.4 *m.*, named for an early settler, Chris Dobie, who staked his claim on the site during the run for the Cherokee Outlet lands. The town of Buffalo

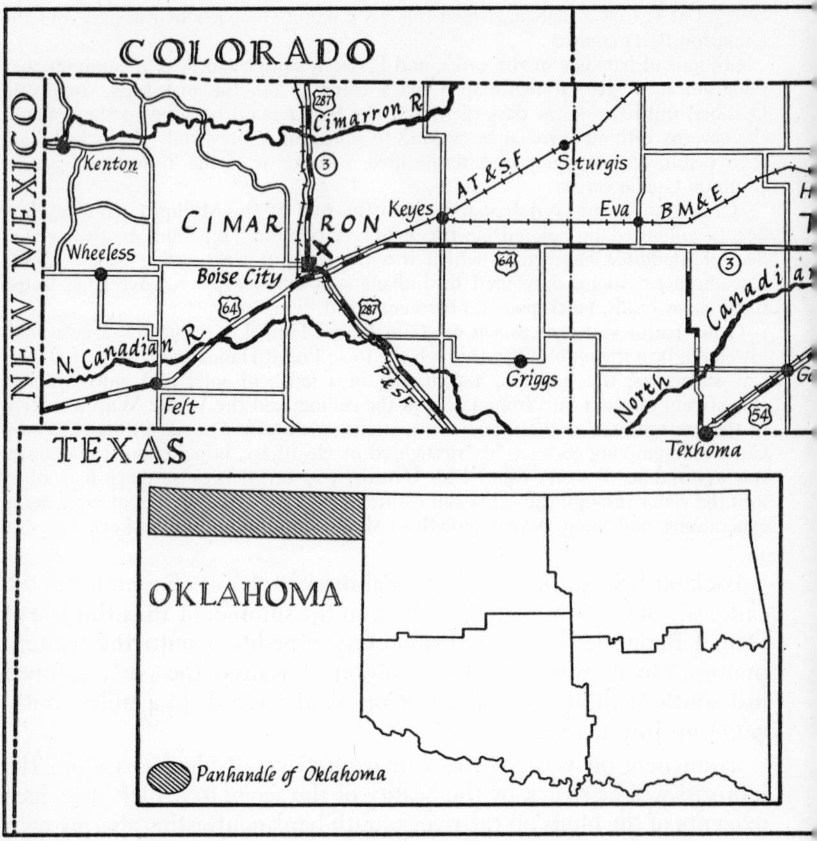

acquired the site several years ago, naming it Doby Springs Park. Some of the artesian springs provide the town's water supply. Others have been dammed to create a small lake which is stocked with fish. Prior to 1874, when buffaloes were common, this was a favorite watering place for many herds.

At 144.2 *m.* is the junction with US 283 (*see Tour 13*), which is united westward with US 64 for 4.2 miles.

GATE, 154.1 *m.* (2,230 alt., 197 pop.), lies on the western slope of a basin, which perhaps held an ancient lake. Northeast of Gate, extensive deposits of silica (Pearlette ash), nine feet deep in places, support the theory that a volcano was once active in this area (probably in the Mt. Capulin region in New Mexico). Approximately one hundred carloads of the mineral are shipped yearly.

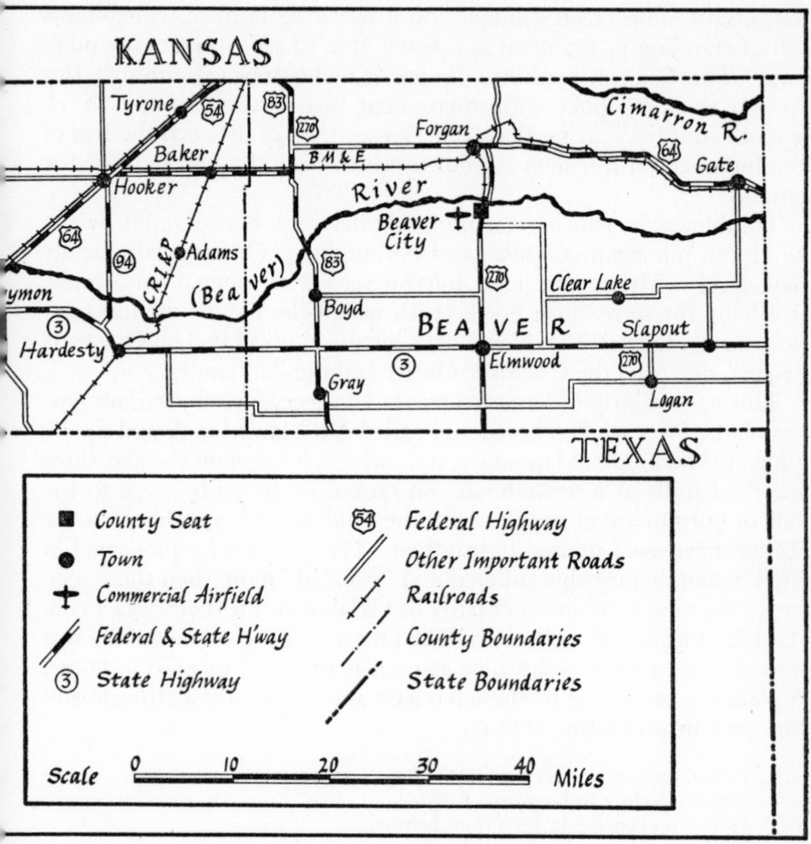

North of Gate is Horse Creek, where what might have been an ancient irrigation canal—about twenty-five feet wide and five feet deep—runs parallel with the stream. The ditch ends abruptly without an outlet, the method of irrigation evidently having been to allow the canal to fill and overflow the adjacent cultivated fields. Some authorities believe that the system was built by prehistoric peoples.

US 64 traverses the Panhandle strip where the land is fertile, but crops are at the mercy of the elements. Wheat, broomcorn, and forage yields are large when drought and winds temper their fury. Many of the acres, particularly the broad plateaus with their terraced canyons, are used as grazing land for cattle. The familiar "short grass" carpets the level tablelands. Between Guymon and the western border, the flat, even terrain creates mirages on a wavering horizon. Inhabitants tell of standing in the open and being able to see towns many miles away. The Spanish explorer, Coronado, who traveled through this section in 1541, spoke with amazement in his report of the "level, smooth country," saying that "one can see the sky between the legs of the buffalo, and if a man lay down on his back, he lost sight of the ground."

Tumbleweeds, which grow profusely here, are blown about by the wind and pile against houses and outbuildings. On especially windy days, sand swirls over the fields, burying seeds and young plants deeply, justifying the term "dust bowl," with which the Panhandle has been periodically tagged. *Tumbleweeds*, a historical novel by Hal G. Evarts (1923), describes the Cherokee Outlet and the Panhandle.

This narrow strip of land was possessed successively by various governments, for a while ignored and called No Man's Land, and finally added to Oklahoma. Maps of the state which, for economy's sake, show the Panhandle as a separate section tacked on in waste space to the side or bottom are unpopular with the residents. Many schools in the section have even refused to use them. The people who pioneered in the Panhandle probably suffered and "sweated" more than those who broke the virgin sod in other parts of Oklahoma, for theirs was a constant fight against the elements. The progress of the whole section was measured by inches of advance as each man toiled to make a home. A plaintive verse sung by these pioneers shows both their struggle and the spirit in which they met it:

> Pickin' up bones to keep from starving,
> Pickin' up chips to keep from freezing,
> Pickin' up courage to keep from leaving,
> Way out West in No Man's Land.

The "bones" and "chips" referred to are relics of the buffalo.

At 181.6 *m.* is the junction with paved US 270 (*see Tour 5*), with which it joins for the next 20 miles. A MONUMENT TO CORONADO (L), a three-ton granite boulder, has been erected here by the Colonial Dames of America.

FORGAN, 182.8 *m.* (2,565 alt., 410 pop.), which looms up on the clear, unbroken prairie from miles away, is a center for the scattered farms and ranches lying between the Cimarron and the North Canadian rivers. The town was named for James B. Forgan, a Chicago banker who helped finance the Wichita Falls & Northwestern Railway (now operated by the Missouri-Kansas-Texas), the first railroad to enter Beaver County (*see Tour 5*). The townsite was laid out and promoted by the rail company.

TURPIN, 204.6 *m.*, BAKERSBURG, 213.6 *m.*, and HOOKER, 223.2 *m.* (2,984 alt., 1,842 pop.), are farm communities surrounded by miles of level wheat fields and isolated houses. But Hooker has almost doubled its population in the past decade and a half, thanks to the tremendous wealth that lies underneath those wheat fields. For the Hugoton Gas Field—which begins seven miles to the east of Hooker and extends west for approximately fifty miles—is probably the largest single gas field in the world, with reserves running into the trillions of cubic feet. In Hooker is the junction with US 54, which is united southwestward with US 64 for 19.3 miles.

At 226.4 *m.* is the sprawling DORCHESTER CORPORATION gasoline plant (R).

At 230.4 *m.* is the OLD BUFFALO historical marker (L), the only physical sign that remains of one of the first towns in No Man's Land, organized as the "Seventh County" of Oklahoma Territory in May, 1890. The Buffalo post office itself was established March 18, 1888.

OPTIMA, 234.5 *m.* (3,090 alt., 97 pop.), is the site of a prehistoric village representing an ancient culture about which little is known. Within the vicinity are the privately owned ruins of at least six slab-lined pit houses. Considerable study has been given to the largest of these by the department of anthropology of the University of Oklahoma, and a large collection of fossil bones is in the university's Stovall Museum (*see Norman*).

GUYMON, 242.6 *m.* (3,125 alt., 4,718 pop.), on a flat plain in the approximate center of the Panhandle, is the seat of Texas County. It is also northwest Oklahoma's largest and fastest growing city, booming on the strength of its seemingly unlimited underground wealth. Gas and oil are responsible for nearly a dozen industrial installations in the area, including compressor stations, extracting plants, and transmission plants. (In 1956 Texas County alone had approximately 1,400 gas wells in production.) And deep-well irrigation is now supplementing the area's always scanty and unpredictable rainfall on nearly 50,000 acres of farm land. (The county's total acreage under irrigation is second only to that of Jackson County in southwestern Oklahoma.)

Guymon's most colorful annual event is its Pioneer Day celebration, held the first weekend in May, the anniversary of the passage of the Organic Act of 1890, which made the Panhandle a part of the Territory of Oklahoma. Pioneers from the entire region, and many from Kansas and Texas, gather for the chuck-wagon breakfast, parade, street entertainment, and rodeo. City Section is a park area that includes a lake, nine-hole golf course, game refuge, and recreational facilities.

Left from Guymon on paved US 54 is GOODWELL, 11 *m.* (3,218 alt., 714 pop.), home of the Panhandle Agricultural and Mechanical College, established as an agricultural school in 1909. By 1925 full four-year college work was being offered and today the physical plant includes nine major buildings and five dormitories, plus extensive recreational facilities.

The college owns 2,275 acres of land, of which 500 acres are under irrigation. A United States Department of Agriculture experiment station in connection with the college seeks improved techniques to cope with the problems of dry-land and irrigation farming. Of particular interest to the visitor is the No Man's Land Museum (*free*), which was opened in 1951 to exhibit data and collections relating to the history of the Panhandle from pre-Coronado days down to the present.

TEXHOMA, 21 *m.* (3,486 alt., 1,761 pop., including 297 Texas residents), with a 153 per cent increase in population from 1940 to 1950, claims to have been Oklahoma's fastest growing town in that decade. With the sale of 96,421 head of cattle in one year (1954) it also claims to have the state's largest weekly livestock auction. Ranching, increased well-water irrigation, and expanding oil and gas production in the area all contribute to the town's prosperity.

Westward from Guymon the tops of towering grain elevators to the right trace the hesitant course of the Panhandle's single east-west railroad, a line which improved highways have pretty much relegated to the once-a-year chore of hauling out the area's June wheat harvest. At 277.1 *m.* US 64 leaves Texas County and enters Cimarron, the only county in the United States that is bordered by four states other than its own—Kansas, Colorado, New Mexico, and Texas.

The approach to BOISE CITY, 304.6 *m.* (4,164 alt., 1,902 pop.), Oklahoma's westernmost town of appreciable size, is marked by the sudden appearance of the two-story, red-brick Cimarron County Courthouse, looming up out of the plains in the center of the road. As the highway loops around the courthouse square, paved side roads lead off to the county's principal scenic and historical attractions.

On the north side of the square, paved US 283 turns right.

Right (north) on US 283 to the intersection with the old SANTA FE TRAIL, 8.7 *m.* Hardy early-day pioneers broke the trail to connect Santa Fe, New Mexico, with Independence, Missouri, the starting point for overland travel to the West.

Impatient at its length, Captain William Becknell set out in 1822 to find a short cut, accompanied by thirty men and a caravan of mules, horses, and "prairie schooners" loaded with merchandise. He was warned of the danger of the Cimarron desert—the stretch between the Arkansas River in southwestern Kansas and the Cimarron River in Oklahoma—which was waterless except in the rainy season, when the shallow creek beds carried their temporary burden to one of the two wide, sandy channels. The party's water supply became exhausted soon after leaving the Arkansas. The men and animals were slowly dying of thirst when Becknell shot a buffalo and on cutting into its stomach found about three gallons of fresh water, indication that the animal had drunk recently. After an hour's ride, the caravan reached the Cimarron, filled their water kegs, and returned to the Arkansas River and the regular route. However, other travelers and wagon trains soon began using the short cut.

The government surveyed the Santa Fe Trail and found that by 1860—the peak year of traffic over it—three thousand wagons, seven thousand men, and sixty thousand mules were using the route annually. Heavy traffic continued until after the Civil War.

Ruts made by wagons, driven three abreast as a defense against possible surprise attack by Indians, are still visible along portions of the old Trail. Near Fort Nichols, three paths—ten feet in depth and twenty feet wide—run side by side, cut by the passage of thousands of heavily laden wagons. In 1875, upon completion of the Santa Fe Railway line through Kansas and Colorado, partially paralleling the trail, use of the route was discontinued. The old Trail is described in *Commerce of the Prairies* (1844), by Josiah Gregg.

On US 64 to the west side of courthouse square, in Boise City, an unmarked paved road leads to the right. This is the former US 64.

Westward (right) on this side road the level Panhandle begins to give way to a more rugged terrain characteristic of New Mexico. At 15.1 *m.* is a junction with a paved section-line road.

Left on this road to a junction with a second paved road, 1 *m.*; R. here through WHEELESS POST OFFICE, 6 *m.*, an isolated postal station serving the few residents of the surrounding area, to a junction with a paved road, 8 *m.*; R. here (only partly paved) to the SITE OF FORT NICHOLS, 10.2 *m.*, established by Kit Carson in 1865, by orders of the War Department. Carson was directed to locate the fort in New Mexico near the 103d meridian as a protection for the users of the Santa Fe Trail. Instead, he selected a site (L) on a high knoll, on the banks of Carrizzo Creek, about four miles east of the present Oklahoma–New Mexico boundary. Rocks for the walls and barracks were brought from the creek bed; the stone floor of the barracks building and of the headquarters building are still visible. Part of the rampart wall is also standing, although farmers have carried away many of the smoothed stones for their own use. A pile of rocks outside the eastern wall identifies the sentry tower which commanded a wide sweep of the plains and of the Santa Fe Trail.

At 26.4 *m.* on the main side road is a junction with an improved dirt road.

Right on this road to HALLOCK PARK, 8.1 *m.*, consisting of ten thousand acres of canyons and mesas, part of which has been developed for recreation purposes. Of the 120 springs which gush forth here, several are the source of streams, affording abundant water for the camp sites. Along the face of a sandstone bluff (six feet high and more than a quarter of a mile long), facing northeast, is a series of PICTOGRAPHS, startling in their color contrast of blue paint against the sandy rock. In crude fashion they depict Indians at their various daily activities. There are also many figures of animals. Deer, bears, antelope, coyotes, and beavers can easily be discerned.

At 27.3 *m.* again on the main side road, is a DINOSAUR QUARRY (R), burial ground of many mighty monsters who roamed the earth during the Jurassic age, more than ten million years ago. Erosion uncovered the spot sufficiently so that workers have been able to remove many fossils intact. Many of these have been shipped to the University of Oklahoma (*see Norman*), where they are reconstructed into skeletons for classwork and display. It constitutes one of the most complete dinosaur collections in the United States. (Altogether, the quarry yielded 6,000 bones weighing more than eighteen tons.) Four types of the prehistoric animals have been excavated, of which the *Brontosaurus*—measuring seventy feet in length and about sixteen feet in height and weighing some thirty-six tons when alive—is the largest. This species, together with the *Stegosaurus*, almost its equal in size, and a giant lizard of the order *Ornithopoda*, were herbivorous. The *Allosaurus*—the fourth type uncovered—was a flesh-eater. Surmounting the entrance to the quarry is a concrete cast of the six-foot long femur (upper thigh bone) of a Brontosaurus.

The SPHINX OR OLD MAID ROCK, 28.3 *m.*, 200 yards (R), is a curious formation, carved by the elements from the point of a sandstone bluff. A magnificent figure, it stands out boldly against the blue sky above the mesa in the background.

At 30.7 *m.* is a junction with an unimproved dirt road.

Right on this road is the NATURAL ARCH, 3.7 *m.*, in the bottom of a wide canyon north of the Cimarron River. The opening of this white sandstone arch—twenty feet high and eight feet wide—was probably formed by the constant battering of wind-blown sand. There are no other rocks or ledges of similar color or composition within a radius of eight miles. From here the tour returns again to the main side road.

KENTON, 36.1 *m.* (4,349 alt., 250 pop.), nestles in a high valley under the shadow of lava-capped Black Mesa to the northwest. Before statehood, Kenton was a roistering saloon town known as the Cowboy Capital. It was platted and laid out as a townsite in 1892 by a nephew of P. T. Barnum. The name, Kenton, is a variation of Canton (Ohio), for which this settlement was named.

Right from Kenton on an improved dirt road to a junction with a second dirt road 2 *m.*; L. here to BLACK MESA, 3.9 *m.*, a plateau capped by a lava deposit from an extinct volcano. This lava cap, underlain by Dakota sandstone, ranges from twenty to seventy feet in thickness and extends some four miles into Oklahoma from the New Mexico Line. In the center of the mesa is the highest point in Oklahoma, 4,978 feet above sea level, designated by a marker of lava fragments and concrete, and topped with a piece of rose-colored granite from the quarry at Granite (*see Tour 13*). The summit of this almost mile-high plateau was formerly a camping place for Indians, and many arrowheads have been found here.

The old Penrose Trail to Fort Lyon, Colorado, began at Black Mesa and extended northwest into Colorado. In the fall of 1863, General W. H. Penrose surveyed this route for the purpose of transporting a fieldpiece for an assault against a bandit fortification near the Mesa, known as ROBBER'S ROOST. Later the Penrose Trail was used by adventurers, and in the 1870's, by cattlemen who had settled in the valleys of the Arkansas and Cimarron rivers. This trail and others of its kind did much to facilitate the settlements of the West. Along their route were fresh-water holes and sheltered spots, without which neither man nor beast could have endured the long marches over the untamed and ruthless lands.

At 4 *m.* is the DEVIL'S TOMBSTONE, a towering slab of brownish sandstone twenty feet high, eighteen inches thick, and twelve feet wide. A hole, worn by constant battering of the elements, is at the bottom of the huge formation and exactly in the center. Sightseers frequently photograph each other peering through the opening, the finished picture making it appear that the face is imbedded in the rock. The rock is, according to compass findings, set in true directions; the flat sides face north and south.

At 38.6 *m.* on the main side road is the New Mexico Line, ninety-eight miles east of Raton, New Mexico (*see New Mexico Guide*).

Back on the square at Boise City, US 64 continues southwest. It crosses the BEAVER (N. Canadian) RIVER at 316.8 *m.* Off to the west, beyond Oklahoma, the motorist suddenly sees RABBIT EARS MOUNTAIN, that eagerly sought-out landmark for wagon drivers on the Santa Fe Trail. Then at 337.1 *m.*, US 64 crosses the New Mexico Line, twelve miles from Clayton, New Mexico (*see New Mexico Guide*).

TOUR 2A

Keystone—Oilton—Yale—Stillwater; State 51, 73.2 m.

Roadbed asphalt-paved throughout.
Accommodations limited, except at Stillwater.

Except for the inevitable oil fields, State 51 crossing the northwestern corner of the former Creek Nation, is a road through history, past and immediate. The region was first visited and thoroughly described by Washington Irving, whose 1832 expedition roughly paralleled the eastern two-thirds of this route. But it also figures in immediate events by virtue of the KEYSTONE DAM over the Arkansas River, under construction in 1957 (*see Tour 2*). When completed, backed-up water will flood out the towns of Keystone and Mannford, the first ten miles of this highway, and many historical points of interest.

State 51 branches southwest from its junction with US 64 (*see Tour 2*) in KEYSTONE, 0 *m.*, (684 alt., 228 pop.) (*see Tour 2*).

Taking its name from Mann's Ford on the Cimarron River, MANNFORD, 6.6 *m.* (740 alt., 426 pop.), was built on land formerly owned by Tom Mann, who established the ford. The old BERRYHILL FARM, near the southern edge of town, was at one time a hide-out for the outlaw Dalton gang. It is believed locally that large sums of money taken from banks by the Daltons are still buried on the farm.

A large projecting shelf of rock (R) is known as DALTON CAVE, 7.4 *m.* It was, according to local belief, the place where a half-blood Creek Indian named Tom Bartee hid and fed the Daltons when they were pursued by United States deputy marshals after their raids. North and west, across the Cimarron River on House Creek, is the spot where authorities believe the Irving party camped the nights of October 16 and 17, 1832, and shot their first elk. (The site can be reached by driving north from Mannford, on Cimarron Street, crossing the river, and then veering west and south on a series of dusty country roads 4.3 miles to a ranch house (L). From here one has to walk the rest of the way.

At 21.9 *m.* is the southern junction with State 99 (*see Tour 14*), which unites with State 51 for 3.2 miles.

To the left at 22.3 *m.* is the business district of OILTON (818 alt., 1,109 pop.). This town marks the approximate northern limit of the famous Cushing Field (*see Tour 1A*). The first river-bed oil well in Oklahoma was drilled in the near-by Cimarron.

The site of Oilton was a cornfield in 1915 when it was platted, as the oil boom was reaching its crest. Lots sold at first for $500 each, and within a week one hundred houses had been erected. Owners of lots on Main Street boosted their asking price to $4,000. But even the most optimistic businessmen considered this excessive, so they sought lots a block north and there most of the development centered.

At 23.3 *m.* the Cimarron River is crossed (*see Tour 14*) and at 25.1 *m.* State 51 leaves State 99. (Right on State 99 is the bridge over LAGOON CREEK, 0.6 *m.*, near where Irving is believed to have spent the night of October 18, 1832.)

YALE, 32.2 *m.* (793 alt., 1,359 pop.), is another small town sustained jointly by Oklahoma's two principal industries: agriculture and petroleum. Oil derricks dot the sparsely wooded hills to the north and west.

At 37.1 *m.* is a tall stone monument (L) marking the first battle of the Civil War on Oklahoma soil. Known as the BATTLE OF ROUND MOUNTAINS, it took its name from two flat-topped hills, now called TWIN MOUNDS, which dominate the skyline a mile to the south. Here on November 19, 1861, Opothle Yahola, leading a band of approximately two thousand Creeks loyal to the Union government, was overtaken and attacked by 1,400 Confederate troops under Col. Douglas H. Cooper of Mississippi. Opothle Yahola managed to escape under cover of darkness. But in the flight for Kansas and refuge, many of his band—which included women and children—died of starvation and disease. As winter closed in, others froze to death. It was not until the middle of January, 1862, that the destitute refugees, greatly depleted in number, reached the safety of southern Kansas.

Western Oklahoma can be said to begin at 40.4 *m.* Here in the roadcuts may be seen clearly the Permian redbeds of the state's western half overlapping the older sandstones of eastern Oklahoma. Westward, the motorist will be increasingly aware of the predominantly reddish soil so characteristic of western Oklahoma.

At 44.6 *m.* is the historical marker (R) that records the outlaw battle of September 1, 1893, in near-by Ingalls, which saw U. S. Marshals Dick Speed, Tom Houston, and Lafe Shadley felled by the Dalton-Doolin gangs. Here is the junction with State 108.

Left on this graveled road 2 *m.*, then left again on dirt road to a section-line crossroads, 3 *m.*

Straight ahead (east) from this corner to the near-ghost town of INGALLS, 3.7 *m.*, named for John J. Ingalls, U. S. senator from Kansas (1873–91). Only a few of the original buildings remain and grass is spreading over many of the ruins. It was to this once-lively town that the Doolin and Dalton gangs of outlaws sometimes retreated after their raids. Following the attempted robbery of two banks at Coffeyville, Kansas, in 1892, when three of the bandits were killed, Bill Doolin and Bill Dalton came to Ingalls and then reorganized their forces in a cave near the Cimarron River. The bronze plaque on a stone monument (R) erected in 1956 contains the names of the three marshals (*see above*) who "fell in the line of duty" a year later.

From the above crossroads, right (south) to IRVING CASTLE (R), 4.7 *m.*, a cedar-lined outcrop of red rock on the crest of a low hill that Washington Irving and his party described October 20, 1832, as resembling a Moorish castle.

At 53.7 *m.* is the junction with State 40, in downtown Stillwater (*see Stillwater*). At 54.1 *m.* is Knoblock Street and the entrance (R) to OKLAHOMA A. & M. COLLEGE.

State 51–C leaves the highway at 62.3 *m.*

Right on this paved road to LAKE CARL BLACKWELL (*swimming, boating, fishing, hunting, picnicking*), 2 *m.* Formerly owned by the U. S. Department of

Agriculture, the 3,380-acre lake was turned over to Oklahoma A. & M. College in 1955. It is a recreation center for much of north-central Oklahoma, and offers seventeen stone cabins, a new restaurant, and other service facilities.

State 51 joins US 77 (*see Tour 10*) at 73.2 *m.*

TOUR 3

(Fayetteville, Ark.)—Muskogee—Oklahoma City—Chickasha—Anadarko—Hollis—(Childress, Tex.); US 62, Arkansas Line to Texas Line, 411.8 m.

Roadbed paved throughout.
Route is roughly paralleled between Muskogee and Taft by the Midland Valley R. R.; between Boynton and Henryetta by the Kansas, Oklahoma & Gulf Ry.; Harrah to Oklahoma City by the Rock Island Ry.; between Chickasha and Lawton by the Rock Island Ry.; between Lawton and Altus by the St. Louis–San Francisco Ry.; and between Altus and the Texas Line by the Missouri-Kansas-Texas R. R. Good accommodations in all but the smallest towns.

Perhaps no other route across Oklahoma passes through areas settled by so many different nationalities as does the twisting path made by US 62. In the east around Tahlequah are the hills where for sixty years the Cherokees maintained a self-governing Indian nation and built a culture of their own. At Fort Gibson, in the Cherokee Nation, was written much of the military history of eastern Oklahoma from the initial appearance of the Five Civilized Tribes, through the troubles with the so-called wild tribes of the western plains, to the turbulent Civil War years when the Five Tribes were split into factions and both Union and Confederate forces at different times occupied the post.

Along this route, too, is seen a curious aftermath of the Civil War—the all-Negro settlements made by slaves freed by their Indian owners. For these freedmen, in the final liquidation of tribal governments, shared equally in the allotment of land. Crossing the old Creek Nation—and passing through its capital, Okmulgee—US 62 skirts the northern boundary of yet another former reservation, that of the Seminoles, who were moved to it from Florida.

The route, like most long highways across Oklahoma, taps rich oil fields and fine farm lands. In its western section, before leaving the state at its southwestern corner, US 62 passes through regions of red earth, rock-pitted breaks and canyons; granite-topped mountains, high prairies, and short-grass pastures. These were once the hunting grounds of the Kiowas, Comanches, Apaches, and Wichitas. Here, if anywhere in Oklahoma, may be seen the Plains Indian not too far removed from his native condition. And here, too, are the evidences of his capacity to adopt the highest type of civilizations. And here, too, as evidenced by the annual Anadarko Indian Fair, the Plains Indian, under capable exposition management, has been able to provide striking ceremonials preserving his ancient culture. That he realizes a modest profit from it is important to his welfare.

Section a. ARKANSAS LINE *to* OKLAHOMA CITY, *209.0 m. US 62*

US 62 crosses the ARKANSAS LINE, 0 *m.*, twenty-nine miles west of Fayetteville, Arkansas (*see Arkansas Guide*).

WESTVILLE, 2.3 *m.* (1,128 alt., 781 pop.), is an important lumbering town on the edge of the heavily wooded Cherokee Hills. Fish abound in many near-by creeks, but it is advisable to employ a local guide (*$5.00 to $100.00 a day*) to find the best holes.

At 2.9 *m.*, on the southwestern edge of Westville, is the junction with US 59 (*see Tour 15*).

CHRISTIE, 10.7 *m.* (834 alt., 100 pop.), is off the highway to the left. Just beyond (L) is an excellent, well-kept example of the "open gallery" (or "dog-trot") type of house so characteristic of the Ozark-Ouachita hill country of eastern Oklahoma.

PROCTOR, 15.7 *m.* (788 alt., 55 pop.), is a small settlement, named for Ezekiel Proctor, a Cherokee.

At the Goingsnake Schoolhouse, which stood on the bank of Baron Fork Creek, south of Proctor, Ezekiel Proctor was tried, in May, 1872, in a tribal court for the murder of Polly Chesterton (*see Tour 15*). This trial precipitated the Goingsnake Massacre. Proctor had surrendered after the killing to the sheriff of Goingsnake District of the Cherokee Nation, and Blackhawk Sixkiller had been appointed to try the case. Dissatisfied with the Cherokee system of prosecution, Chesterton, the husband of the victim, filed charges against Proctor in the United States Court at Fort Smith, Arkansas. Since provisions of their treaty with the government had guaranteed to the Cherokees the right to try and punish their own people, this action was deeply resented. When word was received that Fort Smith officers were coming to arrest Proctor, the Cherokees immediately prepared to defend their treaty rights by force, if necessary. Everyone present at the trial in the schoolhouse—chosen because it could be more easily defended than the courthouse—was armed for attack. Without warning, a posse of Fort

Smith marshals charged. Seven officers were killed, the prisoner and the judge were wounded, and the clerk was slain at his desk.

In reprisal, indictments were returned by a federal grand jury at Fort Smith against twenty Cherokee citizens who had been present at the trial, and all the officers of the tribal court. The Cherokees in turn issued warrants for a number of their own tribesmen. Later all indictments were dismissed by the United States government. After Proctor recovered from his wounds, he lived a law-abiding life, even to the extent of being elected sheriff of the Flint District of the Cherokee Nation, and a member of the Cherokee Council.

From Proctor to ELDON, 22.0 *m.* US 62 swings easily through vegetation that is thick and green, then descends scenic Eldon Hill to the lush valley of the Illinois River. Left from Eldon on State 51 and an unnumbered graveled road, it is approximately nine miles to BIDDING SPRINGS and Oklahoma's only remaining gristmill (*see Tour 15*).

West of the ILLINOIS RIVER (*see Tour 16*), 27.6 *m.*, the highway loops over still more rugged hills to offer the motorist some of the state's most beautiful scenery. Along the way are roadside stands and shops—including that of the SEQUOYAH INDIAN WEAVERS (R)—which offer genuine Cherokee handicrafts, as well as jellies and other products made from local wild fruits.

TAHLEQUAH, 30.8 *m.* (864 alt., 4,750 pop.), became the permanent capital of the Cherokee Nation on September 6, 1839, when the East and West Cherokees met on the site of present square to sign the new constitution. This date is now celebrated each year as a Cherokee national holiday, with Cherokee handicrafts displayed on the courthouse square. Dancers and choral groups present programs. But perhaps the climax of the day's celebration is the world championship cornstalk shoot, a contest recently revived in Tahlequah and conducted by the CHEROKEE NATIONAL CORNSTALK SHOOTING ASSOCIATION. For this contest bundles of cornstalks are set up at a certain distance from the shooters, who are armed with bows and arrows. The winner is the bowman whose arrow has pierced the most stalks in a bundle. The game is one of the most ancient played by the men of the tribe.

Until 1843, when the present town of Tahlequah was first platted, the capital consisted of a council ground, with a large shed in the middle, and a camping site for the delegates of the eighteen tribes that attended the council meetings. On January 8, 1845, a measure was enacted ordering all houses then standing on the PUBLIC SQUARE to be moved before September 1. On their removal, the main streets were laid out and a brick building was erected for the Cherokee Supreme Court. The *Cherokee Advocate* (*see Newspapers*), official publication of the Cherokee government, was printed here. During a fire in 1874, the old building was partly gutted but was rebuilt shortly after; the *Advocate* was housed in the Cherokee jail during the interim. Located just across the street from the southeast corner of the public square, the first SUPREME COURT BUILDING still contains part (mostly the outside walls) of the original materials used in its construction in 1845. In the square also stands the old CHEROKEE CAPITOL, completed in 1869. It now serves as the COUNTY COURTHOUSE for Cherokee County. West of the courthouse and on the grounds of the old square are STATUES of W. P. Adair and Stand Watie, prominent in Cherokee politics and war, respectively.

A present-day hotel, across the street (N) from the courthouse square, is on the SITE OF THE NATIONAL HOTEL, erected in 1848 as an inn for the convenience of the representatives attending council sessions. The hotel was built by a Mormon bishop and two of his followers, who arrived here on their way to Texas in 1847. The Mormons were being driven out of the East at that time, but these three men had chosen not to accompany the main body headed for Utah. The bishop's attempt to carry on his church work in Tahlequah, however, was so deeply resented that he soon left. In another building (immediately across from the northwest corner of the square), erected in the same year by Mormons, was installed in 1886 one of the first telephone lines in Oklahoma. It ran from Tahlequah to Fort Gibson. Ed Hicks, a Cherokee citizen, built the line.

Down Tahlequah's main thoroughfare, Muskogee Avenue, in November, 1855, marched the famous Second Cavalry. Numbering 750 troopers, it was on its way from Jefferson Barracks, at St. Louis, to Texas, where the regiment was engaged in fighting Indians until the outbreak of the Civil War. In command was Colonel Albert Sidney Johnston. Lieutenant Colonel Robert E. Lee, second in command, had been detained at Leavenworth, Kansas, on court-martial duty and did not rejoin the regiment until after its arrival in Texas. Other officers of the regiment included Captain Edmund Kirby Smith, Lieutenant John B. Hood, and Lieutenant J. E. B. Stuart.

In 1846, the Cherokees established two schools of higher learning—one, a Male Seminary just southwest of Tahlequah, and the other, a Female Seminary at Park Hill, approximately four miles south of Tahlequah. Both buildings were destroyed by fire—the school for boys in 1910, and the female institution in 1887. The latter school, relocated at Tahlequah in that year, was purchased in March, 1909, by the state of Oklahoma to form the nucleus of NORTHEASTERN STATE COLLEGE. Present enrollment at Northeastern exceeds 1,500 and the physical plant includes 18 permanent buildings on a wooded campus of outstanding natural beauty. (Interestingly enough, this educational history is relived each spring in early May at the CHEROKEE SEMINARIES HOMECOMING, attended by hundreds of former graduates.)

The CHEROKEE MUSEUM occupies part of the first floor of the new JOHN VAUGHAN LIBRARY and contains many unusual Cherokee items which are closely linked with the history of the Cherokee Nation. Some of the articles (a plow and an ox yoke) were brought over the "Trail of Tears" from Georgia. (Only items of authentic Cherokee origin or ownership are displayed.) The library itself has a large collection of Cherokee books and manuscripts, including several volumes of the *Cherokee Advocate*, the tribal newspaper, and many first editions of books on the Cherokee Nation.

At 34.2 *m.* is the PARK HILL historical marker (L).

Left from US 62 on a graveled road (following official markers) to the SITE OF PARK HILL MISSION, 2 *m.* established in 1836 by the Presbyterians as a religious and educational center for the mission and the schools. It included homes for missionaries and teachers, a boarding hall, gristmill, shops, stables, and a printing office and book bindery. Samuel Austin Worcester, the first missionary here, brought his printing press from Union Mission (*see Tour* 8) in 1836 and published many works for both Cherokees and whites. Millions of pages of tracts, school books, and extracts from the Bible (mostly translated into Cherokee by Worcester) came from this press before the Mission ceased to exist, near the end of the century.

Just north of Park Hill are the ruins of the CHEROKEE FEMALE SEMINARY, which was established by the national council in 1846. A disastrous fire in 1887 left only parts of the walls and the foundation.

Straight ahead on the graveled road is the MURRELL MANSION (*open daily* 9–5), 2.2 *m.*, standing in a grove (R) of maples and catalpas. The stately old building was considered the finest residence in the vicinity in Civil War days. All the lumber and finishing materials were cut from near-by trees, but most of the furniture was imported from France or bought in New Orleans and shipped up the Arkansas and Illinois rivers by steamboat. George Murrell, the original owner, was a prominent merchant and a member of the Ross faction of the Cherokees. Before, and during, the Civil War, the house was the center of social activities for near-by Fort Gibson. Later it passed rapidly from one owner to another, serving for a time as a school. Today it is owned by the State of Oklahoma, and is being restored as a historical monument.

Southeast of the Murrell Mansion, a quarter of a mile through a field, is the WORCESTER MISSION CEMETERY, where Samuel and Ann Worcester, founders of the mission, are buried. The old burial ground, long abandoned, has recently been fenced and restored by the State Historical Society. The monuments to the Worcesters still stand, enclosed by an iron fence. The inscription for Samuel Worcester reads: "To his labors, the Cherokees are indebted for their Bible and hymn book."

At 2.5 *m.* is the GROVE (L) where the Cherokee Confederate Treaty was signed in 1861.

In the ROSS FAMILY CEMETERY, 3 *m.*, stands the JOHN MCDONALD ROSS MONUMENT (L), enclosed by a three-foot stone wall surmounted by iron pickets.

A circular shaft of white marble—broken at the top to represent life interrupted at its prime (he died at the age of twenty-one)—marks the grave of a nephew of John Ross, leader of the Union faction of Cherokees, who is also buried here. The story is told that Confederate General Stand Watie, needing ammunition, remembered the lead balls which decorated the iron palings atop the burial wall of the nephew's grave and ordered his men to remove them to make bullets. Thus the lead from a Ross grave was used to bring death to members of the Ross faction. A few of the ornaments which Watie's men overlooked still remain.

The SEQUOYAH VOCATIONAL SCHOOL, 35.5 *m.*, is a government-maintained institution for Indian orphans. By an act of the Cherokee council in 1872, the Cherokee Orphan Asylum was created and established near Salina (*see Tour* 8). In 1904, following a fire, it was moved to this site, and in 1914 it was sold to the federal government. From the original building and forty acres (occupied by the Cherokee Insane Asylum prior to 1904), the present Sequoyah institution has grown to a modern plant of forty major buildings and 752 acres of land. The 380 students now enrolled are mostly members of the Five Civilized Tribes from eastern Oklahoma. There are also some Mississippi Choctaws and Florida Seminoles. The school offers fully accredited work in Grades 1–12.

From ZEB, 36.8 *m.*, an improved road leads south two miles to the 32,000-acre CHEROKEE GAME MANAGEMENT AREA (*visitors welcome*), which abounds with deer, quail, and other wildlife. The northern half is open to hunting in season.

At 51.2 *m.* is a junction with a paved road.

Right on this road to FORT GIBSON NATIONAL CEMETERY, 0.7 *m.* In the circle of officers' graves is that of Diana Rogers, Cherokee wife of Sam Houston. The inscription, perpetuating an old error, gives her name as Talihina.

Another woman who lies in the officers' circle—in a grave marked simply "Vivia"—still retains an aura of mystery, for her real story has never been told. The legend—probably true—tells of a teen-age girl in love with a soldier, and of her pursuit of him to his post at Fort Gibson, where she masqueraded as a young lieutenant. Her sex was not known until after her death. It is said that Fort Gibson officials consulted with Washington headquarters as to her disposal and were told, "Bury, and say nothing."

Captain Billy Bowlegs, famous Seminole warrior, lies in this circle of men and women who made frontier history. Montford Stokes, governor of North Carolina (1830–32), chairman of the Indian Commission (1830–34), and the only known Revolutionary War veteran to be buried in Oklahoma, is also interred here.

FORT GIBSON, 52.1 *m.* (542 alt., 1,496 pop.), a rural community on the bank of Grand River, stands on the site of the frontier post, Fort Gibson. This was one of the strongest links in the chain of fortifications stretching from the northern to the southern border of the United States. Until 1857 it served as the chief military center for the whole of Indian Territory, and many treaties with the Indians were concluded here.

In October, 1806, Lieutenant James B. Wilkinson, second in command of the Zebulon M. Pike expedition, was detailed to explore the Arkansas River. With five enlisted men, he set out from the site of the present Larned, Kansas, in an attempt to float down the river to its mouth. Freezing over of the river forced the group to follow the banks on foot. At last the party reached the mouth of the Verdigris River; then, on December 6, they came to an Osage village, situated on the east bank of the Grand River, which joins with the Arkansas and Verdigris at this point. This site, recommended by the lieutenant in his report as suitable for a garrison, was chosen for Fort Gibson in 1824, when a military post was needed to halt Osage depredations and to establish peace along the frontier. Colonel Matthew Arbuckle, who came with a part of his troops by boat while others had traveled overland, was in command of the building of the fort, which was to serve as a communication and transportation link between Fort Leavenworth, Kansas, and Fort Smith, Arkansas.

In 1834 an important intertribal Indian council was held here. The fort was abandoned in 1857, but was reoccupied by Union soldiers during the Civil War. Toward the close of the war, six thousand refugee Creeks encamped here on their return from Kansas, where they had fled to seek haven with the Union forces. The Fort also sheltered some ten thousand other refugees in the immediate neighborhood, most of them Union Cherokees who had been harried by the guerrilla tactics of the Confederate Cherokee general, Stand Watie. Watie, master of this type of warfare, took their food and stock, pillaged their homes, and even at one time stripped them of their clothing so that the destitute women and children of his own group might have sustenance and cover.

During its heyday, Fort Gibson was a busy and active place, frequented by many whose names are now famous. Jefferson Davis, later president of the Confederacy, served here under General Zachary Taylor, who was inaugurated President of the United States in 1849. Washington Irving, accompanying an exploring expedition in 1832, camped here, and it was from this spot that he started the trip (*see Tour 2A*) described in his book, *A Tour on the Prairies*. The supposed site where his tent was pitched is marked by a slab made from two stones, one said to have come from the original barracks building and the other from the old Jefferson Davis house, now a U.D.C. museum.

The old Texas Road, with its constant traffic of cattlemen, emigrants, freighters, and traders, passed near the fort, but the main communication for the troops and the residents of the surrounding country was by means of steamboat navigation on the Arkansas River. French fur traders of the Southwest made it a center for their business transactions, and supplies for a large area were imported and dispersed at this point.

Fort Gibson was finally abandoned in 1890, but many of the old buildings have now been restored and opened to the public. The four-sided, square stockade was rebuilt by the National Fort Stockade Commission, and the barracks by the Oklahoma Historical Society. The stone barracks constructed during the Civil War are on a hill overlooking the stockade.

Right from Fort Gibson on State 80, a graveled road winds around the ruins of the old FORT GIBSON COMMISSARY, then follows the left bank of the Grand River to FORT GIBSON DAM, 5.8 *m.* Completed in 1953 at a cost of $46,-000,000 as a power-flood control project, the FORT GIBSON RESERVOIR is more than 25 miles in length, has a normal surface area of 19,100 acres and a shore line of 225 miles. The dam itself is 110 feet high, 2,850 feet long, and the focal point for rapidly expanding sport and recreational facilities. Special feature: more than a dozen of the newly conceived heated fishing docks (*see Tour 15*).

At 53.8 *m.*, State 10 turns left (south) to GREENLEAF LAKE STATE PARK and TENKILLER LAKE STATE PARK (*see Tour 2*).

At 55.5 *m.*, the ARKANSAS RIVER is crossed. A few hundred yards south of the bridge is the approximate SITE OF THE OLD STEAMBOAT LANDING. The first river boats here were canoes and pirogues (hollowed-out logs); these were succeeded by keelboats which were moved along by manpower, applied from the bank. The early steamboats coming up the Arkansas to this region usually stopped at Fort Smith and reshipped their cargoes upstream by keelboat. In 1824, however, the sixty-ton steamboat, *Florence*, carrying one hundred recruits for the new military post, Fort Gibson, ventured this far. Three Forks, as the region was known where the grand and the Verdigris flow into the Arkansas, became a busy trading area for the next fifty years, owing to the advance of river traffic. Because of many shoals in the river bed, this particular landing was much used since here the water was deeper. In February, 1828, the steamboat *Facility* (117 tons) ascended to this point towing two keelboats laden with 780 emigrant Creek Indians for the new Creek agency which had just been established at Three Forks (*see Tour 8*).

River traffic continued to increase, with only a slight interruption during the Civil War, and in February, 1870, a government engineer said in his official report: "Twenty steamboats now ply between Fort

Gibson, Fort Smith, Little Rock, and New Orleans, Memphis, St. Louis, and Cincinnati. The amount of the up and down the river trade received and shipped at Fort Gibson is about 25,000 tons annually . . . and merchants expect traffic to double. . . ." Two years later, however, the Missouri-Kansas-Texas Railroad built tracks to Muskogee and gradually absorbed the traffic which had been carried by the river and the Texas Road. Down to the present day there continues to be some serious talk of constructing a deeper and more permanent river bed for the Arkansas, but use of much of the upstream water for irrigation purposes tends to make the plan impracticable.

At 57.7 *m.* (large glass factory to left) is the junction with a paved road.

Right on this road onto the campus of BACONE INDIAN COLLEGE, 0.7 *m.* The school was named for Professor Almon C. Bacone, the founder, who came to Indian Territory to teach in the Cherokee Male Seminary at Tahlequah (*see above*). In 1879 he received permission to establish a university for Indians of all tribes under the supervision of the American Baptist Home Mission Society. The Baptist Mission House in the Cherokee capital served as the university's first home.

The school, a junior college, is supported by the American Baptist Home Mission Society, by gifts from churches, individuals and other groups, and student fees. In 1885, with the consent of the Creek tribal council, the school was moved to its present location near Muskogee, the governmental center for the Five Civilized Tribes.

Bacone occupies a unique place in state education. In addition to the regular curriculum, it strives to keep alive the ancient Indian arts. Patrick J. Hurley (*see Tour 9*), secretary of war (1929–33) under President Hoover, graduated here in 1905.

The plant is on a campus of three hundred acres, eighty of which are under cultivation. The fourteen college buildings (*open during school hours*) include SAMUEL RICHARDS MEMORIAL HALL, a three-story brick building of Norman design, erected in 1921 by an oil-rich Creek; the SALLY JOURNEYCAKE MEMORIAL, constructed of native stone by student labor and named for a famous Delaware Indian woman; the native-stone ARTS AND CRAFTS BUILDING; MEMORIAL CHAPEL, on the site of the first school structure; the INDIAN COTTAGE, a typical modern log cabin of the type recently built by many Indians on their rural holdings; and the INDIAN ART LODGE (*open to visitors by appointment*), which serves as the school recreational center. The lodge is built of native stone and lumber and is furnished throughout with handmade Indian furniture and rugs. In the Museum Room, relics, beadwork, wood carvings, and pottery are displayed. The fireplace was constructed of hundreds of stones gathered from various Indian reservations and places of historical interest.

The MILLY FRANCIS MONUMENT, in front of the Art Lodge, was erected in 1933 by the faculty and students of Bacone in honor of "Oklahoma's Pocahontas," the Indian woman who was awarded the first Congressional medal ever granted to a woman. Milly saved the life of Duncan McKrimmon, a Georgia militiaman stationed at Fort Gadsden, Georgia, during the border warfare between the United States and Spanish Florida (1817–18). Captain McKrimmon had been captured by Seminole Indians and was about to be killed when Milly's eloquent pleading saved him, on condition that he shave his head and live among his captors. Two years later he was sold to Spanish traders for a barrel of whiskey. It is said that the young soldier returned shortly thereafter and asked Milly to become his wife, but she refused. Later Milly Francis was captured, along with a number of Seminoles, and finally came west to live in the vicinity of Fort Gibson, where Colonel Ethan Allen Hitchcock learned her story. He petitioned Congress to recognize her deed, and an act was passed on June 14, 1844, granting her an annual pension of $96. The act further provided for a medal, but official Washington did not push the matter and Milly died in 1848 without having received it. Her heirs, however, later were given the award.

The MURROW INDIAN CHILDREN'S HOME, on the campus, consists of three modern cottage-type brick buildings. The institution was moved here from Atoka, where it was known as the Atoka Baptist Academy.

The SITE OF FORT DAVIS, a Confederate fort established for a short time during the Civil War, is near the college grounds. A tract approximately 550 feet square has been given to the Fort Davis Memorial Association, which plans to restore the site. At the top of a mound is the place where the flagstaff stood, and near by is an old well which served the fortification.

At 57.9 *m.* is the junction with paved State 16.

Right on this road past the western entrance to BACONE COLLEGE, 0.9 *m.*, to a bridge over the ARKANSAS RIVER, 1.2 *m.* South of here is the site (R) of the council which Bernard de la Harpe, the French explorer, held on September 3, 1719, with some seven thousand Indians, representing Tawakonis and the Wichitas and allied tribes (*see Tour 2*). In his report of the expedition, which crossed from the southeastern section of what is now Oklahoma to this point, he stated that he gave away fifteen hundred pounds of gifts to the Indians that day.

Northward, State 16 parallels the Verdigris River where, before the Civil War, numerous trading posts stood on both banks. For a few miles the highway follows an almost identical route with that of the old Texas Road (*see Tour 8*), a branch of which went southeasterly six miles to Fort Gibson. Midway on this road was the SITE OF WIGWAM NEOSHO, the log house built by Sam Houston in 1830 and occupied by him until 1832, when he started on his Texas adventure. It was here that he lived with his Cherokee wife, Diana Rogers.

A narrow one-way steel bridge spans the VERDIGRIS RIVER, 5.0 *m.* At the east end of the bridge the Daughters of the American Revolution have erected a THREE FORKS MARKER (L), commemorating "the important and ancient trail," the Texas Road, which crossed at this spot; the old Chouteau trading post and the Three Forks landing; the Osage and Creek agencies; the arrival of the first party of emigrating Creek Indians in February of 1828; Washington Irving's visit in 1832; and the near-by home of Sam Houston.

OKAY, 5.8 *m.* (510 alt., 427 pop.), is approximately a half-mile north of the site of one of the oldest white settlements in Oklahoma. The firm of Brand and Barbour set up a trading post at this point in the first years of the nineteenth century and in 1822 sold their property to Colonel A. P. Chouteau, who had already established a post at Salina. Creole carpenters were brought from New Orleans and St. Louis to build the keelboats in which the French traders shipped their furs down the Arkansas and Mississippi rivers to New Orleans, where the boats and peltries were exchanged for supplies. The site was a busy shipping and trading point for it stood at the confluence of the Arkansas, the Grand (Neosho), and the Verdigris, whereby it gained the name Three Forks. At one time the Osage Indians claimed the section; later it was transferred by treaty to the Cherokees, and finally the Creeks settled on a part of the area. In 1828, Chouteau's holdings were bought by the government for use as a Creek agency.

When Washington Irving made the trip described in his *Tour on the Prairies*, he stopped overnight here. He wrote of the stern Osages, the gay Creeks, trappers, hunters, half-bloods, Creoles, Negroes, and frontiersmen, who made the place one of "complete bustle."

The busy little settlement was known by several names—Falls City, Verdigris Falls, Verdigris Landing, Three Forks, Creek Agency, and Sleepyville. The buildings were burned in whole or in part half a dozen times in the first half of the nineteenth century. And the bitter guerrilla fighting between the northern and southern factions that divided both the Creeks and Cherokees devastated the area during the Civil War. With the coming of the railroad in 1871, the settlement moved north to the present site and was known successively as Coretta Switch, North Muskogee, Rex, and finally Okay.

Even this last change was not enough to halt the successive blows of hard luck that struck the town following World War I. Attempts to manufacture gas stoves, plows, OK trucks, and airplanes all failed. And then the elements turned against Okay: in 1911 the town was swept by a devastating tornado, in 1927 by wind and flood, in 1936 by fire. But the construction of Fort Gibson Dam (*see above*) from 1942 to 1953 provided a mild boom, and the town now serves the many sportsmen and vacationers who use the huge reservoir. State 16 east from Okay winds over beautifully wooded hills to an impressive, landscaped Overlook, then drops down a steep bluff to the west end of the dam itself, 11 *m.*

The OKLAHOMA SCHOOL FOR THE BLIND, 61.2 *m.*, is attractively situated on a campus (L) of ninety-nine acres. A coeducational school with an enrollment of 106 with 18 teachers, it offers instruction through the twelfth grade, and in chorus, band, piano, and pipe organ. Emphasis is placed on physical and industrial training; and it has been found that students are especially apt at weaving and piano tuning. There is also an orchestra.

The school plant of twelve buildings includes four large cottages, two each for boys and girls, where the students live during the nine-month school year. Visiting groups are always welcome.

On the west edge of MUSKOGEE, 62.9 *m.* (617 alt., 37,289 pop.) (*see Muskogee*), are junctions with US 69 (*see Tour 8*) and with US 64 (*see Tour 2*), which unites westward with US 62 for 15.4 miles.

TAFT, 70.8 *m.* (605 alt., 541 pop.) (*see Tour 2*).

At 76.5 *m.*, US 62 turns sharply to the left (south).

In OKMULGEE, 104.9 *m.* (670 alt., 18, 317 pop.) (*see Okmulgee*), is the junction with US 75 (*see Tour 9*), which unites southward with US 62 for 21.8 miles.

Right from Okmulgee on paved State 56 is LAKE OKMULGEE, 7 *m.*, the city's water supply. The lake (L) covers 720 acres and provides fishing, camping, and picnicking facilities. Along the shore is a 5,360-acre public shooting area—one of thirteen in the state—on which quail, squirrels, furbearers, and waterfowl may be hunted.

At 14 *m.* is a junction with a graveled county road. Right on this road is NUYAKA, 16 m., a small settlement where NUYAKA MISSION was established by the Presbyterians in 1884, when the village was a fullblood Creek settlement. Miss Alice Robertson, pioneer state educator, secured funds from church women in the East to build the structure and carry on the religious and educational work. Although the Nuyaka school was sponsored and partly supported by the Creek Nation, it remained under the auspices of the Presbyterian church until all Indian schools were taken over by the federal government in 1898. It was later discontinued as an Indian school, and the buildings were sold. One is still standing and is used as a residence.

In 1790, when the Creek Confederation occupied what is now Alabama and a part of Georgia, both Spain and the United States were seeking its friendship and commerce. Spain was planning to use the Creeks as a buffer state between her possessions and the boundary of the United States. Eager to obtain a treaty and also a cession of land, President Washington invited twenty-six Creek dignitaries to New York for a conference. They were so impressed with the city that, after their return to the Creek land, they named a town New Yorker. Since the Creeks soften and scarcely pronounce the consonant "R," the white man transcribed the name as Nuyaka. After the removal to the West and the naming of Nuyaka Mission, the same spelling persisted, but it still refers to New York.

Nuyaka's square was the scene of prolonged councils in the fall of 1880 and, in the summer of 1882, insurrection threatened in the Creek Nation, with this the starting point. The administration of justice by the ruling party and the cession of a small tract of land to the Seminoles was the source of friction, with a group composed mostly of full bloods responsible for the rebellion. Creek soldiers and lighthorsemen, sent to quell the disturbance, were so inadequately provided with food that they helped themselves liberally to the fruit from surrounding peach orchards—hence the fray became known historically as the Green Peach War. No real battles occurred and, although most of the insurrectionists were finally captured, they were soon freed.

Surrounded by low hills, HENRYETTA, 118.7 *m.* (691 alt., 7,987 pop.), was founded in 1900 when the Frisco Railway built to this point and named its station for Indian Hugh Henry and his wife Etta. Predominantly industrial, the town boasts the largest flat-glass plant west of the Mississippi River. Other important industries include zinc smelting (which uses up to ten million cubic feet of gas daily), cadmium and germanium refining, and coal mining. As a symbol of eastern Oklahoma's recently acquired wealth in sprawling man-made lakes, Henryetta also has a plant which manufactures decoys for wildfowl hunting.

Left from Henryetta on paved State 52 is the mile-square JACK NICHOLS PARK, 1.5 *m.*, which provides a sand swimming beach and year-round picnic facilities.

A few miles to the east is Lake Henryetta, the town's water supply, where fishing and boating are part of the recreational facilities.

At 126.7 *m.* is the southern junction with US 75 (*see Tour 9*).

OKEMAH, 137.3 *m.* (882 alt., 3,454 pop.), lies on ground declared surplus after the allotment of the Creek lands. It was opened to white settlement in 1902, when lots were offered for sale at an auction attended by three thousand people. Tents were the only buildings for months and drinking water was hauled in and sold at twenty-five cents a barrel. In the early days a barbed-wire fence was erected around the town to protect it from the thousands of free-grazing longhorn steers on the surrounding prairies. But today these prairie lands produce heavy yields of pecans, corn, sweet potatoes, and cotton to make Okemah a thriving agricultural center. The town qualifies as an angler's paradise on the strength of twenty-one lakes—ranging from 10 to 171 acres—located within a half-hour's drive from the center of town. Eight of these, including Okemah Lake itself, the largest, are open to the public (*fee: fifty cents a day*).

At 146.8 *m.* there is a good example of one of the state's few remaining sorghum mills (L). Although the juice press is powered by mules, the full process also calls for many long man-hours of hot and painstaking labor. The sorghum molasses taffy pull, of course, is no longer the high social event it once was to an earlier generation, but city-bred housewives still prize its rich, sweet flavor and create a lively demand for it.

At 148.0 *m.* is a junction with an improved road.

Left on this road is the State Training School for Negro Boys, 0.7 *m.* Seventeen brick buildings house the classrooms (grades 1–12) and dormitories, the cafeteria, gymnasium, and shops for cobblery, tailoring, barbering, carpentry, auto mechanics, and other trades. The boys (ages 9–19) make their own clothing, receive training in cooking and dairying, and raise much of the institution's food on the adjoining farmland.

BOLEY, 148.5 *m.* (859 alt., 646 pop.), is another of the state's all-Negro towns. The idea was advanced by the president of the Fort Smith and Western Railway townsite company in 1903, when the road was being extended westward toward Guthrie. The Fort Smith and Western roadmaster, W. H. Boley, was greatly responsible for carrying out the plan and was honored in the naming of the town. The location of Boley was particularly chosen because much of the surrounding area had been allotted to Negro freedmen listed on the rolls of the Creek tribe at the time of the division of the Indian lands.

PRAGUE, 161.6 *m.* (992 alt., 1,546 pop.), a clean and prosperous looking farm center, was established in the early part of the twentieth century by a group of Bohemians (Czechoslovakians) with the idea of creating a village like those of their homeland. Although the inhabitants have become completely Americanized in most respects, many Bohemian customs have been retained, largely by members of such organizations as the Sokol Society and the Western Bohemian Association. Prague resembles a "Little Bohemia" when these groups hold the annual Kolache Festival, usually in May. The "kolache" is a fruit roll and as many as 3,000 dozen are sold or given away during the celebration. For the occasion, residents appear in their colorful native costumes for a day of fun and merrymaking, ending it with native dances. On July 4, everyone takes a picnic lunch to the park for a day of visiting, races for the children, swimming, and fireworks.

Prague is at the junction with State 99 (*see Tour 14*).

MEEKER, 173.8 *m.* (874 alt., 672 pop.), is a trading center for the surrounding fertile farm lands, forming the divide between the North Canadian River and its tributary stream to the north, the Deep Fork. Meeker is the home town of Carl Hubbell, onetime pitching star for the New York Giants baseball club.

HARRAH, 189.6 *m.* (1,080 alt., 741 pop.), is the birthplace of Paul and Lloyd Waner, also star baseball players of the 1930's. Paul (Big Poison) and Lloyd (Little Poison) received their nicknames because, as heavy Pittsburgh Pirate hitters, they were "poison" to opposing pitchers.

Harrah is at the junction with US 270 (*see Tour 5*), which unites westward with US 62 for 20.1 miles.

At 191.7 *m.* is a junction with a paved road.

Right on this road is HORSESHOE LAKE (*free fishing*), 1.2 m., so named because of its shape. The lake, in a verdant setting which has been made a game preserve, furnishes water for an Oklahoma Gas & Electric Company steam generating plant.

At 207.3 *m.* is the junction with Eastern Avenue on the east edge of Oklahoma City.

Right on Eastern Avenue to LINCOLN PARK, 0.8 *m.*, Oklahoma City's largest public recreation center (*picnic facilities, children's playground, hiking and bridle trails, golf, and zoo*). This park, with its low, tree-covered hills and spring-fed lake, was purchased by the city in 1908 but remained unimproved until 1925, when a zoo was moved here from another city park. The Zoo covers fourteen acres and contains more than five hundred animals. Extensive work on improvements, including construction, and posting of classifications for the large collection of animals has been done in recent years by the "Friends of the Zoo," a voluntary organization. Monkey Island is one of the most popular spots, for its chattering population furnishes entertainment against a background of an old ship's bow projecting above the surface of the ground. The animals perch in the rigging and portholes and promenade on the inclined deck. Other attractions include the alligator swamp, the bird and reptile cages, and the bear pits. As nearly as possible, abodes have been constructed to resemble the natural habitat of the animals. A new, modern primate building has just recently been completed. A steam-whistling excursion train makes regular runs through the park.

In OKLAHOMA CITY, 209.0 *m.* (1,194 alt., 243,504 pop.; 1956 est., 317,500) (*see Oklahoma City*), are the junctions with US 66 (*see Tour 1*), US 77 (*see Tour 10*), and US 270 (*see Tour 5*).

Section b. OKLAHOMA CITY *to* TEXAS LINE, *202.8 m.* *US 62*

Southwest of OKLAHOMA CITY, 0 *m.*, the land is gently rolling and to a large extent cultivated. Consolidation of farmlands over the past two decades has resulted in fewer farmhouses, but more prosperous ones. The red soil—peculiar to this section of the state, and familiar to all who have seen the stage or movie version of the popular Rodgers & Hammerstein production "Oklahoma!"—is quite rich. Newly discovered oil fields continue to make it even richer.

At 11.4 *m.* is WILL ROGERS FIELD (R), the Oklahoma City municipal airport (*see Oklahoma City*).

The long NEWCASTLE BRIDGE, 17.5 *m.* spans the South Canadian River. Except in rare flood stages, when swirling silt-laden waters make it extremely dangerous, the Canadian is a sleeping giant, its wide sandy bed broken only by placid pools and peaceful meanders. Thick growths of cottonwoods line the banks and often cover much of the bed itself.

Southward, near the junction with State 9, at 27.3 *m.*, there is much recent oil development to be seen. Two wells to the northeast have produced more than 18,000 barrels since their discovery in December, 1953. Production here is from around 10,000 feet underground.

BLANCHARD, 31.9 *m.* (1,239 alt., 1,311 pop.), was named for W. G. Blanchard, who assisted in laying out the site at the founding of the town in 1906.

Near the Washita River crossing, 48.1 *m.*, is the spot where the old Chisholm Trail crossed the river in the nineteenth century. The Trail is practically paralleled today by US 81 (*see Tour 11*). During the 1870's a trading post, known as Fred (named for Colonel Frank Fred, who ran a series of such posts), was established here.

CHICKASHA, 50.1 *m.* (1,116 alt., 15,842 pop.), seat of Grady County, is a market place for a wide and prosperous region. Diversified crops, some forty medium-sized industries, soaring dairy production (Grady County leads the state in dairy income), and a revived oil and gas play, all share in the economic development of the pleasant, tree-shaded college town. The downtown streets are wide, and flanked by substantial business buildings, old and modern. To the west and south, the gently up-sloping residential streets are lined by elms dating back to the 1890's. The Washita River bottom marks the northern limits of the town.

Even before there was a town, the Rock Island had a train stop here (1892). The site of Chickasha was included in the "Swinging Ring" cattle ranch owned by an intermarried citizen of the Chickasaw Indian Nation, the western boundary of which was within a few miles of the place.

The first considerable industrial development at Chickasha was a cottonseed oil mill, and the next was cattle feeding pens where the residue from the mill, called "cake," was the chief fattening feed for the thousands of steers shipped out every month. Today the Chickasha Cotton Oil Company has spread its operations throughout Oklahoma (where it buys 15 per cent of all the cotton produced) and into Texas, New Mexico, and Arizona.

When the new town was only a straggling handful of stores and shacks in the middle of a cornfield, and street-corner sports were betting on whether or not a team would "pull" the slough at the western edge of the field, the *Chickasha Express* began publication as a four-page weekly in a leaky shack. But ten years after its founding, Chickasha had a population of 6,370 and had become a city of the first class. Its growth was greatly stimulated by the opening to white settlement in 1901 of the Kiowa-Comanche reservation, which adjoined the former Chickasaw Nation on the west. The Rock Island made the city a division point and established shops there. More cotton processing plants —gins, mills, and a compress—were located in Chickasha.

After statehood, the growth of the city was steady, if not spectacular. But only two small oil fields, the Cement and Carter Knox pools with some three hundred oil wells, and the Chickasha gas field with 272 wells were developed by 1941. Since the early 1950's, however, there has been greatly increased activity to the southeast as the fabulous Golden Trend (*see Tour 10*) has extended into Grady County.

Recreation is provided by SHANNOAN SPRINGS PARK in the southwest part of the city (lake, golf course, zoo, and a pioneer museum housed in the old Territorial jail), and the 130-acre BORDEN PARK (gymnasium, stadium) in the northwest.

OKLAHOMA COLLEGE FOR WOMEN, at the southwestern edge of Chickasha, is one of the seven state-supported women's colleges in the United States. Founded in 1908 by an act of the first state legislature, the college grants degrees in liberal arts, fine arts, and sciences, and offers courses leading to teachers' certificates and preprofessional work in medicine, dentistry, nursing, and law. The school rates high with accrediting agencies and boasts one of the nation's best teacher-student ratios. Classes average only twelve students each.

The 75-acre, tree-shaded campus contains twenty-seven modern buildings, including a new Student Union (1949), Gymnasium and Pool, library (1950), college theatre (1953), and home management house. The students, numbering about seven hundred, live in modern dormitories. Nearing completion is a new $400,000 home economics building.

Chickasha is at the junction with US 81 (*see Tour 11*).

VERDEN, 59.2 *m.* (1,136 alt., 508 pop.), stands on the site of a cottonwood grove near the Washita River where in May, 1865, an important intertribal council was held. Because a majority of members of the Five Civilized Tribes had sided with the Confederacy, a reckoning had to be made with the Union. Too, fresh outbreaks of trouble with white outlaw bands and with groups of Plains Indians on the warpath made the calling of the council almost a necessity.

The large encampment where the historic council meeting took place was called Camp Napoleon. Attending delegates were Confederate-sympathizing members of the Five Civilized Tribes, and allied bands of Caddoes, Osages, and Comanches, as well as representatives of the Plains Indians—Kiowas, Arapahoes, Cheyennes, and some Comanches, Caddoes, and Anadarkos. The peace pipe was passed, ceremonial tokens were exchanged, and a compact was adopted and signed. What might have been originally intended as a military alliance, however, turned out to be more a league of peace, for the Indians present realized that their greatest need was to establish strength and unity within their own race in order to combat further white aggression. Solemnly, in their compact, they recognized that "our vast and lovely country and beautiful hunting grounds, given to us by the Great Spirit, and knowing no limit but the shores of the Great Waters and the horizon of the heavens, is now, on account of our weakness, being reduced and hemmed in to a small and precarious country that we can scarcely call our own." Finally and inevitably, they agreed that if they were to survive, "an Indian shall not spill an Indian's blood."

This event has been commemorated by the MARKER on the Verden school grounds (L) facing on US 62. Erected by the Oklahoma College for Women in 1931, it reads: "Ancient council fires shall be kept kindled and burning."

ANADARKO, 68.5 *m.* (1,190 alt., 6,184 pop.), seat of Caddo County, was named for the Anadarkos, the Nadako tribe, a branch of the Caddoan group.

The city was founded on August 6, 1901, when the surrounding Kiowa-Comanche and Wichita reservations were opened to white settlement. On that day, some twenty thousand people arrived at the previously surveyed townsite to await their chance of occupation of the adjacent lands. At least ten thousand remained for several months, after which the population shrank to three thousand. Probably the first business establishment on the townsite was a bank, set up in a tent three weeks before the official land opening. It announced its mission on a large piece of canvas hung in front of the tent on which the names of the directors were painted. Several days before the opening, trainloads of liquor had been shipped into the town on the Rock Island Railway, which had built through while the site was still a reservation. For a time saloons and gambling establishments flourished, but the citizens soon tired of being bilked, and the gamblers were chased away. Business then adjusted itself and proceeded normally until the early 1920's when the development of near-by oil fields caused the population to double. The present business section has many modern structures that contrast sharply with older buildings like the red-brick CADDO COUNTY COURTHOUSE, Broadway and 2nd Street, erected in 1907.

Anadarko is an important trading center for farmers of the Washita valley. Alfalfa, cotton, wheat, corn, peanuts, and watermelons are the chief products. Stock-raising, cotton-ginning, cottonseed-oil milling, oil production and associated businesses are the main industries.

Anadarko is also becoming one of Oklahoma's leading tourist cities. On June 26, 1955, INDIAN CITY, U.S.A. was dedicated two and one-half miles southeast of Anadarko in the Tonkawa hills. Built to retain and preserve the cultural history of the American Indian, Indian City is an authentic reproduction of Indian villages grouped into a single city-like cluster. At present there are six villages (more are planned), each constructed so that it is completely separated from the others. The homes are furnished with authentic Indian furnishings, either made by Indians or donated by collectors. Indian City, U.S.A. was built with $100,000 subscribed by the people of Anadarko. During its first year of operation over 70,000 visitors toured the outdoor museum, an intelligent preservation of much of the Southwest's colorful Indian heritage.

In 1878, the Kiowa, Apache, and Comanche agencies were consolidated here with the Wichita office. The combined office is still maintained as an active Indian field office serving more than 10,000 Indians. In Anadarko, too, is the Bureau of Indian Affairs area office for western Oklahoma and all of Kansas, with jurisdiction over more than 26,000 Indians.

The area office is located at OLD TOWN, at the north edge of Anadarko on the south bank of the Washita River. (The first Kiowa agency was founded here in the late 1880's. Near by is an old jail cell once occupied by the mighty Geronimo.) The field office is located in the buff-brick FEDERAL BUILDING, the main floor of which features murals of Indian scenes and peoples drawn by the well-known native Kiowa artist, Steve Mopope.

One of the nation's outstanding Indian events is staged in Anadarko—the American Indian Exposition (*adm. $1.85*), usually held the second week in August. The Southern Plains Indians of Oklahoma, as well as members from tribes throughout the nation, stream into Anadarko for these eight days of colorful Indian pageantry. Many build their own Indian camp on the east edge of town, a camp which often has a week-long population of better than 10,000.

The Exposition presents the cultural and domestic life of the Indian in its mystic, ceremonial, and religious phases. Dressed in their native costumes, the Indians compete in pony races and bow-and-arrow shoots, go through ceremonial dances and rituals, display some of the nation's finest native arts and crafts, and hold traditional powwows and dances that last through the night.

On U.S. 62, adjacent to the exposition grounds is the excellent SOUTHERN PLAINS MUSEUM. It displays articles of ancient Plains Indian cultures and sells authentic Indian crafts. In the downtown CITY HALL, there is also a pioneer museum.

Right from Anadarko on paved US 281, across the Washita River, is the RIVERSIDE INDIAN BOARDING SCHOOL, 1.5 *m.*, founded in 1872. It has 2,200 acres of land (L) and 290 students from Oklahoma, New Mexico, and Arizona. Riverside is a miniature college campus with fine brick buildings, playgrounds, and well-equipped dormitories. Visitors are always welcome.

ST. PATRICK'S MISSION SCHOOL, 70.7 *m.*, is a Catholic school for Indian children. It was established in 1892 by Father Isidore Ricklin, a Belgian, who was adopted by the Comanche tribe the same year. It contains a number of Indian paintings and other art objects.

Near the mission and along the Washita River (R) is the area called TONKAWA VALLEY because it was the site of the gruesome massacre of the Tonkawa Indians. In 1862 this tribe was encamped along the river just south of Fort Cobb, the original Wichita Agency some seven miles to the northwest. The other tribes, served by the agency and encamped in the region, abhorred the Tonkawas because they were suspected of cannibalism. After finding the dismembered body of a Caddo child, who had wandered away from his tipi, they made secret plans to exterminate the Tonkawas.

On the night of October 23, Osages, Shawnees, and Delawares—who had come down from Kansas—together with Caddoes from the agency, started on the warpath. It ended in the near extermination of the Tonkawas and the complete destruction of Fort Cobb. Confederate officials at the fort were killed. Since most of the agency Indians had remained loyal to the Union, they felt no compunction against aiding the Kansas Indians in wiping out the southerners. The whites (except for some who escaped) were killed and thrown into the buildings, which were then set afire. The Tonkawas, who had been alarmed, fled that morning, but they were pursued to their camping place along the Washita, near the present Catholic Mission, and attacked at dawn. The camp was completely obliterated except for the bones of the massacred that lay blanching in the valley for years. Fort Cobb was never rebuilt—although the site was occupied by General Philip Sheridan and his troops for a short time in 1868 (*see Tour* 3A)—but the present town near by bears its name.

APACHE, 87.2 *m.* (1,300 alt., 1,190 pop.), is in the center of a rich agricultural area through which Cache Creek flows. The principal crops raised are wheat, corn, alfalfa, and cotton. About a third of the rural population are Indians. In the past decade and a half it has been the center of rather extensive oil development.

South of Apache the land is rolling prairie, with only a few trees along the creek bottoms. The blue of the Wichita Mountains dominates the horizon to the southwest.

RICHARDS SPUR, 98.3 *m.* (1,199 alt., 150 pop.), is a company village for the near-by limestone quarry. Small company houses line the highway, and in the distance (R) is a great crusher cutting down a rounded limestone foothill of the Wichitas. Exposed here are great tilted ledges of limestone that indicate the extensive deformation of the mountain mass.

At 101.5 *m.* is the junction with State 49 (*see Tour 3B*). Between 101.9 *m.* and 106.1 *m.*, US 62 passes through the FORT SILL MILI-

TARY RESERVATION (*see Tour* 3A), which extends for several miles on both sides of the highway.

At 104.9 *m.* is the junction (R) with the paved Fort Sill Road (*see Tour* 3A).

The FORT SILL INDIAN SCHOOL and the UNITED STATES INDIAN HOSPITAL, 107.3 *m.*, lie within a thousand-acre tract (L) of farm and pasture land used by both institutions. Established in 1871 under President Grant's "peace policy," the school served as a branch of the Kiowa-Comanche Agency, operated at that time by the Quaker agent, Lawrie Tatum. It is one of ten Indian boarding schools now operating in Oklahoma. The 1956–57 enrollment (Grades 1–12) was 192, including 110 Navajos. Most of the pueblo-type buildings are of brick and native stone. Many of the interior walls are decorated by murals painted by Kiowa Indian artists.

The Indian Hospital, north of the school, consists of three red-brick buildings, trimmed in white. They are modern and well equipped, and contain a solarium for the use of tubercular patients.

At the northern edge of LAWTON (*see Lawton*), 107.6 *m.*, US 62 turns west (R) to CACHE, 121.6 *m.* (1,260 alt., 620 pop.), in the foothills of the Wichita Mountains.

Right from Cache on an improved road to CRATERVILLE PARK (*cabins, swimming, fishing, skating, bridle paths, other resort facilities*), 3 *m.*, a large natural amphitheater in the hills, covered with grass and timber and watered by sparkling springs. Here in 1924 was organized the first All-Indian Fair and Exposition, which was moved to Anadarko (*see above*) in 1935.

Expansion plans of near-by Fort Sill, scheduled for 1957, will cause the removal of all Craterville facilities to a new site near Quartz Mountain State Park (*see Tour* 13).

Left from the entrance to Craterville Park is the HOME OF QUANAH PARKER, 1 *m.*, last chief of the Comanches. Quanah was the son of Cynthia Ann Parker, a white woman, and Peta Nokoni, a Comanche chief. Cynthia's story has been told in literature and song. When nine years old (1836), she was kidnaped by the Comanches who destroyed the Texas frontier fort where her family had settled. Years later Cynthia was identified and urged to return to her own race. By this time, however, her marriage and the birth of her half-Indian children had made her a true Comanche at heart. Texas Rangers forcibly returned her to her family, but she died soon after.

Quanah, who had been born about 1845, was of superior intelligence and character. While principal chief of his tribe, he led his warriors in the battle on Adobe Walls in Texas, the last great Plains Indian fight against white buffalo hunters. He rode at the head of his tribe when they surrendered tribal rule at Fort Sill in 1875, marking the close of Indian warfare in southwestern Oklahoma. Quanah was later allotted this tract of land on which he lived with his five wives. A single story serves to illustrate his native shrewdness. On one occasion the old chief was being given advice by Theodore Roosevelt on "how to walk the white man's road."

The gist of the counsel was that Quanah should end his bigamous status by giving up all his wives but one. The Comanche's reply was, "You tell 'em which one I keep!" The old eight-room house, which he built in 1890 and lived in until his death in 1911, is now occupied by his daughter, Mrs. Neda Birdsong.

Right (north) from the entrance to Craterville Park is (1956) the South Gate, 0.5 *m.*, of the WICHITA MOUNTAINS WILDLIFE REFUGE (*see Tour 3B*).

On the main route is INDIAHOMA, 128.9 *m.*, (1,335 alt., 319 pop.), a trade center for near-by Indian and white farmers.

Right from Indiahoma on an improved road to a junction with a second road 2 *m.*; L. on this road (1956) to the old POST OAK MISSION, 5 *m.*, founded in 1894 by the Mennonite Brethren Home Mission Society. Lumber for its construction was hauled from Marlow, some sixty miles distant and the nearest railroad station at that time (*see Lawton*).

In the mission cemetery are the GRAVES OF CYNTHIA AND QUANAH PARKER. Cynthia Ann had first been buried at Stevens, Texas. At her son's request, her body was brought here for reburial in 1910. And according to his wish, Quanah Parker was buried beside his mother in 1911. On May 30, 1930, before a crowd of five thousand people, a seventeen-foot granite monument—purchased with a Congressional appropriation—was raised above the chief's grave. (In October, 1956, the six surviving children of Quanah Parker voted to move the two graves to the Fort Sill Military Cemetery to make way for the base's expanded artillery range. The new Parker plot will lie just inside the Military Cemetery gate. The rest of the Post Oak Mission Cemetery, together with the mission building itself, will be relocated near Indiahoma.)

SNYDER, 141.1 *m.* (1,360 alt., 1,646 pop.), is the center of a diversified farming area. Three years after its founding in 1902, Snyder was almost completely demolished by a tornado that killed ninety-seven persons and caused extensive property damage. As a precaution against a similar loss of life, many of the town's homes now have storm caves or cellars. Granite characterized by a distinctive pinkish coloration is quaried and processed in the area.

At 145.2 *m.* is the entrance (R) to the ROOSEVELT GRANITE COMPANY quarry. The pink granite is clearly visible at the east abutment of the bridge over the North Fork of the Red River, 149.6 *m.*, and in the road-cut through the hills on the west side of the river.

Near HEADRICK, 152.3 *m.* (1,361 alt., 144 pop.), a small farm community, the hills rising abruptly (R) from nearly level fields mark the southwestern edge of the Wichita Mountains.

Entrance to ALTUS AIR BASE (R), one of the Strategic Air Command's important permanent installations, is at 161.7 *m.*

ALTUS, 163.8 *m.* (1,389 alt., 9,735 pop.), thanks to irrigation and the nation's military build-up, is rapidly becoming southwestern Oklahoma's most important city. Yet it owes its existence, somewhat ironically, to a near tragedy—a flood in the spring of 1891 which drove early settlers from a location on near-by Bitter Creek to the higher ground which is now Altus. The name was bestowed on it by one of the refugees because it meant "higher ground."

Inured to hardship, these first residents lived in dugouts until lumber could be hauled over the rutted wagon roads and "rustled" wood for their fuel from the Indian reservation across the North Fork, some fifteen miles away. Church services were also held in dugouts or under brush arbors. School children met wherever it was convenient—once in a livery stable—and the length of the academic term was governed by the length of time the settlers could provide a teacher with board, room, and a little cash. Today, as a dramatic symbol of its progress in little more than six decades, Altus boasts one of the state's most modern school systems. Facilities range from eight grade schools, through three high schools, to a fully accredited municipal junior college. Completed in 1956 as a part of a one-million-dollar expansion program, the new PHYSICAL EDUCATION BUILDING seats 3,100 people and is the second largest of its kind west of Oklahoma City.

In the city square is a granite marker designating the spot where the COMMUNITY PUMP once stood. Today water is supplied by the Lake Altus waterworks at Lugert (*see Tour 13*) on the North Fork of the Red River. Altus also has two large reservoir lakes within the city limits which provide fishing and sail and speed boat facilities.

Two hundred bales of cotton were ginned here in 1897 by a sixty-saw gin run by a threshing machine engine, and a maximum of 124,000 bales has been produced in a single year. But wheat is now equally important and alfalfa seed production has recently been climbing. Diversification and a certain stability of farm income have been made possible in recent years by irrigation, both from the 70,000-acre Lugert-Altus irrigation district and the nearly two hundred wells in operation in Jackson County by the end of 1956.

Altus, the seat of Jackson County, is at the junction with US 283 (*see Tour 13*).

Westward across the Salt Fork of the Red River, 171.1 *m.*, US 62 runs through a rolling, sandy land of mesquite and cactus, short-grass pastures, and occasional irrigated fields. Just northeast of GOULD, 189.3 *m.* (1,621 alt., 303 pop.), are the base marks used by the United States Geological Survey in determining the location of the one hundredth meridian, Oklahoma's western boundary. Between Gould and Hollis the terrain becomes more barren, and where there is no irrigation wind-swept tumbleweeds often pack against the fences in great, bushy walls.

HOLLIS, 197.7 *m.* (1,615 alt., 3,089 pop.), is the seat of Harmon County. It is situated in the extreme western part of old Greer County, the Red River territory which Texas claimed (*see Tour 13*) prior to a Supreme Court decision in 1896. A cotton-oil mill, at the southeast corner of Hollis, is the town's biggest industry. Near by is a characteristic symbol of cotton production—the sheet-iron-covered migrant worker camp. LEGION PARK, in town, provides swimming, while recently opened LAKE ARTHUR HALL, nine miles north, off State 30, offers forty-two acres for fishing.

At 202.8 *m.* US 62 crosses the Texas Line, twenty-nine miles northeast of Childress, Texas (*see Texas Guide*).

TOUR 3A

Junction US 62—Fort Sill—Junction US 62; Fort Sill Blvd., 6.2 m.

Roadbed paved throughout.
No accommodations in Fort Sill; available at near-by towns.

The inhabited part of the FORT SILL MILITARY RESERVATION is always open to visitors except during times of national emergency. The reservation proper covers more than 100,000 acres, varying in topography from rolling open prairie, marked by several abrupt hills on the east, to the rugged, granite peaks of the Wichita Mountains on the west. The area is watered by Medicine Bluff and Cache creeks. Medicine Bluff (R) is a granite and porphyry formation about three hundred feet high. Indians once invested it with supernatural powers, often leaving their sick on its top either to recover or die.

The Wichita Indians were the first people known to have inhabited the region. In the latter part of the eighteenth century a group of them built a village near the point where Medicine Bluff Creek flows into Cache Creek. Some of their grass houses stood where Lucas Field, the post parade ground, is today. Osage depredations and attacks caused them to move to a site on the North Fork of the Red River west of the Wichita Mountains. It was there that they were found by Colonel Henry Dodge and his regiment of dragoons in 1834. Dodge and his men had been sent out from Fort Gibson (*see Tour 3*) to establish friendly relations with the wild Plains Indians so that Santa Fe Trail travelers might be protected and peace assured to the Five Civilized Tribes following their removal from the East. Treaties with the United States were signed the following year as a result of Dodge's friendly expedition. On the trip he made successful overtures to the Wichitas and also to a band of Comanches who were then occupying the site of the former Wichita village on the western half of the present fort. The Colonel first saw the Comanche village when he and his company topped a hill, later named after him, in the northeastern part of the present Fort Sill area. The dragoons camped on the east side of Cache Creek across from the Comanches, not completely trusting their hosts. But soon after making camp, they were amazed to see the Stars and Stripes raised over the lodge of the Indians' chief.

The only white habitation in this region during this period was the trading post established by an agent of the Chouteau interests in 1837. Nothing is known about it except that it was located on the west bank of Cache Creek a little south of where the present road leading from Post Field joins US 62.

Since the Dodge expedition also established peaceful relations with the warring Osages, the Wichitas were enabled to move back to the site of Fort Sill. Here they lived until 1850 when, because of a malarial infection, they migrated east to near the present site of Rush Springs (*see Tour 11*). The region of Fort Sill was deserted for several years although, in 1852, the military and exploratory expedition of Captain R. B. Marcy arrived and camped for a few days where the post now stands. Marcy had been told to explore the country north of the Red River, and his company accomplished their task in a systematic manner, making a geological survey, classifying the natural life, marking the meridians, and making a map. The captain noted the desirability of the Fort Sill site for use as a military post, but it was not until 1868 that a fort was established there.

General Philip H. Sheridan, of Civil War fame, was assigned the task of pacifying the Plains Indians and placing them on reservations. At the start of his campaign, in 1868, he established his troops at the site of the burned and abandoned Fort Cobb (*see Tour 3*), some thirty miles to the north of present Fort Sill. His purpose was also to protect the agency there and to keep the peaceful Indians away from the warring ones so that what had been gained toward final harmony might not be lost. The lack of adequate food and shelter in this camp became so acute that, late in 1868, Sheridan sent Colonel Benjamin H. Grierson on a reconnaissance trip to Medicine Bluff to decide on a new camp site. Grierson had explored there before and now confirmed his former recommendation. When Sheridan arrived in January, 1869, he decided to erect a permanent fort at Camp Wichita, as it was then called.

At first the troops—the Tenth and Seventh (Custer's) Cavalry, and the Nineteenth Kansas Cavalry (Volunteers), lived at various places over the post area in brush-roofed dugouts. Headquarters for the Fort

Cobb Indian agency were moved to Camp Wichita, and many of the roaming Indians were brought in to live on the reservation. Sheridan left Camp Wichita in February, eventually to rise to the position of Commander in Chief of the United States Army in 1884. Grierson, the new post commander, aided by the troops left at the fort after Sheridan's departure, began construction of permanent buildings. Logs were cut from the surrounding stand of timber.

On July 2, 1869, the post was officially named Fort Sill. General Sheridan ordered the change to honor Brigadier General Joshua W. Sill, his classmate at West Point and a fellow officer during the Civil War. By 1870, the building program was well under way. Stone was found in Quarry Hill, southeast of the post, and lime for mortar was prepared in rude ovens along the banks of Cache Creek. Most of the work was done by the soldiers, though some skilled workers were imported. In early 1871 the quarters were finished and a lookout post, the BLOCKHOUSE (*visible from the highway*), was erected on Signal Mountain in the western section of the reservation. The remaining construction work was carried on intermittently for the next five years.

The careers of three Kiowa warrior chiefs—Satanta, Satank, and Big Tree—interlaced closely with the development of Fort Sill during this time and for several years after. The quick-witted Satanta, called the "Orator of the Plains," first came in contact with the military when he was arrested in 1868 after the Battle of the Washita. He was released by Sheridan at Camp Wichita in 1869 after promising to keep his followers at peace. In 1871, he played a leading part in the Warren wagon-train massacre in Texas, an event which brought swift reprisal from General W. T. Sherman, who was visiting Fort Sill on an inspection tour at the time. Satanta, whose moral outlook was that of a statesman at war but whose keenness was sometimes exceeded by his vanity, boasted in connection with the massacre, "I did it. If any other Indian claims the honor, he will be lying; for I did it myself," thereby practically placing a rope around his own neck.

Satanta, Satank, and Big Tree were arrested and placed in a cell under the barracks at the southwest corner of the parade ground. The three were loaded into wagons and sent for trial to Texas, where the massacre had occurred. Satank was killed along the way as he made a desperate attempt to escape. The others were sentenced to hang, later given commutations to life imprisonment, and were finally promised pardons at a conference in Washington, D. C., on condition that their people should fulfill certain peace agreements. Following parole in 1873, after being again lodged at the Fort Sill guardhouse, Satanta immediately reverted to his warrior's role and took part in several raids.

Finally he surrendered and was brought to Fort Sill in 1875 in chains, to be returned once again to the prison in Huntsville, Texas. When he found that there was no chance of being set free, he committed suicide by plunging head first from his second-story cell—the fulfillment of an early and prophetic utterance made by him, "When I settle down, I grow pale and die."

Indian outbreaks continued, though usually on a much smaller scale than in the days before Sheridan's campaign of dissuasion. The forays finally led to a discontinuance in 1874 of the Quaker Peace Policy (*see Tour 1*) of handling the Indians at Fort Sill. Finally, by use of sterner methods and under military command, Indian resistance was virtually broken in 1875. After 1876, the Fort Sill garrison found it necessary in many instances to protect rather than fight the Indians, for swarms of unscrupulous whites drifted into the section to plunder the subdued foe.

Agriculture had been introduced meanwhile to the Indians camped at Fort Sill. The Wichitas and the Caddoes needed little training in farming for they had been in the habit of raising much of their foodstuff. The Kiowas and Comanches, however, found it difficult to learn even the rudiments of agriculture, although they liked its products. Logically enough, to them, their method of plunder seemed much more convenient than the orthodox routine of growing. The agent once sent a party of Comanches to the agency at Anadarko to drive back eleven head of cattle, to be used for rationing at Fort Sill. On their return, the wily Indians passed a melon field and promptly traded five of the beeves for some of the melons. When the agent took the group to task, the Comanches, both hurt and surprised, explained that they had only been trying to act in the "white man's way" by paying a good price for what they wanted rather than stealing it. The agent perforce exonerated them.

When the last Indian disturbance occurred in 1891, quartermaster Lieutenant Hugh L. Scott and a faithful Kiowa assistant, I-see-o, managed to keep the Fort Sill Indians from taking the warpath. This near-rebellion—the Ghost Dance or "Messiah Craze"—covered most of the western part of the United States and was in part an outgrowth of the misfortunes which had befallen the Indians. John Wilson, a Piute Indian of Nevada, had fathered the religion which involved a mystic conception of a Messiah who had thrown over the white people for the red, and whose coming would be synonymous with the return of the almost-extinct buffalo. Many self-appointed prophets sprang up and acquired converts and tribute through a type of spiritual mesmerism. The Ghost Dance, the main ceremonial of the faith, began with the believers forming a circle in which they moved slowly while chanting. The medicine man in the center strove by exhortation to induce a hypnotic trance in which the dancer would fall in a stupor and experience visions of the Utopia to come. An Arapaho named Sitting Bull agitated the craze among the Fort Sill Indians. To deal with a situation that promised to develop into an uprising, Scott kept watch unobtrusively through I-see-o and allowed the obsession to fall of its own weight. Scott later appointed I-see-o a sergeant for life. At his death the respected old Indian was given military burial with full honors.

Fort Sill was a busy and crowded place in 1901 when the surrounding land was thrown open to white occupation. While awaiting the results of the drawing at El Reno, people converged from all directions to camp at the post. Finally in 1909, after the fort had been in danger of abandonment, work was begun on the construction of a new post, northwest of the group of old buildings. A School of Fire for field artillery was established here in 1911, and in 1917 the field artillery unit and its equipment was increased tremendously for the duration of World War I.

The War Department changed the school's designation to the "Field Artillery School" during the 1920–39 period. A building program begun in 1934 expanded the post to its present size. Following the outbreak of World War II in Europe and the enactment of this country's first peacetime draft law in 1940, conscripts began to stream onto the post. The four years following the Japanese bombing of Pearl Harbor saw training at Fort Sill reach its feverish peak. And by the end of World War II, the school's total graduates exceeded 110,000 officers and men.

The postwar years have seen many changes as the nation has sought to adapt itself to the changing conditions of the so-called "cold war." In 1946 the War Department changed the post's main designation to "The Artillery Center," the "Field Artillery School" to the "Artillery School." All types of artillery training were consolidated at Fort Sill. During the Korean conflict courses in the curriculum were expanded from ten to forty-three, the number of students from less than two thousand to nearly fifteen thousand. The final change in designation came early in 1955 when yet another fact of mid-twentieth-century military life was recognized. Fort Sill became the nation's "Artillery and Guided Missile Center."

But the artilleryman's motto—*Cedat Fortuna Peritis* ("let fortune yield to experience")—is unchanged. Today it stands as the tried standard of intelligence and valor which has made the American artilleryman respected in military circles throughout the world.

Fort Sill Boulevard branches right (N. W.) from its junction, 0 *m.*, with US 62 (*see Tour* 3), 17.7 miles south of Apache (*see Tour* 3).

The OLD CORRAL, 0.3 *m.*, is a loopholed, stone-walled structure (R), built by Colonel Grierson in 1870 to protect the fort livestock from the Indians.

The buildings in the square comprising the OLD POST, 0.6 *m.*, are of white stucco and limestone. The OLD CHAPEL, 0.8 *m.*, is a small ivy-covered structure (R) of native stone with six windows and a heavy, iron bell with a pull rope. Built in 1870, the chapel has a fine fireplace and is furnished with dark, wooden pews. A reed organ occupies the choir at the rear. It is now used by the Episcopalians of the post.

Between the Old Post and US 62 is the SITE OF THE PRISON in which some one hundred Indians were incarcerated from December, 1874, to March, 1875. These were the captives taken in the last big campaign during which Indian resistance was finally broken. The prisoners were mostly subchiefs and warriors who had taken an active part in the battles. They were moved from here to the military prison at St. Augustine, Florida, from which they were released in 1878. Only the floor of the old structure, later used as an icehouse and a blacksmith shop, is still visible.

A white stone, two-story residence on the north side of the square has been used as the POST COMMANDANT'S QUARTERS since the early days, although new quarters were built in 1936. It was here that an attempt on the life of General W. T. Sherman was made by an Indian named Stumbling Bear.

Opposite the southwest corner of the Old Post parade ground is the MUSEUM (*open 10–5 Wed. through Sat.; 12–5 Sun.; closed Mon. and Tues.*), 1 *m.*, in the old guardhouse, where Geronimo was sometimes confined while at the post. A Cannon Walk leads to MCLAIN HALL, an artillery section of the Museum. The Apache chief Geronimo and other prisoners of his band had been sent here in 1894 after being quartered in Florida and Alabama following their capture in 1886. At Fort Sill, Geronimo was subject to military control, but was free to roam at will over the reservation. The old chief, who was addicted to spirits, was of necessity often confined to the guardhouse in an effort to sober him. Fort Sill inhabitants of those days grew accustomed to the sight of the notoriously bloodthirsty Indian recovering from a hangover while splitting wood at the rear of the jail. Geronimo was much in demand for traveling fairs and shows, and since he liked being stared at, he obtained leave for this purpose as much as possible. He died of pneumonia on February 17, 1909, and was buried in the Apache cemetery near Cache Creek on the post grounds. In 1913 the majority of the Apaches were returned to Arizona.

The museum was founded in 1934 and contains a comprehensive collection of old carbines, field guns, uniforms, medals, flags of various epochs and units, Indian weapons, dresses, and peace pipes.

McNAIR HALL, 1.2 *m.*, a large three-story brown stucco structure (R) is headquarters of the Artillery and Guided Missile Center. To the north are the STATION HOSPITAL (*visiting hours, 2–4* P.M. *and 6–8* P.M.), NURSES' QUARTERS, OFFICERS' QUARTERS, and the ACADEMIC AREA where the brown stucco officers' quarters line both sides of a wide parked driveway. Southwest of McNair is SNOW HALL, headquarters of the ARTILLERY AND GUIDED MISSILE SCHOOL.

The route, which follows the four sides of the NEW POST PARADE GROUND, turns right on Fort Sill Boulevard at 1.9 *m.* to parallel the east side.

Used by the Protestants, the NEW POST CHAPEL, 2 *m.*, is a narrow, brown-brick structure (R) designed in a pseudo-Gothic style. The tile-roofed structure near by (R), of white stucco, is the POST THEATER (*civilians not admitted*).

At 2.2 *m.* Fort Sill Road turns left to parallel the north side of the Parade Ground, with quarters for officers to the right. Near Medicine Bluff Creek, to the northeast, is the site on which Custer and the Seventh Cavalry camped at the founding of the fort in January and February of 1869. Depressions marking the sites of their brush-roofed dugouts are still visible.

Turning left again, 2.7 *m.*, the route passes along the west side of the Parade Ground, which is bordered (L) by the cream stucco barracks of several FIELD ARTILLERY BATTALIONS, and (R) by the gun sheds and garages of the same units.

Again turning left, at 2.9 *m.*, the route (here called Randolph Road) runs along the south side of the Parade Ground. On the left are more field artillery barracks. Additional barracks, the POST EXCHANGE (*sales made only to post personnel*), the GUARDHOUSE, SIGNAL OFFICE, and FORT SILL NATIONAL BANK are to the right. Gun sheds for field artillery units are south of these buildings.

Leaving the Parade Ground, the route—again Fort Sill Blvd.—turns right 3.4 *m.*, and passes (L) a quarry, 3.7 *m.*

Between the quarry and Post Field is the former summer camp site of the Oklahoma National Guard (R). The area (approximately a square mile) is now ocupied by units quartered here and the OFFICERS CANDIDATE SCHOOL.

Fort Sill Blvd. passes by Post Field (L), 5.2 *m.*, the aviation field established in 1917. It was named for Lieutenant Henry B. Post, twenty-fifth Infantry, who was killed in 1914 while attempting to set an altitude record at San Diego, California.

At 6.2 *m.* is the South Gate of the Fort Sill reservation and the junction with US 62 (*see Tour 3*).

TOUR 3B

Junction US 62—Medicine Park—Wichita Mountains Wildlife Refuge—Indiahoma; State 49, Meers Highway, Scenic Highway, 31.8 m.

State 49 asphalt-paved; Scenic Highway and Meers Highway graveled.
Good resort accommodations at Medicine Park; camping and picnicking facilities within Refuge. No food, service station, or garage concessions within Refuge.

This route passes through the resort town of Medicine Park and the Wichita Mountains Wildlife Refuge, both in the Wichita Mountains, a region abounding in low but rugged mountains, clear streams, vistas of prairie grass, and a series of man-made lakes. All visitors are cautioned to be extremely careful with fires, as a carelessly tossed match can destroy thousands of acres of valuable recreational and scenic refuge lands.

State 49, a paved highway branches west (R), 0 *m.* from its junction with US 62 (*see Tour 3*) at a point 14.3 miles south of Apache (*see Tour 3*).

At the beginning of the mountainous area is MEDICINE PARK, 6.6 *m.* (1,765 alt., 830 pop.), a popular summer resort. LAKE LAWTONKA (*fishing, boating*), extending from the northern edge of town, covers approximately fourteen hundred acres. A dam, 60 feet high and 375 feet long, was constructed across Medicine Bluff Creek at the mouth of a deep gorge to form this reservoir for the city of Lawton and the Fort Sill Artillery and Guided Missile School (*see Tour 3A*).

West of Medicine Park, at 7.4 *m.*, the route passes through the East Gate of the WICHITA MOUNTAINS WILDLIFE REFUGE (*adm. free; no guides necessary*), an area comprising 59,099 acres. The Wichita Mountains extend northwest from Fort Sill for a distance of sixty-five miles to a point four miles northwest of Granite. The greatest width of this mountain system, located mainly in Comanche County, is twenty-eight miles. The weather-sculptured domes and boulders of the Wichitas—averaging 650 to 700 feet in height—show their great age and prove them to be one of the oldest ranges in the United States.

A three-mile paved highway spirals upward a thousand feet, past the "River of Boulders" to the summit of Mount Scott (2,467 feet), overlooking a magnificent sweep of country. More than three-fourths of a million people visit this area annually and the number is increasing. Fifty miles of paved and graveled roads lead to fish-stocked lakes, to swimming beaches, and to free camp and picnic sites. The hills are covered with low forests of blackjack and post oak, while the intervening valleys are covered with native prairie grasses. Herds of buffalo and longhorn cattle, as well as wild turkeys and deer, can be seen from the roads. Almost two hundred kinds of birds are in the refuge including the cardinal, titmouse, chickadee, bluebird, and several different wrens. Bobwhite quail and mourning doves are common nesters in the area.

Until the middle of the nineteenth century, the only inhabitants of this area were Indians. The onetime presence here of a tribe of Wichita Indians has been substantiated, and remains of other tribal lodges have been found. In the extreme northwestern section of the Refuge is CUTTHROAT GAP, scene of the hideous massacre of a band of Kiowas by Osages in 1833. The Kiowa camp was occupied on this tragic day only by the young and old, for the warriors were all away hunting. The Osages struck suddenly, first slitting the throats of their victims, then cutting off their heads, which they placed in the convenient buckets of the Kiowas as an offering to their gods. One of these buckets, found standing in the ruins of the village after the disaster, is in the Fort Sill Museum (*see Tour 3A*).

When this section of Indian land was opened for white settlement in 1901, Congress set aside the Wichita Mountains as a forest reserve under the jurisdiction of the Department of the Interior. When it was transferred to the Forest Service of the Department of Agriculture in 1905, along with all national reserves, it was designated a game preserve by proclamation of President Theodore Roosevelt. After several changes of name and jurisdiction, the area was given its present name —the Wichita Mountains Wildlife Refuge—in 1935. Five years later it was placed under the jurisdiction of the Fish and Wildlife Service of the Department of the Interior.

The alarmingly rapid disappearance of the buffalo was responsible for the Roosevelt proclamation of 1905. A herd of fifteen buffaloes was donated to the government by the New York Zoological Society, which had been making a determined effort to perpetuate the breed, and Congress appropriated $15,000 to fence eight thousand acres in the Wichitas as a pasture for the animals. By 1956 the original fifteen buffaloes had increased to over a thousand head. The buffalo—also known as American Bison—now range over the entire 59,000 acres of the refuge, and many of them have helped to stock zoos over the nation and in some foreign countries. The buffalo feed upon the grasses of the refuge, the big and little bluestem, Indian grass, switch grass, and buffalo grass. The rocky hills and oak timber furnish shelter for the herd from the "northers" that sweep in from the plains during the winter months.

Other wildlife protected in the refuge include elk, white-tailed deer, Texas longhorns, wild turkeys, and prairie dogs. In 1956 the elk numbered 270; the deer about 2,200; the longhorns, 385; and the turkeys, 400. The city of Wichita, Kansas, donated a bull elk in 1908. A shipment of five elk was received from St. Anthony, Idaho, in 1911. In 1912, an additional fifteen were brought in from Wyoming—the same year the first turkeys were placed in the Wichitas. The longhorn cattle are descendants of domesticated animals brought to this continent by the Spanish in 1521. By the close of the Civil War, Texas was overrun with this type of cattle that had been allowed to run wild. With settlement of the range and consequent increase in value of land, the longhorns had to give way to improved breeds and were rapidly becoming extinct. Upon the government's initiative, a few were found along the Rio Grande and the Gulf Coast and brought to the Wichita Refuge in 1927, where they have since increased to their present number.

The annual rainfall of the refuge has varied from a low of just over 15 inches (1910) to a high of over 57 inches (1908). The average rainfall is between 30 and 31 inches. In years of good winter and spring rains, many wildflowers can be seen. In the autumn the fall colors of the oaks, elms, walnuts, persimmons, and other trees attract thousands of tourists.

State 49 passes through the tree-shaded MOUNT SCOTT CAMPGROUNDS (*tables, fire grates, and water*), 8.4 *m.* A quarter of a mile south of the campground is LAKE ELMER THOMAS (*swimming, fishing; boats available from concession headquarters just east of East Gate to refuge*).

At 9.5 *m.* is the junction with the paved Mount Scott Scenic Road.

Right on this winding, looping road, 3 *m.*, to the summit of MOUNT SCOTT (2,400 alt., 1,000 ft. above the base), named for General Winfield Scott, of Mexican War fame. Scott also conducted a part of the removal of the Cherokee Indians from the East to their new home in what is now Oklahoma. Construction of the scenic highway, completed in 1935, necessitated blasting through rock walls twenty to sixty feet high. From LOOKOUT POINT on the top there is a wide view of the surrounding country. A foot trail winds over the summit.

The Indians say that the Great Spirit appeared on Mount Scott after a devastating flood. Here He called all Indians to Him and provided them with the means to survive. Other legends tell of the gold which Spaniards supposedly mined here in the seventeenth century. An old trail, connecting the Spanish possessions east of the Mississippi with their southwest holdings, is said to have skirted the base of this mountain. Rusty knives, pieces of armor, and other relics have been found here, giving some credence to the tale.

At 12.1 *m.* is the junction with the Meers Highway (paved to the north entrance of the refuge, 2 *m.*).

Right here to MOUNT ROOSEVELT, 1.1 *m.*, named for President Theodore Roosevelt. On the south flank of the mountain is the Easter Holy City (*see below*).

At 1.8 *m.* is the junction with a dirt road.

Right here to CEDAR PLANTATION, a seventeen-acre planted grove. At times in some winters thousands of robins and, later in the season, hundreds of blackbirds roost in the trees. The flight into the roost just before dark is extraordinary to watch.

At 2 *m.* is the North Gate to the Refuge.

Left on Meers Highway, now the main route, to the junction with Rush Lake road, paved, with some gravel near Rush Lake, 12.3 *m.*

Right on this road to the EASTER HOLY CITY, 0.8 *m.*, site of the annual Easter Pageant and Passion Play (*3:30 A.M. to dawn; free adm.*), presented by the citizens of Lawton. On the slope of the small hill is a natural amphitheater which seats an audience of approximately 150,000. Buildings of red sandstone, constructed by WPA workers on the flank of the opposite hill, are used as dressing rooms by the two thousand persons who participate in the pageant. The Garden of Gethsemane, the Tomb, and the Court of Pilate have all been reproduced out of natural rock as the setting and are an effective background for the floodlighted performance.

At 2.1 *m.* is LAKE RUSH (*fishing*).

At 12.5 *m.* on Meers Highway is the junction with a graveled road.

Right here is LAKE JED JOHNSON (*picnicking; no camping*), 0.2 *m.*, one of the many artificial lakes which have been created in the Refuge.

At 15.2 *m.* is the junction with a dirt road.

Left on this road to CRATER LAKE, 0.5 *m.* On a rock butte, which projects from a near-by hill into the water, are traces of rock fortifications said to have been erected by Indian war parties.

At 15.7 *m.* is the "Y" paved junction with the Scenic Highway.

Left here to the PECAN SPRINGS CAMPGROUND, 0.2 *m.*

The route passes through the South Gate of the Refuge, 1.9 *m.*, and proceeds to CRATERVILLE, 0.5 *m.* (*ranch resort*), and CACHE, 5.4 *m.* (1,260 alt., 1,000 pop.) (*see Tour 3*), at the junction with US 62 (*see Tour 3*).

Right from the "Y" junction on Scenic Highway, now the main route, to a junction with a graveled road, 16.1 *m.*

Left here to the QUANAH PARKER DAM AND LAKE, 0.8 *m.*, named in honor of this last Comanche chief, whose home and grave are not far from here (*see Tour 3*). The dam, the largest in the Refuge, is semicircular, with a siphon spillway, and measures seventy feet from summit to base. Steps at each end enable visitors to walk across the top. Below the spillway is a small auxiliary dam. The lake covers eighty-six acres.

At 16.6 *m.* on the main route is the junction with the Seminole Beach Trail.

Left on this trail to the QUANAH PARKER CAMPGROUNDS, also named for the Comanche chief, and SEMINOLE BEACH, 0.3 *m.* All work on the extensive beach, the one-hundred-foot diving pier and the surrounding native-stone buildings, was done by the CCC. Some of the large, flat slabs of red granite used in the construction of the buildings are ten feet in height. The tawny red of the igneous rock is colorfully highlighted by the velvetry green of clinging moss and lichens. The main structure, the COMMUNITY HOUSE, has an arched ceiling of white pine, scorched to reveal the beauty of the grain. The walls are finished with rough plaster, and the huge fire place carries out the prevailing theme of granite. The fifteen-foot mantel is inlaid with an Indian pictograph of arrowheads and pines. The near-by bathhouses are square stone structures built in Spanish style. Their dressing rooms (*no charge*) open into a patio.

A footbridge spans the western arm of Quanah Parker Lake here, and a foot trail leads one mile west over Mount Baldy to LAKE OSAGE. On the eastern shore a large mound of rock rises almost perpendicularly from the water to form a jagged peninsula.

At 19.3 *m.* on Scenic Highway is the junction with the Lost Lake–Boulder Campgrounds Trail.

Left here to LOST LAKE, 1.1 *m.*, which legends say was at one time the site of a natural lake. Once, after an absence of three years, Indian hunters returned to find that the body of water had completely dried—hence, its name. Lawton citizens subscribed funds for the creation of the present artificial lake and campgrounds and dedicated the recreational improvements to the National Forest Service on May 31, 1926. Upstream there is a chain of dams.

At 2 *m.* is a junction with a foot trail.

Left here over a cement bridge and up a steep hill to BOULDER CANYON VIEW, 0.3 *m.* This point provides a thrilling view of the Narrows, the sheer one-hundred-foot granite walls which imprison West Cache Creek just before it breaks through into the plains. Red-tailed hawks build their nests high on the steep cliffs and in the morning and evening skim up and down the canyon in their search for food. The rugged, massive walls, reflecting the ever changing colors caused by the play of light and shadow on the stream below, make the canyon a miniature Garden of the Gods.

CAMP BOULDER (*shelterhouse, tables, benches, fire grates*), 2.5 *m.*, is the scene of many group picnics and camping parties. It is especially favored by girl and boy scout organizations.

In PRAIRIE DOG TOWN, 20.5 *m.*, where some four thousand prairie dogs have dug their dens, the little brown animals—about the size of small puppies—whisk in and out of their holes so rapidly that they defy observation. They usually emerge at dusk or early in the morning to seek food, but dodge back into their holes at the slightest sound. They are strictly vegetarians, and because of their proclivity for burrowing and the consequent destruction of crops, farmers regard them as nuisances.

Westward, the EXHIBITION PASTURES (L) cover a large area of gently rolling prairie land surrounded by high, round-topped hills and red granite cliffs and ridges. Small groups of elk, bison, deer, and Texas Longhorns are pastured here so that visitors may watch them graze. The majority of the animals making up the vast Refuge herds roam far from the traveled roads, but magnificent specimens may be seen here. The pastures, extending along the route for about a mile, are covered with an abundant growth of mesquite, buffalo grass, and bluestem. Groves of blackjack and post oaks grow at the bases of the hills and cliffs. Visitors are forbidden to enter the exhibition pens, and any molestation of the animals is rated a federal offense.

At 21.4 *m.* is a "Y" junction with a paved road.

To the right on this road is REFUGE HEADQUARTERS (*maps and descriptive pamphlets*) 0.2 *m.*, which comprises the main office. Straight ahead this road passes through the residential area of the Refuge personnel.

At 1.6 *m.* is a junction with a dirt road.

Left on this road is FRENCH'S LAKE, 0.4 *m.*, named for a former superintendent of the Refuge. There is a large spiral fish ladder at the dam, and downstream from the lake proper is a long line of ponds extending as far as Lost Lake. A hiking trail, beginning on the left side of French Lake, follows the stream to that point.

The main route turns sharply right (follow the pavement) to the junction with the graveled Treasure Lake road, 24.1 *m.*

Right here, 0.2 *m.*, to the POST OAK CAMPGROUND (*tables, fire grates*). Road continues 0.6 *m.* where two artificial lakes (TREASURE and POST OAK) afford a beautiful view with boulder-strewn mountains as a backdrop. Fishing is permitted in the lakes.

The main routes pass ELM SPRINGS CAMPGROUND (*water, tables, grates*) and then proceed easterly to the Refuge Gate, 24.6 *m.* The pavement ends here. The graveled road proceeds southward to INDIA-

HOMA, 31.8 *m.* (1,335 alt., 337 pop.) (*see Tour 3*), at the junction with US 62 (*see Tour 3*).

TOUR 4

(Seneca, Mo.)—Bartlesville—Ponca City—Enid—(Canadian, Tex.); US 60, Missouri Line to Texas Line, 358.1 m.

Roadbed paved all the way.
The Frisco Ry. roughly parallels US 60 between Seneca, Mo., and Vinita; the Katy between Bartlesville and Pawhuska; the Rock Island between Ponca City and Tonkawa, and between Pond Creek and Meno; and the Santa Fe between Cleo Springs and Fairview.
Good accommodations at all of the larger towns along the entire route.

Crossing from Missouri, US 60 continues for a short distance among the rocky, wooded ridges and narrow valleys of the northwestern slopes of the Ozark range, a region where in mid-April dogwood blossoms make vivid white splashes against the dark leafless oaks. It then passes through a section of alternating forest and grassland, where the remnants of a number of small Indian tribes live. The route crosses Grand River, then traverses open country fairly evenly divided between farms and pastures.

To the west is the northern portion of the former Cherokee Nation. Here scattered wells of the first extensive shallow oil fields developed in Oklahoma were still producing in 1956.

Beyond the country of the Osages the route touches the lands of the Ponca and Tonkawa Indians. North and west of Enid it crosses what has been called Oklahoma's "ocean of wheat." Then beyond the Cimarron River lies a stretch of rough, arid high plains broken by gypsum-crusted formations that suggest, on a giant scale, the glitter of five-and-dime-store decorations. And finally, as US 60 nears the Texas Line, the desert motif is suggested by the appearance of the graceful, drought-resistant yucca.

Section a. MISSOURI LINE *to* BARTLESVILLE, *89.8 m.* *US 60*

US 60 crosses the MISSOURI LINE, 0 *m.*, at a point 0.8 miles west of Seneca, Missouri (*see Missouri Guide*), and winds for a few miles through the Oklahoma Ozarks. A historical marker (R), 1.5 *m.*, calls attention to the first Seneca Agency, established July 4, 1832, about twelve miles to the south. Numerous streams have cut narrow, V-shaped valleys through this plateau, and the valleys and gentle hills are covered with abundant stands of post oak, hickory, cottonwood, and walnut. In the spring, dogwood, redbud, and wild plum blossoms splash the woods with color.

Northwest of here are large deposits of tripoli, a rock which is ground into a flour and widely used as an abrasive and a polisher. Most of the refining of the raw material is done at mills in Seneca, Missouri.

At 5.2 *m.* is the junction with State 10.

Left on this road, past numerous resorts along the upper arms of GRAND LAKE (*see Tour 1*), to GROVE, 19.3 *m.* (757 alt., 928 pop.) (*see Tour 15*). Rapidly being improved, this stretch of State 10 is one of the state's most pleasant scenic byways.

WYANDOTTE, 7.5 *m.* (754 alt., 242 pop.), was named for the Wyandotte Indians, whose reservation included this area after the land was turned over to the United States by the Senecas in 1867. (The 900-odd tribal members made nationwide headlines in 1956 when an Act of Congress returned to them an ancient two-acre cemetery in Kansas City's downtown Huron Park. The burial ground, ceded to the United States in 1855 when the tribe was moved to Oklahoma, is worth an estimated one and one-half million dollars!) Indians make up the greater part of the population of the village and surrounding area. But most of the town's activities are dependent on the near-by SENECA INDIAN SCHOOL (*visitors welcome*). Founded by the Quakers in 1869, the first building was a log cabin north of the present site. Now a dozen brick and frame structures comprise the plant, occupying a high bluff overlooking the Lost Creek arm of Grand Lake. The government-supervised institution is open to members of all the northeastern Oklahoma tribes coming under the jurisdiction of the Quapaw Agency.

US 60 is lined with resorts just west of Wyandotte as it crosses the Spring and Neosho rivers, the two northernmost arms of Grand Lake. High bluffs line both streams, which join just south (L) of the highway.

The town of FAIRLAND, 15.6 *m.* (828 alt., 699 pop.), was named for an early-day storekeeper. Long the center of a rich cattle-raising section, it has become increasingly resort conscious since the creation (1941) of Grand Lake.

At 23.6 *m.* is the junction with US 59 (*see Tour 15*) and with US 66–69 (*see Tours 1 and 8*), with which US 60 unites southwestward for the next 23.4 miles. Here, too, is the Afton interchange for access to the Will Rogers Turnpike (*see Tour 1*).

At 25.6 *m.* US 59 turns left for Grove (*see Tour 15*)

AFTON, 26.0 *m.* (790 alt., 1,252 pop.) (*see Tour 1*).

VINITA, 41.6 *m.* (702 alt., 5,518 pop.) (*see Tour 1*).

At 45.6 *m.* is the western junction with US 69; at 46.8 *m.* that with US 66.

COODY'S BLUFF, 65.8 *m.* (648 alt., 64 pop.), just across the Verdigris River, was named for a Cherokee Indian family.

An interesting method of oil extraction has been used in this area since 1937—the use of injected water pressure in order to produce enough oil from stripper wells to warrant their being operated. Water is forced down several wells drilled to the same depth as a centrally located oil well. This water then makes its way through the minute crevices and channels of the oil sand in which pockets of crude oil have been left in the normal process of production and pushes that crude toward the central well, from which it can easily be brought to the surface by pumps. This repressuring method has brought about a "five-spot" appearance to the fields, since the original wells were fairly regularly spaced, one to every ten acres of drilling land. Now an oil well usually occupies the center of each forty-acre tract. A central warehouse and reservoir furnishes water and power for these artificial water-flood projects. The process was first instituted because geologists estimated that only two thousand barrels had been removed from each potential forty-thousand-barrel tract. Since 1937 the process has been widely used. In 1956, near-by Osage County (*see below*) alone had twenty-five water-flood projects in operation. And the Nowata-Childers water-flood setup is one of the largest of its kind in the world.

The turreted and spired houses of NOWATA, 69.1 *m.* (707 alt., 3,965 pop.), with their ornamental lattices, carved banisters and porch posts are typical of turn-of-the-century "gingerbread" architecture. In 1868, this area was included in the land sold by the Cherokee Indians to the Kansas Delawares. From the trading post, which was established a short time later, a settlement grew up to become the town of Nowata. When the railroad arrived, two company surveyors are said to have named it Noweta at the suggestion of a Cherokee woman who said that the word meant "We welcome you to come." The spelling was changed later in Post Office Department records.

Nowata is at the junction with US 169 (*see Tour 9A*).

At 88.2 *m.* is the junction with US 75 (*see Tour 9*). US 60 turns right here, following US 75 for 1.6 miles before turning left onto Frank Phillips Blvd., the principal east-west street through BARTLESVILLE, 89.8 *m.* (694 alt., 19,228 pop.) (*see Bartlesville*).

Section b. BARTLESVILLE *to* ENID, *135.9 m.* US 60

Between BARTLESVILLE, 0 *m.*, and Ponca City, US 60 traverses the confines of the old Osage Nation, now Osage County. Indian tipis once dotted the rocky hills, but today they have been replaced by "stripper wells" and "pumping jacks." The high-rounded Osage Hills encompass well-watered valleys, both blanketed in the spring and summer with many wild flowers.

In 1871, the Osage Indians were removed from Kansas to Silver Lake (*see Tour* 9), and then in 1872 to this tract of almost 1,500,000 acres, which they purchased from the Cherokee Nation. They had been paid $9,000,000 by the federal government for their Kansas land, and since they lived on the interest from their money, they were known as the wealthiest Indians in the country. Their new lands were composed of hills and prairies, which was much to their liking, for they were naturally hunters and fighters rather than farmers. Many leased their lands for pasture; others adopted the white man's way and became ranchers themselves.

The Osage roll, which was approved in 1908, listed 2,229 persons receiving an allotment of 657 acres. All mineral rights were reserved for the benefit of the tribe, each individual headright to receive a pro rata share of the income. The discovery of oil and gas in the extreme east-central part of the Nation in October, 1897, and the subsequent development of the vast field catapulted the Osages into an even greater luxury. By 1916, each member of the tribe was receiving annual amounts ranging upwards from $2,200. By 1926, the peak year, this figure had reached $15,000. And those who had inherited headrights had a still larger income. During this period yearly lease sales ranged from one to fourteen million dollars and total royalty and lease payments received by the tribe for their oil by 1934 amounted to some $252,700,000.

During the period of luxury for the Osages, it was not unusual to see a blanketed Indian—braids down his back and a Stetson on his head—at the wheel of an expensive automobile, while his wife and family, also colorfully blanketed, occupied the back seat. Today the Osage has become more accustomed to his wealth, while the value of his headright itself, due to a partially depleted oil basin, is somewhat reduced. Improved recovery methods, however (*see above*), has increased oil production in recent years. For the fiscal year 1955–56, the Osage area produced approximately one per cent of the nation's oil, and 12 per cent of Oklahoma's. Thirty-seven per cent of this was due to recovery by water flooding. As of September, 1956, there were 2,658 participants in Osage royalties, and the income on each headright for the same period was $8,000, appreciably larger than that of the average white citizen. The value of the Osage headright was estimated in 1956 to be worth about $30,000.

At 2.2 *m.* is the junction (L) with paved State 23.

Left on State 23 to the FRANK PHILLIPS RANCH, 12 *m.* A rustic arched gateway (R) marks the beginning of the winding drive through the ranch grounds to WOOLAROC MUSEUM, 14 *m.* (*adm. free; open 10–5 except Mon.*), synthetically named for "woods," "lake," and "rock." The 4,000-acre ranch (the onetime country home of the founder and president of Phillips Petroleum Company) is a private game preserve containing American bison (buffalo), elk, deer, and other animals, both native and foreign to Oklahoma. There are also seven fish-stocked lakes. The museum, owned and operated by the charitable Frank Phillips Foundation, was established by the late Mr. and Mrs. Phillips and dedicated to ". . . the boys and girls of today, the fathers and mothers of tomorrow. . . ."

The air-conditioned museum is a 300-foot-long stone building with a permanent display of some 50,000 items. It is noted for its priceless archaeological collection, its superb gallery of Western paintings and sculptures, and one of the world's finest collection of Indian blankets.

Among artifacts and ornaments of seven different prehistoric cultures of the Southwest are many outstanding pieces from the Great Temple Mound near Spiro (*see Tour 7*). Represented among Woolaroc's original paintings are the famed "triumvirate" of Western painters—Remington, Russell, and Lee—along with such other well-known artists as Johnson, Sharp, Couse, Balink, Berninghaus, and Phillips. Woolaroc sculptures include the twelve original models from which Ponca City's Pioneer Woman (*see Tour 10*) was chosen, and the original model of the Lincoln Memorial in Washington.

OSAGE HILLS STATE PARK (*cabins, picnicking, swimming, fishing*), 12.6 *m.*, is a rolling 850-acre wooded area (L) that shelters coyote, fox, otter, raccoon, and opossum. There are bridle paths and a number of attractive hiking trails, including one to the old stone water tower atop "Osage Lookout," which gives the visitor his best panoramic view of the park. There is also a small lake. Perch, crappie, and catfish can be taken from it, as well as from bluff-lined Sand Creek (*boats $2 per day*), a clear-water stream that winds through the park. A new swimming pool was opened June 1, 1956.

At 20.4 *m.* is the junction with State 99 (*see Tour 14*), which unites with US 60 to Pawhuska.

At 24.9 *m.* is the junction with a graveled road.

Left on this road to PAWHUSKA INDIAN VILLAGE, 0.8 *m.*, home of many members of the "Dwellers-in-the-Thorny-Thickets" (*see Tour 14*) division of the Osage tribe. Here until he died in 1932 lived Bacon Rind, or Wah-she-hah, one of the Osage's best-known leaders. (Since his tribal election was never confirmed by the Secretary of the Interior, he was not a chief in fact, though he has been widely so called.) Born in 1853, Wah-she-hah possessed a physique "like something in bronze by Praxiteles"—to quote John Joseph Mathews. And his oratory, though he spoke almost entirely in the Osage tongue, was equally impressive. After his death, Bacon Rind lay in state in his home here, face painted in ceremonial fashion, and body clothed in Indian costume. The funeral was a strange mixture of traditional Christian and Indian burial rites. His grave is located on the hilltop (L) in traditional Osage fashion. Farther east on another hill is the grave, also marked, of Chief Lookout, well-loved leader of the Osages for many years.

A dance to commemorate the removal of the Osages from Kansas is held in the village in the latter part of September (*visitors welcome*). Invitations to attend the ceremonies are sent to neighboring tribes. The dancing continues for four days with rites honoring past chiefs. Other dances and feasts are held here in the arbor during fair weather, in the "round house" during rainy spells. One annual dance, around the American flag, honors all Osage soldiers, especially those taking part in World War I and II.

The use of peyote, a dried cactus "button," as a sacrament figures in the elaborate night-long Osage religious ceremonials. Before the Spanish conquest, certain Mexican tribes employed peyote in religious rituals. Gradually its use spread northward until the end of the nineteenth century when it became popular among the Indians of Oklahoma. It was introduced on the Osage reservation in 1898 by John Wilson, a Caddo-Delaware. In 1911, a charter for the incorporation of the Native American Church was obtained from the state by Oklahoma Indians—the articles specifying the use of peyote as a sacrament.

The Osages hold their church meetings on Saturday nights in octagonal lodge houses with earthen floors and cement altars. About sixty feet from the church door is a sweatbath house in which the ceremonial participants purify themselves physically with a buckeye root emetic while taking the bath. After purification, the Indians are led into the clean-swept church by the "Road Man," or leader. All seat themselves on blankets placed on the dirt floor and observe silence while the leader makes and lights a corn-shuck cigarette and prays aloud for the whole world. After the prayer the cigarette is placed on the "Road," and the "Road Man" continues during the night, admonishing, exhorting, and pointing out the right road to the worshipers, who throughout the ritual use the peyote both in its original form as a cactus button and steeped in a tea. The rhythms of a drum and gourd heighten the emotions until the end of the services on Sunday morning when the participants partake of a feast.

PAWHUSKA, 26.0 *m.* (885 alt., 5,331 pop.), is the seat of Osage County, the largest county in the state, and the tribal capital. The town, which still has the traditional Indian atmosphere, was named for a famous Osage chief. Paw-Hu-Scah, or White Hair, received his name from an incident in the battle known as St. Clair's Defeat, fought during Washington's administration. The Osage, then a youth, wounded an officer wearing a powdered wig. He started to scalp his quarry when, to his amazement, the whole scalp came off and the victim escaped, leaving the Osage standing with a fluffy, white wig grasped in his fingers. Believing that the wig had supernatural powers, the warrior henceforth wore it fastened to his own hair.

The original White Hair was chief of the Osage tribe at the beginning of the nineteenth century, a position which he is said to have usurped from the lawful heir, Clermont, through the influence of the Chouteau family (*see Tour 8*). This action brought about a division of the Osage Nation, Clermont's band separating entirely. Both White Hair and his son, also known as Chief White Hair, were presented with medals by Lieutenant Zebulon M. Pike (*see Tour 3*).

On the site of the first station here for the disbursing of funds to the Osage tribe is the TRIANGLE BUILDING, Ki-he-kah Avenue and Main Street. A hitching rail originally enclosed the area, which included the traditional bandstand. Pawhuska businessmen later purchased the triangular plot to erect the modern building. Rising above the business district is AGENCY HILL. At its foot is the CITY HALL, Main and Grandview Streets, formerly the Osage Council House. Atop the hill are the stone and frame buildings of the OSAGE AGENCY, on a 104-acre tract. Here the tribal business is conducted by the superintendent, aided by a council composed of the chief of the Osages, assistant chief, and eight councilmen and a secretary elected by the tribe.

The OSAGE TRIBAL MUSEUM AND AUDITORIUM (*adm. free 8–5 daily*), constructed of native sandstone, occupies the site of the old Osage Boarding School Chapel. Its erection in 1938 was sponsored by the Osage tribal council in order to preserve linguistic and mythological data and artifacts relating to the Osage Indians. The museum houses several extensive collections, the most outstanding of which are the Chief Bacon Rind and the John Bird accumulations of tribal costumes, paintings, bead and feather artcraft, treaties, and valuable documents. Bacon Rind's collection was willed by him to the Smithsonian Institution at Washington, D. C. With the building of the Osage Museum, however, the Smithsonian loaned the historical objects to the tribe for an indefinite period. There are also old photographs, voice recordings in the tribal language, and other materials necessary to trace a complete history of the tribe.

Pawhuska claims the distinction of having the first Boy Scout Troop in America, organized by the Rev. John Mitchell in May of 1909. A granite marker lists the nineteen charter members, two of whom were still living in Pawhuska in 1956. Pawhuska is also the home of May Todd Aaron, a contemporary Oklahoma artist now living in Paris; and of John Joseph Mathews (*see Literature*), of Osage blood, whose writing has received wide notice. Herbert Hoover, President of the United States (1928–32), spent several boyhood summers here with his uncle, Major Laban J. Miles, who became Osage agent in 1878. Some Pawhuskans remember the interest of the orphaned boy visitor in the rocks of the surrounding Osage Hills—an interest which later blossomed into a mining and engineering career.

In the hills near the city are widespread grazing lands on which as many as 250,000 cattle are pastured in one season. Approximately two-thirds of the herds are owned by Osage ranchers. The remaining third is shipped in from Texas and other states, during March and April, to be fattened for July and August markets. Agricultural products of Osage County include corn, cotton, oats, hay, fruit, pecans, and berries.

Right from Pawhuska on the graveled Osage Highway to the BARNARD-CHAPMAN RANCH (*visitors welcome*), 15.4 *m.*, which covers 110,000 acres of rolling, prairie hills on which more than sixteen thousand head of Hereford cattle graze. The ranch house is a sprawling, twelve-room, brick building with a tile roof and many porches. The ranch has its own shipping pens and station located on the main line of the Midland Valley Railroad, which runs through the far-flung spread. When the ranch was first established, cattle were allowed the right of way and gates were put up across the highway so that they might saunter from one side to another at will. There were some thirty-seven gates across roads leading from Tulsa to the Barnard-Chapman Ranch at that time. With increasing travel, however, the gates were removed and notices of the cattle crossings posted, warning the motorist to slow down. In addition to the grass-covered pastures, Sand, Dog, Buck, and Bird creeks cut across the ranch and afforded a plentiful supply of water. It is said that there are more grass-fattened cattle shipped from here annually than from any other point in the United States. Of Osage County's 1,467,520 total acres, 1,218,000 acres are in permanent grasslands.

Right from Pawhuska on an unimproved dirt road is the CHIEF SAUCY CHIEF HOMESTEAD, 3.6 *m.* Nellie, the daughter of the chief, was the first Osage to be given Christian burial. She contracted pneumonia in 1885 at the Carlisle Indian School in Pennsylvania and was sent home, where she died. Major Laban J. Miles, the Osage agent at that time, persuaded her parents to conduct the Christian rites rather than their customary procedure of burying the dead in a sitting posture on the summit of a hill. The Indians kept their own mourning customs, however, the chief wearing only a white sheet, moccasins, and breechclout for a three-and-a-half-month period, despite the snow-covered ground. In preparation for the three-day dance which was to end the mourning observance, the funeral party rode out solemnly to capture the scalp of a town merchant who had ingratiatingly decided to submit himself to a mock scalping. He allowed the Indians to cut off his forelock, minus the traditional accompaniment of skin. Major Miles was accorded the honor of leading the group—much to the amazement of Pawhuska citizens, who saw him riding into town holding the scalp-pole with the hair flying from its top. After Saucy Chief had been bathed and dressed in warm blankets, the dance began. Nellie's death had been properly observed, and her spirit sent on its journey with the blessing of both the white and red man's ritual.

At 47.1 *m.* is the western junction with State 18, a hard-surfaced road.

Left on State 18 to FAIRFAX, 9.6 *m.* (841 alt., 2,017 pop.), located in the center of large oil fields. At the southwest corner of the town is the GRAVE AND

STATUE OF CHIEF NE-KA-WA-SHE-TUN-KA, the last Osage chieftain to receive the complete Osage burial ceremony. This included the killing of his favorite horse and the placing of a human scalp on his grave at the end of the mourning period to allow his spirit to enter the Happy Hunting Ground. The scalp secured in this case was that of a Wichita chief, A-sa-wah, and its taking precipitated an intertribal incident which caused the government to forbid all future scalp-hunting. The Osages finally settled the score by making large payments of money and goods to the Wichitas.

Left from Fairfax on a graveled county road to GRAYHORSE, 4.5 *m.*, where the "Dwellers-on-the-Hilltop" division (*see Tour 14*) of the Osage Indians hold tribal dances and gatherings in the "round house." Near by is an interesting all-Indian cemetery.

State 18 continues south from Fairfax to the SITE OF AN OLD OSAGE RIVER FORD, 15.7 *m.*, on the east bank of the Arkansas River, just across from the small town of RALSTON, 15.9 *m.* When the river at this point divided the Osage and Pawnee Nations, charges of stealing and the raids of scalping parties caused many skirmishes between the two tribes at the ford.

In the early history of Oklahoma, there were many attempts to establish a trade route up the Arkansas River past Fort Gibson (*see Tour 3*), at which point ascending navigation became dangerous. In 1878, one small steamer managed to go as far as the mouth of the Walnut River in Kansas. And in the 1880's, a flour carrier, "Kansas Millers," successfully made the trip from Arkansas City, Kansas, to the Arkansas Line. In 1884, a steamer unloaded merchandise at the Kaw Indian Agency (northwest of this point), and in 1898, the "Minnie" made the last attempt to ascend farther than this landing. Loading with walnut logs to fill a contract for gunstock lumber, she went aground on a sand bar just southwest of this ford. Her cargo was unloaded and hauled to its destination by wagon. In the early 1900's, a small steamboat made several trips between Ralston and Tulsa. Though the ship, using a threshing machine engine for power, was not much more than a flatboat, it provided a means of transporting merchandise to towns having no transportation facilities other than freight wagons and stage coaches.

BURBANK, 49.8 *m.* (935 alt., 268 pop.), until the discovery of oil brought a brief boom to the town, was primarily an Osage settlement. The near-by bluffs—on which cockleburs grow in profusion—are said to have furnished the inspiration for the town's name. It was suggested by railroad men when the Santa Fe established a station here in 1903. Today it is a cluster of weather-beaten houses set on the edge of a forest of tall, black pumping jacks silhouetted against the sky.

At the opening of the BURBANK FIELD in May of 1920, the sale of leases brought less than $10 an acre. After production was well under way, leases sold for as high as $10,000 an acre. The rush for leases in the Burbank boom brought fabulous prices for land which, prior to 1920, had sold for as little as $800 a quarter section. In June of 1921 the sale of fourteen leases brought $3,256,000, while in December of that year eighteen leases sold for $6,250,000. Two lease sales in 1922 brought perhaps the top individual prices: $1,335,000 and $1,160,000. In addition to the bonuses paid to the Indians for the right to drill, all contracts with them call for a special royalty on the production. The ordinary royalty is one-eighth of the oil and gas produced. The Osages, however, receive one-sixth on leases producing less than one hundred barrels a day, one-fifth where the yield is more. (Production from the above-mentioned water-flood projects is the exception. On this oil—which costs more, of course, to recover—the Osages have agreed to accept the ordinary one-eighth royalty.)

At 68.5 *m.* US 60 crosses the Arkansas River.

At 69.1 *m.* is the junction with US 77 (*see Tour 10*)—which unites westward with US 60 for 3.9 miles—at the southeast corner of PONCA CITY, (1,003 alt., 20,180 pop.) (*see Ponca City*).

At 81.1 *m.* is the junction with US 177.

Right on this road to BLACKWELL, 8.5 *m.* (1,020 alt., 9,199 pop.), the second largest city in Kay County and center of the extremely rich (reputedly the second finest in America) Chikaskia River farming area. The town began with the opening to settlement of the Cherokee Outlet in the Run of September 16, 1893. A group of families from Winfield, Kansas, were the first permanent residents. Prior to this date, however, a tent city of some fifteen hundred of Payne's "boomers" (*see History*) was established up the river from the present city. The trespassing colonists lived here the summer of 1884, even publishing a little newspaper called the *Oklahoma War Chief* (*see Newspapers*) before United States troops drove them out.

The town got its name from A. J. Blackwell, an adopted citizen of the Cherokee Nation, who took over the land, platted the townsite, sold lots, and set up a despotic one-man government. As a self-ordained Baptist preacher, he earned the title of "prophet." As a hot-tempered frontiersman, he was twice indicted (but never convicted) for murder.

With the passing of the "Blackwell Era," however, the town settled into a period of steady growth, and today it prospers on a healthy balance between agriculture, oil, and industry. Six grain elevators provide storage for 1,250,000 bushels. One of the state's largest independent meat processing companies serves as a ready market for the area's livestock. Blackwell's principal payroll, however, is that of the BLACKWELL ZINC COMPANY (west edge of the city), which operates what is said to be the world's largest retort-type smelter. Here up to one thousand men process each month some fifteen thousand tons of zinc, most of it imported from mines in Mexico.

Blackwell's excellent PUBLIC LIBRARY, built in 1931 at a cost of $35,000, grew out of a small Chautauqua collection of books housed in a single room over a bank in 1903. In 1956 it contained twenty-two thousand volumes (many of them autographed copies of books by Oklahoma writers), a valuable collection of material on the state's history, and a considerable number of originals by Oklahoma Indian artists.

Symbolic of Blackwell's progressive attitude is the difficulty the casual visitor has in discovering traces of the devastating tornado which razed twenty-nine blocks at the northeast corner of the city on the night of May 25, 1955, leaving twenty-one dead, seventy injured, and damages in excess of ten million dollars. Of the industries destroyed or seriously damaged, only a glassware manufacturing plant was not rebuilt by the same date in 1956.

Along with complete sport and recreational facilities, the city has—in MEMORIAL PARK—a $135,000 swimming pool that is the scene of the annual Olympic tryouts. Blackwell kennels train many of the nation's finest racing greyhounds. And the KAY COUNTY FAIRGROUNDS (just south of the business district on Main Street) are among the state's most impressive.

Named for the Tonkawa Indians who once owned the land surrounding it, TONKAWA, 82.5 *m.* (1,003 alt., 3,643 pop.), is today a busy oil city. Wells in the vicinity have been producing since 1921.

In 1879, Chief Joseph and his band of Nez Percé Indians were brought as prisoners and exiles from their home in Idaho and placed on a reservation located at the Yellow Bull Crossing on the Salt Fork of the Arkansas River, just a few hundred yards west of the present main street of Tonkawa. The crossing received its name from the Nez Percé chief, Yellow Bull, who built a log house near by. Here they stayed for several years, always longing for their former home. Finally they were allowed to return.

The Tonkawas, who were always few in number, seem to have originated in Texas. Then during the Civil War, while encamped on the Washita River near Anadarko (*see Tour* 3), they were suspected of cannibalism and the tribe was almost exterminated. During their wanderings, these so-called "Ishmaels of the Plains" were successively thinned by war, massacre, and disease, before finally finding a home here on the Salt Fork of the Arkansas. It is said that the meaning of the name Tonkawa is "They all stay together." In 1891 they accepted allotments, selling the remainder of their land to the United States. It was opened for settlement along with the Cherokee Outlet in 1893. In 1941, Tonkawa lists showed only eighteen tribesmen.

Tonkawa was platted the year after the Run, and in 1901 it was chosen by the Territorial legislature as the site for the present NORTHERN OKLAHOMA JUNIOR COLLEGE. The state-owned institution is housed in ten buildings on a tree-shaded, twenty-acre campus (on US 60). Ivy-covered CENTRAL HALL is the college's oldest structure. WILKINS HALL, one of the more recent buildings, has an imposing entrance supported by two massive Corinthian columns. HAROLD HALL has an interesting third-floor museum featuring animal life displays, as well as many Indian and pioneer exhibits.

Since the area was included in the Cherokee Outlet opening, Tonkawa joins with a number of other Oklahoma towns in a rousing celebration of the September 16 anniversary of the Run. The traditional parades, pageants, and Indian dances usually feature the nostalgic affair as citizens turn out in costumes suggesting the days of 1893. As for the workaday present, a Tonkawa farm-equipment manufacturing firm ships hammer mills for grinding stock feed all over the United States, as well as to twenty-seven foreign countries.

LAMONT, 97.3 *m.* (997 alt., 594 pop.), named for Daniel Lamont, former secretary of war (1893–97), is near the sandy lowlands of the Salt Fork (L), where unusually large and meaty watermelons are grown. Up to 1955 an annual Watermelon Festival was held each September, at which time citizens celebrated their harvest by serving as much as ten tons of the fruit free to visitors.

POND CREEK, 112.1 *m.* (1,050 alt., 1,066 pop.) (*see Tour 11*), is at the eastern junction with US 81 (*see Tour 11*), which unites southward with US 60 for 23.8 miles.

At 116.3 *m.* is the junction with US 64 (*see Tour 2*), which unites with US 60 and US 81 to Enid.

ENID, 135.9 *m.* (1,246 alt., 36,017 pop.) (*see Enid*), is at the southern junction with US 81 and US 64. US 60 again turns sharply west.

Section c. ENID *to* TEXAS LINE, *132.4 m. US 60*

West of ENID, 0 *m.*, US 60 passes through wide-stretching wheat fields, where towering concrete elevators break the horizon in every direction, looming up like skyscrapers above the level land. In the high, red-tinted country west of the North Canadian River—beyond the sandy Cimarron and past the Glass Mountains—towns are seen at greater distances because of the clarity of the atmosphere. Here overgrazing and overcultivation, plus persistent droughts, have caused considerable economic belt-tightening in the past two or three decades. But larger and better managed landholdings, together with the conversion of much marginal farming acreage to cattle-sustaining grasses, seem to have pulled the region out of an economic slump. Though reduced in numbers, the citizens who remain are better off than their pioneering fathers and grandfathers. And perhaps, in meeting the new challenges of the mid-twentieth century, they are fully as courageous.

At 8.1 *m.* is the junction with a paved road.

Left on this road to DRUMMOND, 6.7 *m.* (1,213 alt., 314 pop.). Just west of the tiny farm center are flats which fill with water during the (occasional) rainy season in the fall to offer excellent hunting for migratory wild fowl.

The largest community of Mennonites in Oklahoma live on farms near MENO, 16.2 *m.* (1,300 alt., 76 pop.), which serves as a trade, educational, and religious center. Founded by Menno Simons (1492–1559)—a Dutch priest who discarded the Roman Catholic faith in the early days of the Reformation to form a new Anabaptist church which eventually took his name—the sect is composed primarily of descendants of German-Russian immigrants who came to this country in the nineteenth century. Though this particular branch has never held to the strict customs as to dress and appearance so commonly thought of in connection with Mennonites (*see Tour* 5), the members' predilection for plain living and hard work is reflected by the neatly kept farmyards and the well-cared-for land. The group maintains a large church here (R), with 308 members, and the Oklahoma Bible Academy (high school).

At 20.2 *m.* is the junction with State 58, a graveled highway.

Left on State 58 to RINGWOOD, 1 m. (1,307 alt., 331 pop.), named for the ring of woods encircling the town. The site was homesteaded in 1895, and the township platted and lots sold at auction in 1901. In September there is an annual Watermelon Festival, complete with Watermelon Queen and free watermelons.

Right on State 58 to HELENA, 12 *m.* (1,397 alt., 484 pop.), home (since 1956) of Oklahoma's State Training School for Boys, formerly located at Stringtown (*see Tour 8*). On the west edge of town, the institution's fourteen brick buildings can accommodate 250 inmates.

At 31.3 *m.* is the junction with paved State 8. US 60 swings southwestward here to cross the wide, sandy CIMARRON RIVER, 32.3 *m.*, typical of most streams in western Oklahoma in that the shifting sands of the river bed allow the usually meager channel to change its course frequently. Gypsum deposits give the banks an added air of barrenness and desolation.

ORIENTA, 34.2 *m.* (1,245 alt., 20 pop.), is at the junction with State 15, a partially paved road.

Right from Orienta on State 15 are the gypsum-covered buttes of the GLASS MOUNTAINS, 5 *m.*, so named because their surfaces are covered with millions of sparkling selenite crystals. (Some maps still call these the *Gloss* Mountains. One explanation is curiously simple—they were named and first described by an English engineer when the region was surveyed in 1880. He remarked that they looked like "Glaws.") The hills, abruptly rising and fancifully shaped, are a part of the Blaine Escarpment, a great gypsum formation which extends across most of western Oklahoma. Geologists believe that water, through the centuries, has worn away the softer shales and clays, leaving the resistant gypsum to form a hard, protecting top. Gradual erosion has left strange formations—appearing to be feudal castles, minarets, and human profiles—carved in solid caps of the gypsum, four to five feet thick. Large quantities of the selenite crystals and bands of satin spar cover the "mountains," which range in height from a few feet to three hundred feet above the valley floor. Chunks of the crystal, clear as processed glass, may be picked up. They crumble, however, into powder when light pressure is applied.

One towering, 300-foot crystalline rock, CATHEDRAL MOUNTAIN, 5.8 *m.*, stands out from the rest—its portals and towers giving it the shape of a great cathedral. From a distance its thick layer of gypsum, streaked a gray-green by the weather, gives the appearance of varicolored and mullioned windows. Westward from here, sand dunes have piled upon the edges of the mountains, covering some of the smaller peaks. The area is extremely desert-like, and there are few houses.

US 60 is the main street of FAIRVIEW, 40.5 *m.* (1,302 alt., 2,400 pop.), the seat of Major County. The town is located on a flat plain in an agricultural section, with the Glass Mountains to the northwest and the Cimarron River valley to the east, making a setting of natural beauty. Because of the presence of gypsum in the water underlying the townsite, the city supply is piped from a source northeast of the Cimarron River. The water and electrical systems are both municipally owned. South and west from Fairview, approximately seventeen miles on State 58, is the popular recreation area surrounding Canton Lake (*see Tour 5*).

West of Fairview, many of the farms seen for the first few miles belong to members of another sect of the Mennonites (*see above*), the Church of God in Christ Mennonites. Their emblem is the cedar tree —chosen for its sturdy and resistant qualities—and evergreen-dotted farmyards make their homes easy to distinguish. The simple life is their creed, and they believe in a doctrine of nonparticipation in military activities. They boast that none of their members has ever registered as a relief client. Since the financial status of each individual has long been under supervision of the church as a whole, its approval is necessary before debt can be incurred.

SEILING, 71.5 *m.* (1,760 alt., 700 pop.), was named for the original homesteader of the townsite. It is located in the fertile valley between the North and South Canadian rivers, with ranching and wheat-raising as its main agricultural activities. Amos Chapman, famous army scout in the days of the settlement of Oklahoma, lived at Seiling after his retirement and was buried in the family cemetery east of town. Chapman was the hero of the Buffalo Wallow fight (*see Texas Guide*) when he lost a leg attempting to save a soldier. His wife was a relative of Chief Black Kettle of the Cheyennes (*see Tour 13*). General W. T. Sherman's aide-de-camp, Colonel Richard Irving Dodge, said in his book, *Our Wild Indians*, that Amos Chapman was "one of the best and bravest scouts . . . I have ever known."

Seiling was also for a time the home of the prohibition-crusader, Carry A. Nation. It was probably from here that she started many of her lecture tours and hatchet-wielding forays through the saloon-infested parts of Oklahoma Territory. Later she moved to Guthrie, where in 1905 she began to publish her newspaper, *The Hatchet* (*see Tour 10*).

In Seiling are the junctions with US 270 (*see Tour 5*), and US 183 (*see Tour 12*) which unites with US 60 for two miles. The route continues almost due west from this point to the Texas Line, traversing a high, flat country in which timber grows only along the streams. Cattle-raising is once again becoming the dominant activity of the section.

Near VICI, 92.5 *m.* (2,253 alt., 620 pop.), a cattle and farming center, are large quantities of bentonite, a clay used in the manufacture of cosmetics. The substance is also used in refining crude oil.

Westward, the rolling plains are covered with tumbleweed and yucca, or soapweed—a sturdy plant of many sword-shaped leaves thrusting skyward abruptly from the earth, and adorned with tall spikes of creamy, drooping, bell-shaped flowers. The yucca withstands the most adverse weather conditions because of its long, tough roots. Pioneers used to dig these roots and boil them to make a thick soap. Here, for perhaps the first time on US 60, the motorist begins to get the "feel" of the West. Red-clay hills and scattered clumps of scrub oak lend the landscape a picturesque, if somewhat barren, charm.

At 119.0 *m.* is the eastern junction with US 283 (*see Tour 13*), which unites westward with US 60 for 6.6 miles.

In the center of the town square at ARNETT, 119.5 *m.* (2,460 alt., 690 pop.), is the ELLIS COUNTY COURTHOUSE, with the PUBLIC LIBRARY near by. The town still preserves a hut built of hand-hewn cedar logs, dating back to territorial days, but Arnett itself is remarkably clean, alert, and progressive. Near here are several large ranches; one, the Berryman Ranch, has a herd of purebred cattle and a wildlife refuge stocked with quail, prairie chicken, and buffalo. Broomcorn production is also important. And as a further hedge against the cyclical lean-and-fat years caused by the area's always scanty rainfall, dairying has recently become a $600,000-a-year "cash crop" for Arnett farmers.

At 120.4 *m.* US 60 crosses the old INDIAN BUFFALO TRAIL, which ran from old Fort Supply (*see Tour 12*) to a huge buffalo wallow northeast of the Antelope Hills (*see Tour 13*) in a bend of the South Canadian River. Many Indian hunting parties once filed along this trail, and General George A. Custer and the Seventh Cavalry marched south on it from Fort Supply to the Washita River when they met the Cheyennes and allied tribes in the Battle of the Washita (*see Tour 13*).

At 125.6 *m.* is the western junction with US 283.

Left at this point on a series of graded dirt roads; R. at 5.4 *m.*, L. at 6.4 *m.*, R. at 7.5 *m.*, and L. again at 8.3 *m.* to the BURNETT GRISTMILL, 12.8 *m.*, built by W. F.

Burnett on his homestead about 1900, and run by the waters of near-by Little Robe Creek. The mill was abandoned in 1925, then used for several years as a canning factory. Today the board walls are warped and peeling, the floor is sagging with the weight of stored baled hay and rusty mill machinery, and the huge paddle wheel is broken. The sturdy axle, which turned the wheel for many years, was originally hewn from a single tree and still is in place.

A story is told of a battle between Texas Rangers and a band of Comanches that supposedly took place near the site of the old mill. In the late spring of 1858, a detachment of Rangers, accompanied by friendly Tonkawa Indian scouts, came up the Red River and attacked a Comanche village which was then on Little Creek. Prohebits Quasho (Iron Jacket), the band's war chief, rode out to greet the attackers, mounted on an iron-gray horse and wearing a rusty coat of mail—armor which had probably been taken from a Spanish explorer some generations before and handed down to each succeeding Comanche chieftain as an insignia of leadership and invulnerability. Iron Jacket courageously braved the fire of the rangers, the bullets having no effect other than to cause him to swerve back and forth. He passed unscathed through the barrage, warranting—even to some of the Rangers—the Comanches' belief that he bore a charmed life. But the bullet of one of the Tonkawa scouts found its mark in his neck, exposed for a moment as he abruptly turned his horse, and Iron Jacket fell dead. The Comanches were easily routed after the death of their leader.

US 60 crosses the Texas Line at 132.4 *m.*, twenty-five miles northeast of Canadian, Texas (*see Texas Guide*).

TOUR 5

Arkansas Line—Wilburton—McAlester—Seminole—Oklahoma City—Watonga—Woodward—Beaver City—Kansas Line; US 270, 487.7 m.

Roadbed paved but for brief initial stretch (scheduled for 1957).
The Rock Island Ry. parallels the route between Wister and Watonga.
Accommodations in all but the smaller towns.

The almost 500-mile southeast-to-northwest course of US 270 through Oklahoma makes it another Sooner State "panorama tour." It enters the state from Arkansas amid the pine- and oak-forested slopes of the Winding Stair Mountains, where the annual rainfall is around fifty inches. It cuts through the fertile valleys of the state's heartland, serving busy cities that have grown steadily from Territorial villages or that shot up abruptly with the discovery of oil. And it climbs over the rolling short-grass country of the northwest to enter Kansas from virtually treeless high plains, where the annual rainfall is well below twenty inches.

Constantly changing, too, are the racial strains of the people. To the east is the former Choctaw Nation. Here early French explorers left

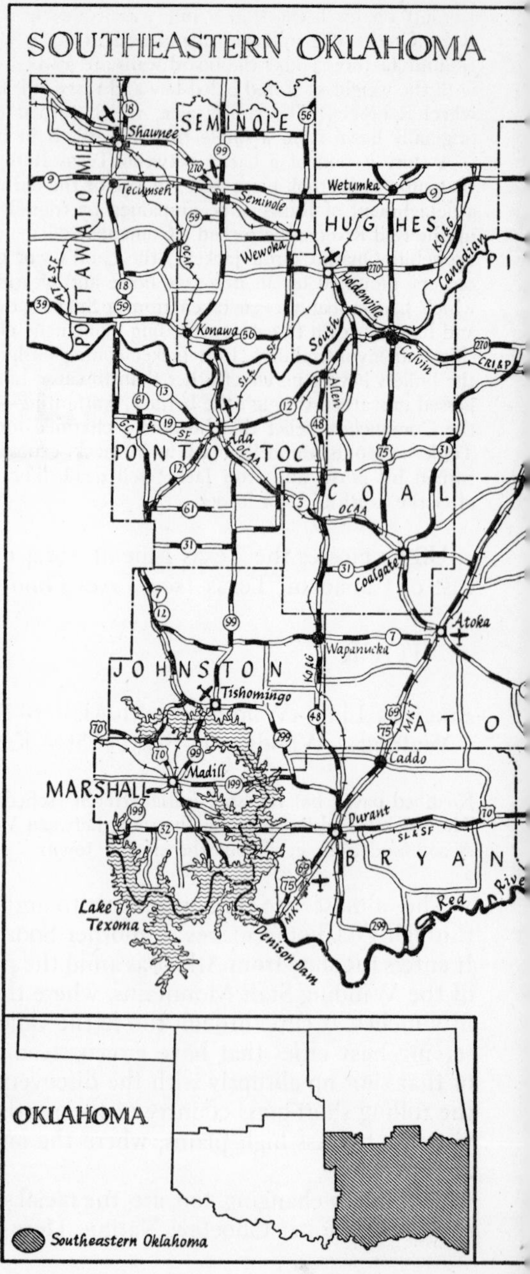
SOUTHEASTERN OKLAHOMA
SEMINOLE
POTTAWATOMIE
Shawnee
Tecumseh
Seminole
Wewoka
Wetumka
HUGHES
Holdenville
Canadian
Konawa
South
Calvin
Allen
Ada
PONTOTOC
COAL
Coalgate
Atoka
Wapanucka
JOHNSTON
Tishomingo
ATO
Caddo
Madill
MARSHALL
Durant
BRYAN
Red River
Lake Texoma
Denison Dam
OKLAHOMA
Southeastern Oklahoma

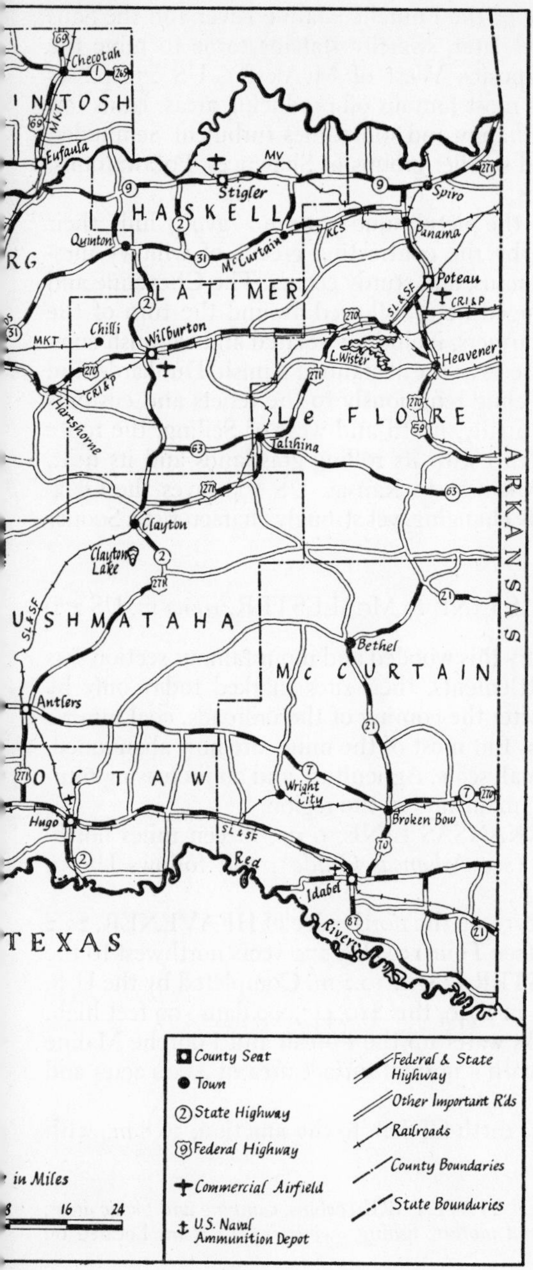
Checotah
INTOSH
Eufaula
MKT
MV
Stigler
Spiro
HASKELL
Panama
Quinton
McCurtain
KCS
RG
LATIMER
Poteau
CRI&P
SL&SF
Chilli
MKT
Wilburton
L. Wister
Heavener
CRI&P
Hartshorne
Le FLORE
Talihina
ARKANSAS
Clayton
Clayton Lake
USHMATAHA
SL&SF
Bethel
McCURTAIN
Antlers
OCTAW
Wright City
Broken Bow
Hugo
SL&SF
Red River
Idabel
TEXAS
County Seat
Town
State Highway
Federal Highway
Commercial Airfield
U.S. Naval Ammunition Depot
Federal & State Highway
Other Important R'ds
Railroads
County Boundaries
State Boundaries
in Miles
8 16 24

their stamp in the naming of the Fourche Maline River and the Sans Bois Mountains. Centuries later, swarthy Italians came to mine the section's valuable coal deposits. West of McAlester, US 270 passes through one of the state's most famous oil-producing areas, lands formerly belonging to the unhappy and sometimes turbulent Seminoles, the hospitable Creeks, and smaller groups of Shawnees, Potawatomis, and recalcitrant Kickapoos.

Northwest of Geary are the picturesque gypsum ("gyp") hills, their rocky barrenness relieved by the contrasting greens of willowy mesquite, squat prickly pear cactus, and sturdy cedars. The Cheyenne and Arapaho Indians once ranged here, followed around the turn of the century by hard-working farmers, including isolated and clannish communities of such religious sects as the abstaining Amish, Dunkards, and River Brethren, who still cling tenaciously to the tenets and customs of their forefathers. And finally, north and west of Seiling, the route emerges onto the high plains with its rolling grasslands and its neat, efficient ranches. From Arkansas to Kansas, US 270 gives the Oklahoma motorist a constantly changing, yet strongly characteristic Sooner State cross section.

Section a. ARKANSAS LINE *to* McALESTER, *100.4 m. US 270*

In the nineteenth century this wooded and mountainous section was dotted with Choctaw settlements, their sites marked today only by scattered piles of stone. After the coming of the railroads, coal mining was an important industry. But most of the mines are now abandoned, or are worked on only a small scale. Agriculture and an increasing tourist trade are the economic mainstays of the region.

US 270 crosses the ARKANSAS LINE, 0 *m.*, fifteen miles northwest of Mena, Arkansas (*see Arkansas Guide*), and follows US 59 (*see Tour 15*) for 23.2 miles.

At the junction with US 59 on the north edge of HEAVENER, 23.2 *m.* (561 alt., 2,103 pop.) (*see Tour 15*), US 270 veers northwest to the Overlook (L) above WISTER DAM, 30.2 *m.* Completed by the U.S. Army Corps of Engineers in 1949, this $10,447,000 dam (99 feet high, 5,700 feet in length) backs water up the Poteau and Fourche Maline rivers to form a reservoir with a normal surface area of 4,000 acres and a shore line of seventy-five miles.

The highway crosses the earth-fill dam to the junction, 30.8 *m.*, with an improved road.

Left here to LAKE WISTER STATE PARK (*cabins, camping and picnic areas, cafe and store, rental boats and motors, fishing, swimming*), 0.4 *m.* Located on

Agriculture

Typical Cattle Farm Scenes.

On the Robert Adams Farm, near Tulsa.

Wheat Fields at Harvest Time.

Modern Farm Homes.

pine-dotted Quarry Isle—actually a narrow peninsula jutting westward into the lake—the park is one of the state's newest, and one of its most scenic. Bass and crappie fishing is especially good, and the surrounding hills offer better than average hunting (*see below*).

In WISTER, 33.6 *m.* (510 alt., 729 pop.) (*see Tour 7*), is the junction with US 271 (*see Tour 7*), which US 270 follows for 6.4 miles, paralleling the north shore of Lake Wister.

South (L) of the tiny community of FANSHAWE, 43.9 *m.*, is the 18,000-acre WISTER PUBLIC HUNTING AREA. On the Fourche Maline arm of Lake Wister, it offers dependable hunting, in season, for quail, squirrel, rabbit, waterfowl, and deer.

RED OAK, 54.1 *m.* (590 alt., 568 pop.), was named for a large red oak tree that stood in the center of the town when this region was the Choctaw Nation. The Indians held district court there and used the oak as a whipping post.

The most serious political disturbance in the history of the Choctaw Nation had its finale at Red Oak when Silan Lewis was executed for his part in the Nationalist uprising (*see Antlers, Tour 7*), following the election of 1892. The fullblood Lewis, who had once been sheriff of his own district, upheld the traditional Choctaw honor when he came striding in from his woodland home on the appointed execution day—November 5, 1894—and sat quietly with his back to the tree to await the firing squad.

Right (northeast) from Red Oak on a graveled county road to the NARROWS, 2 *m.*, a scenic pass on the road laid out in 1838 for Chickasaw immigrants leaving Fort Smith, Arkansas—via the Choctaw Agency, near present Spiro (*see Tour 7*)—on their way southwest to Old Boggy Depot (*see Tour 8*). On October 27, 1858, the Choctaw Council granted William Holloway the right to build a turnpike and establish a tollgate on this well-traveled route. Jackson McCurtain (*see Tour 7*) was given the same privilege in 1867. After the first Butterfield Stage was run west from Fort Smith on September 19, 1858, a meal stop was made at Edwards' Store, about three miles east of the Narrows. The old log building—the first post office (1868) for Red Oak—was still standing in 1956, as a private residence. Several stretches of the old toll road can also be seen. Both stage stop and turnpike will become visitor attractions in 1957 when the Overland Mail Centennial is celebrated.

WILBURTON, 67.6 *m.* (657 alt., 1,939 pop.), the seat of Latimer County, was named for Will Burton, a contractor who helped build the Choctaw, Oklahoma, and Gulf Railroad (now the Rock Island) through this area in 1890. In its early years Wilburton was an important coal shipping point.

Right from Wilburton on paved State 2 is ROBBERS CAVE STATE PARK (*cabins, picnic and play areas, rental boats, swimming, fishing, hiking*), 4.3 *m.* This

8,400-acre recreation area—one of the largest in the state—lies in the heart of the Sans Bois Mountains. Its canyons, pine-covered hills, rock-bottomed streams, and huge rock formations are visible from the winding highway and from the many foot trails and bridle paths. Within the park are six miles of sparkling Fourche Maline Creek, which has, in places, cut deep rock-walled gorges. A dam forms 52-acre Lake Carlton to provide swimming, boating, and fishing. Picnic and camp facilities are spread along the eastern border of the lake and along the creek itself.

In the center of the park is the TOM HALE BOY SCOUT CAMP, 7.6 *m.*, named for the philanthropist whose contributions helped to develop the 140-acre tract adjoining the Fourche Maline.

Just north of this camp is ROBBERS CAVE itself. Steps have been carved to the entrance, one hundred feet up the side of an imposing sandstone cliff. The cave is said to have been used as a hiding place by the James Brothers and other outlaws. Legend has it that loot once cached by early-day robbers and highwaymen is still buried in the cave. One of the more fanciful stories still told concerns "Fiddlin' Jim," an admirer of the notorious Belle Starr (*see Tour 2*), who was slain here by a jealous rival as he sat playing his fiddle at the entrance to the cave. Some of the natives say that when the harvest moon shines they can still hear his weird melodies.

Even more so than most parks in this part of the state, Robbers Cave is a show piece of Oklahoma *flora*. A few of the most common trees are southern yellow pine, red cedar, black walnut, scaly-bark and white hickory, blackjack, chinquipin, post oak, hackberry, black locust, redbud, dogwood, Chickasaw plum, and deciduous holly. Among the shrubs are the black haw, sumac, wild rose, summer huckleberry, elderberry, plum, and spice bush. Honeysuckle, wild grapes, Virginia creeper, and poison ivy are characteristic vines.

Some of the more conspicuous wild flowers are anemone, phlox, blue and dog-tooth violet, arum, cardinal flower, verbena, spiderwort, goldenrod, and aster. Many of the shrubs and trees, of course, also sprinkle the park with vivid color. Best known of these—and frequently the object of organized tours and caravans (*see Tour 15*) —are the dogwood and redbud. Foliage tours are also made in the fall when the red and black haw, wild cherry, and other smaller plants, add their brilliant colors to those of the oaks, maples, and hickories.

At 68.3 *m.*, on US 270, is the western junction with State 2.

Left on this paved road to SPANISH WAR VETERANS' COLONY (L), 8 *m.*, founded in 1936 by the Oklahoma group of the United Spanish War Veterans. The 800-acre rustic retreat is now open to veterans of all wars, and a tax-free, one-acre home-site is available for $15. Living costs are low, recreational opportunities in the near-by Winding Stair Mountains virtually unlimited. The colony includes more than three dozen homes, and administration and central office buildings.

State 2 south to Clayton (*see Tour 7*) and State 2 and 63 southeast to Talihina (*see Tour 7*), both paved, are among the most scenic byways in southeastern Oklahoma.

EASTERN OKLAHOMA AGRICULTURAL AND MECHANICAL COLLEGE, 69.5 *m.*, is a coeducational state junior college which was founded in 1909 as a School of Mines and Metallurgy. Wilburton citizens gave sixty acres of land to establish the institution, which has had a somewhat checkered career. After being closed for two years during World War

I, it was operated for a while by the federal government as an industrial training school for disabled veterans. It became Eastern Oklahoma College in 1927, when a general college curriculum was established in addition to vocational secondary work. In 1935, the state legislature authorized the school to care for and educate dependent youths and orphans who were otherwise unable to obtain an education. Finally, in 1939, the present name and its regular, fully accredited college program were established. Since World War II, it has enjoyed a steady growth, and five new buildings have recently been constructed. It is one of six institutions in the state that offer Air Force ROTC training.

GOWEN, 76.7 *m.* (691 alt., 450 pop.), was once the home of the popular Negro screen actor, Step'n Fetchit (Lincoln Perry). The one-mile walk from his home to the school here was "jes too much," so the story goes, and he rarely attended. But he capitalized so successfully on his laziness that he rose from a $3-a-week job with a medicine show to his long-time status as a well-known—and well-paid—character actor. His screen name evolved from the consistent answer he made to requests for action, "I'll step'n fetchit purty soon."

At 85.5 *m.* is a junction with a narrow lane.

Right on this lane to JONES ACADEMY, 0.5 *m.*, an Indian boys' school established by the Choctaw tribe in 1891 as a companion school to Tuskahoma Female Academy (*see Tour* 7). Named for Wilson N. Jones, then principal chief of the Choctaws, it became the most important of the tribal schools for boys after Spencer Academy, located near Soper (*see Tour* 6), burned in 1896. The Choctaws still own the buildings, but the government owns the land and supports the academy with federal appropriations. On September 5, 1955, Jones was made coeducational, although actual class work was discontinued. The boys and girls now attend the Hartshorne public school where, it is believed, their mingling with non-Indian children will accelerate their assimilation into the white man's society. The grades which the Indian children are making and their participation in extracurricular activities have already made the plan a provisional success.

In this vicinity, Bernard de la Harpe, the French explorer, camped in 1719 (*see Tour* 3), during his expedition to the Arkansas River, where he hoped to make treaties with the Indian tribes he encountered.

The Twin Cities of HARTSHORNE, 83.9 *m.* (705 alt., 2,330 pop.), and HAILEYVILLE, 86.2 *m.* (612 alt., 1,107 pop.), were both established about 1890 and platted in 1902. Both have always had coal mining as their principal industry. With the decline of large-scale mining activities, populations and economic health have tended to sag proportionately, but farming, lumbering, and livestock-raising have to a certain extent taken up the industrial slack. Homes and businesses line the highway between the two towns.

Hartshorne was named for a Dr. Hartshorne, an early settler, and Haileyville for Dr. David Morris Hailey (1841–1919), who came to Oklahoma from Louisiana after the Civil War. He assisted in sinking the first coal mine shaft in the McAlester district of the important Pittsburg County field. His portrait hangs in the State Confederate Memorial Hall of the State Historical Society building in Oklahoma City.

A pioneer coal-mining settlement, ALDERSON, 94.9 *m.* (680 alt., 311 pop.), was the scene in 1894 of a unique labor dispute. The Choctaw Nation required the mining corporations to pay a small monthly tax for each employee. But when a strike over a 25 per cent wage reduction left most of the miners idle, the company refused to pay the tax. The Choctaw chief countered at once by insisting that the miners be removed from his nation. Nonpayment of the head tax, he reasoned, automatically made them intruders. The appeal passed through the offices of the Commissioner of Indian Affairs, the Secretary of the Interior and finally to President Cleveland, who approved it. Three companies of infantry and two of cavalry were dispatched to deport the group. Alderson was designated as troop headquarters and all arrested miners were brought here. Approximately two hundred workers and their families were loaded into boxcars and taken to Jenson, Arkansas, the nearest town outside of Indian Territory.

The governor of Arkansas protested against the action, as did the governments of Italy and Great Britain, since many of the evicted miners were citizens of those countries. But the strike was broken. The mines reopened and royalties once again began to pour into the Choctaw treasury.

KREBS, 97.6 *m.* (715 alt., 1,532 pop.), was built in the midst of coal mines that are now abandoned, and great piles of waste rock still pock the town. Many Italian miners, who first came when the mines were flourishing, have now become farmers.

Wide differences in the background of these early settlers and the confusing circumstances of rule by Choctaw law, federal courts, and the Indian agent combined to give the town an unsavory reputation during Territorial days. Varying legal restrictions regarding the importation, sale, and manufacture of liquor allowed so many loopholes for violation that Krebs became known for its production of Choctaw or "choc" beer, made of hops, tobacco, fishberries, barley, and alcohol. In 1895, a law sufficiently comprehensive to override all previous judgments was passed by Congress, and "choc" was finally made illegal. This it may be, but the legal bar has served merely to make the concoction more difficult to produce, and to consume.

A drugstore, established here in 1888, is still operating. And in Indian Territory days, when there were no hospitals—and gas burns, explosions, and other mine accidents occurred with frightening regularity—it had to cope with many an emergency. Vaseline was stocked in five-hundred-pound quantities, raw linseed oil in fifty-barrel lots, and iodoform in ten-pound lots. One particular explosion caused by blackdamp in 1892 kept the store open day and night for two weeks. And the story is still told about the tattered clothes of an Italian victim of this tragedy. In their haste, rescuers hung the articles on a fence, where they flapped in the wind for days until the brother of the man identified them and, upon examination, found $975 sewed in the ragged jumper.

McALESTER, 100.4 *m.* (718 alt., 17,878 pop.), started in 1870 as a tent store at the crossroads of two well-traveled Indian Territory roads, the California Trail and the Texas Road. The heavy traffic of the Texas Road, used until 1872 when the Missouri-Kansas-Texas Railroad built tracks almost parallel with it, and the influx of adventurers along the California Trail after the discovery of gold in 1849, made a flourishing business for James J. McAlester, the store's owner.

McAlester is also given credit for the discovery of coal in Pittsburg County. A geologist's memorandum book, telling of rich deposits of the mineral, had fallen into his hands and this resulted in his coming to Indian Territory. After his arrival, McAlester married a Chickasaw girl. This made him a citizen of the Choctaw Nation. (By the treaties of 1837 and 1855 the two tribes owned their land in common and enjoyed full citizenship rights in either nation.) When the coming of the railroad made mining operations possible, he and other Choctaw citizens began extracting the coal under a Choctaw constitutional provision allowing a citizen the right to mine for a mile in every direction any mineral discovered by him. Controversy resulted when the Choctaw government claimed the royalty which McAlester's group began to receive from the lessees. Legality of the transaction was approved by the tribal court, but Chief Coleman Cole expressed his opposition to the mines by sentencing McAlester and three of the co-owners to death. The men escaped, however, with the aid of their guard, and a compromise later settled the affair by giving half the royalty to the Choctaw Nation and the other half to the mine owners. McAlester later became lieutenant governor of Oklahoma (1911–15).

The town which grew up around the founder's store is now called North McAlester. The main part of present-day McAlester developed later when the Rock Island Railway built to a junction with the Missouri-Kansas-Texas line. The city is laid out over a series of hills, with the main business district on one hill. Along Grand Avenue, one of McAlester's important thoroughfares, are the PITTSBURG COUNTY COURTHOUSE (at 2nd Street) and the chief hotels. The red-brick courthouse is constructed in a U-shape around an elevated concrete court and sits flush with the street.

The massive, block-long INDIAN SCOTTISH RITE CONSISTORY, Adams Avenue and 2nd Street, is one of two such consistories in Oklahoma. The cream-colored brick and stone building is elaborately decorated with algonite and Carthage stone. A great copper sphere, rising fifty feet above the roof, contains multicolored lenses and, when lighted, may be seen for several miles. It was here the Will Rogers received Scottish Rite degrees in 1908.

The OHOYAHOMA CLUBHOUSE, North Main Street and Park Avenue, is an unpretentious frame building with the traditional pair of center doors, flanking windows, and overhanging porch roof. It was built in 1876 and served as the Tobucksy County Courthouse in the days of the Choctaw Nation. After the absorption of the Choctaws into United States citizenry, the building fell into disuse. Purchased and restored by the Ohoyahoma Club, a local organization of Indian women, it now houses a MUSEUM (*free*) of authentic Indian articles.

A fairly stable commercial and industrial town, McAlester maintains its economy with meat packing, cotton-oil milling, coal mining, lumbering, and the manufacturing of women's sportswear and lingerie. A U.S. Naval Ammunition Depot is eight miles southwest of the city.

McAlester is at the junction with US 69 (*see Tour 8*). A mile west from this intersection, in downtown McAlester, is the junction with the paved Rainbow Highway.

Right on this road, past the MCALESTER GENERAL HOSPITAL (L) and the State Highway Patrol district headquarters (L), to the OKLAHOMA STATE PENITENTIARY (*8–9* A.M. *and 12:30–2* P.M. *Mon. through Fri.*), 1.2 *m.* Here in a ten-acre tract enclosed by a fourteen-foot concrete wall are confined more than 2,200 prisoners. The main prison structures spread out fanwise from a large Administration Building. To the south, outside the walls, are the trees and green lawns surrounding the warden's home. Here too, at the main gate, is the prison's Arts and Crafts Shop. West of the penitentiary are the brick yard and 1,985 acres of pasture land. Isolated prison camps are used for crop and vegetable farming.

Rainbow Highway parallels the east wall of the penitentiary and curves around a long hill to a gateway, 2.4 *m.*

Right through this gateway to LAKE NO. 1 (*camp sites, fishing*), 0.2 *m.* LAKE NO. 2 is separated from it by a small dam.

The main side route continues to a junction with a blacktop road, 8.0 *m.* Left here, 0.9 *m.* are the RAINBOW GARDENS (*adm. by courtesy card from Supreme Assembly Office, 319 E. Grand Ave., McAlester*), at the top of a steep hill overlooking Lake McAlester. The 75-acre estate is owned by the Order of the Rainbow, an international character-building society for girls (thirteen to twenty years of age) founded in 1922 by the Rev. W. Mark Sexson, of McAlester, under the sponsorship of the Order of the Eastern Star. The supreme office of the Rainbow Order is in McAlester. The buildings and landscaped grounds serve as a retreat for the girls and as the scene of initiation rites.

From Lake McAlester Dam, 9.1 *m.*, back on the main side road, a gravel and blacktop road encircles the thirty-five-mile shore line of LAKE McALESTER (*fishing: fifty cents a day*). The road is fringed with cabins, stores, and bait houses. The 2,500-acre lake is stocked with several varieties of game fish by the city of McAlester.

Section b. McALESTER *to* OKLAHOMA CITY, *130.2 m.* *US 270*

From McALESTER, 0 *m.*, US 270 angles to the northwest, passing through a region dominated by oil. Here are two of the state's largest fields—Greater Seminole and Oklahoma City—which for a time provided an even seventy per cent of Oklahoma's total oil production. Drilling rigs, field shacks of corrugated iron, storage tanks, tool shops, supply houses, and the other symbols of oil exploration and production are scattered along both sides of the highway.

The huge, whitewashed stone chimney of White Chimney, 16 *m.*, a traditional log house (L), consisting of two rooms and open gallery, is said to have been constructed in 1828. It served as a guidepost for travelers on the old wagon road running through this area. An Indian named Honubby (Choctaw for "woman-killer") built it—the near-by town of Stuart was called Honubby until the early 1900's—but after he moved away it became a rendezvous for outlaws. Numerous bullet holes are visible in the walls and posts, helping to substantiate the many stories of crimes committed in the house. One tenant is even credited with having unearthed human bones while digging a cellar.

At CALVIN, 30.0 *m.* (*see Tour 9*), is the southern junction with US 75, which unites with US 270 as the route makes an abrupt turn north. At 39.3 *m.*, the northern junction with US 75, US 270 turns sharply westward.

HOLDENVILLE, 48.3 *m.* (866 alt., 6,192 pop.), the seat of Hughes County, is on the eastern edge of the Greater Seminole oil field. Products manufactured here range from women's clothing to fishing tackle. Farm produce and trade also contribute to the town's economy.

Holdenville has had two sites and three names during its existence. The earliest village was named Echo and was located some two miles to the south of the present town. About 1890 it was officially designated as a post office under the name of Fentress. The present townsite was surveyed in 1895 at the junction point of the Choctaw, Oklahoma, and Gulf Railroad (now the Rock Island) and the Frisco Railway. Fentress moved to the new site and the name of Holdenville was added shortly afterward.

Left from Holdenville on paved State 68 to LAKE HOLDENVILLE (*fishing, boating, water skiing*), 4.5 *m.*, a 550-acre municipal reservoir (L) with a well-timbered shore line fourteen miles long.

The SITE OF FORT HOLMES (R), 6.0 *m.*, is on the south bank of Little River near its confluence with the South Canadian. Fort Holmes, later known as Fort Edwards, was established in 1834 under the supervision of Lieutenant Theophilus Hunter Holmes, an officer of the dragoon expedition that had been sent out from Fort Gibson (*see Tour 3*) to make treaties with the Plains Indians. Although Fort Holmes was soon abandoned, a firm of traders, Edwards and Shelton, established a trading post just across the river and for years it flourished as Edwards' Settlement and Trading House or Fort Edwards. Jesse Chisholm, the half-blood Cherokee freighter (*see below*), for whom the well-traveled Chisholm Trail (*see Tour 11*) was named, married Edwards' daughter and lived for a time at the post. It was on the busy California Trail and was also a favorite trading place for many of the southwestern Indian tribes. Some of these latter brought in not only furs and pelts to trade, but also white prisoners. The Comanches, in particular, trafficked in human beings, usually kidnaping the whites at isolated settlements in Texas and exchanging them for merchandise at trading posts or for ransom at Fort Gibson.

At 54.4 *m.* a historical marker notes the SITE OF EMAHAKA MISSION northeast of this point. This well known school for Indian girls was established in 1894 by the Seminole Nation. In 1908, the superintendent was Mrs. Alice Brown Davis, who later became the first woman chief of the Seminoles. Emahaka was abandoned in 1914 and the imposing building was destroyed by fire in 1927.

Between Holdenville and Wewoka are signs of increasing development of the Greater Seminole Field. Because the wells are comparatively shallow, drilling rigs are generally shorter than those in the Oklahoma City Field (*see Oklahoma City*).

WEWOKA, 59.2 *m.* (788 alt., 6,747 pop.), the seat of Seminole County, was named for one of the former Creek tribal towns in the East. When the Seminole Indians, who were affiliated for a time with the Creek confederacy, branched from the league, they also had an eastern Wewoka town. They transferred the name to this site in Indian Territory at the time of their removal.

A controversy developed in 1845 over the Seminoles' migration to the Territory. They agreed to settle on Creek land and under Creek government. But the comparatively free status of their Negro slaves was distasteful to the Creeks, whose own slaves were held in stricter bondage. The Negroes among the Seminoles had a status similar to that of renters or sharecroppers of today. They lived in separate villages and enjoyed equal liberty, paying a portion of their crops for the use of the Seminole land. They could even own land on which their masters made no claim. When the United States General Thomas S. Jesup was conducting his campaign to subdue the Seminole tribe in Florida, he had promised the Creek Indians that they might have all the Seminole slaves they could capture. But the federal Attorney General later ruled that all Negroes taken under Jesup's order were to be restored to the Seminoles, and 286 Negroes from Florida were accordingly delivered to a group of Seminole chiefs at Fort Gibson in January, 1849.

The Creek Indians were resentful over the decision and passed a law declaring that no town of free or limited-slavery Negroes could exist in their country and also forbidding the possession of arms by slaves. The Negroes had already settled in the vicinity of present Wewoka and, aware of the hostility of the Creeks, had armed themselves. On June 24, 1849, an armed party of Creeks, with some whites and Cherokees, came to Wewoka to seize several Negroes whom they claimed were rightfully their slaves. Many of the Seminole Indians prepared to aid in the defense of the Negro town, but troops from Fort Smith, Arkansas, intervened in time to stop the battle. A council was held, a few of the Negroes claimed by the Creeks were turned over to them, and the threat of a real war between the two tribes subsided.

As an aftermath of the dispute, a treaty in 1856 assigned the Seminoles a separate reservation. But a surveying mistake in 1866 resulted in Wewoka, the Seminole capital, being laid out astride the boundary between the Creek and Seminole nations. This was the source of friction for a long time, mainly because of schools and other public improvements which were built by the Seminoles on land found later to belong to the Creeks. Present-day Seminole Street (one-half block east of Main Street) in Wewoka was the last-named true boundary between the two nations.

The government set up by the Seminoles in their new land in 1866 was the most primitive of those of the Five Civilized Tribes. The principal chief, his assistant, the treasurer, and the superintendent of schools were elected by the people; a council composed of fourteen band chiefs assumed both the legislative and judicial duties. The only record of law was written in a book kept by the chief. Twenty "lighthorsemen" performed police duty and also officiated at floggings and executions. The chief and the treasurer personally owned trading posts where they extended credit to enrolled citizens against the per capita payments due them.

The present Rock Island railroad through Wewoka was constructed in 1899. A townsite was soon laid out, and in 1902 white settlers began to arrive. The town became an important Indian trading post and merchants and traders for many miles around ordered supplies shipped to this new rail siding, where they were picked up in wagons. In 1926 the fantastically rich Greater Seminole Field (*see below*) was discovered and Wewoka's population doubled within sixty days. For several years it ranked as one of the principal oil towns of the state.

The name of a recently built (1956) motel—the Wewoka Switch—recalls much of this early history, especially in its more hectic aspects. Back in trading post days, merchants of the area used the rail siding as a convenient excuse for any and all commercial shortcomings. Whenever they were unable to produce an item a customer asked for, they had a ready excuse: "I've got it, but it's in the Wewoka Switch." In 1926, when Wewoka became overnight an oil boom town, field supplies began to flood this same switch. Lost freight bills, poor telephone service, and inadequate freighting facilities congested the traffic. Shipments often thought to be lost in transit were frequently found, in fact, in Wewoka Switch. Oil field slang—always colorful, if not always printable—promptly adopted, and adapted, the term. To "get caught in a Wewoka Switch" grew to mean that one had suddenly found himself in a trying situation. Oil men carried the expression to new fields over the world and it has now been immortalized, after a fashion, in neon.

The COUNTY COURTHOUSE, Wewoka Avenue on Courthouse Square, is a modern three-story brick building, similar in design to the CITY HALL, 204 South Wewoka Avenue. On the Square an old pecan tree was used as a TRIBAL WHIPPING POST from 1899 until statehood (1907). It replaced the original "execution tree," the stump of which is on exhibition in the Oklahoma Historical Society Building (*see Oklahoma City*).

Right from Wewoka on paved State 56 is the last COUNCIL HOUSE OF THE SEMINOLES, 1.0 *m.*, now used as a residence on the Youngblood farm. It was built about 1800 and replaced the brush-covered arbor that had previously served as the tribal capitol. Here, too, were the campgrounds and the big spring of the Seminoles.

At 60.8 *m.* is the junction with an improved road.

Right on this road is LAKE WEWOKA (*swimming, fishing, boating, picnic and camping areas, recreational facilities*), 1.4 *m.* The 260-acre municipal reservoir, three miles long, is the scene of boat races every June. Near by, is the 344-acre LAKE SEMINOLE project started in 1957. Plans have been made by the Wewoka Creek Water and Soil Conservation District No. 2 for the building of sixty lakes in Seminole and Hughes counties, under approval of the Department of Agriculture and the United States Congress.

In the valley midway between the North and South Canadian rivers is SEMINOLE, 71.1 *m.* (863 alt., 11,863 pop.), named for the Indians on whose allotted lands the town was located. Originally a branch of the Creek confederation, the tribe's habit of living apart gave them the name Seminole, meaning "wild" or, literally, "those who camp at a distance." (Some of them still "camp" in Florida, their traditional home.) The Seminoles are one of the Five Civilized Tribes.

When the Mekusukey Mission was built four miles southwest of present-day Seminole in 1890 (*see below*), shipments of freight for the mission were billed to a "Mr. Tidmore." The community was known as Tidmore until 1906 when it was officially named Seminole by the Post Office Department. In 1926, Seminole had grown to only about 1,000 population, with stockmen and farmers using it for a trading center. Then in July, 1926, one of the greatest oil pools in history was discovered at Seminole. The town became the center of the Greater Seminole Field, a bonanza that for a time produced as high as 527,000 barrels of high-grade crude oil daily. By 1950 gross production had topped the billion-barrel mark and by 1956 an average of three hundred new wells were being completed each year.

The 1926 oil boom caught Seminole by surprise. From 1,000, the city's population grew to 35,000 within a year. People lived in shacks, covered wagons, and hastily built "shotgun" houses. They slept under pool tables while the balls clicked on above them. Prices on everything, even drinking water, reached fantastic heights. A small basement rented for $400 a month, an old barn for $200, a smokehouse for $50. Farm produce became scarce as farmers quit plowing and took to "roughnecking" on near-by rigs. Rock Island freight income for six months in 1926 was more than a million dollars, exceeded only by Chicago, it is said, for that same period.

Vice and corruption quickly followed the oil boom. Bishop's Alley, mushrooming on land at the edge of the city owned by W. A. Bishop, a quiet attorney, soon attained almost national fame for its "49er's Dance Hall," the "Big C," and the "Palace." Bootlegging, dope-peddling, hijacking, brawling, and an occasional murder became more and more common. The climax came with the killing of a state peace officer, after which residents went on a crusade and quickly cleaned up the area.

Today Seminole is the center of a diversified industrial area, although oil-field service and supply is still the predominant activity, since oil continues to be the main industry of the county. But agriculture is becoming increasingly important, with the development of conservation plans (*see above*) to restore natural fertility to the Wewoka Creek watershed.

Seminole has a modern nine-hole golf course, several excellent parks, a municipal swimming pool, and a professional baseball team. Lake Seminole, to the southeast (*see above*), offers many recreational facilities. Hunting in the area includes squirrel, quail, and waterfowl.

In sharp contrast to conditions during the oil-boom days, Seminole also maintains a strong position in the field of education. The SEMINOLE HIGH SCHOOL, 501 N. Timmons Street, has included since 1931 a fully accredited Junior College with an average enrollment of seventy-five students. The main building of buff brick, concrete and stone, completed in 1931, was extensively modernized in 1955.

Seminole is at the junction with State 99 (*see Tour 14*). A marker at the junction calls attention to the SITE OF THE MEKUSUKEY ACADEMY, a school for Seminole Indian boys which was established by the tribe four miles to the southwest in 1891. It was named for one of the "war towns" of the old Seminole Nation, whose people were noted for their bravery. The red sandstone blocks used in the construction of the buildings were hauled overland by oxen from Muskogee. The academy was closed in 1930, but it yielded an unexpected bonus four years later when oil was discovered on the school grounds (to which the Seminoles had retained title) and each enrolled member of the tribe received $35.

SHAWNEE, 89.1 *m.* (1,008 alt., 22,948 pop.) (*see Shawnee*).

Left from Shawnee on paved State 18 to a cluster of buildings, 2.5 *m.*, the SHAWNEE INDIAN SANATORIUM (L), the SHAWNEE INDIAN AGENCY (R), the old SHAWNEE QUAKER MISSION (L), and the MISSION CEMETERY (R). The entire center started when the Society of Friends built the tiny, white, frame Shawnee Quaker Mission in 1885. Their missionaries had previously held services in log cabins in the Shawnee lands until one of them, Franklin Elliott, completed this single-room church, set facing east on a hill. The lumber was hauled from Independence and Coffeyville, Kansas, over a route that was unbroken much of the way. The heavy iron bell, still hanging in the open belfry, was brought overland in the same manner. After white infiltration into the surrounding vicinity, the two races worshiped in the old mission until it was abandoned in 1924. It was opened for services only once after that—for the wedding of the granddaughter of Anthony Bourbonnais, one of the three Indian men who hauled the original lumber. In 1940 the Pottawatomie Historical Society bought the three and one-half acres of land from the Quaker Church and restored the old landmark. It was made a museum in 1950. The nearby Mission Cemetery is now a part of the Tecumseh Cemetery, which is located directly across the highway from the Mission.

A school was conducted as a part of the early work of the old Quaker Mission. Supervision was later transferred to the government, which continued to maintain it as an educational institution until 1918. In 1925, the Department of the Interior decided to utilize the plant as a sanitarium to combat the ever growing prevalence of tuberculosis among the Indians. Accordingly, the Shawnee Indian Sanatorium was established on the site of the school and the 240 acres of surrounding land. Materials from the old buildings were used in construction of the present plant of fifteen units, centering around a large, fireproof, brick infirmary.

The white frame structures of the Shawnee Indian Agency, which ministers to the approximately 1,500 enrolled Indians, include an administration building, stores, and living quarters for employees. The Pottawatomie County Historical Society planned in 1956 to open up a road to the SITE OF THE OLD SHAWNEE TRADING POST, located one-quarter mile west of the Agency offices.

At 92.1 *m.* on US 270 is the junction with a graveled drive.

Right on this drive is ST. GREGORY'S COLLEGE, 0.3 *m.*, an institution operated by the Benedictine Fathers. The most prominent structure on the 800-acre campus, the Administration Building, is also the oldest. A massive six-story affair of red brick and white stone, with turrets surmounting the four corners of the square tower, it is considered one of the best examples of Tudor Gothic design in the Southwest. South and east of the Administration Building, and blending with it in materials and design, is the Abbey Church, erected in 1942. It is impressive for its majestically simple interior. Attached to the rear of the church by an enclosed arcade is the four-story Monastery, where the Benedictine monks, in silence, live out their lives in prayer, study, and work.

In 1956 the school offered accredited junior college and high school courses to approximately 240 students, many of them preparing for the priesthood. It is an outgrowth of the work of the Benedictine Fathers of Sacred Heart Abbey (*see Tour 14*) in the southern part of Pottawatomie County. The early school work of the order was perpetuated in the founding of St. Gregory's here in 1915.

The ST. GREGORY MUSEUM AND ART GALLERY (*open to public during school terms, 1–5 Sun., other times on request*) has an outstanding display of paintings and art objects which were collected over a period of twenty-five years by the late Rev. Gregory Gerrer. Father Gregory, a distinguished artist who died in 1949, painted the official portrait of Pope Pius X, an exact replica of which hangs in the Vatican at Rome. Although he was the youngest of the six famous artists invited to paint the Pope's portrait in 1902, his work was chosen as the finest and the original is prominently hung in the St. Gregory gallery. Displayed in a near-by glass case is a zuchetto (skullcap) personally presented to Father Gregory by Pope Pius.

The gallery has priceless canvases by the Renaissance artist Il Guercino, Raphael, Murillo, Aretino Spinello, Guido Reni, José de Ribera, and others. One is the famous painting, "The Adoration of the Magi," by Giulio Romano, pupil of Raphael. Whistler and Rembrandt are among those represented in the group of etchings. Several works by the Kiowa Indian artists—Mopope, Asah, and Auchiah, of Anadarko (*see Tour 3*)—are also on display.

The museum contains a comprehensive and varied collection of four thousand specimens, art objects, and curios gathered from all parts of the world. Egyptian mummies; skulls; strange and ancient seeds and nuts; old copies of newspapers; specimens of minerals (many representative of Oklahoma formations); native and foreign woods, shown in cross section; mounted and classified rare birds, mammals, and reptiles; antique and modern firearms and medieval armor; primitive utensils; Indian handicraft; rare Oriental art works and antiques of Babylonian, Greek, Roman, Aztec, and Toltec origin are included in the various sections.

DALE, 98.1 *m.* (1,037 alt., 378 pop.), was first established in 1889 as King's Post Office, since it was located on the allotment of an Indian named John King. In 1890, it was moved two miles east and named Dale in honor of Judge Frank Dale, a Territorial judge of Guthrie (*see Tour 10*) noted for his stern treatment of Territorial bad men. When the present Rock Island Railroad arrived in 1895, the town moved again—buildings were loaded on wagons and transferred intact—to its present location.

On a hilltop one mile from Dale is said to be the site of a Civil War encampment from which Confederate raiders made forays into Kansas. Well-defined trenches of the earthwork fortification still remain. Cartridge cases have been found near by.

McLOUD, 102.7 *m.* (1,058 alt., 718 pop.), was established at the time of the extension of the railroad and named for railway attorney John W. McLoud. The town lies in the middle of a rich farming section on the bank of the North Canadian River. This fertile region is the principal source of Pottawatomie County's record production of blackberries.

Many Kickapoo Indians live on allotments near McLoud and, although the location and time vary from year to year, their annual celebration (*make local inquiry*) is often held in the McLoud area. The Kickapoos, closely related to the Sac and Fox tribe, were driven out of their former home in Illinois to the Southwest by the inexorable advance of the white man about the middle of the nineteenth century. When a band of them drifted into Mexico and began to make border raids into Texas, an international problem was posed. To solve it, the United States persuaded them to return, settling them on a small reservation in this vicinity in 1873. Here they became the peaceful neighbors of the Sac and Fox, the Seminoles, the Potawatomis, the Shawnees, and the Iowas. But trouble threatened again, briefly, in 1889 after the opening of near-by Old Oklahoma. White settlers began to cut timber and graze cattle on the Kickapoo reservation. When the Indians complained, wild rumors of an impending warpath reached the citizens of newly founded Oklahoma City to the northwest and for a few frenzied days preparations were made to defend the sodhouse and tent settlement. A federal order prohibiting white men from encroaching on Kickapoo land soon restored order. The tribe became angered again in 1895, when the government proposed to open their land for settlement. They protested strenuously—since their treaty had made no provision for such action—but all they got for their pains was the subsequent name, the "Kicking Kickapoos." Most of the remaining tribesmen now live on their assigned allotments on the old reservation.

HARRAH, 110.3 *m.* (1,080 alt., 741 pop.) (*see Tour 3*), is at the junction with US 62 (*see Tour 3*), with which US 270 unites for the next 19.9 miles.

OKLAHOMA CITY, 130.2 *m.* (1,243 alt., 243,504 pop.; 1956 est., 317,500) (*see Oklahoma City*), is at the junction with US 77 (*see Tour 10*), US 62 (*see Tour 3*), and US 66 (*see Tour 1*), with which US 270 unites westward for 36.5 miles.

Section c. OKLAHOMA CITY *to* KANSAS LINE, 257.1 *m.* *US 270*

West of Oklahoma City, US 270 continues its northwesterly course up the fertile valley of the North Canadian River. For nearly one hundred miles beyond Geary the route roughly parallels the Gypsum Hills. Where erosion has worn away the top soil, ledges of dead-white gypsum stand out as though drawn with chalk. The hills raise their bold, flat-topped knobs intermittently across Blaine, Dewey, and Woodward counties. The Cheyenne and Arapaho Indians roamed this section, before it was assigned to them as a reservation (*see Tour 1*). Today it is the home of conservation-minded farmers, prosperous ranchers, and lazy rattlesnakes (*see below*).

West of OKLAHOMA CITY, 0 *m.*, US 270 unites with US 66 (*see Tour 1*) to CALUMET JUNCTION, 36.5 *m.*, where it turns abruptly north (R).

CALUMET, 42.3 *m.* (1,400 alt., 339 pop.), is a small agricultural community in the North Canadian River valley.

At 50.5 *m.* is the junction with a dirt road.

Right on this road is COYOTE HILL (R), 0.8 *m.*, a red sandstone butte capped with dolomite that affords an excellent view (*hiking only*) of the valley of the North Canadian. Since dolomite is harder and more resistant than sandstone, the butte is striking evidence of erosion over the centuries. This spot was a favorite meeting place for the Cheyenne and Arapaho Indians, whose present tribal center is only a few miles east at Concho (*see Tour 11*), and many gatherings took place here in 1890 during the "Ghost Dance" or "Messiah" craze (*see Tour 3A*). The fanatical belief of the cult's followers was that the Indian Messiah would soon be coming to free them of white domination. And to prepare for the great event, the group meeting here placed an iron bedstead, equipped with springs, mattress, and blankets, on the summit of the butte. The Indians' explanation was forthright and logical: "When the white man's God came to visit His children, He was a poor man. He had no house. He had no bed. He had no money. The little bird had a nest in the tree, the coyote had a hole under a rock, but white man's God had no place to sleep. We are better than white man. When our God comes He will find that we, his people, have bed ready for Him."

GEARY, 53.2 *m.* (1,499 alt., 1,614 pop.), was named for Ed Guerrier, a pioneer settler, but the name of this stable farming community was promptly corrupted to Geary. The town was started in 1898 (the year the railroad arrived) on land which had belonged to the Cheyenne and Arapaho Indians until it was thrown open to settlement on April 19, 1892.

Since it is the center of an important wheat-growing region, a grain elevator dominates the skyline. On the west edge of town, in a wooded canyon, is the L. A. HOLMES PARK (*swimming, picnic and recreation facilities, stadium*). In Geary is the office of the North Canadian Soil Conservation District, established in 1938, one of the oldest and largest of the more than eighty soil-conservation groups working in Oklahoma.

From Geary, US 270 drops quickly into the flat, fertile valley of the North Canadian River, where plans are under way to irrigate sixteen thousand acres with water stored in Canton Reservoir (*see below*). Memorial Tree Lane (R) honors Jesse Chisholm. A marker, 55.2 *m.*, at the end of the lane, notes that Jesse Chisholm was an Indian trader, a manufacturer of salt in Blaine County before 1861, and a noted pathfinder. Returning from Kansas in 1865, he first traveled the path of what later became the famous Chisholm Trail, now followed approximately by US 81 (*see Tour 11*). His last camp (*see below*) was at Left Hand Spring, where he died in 1868.

At 58.5 *m.* is the junction with a graveled road.

Right on this road, across the North Canadian River, to junction with a dirt road, 4.6 *m.*; L. here to another dirt road, 6.8 *m.*; L. again to a farmhouse, 7.3 *m.* In the pasture southwest of the house (*make local inquiry*) is the GRAVE OF JESSE CHISHOLM, on the side of a sloping knoll overlooking the North Canadian. The pioneer freighter was born in Tennessee in 1805. His father was a Scotchman, his mother a Cherokee. As a trader with the Indians, he was known as a man with a straight tongue, and his honesty and fairness frequently made him a peacemaker. At his death March 4, 1868, he was the adopted brother of a dozen Indian tribes.

GREENFIELD, 60.8 *m.* (1,455 alt., 191 pop.), was named for William Greenfield an early settler.

Between Greenfield and Watonga, the route lies close to the North Canadian River (R) and makes a long curve to pass beneath the east face of the Red Hills, an abrupt outcropping of white dolomite and shale. At 67.7 *m.* the winding, sandy-bottomed, river is crossed.

Named for an Arapaho chief, WATONGA, 69.7 *m.* (1,515 alt., 3,249 pop.), is the seat of Blaine County. It was settled in 1892, the year the Cheyenne and Arapaho reservation was opened to settlement, and many Indians still live in or near the town (R). Until recently the streets of Watonga—as well as those of Geary and Canton (*see below*)—were brightened by the older tribal members who still retain their traditional dress, the women in colorful blankets and moccasins, the men with their long black braids interwoven with gay ribbons. But most of these older ones are gone and the distinctive Indian regalia is rarely seen. Black Coyote's town owes, however, much to its long Indian tradition, even though the youngsters of Indian blood can now be distinguished only by color of skin, sharpness of features, and a lingering springiness of step.

An important feature of the early history of Watonga was the publication of its first newspaper, the *Watonga Republican* (*see Newspapers*). Its editor, Thompson B. Ferguson, was appointed by President Theodore Roosevelt as governor of Oklahoma Territory in 1901.

The grain elevators beside the highway symbolize the town's principal economic asset, the fertile farmlands, which comprise the Watonga trade area.

North from Watonga (straight ahead) on paved State 8 to junction with second paved road, 4.4 *m.;* L. here to ROMAN NOSE STATE PARK (*lodge, cabins, fishing, swimming, boating, hiking, camp and picnic areas*), 6.9 *m.* The 540-acre park was named for the last warrior-chief of the Cheyennes, Henry Roman Nose, a steel-and-concrete silhouette of whom guards the park entrance. The great chieftain used the park site as a winter encampment for his braves and later, when the land was opened to settlement, he claimed it for his allotment. The same rugged, heavily wooded canyons and dependable springs that make the park northwestern Oklahoma's finest playground offered the Indians in early days protection from winter winds and pleasant relief from summer heat, a convenient source of wood, and an abundant supply of fresh water. Roman Nose, who had taken part in the Battle of the Washita (*see Tour 13*) as a member of Black Kettle's band, lived here until his death about 1917. A number of his grandchildren still live in Watonga.

The deep red clays of the Permian Red Beds (*see Tour 2A*) give the park's main canyon its distinctive charm. Lying on the broken rim of the "Gyp Hills" (*see above*), this canyon opens out onto the fertile farmlands that stretch away to the east. Near the site where Roman Nose had his dugout, the "Spring of Everlasting Water," an icy gusher of four hundred to six hundred gallons a minute, supplies a large concrete swimming pool, 18-acre Boecher Lake (one of the few in Oklahoma to offer trout fishing), and the 55-acre Lake Watonga. (Most of the land surrounding this lake is owned by the State Game and Fish Department and hunting, forbidden in Roman Nose Park itself, is permitted in accordance with its regulations.) Twenty-room Roman Nose Lodge overlooks Boecher Lake. Many squirrels and opossums inhabit the elms, cottonwoods, and cedars dotting the canyons, and native shrubs afford shelter for wild fowl. The Cat Canyon Trail (*make local inquiry*) leading from Roman Nose north into the Salt Creek Canyon country is one of the state's interesting scenic drives.

In the early days an old military trail from Fort Reno (*see Tour 1*) to Fort Cantonment, northwest of the park, passed through this area. The same sparkling spring that attracted the Indians also appealed to the federal troops and it was usually chosen as a camp site. Local legends also tell of several Territorial outlaw bands who found the hills and canyons an ideal hiding place for both themselves and their loot.

Given to the state by the people of Watonga, Roman Nose was developed by the National Park Service in co-operation with the Oklahoma Planning and Resources Board. Civilian Conservation Corps workers constructed the first facilities, and the park was opened to the public in 1937.

West of Watonga, US 270 again crosses the North Canadian River, 72.3 *m.*, bordered here by brush-covered sand dunes. Beyond, and for the next forty miles or more, the route rolls over a gently undulating plain broken by scattered stands of scrub oak and blackjack. Here in the winter—as along other highways serving Oklahoma's "short grass" country—the motorist will see snow fences a short distance back from the road. Although snowfall is comparatively light and rarely covers the ground for more than a few days at a time, strong winds often whip up much of the snow that does fall, to deposit it in the first convenient depression, which is likely to be an unprotected road cut. The rust-red fences resemble grass matting, so closely are the thin laths placed together. In summer they can easily be rolled up for storage.

At 79.1 *m.* is the junction (R) with State 58, which leads to Canton (*see below*), and State 33, which leaves US 270 at this point.

Left on this paved road is THOMAS, 12.5 *m.* (1,513 alt., 1,171 pop.). This prosperous agricultural community was platted in 1902 on land homesteaded by Joseph W. Morris in the run which opened the Cheyenne and Arapaho reservation ten years before. Extensive sweet potato production (up to 250,000 bushels a year) furnishes Thomas with an unusual industry, for the plants grown in the area (often with the help of deep-well irrigation) are of such excellence that seedlings are shipped from here to all parts of the United States. A fringe of towering grain elevators that provide storage for two million bushels of wheat—the greatest capacity between the terminals at Enid and Amarillo, Texas—indicate the area's other principal crop.

On the fertile farmlands south of Thomas are communities of four religious groups: the Amish, the Old Mennonites, the Dunkards, and the River Brethren. In their pacifism, abhorrence of ostentation, and otherworldly conservatism, all are similar in general character and purpose to the Mennonites, although the latter two are not actually branches of that sect (*see Tour 4*).

The Amish—popularly called the "Hook-and-Eye Dutch"—first came to America from Holland and Switzerland in the seventeenth century, hoping to settle where they might be free to follow their customs and institutions without hindrance. They emigrated to New York and Pennsylvania, settling first near the Quakers. Later, when this area became more heavily settled, some of them came to their present home in Oklahoma. The forefathers of the Amish were among the first in this country to protest against slavery. Originally, the Amish did not permit private ownership of land. This is countenanced today, but the group remains a closely knit clan. They tend to marry within their sect. Worship services, still conducted in German, are held in small groups in the various homes.

Changes are taking place, however, though slowly and often with extreme reluctance. Tractors have now become commonplace, and within the past few years the first pickup trucks have appeared. However, rural electrification and telephones are still forbidden, as are passenger autos. Too, the Amish consider color and style in clothing ostentatious. Both men and women wear clothes of drab, solid colors, all cut to virtually the same pattern. The women wear long, full-skirted, high-necked, long-sleeved dresses and modest poke bonnets of the same color; the men wear straight sack coats, "barn-door" pants, blunt-toed high shoes, and flat wide-brimmed hats with uncreased crowns. Neckties are never worn, nor are buttons used. (The use of the hook-and-eye fastener began in Europe as a protest against what the Amish considered an unfair tax on buttons.) Similarly, the absence of whiskers on the smooth faces of the Amish men—with the exception of the distinctive fringe around the chin—began as a protest against taxation. (A sure sign that a clean-shaven youth is seriously considering matrimony is the scraggly appearance of his chin whiskers.) The children are miniature counterparts of their parents in appearance. Thomas streets, especially on weekdays (there are too many automobiles on Saturdays), will usually contain a scattering of horse-drawn Amish vehicles as whole families come to town to trade.

The Old Mennonites are considerably less conservative in their customs. Though their religious tenets are quite strict, they hold their worship service in a regular church. They shun ostentation in dress (even to banning rings and other jewelry), and the women wear a "prayer covering" (a tiny black cap), but their clothes are conventional, if plain. Generally they own modern machinery and autos, and their homes are wired, though television is not yet generally accepted.

The Dunkards—or the Church of the Brethren, as they prefer to be known—are an outgrowth of the widespread church-reform movement in Europe in the early eighteenth century. This sect originated in Germany, later emigrated in a body to the United States. Central in the group's religious observances is the Feast of Love, which follows closely the acts of Christ and His disciples at the Last Supper The distinctive rituals of washing one another's feet and the kiss of charity are followed by the supper itself (a simple meal), climaxed by the conventional Communion service. The sect is not as strict in matters of dress and custom as are the two Mennonite groups, but the women observe certain conventions of dress; they use no cosmetics, little if any jewelry. The Dunkards are progressive farmers and use modern farm methods and machinery.

The River Brethren—or Brethren in Christ—probably originated in Pennsylvania when the first group began the practice of immersion in the Susquehanna River. The sect has no definite creed, but stresses plain living, spiritual regeneration, and sanctification. The church at Thomas was founded by a missionary from Indiana, who also helped establish the Jabbok Bible School and Orphanage one mile southwest of Thomas. The school continued caring for orphans, both Indian and white, until 1925, when this part of the work was dropped. The school itself was closed in 1955.

At 99.2 *m.* on the main route is the junction with paved State 51.

Right on this road to the junction with a graveled road, 11.2 *m.*

Left on this road to the SITE OF OLD FORT CANTONMENT (R), 2.8 *m.* The fort was established in the spring of 1879 and troops were billeted here to control the Cheyennes during the Plains Indian campaign (*see Tour* 3A). It was located just sixty miles due northwest of the old Darlington Agency (*see Tour* 11) near the present Fort Reno (*see Tour* 1), which also served the Cheyennes and Arapahoes. But the establishment of Cantonment was considered necessary because of the hostile feeling between the Southern Cheyennes, who were in home territory, and the Northern Cheyennes, who had been brought south from Nebraska and the Dakotas. Not long after the fort had been founded, a number of stone buildings were erected, one of which is still standing. After the dissatisfied Northern Cheyennes returned to their original home, the necessity for Fort Cantonment's existence decreased, and it was abandoned in 1882. The plant was then turned over to the Department of the Interior, which contracted with Mennonite missionaries to open a school for the Plains Indians.

The Mennonites conducted the school for a few years before erecting a private institution, and in 1898 the government took over the supervision of the Cantonment school, which it maintained until 1949. The Cheyenne-Arapaho Business Committee (*see Tour* 11) planned in 1956 to make a museum of the building.

A CHEYENNE-ARAPAHO SUBAGENCY was established here in 1903, when the jurisdiction of the old Darlington Agency was divided, but it has been discontinued. The construction of Canton Dam (*see below*) made it necessary to move the Cantonment cemetery to ground near the construction project office. Many Cheyennes and Arapahoes still live in this area south and west of Canton Lake and ceremonial dances of the two tribes are frequently held here. Even two of the rituals officially frowned upon—the Peyote Dance and the grueling Sun Dance (*see Tour* 11)—are still observed.

Straight ahead on State 51 to the junction with a paved road, 11.2 *m.*

Left on this road to CANTON DAM, 1.4 m. Constructed by army engineers primarily for flood control and irrigation, this $10,327,000 structure (completed in 1948) consists of an earth embankment 14,300 feet long and a concrete spillway 778 feet wide. Maximum height is seventy-three feet; normal surface area of the reservoir is 7,720 acres with a shore line of 44.2 miles. More than three hundred thousand visitors a year come to fish (principally for catfish, bass, and crappie) and to hunt. The state maintains a 13,000-acre public hunting area along the northern perimeter of the reservoir. Boating and camping facilities are available.

Straight ahead once again on State 51 is CANTON, 13.2 *m.* (1,590 alt., 959 pop.), a trading center and supply point for vacationers.

At 18.6 *m.* is the junction with paved State 51A.

East (straight ahead) on this road is SOUTHARD, 0.8 *m.*, the location of the quarries and mills of the United States Gypsum Company, which has operated here since 1905. Although totals vary according to business conditions, the plant annually produces a hundred million square feet of gypsum wallboard, lath, and sheathing, along with a quarter of a million tons of gypsum rock and plaster. The company employs about three hundred people.

State 51 veers north and east from Southard, skirting the edge of the "Gyp Hills."

OKEENE, 30.1 *m.* (1,203 alt., 1,170 pop.), with its massive grain elevators to the east and west, is the prosperous center of a rich wheat-growing area. Its principal industry is a flour mill, while its most important "non-commercial" activity is serving as headquarters for the International Association of Rattlesnake Hunters. Billed as "the nation's most unusual sporting event," Okeene's annual Rattlesnake Roundup (held on a Sunday in early April) is a day-long trek into the near-by gypsum hills in search of lazy diamondback rattlers. Hunters go armed with a forked stick, a game bag, and an emergency first-aid kit. The live snakes brought in—there is no market for dead ones—are milked of their venom for medical laboratories and sold to zoos and canneries. Veteran hunters make more than expense money; the market usually steadies at around fifty cents a pound. Crowds of up to twenty thousand have turned out for the roundup, held annually since 1939, and rattlesnake meat is traditionally served at the Saturday night banquet for association members. Sunday's activities follow the usual carnival pattern, with such added attractions as a "snake pit" and a rattlesnake derby. This concludes State 51 side tours, returning to US 270 for the main tour.

SEILING, 107.5 *m.* (1,760 alt., 700 pop.) (*see Tour 4*), is at the junction of US 270 with US 60 (*see Tour 5*).

At 110.2 *m.* US 270 unites with US 183 (*see Tour 12*), which it follows for the next 47.1 miles.

West of FORT SUPPLY (*see Tour 12*), 157.3 *m.*, US 270 strikes west to enter the Oklahoma Panhandle.

SLAPOUT, 188.1 *m.*, is of interest primarily for the derivation of its name. Allegedly, it evolved from the unvarying response of an early-day storekeeper to every call for an item he did not have in stock: "I had it yesterday, but I'm slap out today."

At 210.1 m., more than midway across the state's longest stretch of highway—sixty-seven miles—without a single curve, US 270 leaves State 3 and turns sharply right (north).

BEAVER CITY, 224.0 *m.*, (2,493 alt., 1,495 pop.), is the seat of Beaver County and onetime capital of the "Territory of Cimarron." A sod building, erected here in 1879, served as a store for cattlemen driving their herds across Beaver (North Canadian) River on the way to market in Dodge City, Kansas (*see Kansas Guide*).

The peculiar conditions which left the Panhandle without legal government brought about the formation of the "Territory of Cimarron" in 1887—an earnest effort by the people who had settled here to bring a semblance of law and order to No Man's Land. The convention for its formation was held at Beaver City and the town was named its capital. But the federal government never recognized the territorial organization, and the Organic Act of 1890 automatically dissolved it, adding the entire section to Oklahoma Territory as Beaver County. When Oklahoma became a state, the Panhandle was divided into three counties, with the eastern one retaining the name of Beaver and Beaver City as its county seat. The *Beaver City Pioneer* (*see Newspapers*), one of the earliest white man's newspapers published in Oklahoma—and the first in this section of the state—appeared here in 1886.

In 1910, the Wichita Falls & Northwestern Railroad bought options on land six miles north of Beaver City, intending to extend its line to that point and found a town at the terminus. This the company did, creating the present town of Forgan. But in the meantime Beaver City citizens, hoping to forestall the devastating effect the new town would have on their settlement, began to build a railroad of their own. The plan was to connect it with Meade and Englewood, in Kansas. But construction, carried on with small contributions of both money and labor from practically every local citizen, was painfully slow. Many months were required to cover the six miles to Forgan, and several times the project was offered as a gift to the Missouri-Kansas-Texas Railroad, which had taken over the Wichita Falls & Northwestern. The offer was always refused. But when the transportation of wheat during World War I brought prosperity to the struggling Beaver, Meade & Englewood Railroad, it was, somewhat ironically, sold to the Katy for more than $2,000,000.

Beaver City is still an important wheat-growing area. And the BM&E still connects it with the Katy at Forgan.

At 230.4 *m.* is the junction with US 64 (*see Tour 2*), with which US 270 joins westward for 19.8 miles. It turns right (north) sharply at 250.2 *m.* and reaches the Kansas Line, 257.1 *m.*, five miles southeast of Liberal, Kansas (*see Kansas Guide*).

TOUR 6

(De Queen, Ark.)—Hugo—Durant—Ardmore—Waurika—(Vernon, Tex.); US 70, Arkansas Line to Texas Line, 293.0 m.

Roadbed paved throughout.

Texas, Oklahoma & Eastern R. R. parallels route between Arkansas Line and Broken Bow; St. Louis–San Francisco between Idabel and Ardmore; Santa Fe,

between Ardmore and Ringling; Missouri-Kansas-Texas between Deval and Grandfield.
Good accommodations in the larger towns.

US 70 is a 300-mile-long tour through the heart of Oklahoma's "Little Dixie," a humid, wooded section that contrasts sharply—in climate, topography, philosophy of life, and in religious and political affinities—with the high and dry prairie section of the state far to the northwest. Yet there is at least one common denominator, the Indian. For the highway parallels to a great extent the trail beaten out by the Choctaws as they pushed westward into the new land to which they were exiled from their Mississippi homes in 1831–33. Passing through rich cotton lands and still profitable pine and hardwood forests, the route bisects the oldest Choctaw settlements in Oklahoma.

Between Idabel and Durant, US 70 follows, in general, the wide bottom lands of the Red River. To Madill, it arches across huge Lake Texoma, one of the nation's most popular recreation areas. Continuing westward, the highway crosses the old Chickasaw Nation and plunges through the onetime reservations of the Kiowas, Comanches, and Apaches.

Thus US 70, throughout its course in Oklahoma, is reminiscent of Indian history. Along its route were established the first schools and churches for the immigrant Choctaws and Chickasaws, their first mills and trading posts, and the occasional big plantations owned by enterprising mixed bloods. Beside it still live many of their descendants, and those of their Negro slaves who were freed by the Civil War. And here—if anywhere in Oklahoma—in cut-over sections of southern Kiamichi mountain slopes, on fertile Red River farm lands, in isolated and half-forgotten villages can still be found relics of a way of life more than a century old, a way of life shared as it always has been by Negroes, whites, and Indians of the Five Civilized Tribes.

US 70 crosses the ARKANSAS LINE, 0 *m.*, eight miles west of De Queen, Arkansas (*see Arkansas Guide*), and passes for several miles through one of the state's finest pine forests.

EAGLETOWN, 6.5 *m.* (400 alt., 600 pop.), which saw its first settlers arrive in about 1820, was long an important Choctaw town. Stockbridge Mission was established in 1837 by the Rev. Cyrus Byington, who produced here his monumental "Dictionary of the Choctaw Language." In 1842, the Choctaw General Council founded the Iyanubbee Seminary for Girls at the mission. None of these first buildings remains, but the town (L) does have an interesting old home (to the right of the main road leading in from US 70) with a rare T-shaped open gallery.

The town was given added importance as the first station west of the Arkansas line on the military road from Little Rock to Fort Towson (*see below*). Its Choctaw name, Apukshunubbee, was that of a chief who died before the tribe's removal from Mississippi.

At 8.6 *m.* US 70 crosses the tree-lined Mountain Fork River, a well-stocked fishing stream, one of the clearest and most beautiful of the entire Kiamichi mountain region. Just beyond is the junction, 8.8 *m.*, with a farm lane.

Right on this lane to a two-story, elaborately designed farmhouse, 0.3 *m.*, (*adm. twenty-five cents*). Built in 1884 of hand-cut boards by the Choctaw chief, Jefferson Gardiner, the gracefully curved upstairs porch and the ornate woodwork strongly suggest the builder's love for the Mississippi River showboats. The site, called "Old Eagletown" (*see above*), was the first location of Bethabara Mission, established in June of 1832 as the first mission station for the exiled Choctaws. Presbyterian missionary Loring S. Williams also served as the postmaster when the first post office, called Eagle Town, was opened on July 1, 1834. The Choctaws maintained a log courthouse here from 1850 to 1907. Near by was a giant pin oak to which offenders were bound and whipped. (Both were destroyed by a storm some thirty years ago.)

From the farmhouse (which is also an informal museum) a foot trail leads to a CYPRESS TREE, 0.4 *m.*, on the west bank of Mountain Fork River at the old Bethabara Crossing, which marked the end of the Choctaws' "Trail of Tears" from Mississippi. Reliably estimated to be more than 2,000 years old, the tree is more than one hundred feet tall and has a circumference of forty-five feet, making it one of the largest known cypresses in this country. A lightning rod has been fixed in its already shattered top to preserve it from future storms.

BROKEN BOW, 15.6 *m.*, (467 alt., 1,838 pop.), in the center of Oklahoma's largest timbered area, was named by the Dierks brothers, pioneer lumbermen, for their Nebraska home. The mill they erected (L) still turns out its daily thousands of feet of pine and hardwood lumber—shortleaf oak, walnut, and gum. Throughout the year, the aroma of fresh-cut pine fills the air and mingles with the smell of smoke from the mill's tall stacks to provide a reliable barometer of the town's economic climate. Logically enough, Broken Bow's biggest annual event is the early-June Forest Festival. Sponsored by the State Forestry Service, it features log-sawing, women's nail-driving, and other contests and exhibits. On the north edge of town is the Forestry Service's tall steel lookout tower (*visitors welcome*).

Broken Bow is at the junction with State 21 (*see Tour 15A*).

Southward, cotton fields alternate with forests. In the fall, families of cotton pickers—Indian, Negro, and white—may be seen at work between the white-bolled rows, or camped near by. Here and there "clearin's" or "burnin's," new fields carved out of the forest, border these cotton patches. High up among the branches of many of the surrounding trees—elm, hickory, gum, and cottonwood—the mistletoe, Oklahoma's state flower, grows in such abundance as to provide Christmas money for the farmer willing to gather and ship it to the city markets. But the forest, generally, dominates the cotton fields. Near Little River, which US 70 crosses at 21.4 *m.*, a lone cypress sticking up here and there above the other trees suggests to the motorist the swamp-filled eeriness of the Deep South. And an occasional roadside creosoting mill reminds him that he is in the heart of Oklahoma's three million acres of commercial timberland.

IDABEL, 27.5 *m.* (504 alt., 4,671 pop.), seat of McCurtain County, is on the divide that separates the valleys of the Little and Red rivers. The town was named for the daughters, Ida and Belle, of the Choctaw citizen on whose land it was built. Farming and lumbering are the principal supports of the town, but Idabel is attracting an increasing number of sportsmen. Many streams and natural lakes in the area provide excellent fishing, while the forests to the north shelter a disproportionate number of the state's deer.

A marker at 28.1 *m.* calls attention to MILLER COURT HOUSE and Oklahoma's FIRST POST OFFICE, about nine miles to the south. The date was September 7, 1824. The post office was abolished in October, 1828, when this part of Arkansas Territory County was ceded to the Choctaw Nation. And the courthouse itself was destroyed by fire a month later.

Near Shawneetown, about three miles southwest of here is a plain wooden marker that notes the first cultivated farm in what is now Oklahoma. Ground was broken in 1804.

GARVIN, 36.2 *m.* (500 alt., 155 pop.), laid out when the Frisco railroad built through this region, saw the opening of the county's first bank. Here, too, sat the first U.S. Commissioner's Court in southeastern Oklahoma.

MILLERTON, 40.8 *m.* (519 alt., 250 pop.), is one of the first towns established in the Choctaw Nation.

Right from Millerton on a graded road to the empty buildings of WHEELOCK ACADEMY, 1.9 *m.*, founded in 1832 for the education of Indian girls by the missionary Alfred Wright, who helped to reduce the Choctaw language to writing. On top of a small hill near the old school—merged with Jones Academy near Hartshorne (*see Tour* 5) in 1955, after one hundred and twenty-three years of continuous service to the Choctaw people—are the ruins of one of the original log buildings occupied by the United States soldiers who conducted the first Choctaw exiles from their homes in Mississippi.

The academy was named for Eleazer Wheelock, founder and first president of Dartmouth College, Hanover, New Hampshire. South of the academy site is the stone Wheelock Mission Church, said to be the oldest church building in the state. It was erected by Presbyterian missionaries in 1842. Near by is the old missionary cemetery where Alfred Wright was buried.

Since its founding Wheelock Academy has been rebuilt, added to, and remodeled. The plain wooden buildings, attractive in their simplicity, housed, until 1955, one of the most complete institutions of its kind in Oklahoma—a school for orphan Choctaw girls, maintained by the federal government.

VALLIANT, 45.6 *m.* (522 alt., 661 pop.), gateway to excellent fishing and deer-hunting country along near-by Glover and Little rivers, is a trade center for corn, cotton, and peanut production, large peach and apple orchards, and (thanks to enlightened reforestation) pine pulpwood and hardwood forests.

Before and after the arrival of the Choctaws, the hill country to the north—the famed "Kiameesh"—was a favorite refuge of fugitives from other states, and Fort Smith's "Hanging Judge" Parker drew many of his victims from south of the Poteau River. Most of this outlawry, however, is now in the past. "Today," says one local observer, "there are seldom more than three illicit whisky stills found annually. No longer is 'wildcat' trucked to market. Killings are no more frequent than in the other sections of the state."

Right from Valliant on paved State 98 is WRIGHT CITY, 9.0 *m.* (520 alt., 1,121 pop.), home of another large lumber mill, owned (as is the one at Broken Bow) by Dierks Forests. The two together have a capacity of more than three hundred thousand board feet of lumber daily. North of Wright City, on a series of unnumbered gravel roads, is ALIKCHI, 18.3 *m.*, where it is said that the last tribal execution of an Indian in McCurtain County took place in 1902. Tried by a jury of fellow Choctaws, he was convicted of murder and then, according to custom, allowed to go home until the day of his execution. On the appointed day he turned himself in and was shot to death.

At 55.6 *m.*, on US 70, is the Fort Towson Historical Marker, at the junction with a graveled road.

Right on this road are the Ruins of the Original Fort Towson, 0.5 *m.* The fort was established in 1824 to protect the Choctaws—who were induced by the federal government to emigrate from their Mississippi homes—both from the raiding western Plains Indians and the outlaws that made their headquarters along the north bank of Red River. Soldiers sent to Fort Towson had little military work to do and were occupied mainly in building roads. The post was abandoned in 1829, then re-established when enforced removal of the Choctaws began in 1831. Abandoned once again in 1854, it was used as a Choctaw Indian agency until the outbreak of the Civil War, when it was taken over by the Confederates. In 1864 the fort was headquarters for General S. B. Maxey. And here, in June of 1865, two months after the official ending of the war, the Cherokee Confederate General Stand Watie surrendered.

It is said that Sam Houston met representatives of the Pawnee and Comanche tribes at Fort Towson in December of 1832, to negotiate treaties of peace between them and the tribes then being removed from east of the Mississippi. From this meeting Houston, allegedly, went on to begin the four-year campaign that ended with the wresting of the Province of Texas from Mexico.

All that remains of the commodious hewn-log barracks of Fort Towson and the lathed and plastered officers' quarters, ample for the accommodation of four companies, are scattered stones and traces of a few foundations.

FORT TOWSON, 56.2 *m.* (448 alt., 713 pop.), was named for the old military post.

Right from Fort Towson on a dirt road is the SITE OF DOAKSVILLE, 1 *m.* Established in 1821 by the Doaks brothers, who were fur traders, the settlement became an important center for trappers and Indian and white settlers as the frontier pushed farther and farther west. Shallow-draft Red River steamboats and overland freight served the settlement. In 1833, seventeen boats discharged cargoes for Doaksville—such varied items as powder and shot, churns, and cloth. Furs and cotton were loaded for the return trips.

By a treaty made at Doaksville in 1837, the Choctaw Nation agreed to grant (for $530,000) equal rights in their country to the Chickasaws, and the boundaries of the Chickasaw District were defined. In 1855 the tribes agreed to formal separation and the Chickasaw District became the Chickasaw Nation. From 1850 to 1863, Doaksville was the Choctaw capital. Its decline and eventual disappearance were due to the war, discontinuance of river traffic, and finally the removal of the capital itself. Nothing remains today but two ruined log buildings and the cemetery, which contains many pre–Civil War gravestones. Near Doaksville were located two girls' schools: Goodwater, founded in 1837 by the missionary Ebenezer Hotchkin; and Pine Ridge, opened in 1845.

SAWYER, 61.9 *m.*, came into existence about 1900 when the Arkansas and Choctaw Railroad (now the Frisco) built its branch line between Texarkana, Arkansas, and Ardmore. Approximately eight miles north is the SITE OF SPENCER ACADEMY, long a noted school for boys. It was established by the Choctaw Nation in 1841 and named for John C. Spencer, U.S. Secretary of War (1841–43).

US 70 crosses the KIAMICHI RIVER, 63.0 *m.*, and at 68.3 *m.* is the junction with a graveled road.

Left on this road, 1.5 *m.*, is ROSE HILL CEMETERY (R). In 1956 a monument was placed here marking the grave of Joseph T. Thoburn (1866–1941), one of Oklahoma's best-known historians. Here, too, is buried Robert M. Jones, one of the most remarkable figures in the history of the neighborhood. A half-blood Choctaw, Jones established a store here and at Scullyville (*see Tour 7*). But these were only two of his many enterprises. In all he owned five hundred slaves and six plantations, one of which, Lake West, included five thousand acres of rich Red River bottom land planted to cotton. The others, strung out along the river, were called Boggy, Rose Hill, Root Hog, Shawneetown, and Walnut Bayou. To carry his produce to market and bring in stocks for his stores, he also owned and operated two steamboats.

The cemetery is on the site of the old Rose Hill plantation, which was Captain Jones's home in the days when he lived in truly southern opulence. The house was elaborately finished in oak, maple, walnut, and mahogany, furnished largely from France (as was customary among rich ante bellum plantation owners). It burned in 1912—long after it had been abandoned and had fallen into decay—and today only a small tenant house and a few cedar trees remain. Jones was ruined by the Civil War and died at Rose Hill in 1873. The cemetery, with its impressive tombstones, is enclosed by a rock wall.

HUGO, 71.1 *m.* (549 alt., 5,984 pop.), symbolizes the kind of success story that probably would have delighted its namesake, Victor Hugo. The seat of Choctaw County, it was named by Mrs. W. H. Darrough, whose husband surveyed the original townsite, in honor of her favorite author. And with the coming of the railroads in the early 1900's, it enjoyed a brief boom. But following World War II, there was the inevitable loss of population that hit most of Oklahoma's predominantly agricultural towns. It was then that Hugo launched one of the state's first—and, to date, one of its most successful—drives for industrial development. Its industries include food processing and the manufacture of gloves, furniture, and other wood products.

With access to four rivers, eight streams, and ten lakes, Hugo is also a popular resort center for hunters and fishermen. It substantiates its claim to being "The Sarasota of the Southwest" by serving as winter headquarters for the Al G. Kelley & Miller Bros., George W. Cole, and Tex Carson circuses. (Visitors are welcome from October to April.) Pittman's Coonhound Kennels, two miles east of Hugo, is one of the largest in the Southwest. And the old Hugo Indian Territory Trading Post proudly proclaims "We buy and sell anything from chiggers to elephants; false teeth to steam engines."

Hugo is at the junction with US 271 (*see Tour* 7), which unites westward with US 70 for 7.2 miles. Along the way (provided it is not the circus season) the motorist will see gayly painted circus vans, vacationing elephants, and occasionally a camel getting awkwardly to its feet from a near-by pasture.

BOSWELL, 92.8 *m.* (580 alt., 875 pop.), grew up on the site of a much older settlement of Choctaws and the region has remained largely Indian in character. Here in a modified form is still followed the old custom of holding a Funeral Cry twenty-eight days after the burial of a Choctaw. Formerly, on the day of the burial, the surviving head of the family cut twenty-eight small sticks representing the duration of the lunar month, and each morning one stick was taken from the bundle and broken. When only seven sticks remained, he sent invitations to kinsmen and friends to come for the cry on the day the last stick was broken. Each family brought its own provisions of corn meal, flour, beef, and vegetables and camped near the burying ground. The cry began with the recital by a close relative of the good qualities of the deceased, and as he proceeded the mourners, gathered around the grave with heads covered, started to cry. This ceremony sometimes lasted several days. In bad weather, it was held in the church, lighted at night by candles.

Right from Boswell on a dirt road is the SITE OF MAYHEW COURTHOUSE, 4 *m.*, where the Choctaws held tribal court, generally four sessions each year. The courthouse was a one-room building in which offenders received whipping or death sentences. All that remains is an old picket fence and a four-room house of logs and slabs.

BENNINGTON, 102.3 *m.* (615 alt., 361 pop.), is another old Choctaw settlement. On the original road from Doaksville to the west, the town grew up around a church organized in 1848 by the Presbyterian Mission Board. Still standing on the spot known locally as Old Bennington, the church (now remodeled) has a well-cared-for cemetery near by.

Best remembered of the old church's ministers was Rev. W. J. B. Lloyd, who preached there after the Civil War. It was Mrs. Lloyd who told the following story to illustrate early banking practices. One day in the seventies she rode on a visit to the home of Wilson N. Jones, later chief of the Choctaws. As she prepared to return, Jones came out and tied a small, heavy bag to her saddle. His instructions were simple. "This is $10,000 in gold. Take it home and keep it until I come for it. I'm afraid of being robbed here, but no one would think of robbing a preacher!" Mrs. Lloyd is said to have kept the gold for five years, hidden in the foot of a feather bed, until Jones finally claimed it.

BOKCHITO, 109.3 *m.* (650 alt., 643 pop.), is a farming center.

Right from Bokchito on a graveled road are the ruins of ARMSTRONG ACADEMY, 2.3 *m.* In 1844, two years after the Choctaw Nation had provided for a school system, the academy was built to serve the western portion of the Pushmataha District. It was placed under the supervision of R. D. Potts, a Baptist missionary, and named for the popular Choctaw agent, William Armstrong.

Instruction for adults was undertaken on weekends, and toward sunset on Friday evenings wagons bearing families began arriving at the campground in the clearing around the school. From Saturday morning to Sunday evening, classes for men and women were held in which reading, writing, and arithmetic were taught, along with religious instruction.

The academy site, renamed Chata Tamaha (Choctaw Town), served as capital of the Choctaws from 1863 to 1883, when the tribal lawmakers removed it to

Tuskahoma (*see Tour* 7). Closed during the Civil War, Armstrong Academy was reopened in 1882 by the Presbyterians, under contract with the Choctaw Nation, and continued as a school for orphan boys until it was burned in 1921.

DURANT, 123.1 *m.* (643 alt., 10,541 pop.), is the seat of Bryan County and the principal agricultural center of Oklahoma's Red River valley. It was first settled in 1870 by the Choctaw family of that name and built on the Dixon Durant ranch. The name Durant Junction, given the community by the Missouri-Kansas-Texas Railroad when it entered the Choctaw Nation in 1872, was shortened to Durant ten years later.

Bryan County's rich black soil continues to make the town dependent primarily on its surrounding farm lands. The once lordly cotton boll, however, has been pushed into second place in recent years by the lowly peanut, a consistent million-dollar cash crop for the area. Some 20,000 acres of peanuts are harvested each year and three peanut processing plants operate in Durant. Also reflecting the area's agricultural production are a cottonseed mill, meat packing plant, and a feed milling industry. Manufacturing has become more important, too, in recent years. A plant making bodies for school buses gives the town its top industrial payroll.

Durant has other important, if less tangible, assets. OKLAHOMA PRESBYTERIAN COLLEGE (a preparatory school specializing in Christian education for girls) occupies a twenty-two acre campus at the western edge of the city. And SOUTHEASTERN STATE COLLEGE, one of Oklahoma's six state-supported teachers colleges, has a fifty-eight-acre "campus of a thousand magnolias" adjoining the city on the north. Opened in June of 1909, the college has expanded greatly since World War II. The latest addition to its physical plant is a $600,000 Health and Physical Education Building, completed in early 1957. An Amphitheater seating three thousand persons is constructed on a beautiful natural site just north of the Education Building. In 1956 the school had a faculty of seventy-one, with an enrollment of 1,600. Significantly, considering its historical setting, Southeastern State College is also a center of study of Choctaw and Chickasaw Indian tribal history and culture.

Although it is a modern college town, Durant still retains from its past some of the grace and charm of the Old South. Magnolias add beauty to many lawns and gardens, and along the quiet tree-lined residential streets can still be found handsome galleried homes, their high ceilings and big windows reflecting the influence of the old plantation style of architecture.

In the construction of sprawling Lake Texoma to the west and south (*see Tour 8*), Durant, as the largest Oklahoma town close to the site of Denison Dam, served as supply base for the builders. Since then it has been a convenient access point for many of the millions who visit Texoma's numerous resort areas each year (*see below*).

Just west of Durant, US 70 crosses the boundary line between the former Choctaw and Chickasaw nations, and the motorist passes quickly from the mid-nineteenth into the mid-twentieth century. An increase in the number of resorts indicates the approach to Oklahoma's biggest playground, the octopus-like, 95,400-acre LAKE TEXOMA. Formed in 1945 by DENISON DAM (*see Tour 8*), it ranks ninth among the nation's man-made lakes in surface area (a maximum of 144,100 acres) and sixth in capacity (5,719,000 acre-feet). Oklahoma's largest and most popular resort, Texoma has also outdrawn the nation's other federal lakes, as well as parks and monuments, with a 1954 visitor count of 5,108,000 and a record 6,598,000 visitors in 1955.

Crossing a high earthen fill—with oil derricks sticking up out of the water to the right—US 70 touches the east end of ROOSEVELT MEMORIAL BRIDGE, 138.0 *m.* (The Lake Texoma Information Center here is maintained by the Oklahoma Game and Fish Department.) The 4,920-foot concrete span, Oklahoma's second longest, is flanked on either side by raised sidewalks for the convenience and safety of anglers who often line its entire length. Recently installed lights have now made night fishing possible.

At the west end of the Roosevelt Memorial Bridge is the junction with a paved road, 138.8 *m.*

Left on this road to LAKE TEXOMA STATE PARK (*lodge, cabins, campgrounds, picnic areas, boating, fishing, hiking, swimming*), 0.5 *m.*, a 2,600-acre playground on Catfish Bay. A two-million-dollar expansion program, completed in 1956, has added an ultramodern 106-room lodge, fifty cabins, and a 20-room fishing lodge, along with complete dining, swimming, and other recreational facilities. There is a unique fish-a-ring floating dock for anglers. The lake also has an excursion boat.

KINGSTON, 144.0 *m.* (791 alt., 677 pop.), is another of the many small towns in the area that depend largely on Lake Texoma for economic stability. In addition to these towns, more than two dozen recognized resort areas dot the coves and inlets around the sprawling reservoir. These are served by US 69 (*see Tour 8*) and US 75 (*see Tour 9*) on the east, by State 99 (*see Tour 14*) on the north, and US 77 (*see Tour 10*) on the west, as well as by US 70 and feeder routes (from east to west) like State 75A, 70A, 70B, 32, and 199.

A historical marker in Kingston notes the site of CAMP LEAVENWORTH, about two miles to the south. It was named for General Henry Leavenworth, who died near here an July 31, 1834, while en route from Fort Gibson to Wichita Village in western Oklahoma for a peace conference with the Plains Indians. The expedition continued under the direction of Colonel Henry Dodge. In the party were Lieutenant Jefferson Davis and George Catlin, the artist famed for his portrayal of Indian life.

MADILL, 151.5 *m.* (775 alt., 2,791 pop.), the seat of Marshall County, has changed greatly since the development of Lake Texoma (*see above*). The first bank was known locally as the Cottonwood National, because it was built of boards sawed out of near-by cottonwood trees. For a long period the town was dependent primarily on its surrounding farm and ranch lands. Flooding of thousands of its most fertile agricultural acres, however, made it topographically the "Heart of Texomaland," and it promptly set out to become a recreational center for the vast new playground as well. Small industries and an increased oil play in the area have also contributed to its prosperity.

Madill is at the junction with State 99 (*see Tour 14*).

At 173.0 *m.* is the junction with an improved road.

Right on this road to the three-thousand-acre OAK HILL FARM (*visitors admitted*), 2.5 *m.*, one of the largest establishments in the world for the breeding of show ring horses, especially three-gaited and five-gaited saddle horses. About fifty colts a year are foaled here and given show ring training. In addition, entries in the harness classes are sent to the annual shows throughout the Southwest and at Kansas City, St. Louis, and Louisville.

At 173.5 *m.* is the nationally recognized SAMUEL ROBERTS NOBLE FOUNDATION, set up in 1945 by the late oilman Lloyd Noble (*see Ardmore*), who died in 1949. The foundation engages in extensive research into cancer and degenerative diseases, and operates three experimental farms in Marshall and Carter counties for agricultural research.

ARDMORE, 177.6 *m.* (872 alt., 17,890 pop.) (*see Ardmore*), is at the junction with US 77 (*see Tour 10*).

US 70 west of Ardmore skirts a half-dozen productive oil fields to RINGLING, 202.7 *m.* (846 alt., 1,092 pop.), named for one of the brothers who operated the old Ringling Brothers–Barnum and Bailey circus. The story is that in the early 1900's a young lawyer named Jake L. Hamon boarded the circus train that lay on a siding at Ardmore and presented his card to John Ringling. "I'm afraid we can't do anything for you," Ringling began. "Our legal business is already taken care of." Hamon answered, "I don't want your legal business. I want three dollars. Several years ago I worked as a roustabout for this circus, and when I was paid off you beat me out of that amount."

Ringling liked the young man's nerve and invited him to stay for dinner. They became friends, and in 1914, when oil was found on leases Hamon held west of Ardmore, he induced Ringling to enter the field and build twenty miles of railroad to their holdings. The road was extended, and at its western terminus is the town named for the circus man. Expanded development of the rich Healdton oil field northeast of Ringling has caused considerable growth in the town during the past decade.

Until 1916, Cornish was a small town one mile to the south. In that year most of its residents moved to Ringling, leaving only an orphans' home on the old site. Established in 1903 by Moses E. Harris as a private philanthropy, the home gave approximately two thousand orphans a start in life before it was closed in 1956 by its eighty-five-year-old founder.

At 225.2 *m.* is the Y junction with US 81 (*see Tour 11*).

WAURIKA, 226.6 *m.* (873 alt., 2,327 pop.), is a town which in layout resembles a stadium. Its residential sections spread out to overlook an arena of business buildings. Like many other Oklahoma towns, Waurika has had more than one name in its brief history. When first laid out in 1892, the railroad station was called Monika. It became the seat of Jefferson County in 1908 after a year's fight with near-by Ryan (*see Tour 11*). Besides farm trade, Waurika is also dependent on the Rock Island shops at the town's southern edge.

During the days of the Chisholm Trail cattle drives the site of Waurika was a favorite camping spot. West of Waurika are hill pastures covered with nutritious buffalo grass. In the days of the trail drives, cattle were allowed to linger here in order to put on fat more quickly. "Monument Hill," to the northeast (*see Tour 11*), dates from this period.

This range and farm country was part of the Kiowa-Comanche reservation, which was opened to white settlement by land lottery in 1901. Where stolen Comanche ponies once ranged, registered cattle now graze. And stretches of alkali-whitened land alternate with rolling pastures, wheat and cotton fields, and the thin timber borders of small creeks. Where the route comes close to the Red River bottoms there are patches of heavier timber and mesquite and tamarisk.

RANDLETT, 252.9 *m.* (1,238 alt., 396 pop.), is a small farming community (R) lying in the southern part of Cotton County. The county was established by a proclamation by Governor Cruce on September 14, 1912, following an overwhelmingly favorable vote of the people in the southern townships of Comanche County, who had made two previous but unsuccessful efforts to secede.

Westward through GRANDFIELD, 267.5 *m.* (1,113 alt., 1,232 pop.), US 70 roughly parallels the Red River. Bottom-land pastures alternate with wheat and cotton fields.

At 289.6 *m.* is the junction with US 183 (*see Tour 12*), 0.5 miles north of DAVIDSON (1,160 alt., 490 pop.) (*see Tour 12*). US 70 crosses Red River and the TEXAS LINE, 293.0 *m.*, twenty miles northeast of Vernon, Texas (*see Texas Guide*).

TOUR 7

(Fort Smith, Ark.)—Poteau—Talihina—Antlers—Hugo—(Paris, Tex.); US 271, Arkansas Line to Texas Line, 161.8 m.

Roadbed paved throughout except two short stretches of gravel scheduled for hard surfacing in 1957.
Kansas City Southern Ry. parallels route between Spiro and Poteau; the Frisco Ry. between Poteau and Paris, Tex.
Accommodations limited to the larger towns.

> "*Ch at ta Okla i Minko sia hash himaka okla kana hokeya, pi yakni illappa ietanowvt nine chito micha boke oka achukma, yakomi ka okla pisat itanowa chi ka ashila illappa pit achile hoke.*"
>
> Translation: "As chief of the Choctaw people, I do hereby extend a welcome and an invitation to all who wish to visit the Indian country and view the mountains and the many beautiful fishing streams."
>
> —W. A. Durant, Principal Chief of the Choctaws in 1941.

US 271 winds through the rugged hills and narrow valleys that were once the home of the Choctaws. Driven from the East, they labored to re-create the traditional strength of their nation in this area of verdant beauty. Log and brick buildings and forgotten piles of stone, now standing amid the upland forests of pine and oak, testify to tribal decisions that school children of today recite as history.

For a few miles along the most eastern portion of US 271 in Oklahoma the Chickasaws, too, once beat out their Trail of Tears. And not long afterwards there passed over it the turbulent remnant of the fierce Seminoles, who had fought so desperately in Florida to protect their homes against white aggression.

The old Fort Towson Road, along which flowed processions of troops and supplies from Fort Smith to Fort Towson, nearly parallels US 271. Deep ruts made by the heavy wagon wheels are still visible in places. Piles of stone, from chimneys long in disuse, indicate the buildings that once were havens of rest and refuge for hardy early-day stagecoach passengers. Across this region from the southeastern corner of the state, up the divide between the Little and Kiamichi rivers, across the latter stream near Tuskahoma, and on to the northwest went Bernard de la Harpe, exploring for the glory of France in 1718.

Yet another important early-day road through this region was the one followed by the Butterfield Overland Mail from Fort Smith to Colbert's Ferry on the Red River (*see Tour 8*). It was on September 19, 1858, that this first transcontinental mail coach (carrying one passenger) forded the Poteau River near the north end of US 271.

The highway skirts new and popular Lake Wister, crosses cool mountain streams that offer excellent fishing, loops its way through beautiful Ouachita National Forest. Up and over the Winding Stair and Kiamichi mountains and through the regular rows of the Potato Hills, US 271 twists and dips, Oklahoma's one sustained mountain wilderness road.

US 271 crosses the OKLAHOMA LINE, 0 *m.*, seven miles south of Fort Smith, Arkansas (*see Arkansas Guide*). Cutting through excellent farmlands, the highway crosses POTEAU RIVER at 3.9 *m.* This river —the only one in Oklahoma to flow from south to north—joins the Arkansas a few miles to the right.

OAK LODGE CHURCH (R) marks the almost completely deserted village of SCULLYVILLE, 8.2 *m.* It was established in 1832, when the Choctaws were being removed from their eastern homes. The site was chosen by the Indian agent as a center where annuities due the Choctaws were to be paid—hence the name, derived from the Choctaw word *iskuli*, meaning money. Traces of the old AGENCY BUILDING, erected from hand-hewn logs on a four-foot stone foundation, can still be found. Appropriately and succinctly, the Choctaws called it the "pay house."

It was here that Moshulatubbee, important political figure of the Choctaw Nation, lived while serving as chief of the northern district, of which Scullyville was the capital.

Although little remains but the church of Scullyville, a century ago it was an educational, social, and political center for the Choctaw Nation. The artist George Catlin visited there in 1834 and painted his virile canvas, "Tullock-chisk-ko," using as a model the most distinguished ballplayer in the nation. This picture is now in the Smithsonian Institution at Washington, D.C. Catlin told of watching a ball game (the subject of another of his famous paintings) on a site southwest of the town, with some three thousand cheering and betting Indians in the crowd. The games were usually played between teams of the different districts, with much rivalry and sometimes even a riot. The game is still played by Choctaw boys in various Indian schools.

In 1844, New Hope, the most noted of the schools established for Choctaw girls, was located here. The institution was closed during the Civil War, reopened in 1870, and stayed in operation until it was burned in 1897. The custom of the Choctaws at the time was to send some of this school's graduates to an eastern college at the expense of the nation. Only fragments of the foundation of this important seminary remain.

When the famous Butterfield Overland Mail route was established between St. Louis and San Francisco in 1858, Scullyville was made one of the stations on the line. The nearness of the town to the Arkansas River (some five miles to the northwest) also made it a busy trading post for river traffic, and the Scullyville boat landing served both this settlement and Fort Coffee. In 1863, Union forces captured Scullyville and held it until the end of the Civil War, leaving devastated fields and ruined homes behind them and contributing to the early decline of this once important town.

At 9.4 *m.* is the junction with a graveled road. Official historical markers (R) summarize much of the area's rich history.

Right here to the SPIRO INDIAN MOUNDS, 1 *m.*, the best-known archaeological site in Oklahoma (*200 yds. L*). Excavated under the direction of the University of Oklahoma's department of anthropology in 1936–38, the mounds yielded up spectacular archaeological discoveries which reflect the state of development, the crafts, and the culture of people who lived in this region in prehistoric times. Articles taken from the mounds include ornaments with intricate carvings, vases in the shapes of owls and frogs, ceremonial maces, arrowheads, bone fragments, and pieces of woven cloth. Exhibits from the Spiro Mounds may be viewed at the museum of the University of Oklahoma (*see Norman*), the Oklahoma Historical Society Museum (*see Oklahoma City*), and the Philbrook Museum (*see Tulsa*).

At 5 *m.* on the main side route is the junction with a second graveled road. R. here to a farmhouse, 0.5 *m.*, which has been built (L) on the SITE OF THE QUADRANGLE OF FORT COFFEE. The post was established June 16, 1834, and named in honor of General Coffee of Tennessee, close friend of President Andrew Jackson, who aided in the removal of the Choctaws from the East. Fort Coffee was a busy and important military post during the removal years. Built on a high bluff overlooking the Arkansas River, with a watchtower perched atop a rocky promontory on the south bank, its one-story buildings were grouped to form a hollow square in the manner of pioneer fortifications. The barracks were constructed of rough slabs, with battened doors and window shutters, a natural-stone fireplace and chimney at each end. The Scullyville boat landing was also located at this strategic river point.

Fort Coffee was abandoned in 1838 and in 1842 the Choctaw Council established the Fort Coffee Academy for boys. The school closed after the outbreak of the Civil War, when Confederate and Union troops occupied the old fort successively, and the principal buildings were finally burned. Today little remains of them except the large blocks of sandstone which formed the foundations. Even the old Choctaw cemetery has virtually disappeared, although it is the final resting place of many of the early leaders of the nation, including members of the McCurtain, Folsom, and Ward families. Some lie in unmarked graves, others in graves with half-fallen stones that date back to 1830. Here, too, lies Major F. C. Armstrong, the first Choctaw agent at near-by Scullyville (*see above*) in 1832. In North Building, the first agency structure, the Choctaw Nation in 1857 adopted its new constitution.

SPIRO, 11.0 *m.* (494 alt., 1,365 pop.), was founded about 1895 when the Kansas City Southern Railway was built through this region. At that time, the majority of Scullyville's few remaining inhabitants left their war-devastated town and moved to this new one. Spiro's business district (L) is an authentic museum piece of turn-of-the-century commercial architecture. The town remains primarily an agricultural center, with a local cannery taking care of the green beans, peas, and other vegetables raised on the near-by truck farms.

At 14.4 *m.* is the northern junction with US 59 (*see Tour 15*), which unites with US 271 for the next 16.9 miles.

PANAMA, 19.3 *m.* (490 alt., 1,027 pop.), like Spiro, was established about 1895 as a by-product of the Kansas City Southern Railway. Construction of the Panama Canal at that time suggested the town's name. With the decline of coal mining in the area, farming and stock raising have become increasingly important.

SHADY POINT, 21.6 *m.*, is an outgrowth of an early Choctaw settlement about one mile to the west. Farther west, in the days of the stage coach route on the military trail to Fort Towson, was a stop called Brazil Station.

POTEAU, 28.4 *m.* (483 alt., 4,776 pop.), seat of LeFlore County, was founded in 1898 and named for the near-by Poteau River. The town is located in a picturesque valley between Cavanal Mountain (2,369 feet above sea level, with a road leading to a park on its crest) and Sugar Loaf Mountain (its 2,600-foot elevation making it one of the highest in the Ouachita region). As a result of this mountainous terrain, Poteau's narrow streets wind and dip, paying little attention to compass directions.

With the decline of coal mining, Poteau has depended more and more on lumbering, truck farming, and small industries. However, with more than a dozen large lakes and streams within a few miles of the city—all of them well stocked with game fish—as well as heavily forested areas to the south and west, Poteau has also become increasingly popular as a year-round sports center. Within the city itself are ample facilities for swimming, golf, tennis, and picnicking.

At 31.3 *m.* is the southern junction with US 59 (*see Tour 15*).

WISTER, 36.9 *m.* (510 alt., 729 pop.), was first known as Wister Junction because two railroads, the Rock Island and the Frisco, crossed at this point. In Wister is the junction with US 270 (*see Tour 5*), gateway to LAKE WISTER (L) and LAKE WISTER STATE PARK (*see Tour 5*). US 270 and US 271 are united west from Wister for the next 6.4 miles.

CASTON, 43.3 *m.*, is at the junction of the two highways. US 271 turns left here, crossing a flat, denuded area that marks the upper reaches of the Lake Wister flood basin (actually the bed of the Fourche Maline River), then climbs immediately into the pines of the Ouachita National Forest, 50.8 *m.*

The next twenty miles are among the most scenic on all of Oklahoma's highways. The dark-green pines contrast sharply with the lighter-hued oaks against a background of red-tinged soil. Looping and twisting to gain altitude, the road offers an ever broadening panorama of valleys and mountain ridges stretching ahead.

At 57.4 *m.* is the junction with a forest service road.

Left here, on the HOLSON VALLEY ROAD, it is approximately seventeen miles along the mountain foothills to the junction with US 59 and US 270 (*see Tour 5*). This is only an improved National Forest Service road, but it is one of the most picturesque drives in the state, particularly in the spring when wild plum and serviceberry bushes mingle their white blossoms with the brilliant fuchsia tones of the redbuds.

WINDING STAIR SUMMIT, 61.1 *m.*, with its 1,287-foot elevation, offers a superb panorama of forested mountains and valleys. SKYLINE DRIVE, another graveled forest service road, runs along the top of the ridge to the left. Like the Holson Valley Road (*see above*), it connects US 271 with US 59 and US 270, offers the motorist a sweeping view of southeastern Oklahoma's mountains, forests, and fish-filled streams. The road serves Sycamore Tower (2,428 feet), just east of US 271, and Winding Stair Tower. Visitors are welcome to both of these fire lookouts. (Information on all roads, fire towers, and recreation facilities in the Ouachita National Forest can be obtained from the division office of the Kiamichi Ranger District in Talihina.)

TALIHINA, 69.4 *m.* (688 alt., 1,965 pop.), was a small, unnamed missionary settlement in this valley of the Winding Stair Mountains when, in 1888, the Frisco Railway built across the mountains from Fort Smith, Arkansas, to Paris, Texas. The name Talihina dates back to this event; in the Choctaw language it means "Iron Road."

As the road crews laid down the shining steel rails, the Indians looked on in superstitious wonder. In the diary of one of the missionaries are recorded the words of a chief who had once been on a train: "I have ridden on the railroads east of the Mississippi. They have little houses on wheels which can be shut up and locked. If we allow these railroads to come, the white men will invite all the full bloods to a picnic and get the men to go off and play ball. Then they will get our women to go into the little houses on wheels and lock them up and run off with them into Texas or Missouri. Then what will we do without our women?"

Despite the objections of the Indians, the railroad was completed and the present Talihina developed. However, it remained almost inaccessible except by rail until 1919, when a road was cut through the near-by forest by convict labor. Since then more highways have been built, but the town remains essentially mountain-locked. It is a popular rendezvous for sportsmen. Near-by streams are well stocked with game fish, and the surrounding oak, pine, and hickory forests offer excellent deer hunting. Much of the business activity at Talihina is dependent on lumbering.

Right from Talihina on paved State 63 to a junction with paved State 63A, 1.7 *m.* Right (*following signs*) to the state's EASTERN OKLAHOMA TUBERCULOSIS SANATORIUM, 1.5 *m.*, opened in 1921. Set down among the oaks and pines on the side of a mountain that protects it from north winds, the sanatorium has the appearance of a summer resort. Its modern brick buildings provide facilities for 360 patients. The last addition was built in 1952 and houses a surgical unit and 150 beds for women.

Straight ahead (*following signs*) to the INDIAN HOSPITAL, operated by the United States Public Health Service. The hospital was first established here in 1916, under federal supervision, with $50,000 furnished by the Choctaw and Chickasaw Indian tribes. Originally only tubercular patients were admitted, but in 1936 Congress appropriated money to enlarge the hospital so that general medical service might be offered. The present $1,000,000 plant includes a huge, rambling main building of native stone, resembling a Mediterranean castle, and a unique motel-like grouping of staff quarters around a patio. The grounds are beautifully landscaped, as are those at the sanatorium.

Southwestward from Talihina, US 271 skirts the southern slopes of the heavily wooded Potato Hills.

At 74.3 *m.* is the junction with a graveled road.

Left on this Indian Service Road thirty-three miles to junction with State 21 at Bethel (*see Tour 15*). Crossing tree-lined Kiamichi River and cutting straight across the Kiamichi Mountains, this forest trail is equal in scenic beauty to any in Oklahoma.

ALBION, 77.0 *m.* (678 alt., 178 pop.), is a lumbering town.

KIAMICHI (Ki′-a mish′-e), 81.0 *m.*, was named from the Kiamichi River, which roughly parallels the highway through this section. In a report made in 1805 by Dr. John Sibley, United States explorer, he speaks of a tributary to the Red River "which is called by the Indians *Kiomitchie*." The waters provide excellent fishing.

At 85.2 *m.* is the site of SPRINGS STATION, a stop on the old Fort Towson Military Road from Fort Smith, Arkansas. It was named for John Springs, an influential Choctaw, whose home was there. In a near-by field is the unmarked grave of William Bryant, principal chief of the Choctaws from 1870 to 1874.

At 87.3 *m.* is the town of TUSKAHOMA (L), which came into existence with the arrival of the railroad. Long before, however, it was the political capital of the Choctaws. Near here, in 1834, the first constitutional law was written in what is now Oklahoma.

By the Treaty of Dancing Rabbit Creek, made in Mississippi in 1830, the Choctaws were promised many things in return for their land. One provision was for funds with which to erect a new council house in the approximate center of the land they were to occupy. The site selected was on a mound about one and one-half miles northwest of the present Tuskahoma. The new capital was called Nunih Wayah, a name that had been brought from the East, where a similarly named sacred mound figured in ancient Choctaw legends. The SITE OF NUNIH WAYAH (*ask direction locally*) is marked today by a pile of rocks that was once the chimney of the old log capitol.

Approximately two miles northwest of Nunih Wayah is the SITE OF THE TUSKAHOMA FEMALE ACADEMY, established in 1891 to serve as a companion school for the Jones Academy, Choctaw boys' institution at Hartshorne (*see Tour 5*). The main building burned in 1927.

Nunih Wayah was not, however, the permanent capital. Because of factional disputes, the seat of government was located at various places until 1883, when the council appropriated funds to erect the present CHOCTAW COUNCIL HOUSE (R), one-half mile north of US 271. Built of wood from the surrounding forests and of red bricks from native clay, this solid rectangular building of two stories and a mansard garret third story remained the capitol of the nation until tribal government was ended in 1906. In 1934, the Choctaws drafted plans to restore the building and provide a landscaped courtyard. In June, 1938—one hundred years after the first council meeting at Nunih Wayah—the Council House, last of the Choctaw capitols, was rededicated as a historical and educational institution.

North of the Council House is an old BURYING GROUND, where many well-known Choctaws rest. In this spot are the graves of Jackson McCurtain, who was chief of the nation when the council building was erected; of his wife Jane, most prominent and capable of the few Choctaw women who took an active part in politics; and of Peter Hudson, brilliant educator and writer, who used his talents to keep alive Choctaw history and tradition. Near the Council House stands the

McCurtain Home, built at about the same time as the capitol, where many prominent tribesmen were entertained while the council was in session.

At 90.3 *m.* is the junction with State 2. US 271 turns left here to CLAYTON, 93.6 *m.* (602 alt., 612 pop.), a small town that serves as headquarters for an increasing number of sportsmen. This is the heart of the state's eight-county southeastern corner, an area sometimes referred to as "Oklahoma's last wildlife frontier." Its rugged mountains and timbered valleys harbor most of the state's deer herds. Wild turkey have been re-established. The region also offers quail, squirrel, fox, raccoon, and bobcat. Its countless springs feed about half of Oklahoma's best fishing streams.

CLAYTON LAKE RECREATION AREA, 98.0 *m.* (R), is set in a picturesque pocket of the hills. It includes 410 acres surrounding 75-acre Lake Clayton. Most of the facilities provided by the state are on a timbered promontory jutting into the lake from the east side. There are tables, grills, and picnic shelter. On the north side of this promontory is a swimming beach (bathhouses) and on the south side is a boat dock (rental boats).

US 271 continues to wind through the sparsely settled rough slopes of the Kiamichi Mountains, in a general way following Cedar Creek, another of the region's fine fishing streams.

FINLEY, 120.4 *m.*, lies in a fertile valley just south of the Kiamichis. Stock-raising and lumbering are the principal industries of the area.

ANTLERS, 130.8 *m.* (511 alt., 2,506 pop.), was so named because of the Indian custom of fastening a set of antlers to a tree to mark the site of a spring. A large spring near the town had been marked in this way. The chief industry of this district is lumbering, although dairying and truck farming are also important. Antlers, too, has benefited from the general increase in vacationing in this corner of the state. Guide and boat services are readily available at various points throughout the area.

During the winter of 1892–93, Antlers was the scene of a political insurrection still known locally as the "Locke War." Congress had voted to pay $2,943,050 in settlement of a land claim to the Choctaw Nation, and bitter strife developed between the citizens as to the handling of this money. The question became the main issue in the election of 1892, when the voters were to cast their ballots for principal chief. The two main political parties—Nationalist and Progressive—had as their respective candidates Jacob B. Jackson, an influential full blood who had received a college education and had held numerous tribal offices, and Wilson N. Jones, a wealthy rancher then serving as chief. The vote was very close, but the party in power, after canvassing the returns, decided in favor of Jones. The Nationalists then formed armed bands, intending to march against the capitol and seize the government. Most of these were dispersed, with little bloodshed, by the tribal militia. Some 150 of the insurrectionists, however, barricaded themselves at Antlers under the leadership of Victor M. Locke, an intermarried white man, and prepared to defy the administration. Chief Jones's militia attacked their stronghold, but few casualties resulted since neither side was willing to engage in a pitched battle. For the first time in the history of the Choctaw people, federal troops were called in to restore order, and a United States commissioner finally persuaded the leaders of the two factions to make peace. Jones served out his term without further incident, but the log stockade in which the Nationalists had barricaded themselves at Antlers remained standing for many years as a grim reminder of the most serious political disturbance in the history of the Choctaw Republic.

At 144.1 *m.* is the western junction with US 70 (*see Tour 6*), which unites eastward with US 271 for the next 6.9 miles. In HUGO, 151.0 *m.* (549 alt., 5,984 pop.) (*see Tour 6*), US 271 turns right, leaving US 70.

At 153.1 *m.* is the junction with paved State 2A.

Right on this road is the GOODLAND SCHOOL, 2.3 *m.*, said to be the nation's oldest Protestant Indian orphanage. Rev. Cyrus Kingsley arrived in the area in 1835, followed by Rev. and Mrs. John Lathrop in 1848. That same year the Indian Presbytery was petitioned by the Choctaws in the vicinity to send a teacher. Rev. O. P. Stark and his wife settled at Goodland in 1850 and established a mission and school in their log cabin. A church was soon built, and the school was conducted in this building for many years. Until 1890, the institution depended largely on the support of the community.

Today the $2,000,000 plant, owned and operated by the Presbyterian church, includes twelve modern buildings on 763 acres of land. Nearly a third of these acres are farmed by the more than two hundred students, who represent fourteen different Indian tribes. (For many years only Choctaw and Chickasaw children were accepted.) Courses are offered from the first grade through high school.

GRANT, 156.1 *m.* (573 alt., 351 pop.), established at the time the Frisco Railway was built through this region, serves the surrounding agricultural lands of the Red River bottom. Southwest of Grant is 350-acre LAKE ROEBUCK, Oklahoma's largest natural lake. It is well stocked with bass, channel cat, and other game fish.

ORD, 161.5 *m.* (422 alt., 206 pop.), was named for a town in Nebraska.

At 161.8 *m.*, US 271 crosses the Red River at the Texas Line, fifteen miles north of Paris, Texas (*see Texas Guide*).

TOUR 8

(Columbus, Kan.)—Vinita—Muskogee—McAlester—Atoka—Durant —(Denison, Tex.); US 69, Kansas Line to Texas Line, 260.9 m.

Roadbed intermittently paved with concrete and asphalt.
The Missouri-Kansas-Texas R. R. parallels the route southward from Vinita.
Good accommodations at short intervals; hotels chiefly in cities; numerous motels.

Probably as significant historically as any route through Oklahoma, US 69 follows almost exactly the old Texas Road, over which fur traders, trappers, freighters, emigrants, and pioneer settlers traveled. From the Kansas Line to the Three Forks district near Muskogee, it follows the old Osage Trace, along which the Osage Indians frequently sent hunting parties into the wilderness region. Records have established the trail's use as far back as the opening years of the nineteenth century.

With the establishment of trading posts, missions, and the military outpost of Fort Gibson, the Trace developed into a road advancing rapidly toward Texas and other points to the southwest. The heavy traffic that followed left ruts that are still visible today. A count taken in March of 1845 showed that one thousand wagons crossed from what is now Oklahoma over the Red River into Texas in a period of six weeks.

Though they lacked twentieth-century knowledge and equipment, the Indians and early pioneers surveyed skillfully. When the inevitable railroad and highway were laid out they followed the rutted old road quite closely. Only recently has a realignment of US 69 north of Muskogee cut off the actual Three Forks section of the Texas Road (*see Tour 3*).

Many Indians still live along the route, for it traverses areas which belonged at various times to the Osages, the Cherokees, the Creeks, the Choctaws, the Chickasaws, and the Caddoes. No longer applicable, of course, is Washington Irving's description of the Osages as ". . . stately fellows, stern and simple in garb and aspect" and the Creeks as "gaily dressed." But much of their former colorful array may still be seen in museums and collections along the way. For the cultural heritage of the Indian—despite such modernities as multi-purpose dams and multi-million-dollar industrial installations—colors and enriches US 69 from Kansas to Texas.

Section a. KANSAS LINE *to* MUSKOGEE, *106.4 m.* US 69

US 69 crosses the KANSAS LINE, 0 *m.*, at a point 13.1 miles south of Columbus, Kansas (*see Kansas Guide*).

Here the route passes through the lead and zinc mines of the Tri-State area (*see Tour 1*). Since 1948, operations have been somewhat curtailed, but the mines are still adding to the many huge piles of chat that are reminders of the boom days of World War I and II. In some places board or stone barricades are necessary to protect the highway from these encroaching man-made hills.

PICHER, 1.6 *m.* (820 alt., 3,951 pop.), is perhaps Oklahoma's most unstable town, in a strictly literal sense. Mine shafts and cavernous chambers honeycomb the earth beneath the town. And since early 1950, two huge underground pillars supporting the intersection of Second and Main Streets have shown signs of collapsing. As a result, a four-block area (R) has been abandoned and, for additional safety, enclosed by a seven-foot-high steel fence.

There are other signs of impermanence in the town. Buildings have been located in a hit-and-miss fashion in the spaces about the great shaft openings and the sprawling chat piles. For the most part, the miners' homes themselves reflect the general instability, for virtually the entire townsite is leased to the mining companies, making all buildings subject to removal when mine operations require it.

Mining in the Tri-State area (the world's largest producer of zinc) is of the shaft type. But the mines are not the narrow-tunneled winding shafts usually thought of in connection with mining. Instead they are high-ceilinged, long, and wide. Tunnels vary from two to four hundred feet in depth and are crisscrossed with roads. One underground "highway" carrying men and material in diesel trucks is a hundred miles long. Ceilings and walls are capped with monolithic limestone and—except in isolated cases like that of Picher (*see above*)—need no artificial support. Many excavated areas underground are large enough for a football field. In recent years the Tri-State area has produced close to three million rock tons of the minerals annually.

CARDIN, 2.7 *m.* (813 alt., 750 pop.), formerly named Tar River, came into existence as a mining camp in the boom years of this area. It was incorporated in 1918 and named for W. C. Cardin, who laid out the townsite.

At 3.7 *m.* is the junction with an improved road.

Left here to the NANCY JANE MINE (*adm. $1.25 for adults, $0.65 for children six to twelve*), an abandoned Eagle-Picher shaft 320 feet under ground, through which tours are conducted. Temperature is sixty-five degrees the year round.

To the left at 4.2 *m.* is the EAGLE-PICHER CENTRAL MILL (*contact safety officer for tours*), one of the largest and most modern in the world. Built in 1932, it replaced more than 250 smaller and less efficient mills that had previously dotted the area. As much as 17,500 tons of ore have been milled here in a single day. The crude ore is hauled in on thirty miles of E–P railroad tracks. Then at the mill it is crushed and the lead and zinc "concentrate" separated from the accompanying rock. The waste chert and limestone thus extracted, crushed into chat, is widely used for railroad ballast, concrete materials, and macadam road building. The "concentrate" itself is shipped to smelters (*see Tour 3, Henryetta*) for refining.

COMMERCE, 5.2 *m.* (805 alt., 2,442 pop.) (*see Tour 1*), is at the junction with US 66 (*see Tour 1*), which unites southwestward with US 69 for the next 38.5 miles.

MIAMI, 10.0 *m.* (800 alt., 11,801 pop.) (*see Tour 1*).

At 12.0 *m.* is the junction (R) with US 50 (*see Tour 15*), which follows this route for the next 10.9 miles.

At 22.9 *m.* is the junction (L) with US 60 (*see Tour 4*), which unites with this route for the next 20.8 miles.

AFTON, 24.1 *m.* (790 alt., 1,252 pop.) (*see Tour 1*).

VINITA, 39.7 *m.* (702 alt., 5,518 pop.) (*see Tour 1*).

At 43.7 *m.* is the western junction with US 60 (*see Tour 4*) and US 66 (*see Tour 1*). US 69 turns sharply south (L).

At 48.4 *m.* is the junction with the WILL ROGERS TURNPIKE (*see Tour 1*). Big Cabin interchange is to the left.

BIG CABIN, 49.9 *m.* (720 alt., 210 pop.), was named for the cabin of the settler who first occupied the site.

Cabin Creek (L), which runs almost parallel here with US 69, was the scene of two important Civil War battles. Where the old Texas Road crossed the creek, approximately eight miles to the east, some fifteen hundred Confederates under Cherokee General Stand Watie attacked a southbound Union supply train of two hundred wagons on July 1 and 2 of 1863. The attack was beaten off and the train reached Fort Gibson (*see Tour 3*) safely with its supply of badly needed food.

General Watie was more successful, however, the following year. In a battle on the same spot, he and Confederate General R. M. Gano captured a Union supply train valued at $1,500,000. The 295 wagons, several ambulances, and 260 men en route from Fort Scott to Fort Gibson and Fort Smith, Arkansas, were attacked by the Confederates at two o'clock in the morning of September 19 by artillery pieces hidden in the timber. Only 130 wagons were taken away. The others, including ricks carrying some three thousand tons of hay, were destroyed by order of General Gano. In addition to clothing and food, the wagons contained a quantity of whisky on which the Confederate troops are said to have become quite drunk after the fighting was over. Watie stopped the drinking by ordering the remaining whisky poured into the near-by creek.

ADAIR, 57.7 *m.* (682 alt., 299 pop.), was named for the prominent Cherokee Indian family of that name.

In July of 1892 the Dalton gang of outlaws (*see Tour 11*) committed one of their most daring robberies at the Missouri-Kansas-Texas Railroad station in Adair. A shipment of $17,000 in currency was being carried by the express due to stop there. But the plans of the Daltons had become known and a posse of deputy marshals was also on the train. Despite the hot gunfire, the gang managed to escape with the money, which they are said to have buried in the Dalton caves near Sand Springs (*see Tour 2*).

Left from Adair on paved State 28 is PENSACOLA, 8.5 *m.* (681 alt., 48 pop.), built on the SITE OF HOPEFIELD MISSION, a branch of the old Union Mission near Chouteau. Hopefield was originally established for the Osage Indians farther south on the Grand River, but the Cherokee-Osage treaty of 1828 placed that site in Cherokee country. The mission was then moved here, where it remained a busy and helpful organization for several years.

East of Pensacola, at the great bend in the Grand River, is the GRAND RIVER DAM (*see Tour 1*). Highways, railroad right of ways, and even entire townsites were moved as the shore line of sprawling Grand Lake lengthened.

PRYOR, 67.1 *m.* (627 alt., 4,486 pop.), is a prosperous and growing symbol of Oklahoma's determined drive for greater industrialization. A purely agricultural community before the building of Grand River Dam, it has capitalized extensively on its abundance of power, water, and natural gas. Two large paper mills and a pair of chemical plants have located recently in the Pryor area. To the southeast is the sprawling PRYOR ORDINANCE WORKS, a tremendous World War II installation now held on a stand-by basis by the federal government. And beyond that a $23,000,000 nitroguanidine plant was begun in 1957, also by the government. Planned for the Grand River, eight miles southeast of Pryor, is the Markham Ferry Dam, which will generate additional electricity. As a result of these expansions, Pryor's population has nearly doubled since 1950.

The city was given its name in honor of Nathaniel Pryor, who served as a scout with the Lewis and Clark expedition and as a captain in the Battle of New Orleans. Honorably discharged from the army, Pryor obtained a license in 1819 to trade with the Osage Nation. Later, he built a trading post southeast of Pryor on the creek which was also named for him. Today, the town has an excellent school system, complete sport and recreational facilities, including an NCAA-approved swimming pool.

Left from Pryor on paved State 20 to SALINA, 10.3 *m.* (618 alt., 905 pop.), a modern town built on the SITE OF THE CHOUTEAU TRADING POST, established in the early nineteenth century by the same famous French family that figured in the founding of St. Louis, Missouri.

In the latter part of the eighteenth century the Chouteaus possessed a license to trade with the Osage Indians, then living in the present limits of Missouri. But in 1802 the Spanish governor canceled their privilege and granted it to Manuel Lisa, a Spaniard. The Chouteau brothers, however, decided to retain the trading business without official sanction. And so in the early part of the nineteenth century, Major Jean Pierre Chouteau set out to establish new posts and cement the family's relations with the Indians. The expedition brought him to this ideal location on a wide, navigable river—the Grand, known as the Neosho in Kansas—bounded by well-wooded hills on the east and level lands to the west. Near by were both clear-water and salt-water springs. He set up a trading post here during the first quarter of the century (exact date is a matter of controversy), but the establishment was not really active under the ownership of the Chouteaus before 1817. Chouteau, from his location in St. Louis, had in 1804 persuaded some three thousand Osage Indians with whom he had traded to move to the Grand River area. He even appointed a new chief for the emigrants—Cashesegra or Big Track—and became something of a benevolent but firm dictator of his self-made empire. Since the country was rich in furs, fowl, tallow, wild honey, and many other marketable products, he enriched the family coffers.

Succeeding his father, Jean Pierre, Auguste Pierre Chouteau moved the Grand River post in 1822 to Three Forks, at the confluence of the Grand, Verdigris, and Arkansas rivers. He built a pretentious home here, which Washington Irving visited in 1832 and described in his *Tour on the Prairies* as a large, two-story log structure filled with valuable furnishings and surrounded with trees, shrubberies, and flowers. Smaller houses dotted the river bank and the woods. Texas Road travelers found gracious hospitality at this frontier palace, where lived Auguste and his numerous children by his two wives (one a cousin, the other an Osage). He also had a large retinue of Indians and Negroes.

Auguste died in 1938 at La Saline while engaged on a government diplomatic mission with the Indians. He was heavily in debt, and his slaves, stock, and merchandise were mostly attached or stolen. John Ross (*see Tour 3*), chief of the Cherokee tribe, and his brother Lewis acquired many of the Chouteau holdings and built a brick mansion on the site now occupied by the Salina High School gymnasium. In one corner of the schoolyard still stands a BLOCKHOUSE, built by Ross, enclosing one of the springs used since the founding of the Chouteau Trading Post.

The settlement then became known as Grand Saline and served as an important point on one of the California trails. A marked depression near the bridge on the west bank of the Grand River is said to have been made by the wagons of the many emigrants who traveled to California in 1849 and later. Traffic became so heavy that a post office was established on June 11, 1849. In 1872, the Lewis Ross home and surrounding farm lands were purchased by the Cherokee Nation for the establishment of the Cherokee Orphans' Home, which operated there until the building was destroyed by fire in 1903 and the institution moved near Tahlequah (*see Tour 3*).

In recognition of the significance of the site, a Stone Marker has been erected on Salina's main street, commemorating the dates of the trading post, the Cherokee town, and the orphan asylum. The state legislature proclaimed October 10, the birth anniversary of Major Jean Pierre Chouteau, as "Oklahoma Historical Day," and in 1940 the first observance of the date was held at Salina. It is still the town's biggest annual event.

Some three miles south of Salina a small creek flows from the east into the Grand River at the foot of a range of rocky bluffs. High on the cliffs is the spot which Cherokee Indian legends say is the home of the "Little People" who have been a part of Cherokee traditional lore since ancient times. When the tribe lived in the East, they believed in the "Little People," who were supposed to be no more than knee high, but well formed, handsome, and exceedingly clever. They lived far back in the mountains and were never seen except at dusk or by solitary individuals.

Some Cherokees, at the time of the Removal, still believed in the legendary figures and moved their "Little People" to the new nation and to this site. Tribal members would stop fishing at a certain spot in the Grand River if stones happened to roll down the bluffs into the water—usually with the remark, "Let's move downstream, I see the 'Little People' live here and want the fish for their own use."

State 20 continues to SPAVINAW, 13.4 *m.* (668 alt., 213 pop.) (*see Tour 15*), and the Spavinaw Hills Park.

Whitaker State Orphans Home, 67.8 *m.*, on the south edge of Pryor, was first established in 1879 for the orphans of Indian Territory. In 1908, the state took over the institution, and in 1956 it represented an investment of $1,750,000, occupying six hundred and eighty acres and providing a home and school for more than three hundred children. Vocational training is emphasized (academic education is taken care of by the Pryor public school system), and the boys and girls may stay at the home until they are eighteen or have finished high school.

CHOUTEAU, 76.3 *m.* (627 alt., 858 pop.), was named for the Chouteau family. East and north of the town is the big $80,000,000 Oklahoma Ordinance Works (*see above*), built as a part of the World War II defense program.

At 81.3 *m.* is the junction with an improved dirt road.

Left on this road, across railroad tracks, 0.9 *m.*; R. here 3.5 *m.*; then L. to the Site of Union Mission, 5.2 *m.*, indicated by a stone marker at the top of a wooded hill near the road. All that remains of the twenty buildings formerly comprising the old mission are a few foundation stones placed around the spring (300 yards southeast of the marker) about which the buildings were originally grouped.

Epaphras Chapman, a Presbyterian missionary, located the site in 1819 and obtained permission from the American Board of Commissioners for Foreign Missions and the Osage Indian tribe to set up a mission here in the Osage territory. On November 5, 1820, Chapman and his caravan of nineteen men, women, and children (two had died along the way) reached the remote wilderness station after suffering much hardship and sickness on the long journey from New York. They cultivated about one hundred acres of the surrounding land, opening the Union Mission school in 1821 and operating it until 1832–33. In addition to the Osages, some twenty Creeks, who were destined to play an important part in tribal life, enrolled in 1830. From this start Presbyterianism spread among the Creeks. The Cherokee-Osage treaty of 1828, however, placed Union in Cherokee country and, since the mission had been established primarily for the Osages, the work was necessarily curtailed. This resulted in the founding of the Hopefield Mission near Adair (*see above*).

In 1835 the Presbyterian minister, Rev. Samuel Austin Worcester, came from Georgia, installing his printing press in Union's vacant buildings. The press had been retrieved once along the way when the boat carrying it sank in the Arkansas River. Worcester printed the first publication issued in what is now Oklahoma, said to be "The Child's Book" or "Ī stutsi in Naktsokv" (Creek or Muskhogean). It was written by John Fleming, of the American Board of Commissioners for Foreign Missions, and James Perryman, prominent Creek Indian, who together reduced the Creek language to writing. In June, 1837, the press was moved to Park Hill (*see Tour* 3), where many publications in the Cherokee, Creek, and Choctaw languages were printed. Several volumes from this press are now preserved in the Library of Congress in Washington, D.C.

A monument here marks this SITE OF OKLAHOMA'S FIRST PRINTING PRESS. Across the road from the marker is the UNION MISSION CEMETERY, where the founder of the mission, Rev. Epaphras Chapman is buried. He died in 1825. In a near-by grove of black locusts is an old FRENCH CEMETERY where growing crops almost cover the toppled and broken headstones that once marked the graves of early French traders.

A short distance north of the Union Mission site is the SALINE SPRING mentioned in a report made by Major Amos Stoddard in 1806 concerning the natural resources of the Louisiana Territory. Later the Osages came here to make salt, frequently borrowing from the Union missionaries kettles in which to boil the water. Two men named Campbell and Earhart later acquired the property and built a furnace—one hundred feet long—to quicken the boiling-water process of extracting the salt. Many people were employed by them to cut the wood necessary for fuel. The spring is still active, but nothing of the old furnace remains. However, one of the huge kettles said to have been used then is set in concrete in Saline Park in Salina.

South of MAZIE, 82.3 *m.* (620 alt., 100 pop.), numerous paved and graveled roads lead off (L) from US 69 to the many resort areas along the west shore of sprawling Fort Gibson Reservoir. Created with the completion of Fort Gibson Dam (*see Tour* 3) in midsummer of 1953, the lake backs up the waters of Grand River for twenty-five miles and provides 225 miles of shore line for recreational development.

WAGONER, 92.0 *m.* (588 alt., 4,395 pop.), now lies 1.5 miles east of rerouted US 69. Established in 1886 when the Arkansas Valley and Kansas Railroad built to a junction here with the Missouri-Kansas-Texas line, it is said to have been named for a popular train dispatcher, "Bigfoot" Wagoner, of Parsons, Kansas. In recent years catering to sportsmen and vacationists has become increasingly important to its once predominantly agricultural economy. In the CARNEGIE LIBRARY (*open weekdays 8:30–5*) is a collection of Indian articles and Civil War relics.

Wagoner is at the junction with paved State 51.

Left on this highway, through Wagoner, to site (R) of prehistoric INDIAN MOUNDS, 9.1 *m.*, now flooded by Fort Gibson Reservoir. Excavation was done in 1936 by a WPA project under the supervision of the Department of Anthropology of the University of Oklahoma. Traces of a fortified village were discovered. Findings include burial bundles, pottery, stone pipes, sheet-copper breastplates, flint knives and scrapers, and other implements now on display at the University Museum (*see Norman*).

The Taylor Ferry resort area is to the left of US 69 as the highway crosses Fort Gibson Reservoir, 9.5 *m.* At 10.5 *m.* is the entrance (R) to SEQUOYAH STATE PARK, one of Oklahoma's newest and most modern recreation areas. Dotted with timber, the rolling 19,500 acres of the park fill a picturesque peninsula jutting into the reservoir. Facilities range from the Western Hills Lodge, completed in 1956 (104 rooms, cabana units, and swimming pool), to modern cottages, boat docks (rental boats), swimming beaches, camp and picnic areas.

From Wagoner south to Muskogee, US 69 has been rerouted. (For this section of the old Texas Road, *see Tour 3*.) The highway crosses the Verdigris River at 97.5 *m.* The WIGWAM NEOSHO HISTORICAL MARKER (L), 101.2 *m.*, is a reminder of Sam Houston's brief sojourn among the Cherokees in Oklahoma (*see Tour 3*).

At 102.4 *m.* the CHIEF PUSHMATAHA HISTORICAL MARKER (L) commemorates the battle of January, 1807, between a Choctaw hunting expedition from Mississippi, led by their famous chief, and a group of men under Joseph Bogy, a French trader to the Osages. Bogy's band was put to rout by the Choctaws.

US 69 crosses the Arkansas River, 102.9 *m.*, and enters MUSKOGEE, 106.4 *m.* (617 alt., 37,289 pop.) (*see Muskogee*), at the junction with US 64 (*see Tour 2*) and US 62 (*see Tour 3*).

Section b. MUSKOGEE *to* TEXAS LINE, *154.5 US 69*

South of MUSKOGEE, 0 *m.*, the route passes through towns and counties bearing the names of chieftains and leaders of the Creek Indians who peopled this area after their removal from the East. Just east of the railroad tracks the ruts of the old Texas Road are still discernible. Herds of cattle being driven north from Texas along this route had to make way frequently for the long lines of emigrants' wagons headed south.

OKTAHA, 13.7 *m.* (591 alt., 207 pop.), is a small farming center

(L) named after Oktarharsars Harjo, leader of a conservative faction among the Creeks. The town began as a station on the Missouri-Kansas-Texas Railroad in 1872.

South of Oktaha (R) on the banks of Elk Creek, 2.4 *m.*, is the SITE OF THE BATTLE OF HONEY SPRINGS (L), the most important Civil War battle in Indian Territory. In the summer of 1863, several thousand Confederates under the command of General Douglas H. Cooper were stationed at Honey Springs, a stop on the Texas Road. It was from this point that they planned to attack Fort Gibson, key to the whole of Indian Territory. Union scouts, however, reported the proposed movement to Fort Gibson, and on the morning of July 17 the Union forces, under General James G. Blunt, marched from the fort and met the Confederates at Honey Springs. Outclassed in equipment and ammunition by the Union troops, the Confederates retreated down the Texas Road, leaving two hundred dead and wounded lying amid the smoking ruins of their warehouses, which they had fired to facilitate retreat. This turning point in the Indian Territory theater of war occurred only a few days after the fall of Gettysburg and Vicksburg, completing the geographical line of defeat resulting in the dissolution of the Confederacy.

The remains (L) of the abutments of an old bridge over which the Texas Road crossed are still discernible. The bridge was the focal point of the battlefield on the day of the Honey Springs rout. This and other bridges on near-by streams were built by citizens of the Creek Nation, who then levied tolls on travelers and freighters using the Texas Road.

CHECOTAH, 21.9 *m.* (638 alt., 2,638 pop.), the trade center for an agricultural and stock-raising area, was named for Samuel Checote, an early fullblood statesman. Checote, who had been educated in a Methodist mission school in Alabama, was elected principal chief of the Creeks when a new constitution was adopted by the tribe in 1867. But the conservatives objected to his introduction of constitutional procedures modeled after those of the white man, and under the leadership of Oktarharsars Harjo they carried on a series of insurrections against the tribal government, culminating in the Green Peach War (*see Tour 3*). The railroad building through the Creek country played the peacemaker, diplomatically naming the stations of Oktaha and Checotah to honor both leaders.

The ODD FELLOWS HOME, for old people and children—a two-story brick structure on a 160-acre tract, given by William Gentry, a mixed-blood Creek—is similar to the Odd Fellows' other institution at Carmen, in Alfalfa County.

US 69 crosses the NORTH CANADIAN RIVER, 32.4 *m.*, where Alexander Lawrence Posey (1873–1908), well-known Creek writer and poet, was drowned. Posey, the son of a Scotch-Irish father and a fullblood Creek mother, spoke only the Creek language until he was twelve. After attending Bacone College, he started on a career of leadership among his people and literary achievement in the white man's language. He held a number of tribal offices, and after the dissolution of the Creek government by the Dawes Commission, he became city editor of the *Muskogee Times* (*see Newspapers*). He is best known for his published poems and for the "Fuss Fixico" newspaper column where in Indian-English dialect he loosed his satirical arrows at members of the Dawes Commission and other federal officeholders in Indian Territory.

NORTH FORK TOWN HISTORICAL MARKER (L), 33.7 *m.*, calls attention to the site, 1.5 miles east, of a once important Creek community at the crossing of the old Texas Road with a branch of the California Road. Taking its name from the North Fork of the Canadian, it was settled by the Creeks shortly after their migration from the East in 1836. It was the scene, in 1861, of the treaty-making between the Confederates and the Creeks, Choctaws, and Chickasaws.

EUFAULA, 35.4 *m.* (613 alt., 2,540 pop.), the seat of McIntosh County, is a few miles west of the confluence of the North and South Canadian rivers. Development of the town began with the coming of the railroad in 1872, when residents of North Fork Town (*see above*) moved here to be near transportation facilities. Northeast of Eufaula is the SITE OF ASBURY MISSION, a boarding school established by the Methodist Episcopal church in 1849 under a contract with the Creek Council. It was housed in a large brick building accommodating one hundred pupils and, until it was destroyed by fire in 1889, it made a definite contribution to the culture and progress of the tribe.

Successor to the Asbury school is the EUFAULA BOARDING SCHOOL (for girls), which was opened by the Creeks in 1892 and is still active. A marble plate on the second floor of the main building reads "Eufaula High School," recalling the early years when the village of Eufaula, lacking an educational system of its own, sent its white boys and girls to a school built and maintained by Indians—an instance perhaps unique in the history of Oklahoma. The boarding school was taken over by the federal government in 1899, and in 1907 the enrollment was limited to girls. The vocational department offers interior decorating and other household arts. But these courses are not recent innovations; pre–Civil War curricula show that homemaking skills were taught the children here as early as 1854.

The oldest surviving newspaper in the state, the *Indian Journal* (*see Newspapers*), is published here. It was founded at Muskogee as a tribal organ in 1876.

At 37.9 *m.* is the junction with paved State 9.

Left on this road to EUFAULA DAM SITE, 18 *m.* Approved in 1956, with preliminary construction under way by 1957, this huge flood control-hydroelectric project will cost more than $150,000,000 and take about eight years to complete. Eventually, the 3,180-foot dam will back waters up both branches of the Canadian River to create a reservoir with a normal surface area of 99,000 acres, making it Oklahoma's largest lake.

US 69 crosses the SOUTH CANADIAN RIVER at 41.3 *m.* The wide, sandy stream formerly served as the boundary between the old Choctaw Nation on the south and the Creek Nation on the north. Southward, one can still see occasionally a sight once common along many Oklahoma highways: the rutted tracks on either side of the pavement made by the wagons of Indians, some of whom still do not own automobiles.

McALESTER, 62.8 *m.* (718 alt., 17,878 pop.) (*see Tour 5*), is at the junction with US 270 (*see Tour 5*).

Between McAlester and the Texas Line the route traverses country cut by many streams and rivers. The towns are small and agriculture and ranching are the main occupations. Throughout the region are sites where events of historical importance took place when the land belonged to the Choctaw Nation. One of the most dramatic, perhaps, was the brief existence of the Butterfield Overland Mail, whose route paralleled that of present US 69 from McAlester to the Red River from September, 1858, to the start of the Civil War. This was America's first transcontinental mail line and the 2,391 miles from St. Louis to San Francisco were covered in a scheduled twenty-five days. To maintain twice weekly departures from both cities, more than one hundred Concord coaches were required, along with one thousand horses, some five hundred mules, and eight hundred men. Today, though modern airlines cover the route in a matter of hours, one curious similarity remains—"free baggage" allowance on the present-day plane is exactly that of the 1858 Concord—forty pounds!

At 68.2 *m.* a marker (R) points out the SITE OF PERRYVILLE, 0.3 *m.* west, a trading post and stage station established on the Texas Road about 1838 by James Perry, member of a prominent Choctaw-Chickasaw family. A post office was opened here in 1841. And in 1858, when John Butterfield was awarded the contract to carry mail in stagecoaches across the continent to California, the route intersected the Texas Road at this station. Colbert Institute, a Chickasaw school, was founded here by the Methodist Church in 1852. (A few years later, when a boundary settlement placed it on Choctaw land, the school was moved about fifty miles southeast and re-established as Collins Institute.) Perryville became the seat of Tobucksy County of the Choctaw Nation in 1855.

During the Civil War the Confederates used Perryville as a military post and supply depot, and it was to this refuge that General Douglas H. Cooper retreated from the Honey Springs rout fifty miles north (*see above*). Brigadier General William Steele met him here with additional forces, but despite the combination they were again beaten by Union forces under Major General James G. Blunt in August of 1863. After several men had been killed in the Battle of Perryville, Cooper realized the futility of resistance and evacuated the town, first dumping salt in the water wells. The Union soldiers confiscated what they could and then completed the destruction of Perryville by burning the buildings.

The U.S. Naval Ammunition Depot (R), 71.2 *m.*, was an important World War II installation.

In 1880, SAVANNA, 71.9 *m.* (679 alt., 525 pop.), was a thriving coal-mining town in the Choctaw Nation. In 1887, however, an explosion killed eighteen miners and caused the operators to close their mines and move their machinery to another location. Evidences of strip mining can still be seen on either side of US 69 south of Savanna.

KIOWA, 79.4 *m.* (650 alt., 802 pop.), was founded in 1872 when the Missouri-Kansas-Texas Railroad was extended southward. The Pine Mountains to the east provide good fishing in several lakes and streams and dependable deer hunting in the fall.

A break in the limestone ridge at this point was responsible for the naming of LIMESTONE GAP, 88.8 *m.* (642 alt., 15 pop.), a virtually abandoned settlement through which the old Texas Road passed before swinging to the southwest. Near-by Buck Creek was spanned by a toll bridge at that time, operated by Captain Charles LeFlore, a member of the prominent Choctaw family. LeFlore's old home (R), a white frame two-story colonial structure, is still standing.

CHOCKIE, 91.2 *m.* (669 alt., 59 pop.), is an old Choctaw village. It was first named Chickiechockie in honor of Captain LeFlore's daughters, who had in turn been named for the respective Chickasaw and Choctaw nationalities of their mother and father. Chickie, who became the wife of Lee Cruce, Oklahoma's second governor, died early in the twentieth century and her name was removed from the depot sign. "Chockie" has remained.

All along this once-lonely route across Indian Territory, railroad trains were subject to frequent depredation by the lawless. From the early 1870's until well into the present century, mounted gangs would block the tracks, "stick up" the train, then seek shelter in the broken hills near by. Two of their favorite ambush points were in this immediate area—Limestone Gap (*see above*) and Stringtown (*see below*). Both were long dreaded by engineers, conductors, and other Katy line officials.

STRINGTOWN, 99.7 *m.* (596 alt., 499 pop.), was first a stage stop on the road from Fort Smith to Red River, later an important lumber-shipping point when the railroad was built through. Now it has a large quarry (L), one of several in this area. But for years Stringtown has been best known for the STATE TRAINING SCHOOL FOR BOYS (R), 103.4 *m.* This institution was transferred to Helena (*see Tour* 4) in 1956 and the facilities are now used in connection with the Oklahoma State Penitentiary at McAlester (*see Tour* 5).

ATOKA, 106.5 *m.* (582 alt., 2,653 pop.), is the seat of the county of the same name, both of which were named for a subchief of the Choctaw Nation. He is buried about twenty miles east of town near the little settlement of Farris. When the section was surveyed, the chief's resting place was found to be in the middle of the road, but the body was never moved.

Rev. J. S. Murrow, a Baptist missionary, founded Atoka in 1867. Shortly afterwards, he established the Atoka Baptist Academy, which eventually was absorbed into the Murrow Indian Orphans' Home on the Bacone College campus northeast of Muskogee (*see Tour* 3).

The Atoka Agreement, breaking up for allotment the lands of the Choctaw and Chickasaw nations, was signed at Atoka in 1897. In many ways the city has changed little over the years. A faded but still legible sign on the side of a three-story brick business building reads "Coffins & Caskets . . . Wagons & Buggies." Another "old" touch is provided by the Chuck Wagon Cafe and the Musical Museum (*free*) with its valuable collection of rare coin-operated music machines, several of which date back to the Civil War era. The museum is located on US 69–75, one block south of the bus station, in downtown Atoka.

Atoka is at the junction with US 75 (*see Tour* 9).

At 107.7 *m.* is the junction with paved State 7.

Right on this road to the junction with a graveled road, 11.3 *m.*; L. here to SITE OF BOGGY DEPOT, 15.1 *m.* Old Boggy Depot (present Boggy Depot is 2.5 miles to the south) was an important Choctaw-Chickasaw town which grew from an Indian log cabin built in 1837 to a flourishing trade center and Civil War army post. The name of the town comes from that of Clear Boggy Creek about one mile west. The Clear Boggy, Muddy Boggy, and North Boggy streams seem to have been given their names by early French traders who called them V*azzures* (*vaseuse,* miry or boggy). Americans adopted the translation probably about the time of the exploratory expedition made in 1805 by Dr. John Sibley, who wrote in his report, ". . . we arrived at the mouth of the V*azzures,* or Boggy River . . ." "Depot" was added after the Choctaw-Chickasaw treaty of 1837, when the Chickasaws emigrated from the East and were paid annuities at the "depot on the Boggy." The Post Office Department officially named the town in 1849, and a boundary treaty in 1855 placed it in the Choctaw Nation.

When a post route was established in 1850, Boggy Depot became an important town and several large two-story residences were erected. The settlement was at the junction of the Texas Road and one of the trails from Fort Smith to the West, and it did a thriving business. The town church, built in 1840 by Rev. Cyrus Kingsbury (the so-called "Father of the Choctaw Missions" who came from Mississippi with the tribe in the 1830's), served as the Choctaw capitol in 1858 when Chief Basil LeFlore ordered the national council to meet there temporarily during a factional dispute. The Confederates made Boggy Depot a military post during the Civil War, and the Confederate banner floated from a flagpole in the center of the town for four years. (There is a long row of Confederate graves in the cemetery.) Incongruously, the Indian troops fighting for the South would gallop at high speed around the flag whooping and yelling and singing the Choctaw war song. One of the first Masonic lodges to be established in what is now Oklahoma was started here by Rev. J. S. Murrow about 1872. When the Missouri-Kansas-Texas Railroad was built through the area, the route missed Boggy Depot, and the town declined.

Traces of the main streets of the old town were still visible in 1956. Tree-choked foundations, abandoned wells, and cement cisterns locate some of the former residences. But the town's last important landmark, the home of Chief Allen Wright, built in 1860, was destroyed by fire in March of 1952. Wright (1826–95) served two terms as principal chief of the Choctaw Nation and translated several books into the Choctaw language. It was he who suggested, in 1866, the name "Oklahoma" for the proposed Indian territory. The word is a Choctaw phrase meaning "Red People" and had occurred frequently in the Treaty of Dancing Rabbit Creek when reference was made to the Choctaws. After that the name was in common use and it was finally given officially to Oklahoma Territory and to the state. Chief Wright, Rev. Cyrus Kingsbury, and other prominent pioneers are buried in the abandoned cemetery here.

CADDO, 126.5 *m.* (591 alt., 895 pop.), located on a small branch of the Blue River, is named for the Caddo Indians who occupied this region before the coming of the Choctaws. It then became a Choctaw court town and was filled on the first Monday of each month with many tribal members who came to air their grievances or to stand trial. (The two-story, fifteen-room courthouse survived until 1956, when it was completely destroyed by fire.) Caddo was later an important station on the trail between Fort Smith and Fort Sill. After the coming of the railroad, it became an even more important junction for traffic to and from the West. It was to this place that Lone Wolf and other chiefs of the Plains tribes were brought overland in 1874 (*see Tour 3*), under military guard, and then sent by train to Florida for imprisonment there.

South of Caddo is a hilly region where a battle was fought in 1806 between the Caddoes, who then occupied the territory, and the Choctaws, who were still living in Mississippi. The latter tribe hunted on the plains of the present Oklahoma long before the nineteenth century and it was on one of these hunting parties that they were surprised by the Caddoes. Many bones and arrows were later found in the hills. It was from these hunting trips that the Choctaws learned much about the land which they selected when removal became necessary. Pushmataha, one of the Choctaw chiefs who made the exchange of territory with General Andrew Jackson at Doak's Stand, boasted that though the western land was supposed to have been unknown to him at the time, actually he knew it well; on "big hunts" he had been chased by the Comanches from one end of the country to the other. The Washita River gained its name from these early expeditions, for the Choctaw words *owa chito* mean "big hunt."

The STATE FISH HATCHERY (*visitors welcome*), 132.9 *m.*, on the Blue River (R), is the largest in Oklahoma. Close to three-quarters of a million fingerlings (bass, channel cat, red-ear, crappie, bluegill, and others) are now propagated each year in its 274 acres of culture ponds.

At 137.2 *m.* is the junction (R) with State 78.

Right here to the junction (R) with State 48, 3.0 *m.*

Immediately north of this junction, near the point where State 48 crosses Blue River, is the SITE OF FORT MCCULLOCH, established on the south bank of the river in 1862 by General Albert Pike and named for Brigadier General McCulloch, who commanded the Confederate forces in Indian Territory the first year of the Civil War. This fort existed only briefly, for soon after its construction Pike resigned his commission and his successors planned other defense outposts. But the places where the bastions and redoubts were erected are still plainly visible.

About a half-mile to the east (R) is NAIL'S CROSSING, where the Texas Road crossed the Blue River. It was named for a prominent Choctaw family, and the old Nail house stood until the 1930's, when it was destroyed by fire. The abandoned family cemetery is near by.

State 78 continues west to a junction with paved State 199 at 11.2 *m.* West on this road and then north (*make local inquiry*) to the SITE OF FORT WASHITA, 15.3 *m.*, on the east bank of Lake Texoma. This important military outpost, the first of a series of forts on the Washita River (*see Tours 3 and 10*), was established in 1842 by General (later President) Zachary Taylor. The purpose of Fort Washita was to protect the Chickasaws and Choctaws from border raids by the wild tribes of the Southwest. The Marcy Trail to California ran through this point, and the site became a refuge where emigrants might gather to await fellow travelers before starting on the more dangerous portion of their trip. The United States abandoned the fortification in 1861, however, and it was never again occupied except by the Confederates for a short time during the Civil War.

Fort Washita is now a ghost fortress overgrown with post oaks, but the well-preserved remains of many of the buildings and sites clearly show the plan of the stronghold. The ruins of massive-chimneyed barracks are still here, for the Goodland limestone, quarried near the site, has successfully withstood the elements. The straight chimneys of the old tavern, built just outside the quadrangle, rise like sentries. Water still flows from the stone springhouse. A move is currently under way to preserve the ruins as a state or national monument.

North of the fort is the old Military Cemetery. A marker notes the grave of General William Belknap, former commander of the southwestern forces of the United States Army, who died here in 1851. His body, however, has since been moved to Washington, D.C.

DURANT, 139.4 *m.* (643 alt., 10,541 pop.) (*see Tour 6*), is at the junction with US 70 (*see Tour 6*).

CALERA, 144.3 *m.* (643 alt., 643 pop.), an agricultural center, was one of the first townsites in which white men could purchase lots and get titles for the land directly from the Indian tribes. The lot sale took place in September, 1899.

COLBERT, 151.7 *m.* (661 alt., 748 pop.), a farming community in the fertile Red River valley, was named for Benjamin F. Colbert, an enterprising and highly successful Chickasaw. Coming to this area from Mississippi in 1846, he soon owned and operated a five-hundred-acre plantation, as well as a steam sawmill, a grist-mill, and a cotton gin. In 1853 he established ferry service on the Red River (*see below*), running it until 1875, when he built a $40,000 wagon bridge across the river. The span was 577 feet long and sixteen feet wide, with a "turn-off" in the center, twenty-four feet wide, for passing teams.

Right from Colbert on paved State 75A to DENISON DAM, 3.5 *m.* Completed in 1944, the $65,000,000 structure, a joint flood control and power project, is 15,200 feet long and has a maximum height of 165 feet. The highway runs across the dam, which is constructed at the confluence of the Washita with the Red River. The hydroelectric installation is open to visitors. Near by are a number of the more than three dozen private resort areas (*see Tour 6*) that ring the huge reservoir. Boating and fishing are the two most popular recreational activities.

The free bridge over the Red River, 154.5 *m.*, was the cause of the so-called Red River Bridge War in 1931. For many years previously the Texas Toll Bridge Company had operated a toll bridge at this crossing, but in 1929, Texas and Oklahoma, with the consent of Congress, began the construction of a free bridge. The toll bridge stockholders then secured an injunction from the Federal District Court to prevent the opening of the free bridge, and the Lone Star governor thereupon ordered barricades erected at its south end. On July 23, 1931, however, William H. "Alfalfa Bill" Murray (*see Tour 14*), having discovered a previous Supreme Court decision placing both banks of the river under Oklahoma jurisdiction, ordered the State National Guard to clear the bridge and let traffic flow undisturbed. He also ordered the highway approaching the north end of the toll bridge plowed up and the paving removed. A judgment against Oklahoma was granted the company, but the Federal Circuit Court of Appeals reversed the decision, and the "War" came to an end. The old bridge, downstream from the present US 69 span is still in service, though it was threatened with condemnation in 1956 as being unsafe for traffic.

US 69 crosses the TEXAS LINE, 154.5 *m.*, at a point five miles north of Denison, Texas (*see Texas Guide*).

TOUR 9

(Independence, Kan.)—Bartlesville—Tulsa—Okmulgee—Calvin—Atoka; US 75, Kansas Line to Atoka, 223.5 m.

Roadbed paved throughout.
The Atchison, Topeka & Santa Fe Railway parallels the route between the Kansas Line and Tulsa; the St. Louis–San Francisco Railroad between Tulsa and Wetumka.
Good accommodations available in the larger towns.

This north-south road through eastern Oklahoma crosses rich range country in the north, skirts the eastern border of the earliest and most extensive shallow oil-field development in the state, bisects the old Creek Nation, and ends in the heart of the former Choctaw Nation. In this last region are coal diggings that began as early as 1880 and declined almost to the vanishing point after the development of Oklahoma's rich reserves of oil and natural gas.

Almost at the route's halfway mark is the first of Oklahoma's famed gusher oil fields, the Glenn Pool. There, in sandy, blackjack-studded hill country, illiterate Creek Indian full bloods were made millionaires by chance and oil-boom towns provided a melodramatic chapter in the state's history.

With its many views of ranches and farms, oil wells and coal mines, and its dips into industrial cities like Sapulpa and Henryetta, and cosmopolitan ones like Bartlesville and Tulsa, US 75 offers a fairly complete panorama of Oklahoma's resources, occupations, and landscapes.

US 75 crosses the KANSAS LINE, 0 *m.*, two miles south of Caney, Kansas (*see Kansas Guide*).

COPAN, 8.1 *m.* (776 alt., 459 pop.), in the northwestern corner of the old Cherokee Nation, grew up in the 1880's around a trading post that served near-by Delawares and Osages, as well as Cherokees. The coming of the railroad in 1898 and the later development of small, shallow oil fields produced only mild and short-lived booms. In Copan is the junction with State 10.

Right on this graveled road to HULAH DAM AND RESERVOIR, 10 *m.* Created in 1951 by a 4,728-foot earth embankment across Caney River, the 3,200-acre lake is well stocked with fish. There are picnic facilities, boat docks, and cabins.

DEWEY, 15.2 *m.* (700 alt., 2,513 pop.), was founded in 1898 by J. H. (Jake) Bartles, who had previously founded Bartlesville (*see Bartlesville*). It was named in honor of Admiral George Dewey, whose victory at Manila Bay was fresh in everyone's mind. The DEWEY PORTLAND CEMENT COMPANY PLANT (L), one of the largest in the state, employs some three hundred workers. The town's biggest event is the annual Washington County Free Fair in September.

Bartles is an interesting example of pioneer ingenuity. When the Santa Fe purchased the grade of the projected Kansas, Oklahoma and Southwestern Railroad—which Bartles had surveyed and constructed from Caney—and began laying rails, this enterprising trader undertook to move his store to Dewey from Silver Lake, four miles south of Bartlesville. (Though it no longer exists, Silver Lake was the site of the Osage Indian Agency until it was moved to Pawhuska, *see Tour 4*). In order to do this, he built a road north from Bartlesville. But the heavy walnut lumber used in the store's construction made it extremely heavy to move, and despite the log rollers it rested on, oxen could only inch it along through the mud of the Caney River bottoms. Yet throughout the five months required for the move, the store remained open for business as usual.

Right from Dewey on improved roads to BAR DEW LAKE, 5 *m.*, a 212-acre reservoir made by damming a branch of the Caney River. At the dam is a ten-acre recreational area. Like Hulah, it provides dependable fishing and hunting.

At 18.4 *m.*, on the east edge of BARTLESVILLE (694 alt., 19,228 pop.) (*see Bartlesville*), is the junction with US 60 (*see Tour 4*), which unites with US 75 for the next 1.6 miles.

State 23A branches off to the right, at 20.9 *m.*, for Wooloroc Ranch and Museum (*see Tour 4*).

OCHELATA (570 alt., 357 pop.), lying two miles west of US 69 at 29.4 *m.*, bears the Indian name of Charles Thompson, principal chief of the Cherokees, 1875–79. Here, in the fertile valleys of Caney River and Double Creek, are numerous fine ranches.

RAMONA, 34.0 *m.* (703 alt., 583 pop.), grew from the depot erected here in 1900 by the Santa Fe Railway. It was named for the heroine of Helen Hunt Jackson's widely read novel about the Indians of California, *Ramona*. The same author's book, *A Century of Dishonor*, did much to awaken Americans to the injustices done the Indian. Three older trading posts—Old Ringo, Austin, and Hillside Mission (*see below*)—were later merged with the town.

VERA, 41.2 *m.* (645 alt., 164 pop.), occupies a site which was once a part of the allotment of W. C. Rogers, the last elected principal chief of the Cherokee Nation. He donated the land to the Santa Fe Railway when a station was established in 1900, and earlier town-builders moved here from a site they had occupied two miles north. Vera now serves the people of an area given over largely to ranches.

At 47.6 *m.* is the junction with an improved dirt road.

Right on this road is the SITE OF HILLSIDE MISSION, 6 *m.*, where a mission was opened in 1884 by John Murdock, a missionary sent out by the Society of Friends (Quakers) of Philadelphia to work among the Osages, Cherokees, and Delawares who lived within driving distance of the place. Substantial buildings of walnut lumber were erected, one of which, a house of twenty-four rooms, still stands. When John Watson was sent to relieve Murdock at the mission, he carried with him a shoot from the ancient elm under which William Penn signed the treaty with the Delaware Indians in 1682. It was planted in the mission grounds and is now a big tree.

In the cemetery across the road from the mission site a stone marks the grave of Chief Rogers (*see above*).

COLLINSVILLE, 49.3 *m.* (621 alt., 2,011 pop.) (*see Tour 9A*), is at the junction with US 169 (*see Tour 9A*), which unites with US 75 for 10.2 miles.

In TULSA, 72.7 *m.* (750 alt., 182,740 pop.; 1956 est., 254,100) (*see Tulsa*), are junctions with US 64 (*see Tour 2*), and with US 66 (*see Tour 1*), which unites southward 13.3 miles with US 75 to SAPULPA, 86.0 *m.* (712 alt., 13,031 pop.) (*see Tour 1*).

South of Sapulpa is the region in which the first spectacularly productive oil field in the state was developed in 1905–1906. The discovery well came in—December 1, 1905—on land southeast of Sapulpa owned by Ida E. Glenn, a Creek citizen, and the field became known as the Glenn Pool. Initial production was from a depth of 1,475 feet and amounted to seventy-five barrels a day. The second well drilled was a "duster," a dry hole. Then things began to happen.

The third well was a gusher—producing a thousand barrels a day. And when production on the fourth shot up to 2,500 barrels a day, the rush was on. Oil men converged on Indian Territory, and because Tulsa had already become headquarters for the companies and individuals developing the Red Fork Field (*see Tulsa*), that city, rather than near-by Sapulpa, benefited most from the rush of thousands of people into the new field. Additional interest was stimulated by the mystery surrounding the discovery well. It had been drilled as a "tight hole" with only the men working on it allowed to approach the rig.

The suddenness—and bountifulness—of the Glenn Pool caught producers with neither sufficient tank storage nor adequate facilities for shipping the crude oil to refineries. As more gushers came in, operators began in desperation to dam near-by ravines to hold this flood they did not know how to control. Much oil was wasted before tanks and pipelines could be built to handle it. Gross production from the field in the half-century since its discovery is 248,000,000 barrels.

Many of the most productive wells of the old Creek Nation were drilled on the land of Indians who, resisting allotment of the communal lands of the tribe, had refused to select allotments themselves and had been arbitrarily given acreage in the worthless blackjack-covered hills which other tribesmen did not want. One of these, whose name became known nationally because of the long-drawn-out litigation following his marriage to a white woman, was Jackson Barnett. An illiterate full blood, he was declared incompetent, and his millions were controlled by the Indian Bureau and doled out to him by his appointed legal guardian. Other Creeks who were made rich from oil royalties include Enos Wilson and Katie Fixio, who was also declared incompetent, and whose money paid for the County Courthouse at Okmulgee. Court-appointed guardianships over these illiterate full bloods became the choicest of plums in a young Oklahoma. They often led to prolonged litigation and occasionally to scandal.

Producers, too, became principals in true stories of quick wealth, men like Robert McFarlin and James E. Chapman. The first was a small-town banker, the second a small-ranch cattleman. From an investment of $700 on a first lease, these partners ran up their holdings in eleven years to an aggregate of leases, wells, stored oil, and pipelines which a major company bought for $35,000,000.

KIEFER, 91.7 *m.* (686 alt., 275 pop.), before the opening of the Glenn Pool, was only a siding on the Frisco. Then, because it was the nearest unloading point for machinery needed in the oil field, houses and stores were built. One of the first casing-head gas-treating plants—for extracting gasoline from wet gas—was located here. In the semi-legendary history of Oklahoma's oil-soaked boom towns Kiefer's position as one of the toughest is quite secure.

BEGGS, 106.0 *m.* (690 alt., 1,214 pop.), gave its name to another of the state's rich oil fields. As development from the Glenn Pool area spread west and south, in the period from 1910 to 1915, Beggs began to boom and by 1920 it was an important supply point for drilling operations. Production from the North Beggs District alone, covering 4,200 acres, reached 58,700 barrels by 1954.

Southwest of Beggs (*make local inquiry*) is the so-called "Giants' Highway," a span of limestone blocks five hundred feet wide. The heavy stones, averaging two feet in thickness, lie in a close-fitting checkerboard pattern. They run in a northeast-southwest direction, and a car can be driven over sections of the "road." Geologists say the highway-like formations are a freak of nature.

OKMULGEE, 118.8 *m.* (670 alt., 18,317 pop.) (*see Okmulgee*), is at the junction with US 62 (*see Tour* 3), which unites southwestward with US 75 for 21.9 miles.

Southward, oil fields begin to give way to coal mines. Then Ben Hur (R), 126.6 *m.*, a slope mine on Henryetta coal thirty-eight inches thick, was opened in 1918 and abandoned in 1936, after producing 395,652 tons. The Whitehead shaft mine (R), 127.3 *m.*, was opened in 1909 and closed in 1929. The Atlas (R), 129.1 *m.*, a drift mine working a forty-inch coal bed, was opened in 1922 and has produced 1,655,800 tons of coal.

At 130.4 *m.* are the tall, smoke-trailing stacks of the EAGLE-PICHER ZINC SMELTER (L), on the northeast corner of HENRYETTA, 132.7 *m.* (691 alt., 7,987 pop.) (*see Tour* 3).

US 75 leaves US 62 at 140.7 *m.*, dropping south into the valley of the North Canadian River.

WELEETKA, 147.9 *m.* (690 alt., 1,548 pop.), is the trade center for a farm area that still contains many Creek families. Watermelons are an important cash crop and the town usually stages a watermelon festival in August.

On the banks of Coal Creek, fifteen miles east of Weleetka, is the site of the OLD HICKORY STOMP GROUNDS, where in 1901 the fullblood Creek leader Chitto Harjo (known to the whites as Crazy Snake) gathered his numerous fullblood faction in a rump session of the tribal council to legislate against division of the Creek Nation by allotment. In justifying his action, he said: "He [the federal government] told me [the Creek Nation] that as long as the sun shone and the sky is up yonder these agreements will be kept. . . . He said, 'Just as long as you see light here, just as long as you see this light glimmering over us, shall these agreements be kept, and not until all these things cease and pass away shall our agreement pass away.' That is what he said, and we believed it." But his faith in treaties was soon shattered. He and a number of his followers were arrested and given suspended sentences for obstructing allotment. Eight years later, after being shot through the hips in another attempt to arrest him, Chitto Harjo died.

WETUMKA, 158.3 *m.*, (770 alt., 2,025 pop.), means noisy or sounding water in the Creek language. The town was settled by a conservative faction of the tribe and named for the town in Alabama from which they had been exiled. Along with the name, the band also brought with them to Wetumka living fire from their old communal hearth. On the weary "Trail of Tears" two of the braves were entrusted with the duty of keeping the fire. At each camping place, the coals were blown up anew for the cooking. When the march was resumed, new coals were carried forward. At the site of this western "Wetumpka," a new communal hearth was dedicated. "Here is our town," said the leader of the band, "we shall go no farther west."

The first trading post was established in 1858, the first post office in 1881. The important tribal settlements of Tuckabatchee and Thlopthlocco were located near Wetumka. Many of the principal Creek chiefs have come from the Wetumka area and it is the home of Principal Chief Roly Buck. Stomp dances and Indian stickball games still figure prominently in the social activities of the fullbloods. Usually staged during the summer months, they are open to white visitors. Visitors are also welcomed at one of the largest quarter-horse ranches in the Southwest, located one mile northwest of Wetumka.

"Sucker Day," on the last weekend in August, is the town's biggest annual event, and one of the country's most unusual. In 1950, one F. Bam Morrison "conned" Wetumka businessmen out of considerable cash while acting as the advance man for a nonexistent circus. Embarrassed but game, the swindled merchants swallowed their pride, declared a holiday, and donated their extra pop, buns, hot dogs—and elephant hay—for a day-long celebration. Since then parades, dances, and water sports contests on near-by Lake Wetumka have drawn crowds of up to five thousand people.

At 168.8 *m.* is the junction with US 270 (*see Tour* 5). The two highways for the next 9.4 miles, across the South Canadian River, and through CALVIN, 177.7 *m.* (716 alt., 557 pop.) (*see Tour* 5).

South of Calvin, US 75 curves, dips, and rises among scrub-forested hills. Farms and ranches are scattered and the region still shelters a few of the more conservative Choctaw full bloods who prefer the old ways of life to the new.

The Whipple Survey historical marker, 181.6 *m.*, recalls the trip made through here in 1853 by Lieutenant A. W. Whipple. Under instructions of Jefferson Davis, U.S. Secretary of War, the party made the first railroad survey from Fort Smith, Arkansas, to the Pacific Coast.

COALGATE, 210.5 *m.* (622 alt., 1,984 pop.), in the words of one outside observer, "should actually be a ghost town, but the civic-minded people just refuse to let it die." Once a thriving and prosperous coal-mining center, the town declined to its present status as an agricultural community when oil and natural gas reduced the demand for coal. Under lease from the Choctaw Nation, the first coal mine was opened in 1882 within one hundred feet of what is now Main Street. The vein was so close to the surface that the overburden could be stripped away with plows and scrapers and the coal removed with sledges, steel coal pins, and shovels. In 1956 in all of Coal County, of which Coalgate is the seat, there was only one coal mine in operation. And Coalgate itself was planning to manufacture overalls.

LEHIGH, 215.0 *m.* (599 alt., 352 pop.), is another mining center in the old Choctaw Nation. Coal was first mined here in 1880, and the settlement was named for Pennsylvania's coal-mining city. Yet it was little more than a company commissary and a huddle of shacks until 1887, when a mine disaster at Savanna (*see Tour* 8) caused the closing of the mines there and the removal to Lehigh of mining equipment and 135 houses. But disaster in turn struck Lehigh in 1912. A destructive fire swept the town and in 1956 only a few gray-black ruins gave evidence of the town's prosperous days when its population was three thousand.

Right from Lehigh on a dirt road to the junction with another dirt road, 2.5 *m.*; L. here, 4.3 *m.*, to the BIRTHPLACE OF PATRICK J. HURLEY, secretary of war (1929–33) under President Hoover and ambassador to China (1944–45) under President Roosevelt. His father was a coal miner and farmer of this district, and young Hurley satisfied his early thirst for books at the home of a neighbor, Ben Smallwood, a cultivated mixed blood who was for a time principal chief of the Choctaw Nation. The old Hurley home was burned some years ago, and a tenant house stands on the site. The new MARY HURLEY HOSPITAL in Coalgate honors his mother, who is buried in the Lehigh Cemetery.

ATOKA, 223.5 *m.* (582 alt., 2,653 pop.) (*see Tour* 8), is at the junction with US 69 (*see Tour* 8).

TOUR 9A

(Coffeyville, Kan.)—Collinsville—Tulsa; US 169, 71.4 m.

Roadbed paved throughout.
Missouri Pacific R. R. parallels route between Kansas Line and Oologah; the Santa Fe between Collinsville and Tulsa.
Good accommodations at the larger towns.

This route passes, for the most part, through an area originally settled by the Delaware Indians who in 1867 used tribal funds to purchase equal rights with the Cherokees in the Cherokee Nation. It is occupied mainly by white farmers and ranchers. This upland prairie region witnessed the development of one of the state's first extensive shallow oil fields, and almost fifty years later, many of them were still producing by the water-flood method (*see Tour 4*).

US 169 crosses the KANSAS LINE, 0 *m.*, 3.8 miles south of Coffeyville, Kansas (*see Kansas Guide*).

SOUTH COFFEYVILLE, 0.6 *m.* (740 alt., 527 pop.), with its scattering of homes, beer, pool, and dance halls, garages, and stores, was once a notoriously wild border town where bootleggers flourished since both Indian Territory and Kansas were dry. When United States marshals arrived to raid the whisky joints their proprietors hastily moved their stock of liquor out of the back doors a few yards across the Kansas Line. At times, outraged Kansans disregarded legal barriers to burn saloons and destroy whisky, but South Coffeyville's defiant bootleggers always restocked and carried on under brush arbors until they could rebuild.

The name of LENAPAH, 10.6 *m.* (759 alt., 328 pop.), is a variation of the ancient name of the Delaware Indian tribe, Lenape. The town is the center of a district formerly occupied by these Indians and their freed slaves.

DELAWARE, 15.8 *m.* (716 alt., 582 pop.), named for the original Indian settlers, is a livestock shipping and trading point for the ranchers west of town and the farmers to the east in the valley of the Verdigris River. Its small business district (R) lies between the highway and the Missouri Pacific tracks.

At the height of the boom in the extensive shallow oil field surrounding Delaware, after 1907, the little town became a highly congested resort of drillers, roustabouts, pipeline workers, pumpers, lease hounds, gamblers, bootleggers, and "entertainers" attracted by the prospect of easy money. In one block were fourteen saloons and gambling joints—all illegal, of course—where brawls were common and killings not unknown. And from this era of Delaware's history comes the story of the teamster who went into an explosives magazine near the town to get nitroglycerin with which to "shoot" an oil well. There was a terrific explosion, and the man disappeared. Months later the man and his mules turned up in New Mexico. As the teller of the tale explains it solemnly, "Him and his team both was blown clean across Oklahoma an' the Panhandle of Texas!"

To the right of the highway is NOWATA, 21.5 *m.* (707 alt., 3,965 pop.) (*see Tour 4*), at the junction with US 60 (*see Tour 4*).

At 38.9 *m.* is the junction with a graveled road.

A marker (L) in the shape of a cowskin framed by poles bears the inscription, "Two miles east is the birthplace of Will Rogers, the Oklahoma cowboy, who by way of Broadway, Hollywood, and the public press won his way to the hearts of the American people."

Left on the graveled road is WILL ROGERS BIRTHPLACE (*open*), 2.6 *m.* His father, Clem V. Rogers, a blood citizen of the Cherokee Nation and a prosperous cattleman prominent in tribal affairs, was one of the pioneers of this region. He settled on the ranch in 1869, and in 1875 he built his home at the foot of an oak-crowned sandstone bluff. From its south windows he could overlook the broad expanse of Verdigris bottom farm land that he put under fence. Later, as open range ceased to exist, the Rogers pastures on the prairie to the west were also fenced.

The house was originally built of logs which later were covered with weatherboarding painted white. With slight additions, it stands as it was when Will was born in 1879, a commodious, dignified, two-story ranch dwelling dominating the group of outbuildings—smokehouse, blacksmith shop and toolhouse, cribs, machinery sheds, and barn—and stock corrals to the east and south.

By 1960, when the $41,000,000 Oologah Dam across the Verdigris River is scheduled for completion, the home site and all but 300 of the 2,000 acres of the Rogers farm will be flooded. The dam site is southeast of the Rogers home. The reservoir, when filled, will back up the Verdigris waters thirty-two miles from the dam, with a maximum width of about three miles.

OOLOGAH, 40.0 *m.* (658 alt., 242 pop.), is Will Rogers' authentic home town and the post office address of the Rogers ranch, although Claremore (*see Tour 1*) is commonly referred to as Rogers' home. Oologah is but a modest cluster of stores and houses that grew up around the depot of the Kansas and Arkansas Valley Railroad (now the Missouri Pacific) when the road built through in 1887. A miniature REPLICA OF THE ROGERS RANCH HOUSE (L) is near the railway station. Beside it is a bust of Will erected by the citizens of Oologah.

COLLINSVILLE, 50.2 *m.* (621 alt., 2,011 pop.), took its name from a Dr. Collins, who, in anticipation of the building of the Santa Fe Railroad through the region in 1900, gave land for a townsite. The railroad, however, passed a mile to the west, whereupon the town moved over to its present site. It is mainly dependent on the near-by farms and ranches, and a shallow oil and gas field that extends northward almost to the Kansas Line.

Collinsville is at the northern junction with US 75 (*see Tour 9*), which unites with US 169 for 10.2 miles.

A trading center for a farm community, OWASSO, 57.3 *m.* (592 alt., 431 pop.), lies like a fringe on both sides of the highway.

US 169 veers right from US 75 at 60.4 *m.* At 61.0 *m.* is the northern entrance to MOHAWK PARK, Tulsa's 3,000-acre recreational area through which Bird Creek flows between high banks overhung by thick tree growths.

At 61.5 *m.* is the junction with a black-top road which leads to Mohawk Park's principal attractions.

Left on this road to MOHAWK PARK POLO FIELD (L), 0.7 *m.*

MOHAWK BOATHOUSE (*boats, recreational facilities*), 1.1 *m.*, a building (R) of native limestone and big beams, is in a grove beside a canoe lagoon. North of the boathouse is RECREATION LAKE (*boating, fishing*).

The Zoo (Refectory), 1.7 *m.*, is a closely grouped series of exhibits. Some of the animals are shown in rough limestone structures with heavy hewn beams and some in small paddocks. The outstanding attraction of the zoo is MONKEY ISLAND, a large artificial hill of rocks surrounded by a moat whose outer walls slope inward to prevent the escape of the monkeys. In the rocks of the island are the dens for the animals. Adjoining the zoo on the south are the birdhouses, the lake refuge for wild fowl, botanical display, and greenhouse.

The road, keeping to the north side of the canoe lagoons, enters the main PICNIC AREA (*stone shelter houses, tables, ovens*), 3.3 *m.*

The site (R) of the MASHED–O RANCH (*private*), 63.7 *m.*, is across Bird Creek in a bend of the stream. This ranch once included a large part of the range northward to Bartlesville and eastward from the border of the Osage reservation to the Verdigris River. It was W. E. Halsell, of Vinita (*see Tour 1*), an intermarried citizen of the Cherokee Nation, who came up from Texas about 1880 with his first herd of longhorns and turned them out on the good grass of this region.

At 65.0 *m.* US 169 crosses a lagoon. On both sides of the highway are free picnic areas.

At 65.8 *m.* is the junction with a graveled road.

Left on this road is the well-kept MOHAWK MUNICIPAL GOLF COURSE (*two 18-hole courses; greens fee 75c weekdays, $1.50 Saturdays, Sundays, and holidays*), 0.6 *m.*

YAHOLA RESERVOIR (*boating, fishing*), 65.9 *m.*, is an auxiliary reservoir for Tulsa's water supply.

In TULSA, 71.4 *m.* (750 alt., 182,740 pop.; 1956 est., 254,100) (*see Tulsa*), are junctions with US 66 (*see Tour 1*), US 64 (*see Tour 2*), and US 75 (*see Tour 9*).

TOUR 10

(Arkansas City, Kan.)—Ponca City—Oklahoma City—Ardmore—(Gainesville, Tex.); US 77, Kansas Line to Texas Line, 261.0 m.

Roadbed paved throughout.
The Santa Fe Ry. parallels the route.
Excellent accommodations at short intervals.

Dividing the state almost exactly in half from north to south, US 77 crosses a greatly varied country. From the farm and range land of the old Cherokee Outlet, it passes into the red orchard land surrounding the first Oklahoma Territory capital, crosses the rich bottoms of the Canadian and Washita rivers where alfalfa, oil, and native pecans predominate. It loops the rocky, rounded heights in the Arbuckle Mountains' cattle-raising region. Then, in its last fifty miles, it dips across pastures, farm lands, and the sandy, timbered approach to the Red River.

Over stretches in the north, now paved with concrete, the white settlers of Oklahoma Territory made their frenzied races for homesteads, first in 1889 and again in 1893. And out of that varied, adventurous population emerged men and women who in unusual and sometimes bizarre fashion left their imprint on the nation's life—showmen, a temperance crusader, an art collector, politicians, movie stars, and outlaw-catchers.

Within the limits of Oklahoma City, US 77 skirts the greatest gusher oil field ever developed in the state. But from Ponca City to Ardmore, oil touches the highway and continues to effect strongly the lives of communities and individuals. With two important schools along the way—the University of Oklahoma, at Norman, and Central State Teachers College, at Edmond—US 77 is in fact, a principal Sooner State artery along which flows nearly everything that is characteristically Oklahoman in setting and population. Farmer, rancher, oilman, politician, educator, and sportsman—all have contributed to the history of the region. Compressed into a comparatively few years, its story admirably epitomizes the young state which, in 1957, celebrated its fiftieth birthday.

Section a. KANSAS LINE *to* OKLAHOMA CITY, *124.3 m. US 77*

Where US 77 crosses the KANSAS LINE, 0 *m.*, four miles south of Arkansas City (*see Kansas Guide*), a granite MONUMENT (R) commemorates the opening to settlement in 1893 of the Cherokee Outlet. Near it is the official INDIAN STATE HISTORICAL MARKER, pointing out that the land in this area was granted to the Cherokee Indians in 1828. Five miles east was the tribal reservation of the Kaw Indians, whose best-known member was the Hon. Charles Curtis, Vice President of the United States, 1928–32.

At 0.8 *m.* is the junction with an asphalt road.

Right on this road, through an arched gate and a double row of trees, is CHILOCCO INDIAN SCHOOL, 1.6 *m.*, one of the outstanding institutions of its kind in the country. Chilocco was established by an act of Congress in 1882 as a nonreservation boarding school for children of the Plains tribes in the western part of Indian Territory. After the breakup of the tribal governments, preceding statehood, and the dissolution of their own educational system, the Five Tribes also began to send many students to Chilocco. Since 1947 it has participated prominently in the stepped-up education program for the Navajo Indians of New Mexico and Arizona. Enrollment for the 1956–57 school year was 830, including 470 Navajos. More than a dozen other tribes were also represented.

Chilocco—called "The School of Opportunity"—stresses vocational training, homemaking courses for the girls, agriculture, and advanced trades for the boys. But the academic side of the curriculum has been strengthened in recent years. Six modern three-story dormitories, set about a quadrangle, house the students. Built of a cream-colored limestone quarried near by, they reflect generally the gabled, turreted, and ivied architecture of the nineties. In addition, the plant includes a dining hall, four-unit shop building, gymnasiums, music studios, auditorium, library, and extensive agricultural buildings. There is also an interesting MUSEUM, which, like all of Chilocco, is open to visitors upon permission of the superintendent. The school is maintained and operated by the federal government. Most Chilocco graduates are placed in near-by communities and industries. Relatively few return to their home community, where opportunities for employment are usually limited.

NEWKIRK, 8.1 *m.* (1,149 alt., 2,201 pop.), seat of Kay County, came into existence after the opening of the Outlet. It profited considerably from the development of shallow oil fields in the area in 1919 and again in 1923. In recent years additional fields have been discovered, and the red-clay soil now sprouts dipping pump jacks along with wheat and corn.

Six miles east of Newkirk, on the bank of the Arkansas River, is the SITE OF FERDINANDINA. Established by the French and boasting perhaps as many as three hundred traders, explorers, and Indians during the decade from 1740 to 1750, it was probably Oklahoma's first white settlement. Only the faint marks of the stockade are visible today, but a collection of relics—some five thousand items—representing both Indian and white cultures in the area, has been turned over to the Oklahoma Historical Society.

At 17.1 *m.* is the junction with a paved road.

Left on this road to KAW CITY, 12.5 *m.* (1,009 alt., 561 pop.), once a center for oil operations in western Osage County and the home of the important LAURA

A. CLUBB ART COLLECTION. A former school teacher who married a cattleman, Mrs. Clubb began buying paintings after oil made the family wealthy in 1922. When she bought her first painting—Van Marke's "In the Pastures," for $12,500—it is said that her husband protested, "I could have bought a trainload of cattle for that!" The collection, now moved to the Philbrook Museum in Tulsa (*see Tulsa*), included more than two hundred paintings and was housed in the Clubb Hotel.

At 20.0 *m.* is the junction with a graveled road.

Left here 1 *m.*, then right to PONCA CITY COUNTRY CLUB (*18-hole golf course, swimming pool*), 2 *m.*

Continue on side road to PONCA MILITARY ACADEMY (R), 2.5 *m.*, which trains boys through the twelfth grade and has a capacity of 120 students.

Beyond (R) is the AMERICAN LEGION HOME. The only institution of its kind in the country, it cares for some 120 boys and girls of deceased and disabled veterans. The plant includes an administration building and three billets, all of Spanish design, and a recreation building. Part of the 120-acre tract is landscaped, the remainder is farmed by the boys. The children attend the Ponca City public schools.

At 21.0 *m.* is the junction with an asphalt road.

At this corner (L) is the PIONEER WOMAN STATE MONUMENT, a heroic bronze statue of a sunbonneted pioneer mother and her child, standing on a broad base of native limestone. In the period of his greatest prosperity (*see Ponca City*), E. W. Marland conceived the idea of this memorial to the pioneer women of the West. Providing for its financing, he asked for models from sculptors throughout the country. After a nationwide tour showing the twelve submitted models in all the principal cities, Bryant Baker's was selected by popular vote. The statue was dedicated April 22, 1930.

At the end of the tree-bordered avenue that extends northeast from the Pioneer Woman is the former Marland Home. Now known as ASSUMPTION VILLA, it is world headquarters for the Order of the Felician Sisters, which conducts a retreat house and loan library for the public.

East and northeast on the main side road is LAKE PONCA (*fishing, boating, water skiing*), 2.9 *m.*, and heavily wooded LAKE PONCA PARK (*picnicking, playground equipment*).

Farther north on the Lake Road is WENTZ EDUCATIONAL CAMP (*cabins*), 3.8 *m.*, and POOL, 5.5 *m.* Given to the people, with the children especially in mind, by Lew Wentz (*see Ponca City*), this 160-acre tract has become a popular resort used by the YMCA and YWCA, the Boy Scouts, the Camp Fire Girls and Girl Scouts, and the general public.

The pool, one hundred by fifty feet, has electric lights at the bottom, elaborate diving tower, wide tiers of stone and marble seats rising from one side and flanked by towers, all brilliantly lighted at night. From the top of one of the eighty-foot towers, reached by ladders, the visitor gets a long view of Ponca and the valley of the Arkansas River beyond. With its lights and convenient seating, the pool is frequently used for water sports, races, and exhibition diving. The camp also includes a small game preserve.

West of PONCA CITY, 23.0 *m.* (1,003 alt., 20,180 pop.) (*see Ponca City*), US 60 (*see Tour 4*) unites with US 77 for 3.8 miles.

At 31.6 *m.* is the 101 RANCH (R), a striking symbol of that changing West which brought fortune to men and took it away with no more than a shrug of regret.

In the early seventies, a shrewd trader named George W. Miller left Kansas with twenty thousand pounds of bacon to exchange for whatever could be sold at a profit. He arrived in San Saba County, Texas, in the spring with enough bacon to trade for four hundred longhorn steers. These he herded back over the good grass trail to a range in the northeastern corner of Indian Territory belonging to the Quapaw Indians, and there he sold them when fat at a handsome profit. In order to obtain more range for the enlarged herds he meant to own, he went out to the Cherokee Outlet and found abundant grassland. His first lease was sixty thousand acres. Then, going back to Texas, he found that he could buy a steer for $3.00 in gold instead of $6.00 in bacon.

Miller's next step was to induce the small tribe of Ponca Indians, then living temporarily with the Quapaws, to accept a reservation near his leased land and allow him to graze his cattle on it for one cent per acre annually. He was a good friend to the Indians, an excellent cattleman, a tireless hustler; and the earnings of his ranch grew enormously. When it became possible to buy Indian land, he acquired more and more. And when his sons, Joe, George Jr., and Zack, grew up, they too joined in pushing forward the enterprise.

George Miller died in 1903, in the dugout that had been ranch headquarters, just before the first "White House"—three stories and a basement—was completed. Before his death, he saw thirteen thousand acres of the ranch sown to wheat, three thousand planted in corn, and three thousand acres devoted to forage crops. He was paying $32,500 annually in rentals to the Indians, and running expenses amounted to $75,000 a year. But income ranged from $400,000 to $500,000 a year, and the problem was how to employ these earnings profitably. This "problem" was made even more complicated by the discovery of oil on the 101 Ranch holdings.

It was the Miller sons who thought of the 101 Ranch Wild West Circus; and the first tryout was staged at Ponca City on April 14, 1908, with two hundred performers. For eight years the show made money. But the Miller sons devoted more and more time to it, less and less time to the legitimate business of the ranch. After 1916 the tide began to turn. By 1921, owing to losses and extravagance, it became necessary to reorganize. Then, in 1927, Joe Miller died of monoxide gas poisoning, and two years later his brother George was killed in an automobile accident. When oil prices dropped, the show failed and Zack Miller found himself facing an indebtedness of $700,000. In August, 1931, the ranch was placed in receivership, and despite Zack's roared protests—backed by a loaded shotgun—a man from the federal courts was placed in charge. The guest register at the "White House," with its scores of names of the well-advertised in almost every line of endeavor, reflects the Miller sons' absorbing passion for publicity. But the house itself is now a bleak square of foundation stones, and the two-story white stucco "Ranch Store" is the only building that remains. The sprawling ranch has long since been broken up.

At 34.8 *m.* is the White Eagle Monument (L), erected by the Miller Brothers in memory of the Ponca Chief their father induced to come to this area (*see above*) in 1879. The monument stands on a hill which was once a signal station of the Indians. Built of native red stone, it is twelve feet in diameter and twenty feet high, topped by the huge white figure of an eagle.

White Eagle was a principal figure in a drama of tribal exile quite as tragic, though not as well known as the "Trail of Tears" traced by the Five Civilized Tribes. In 1868, after the federal government had induced the Poncas to make two cessions of land along the Missouri River in Dakota and had solemnly confirmed them in the possession of what remained, a treaty with the Sioux included a clause giving them every acre of the Ponca reservation. The Poncas refused to give up their ancient homes, and warfare between the tribes followed, in which the more powerful Sioux killed a fourth of the Poncas.

Nine years later, the government acted to save the Poncas, not by giving back their land and otherwise satisfying the Sioux, but by ordering them off. They still objected to removal, whereupon an official from Washington came to escort ten Ponca chiefs to Kansas and Indian Territory so that they could select a new home. They reached the country of the Osages in the fall of 1876. In the words of one of the chiefs, "We . . . found it stony and broken and not a country that we thought we could make a living in. We saw the Osages . . . without shirts, their skin burned, and their hair stood up as if it had not been combed since they were little children."

Arriving at Arkansas City, Kansas, without having induced the Poncas to choose a new location, the government man lost patience with the chiefs and deserted them. So they went back, five hundred miles, on foot. The following summer, in 1877, soldiers gathered up the tribe and marched them to the Quapaw reservation in the northeastern corner of Indian Territory. (It was here that George Miller found them and persuaded them to move to land adjoining his lease.)

In their new reservation—which had been described glowingly by the Commissioner of Indian Affairs as "in all respects . . . far superior to their old location in Dakota"—158 of the tribe died within a short time. To make their situation more bearable, the government gave help in building homes and establishing schools. But in the winter of 1879, Standing Bear led a party back to the Nebraska reservation of the Omahas, their kinsmen, who gave them refuge and supplied them with seed to plant in the spring. Before they could plant, however, soldiers came to arrest Standing Bear. He and thirty of his followers were imprisoned at Fort Omaha.

Through the intervention of citizens of Omaha, led by a newspaperman, the case of the Poncas came to trial on a writ of habeas corpus sworn out to secure their release. They were successful and the Poncas returned to the Omaha reservation, where they were joined later by some two hundred others who came up from Indian Territory. But the greater number of the Poncas, some seven hundred, remained on the land assigned to them in the Cherokee Outlet.

At the trial of Standing Bear, government attorneys contended that an Indian was not entitled to a writ of habeas corpus because he was not a "person within the meaning of the law." An old chief answered them eloquently and well: "The people of the devil . . . have tried to make me believe that God tells them what to do, as though God would put a man where he would be destroyed! . . . They have destroyed many already, but they cannot deceive me. God put me here, and intends for me to live on the land they are trying to cheat me out of."

MARLAND, 35.4 *m.* (1,001 alt., 221 pop.), was named for E. W. Marland (*see Ponca City*), governor of Oklahoma (1935–39), whose extensive oil leases covered the site.

At 43.3 *m.* is the junction with US 177.

Right on this road to THREE SANDS, 4 *m.*, a ghost town once known as the "billion dollar spot." The Three Sands story began in June of 1921 with the first oil strike. Almost overnight the town became a jumble of derricks interspersed with jerry-built shanties. By 1923 the boom was at its height and the camp had an estimated population of six thousand. During its period of peak production the field's more than five hundred wells were gushing out an average of more than one hundred thousand barrels a day. But little more than the post office remains of this once-famous boom town.

In PERRY, 61.2 *m.* (1,005 alt., 5,137 pop.) (*see Tour 2*), is the junction with US 64 (*see Tour 2*), which unites westward with US 77 for 5.4 miles.

At 74.6 *m.* is the historical marker noting the line from which settlers made the Run into "Old Oklahoma" from the north, when it was opened in 1889, and from the south into the Cherokee Outlet in 1893.

ORLANDO, 75.5 *m.* (1,078 alt., 262 pop.), though near a productive (1,413,000 barrels to 1955) oil field, has remained a farm trade center since its founding in 1889. Only twice has its essential calm been broken, once when the mad race into the Cherokee Outlet took place on September 16, 1893, and again in 1896 when swindlers—by "salting" a diggings with ore that assayed $185 to the ton—duped a number of Orlando men into believing that gold had been found on a farm southwest of town.

At 78.2 *m.* is the junction with State 51 (*see Tour 2A*).

MULHALL, 82.1 *m.* (936 alt., 320 pop.), was named for "Uncle Zack" Mulhall, a showman who came into the country in 1889 as a rancher and livestock agent for the Santa Fe Railway. In the prosperous days of "Uncle Zack," it was headquarters for eighty thousand acres of ranch land in "Old Oklahoma" and across the line in the Cherokee Outlet, the home of his rodeo, and a notable center of hospitality. Out of the Mulhall rodeo forces emerged two well-known figures in the entertainment world, his own daughter Lucille, who starred as the world's first "cowgirl," and the even better-known Will Rogers.

Like the Millers (*see above*), the Mulhalls failed in ranching, the family scattered, and the last to occupy the old house was Lucille, who died just after Christmas in 1940. The ranch has been sold and the house torn down.

South from 88.4 *m.* the highway parallels the Cimarron River (L) for four miles where it breaks through the red sandstone region marked by the cliff known as the Palisades. Huge moss-covered boulders, young trees, and a tangle of shrubbery make an interesting background for the wide, and usually sand-choked bed of the river.

GUTHRIE, 95.7 *m.* (1,021 alt., 10,113 pop.), claims to be both "the Birthplace of Oklahoma" and "the Fraternal Capital of the Southwest." The first claim—elaborated on by an excellent series of locally erected markers—is one of historical fact. Guthrie was the capital of Oklahoma from the time of the organization of the Territory in 1890 to 1910, when it was removed to ("stolen by" is the local phrase) Oklahoma City. The second claim is substantiated by an expanding roster of impressive fraternal buildings. But in appearance and population, Guthrie has changed surprisingly little since its political loss. Though progressive and alert, it remains a rather picturesque reminder of the prosperous Oklahoma town at time of statehood.

The city came into existence overnight, attracting some fifteen thousand persons to the site on the day of opening. Within three weeks, what had been only a brown-painted Santa Fe depot had developed into a prairie metropolis with a functioning chamber of commerce and three newspapers. A waterworks system was operating in two months, the streets electrically lighted within four. Schools, churches, and hospitals soon followed.

Among those who have claimed Guthrie as home were such well-known early residents as General J. B. Weaver, candidate for President on the Greenback ticket in 1880; Fred G. Bonfils, later publisher of the *Denver Post;* Cassius M. Barnes, a Territorial governor of Oklahoma; Cora V. Diehl, first woman to be elected to office in Oklahoma; movie stars Lon Chaney, Tom Mix, and Will Rogers. William Wrigley made his first package of chewing gum at 113 North Division Street. Bill Tilghman, the marshal who ruled Dodge City, Bill Fossett, secret service operator and the Southwest's first G-man, and Chris Madsen, soldier of fortune and Indian fighter, were all early-day settlers in Guthrie. Edward P. Kelly, later vice-president of the Rock Island Railway, was the first city marshal.

Guthrie was also for a time the home of hatchet-wielding Carry (the family's spelling) Nation. She began her magazine-publishing experience at Guthrie in July, 1905, with *The Hatchet,* after being divorced by David Nation (lawyer, preacher, editor) on the grounds of desertion. From Guthrie, Carry sallied out to smash saloon bars, attain wide notoriety, and tour Europe with the announced intention of suppressing liquor, beer, narcotics, and tobacco in all foreign countries.

As a pleasant trade and residential center, Guthrie has become the capital of Masonry. The SCOTTISH RITE TEMPLE (*open 8–5 weekdays; 10–5 Sundays*) is the largest structure of its type in Oklahoma and said to be the largest in the world devoted exclusively to Masonic uses. Designed by J. O. Parr, Oklahoma City, and built at a cost of $2,500,000, this light-yellow brick structure of Greek Doric design is set in a ten-acre park near the eastern edge of the city. Its auditorium, with a stage sixty-two feet wide and ninety feet deep, has seats for 3,500. Its dining room accommodates fifteen hundred.

In Guthrie, too, are the STATE MASONIC HOME FOR THE AGED, Harrison Ave. between Broad and Ash Sts., the STATE MASONIC HOME FOR CHILDREN, Elm and College Sts., and the newest Masonic structure (completed in 1956), the GRAND LODGE TEMPLE, Broad St. and Oklahoma Ave.

The CITY HALL, 304 W. Oklahoma Ave., replaced (in 1955) the the old red-brick, three-story City Hall erected on the spot in 1902. (The cornerstone, topped by the old bell, remains.) The hall on the second floor of this ornately towered structure was the meeting place of the constitutional convention of 1906–1907. During the time when the Territorial and the state capital was at Guthrie, it was the scene of many official balls and banquets.

The old FEDERAL JAIL, corner of Noble Ave. and Second St., was built as a private investment and rented to the government. It has been remodeled and is used by the Nazarenes as a church building.

The CARNEGIE LIBRARY, 402 E. Oklahoma Ave., constructed of brick, stone, and marble—with a silver dome to draw the eye—was a gift from Andrew Carnegie. On its front steps C. N. Haskell, the state's first governor, took the oath of office. There, too, a symbolic marriage ceremony took place, uniting Oklahoma and Indian Territories.

JELSMA FIELD AND CITY STADIUM, Harrison Ave. and E. Springer St., is one of the largest municipal athletic plants in the state. The stadium seats five thousand.

Four city parks provide picnic and recreational facilities for Guthrie citizens. Highland, the largest of the four, contains the municipal swimming pool. Mineral Wells, on the southern edge of the city, has been the scene of speeches by two of history's more colorful figures: William Jennings Bryan, who twice addressed large audiences here; and (in 1893, when the park was only a grove of trees) Jacob S. Coxey, who later led "Coxey's Army" in a march on Washington, D.C.

East of Guthrie, three miles on State 33, is the Guthrie Golf and Country Club (*9-hole course*). Four miles southwest of Guthrie is the two-hundred-acre LAKE GUTHRIE (*daily fishing fee: 50 cents; rental boats, $2.00*).

Also east from Guthrie on State 33 (*see Tour 1A*) is BENEDICTINE HIGH SCHOOL, 2 *m.*, housed in a four-story red-brick building set in the middle of a tree-shaded seventy-acre campus. Here, until 1955 (when it was moved to Tulsa), was the Catholic College of Oklahoma, a Benedictine institution for women, founded in 1892.

Guthrie recalls its colorful and sometimes boisterous past with an annual Eighty-niner's Day celebration, held on April 22, a tribute to the hardy pioneers who settled here on that date in 1889. Festivities include street dancing, a rodeo, carnival, and an elaborate historical parade. As many as 100,000 people have lined the streets for this spectacle.

At 111.4 *m.* is the junction with US 66 (*see Tour 1*), which unites with US 77 for 10.3 miles. Right on State 77 to EDMOND, 3 *m.* (1,200 alt., 6,086 pop.) (*see Tour 1*).

At 114.9 *m.* is the western terminus (L) of the Turner Turnpike (*see Tour 1*).

In OKLAHOMA CITY, 124.3 *m.* (1,194 alt., 243,504 pop.; 1956 est., 317,500) (*see Oklahoma City*), are junctions with US 62 (*see Tour 3*) and US 270 (*see Tour 5*).

Section b. OKLAHOMA CITY *to* TEXAS LINE, 136.7 *m.* US 77

South of OKLAHOMA CITY, 0 *m.*, US 77 crosses the southern portion of old Oklahoma Territory and continues through the former Chickasaw Nation. Along the way it skirts the famed Oklahoma City oil field (L). Discovered in August of 1926 (*see Oklahoma City*), the field had 570 producing wells in 1956, with cumulative production to that time in excess of 690,000,000 barrels of oil. The highway passes the state's largest university (R), then cuts through increasingly fertile farm lands and some of Oklahoma's best ranching areas. Intensive oil-producing and refining operations line this entire section of US 77, which is featured scenically by the Arbuckle Mountains and Turner Falls.

Established in 1887, MOORE, 12.0 *m.* (1,250 alt., 942 pop.), was named for an engineer of the Santa Fe Railway. On the grounds of the consolidated school (on old US 77) is a monument to Washington Irving who, it is said, camped on the spot when he visited this region in 1832 (*see Tour 2A*).

NORMAN, 21.2 *m.* (1,160 alt., 27,006 pop.) (*see Norman*).

LEXINGTON, 37.6 *m.* (1,030 alt., 1,176 pop.), on the east side of the South Canadian River and almost in the shadow of Purcell, is a local supply point for the fine farms of the river valley.

Historically, the neighborhood is interesting as the site of one of the first military camps and trading posts established so far west in Indian Territory. Here, in the late summer of 1835, at a place called Camp Mason, was held the great council between the Five Civilized Tribes and the Plains Indians to agree on terms of peace. Five thousand met together and worked out a treaty which lasted until the Civil War. Nothing remains of either the camp or the trading post which the Chouteaus established after the great council of 1835.

After the opening in 1889, the Sand Bar Saloon was built on stilts as near as possible to the Indian Territory (prohibition) side, and a long footbridge led to dry territory. At flood stages, the saloon was washed away, but it was always rebuilt. North and east of Lexington is a reserve of 6,000 acres comprising a game-management area (quail primarily, also squirrel, dove, waterfowl), another of Oklahoma's thirteen public shooting areas.

US 77 crosses the Canadian River into PURCELL, 39.0 *m.* (1,029 alt., 3,546 pop.), on a bridge built in 1938. The first bridge, put across in 1910, was a toll affair and for a time the toll was $10. With increased traffic, it was lowered finally to $1. In 1931, when the operating company's charter expired, the legislature refused to renew it. The state took over and the toll was abolished. The town tops the steep red bluff beside the river, and its streets, shaded by fine mistletoe-hung maples, elms, and gnarled cottonwoods, slope toward Walnut Creek on the south. Purcell City Lake, in Chandler Park, provides good fishing (*fee: fifty cents a day*).

At Purcell, the river marks the northern boundary of the old Chickasaw Nation. Few Indians lived in this portion of the nation, however, and even before statehood the country was occupied mainly by white men and their families who leased land from the Chickasaws. The town was settled in 1887 when the Santa Fe came through, and was named for the engineer who surveyed the railroad's right of way through the region. The railroad's extensive switching yards lie under the highway bridge along the bank of the Canadian.

At 41.0 *m.* is the junction with State 74.

Right on this road to MAYSVILLE, 12.4 *m.* (944 alt., 1,294 pop.), long known as one of the state's principal broomcorn-producing centers. It calls itself the "Heart of the Golden Trend," after one of Oklahoma's more important recent oil discoveries.

Right (west) from Maysville on State 19 is LINDSAY, 21.4 *m.* (977 alt., 3,021 pop.), a close rival to Pauls Valley (*see below*) for the lead in development of the "Golden Trend" area. With Garvin County first in Oklahoma's production of broomcorn, and near-by Grady County (*see Chickasha, Tour 3*) second, the offices of Lindsay's broomcorn buyers are bustling financial centers at harvest time, and the world market for the crop is largely determined by the prices they pay.

At 47.0 *m.* is the junction with State 59. A marker here (R) notes the crossing of the California Trail. Caravans of gold-seekers in the rush for California traveled this trail in the spring of 1849 under a military escort commanded by Captain Randolph B. Marcy. Three miles to the west was a well-known campground and spring.

At 59.4 *m.* the route crosses the Washita River. Five miles southeast of here wagon trains on the old Boggy Depot–Fort Sill road, carrying great quantities of supplies to the western Plains Indians, forded the stream. Cattle drives to the east also used the ford from 1874 until 1887, when the Gulf, Colorado and Santa Fe Railroad reached this area.

PAULS VALLEY, 61.4 *m.* (880 alt., 6,896 pop.), is the seat of Garvin County, one of the leaders—with Stephens County (*see Tour 11*)—of Oklahoma's seventy (out of seventy-seven) oil-producing counties. The fertile Washita River valleys make Garvin County a leading producer, too, of corn, broomcorn (*see above*), alfalfa, and native pecans.

Smith Paul, the first white settler, came to the valley in 1847. He farmed thousands of acres of Indian land and the settlement became known as "Smith Paul's Valley." When the railroad arrived and the town was incorporated in 1899, the name was shortened to Pauls Valley. Trees arch over the residential streets and the town has a permanent and prosperous appearance. Wacker Park and the Old Cemetery are special points of interest. Only recently restored, the latter was used from 1868 to 1901.

One of the most colorful of Pauls Valley's early-day citizens was Moman Pruiett, the famous criminal lawyer. In his flamboyant career Pruiett defended 343 persons charged with murder, secured 303 acquittals, usually by virtue of his showmanship. The one client to receive a death sentence was eventually saved by presidential clemency.

The PAULS VALLEY STATE HOSPITAL, 65.0 *m.* (L), is an institution for mentally retarded children. Originally built as a boys reformatory in 1915, the plant was later used as an epileptic hospital. Many of the old buildings on the four-hundred-acre tract have been replaced and the present institution (established in 1953) was planned to house eventually one thousand patient-students.

WYNNEWOOD, 70.1 *m.* (847 alt., 2,423 pop.), is the center of a diversified farming region and a shipping point for livestock and pecans. The Kerr-McGee refinery (R) is Garvin County's second largest industry. In addition to ordinary refinery products, asphalt by-products for industrial use are also manufactured here.

DAVIS, 80.8 *m.* (838 alt., 1,928 pop.), on the east bank of the Washita River, was settled when the Santa Fe Railway came through in 1887. It is set at the foot of the rocky northern foothills of the Arbuckle Mountains and is the center of a good range country. The two-story NELSON CHIGLEY HOUSE (*privately owned*), on the northeastern edge of town, is a fine example of the best dwellings built by prosperous Chickasaws in Territorial days. It is a gracious colonial structure surrounded by fine old trees.

In Davis is the junction with State 7 (*see Tour 10A*).

Right on paved State 7 to the RHOADY STORE, 7 *m.*, where a cement marker (R) indicates the location (one mile south) of the INITIAL POINT, the spot from which all post–Civil War surveys of Oklahoma, except those in the three Panhandle counties, were made. The north-south line through that point is called the Indian Meridian, the east-west line the Base Line. The Initial Point marker itself is a large boulder and a pile of stones, difficult to find without a guide.

Right from this intersection on graveled State 19A to the SITE OF FORT ARBUCKLE, 7.1 *m.* Turn left across a cattle guard where a concrete marker stands. (*Visitors permitted upon request.*) Although none of the structures of the fort remains, two stone fireplaces and chimneys mark the site of the Bachelor Officers' Quarters.

This fort was established to keep order among the Plains Indians, to protect immigrant Chickasaws from their raids, and to provide assistance to California-bound travelers. Its construction was supervised by Captain Randolph B. Marcy, who escorted parties of California gold-seekers across the plains (*see above*). Completed in 1851, the fort was named for General Matthew Arbuckle, who commanded in the Indian country for many years, and for whom the low mountain range to the south was also named. Troops from Fort Towson (*see Tour 6*) were sent to Fort Arbuckle soon after it was built. Some relics and other articles from the original fort are in the possession of the Grant families, whose four modern homes occupy the site.

South of Davis, US 77 winds across the Arbuckle Mountains, a low range of limestone hills, rather sparsely covered with red cedar, soapberry, and blackjack oaks, and providing excellent short-grass pastures. This section was part of the former Chickasaw Nation, and its earliest white settlers were cattlemen who leased rangeland from the Indian owners.

Because of their age and unique formations, the Arbuckles are exceptionally interesting to geologists, providing them with the opportunity to study the types of rock formations encountered in drilling for oil in other parts of Oklahoma, as well as in Kansas and Texas. The upthrust rows of limestone and other kinds of rock have been worn away until the edges of formations, located deep beneath the earth in other areas, are exposed here for easy study.

At 85.2 *m.* is the junction with a surfaced road.

Right on this road to CAMP CLASSEN, 1.5 *m.* Built by the YMCA in 1941, it occupies a wooded tract of 220 acres. A 35-acre lake, created by damming Lick Creek, provides swimming, boating, fishing, and water sports. Marked trails for hikers crisscross the hills. There are twenty native-stone cabins for the boys. The central dining hall has two enormous fireplaces constructed of geological specimens, fossils, and petrified wood from the Arbuckle region.

Left from US 77 on a surfaced road to a Y junction, 0.1 *m.*; R. here to PRICE'S FALLS (*camping, picnicking, fishing, cabins*), 2.7 *m.*, a popular resort from which such other points of interest as Seven Sisters Falls, Burning Mountain, White Mound, and Oil Springs may be visited (*make local inquiry*).

Right from Price's Falls on an improved road to SWIMMING POOL, 3.7 *m.*, a clear basin in the rock bed of a small stream, sixty feet long and about fourteen feet wide. Below the pool is a lake created by a group of sportsmen. Certain small feeders of this lake are called spouting springs.

At 4 *m.* is the FALLS CREEK ASSEMBLY GROUNDS (*cabins, tents, lots for rent, tennis courts, swimming pool, post office*), the site of what is said to be the largest Baptist assembly in the world. The 180-acre tract contains an open tabernacle for summer meetings, which are attended by as many as twenty thousand people at a time.

CEDARVALE, 87.0 *m.*, is a resort (*cabins, swimming pool, store, shops, cafes, skating rink*) under the shadow of the high, sheer bluff (L) of Honey Creek.

The METHODIST ASSEMBLY GROUNDS (L) (*cabins, dining hall, dormitories, pavilion, swimming pool*), 87.5 *m.*, was a gift to the church by a citizen of Davis. The grounds are used by various church groups during the summer season. Hiking trails lead out over the Arbuckles toward the east. VESPER HILL and INSPIRATION POINT on its summit, where a cross has been erected, is the site of many outdoor religious services.

At 87.9 *m.* is the junction with a graveled road.

Right on this road into TURNER FALLS PARK (*cabins, free camp and picnic areas*), owned by the city of Davis and maintained in part by the State Park Service. The first primitive road into this area was begun by convicts in 1926. CCC boys finished it and constructed trails in the 1930's.

BLUE HOLE, 0.1 *m.*, has been blasted from the rock bed of Honey Creek and is filled with the cool water of that stream.

The road continues along the creek between high steep cliffs dotted with cedars to a parking place (L), 0.4 *m.* From this point a footpath with steps cut in the rocks leads to TURNER FALLS, 0.6 *m.*, where the water of Honey Creek tumbles through a rock gorge into a clear deep pool.

From another parking place, 0.9 *m.*, above the falls, there is a fine view of the surrounding mountain country.

At OBSERVATION HOUSE (*cafe, aerial cable car*), 88.8 *m.*, also overlooking Turner Falls, may be seen the peculiar striped effect on nearby hillsides of the uneven weathering of rock strata so characteristic of this region. South from this point, roadside signs indicate the various geological formations—from the Pennsylvanian and Mississippian to the Ordovician and Cambrian—that have been exposed by uplift and erosion.

At 93.8 *m.* is the junction with paved State 53.

Right on this road to WOODFORD, 8.1 *m.* (1,014 alt., 100 pop.). Right from Woodford on a mountain road to ARDMORE MOUNTAIN LAKE (*overnight or week-*

end camping not allowed), 9.3 *m.* Locally called Hickory Creek Lake, this 215-acre reservoir supplies water for the city of Ardmore (*see Ardmore*). The State Game and Fish Commission keeps it stocked with largemouthed and small-mouthed bass, bream, crappie, and perch.

US 77 now leaves the mountain country to descend to rolling pastures dotted with grazing Hereford cattle.

At 95.9 *m.* is the junction with State 77C. East on this road six miles is the ARDMORE AIR FORCE BASE. On the southwest corner of the intersection is the Ardmore Airport (*see Ardmore*).

Near the Caddo Creek bridge, 100.0 *m.*, is the PECAN RESEARCH FARM, established by the Noble Foundation (*see Tour 6*), a philanthropy of the late Sam Noble, well-known Oklahoma oilman.

At 103.0 *m.* is the junction with a graveled road.

Left on this road is CARTER SEMINARY, 0.6 *m.*, a group of gray stone buildings. Founded near Durant (*see Tour 6*) in 1852 by the Chickasaws, it was originally known as Bloomfield, a name suggested by a former Chickasaw chief because of the profusion of flowers in the surrounding fields. But the school might well have been named George Washington, for at one time it annually received $1,000, a portion of the interest derived from funds appropriated by the First Congress of the United States to pay General Washington for his Revolutionary War services. When Washington refused to accept the money, it was set aside for educational purposes.

The school was officially opened in the fall of 1852, and twenty-five girls were enrolled. They were taught English, botany, spelling, reading, and history during the regular school hours, and sewing, cooking, baking, housework, drawing, painting, and singing in the afternoons. During the Civil War, Chickasaw soldiers camped near by, using the schoolroom as a hospital and a small building in the yard as a doctor's office. Closed in May of 1863, the seminary was reopened in 1876 as a girls' high school. The government took it over, along with all other Chickasaw tribal schools in 1906. After a fire had destroyed most of the buildings in 1914, Bloomfield was moved to Ardmore. Supported by federal funds, the school is quartered in ten buildings—part of the old Hargrove Methodist College, which the government purchased in 1916—and has a student enrollment of 130. As do the children of Jones Academy (*see Tour 5*), the girls at Carter attend the Ardmore public schools.

ARDMORE, 104.7 *m.* (872 alt., 17,890 pop.) (*see Ardmore*), is at the junction with US 70 (*see Tour 6*).

Right from the corner of Main and Washington Streets, in Ardmore, south on Washington Street, to LAKE MURRAY STATE PARK (*26-room lodge, 78 cabins, swimming, boating, fishing, camp and picnic areas*), 3.9 *m.* Centered around 6,000-acre Lake Murray, this wooded park covers 21,000 acres and is the largest and most completely equipped of the thirteen areas in the State Parks system. A full-time recreational director presides over vacation activities that range from hiking, riding, and badminton to speedboating, sailboating, aquaplaning, swimming, and fishing. The boat-dock sector is well equipped to serve all fishing needs.

At the entrance gate is a Y junction. The park road to the left leads to the group camps. The road to the right serves access roads leading to the lodge and cabin area, the stables, the boat docks, and other park facilities. TUCKER TOWER (*museum*), 13.7 *m.*, set on the top of a rocky crag that juts into the lake, is one of the most beautiful spots in the park. Eighty-five feet of water lie directly under the long porch of the tower building. South of the tower, and northeast of LAKE MURRAY DAM, 15.2 *m.*, is the lake area where motorboat races are held.

The OKLAHOMA VETERANS HOME, 105.4 *m.*, was established (R) in Territorial days at McAlester, under the sponsorship of Dr. D. M. Hailey, founder of Haileyville (*see Tour 5*), and J. J. McAlester, founder of McAlester (*see Tour 5*). When public subscriptions proved inadequate, it became a state-supported institution. It was moved to its present site in 1910. A broad, tree-lined drive leads across the well-improved grounds to the home.

At 11.8 *m.* is the junction (L) with State 77 leading to Lake Murray State Park (*see above*).

MARIETTA, 121.4 *m.* (846 alt., 1,875 pop.), a farm center, is the seat of Love County. The nucleus of the town was a little shack that served as the station of the Santa Fe Railway, which built its tracks through in 1887. The site of Marietta, and the surrounding area, was then in the possession of two Chickasaws, Jerry and Bill Washington. Jerry Washington's wife was named Marietta, and it was in her honor that the Santa Fe named the town.

South of Marietta two types of roadside "attractions" beckon. The first is a characteristic phenomenon of legally dry Oklahoma: the beer tavern. Common throughout the state, they are particularly numerous on the Sooner State side of the boundary with near-by Texas counties that are (by local option) totally dry. The second attraction—and one that also offers liquid refreshment—is the open roadside stand with its bottles of apple, cherry, and grape ciders gleaming cheerfully in the sun.

At 134.8 *m.* is the junction with an improved road.

Right on this road is the old REFUGE SPRING, 1.2 *m.*, the burial ground of many early Texas outlaws. The white cedar trees, set out about 1840, formed an approximate boundary between Texas and Oklahoma. When an outlaw, fleeing from Texas, reached this spot, he was presumably safe. For many of them, however, especially those who had been wounded by pursuing posses, it proved only a temporary sanctuary.

US 77 crosses the Red River to the TEXAS LINE, 136.7 *m.*, on a long bridge, eight miles north of Gainesville, Texas (*see Texas Guide*).

TOUR 10A

Davis—Sulphur—Platt National Park—Junction US 70; State 7, State 18, Perimeter Blvd., 38.9 m.

Roadbed asphalt paved.
Jordan Transportation Co. Bus Line follows route between Davis and Sulphur.
Excellent accommodations at Sulphur; free campgrounds in park, but no cabins.

East of DAVIS, 0 *m.* (838 alt., 1,928 pop.) (*see Tour 10*), State 7 proceeds eastward from its junction with US 77 (*see Tour 10*) and passes through rolling hilly country to SULPHUR, 8.3 *m.* (976 alt., 4,389 pop.), a pleasure and health resort with something of the appearance of a continental spa. Rock Creek flows through the town and divides it into East and West Sulphur, each section having its own business and residential sections. In East Sulphur are the city hall and the larger hotels. In West Sulphur are the Murray County Courthouse and county offices. Mineral water—with sulphur and iron content—is plentiful and is used in many of the numerous swimming pools, and in the Artesian Bath House. But the town's entire water supply comes from deep, flowing wells. Aside from health and recreation facilities, Sulphur also depends economically on its famed Hereford Heaven ranches and its surrounding dairy farms.

In Sulphur is the OKLAHOMA SCHOOL FOR THE DEAF, where the state provides instruction through high school for boys and girls whose lack of hearing makes impossible attendance at regular public schools. Academic work is supplemented with industrial and vocational training.

At 8.7 *m.* is the junction with State 18, which the tour follows south (R) through PLATT NATIONAL PARK (*three campgrounds*). The park, lying south of the junction, covers an area of 912 acres and accommodates more than one million visitors annually, giving it a third-place ranking among the national parks in travel popularity. There are thirty-one of the larger springs in the park (water is free)—eighteen sulphur, four iron, three bromide, and six fresh water. There are also several smaller springs. The tract was formerly included in the territory of the Chickasaw Nation, and a large part of it was purchased from the Indians by the federal government in 1902, the year the park was established. First named Sulphur Springs Reservation, it was renamed in 1906 for U.S. Senator Orville Hitchcock Platt, of Connecticut, member of the Senate Committee on Indian Affairs (1879–1905).

From early spring to late fall, colorful wild flowers are abundant here—Spanish larkspur, Virginia creeper, primrose, blue salvia, goldenrod, redbud, and the briery, pink-flowered cat's-claw, locally known as gander's teeth. Five or six varieties of cactus, native to the state and the Southwest, grow among the rocks on the hillsides, and in the creek valleys are many varieties of trees. Wrens, herons, cardinals, meadow larks, horned larks, sparrow hawks, brown thrashers, and many other birds frequent the region seasonally. Raccoons, opossums, skunks, rabbits, and squirrels are found in or near the park.

TRAVERTINE CREEK, 8.9 *m.*, is crossed on a stone bridge.

At 9.0 *m.* is the junction with Perimeter Boulevard, over which the route continues due west (R), making an elongated circle through the park and returning to this junction.

Travertine Creek (R), which parallels Perimeter Boulevard for a short distance, is spanned by LINCOLN BRIDGE, 9.1 *m.*, a footbridge constructed of white limestone blocks, with turrets at each end. Across the bridge is FLOWER PARK, comprising five acres of cleared land. A small, shallow stream, formed by diverting the overflow from Vendome Plunge, a swimming pool near by, flows through the area.

The boulevard crosses ROCK CREEK, 9.2 *m.*, the largest stream in the park. On the summit of a small knoll (R), just west of the Rock Creek bridge, are BLACK SULPHUR SPRINGS, which have an extremely strong sulphur content. The spring's pavilion, constructed of stone covered with rough stucco, is hexagonal in shape, with open sides and slender pillars supporting the sloping roof.

A large open pavilion (L) at BROMIDE SPRINGS AREA, 10.0 *m.*, houses medicinal springs. CCC workers built the stone structure surrounded by a flagged terrace. The varieties of mineral water obtainable here are indicated by labels on the faucets. There is a small museum near the Bromide pavilion.

ROCK CREEK CAMPGROUNDS (*trailer and tent accommodations, picnic facilities*), within the area, is well shaded.

South of the pavilion, a trail leads to the bottom of BROMIDE CLIFF (1,050 alt.), which rises 140 feet above the creek. Trails, with bridges and retaining walls, lead from this point along the sides and to the summit of the cliff. Near by are three springs that supply water to the pavilion. A larger spring boils up in the center of Rock Creek.

Perimeter Boulevard again crosses Rock Creek, 10.1 *m.*, winds around the western side of the cliff, and ascends to the top of the hill which forms the precipice.

At 10.4 *m.* is a junction with a paved road.

Right on this road to VETERANS LAKE (*state fishing license required*), 0.1 *m.*, which covers 115 acres and has a maximum depth of eighty feet. The lake is restocked each year.

A PARKING AREA (L), 10.5 *m.*, is near the highest point in the park. Several foot trails from here across the summit of Bromide Cliff to COUNCIL ROCK, locally called Robbers' Roost, offering a wide view of the park and the town of Sulphur. Here various Indian tribes lighted their signal fires or held councils of war or peace. A hiking trail leads from the rock down the cliff to Bromide Springs Pavilion.

The BUFFALO PASTURE (*no trespassing*), 11.5 *m.*, is a large area (L) where a small herd of buffalo is maintained.

At 11.7 *m.* is the junction with State 18. The route continues east on Perimeter Boulevard and climbs a ridge. At the top, 12.0 *m.*, is a view of the STATE VETERANS HOSPITAL (R), a group of brick, cottage-like buildings trimmed with white, except for the administration building, which is a square limestone structure. The grounds are landscaped, with well-kept lawns and cedars.

The road descends a slope to Travertine Creek (L), which it parallels for two miles. Wild flowers grow in profusion and dense growths of oak and elm trees shade the valleys.

TRAVERTINE ISLAND (L), 13.4 *m.*, was formed by the "looping" of Travertine Creek. At the eastern end of the island is LITTLE NIAGARA, a waterfall over a rock formation in the creek.

BUFFALO SPRINGS (*picnic facilities*), 14.3 *m.*, is one of the two sources of Travertine Creek. The springs (L) boil up through a bed of sand, flecked with patches of green moss. Curving to the left in a hairpin turn, Perimeter Boulevard rounds the springs to parallel the north side of the creek and continues westward. ANTELOPE SPRINGS, 14.7 *m.*, the other source of Travertine Creek, flows from a small rock hill (L). Both Antelope and Buffalo Springs are fresh-water sources and are often dry, though normally they flow about five million gallons daily.

Travertine Island, 15.4 *m.*, is passed again (L) as the road proceeds southwestward.

Two adjoining SWIMMING POOLS, 15.8 *m.*, have been made by damming the creek. Near-by COLD SPRINGS CAMPGROUNDS, 15.9 *m.*, has floodlight illumination.

At 16.8 *m.* is the junction with State 18, which now again becomes the route.

Left on State 18 to PAVILION SPRINGS, 17.0 *m.*, where there is a pavilion (L) of native stone and handhewn timbers used for community gatherings. North of the winding, flagged walk leading to the building are HILLSIDE SPRINGS, from which a large volume of water flows.

South of the South Gate, 17.6 *m.*, of Platt National Park, State 18 continues to a junction with US 70 (*see Tour 6*) at 38.9 *m.*

TOUR 11

(Caldwell, Kan.)—Enid—El Reno—Chickasha—Duncan—(Ringgold, Tex.); US 81, Kansas Line to Texas Line, 230.7 m.

Roadbed paved throughout.
Rock Island Ry. parallels the route.
Good accommodations all along the way.

Throughout its course in Oklahoma, US 81 has for historical background the old Chisholm Trail, the best known of the several trails beaten out by the millions of Texas longhorns driven to Kansas railroads and more northern Indian reservations in the two and one-half decades following the Civil War. Beginning with a mere thirty-five thousand head of cattle sent up the trails in 1867, the number rose year by year to a peak, in the eighties, of more than five hundred thousand a season. An estimated ten million cattle passed over the Chisholm Trail during the quarter of a century it was in use.

Much of the trail was first cut by a trader named Jesse Chisholm who, in 1865, conducted a trading expedition from Wichita, Kansas, to the Indians living in the Wichita Mountains area of Indian Territory. When the northward flood of cattle began a few years later, Chisholm's trail proved to be the most feasible for drivers who needed plentiful water and good grazing for their herds. Then, too, as an 1871 advertisement pointed out, the Chisholm Trail was shorter than the others, the streams were "narrow and more easily forded . . . and as the trail is through thinly settled country, drovers are not subject to molestation by settlers, have no taxes to pay, and . . . no ferriage is necessary."

So long was this trail used that a great body of tradition grew up around it. And there was hot controversy—long after trail driving had become history—as to its exact route and the man for whom it was named. (Much of the confusion stems from the fact that a Texas–New Mexico cattleman, John Chisum, also pioneered trails that bore his name.) But the original Chisholm Trail remains, in fact as well as in fancy. For that favorite cowboy song which opens with the couplet,

Come along, boys, and listen to my tale,
I'll tell you a story of the old Chisholm Trail,

is known wherever cowboy lore is known and loved. And that, thanks to an apparently undying juke-box popularity, is throughout the country. Two other couplets of that endless jog-trot classic express the ambition of the tired cowboy after the herd had been loaded on the cars in Kansas,

I'm goin' down south, not a-jokin' nor a-lyin'
I'm goin' down south just a-whoopin' an' a-flyin'

I'm goin' down south for to marry me a squaw,
An' live on the bank of the Little Washitaw.

With the opening to settlement of Old Oklahoma, in 1889, and the southward building of the Rock Island Railway, which reached Texas in 1892, the trail ceased to function as a cattle highway. Yet even today, eroded and weed-grown traces of these wide-spreading and rutted paths made by the longhorns can still be found.

But US 81 has more than historical interest. It also serves a varied and prosperous section of Oklahoma. In the old Cherokee Outlet to the north are the broad, level wheat fields that justify the description of the area around Enid as the state's breadbasket. Farther south is the territory in which many of the border disputes between white pioneers and Indians led to battles and skirmishes, where the farmer gained a foothold against the ranchman and finally supplanted him. Somewhere in the neighborhood of Chickasha, wheat begins to give way to cotton, corn, sorghum grains, orchards, alfalfa, and vineyards. Then, after a stretch of rough country between the Arbuckles and the Wichitas, the route approaches the Red River bottom lands where cotton and other crops again take over.

It has taken little more than a half-century to change completely the character of the country and of the people along US 81. The Indian-Pioneer phase has passed and is already only a dramatic memory.

US 81 crosses the KANSAS LINE, 0 *m.*, 2.7 miles south of Caldwell, Kansas (*see Kansas Guide*), and cuts south across the west-central portion of the state.

MEDFORD, 14.9 *m.* (1,087 alt., 1,305 pop.), seat of Grant County, is at the northern edge of the most productive wheat-growing region in the state.

Out of the town and into national prominence as fliers came the brothers Apollo and Zeus Soucek. About 1918, as boys of ten and twelve, they constructed a homemade glider plane and started it in flight by mule power. In 1930, as an officer of the naval air force, Apollo established an American record for altitude, 43,165 feet. His brother Zeus, also a navy flier, designed some of the equipment used in his flights.

The small farming center of JEFFERSON, 21.9 *m.* (1,047 alt., 179 pop.), was originally called Pond Creek. The name was changed when the settlement four miles to the south proved its claim to being the site of Pond Creek station on the old stage route from Kansas to Fort Sill.

At 22.4 *m.*, the tall elm and cottonwood trees (L. one-quarter of a mile) marked the site of ROCK ISLAND PARK. Originally it was an eighty-acre allotment taken by a Cherokee in the outlet and later turned over to a townsite company. When the railroad came, however, the station was built too far away to make the townsite valuable, and its few residents moved to Jefferson.

A marker, 22.6 *m.*, indicates the SITE OF SEWELL'S STOCKADE (L. three-fourths of a mile), which was one of the stopping places for trail drivers. (At near-by Round Pond are perhaps the most clearly visible signs of the Chisholm Trail.) Sewell built the stockade in the early 1870's for protection against Osage Indian mourning parties and war raiders. The Osage Black Dog war trail crossed the Salt Fork of the Arkansas just one mile south of here.

It was an Osage custom to bury with a tribesman the scalps he had taken. To send a warrior into the next world without at least one scalp was considered a tragedy. But as intertribal warfare waned, scalp-taking became more and more uncommon, and the problem of getting the necessary trophy to bury with the dead man more and more acute. And so arose the custom of sending out secret "mourning parties" to bring in the all-important scalp. And since the killing of a Pawnee or other Indian could easily lead to war, the scalps of isolated white men were in steady demand.

US 81 crosses the SALT FORK of the Arkansas River, 23.8 *m.*, which drains the Great Salt Plains (*see Tour 2*).

At 25.1 *m.* is the junction with an improved dirt road.

Left on this road, across the railroad tracks, 0.3 *m.*; in a field (L) is the SITE OF THE POND CREEK STAGE STATION on the Chisholm Trail. In the days of the cattle drives there was a broad, deep lake here. But a short time before the opening of the Cherokee Outlet (1893) to settlement, cattlemen who had the area under lease drained the lake. Still later, it was filled in.

On a little knoll about two hundred yards to the right of the stage station site are the GRAVES OF TWO PIONEERS. One of them, Tom Best, was slain by an Osage funeral party in 1872. The other, a man named Chambers, was an Osage victim in 1874. Their graves were marked in 1889.

POND CREEK, 26.1 *m.* (1,050 alt., 1,066 pop.), at the time of the opening of Old Oklahoma to settlement in 1889 was the southern terminus of the Rock Island Railway and was known as Round Pond. As the April 22 opening day drew near, the Rock Island engaged D. R. Green, owner of a half-dozen rickety old stagecoaches, to carry those who meant to make the Run to the border. One of the last trains to arrive before the opening was from Chicago, and Green, in his "Leadville Cannon Ball" stagecoach, with a long caravan of coaches, wagons, hacks, buggies, and buckboards drawn up behind him, awaited the unloading of the train. Then at last came the rush to the border, nearly forty miles away. And though railway workers had repaired somewhat the rutted prairie road, the ride was a memorable experience.

In Pond Creek is the northern junction with US 60 (*see Tour 4*), which unites with US 81 for 23.8 miles. At 30.1 *m.*, four miles west of Pond Creek, is the junction with US 64 (*see Tour 2*), which unites with US 81 for 18.7 miles.

South of Pond Creek the highway crosses a long stretch of gently rolling land that is the center of the state's greatest wheat-growing district. On these nearly level, deep-loam acres, the stretches of wheat are like a vast carpet through the winter. With the coming of spring they grow quickly to a knee-deep luxuriance of green. And by harvest time in June they are a tapestry of golden yellow. Only around the farmhouses are there any trees. To the south, the solid gray towers of Enid's terminal elevators loom up impressively out of the flat landscape.

ENID, 49.9 *m.* (1,246 alt., 36,017 pop.) (*see Enid*), is at the southern junction with US 60 (*see Tour 4*) and with US 64 (*see Tour 2*).

WAUKOMIS, 57.3 *m.* (1,264 alt., 537 pop.), is the center of another wheat-growing area.

At 61.8 *m.* is the old BUFFALO SPRINGS water hole (R), another favorite stopping place on the Chisholm Trail.

HENNESSEY, 69.9 *m.* (1,162 alt., 1,264 pop.), was laid out in 1889 and named for Patrick Hennessey, a freighter on the Chisholm Trail. On July 4, 1874, Hennessey's three-wagon outfit was attacked by Indians at what is now the northwest corner of the town. Hennessey, George Fand, Thomas Caloway, and Ed Cook were killed, and their wagons, loaded with coffee and sugar for the Kiowa-Comanche Agency, were burned. His grave (R), three blocks from the highway, is enclosed by an iron fence, and a rough-stone memorial in the form of a lighthouse twenty-four feet high has been erected. Three blocks south of Hennessey High School is the SITE OF BULL FOOT STAGE STATION. The building was burned the day Hennessey was killed.

Roy Cashion, of Hennessey, a trooper in the First United States Volunteer Cavalry (Rough Riders) in the Spanish-American War of 1898, was one of the first young men of Oklahoma to give their lives for their country on foreign soil. He was killed in the battle for San Juan Hill and a towering monument to him is in Memorial Park.

Known for a time during the trail drives as Red Fork Ranch, DOVER, 79.2 *m.* (1,033 alt., 400 pop.), was a stage station where freighters on the Chisholm Trail changed teams. It was then no more than a stockade inside of which lived a stock tender named Chapin. Among those who stopped here was General Philip H. Sheridan on his way to Fort Supply (*see Tour 12*).

Freighters hauling supplies to Indian Territory forts over the Chisholm Trail were compelled so often to detour to avoid the herds being driven north that a separate freight trail was finally beaten out. It branched southwest at Red Fork Ranch, then dropped south to forts Reno, Cobb, and Sill.

Near the spot where US 81 crosses the CIMARRON RIVER, 81.3 *m.*, occurred in September of 1906 one of Oklahoma's most serious railroad wrecks. A wooden bridge gave way, dumping all but the sleeping cars of a Rock Island passenger train into the river. Some of the train crew and passengers, along with the train itself, were lost. Ordinarily almost dry, with its wide bed little more than a stretch of blowing sand, the Cimarron is like most western Oklahoma rivers, treacherous with quicksands and likely to become a devastating torrent after heavy rainfalls. The bridge which replaced the wrecked one is of steel construction and its piers are sunk to bedrock.

The parents of the notorious Dalton Boys, outlaws whose exploits have been widely publicized in print and on the screen, were among the homesteaders near Dover. The mother was living on the farm at the time two of her sons were killed and a third seriously wounded in the attempted Coffeyville (*see Kansas Guide*) bank robbery on October 5, 1892.

A cattleman named King Fisher gave his name to KINGFISHER, 88.2 *m.* (1,060 alt., 3,345 pop.), where he operated a stage line and maintained a stage station. The name was also selected for one of the five original counties comprising Old Oklahoma. Locally, the town is known as "the golden buckle of the wheat belt."

In the neighborhood of Kingfisher the Chisholm Trail was deeply rutted through the level prairie. At the time of the Run, April 22, 1889, these ruts were still so deep and narrow that, overgrown as they were with grass, vehicles making the race for homesteads were sometimes wrecked and horses' legs broken. An old-timer, describing some of the big herds on the trail, has said that more than once as a boy he watched a single herd passing his father's home from sunrise to sunset.

OKARCHE, 97.8 *m.* (1242.9 alt., 532 pop.), sprang up around a cattle-loading station on the Rock Island Railroad following the opening by run of the Cheyenne and Arapaho reservation on April 19, 1892. As German-speaking Catholics, Lutherans, Evangelicals, and Mennonites moved onto the rich farms in the area the town became—and remains in part to this day—a close-knit German community. Aside from the ubiquitous wheat-country elevators, Okarche's principle structures are church-owned. Both the Catholics and the Lutherans maintain parochial schools.

At 107.4 *m.* is the junction with an asphalt-paved road.

Right on this tree-lined road to CONCHO, 2.2 *m.*, the administrative center of the 5,280-acre Cheyenne and Arapaho Indian reservation. The twenty-six frame and brick buildings comprising the CHEYENNE-ARAPAHO AREA FIELD OFFICE form a rectangular group overlooking a wooded canyon which was once a favorite camping place for freighters because of its springs. First established in 1869 at a point 2.5 miles southeast of the present location and near the North Canadian River, the place was known as the DARLINGTON AGENCY, for Brinton Darlington, a Quaker appointed to administer the affairs of the combined tribes. Darlington also opened a school there for the Arapahoes. Although the Cheyennes and the Arapahoes had been associated in war together, they desired separate schools. For this reason an institution expressly for the Cheyennes, located at Caddo Springs (now Concho), was founded in 1897. The two-story red-brick building (now abandoned) just east of Darlington near the railroad, housed for a time a Cheyenne-Arapaho mission operated by the Mennonites.

Darlington Agency itself was abandoned in 1909 and the office moved to Concho, which had been named by the railroad in establishing a switch there. Its site is now the ninety-five-acre STATE GAME FARM (*visitors restricted to administrative buildings*). In 1955 more than 94,000 quail and 28,000 pheasant were raised here and distributed throughout the state, many of them to be reared by contract with local sportsmen's clubs.

The CHEYENNE AND ARAPAHO BOARDING SCHOOL, near the field office, is reached by following a winding road which crosses the deepest part of the canyon by means of an elevated footbridge. The canyon valley (*visiting by permission of the superintendent*) has been developed into a park and recreation area.

This is the only Cheyenne and Arapaho educational institution operating today. A faculty of forty-six teachers and other workers, all civil service employees, instruct about two hundred Indian boys and girls, many of them in recent years Navajos from Arizona. In addition to the regular school curriculum, trades, home economics, and farming are taught. The school maintains a large experimental farm. Help offered to the adult Indians by the agency includes conservation and farming advice for the men, training in domestic science and nursing for the women. There is a clinic which, in addition to the hospital at Clinton (*see Tour 1*), serves all members of the two tribes.

Symbolic of the Plains Indians' gradual transition to the white man's way of life is the disappearance of most of the traditional tribal assemblies at Concho. Two annual events, a May Day Celebration and a Labor Day Festival, drew thousands of Cheyennes and Arapahoes to the agency until comparatively recent times. At these celebrations the weird Owl Dance, the gay Rabbit Dance, and the light and fast Kick Ball Dance were regular features. Against a throbbing background of tomtoms and clapping hands, the painted bodies and vivid costumes of the dancers made the scene a colorful display of rhythm and grace. Today, however, the Cheyenne-Arapaho Powwow (*visitors welcome*) is usually held in near-by El Reno (*see Tour 1*) in August or September. Concho itself has but one big tribal gathering. It is more in the nature of a modern corporation's annual meeting of stockholders. Held the first Wednesday of October, the all-day affair features the yearly report of the Tribal Business Committee, which then serves beef and other dishes to the members of the tribe.

The legendary Sun Dance, a symbolic religious ritual, has been practiced in various forms by most of the Plains tribes, but because of the self-mutilation which was a part of the original ceremony, its presentation has been prohibited by the government. The Cheyennes, however, still perform a modified Sun Dance in the second week of August on one of their ranches west of Canton (*see Tour 5*). As done today, the dance retains the religious significance but not the torture of the former rite, in which volunteer warriors inserted sticks through open gashes in their skin and then dragged behind them heavy burdens tied to the sticks with lariat ropes. The purpose of the self-sacrifice was to display to the Great Spirit the willingness of the brave youthful warriors to bear the burdens and sorrows for the older and weaker members of the tribe. The chief's call upon the Great Spirit to watch the proceeding was directed to the sun, which served as an intercessor. Seven Cheyenne braves danced two days and three nights at the 1956 Sun Dance.

At 108.4 *m.* is the junction (R) with an improved road. West here two miles to the STATE GAME FARM (*see above*).

EL RENO, 112.0 *m.* (1,363 alt., 10,991 pop.) (*see Tour 1*), is at the junction with US 66–270 (*see Tours 1 and 5*), with which US 77 joins for 2.2 miles.

South of El Reno the country is somewhat more broken as the route approaches the South Canadian River.

UNION CITY, 122.5 *m.* (1,321 alt., 301 pop.), is a trading point (R) for farmers and small ranchers.

At 124.5 *m.* the route crosses the broad red-banked South Canadian River into the old Chickasaw Nation, whose extreme western edge it then skirts. Few of the tribe ever lived so far west, however, and the region was occupied before allotment by cattlemen. Some of the latter had married Chickasaw wives and had thus become adopted citizens. Most of them, however, operated ranches on leases or were simply intruders brazenly defying tribal laws.

MINCO, 128.4 *m.* (1,538 alt., 978 pop.), began in 1889 and the railroad arrived the following year. Three grain elevators emphasize the importance of wheat in the area's agricultural picture. ALTA META

Some Oklahomans

A Favorite Sport.

(*above*) Sunday Morning Service.

(*below*) Saturday Night in Town.

Oil Well Driller.

(*above*) Jet Acrobatics, National Air Show at Oklahoma City.

(*below*) At the Football Game, University of Oklahoma, Norman

(*above*) Easter Pageant, near Lawton.

(*below*) Workers in Electric Products Plant, Shawnee.

(*above*) Excitement at the Rodeo

(*below*) Eighty-niner Celebration, Guthrie.

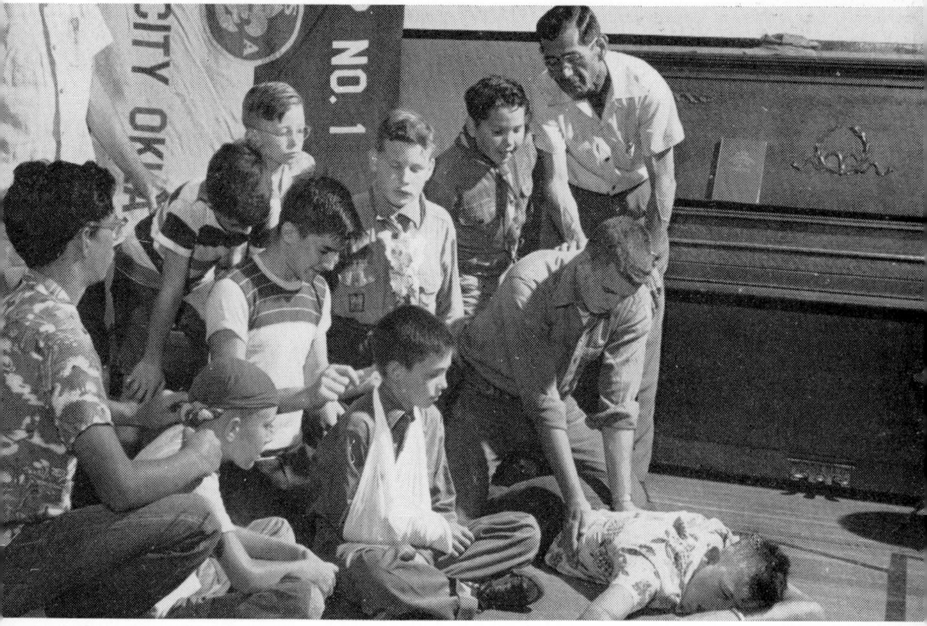

(*above*) In the Little Leagues.

(*below*) First-aid Training, Boy Scout Safety Program.

(*above*) AT THE WOOLAROC MUSEUM, near Bartlesville.

(*below*) STUDENTS, University of Tulsa.

Bond Park honors the college by that name which was located in early-day Minco.

Left from Minco on asphalt-paved State 37 is TUTTLE, 8.6 *m.* (1,296 alt., 715 pop.). A twelve-ton boulder in the schoolyard (L) on the eastern edge of town marks the course of the Chisholm Trail and the Site of Silver City Trading Post. A bronze tablet states that the community's first school and burying ground were two miles north. "Dedicated to ranchmen, cowboys, early settlers, and their descendants," the tablet bears the names of 112 pioneers. It was placed there by the Daughters of the American Revolution.

Left from Tuttle on an improved dirt road to the south bank of the South Canadian River and the Site of Silver City, 1.6 *m.*, one of the important halts and trading points on the old cattle trail. Early ranchers in the neighborhood found it necessary to herd their cattle and horses, and pen them at night, to prevent their being drifted away by grazing buffalo herds. Negro and Indian herders were allegedly hired over white cowboys because of the preference for white scalps on the part of raiding Kiowas and Comanches. Though Silver City once boasted a store, hotel, and post office, only the cemetery remains.

Named for a village in Massachusetts, POCASSET, 136.8 *m.* (1,197 alt., 260 pop.), was the point at which Al Jennings—successively lawyer, train robber, convict, candidate for governor of Oklahoma, amateur evangelist, and author—once led his gang in the holdup of a train. In attempting to blow open the safe in the baggage and express car, the job was bungled and the whole car blown up. Not wanting to go away empty handed, Al and his fellows robbed the passengers of jewelry and some $400 in cash. Then salvaging from the wrecked car a bunch of bananas and a two-gallon jug of whisky, they rode away.

Near the crossing of the WASHITA RIVER, 145.4 *m.*, is the Chickasha Municipal Airport.

At 146.1 *m.* is the junction with US 62 (*see Tour 3*), which US 81 joins (L) for 1.3 miles.

CHICKASHA, 147.4 *m.* (1,116 alt., 15,842 pop.) (*see Tour 3*).

At 151.4 *m.* is the junction with paved State 19.

Left on this road is the Site of the Stage Station, 1 *m.*, where the Boggy Depot–Fort Sill road crossed the Chisholm Trail. This stand, known as Fred, was a trading point and an overnight stop. It was at first located on the Washita River at the Trail crossing (*see Tour 3*).

A favorite camping place for trail drivers, RUSH SPRINGS, 166.8 *m.* (1,291 alt., 1,402 pop.), got its name from the springs which form the source of near-by Rush Creek. One of these fine springs is at the center of the Municipal Park. The town is the market place for a farming district in which watermelons are a principal crop. Rush Springs usually stages an annual watermelon festival in August.

Five miles southeast of Rush Springs, on October 1, 1858, occurred the Battle of the Wichita Village, one of the tragedies of the conflict between the whites and the Indians. At the urging of Wichita Indians, who were friendly with the whites, a considerable body of Comanches were on their way to Fort Arbuckle (*see Tour 10*) to discuss peace terms. While in camp, the Comanches were attacked at dawn by a force of cavalry under Captain Van Dorn from Fort Belknap, Texas, supported by one hundred friendly Indian scouts. Surprised and outnumbered, the Comanches lost practically all of their warriors, seventy in number. Five of Van Dorn's command were killed and a number wounded. In the Captain's defense it was said that he knew nothing of the Comanches' mission and that he was under orders to find and exterminate these tribesmen for their recent raids into Texas.

At 173.0 *m.* MT. SCOTT, highest point in southern Oklahoma (*see Tour 3B*), is visible to the west.

Although MARLOW, 176.1 *m.* (1,308 alt., 3,399 pop.), is now a peaceful, law-abiding center for a prosperous farming community, with wide streets, pleasant parks, good homes, and modern schools, it was named for a family of outlaws. According to local tradition, the five Marlow brothers lived in the brush on Wildhorse Creek near the present townsite. Since this was also near the Chisholm Trail, the Marlow boys developed the nocturnal custom of raiding the herds coming up from Texas and driving off longhorns to the timber twelve or fifteen miles east of the trail. In a day or two they would then drive the cattle back to the herd, claim they had found them straying or in possession of cattle thieves, and collect a suitable reward. Finally becoming suspicious, the cattlemen set a trap for them and wiped out the band.

With the coming of the Rock Island Railway, about 1892, a station was established here and, at the request of men living near by, it was called Marlow. Five oil fields were developed around Marlow in the late 1940's.

In Marlow, in the triangle formed by the junction of US 81 with State 29, is a MONUMENT TO ALL OKLAHOMA PEACE OFFICERS. Its erection was inspired by the killing of Sheriff W. A. Williams near the spot in 1930. The pear-shaped memorial was cut from pink granite quarried in the Wichita Mountains (*see Tour 3*).

DUNCAN, 186.2 *m.* (1,131 alt., 15,325 pop.), was named for a trader, William Duncan, once a tailor at Fort Sill, who settled near by in 1872 after marrying a citizen of the Chickasaw Nation. In 1889, when it became known that the Rock Island Railway was coming through from the north, Mrs. Duncan—acting under her tribal rights—selected as a farm a five-hundred-acre tract in the path of the rails.

Three years later, with the depot built and the townsite laid out, Mrs. Duncan sold lots on the understanding that when it became possible to give title legally she would do so. The promise was carried out after allotment, and when the Kiowa-Comanche reservation was opened to settlement in 1901, an additional tract of 540 acres was added to the original townsite.

If not exactly typical, the Duncan story is at least strongly characteristic of municipal growth and development in oil-rich Oklahoma. In 1920, it was a village of some 3,000 persons, dependent on agriculture. Then in 1921, oil came to Duncan, followed almost immediately by industry. It was here that Erle P. Halliburton originated and developed his now famous oil-well cementing business, a business which now operates in twenty-three states and thirteen foreign countries. Other petroleum industries followed—drilling and pipeline concerns (one local firm owns and operates 330 miles of pipelines), oil-well supply houses, and service and transport companies.

By 1940, Duncan had grown to nine thousand. Then in 1947 new oil discoveries at levels over a mile deep started a new industrial growth cycle. In 1956, four large refineries operated in the Duncan area, employing more than seven hundred people. (Some 4,500 producing oil and gas wells have been drilled in all of Stephens County, which, in 1954, produced 20 per cent of all Oklahoma's vast oil output.) With 1,750 of its four thousand employees living in Duncan, the Halliburton Company is still the city's largest and most important single industry. Many of its vast service facilities and its new Technical Center lie alongside US 81 (L) south of Duncan.

Duncan has also progressed in other respects. During the first half of the 1950's an average of thirty-five new homes were built each month. Schools have been rapidly expanded to take care of more than 4,500 students. Park and recreational facilities have grown with the population. Two lakes to the northeast—Duncan and Clear Creek—provide fishing and boating.

COMANCHE, 195.6 *m.* (983 alt., 2,083 pop.), is a wide-spreading town rimmed on the north and east by an extensive shallow-well oil field. Discovered in 1920, it now includes 4,900 proven acres. Before the coming of the railroad in 1892, Comanche was called Wilson Town in honor of a member of the Chickasaw tribe. It started as a trade center for a large ranching area in both the old Chickasaw Nation and the Kiowa-Comanche reservation in which stockmen leased range for their cattle at the rate of twenty-five cents per head. After allotment, settlers came in and the region became primarily one of farms.

A market town for near-by farmers and ranchers, ADDINGTON,

204.1 *m.* (915 alt., 174 pop.), is made up of a few brick business buildings and scattered residences.

Left from Addington (east) two miles is the 18,000-acre Henry Price ranch, with its imposing white colonial residence surrounded by rich grasslands that were settled upon in 1886 by J. C. Price. The Chisholm Trail cut across what is now the Price ranch, and Price himself drove cattle through the area before settling down to ranching. On the ranch is MONUMENT HILL, a well-known landmark on the Chisholm Trail. A clear spring near by, its position conveniently located at the end of a drive north from the Red River, made the hill a popular camp site with northbound trail drivers. Succeeding campers added rocks to the "hill" until by 1893 they had actually erected a sizable monument.

At 209.8 *m.* is the junction with US 70 (*see Tour 6*).

An old town fighting stubbornly for existence is the way RYAN, 220.8 *m.* (833 alt., 1,019 pop.), has been described. It has never recovered from the year-long fight it lost to Waurika (*see Tour 6*) in 1908 for the seat of Jefferson County.

TERRAL, 229.0 *m.* (849 alt., 616 pop.), was named for a preacher who was responsible for laying out the townsite when the railroad came through in 1892.

At 230.7 *m.* US 81 crosses the Red River and the Oklahoma-Texas Line four miles north of Ringgold, Texas (*see Texas Guide*).

TOUR 12

(Ashland, Kan.)—Woodward—Seiling—Frederick—(Vernon, Tex.); US 183, Kansas Line to Texas Line, 219.8 m.

Roadbed paved throughout.
No train service between the Kansas Line and Arapaho; between Arapaho and the Texas Line the route is paralleled by the Frisco Railway.
Accommodations limited to the larger towns.

US 183 cuts a section of mid-western Oklahoma where the history, by and large, is richer than the soil, where fascinating legends and tall tales are perhaps easier to come by than a sure, dependable cash crop. For here is yet another part of the storied "dust bowl" (*see Tour 13*), a region of generally insufficient rainfall where burning sun and biting wind alike can, at times, spell economic havoc to the hardy sons and grandsons of pioneers who perversely seem to prefer it to any other section of the Sooner State. Yet they have a legitimate case. For the air in this upland country is dry, healthful, and exhilarating. The short grass, when there is sufficient moisture, puts profitable weight on sleek herds of beef cattle. And the red soil, particularly at the southern end of the route, manages with surprising consistency to produce wheat, cotton, and alfalfa, even in years when rainfall is slight.

In common with many other parts of the state, this area is becoming increasingly conscious of small industry as one sure way to hold its population and stabilize its economy. Too, it has begun to rely more and more heavily on the irrigation well, if not to replace the rain cloud, then at least to reinforce it.

South of the Kansas Line, US 183 passes through the old Cherokee Outlet, a thinly settled area of rolling country dotted with sagebrush and soapweed, and broken by deep red-tinged gullies. Farms are generally limited to the fertile flatlands beside the streams. But the uplands produce fine beef on some of the state's largest ranches.

From Seiling south to the Texas Line, US 183 roughly parallels the old Western Trail (*see Tour 13*), beaten out by herds of Texas longhorns after barbed-wire fences and levies of ten cents a head on cattle driven through the Chickasaw Nation made the more famous Chisholm Trail (*see Tour 11*) unprofitable. How many cattle were sent to market over this road is not known. The total varies, with the historian, from as few as two million to as many as seven million for the nearly twenty years it was used. But 1881 and 1882 are believed to have been the peak years, when perhaps a third of a million head of cattle were driven north.

Two large Indian reservations once included the whole area south of the Cherokee Outlet—that of the Cheyennes and Arapahoes, opened to white settlement in 1892, and that of the Kiowas and Comanches, which was opened in 1901. For a fillip, the route has its own echoes of border warfare and its hoary tales of long-lost Spanish treasure.

US 183 crosses the KANSAS LINE, 0 *m.*, twenty miles southeast of Ashland, Kansas (*see Kansas Guide*).

At 10.4 *m.* is the junction with US 64 (*see Tour 2*), which unites with US 183 for 1.4 miles to Buffalo.

Seat of Harper County, BUFFALO, 11.8 *m.* (1,791 alt., 1,544 pop.), was founded in 1907 when Oklahoma became a state. Following the general pattern, the surrounding area is devoted to farms along the creeks, and to wide-spreading ranches of registered cattle on the uplands. The region, too, is well known to sportsmen for its small game—quail, doves, and pheasants. This is one of the areas in the state where antelopes, wild turkeys, and prairie chickens have been re-introduced.

At 30.4 *m.* is the junction with US 270 (*see Tour 5*), with which US 183 unites for the next 47 miles.

SUPPLY, 31.0 *m.* (1,994 alt., 293 pop.), first came into existence in November, 1868, as Camp Supply. It was an army base of operations against the Plains Indians, especially the Cheyennes and Arapahoes. The name was later changed to Fort Supply and, after the post was abandoned in 1893, simply to Supply. At different times the fort was field headquarters for Generals Miles, Sheridan, Custer, and Sully, all well-known commanders in the protracted border warfare following the Civil War.

In 1894, the United States gave the old military reservation to the Territory of Oklahoma. In 1903, the Territory authorized the establishment of the WESTERN STATE HOSPITAL for the mentally ill. Early-day buildings still standing include the original Guard House, now used as a commissary storeroom; the Custer House, now a home for student nurses; and a log cabin near the barns that was once a teamster's cabin. Seven dormitory buildings and a hospital dominate the 120 acres of grounds, 28 acres of which are in shaded lawns. In 1955 the hospital had 1,340 patients and 387 employees. A granite marker on the grounds commemorates the officers and troop units (best known, Custer's Seventh Cavalry) that were stationed at Fort Supply.

Right from Supply to FORT SUPPLY DAM AND RESERVOIR (*fishing, boating, hunting, picnic facilities*), 2.2 *m.* Located on Wolf Creek, a tributary of the near-by North Canadian River, the dam, eighty-five feet high, was completed in 1942 at a cost of $7,500,000. With its 11,325-foot earth embankment, it creates a reservoir of 1,800 acres. South of the lake the State Game and Fish Department maintains a 1,900-acre public hunting area that offers quail, pheasants, doves, and waterfowl.

At WOLF CREEK, 33.3 *m.*, the Cheyennes and Arapahoes were defeated in 1837 by allied forces of Kiowas, Comanches, and Apaches. Two years later permanent peace was made among these tribes.

WOODWARD, 46.1 *m.* (1,916 alt., 5,915 pop.), the seat of Woodward County, which was carved out of the Cherokee Outlet, and the prosperous trade center of a wide farm and ranch area, is also a dramatic symbol of corporate courage and determination. It was here on the night of April 9, 1947, that one of the most savage tornadoes ever analyzed by the U. S. Weather Bureau (its destructive core was 1.8 miles in width) roared in from the southwest, flattened more than one hundred city blocks, and disappeared again into the darkness, leaving behind 107 dead and more than 700 wounded. Property damage ran to more than $8,000,000. Yet only the most observant visitor today, a decade later, can find even a trace of the storm's furious destruction.

Central Park's CITY HALL, COMMUNITY HOUSE, AMERICAN LEGION HALL, and CARNEGIE LIBRARY are now as neat and substantial as ever.

And scars on the modern courthouse in West Park have been healed, with young trees once again beginning to cover the stark nakedness left in the storm's wake. A reminder of this tornado can be found in the main reception room of the handsome WOODWARD MEMORIAL HOSPITAL, constructed in 1951. Here a three-scene bronze plaque, "In Memory of Woodward's Dead," honors not only the victims of World Wars I and II, but Woodward's tornado victims as well.

Woodward's citizens, however, have not been content merely to recover their former status as an agricultural and trade center. Although the city is still an important market for small grains and livestock (the Woodward Livestock Commission handles some two thousand head of cattle a week and holds, each month, one of the state's few regularly conducted horse sales), it has become increasingly active in the small industry field. Approximately three hundred and fifty people are employed in Woodward's two clothing manufacturing concerns. And other Woodward-made products range from print-shop machines to fishing sinkers.

One daily newspaper, the *Daily Press,* and two weeklies survive from this breeding ground for western Oklahoma journalists. Pioneering in the newspaper field, the *Woodward Jeffersonian* appeared seven days after the Opening and reported that "the first man to arrive . . . was David Jones, one of the good men from the Panhandle of Texas whose horse had more wind than the average newspaper man." Four other papers followed shortly afterward.

Like other cities created overnight in the Outlet, Woodward acquired between noon and sunset of September 16, 1893, a population of five thousand. Unlike most, it immediately established a pattern of orderliness that persists today. That first night a voluntary committee on law and order sent around the warning. "If you must shoot, shoot straight up!" All townsite lots were staked instantly by the swarming invaders, but 160-acre homesteads in the new county were less in demand because the land was thought to be too arid for farming. A week after the Opening—in sharp contrast to previous runs—many homesteads had still not been staked, including some that proved eventually to be excellent farms.

Notable among Woodward's pioneer citizens was Temple Houston, son of Sam Houston, the famed liberator of Texas who became its first president and later its first governor. Temple Houston was a lawyer specializing in criminal cases and flamboyant oratory. He wore his hair long, dressed spectacularly, and left a memory of his talents and idiosyncracies sufficiently vivid to make him the principal character in Edna Ferber's well-known Oklahoma novel, *Cimarron.*

Right from Woodward on a paved road to CRYSTAL BEACH PARK (*swimming, boating*), 1.7 *m.*, a 246-acre tract which includes a race track, the scene of an American Legion horse race held July 2–4 annually, and a rodeo arena, the scene of the annual Elk's Rodeo. Lasting usually four days, around the end of August or in early September, the rodeo—held in front of a concrete grandstand seating six thousand—is one of the state's biggest and best. The park's lake is supplied with mineral water from an artesian well.

Left (north) from Woodward on State 34, 1.5 *m.*, then right (east) on paved State 34C to BOILING SPRINGS STATE PARK (*cabins, camping, fishing, boating and swimming facilities, picnic and play areas*), 5.9 *m.*, an 880-acre playground of woods and hills on the north bank of the North Canadian River. Named for the springs that bubble up through the sand, the park was a well-known water hole in pioneer days. The largest of the springs, with a flow of three hundred gallons a minute, supplies a four-acre swimming pool. Many migratory waterfowl visit the area, and visitors in the spring and fall can often see pelicans, cormorants, herons and black gulls, terns and cranes, as well as ducks and geese.

In the thirty miles southeast of Woodward the route passes through the range area south of the North Canadian River and enters a region of small, dry-land farms.

US 183 leaves US 270 at 77.4 *m.*, 2.2 miles northwest of Seiling (*see Tour 4*). At 78.9 *m.* is the junction with US 60 (*see Tour 4*).

A bridge, 86.2 *m.*, now spans the South Canadian River, one of the streams of western Oklahoma particularly treacherous in times of flood because of its many quicksand traps. But before the day of bridges, travelers were often forced to make long detours in order to find safe fords, and many tales are told of horses and wagons that were lost in the five to eight feet of quicksand in the river bed. All but one of the twenty-one spans—each sixty feet in length—of an earlier bridge were washed from their foundation piers by a flood and now lie beneath the smooth surface of the sand.

Twelve miles southwest of this bridge was the well-known WAGONROAD CROSSING, used by early-day freighters from Fort Supply to Fort Sill.

South, for about the next forty miles, the soil is predominantly sandy and, despite steadily improving conservation methods, often shows the effects of serious wind and water erosion.

TALOGA, 86.8 *m.* (1,708 alt., 430 pop.), was made seat of "D" County after the United States government survey of the Cheyenne and Arapaho reservation in 1891, prior to its opening to settlement in 1892. The county did not acquire the name Dewey until after the battle of Manila Bay in 1898.

On the south bank of the South Canadian River, Taloga is the central point of a considerable stock-farming area. Also in the neighborhood are fields that lie in shallow valleys, partially sheltered from the frequent dry winds.

PUTNAM, 99.6 *m.* (1,959 alt., 106 pop.), is a small trading community on the high backbone between the South Canadian and the Washita rivers.

Seat of Custer County, ARAPAHO, 119.4 (1,540 alt., 311 pop.), is known locally for its success in the long-drawn fight made by Clinton (*see Tour 1*)—the metropolis of the county with a population more than twenty-four times as great—to gain the county seat. A modern county courthouse, school, and municipal building testify to the optimism of the town's citizens in the face of a 7.5 per cent loss in population between 1930 and 1940, and an almost 25 per cent drop from 1940 to 1950. Stock raising, wheat farming, and scattered fields of alfalfa represent the resources of the region surrounding the town.

In CLINTON, 123.6 *m.* (1,564 alt., 7,555 pop.) (*see Tour 1*) is the junction with US 66 (*see Tour 1*).

CORDELL, 139.6 *m.* (1,565 alt., 2,920 pop.), the center of an excellent farming area, is the seat of Washita County, with its business district close about the courthouse square. For ten years after the opening of the Cheyenne and Arapaho lands to settlement, Cloud Chief, some eight miles east of Cordell, was the county seat. But when the Frisco Railway built through the region, old Cordell, a mile east of the present city, moved to the rails and soon became the county seat.

City Park, one block east of US 183, provides a swimming pool, picnic tables, and playground equipment, surrounded by landscaped gardens. Cotton gins, grain elevators, and a community sales ground accurately reflect the town's primary dependence on agriculture.

ROCKY, 150.6 *m.* (1,560 alt., 366 pop.), grew from a store building made of rocks hauled to the railroad by a trader among the Kiowas. The town, named when a post office was opened in the store, is a trading point for a diversified farming region. Though small, Rocky is striking for its neat business district, its well-kept homes, and its pleasant tree-lined streets.

Immediately northwest of town is ROCKY LAKE (*fishing permit: 25c a day*), a five-hundred-acre municipal reservoir owned by the city of Hobart (*see below*). Swimming and overnight camping are forbidden, but the lake is one of southwest Oklahoma's top fishing spots.

At 159.1 *m.* is the junction with asphalt-paved State 9A.

Right here is HOBART, 1.7 *m.* (1,550 alt., 5,380 pop.), named for Vice-President Garrett A. Hobart (1897–99), who died near the end of President McKinley's first term and shortly before the opening of the Kiowa-Comanche lands to settlement. The seat of Kiowa County, and known locally as "The City of Iris,"

Hobart serves a rich and highly diversified farming area, especially along Elk Creek, two miles west. Here, on the opening of the reservation in 1901, many Kiowa Indians took their allotments, most of which today are farmed by white men. The valley lands produce heavy crops of alfalfa, cotton, and various forage grains, while dairying and poultry raising are also important. On the uplands wheat, small grains, kaffir, and sorghum crops are raised; and the pastures support many cattle and sheep. Thirty-six producing wells in a shallow (1,000 to 1,100 feet) oil field northeast of Hobart have also helped the town. The field was opened in 1939.

The city centers around COURTHOUSE SQUARE, on which face a modern FEDERAL BUILDING and the CARNEGIE LIBRARY. Four blocks north is the HOBART HIGH SCHOOL, with its attractive campus and athletic field. At the southeastern corner of the city, where the tracks of the Rock Island and Frisco railroads cross, are cotton gins, compresses, and an oil mill. Near by are stock feeding pens.

BABBS MEMORIAL SCHOOL (L), 164.2 *m.*, recalls the Christmas Eve fire in 1924 which destroyed the earlier Babbs Switch School claiming thirty-six lives. The present red-brick building itself in 1956 was slated for extinction, not by fire but by the same changing conditions which have brushed aside virtually all of Oklahoma's country schoolhouses. But the grounds are to be maintained as a permanent memorial to the fire victims. Although thirty-six bodies were recovered from the catastrophe, a thirty-seventh person was missing, three-year-old Mary Elizabeth Edens, who was unaccounted for after more than thirty years. In February of 1957 newspaper stories announced that the missing "child" had presumably been located. A thirty-six-year-old California woman and the Edens family have held a reunion in Hobart. They are convinced that the 1924 mystery has finally been solved.

Named in honor of Colonel Theodore Roosevelt by a man who served with the Rough Riders in the Spanish-American War, ROOSEVELT, 171.9 *m.* (1,460 alt., 679 pop.), is a farm supply point on a branch of Otter Creek.

At 181.9 *m.*, a marker (R) points out the site—at Cold Springs, two miles to the west—of CAMP RADZIMINSKI, established in 1858 by Major Earl Van Dorn and named for a lieutenant of his regiment who had recently died. It was from this palisaded camp (permanent buildings were never erected) that Van Dorn moved his troops to attack the Comanches near the site of present-day Rush Springs (*see Tour 11*). With the construction of Fort Cobb (*see Tour 3*) in 1859, Camp Radziminski was abandoned, though a body of Texas Rangers used the post for more than a year while patrolling the border and indulging in skirmishes with the Indians. The camp area is now under cultivation and only the location of the camp cistern can be seen. But the site still attracts relic hunters searching for "minnie" balls, stirrups, uniform buttons, and insignia markings—and an ever dwindling number of those more credulous ones who still poke the rocks throughout southwestern Oklahoma for buried Spanish treasure.

MOUNTAIN PARK, 184.0 *m.* (1,376 alt., 418 pop.), is dependent on granite quarrying and valley farming in the Otter Creek region. The creek itself is dammed in three-acre Municipal Park (*picnic and recreational facilities*) to provide a free swimming pool.

At Mountain Park is told the story of Anton Soukup, a Bohemian-born citizen, who arrived in 1915 and bought 160 acres of land on the rugged slopes of Mount Radziminski. Though ostensibly a farm, the tract was obviously suited only for goat raising. So Anton acquired goats, buying additional bits of the mountain from time to time—for additional pasture, as he explained it. But when he finally had title to the whole mountain, he wired a fellow Bohemian, Frank Svoboda, a granite-finisher of Omaha, Nebraska, who had financed his purchases. And Svoboda promptly began extensive exploitation of the enormous granite pile that is Mount Radziminski. In the past as many as five hundred granite-cutters have been employed at one time, although shipments in 1956 were down to several carloads a month.

Right from Mountain Park on a series of graded and graveled roads: R. at 5 *m.*, L. at 7 *m.*, L. at 12 *m.*, and R. a short distance at 13 *m.* to the J. C. Brown farmhouse (L). Left here on a road through the farmyard to a GIANT PECAN TREE, 13.5 *m.*, on the north bank of the North Fork of Red River. So far as is known, this pecan tree is the largest of its kind in the world; it is seventeen feet and six inches in circumference (four and one-half feet above the ground) and 112 feet high. Only one other Oklahoma tree of any type—a cypress in McCurtain County (*see Tour 6*)—is larger.

SNYDER, 187.0 *m.* (1,360 alt., 1,646 pop.) (*see Tour 3*), is at the junction with US 62 (*see Tour 3*).

At 191.4 *m.* US 183 enters Tillman County, the last before leaving Oklahoma, and one in which irrigation has, within the past few years, developed into a major industry. In 1956, an estimated ten thousand acres were being watered from more than four hundred wells.

FREDERICK, 205.7 *m.* (1,289 alt., 5,467 pop.), seat of Tillman County, was one of the towns that came into existence when the Kiowa-Comanche reservation was opened to settlement in 1901. Hard durum wheat and cotton are still the staples of the surrounding farm area, as symbolized by three grain elevators, four gins, two cotton compresses (with a combined capacity of fifty-five thousand bales a season), and a stand-by cottonseed-oil mill. The town is characterized by wide streets, substantial homes, a modern business district—and a thirty-one year record of no ad valorem taxes for municipal purposes.

(Local government is supported by revenues from city-owned public utilities.)

As it has to most Oklahoma cities, industry has come to Frederick in recent years. A helicopter corporation and a leather goods company are located at Municipal Airport, two and one-half miles southeast of the business district. The town possesses a Carnegie Library with more than 12,000 volumes, a floodlighted football stadium, and a municipal swimming pool. Its baseball park, meets Class D requirements, and many other recreational facilities are to be found at near-by Murray Lake (*fishing, swimming, boating, surfboarding*) and Burts Lake (*fishing, picnic facilities*).

It was from Frederick on April 8, 1905, that President Theodore Roosevelt started on a wolf hunt that became famous because Jack Abernathy, a young rancher of the region, caught a coyote with his bare hands and Roosevelt wrote about the feat. Later, after leaving his job as United States marshal, Abernathy repeated his coyote-catching stunt for the movies.

At 209.5 *m.*, US 183 skirts the South Frederick Field (L), an oil discovery of 1945. The far more important West Frederick Field was discovered in 1937. With only eleven active oil wells in 1956, its cumulative production to mid-1955 was more than four million barrels.

DAVIDSON, 216.5 *m.* (1,160 alt., 460 pop.), a farming community was called Texawa at its founding when the Kiowa-Comanche reservation was opened. At the north edge of Davidson is the junction with US 70 (*see Tour* 6).

Together for the next 3.4 miles, the two highways cross the Red River on the 5,460-foot Davidson Bridge, the state's longest, and reach the Texas Line, at 219.8 *m.*, sixteen miles northeast of Vernon, Texas (*see Texas Guide*).

TOUR 13

(Englewood, Kan.)—Shattuck—Arnett—Sayre—Mangum—Altus—(Vernon, Tex.); US 283, Kansas Line to Texas Line, 203.3 m.

Roadbed paved throughout.
No railway parallels this route.
Accommodations in the larger towns and at Quartz Mountain State Park.

But for a brief stretch at its southern end, US 283 crosses a high, gently rolling upland, an area of short-grass ranches and dry-land farms, of erosion-cut gullies and occasional low rocky buttes. Trees are scarce.

Rivers and creeks are often dry beds only. But the farm and ranch houses, although scattered, are generally substantial. The towns, few in number and for the most part small, are surprisingly clean, alert, and prosperous in appearance—surprisingly, because here, more than in any other area of the state, the one life-and-death factor that determines its very existence is as fickle and unpredictable as the weather itself. Rainfall—too much of it at rare intervals, far too little (an average of only twenty inches a year) most of the time—is the key to western Oklahoma's joys and woes.

This area was part of the notorious "dust bowl" of the mid-thirties (*see Tour 12*). And in the mid-fifties it has again been disastrously dry. During times like these, hot winds sear the crops and carry away unprotected top soil, native grasses turn brown, and stock tanks evaporate. Yet these harsh conditions of climate have, in a way, served to give strength to enterprise in this area—developing a resolution and resiliency in seeking out new and improved ways of adapting itself to nature.

The seventy-thousand-acre W. C. Austin Irrigation District, near the southern end of US 283, is one example of this adaptation. An increasing use of privately financed irrigation systems is another. Few areas in the state have gone so far in developing methods of watershed control, soil conservation, and improved farming in general. The semiarid section served by US 283, particularly along its southern end, also figures prominently in the federal government's "shelterbelt" program set up in 1935–40. Greer County alone had three hundred miles of these reforested strips, each forty to fifty-five feet wide and containing rows of eight or ten different kinds of hardy, fast-growing trees. Although there was much skepticism at the time, the percentage of tree survival (sixty-five per cent even in the 1935–37 drought years) was higher than expected. There has been general agreement that the thick stands of trees have accomplished their primary purpose of cutting down wind erosion on dry soil, and farmers are continuing to plant shelter belts in western Oklahoma, even though the government no longer subsidizes or supervises the planting.

US 283 crosses the old Cherokee Outlet, penetrates the former Cheyenne and Arapaho reservation, and approaches the timbered breaks of the Washita where the massacre of Black Kettle's band in the dawn of a freezing winter day helped to establish the military glory of General Custer. It ends in once-disputed Greer County, which was finally joined to Oklahoma after the U.S. Supreme Court decided it was not a part of Texas.

Three miles south of Englewood, Kansas (*see Kansas Guide*), US

283 crosses the KANSAS LINE, 0 *m.*

At 12.1 *m.* is the junction with US 64 (*see Tour 2*), which unites eastward with US 283 for four miles.

ROSSTON, 14.1 *m.* (2,139 alt., 85 pop.), is an "elevator town," typical of many tiny farming communities in western Oklahoma and the Panhandle.

At 16.1 *m.* US 283 turns sharply south, leaving US 64.

LAVERNE, 23.3 *m.* (2,104 alt., 1,269 pop.), is a somewhat unexpected oasis on the generally treeless short-grass plains, a shaded and prosperous trade center in the productive valley of the Beaver (North Canadian) River. Wheat, alfalfa, native hay, broomcorn, and sorghum crops, along with registered herds of cattle, provide its economic backbone. Use of shallow underground water sources for irrigation has increased in recent years.

SHATTUCK, 53.6 *m.* (2,237 alt., 1,692 pop.), was settled in 1904 by descendants of German-Russians who first came to the United States in the 1870's. Originally German, these people had lived for a century in Russia, enjoying freedom from taxation and military service. When these advantages ended, they emigrated to America. Farming and the breeding of registered cattle contribute to the area's wealth. Shattuck is also the home of the NEWMAN HOSPITAL AND CLINIC, one of northwestern Oklahoma's best-known medical institutions.

At 63.0 *m.* is the junction with US 60 (*see Tour 4*), which unites eastward with US 283 for 6.8 miles.

ARNETT, 68.8 *m.* (2,560 alt., 690 pop.) (*see Tour 4*).

At 69.8 *m.* US 283 again turns south (R) sharply.

At 81.4 *m.* is the junction with a dirt road.

Right on this road is GRAND, 1.5 *m.*, seat of onetime Day County, now a ghost town whose broad unpaved main street was once busy with the traffic of farmers and merchants. Except for its post office and a store, Grand moved to Arnett immediately after statehood in 1907. Nothing remains today but the vault from the old courthouse, and a small spring-fed lake.

South of Grand, across the South Canadian River, are the ANTELOPE HILLS, six conspicuous, irregular peaks that rise out of the level plain. The river loops around the northern edge of the hills, its bank rimmed with scattered trees and sparse vegetation. From the hill tops there is a panoramic view of much of Ellis and Roger Mills counties. The Antelope Hills were once a prominent landmark for the international boundary between the United States and Mexico.

At 88.3 *m.* US 283 crosses the Packsaddle Bridge over the South Canadian River.

A marker at the junction with State 47, at 93.1 *m.*, notes the crossing of the California Road, first traveled by California gold-seekers in the spring of 1849 under a military escort commanded by Captain R. B. Marcy. On Robe Creek to the northwest, beyond the Antelope Hills, is the site of a battle fought in 1858 between the Comanche Indians and a detachment of Texas Rangers under Captain John S. Ford.

This area through which US 283 passes was once the three-million-acre Cheyenne and Arapaho reservation, thrown open to settlement on April 19, 1892. Because the region was then far from railroads and considered almost too arid for agriculture, the opening failed to attract the flood of homesteaders that made the other runs farther east.

The WASHITA RIVER is crossed at 106.6 *m.*

CHEYENNE, 107.5 *m.* (1,932 alt., 1,133 pop.), came into existence when the federal government laid it off as a county seat (Roger Mills) and opened its town lots to a "Run for Homes" on April 19, 1892 (*see above*).

The famous SANDSTONE PROJECT—a dramatic demonstration of a new upstream approach to flood control and soil conservation—is located on near-by Sandstone Creek, a tributary to the Washita. The watershed is fifteen miles long, six miles wide, and has an area of 65,000 acres. Here the federal government has constructed twenty-four small dams to impound runoff water where it falls. With approved soil conservation practices, the project has virtually eliminated flood damage and cut soil erosion to a minimum. Sandstone seems to point the way to a sure and practical method of controlling the West's great rivers.

Right from Main Street in Cheyenne on paved State 33 to a junction with an improved dirt road, 1 *m.*; R. to a second junction, 1.5 *m.*; R. here to a granite marker (R), 1.8 *m.*, which commemorates the BATTLE OF THE WASHITA. In the bitter winter of 1868, General George A. Custer (*see Tour 3A*), later killed by the Sioux in the Battle of the Little Big Horn, led his cavalry some seventy miles from Fort Supply (*see Tour 12*) to the Washita River and in the night closed in on three sides of Chief Black Kettle's encampment of Cheyennes. At dawn he charged, scattering the totally unprepared Indians. Custer's troopers killed or wounded some two hundred men, women, and children, with only negligible losses to the military force.

SAYRE, 129.3 *m.* (1,810 alt., 3,362 pop.) (*see Tour 1*), is at the junction with US 66 (*see Tour 1*), which unites southward with US 283 for 2.9 miles.

WILLOW (R), 151.5 *m.* (1,735 alt., 223 pop.), was named for Will O'Connell, the town's first settler and postmaster. It lies within a cotton-producing area.

BRINKMAN (R), 154.3 *m.* (1,694 alt., 102 pop.), established in 1910 on the line of the Wichita Falls and Northwestern Railway (now the Missouri-Kansas-Texas), was named for a man who helped to finance the townsite. It is said that more wheat is shipped from Brinkman than from all other markets in Greer County combined.

At 157.7 *m.* is the northern junction with asphalt-paved State 9.

Left on State 9 is GRANITE, 7.0 *m.* (1,618 alt., 1,096 pop.), the center of a quarrying industry. The main streets of the town end abruptly, and picturesquely, against a towering cliff of granite to the north.

The OKLAHOMA STATE REFORMATORY, 8.2 *m.*, a castlelike structure (R) of roughhewn granite, is equipped to house some five hundred persons. These inmates are male offenders under twenty-six years of age who are considered worthy of efforts at rehabilitation. Within the sixteen-foot walls is a ten-acre tract which contains the cell blocks, dormitory, workshops, offices, and a fourteen-teacher, fully accredited high school, perhaps the first of its kind within prison walls in the United States. Outside the walls, beside the tree-shaded highway, are fifty-two homes for officials and employees. The adjoining dairy and 1,800-acre farm produce an average income of $150,000 a year.

State 9 unites southward with US 283 to 161.3 *m.*

Right (west) on paved State 9 is REED, 11.0 *m.* (1,744 alt., 200 pop.). Left from Reed on a dirt road is CAVE CREEK, 2.5 *m.* Along the banks are many tunnels and grottoes known locally as the BAT CAVES because of the thousands of bats that emerge after sunset. One cavern with a six-foot-high ceiling can be penetrated for half a mile. It is necessary, of course, to carry a lantern or flashlight in the cave.

At 23.0 *m.* is VINSON (1,883 alt., 100 pop.), a small back-roads town. Right from Vinson on a dirt road is the NATURAL BRIDGE, 26.4 *m.*, a great rock formation nearly one hundred feet high, that overlooks an area pitted with caves. Many of these contain springs, which keep the interior water cooled on the hottest days.

MANGUM, 163.4 *m.* (1,588 alt., 4,271 pop.), was named for Captain A. S. Mangum, one of the first to apply to the *de facto* government of Texas for land in what was then known as Greer County, Texas. It is now the seat of Oklahoma's Greer County.

Old Greer County, so long a disputed territory (it also included present Harmon and Jackson counties), was reorganized in 1860 under an act of the Texas legislature signed by Governor Sam Houston. In 1881, after the lands of Greer County had been apportioned, one-half to the schools of Texas and the rest to the service of the state debt, certain Civil War veterans were given land here. By 1884, H. C. Sweet, representing Mangum, and J. R. Crouch had arrived in the wake of the cattlemen who used the ranges. The issue was raised that the county was not Texas land, but was in fact a part of Indian Territory. When Oklahoma Territory was created in 1890, however, Greer County was not included. It was not until 1896 that the issue was finally settled by a decision of the United States Supreme Court. Meanwhile, the governor of Texas succeeded in getting the federal government to recognize the titles of the Texas veterans to the townsite of Mangum.

The city is the center of a large farming district lying between the Red River and the North Fork of the Red River.

At 173.9 *m.* is the junction with paved State 44. A marker, "Peace on the Plains," here recalls the first meeting between the United States and the Plains Indians in Oklahoma for the purpose of promoting peace. The date was July 21, 1834. The setting was a Wichita village in rugged Devil's Canyon (*see below*), about five miles southeast of this spot. The United States forces were under the command of Colonel Henry Dodge. To the east, against the side of the mountain, can be seen the main irrigation canal carrying water from Lake Altus to the W. C. Austin Irrigation District (*see Tour* 3).

Left on State 44, across the North Fork of Red River, 1.7 *m.*, to a junction with State 44A, 2.4 *m.*

Left on this road is the newly relocated (1957) CRATERVILLE PARK, 3.3 *m.* Expansion of the Fort Sill reservation (*see Tour* 3A) forced the moving of this well-known recreation facility from its long-time home near Cache (*see Tour* 3).

QUARTZ MOUNTAIN STATE PARK (*lodge, cabins, picnic areas, boating and swimming facilities, fishing, hiking*), 3.5 *m.*, contains 11,000 acres, with 6,800 acres of it covered by Lake Altus, the center of its recreational activities. The highly scenic park road loops past the service facilities, then winds around and over rocky granite hills above the lake to the QUARTZ MOUNTAIN LODGE, 5.5 *m.* Overlooking the lake from a ledge against the side of a mountain, this $750,000 structure (*dining room, swimming pool*) has fifty rooms, half of them facing the water.

Red granite hills, varying in height from six to eight hundred feet, rim the park on the west, their slopes covered with great lichen-crusted boulders. Live oak, white oak, pin oak, cedar, and mesquite cover the hillsides and provide shelter for red fox, quail, cardinals, and other species of native birds and wildlife.

South and east of Quartz Mountain Park (*make local inquiry*), is isolated DEVIL'S CANYON, which Spanish explorers are said to have entered in 1611 under Fra de Salas in search of gold. According to records of the State Historical Society at Santa Fe, New Mexico, they established an Indian mission here which was maintained for ninety years. The Indians grew corn, pumpkins, and squash, which they stored in underground chambers and covered with boulders. Legend has it that extensive gold-mining operations were carried on, and that the Spaniards were finally driven out by the Indians and slaughtered in a near-by canyon. Tending to confirm the tale are ruins of adobe houses, copper and iron implements, and other artifacts. Human bones have also been uncovered in the valley. Plans have been made to add the canyon eventually to Quartz Mountain State Park.

BLAIR, 179.2 *m.* (1,462 alt., 700 pop.), having survived a tornado in 1928 and eleven subsequent years of agricultural depression, prospers modestly as a result of irrigation water from Lake Altus (*see above*).

ALTUS, 188.9 *m.* (1,389 alt., 9,735 pop.) (*see Tour 3*), is at the junction with US 62 (*see Tour 3*).

South of Altus, US 283 traverses an almost level plain for ten miles. The route approaches the Red River—a narrow stream at this point, formerly called Prairie Dog Town Fork—only a few miles above the famed DOAN'S CROSSING on the Western Trail (*see Tour 12*). Here in the 1870's and 1880's great herds of Texas longhorns swam the river to begin the long trek across Indian Territory to the distant railheads in Kansas. The peak year was perhaps 1881 when an estimated 301,000 head of cattle were driven north. Supply point for the trail drives was Doan's, now a sleepy little settlement downstream from the highway on the Texas side of the river.

At 203.3 *m.* US 283 crosses the Red River twenty miles north of Vernon, Texas (*see Texas Guide*).

TOUR 14

(Sedan, Kan.)—Hominy—Drumright—Ada—Tishomingo—Kingston; State 99, Kansas Line to Lake Texoma, 237.3 m.

Roadbed paved throughout.
The Santa Fe Railway parallels the route between Bigheart and Pawhuska, and between Madill and Kingston; the Missouri-Kansas-Texas Railroad between Wynona and Jennings; the Oklahoma City-Ada-Atoka Railway between Konawa and Ada.
Accommodations at frequent intervals.

Starting in the Osage Indian country and touching every phase of that tribe's comparatively brief experience in their present location, State 99 passes successively through the former Creek, Sac and Fox, Shawnee, Potawatomi, Seminole, and Chickasaw reservations. It is edged by missions and churches—most of them now but ruins and sites—erected by zealous friends of the exiled races for their consolation and education.

Agriculturally, this highway from Kansas to Texas is typically Oklahoman. Pastures give way first to corn and wheat, then to orchards and wild pecan groves and peanut fields, and finally to cotton. It is oil-smeared at intervals throughout its course. In the northern third of that course, State 99 splits the first large-area oil pool developed in Oklahoma, beginning in 1912. Toward its southern end it bisects the vast Seminole fields, opened in the mid-thirties.

From rolling, upland, bluestem pasture land, State 99 passes to fertile river bottoms, mounts again to prairie ridges, winds through wooded hills where the motorist may still see an occasional log cabin built by Indians, and emerges near the shore of one of the nation's big playgrounds, sprawling Lake Texoma.

State 99 crosses the KANSAS LINE, 0 *m.*, 8.2 miles south of Sedan, Kansas (*see Kansas Guide*).

CANEY RIVER, 2.2 *m.*, marks the upper reaches of the flood control pool of Hulah Reservoir (*see Tour 9*). Boulanger Landing is on the left.

At 4.5 *m.* the route crosses Pond Creek, a small tributary of the Caney and also a part of the Hulah reserve pool. Pond Creek Landing is downstream approximately one mile. Local legend has it that one of the last funeral parties sent out by the Osages in search of a scalp to bury with a dead warrior (*see Tour 11*) came upon two loggers in camp here, Jack Wimberly and Al Gifford. The Osages were not interested in Wimberly's red hair, but they craved a bit of Gifford's scalp, and offered him twenty ponies for a narrow strip just above the forehead. Gifford, of course, refused to deal with them, whereupon they took the strip by force. Next morning the twenty ponies were duly delivered.

At 6.5 *m.* is the junction with an improved road.

Left on this road to the HULAH PUBLIC HUNTING AREA, 2.6 *m.*, a three-thousand-acre reserve along the south perimeter of Hulah Reservoir. One of the thirteen such areas managed by the State Game and Fish Department, it offers small game and waterfowl.

To the left at 11.4 *m.*, east of State 99, is the community of BIGHEART (832 alt., 13 pop.), once an Indian trading town named for the Osage chief, James Bigheart. This is a region of upland limestone where grass is good and the big summer pastures, leased by stockmen from the Osages, are dotted with registered herds of cattle.

Beyond ROCK CREEK, 12.8 *m.*, the rounded hills rise beside the highway in rugged ledges sparsely clothed by scrub oaks. This nearly worthless timber and the scant grass coverage have caused the section to be called the "strip range."

At 19.2 *m.* the highway begins its descent to the Sand Creek bottoms that lie under the shadow of a range of hills. Among the pecan and persimmon trees that flourish in the sandy loam were camps along the old "Thieves Path," overnight stopping places in the 1890's for men who stole horses in Texas and drove them to Kansas for sale.

At 19.8 *m.* is the junction with US 60 (*see Tour 4*), with which State

99 unites southward to PAWHUSKA, 25.4 *m.* (885 alt., 5,331 pop.) (*see Tour 4*).

The center of a shallow oil field, WYNONA, 34.7 *m.* (887 alt., 678 pop.), is one of many small boom towns that declined rapidly after the peak of development had passed.

Wynona is at the approximate center of the old Osage Indian culture, and here for a long time ancient customs and rites could best be studied. One of these—the "Sending Away the Spirit"—was held the fourth day after the death of a warrior. A tree was selected, the bark of which was cut away by the master of ceremonies and the surviving warriors. The naked trunk was then stained red and, as a symbol of the spirit of the dead man, the tree was bidden to travel with the God of Day on its endless journey.

Another ceremony for the dead warrior took place on the return of the war party to the village. Within sight and sound of the tepees, they sat down in a circle and began to wail for their lost companion. From the town came the master of ceremonies and the people. And in the smoke of fragrant cedar boughs the warriors, their cast-aside clothes, weapons, saddles—even their horses—were purified. All their discarded property was then distributed to those of the three clans of the Osages who took part in the rites. As a final precaution, the returning warriors marched in procession around the encampment in order to establish a line across which the spirit of death could not pass.

At the end of October or the beginning of November, the Wynona area is often the scene of the Osages' annual wolf hunt, which lasts four or five days. (There is no fixed place for the hunt, but it is usually held in the timbered eastern and southern sections of the reservation.) Organized by dog owners, it is primarily a field trial for wolf dogs, and from seventy-five to one hundred owners enter an average of 125 contestants. Five mounted judges follow the dogs, which are sent out to start a wolf at three o'clock in the morning. Dog owners and visitors camp out during the trials, and at night bench shows, fiddlers' tourneys, and cow-horn blowing contests are held. About the same time of year a country-wide roundup is often organized by stockmen and farmers to rid the ranges and pastures of coyotes that kill calves and sheep.

At 43.8 *m.* is an OSAGE INDIAN GRAVEYARD (R), where American flags wave on tall poles set up at the graves. It is said that this custom dates from the death in 1845 of a leader called Tom Big Chief, who wished to be so honored. It was generally adopted after 1873, when the custom of raising the scalp of an enemy on a pole was renounced. According to local history, the last scalp so exhibited was that of a

Wichita Indian chief, and its taking all but precipitated a war between the tribes. Gifts by the government of flags to be displayed at the graves of tribal members who fell in the Spanish-American War and World War I further encouraged the flag practice. Tattered flags are replaced on the Fourth of July. After the coming of oil riches to the tribe, many pretentious monuments were placed in this cemetery. Sometimes photographs of the dead were placed in glass-protected niches in the tombstone itself.

Although some of these burial customs may seem strange to the average American, through these rites the Osages were expressing a deep sincerity in their belief that at death a new and glorious life was beginning. Their ceremonials and their Mourning Dances were demonstrations of this firmly felt faith. Theirs was the natural urge to do something in harmony with such an important and sacred event as the passing of a soul to the other world.

Established as a subagency for the Osages in 1874, HOMINY, 44.8 *m.* (780 alt., 2,703 pop.), became a trading point for the Indians who lived in the southern part of the reservation. (The name is believed to come from that of the Osage leader *Ho Moie,* which means He-Who-Walks-in-the-Dark.) These Osages, according to legend, are descendants of the Dwellers in the Upland Forest; that is, the people who fled into a forest long ago to escape a great flood. (Characteristics of this Wah Ti Ankah Band include hot temper, loudness, foot-stamping oratory, aggressiveness, and bluff.) Other Osages sought safety on a hill and became known as Dwellers on the Hilltop, whose modern center is Gray Horse (*see Tour 4*), in the western part of Osage County. A third band, caught in flight among thorn trees, earned the title of Dwellers in the Thorny Thickets, and Pawhuska (*see Tour 4*) is their central town. The Little Osage, a fourth group, settled to the north along Pond Creek (*see above*) and near-by Mission Creek.

Oil, discovered in 1916, is almost wholly responsible for the growth of Hominy, a modern, predominantly Indian town, with a municipal hospital, country club and golf course, armory, athletic field, and good schools. The tribe's war veterans observe Armistice Day at the ceremonial ROUNDHOUSE in the old Indian section of Hominy with a ceremony called the Feast of Peace. In deference to the elders of the tribe, it has long been conducted in the Osage tongue. The Roundhouse is also the scene of various other tribal rites, dances, and feasts throughout the year.

Between Hominy and Cleveland, State 99 loops through the rugged, wooded hills that line the ARKANSAS RIVER, 52.6 *m.*

CLEVELAND, 54.7 *m.* (740 alt., 2,464 pop.) (*see Tour 2*), is at the junction with US 64 (*see Tour 2*), with which State 99 unites for 6.2 miles westward.

At 60.9 *m.* State 99 turns sharply south (L).

HALLETT, 64.6 *m.* (740 alt., 120 pop.), is another small farming community that had only a brief oil boom.

On the GEORGE FLEMING FARM, 66.5 *m.*, are hundreds of evergreen trees fancifully trimmed into curious shapes—dogs, horses, deer, and even household objects.

JENNINGS, 68.3 *m.* (918 alt., 338 pop.), is in the former Cherokee Outlet near the northern edge of the old Creek Nation. It was named for the allottee on whose land the town was built.

In the triangle formed by State 99 and the Arkansas and Cimarron rivers, which unite twenty miles east of Jennings, are tangled woods, rugged hills, deep gullies, creek bottoms, and natural caves. The area was long the refuge of such bank-robbing outlaws as the Daltons, the Doolins, Matt Kimes, Wilbur Underhill and Ray Terrill, all well known to the people who lived there. As a matter of policy (and enlightened self-intent) the outlaws refrained from committing local robberies.

At 72.8 *m.* is the junction with State 51 (*see Tour 2A*), with which State 99 joins for the next three miles.

The Cimarron River is crossed just north of OILTON, 75.3 *m.* (818 alt., 1,109 pop.) (*see Tour 2A*).

South of Oilton, State 99 climbs to the backbone of a low ridge through a forest of oil derricks marking the approximate northern edge of the famous Cushing Field, discovered in 1912 (*see Tour 1A*).

DRUMRIGHT, 83.1 *m.* (866 alt., 5,028 pop.), began its career as Fulkerson but was renamed for the owner of the land on which the townsite was laid out in 1913. For nearly three years its tents, lean-tos, and ramshackle wooden buildings—set amid three hundred or more richly producing oil rigs—sheltered bootleggers, highjackers, gamblers, and the routine assortment of lawless boom-town hangers-on. Then, in 1916, the decent citizenry made "Fighting Jack" Ary the town's chief of police. He promptly moved against the leader of the criminal element, a half blood Creek Indian named Creekmore. With Creekmore in prison, the situation rapidly improved.

Drumright's Main Street runs over steep Tiger Hill, which holds the distinction of being the state's longest uphill-and-downhill thoroughfare. In the early days of the oil fields, with its crush of mule-drawn trucks loaded with heavy equipment, it was also the scene of many spectacular wrecks. Drumright today bears few scars of the tornado which ripped through the town April 2, 1956, destroying seventy-five homes and killing five people. Two city parks provide swimming and complete picnic and recreational facilities. Two natural gasoline plants in the area are open to visitors.

Drumright is at the junction with State 33 (*see Tour 1A*), which unites with State 99 for 2.9 miles. Immediately west of Drumright, the route enters the former Sac and Fox Indian reservation.

At 86.0 *m.* State 99 leaves State 33, turning south (L).

At 102.1 *m.* the highway passes over the Turner Turnpike (*see Tour 1*).

STROUD, 102.6 *m.* (905 alt., 2,450 pop.) (*see Tour 1*), is at the junction with US 66 (*see Tour 1*).

At 108.1 *m.* is the SITE OF THE SAC AND FOX INDIAN SCHOOL. Established by the Quakers in 1872 with tribal funds, the school was closed in 1919 when the affairs of the tribe began to be administered jointly with those of the Shawnees, Kickapoos, Potawatomis, and Iowas from the combined agency at Shawnee (*see Shawnee*).

At 108.6 *m.* is the abandoned SAC AND FOX AGENCY (L), where the business affairs of the tribe were handled from 1872 until the closing of the agency. The small remnant of a once powerful Indian tribe, the Sac and Fox for a time occupied an extensive territory in northern Illinois and southern Wisconsin. The band was moved to Oklahoma, however, from the neighborhood of Lawrence, Kansas. They made the nineteen-day journey in cold, uncomfortable weather, arriving in this area December 14, 1869. The rest of the winter they lived in tents supplied by the government and worked at erecting permanent homes and putting land under the plow. Only the water tower of the old agency still stands, a lone sentinel above the ruins of two rock and brick buildings. The old Sac and Fox Cemetery lies approximately a mile beyond on the dirt road that runs past the agency ruins. In it are buried some of the old Sac and Fox chiefs, notably Moses Keokuk (*see below*), and the Whistler family.

Across State 99 from the Sac and Fox Agency is the BLACK HAWK RESTAURANT, operated by Guy Whistler and his wife, both members of the Sac and Fox tribe. Squaw bread is an interesting specialty. Also of interest are the paintings, pictures, bows and arrows, and other Indian relics on display in the dining room.

PRAGUE, 121.2 *m.* (992 alt., 1,546 pop.) (*see Tour 3*), is at the junction with US 62 (*see Tour 3*).

At 126.3 *m.*, a marker (R) notes the site of the ghost town of Keokuk Falls, two miles to the east. It was platted near some falls on the North Canadian River at the time of the opening of the Sac and Fox reservation, September 22, 1891. Named for Chief Moses Keokuk, it became a thriving town with a number of taverns, and even a distillery—in "wet" Oklahoma Territory, but on the line of "dry" Indian Territory. Frequent wars between rival saloons caused many bloody battles. The town was abandoned in 1907, the year Oklahoma became the forty-sixth state in the Union—and completely "dry."

In the neighborhood of the North Canadian River, 127.7 *m.*, a number of Caddoan Indian Mounds (*see Early Oklahomans*) have been found. South of the river, State 99 leaves the Sac and Fox country and enters the former Seminole Nation.

SEMINOLE, 138.6 *m.* (863 alt., 11,863 pop.) (*see Tour 5*), is at the junction with US 270 (*see Tour 5*).

BOWLEGS, 144.1 *m.* (840 alt., 450 pop.), was named for a member of the Seminole tribe on whose allotment the town was built. The first oil well drilled in the Seminole Field in 1924 was also on land owned by a Bowlegs, a grandson, according to local report, of Chief Billy Bowlegs who fought against the removal of the tribe from Florida. The Bowlegs Field to the east was discovered in 1922 and by 1955 had produced 135,000,000 barrels of oil.

KONAWA, 158.9 *m.* (962 alt., 2,707 pop.), is surrounded by productive oil fields and fertile farmlands.

Right from Konawa on paved State 39, 4 *m.*; R. on a graveled road to the SITE OF ST. MARY'S ACADEMY, 6 *m.*, a convent school for Indian girls. Founded in 1884 by four Sisters of Mercy from Illinois, who came at the invitation of Benedictine Fathers to run a day and boarding school for white and Indian girls, it received students from practically all of the Five Tribes and from many of the Plains tribes. The school was closed in 1943 and the buildings dismantled.

Established in 1876 by Father Isidore Robot, of the Benedictine Order, SACRED HEART MISSION, which sponsored St. Mary's Academy, occupied a tract of 640 acres in this locality donated by the Potawatomi Indians (*see Tour 5*). The parish church is still active, but the three-story, fifty-room monastery, the old bakery, and a hewn-log building, once the casket shop, are abandoned and in serious disrepair. They are under the jurisdiction of St. Gregory's College at Shawnee (*see Tour 5*), which has offered this "Cradle of Oklahoma Catholicism" to the state as a historical shrine. The old mission school claims a number of distinguished alumni, including the late Jim Thorpe, the internationally famed Sac and Fox athlete, and Patrick J. Hurley, the former statesman and ambassador to China (*see Tour 9*).

At 163.2 *m.* on the main route is the junction with paved State 56.

Left at this point to a historical marker, 8 *m.*, noting the SITE OF THE JOHN F. BROWN HOME. Built by a rich Seminole chief when there was a settlement and trading post near by called Sasakwa, the home was a huge, two-story frame building. Across nearly one hundred feet of its L-shaped front, a first-floor porch and a second-story veranda—both with ornamental balustrades—suggested a strange opulence in the midst of a bleak sand-hill and scrub-oak region.

On the SEMINOLE INDIAN CHURCH AND CAMP-MEETING GROUNDS, 8.4 *m.*, are a score or more large brush arbors under which families and groups camp during the summer religious meetings. In good weather, the meetings, which often last for several days, are held out of doors. A new brick church has been built beside the old frame meetinghouse.

SASAKWA, 10.2 *m.* (839 alt., 365 pop.), superseded the older settlement of the same name near the old Brown home. Left from Sasakwa on a dirt road is SPEARS HILL, 12.1 *m.*, site of the encampment of one hundred or more tenant farmer participants in the so-called Green Corn Rebellion of 1917.

Syndicalist propaganda, and agitation to resist the World War I draft in this general area, led to the formation of the Working Class Union. In August some five hundred members armed themselves and, as a protest against the draft, began damaging railroad bridges, cutting fences, and turning livestock into fields. In camp, this mixed force of whites, Indians, and Negroes lived largely on barbecued beef and the old Indian green-corn dish called "tomfuller." This item of their diet, plus the fact that it was the season of the annual green-corn dance of the neighboring Shawnees, fixed the name on this abortive effort to take over the government of the United States.

Seat of Pontotoc County, ADA, 175.1 *m.* (1,027 alt., 15,995 pop.), is one of the principal cities in southeastern Oklahoma. Jeff Reed, the city's first postmaster (1891), came to the area in 1890 and erected the first building, a combination log store and dwelling. The town was named for his daughter.

Ada grew rapidly into the industrial and trade center for an extensive territory. In 1910, ten years after the coming of the first railroad, its population was 4,349. It almost doubled by 1920, and again by 1940.

With statehood (and state-wide prohibition) Ada began to acquire the reputation of being one of the toughest places in the Southwest. In 1908 there were thirty-six murders in or near the town, few of which received more than cursory inspection by the courts. It was a well-known fact that if a slayer had friends and money he usually went scot free. In 1909 an event took place which carried echoes and repercussions from the career of Billy the Kid.

It was a man called Jim Miller who contrived the death of Pat Garrett after Garrett had slain Billy the Kid. With the murder of Garrett and more than thirty others successfully accomplished, this same Jim Miller shot from ambush and killed Gus Bobbitt, one of Ada's accepted citizens. When it became known that Miller was the hired assassin of an outlaw gang, a committee of townspeople was formed to bring the murderer to justice. They tracked him down and brought him to jail, together with the three men who had planned the murder. After Miller's examining trial it seemed obvious to some that justice might be tempered with too much mercy. Ada had had enough. At 2:30 A.M., on a misty April morning, some forty to fifty masked men, grim and fast moving, slid open the doors of the jail and summoned the desperadoes to their doom. Thirty feet from the jail was an old livery barn beside the Frisco tracks. Inside, ropes were thrown over rafters, and one at a time the four outlaws were hauled up into the air—and left hanging there, a symbol of justice for all to view.

It was the most sensational lynching in Oklahoma's history. Ada breathed a sigh of relief, as did worried citizens in other towns. Oklahoma's courts immediately tightened procedures, and outlaws soon learned that an era had ended.

Ada is an excellent example of the balanced community. Agriculture continues to be an important factor in the city's economic picture, and the beef cattle industry has expanded over the years on the strength of near-by range land, especially to the south and west, that is as fine as any in the state. Two large packing plants and the Ada Livestock Exchange provide a ready market for local cattle, sheep, and hogs.

The largest single industry is the IDEAL CEMENT PLANT on the southwest edge of Ada. A $15,000,000 expansion program, begun in 1957, will raise the plant's total annual capacity from 2,200,000 to 3,700,000 barrels of cement, making it one of the largest operations of its kind in the United States. The necessary limestone is obtained from company quarries at Lawrence, south of Ada. Also making use of near-by raw materials are two other local industries—HAZEL-ATLAS GLASS, using fine silica sand deposits, and SUPERIOR CLAY PRODUCTS, obtaining raw material from the clay pits east of Ada. Other products manufactured here include concrete pipe, steel folding chairs, and milling equipment.

In typical Oklahoma fashion, oil has also played its part in the city's development. The largest and most interesting of the fields that ring the city is the Fitts, ten miles to the southeast. A multiple-pay field (some of its deeper wells have produced from as many as nine different levels), Fitts was discovered in 1933. By 1936 it had more than one thousand producing wells and cumulative production by the end of 1954 had reached 111,000,000 barrels.

EAST CENTRAL STATE COLLEGE, at the east end of Main Street on Francis Avenue, has thirteen permanent buildings on a sixty-acre campus. The school has a faculty of eighty and an enrollment approaching two thousand.

Created by an act of the state legislature in 1909, East Central began as a two-year teacher-training school. The granting of degrees was authorized in 1919, when the school began a four-year college curriculum and the name was changed to East Central State Teachers College. Arts and science courses were added in 1939 and "Teachers" was dropped to give the school its present name. A fifth-year Master of Teaching Degree was offered in 1954 (as it was in all of the state's six former teachers' colleges) and teacher training remains an important function of the college.

At the main entrance to the campus is a giant CALLIXYLON, the fossilized stump of a tree dating back to the Devonian period. It was found by John Fitts, the geologist for whom the Fitts Field was named. Placed by him in its present position, it was dedicated to the memory of David White, noted plant paleontologist and onetime chief geologist of the United States Geological Survey.

East Central's physical plant centers about old (1909) SCIENCE HALL, facing the entrance, a spacious buff-brick, three-story building with a wide white-pillared front. To the north and northeast are the FINE ARTS BUILDING and the MEN'S DORMITORY. To the south are the burnt-brick ADMINISTRATION BUILDING, LINSCHEID LIBRARY, the HEALTH BUILDING, the president's home, and six concrete tennis courts. East of these, overlooking the athletic area, are KNIGHT HALL, where 175 women students live, and the MEMORIAL STUDENT UNION. The KATHRYN P. BOSWELL MEMORIAL CHAPEL is north of the Union. HORACE MANN SCHOOL, located across Francis Avenue southeast of the Science Hall, offers special teacher training under the supervision of the college.

Other public buildings in Ada include an excellent CITY LIBRARY, five modern grade schools, and more than a score of churches. The UNITED STATES POST OFFICE AND COURTHOUSE, East 12th and Constant Streets, has a third-story sun deck from which the visitor can get a good view westward across the city and the hills beyond. The afternoon *Ada News* began publication as a tiny weekly in 1900, the first year of Ada's existence. It has been a daily since 1903.

GLENWOOD PARK, with its municipal swimming pool, is located just west of the city's business district on Main Street. Another pool, with modernized facilities, is at WINTERSMITH PARK, a ruggedly beautiful 137-acre tract on the southeast edge of the city. The lake here, which provided Ada's water supply before Byrd's Mill Spring (*see below*) was acquired, has long been a favorite with fishermen. Bridle paths, hiking trails, and a public lodge building are also available.

In addition to the sport and recreational facilities provided by the city and East Central, the surrounding area also has much to offer the visitor. Blue and Little Blue rivers, and Pennington, Sheep, Delaware, Mill, Clear Boggy, and Jack Fork creeks all drain areas of great natural beauty and offer abundant opportunity for hunting, in season, and year-round fresh-water fishing.

Off State 12 at the east edge of Ada is VALLEY VIEW HOSPITAL, a community institution erected in 1936–37 on a ten-acre tract overlooking a broad valley. The 120-bed hospital, with its separate maternity ward and nurses' home, was made possible by joint contributions of the city and the Commonwealth Fund of New York. These modern facilities are combined with an unusually large number of private physicians and clinics.

Right from Ada on State 12 is the ROY J. TURNER RANCH (*visitors welcome*), 24.0 *m.*, a million-dollar registered Hereford ranch (L) occupying some ten thousand acres in Oklahoma's so-called "Hereford Heaven." At the ranch's last sale (1954) a one-half interest in one of the Turner show herd bulls sold for $45,200. At the same time, 362 sons of the noted herd sire, TR Zato Heir, were sold for more than $1,000,000.

At 187.0 *m.* is the junction with an improved road.

Right on this road is BYRD'S MILL SPRING, 2.7 *m.*, the source of Ada's water supply. Out of this enormous natural spring, protected by a covering of concrete, spouts an almost unbelievable volume of clear, sweet water—from ten to twenty million gallons a day. The spring was a favorite meeting and camping place for the Indians and was named for a former chief of the Chickasaws who operated a gristmill here with water power supplied from the spring. For generations this section, laced with rugged canyons and clear streams, has been a popular recreation area.

FITTSTOWN, 187.9 *m.* (990 alt., 150 pop.), is composed almost wholly of corrugated iron or frame houses occupied by oil-field workers. It was named for John Fitts, the geologist (*see above*) who was responsible for the development of the rich Fitts oil pool.

PONTOTOC, 196.9 *m.*, and CONNERVILLE, 199.9 *m.*, once prosperous trading centers in the Chickasaw Nation, are in the middle of fine ranch country covered with bluestem grass.

At 206.6 *m.* is the junction with paved State 7.

Left on State 7 to the junction with paved State 7D, 8.4 *m.* Left here to BROMIDE, 2.6 *m.* (700 alt., 258 pop.), a sleepy near-ghost town that was, from 1913 to the early 1920's, a flourishing spa. Springs that bubbled "35 million gallons of healing waters daily," according to press agents, brought excursion trains in from Texas. At the height of its resort glory, Bromide boasted four hotels (including the pretentious three-story Galbreath), one bathhouse, a swimming pool, a bank, a theater, and other business. Little remains today to suggest its heyday as a spa but a trickle of water from a pipe at the site of what once was a large fountain.

Continue east on State 7 to WAPANUCKA, 12.8 *m.* (620 alt., 592 pop.), where one of the first schools in the Chickasaw Nation was opened in 1852. It was first called the Wapanucka Female Manual Labor School. Its limestone building was condemned, and the school closed, in 1901. Reopened in 1903 as a boys' school, after the building was repaired, it was again closed in 1907. The building, on the bank of Delaware Creek, was dismantled in 1948.

Near Wapanucka, in June of 1865, occurred a little-known battle between Comanches and Chickasaws. The Comanches, 350 strong, swept in from the west and for four days raided farms and ranches, rounding up a big herd of stolen horses in the process. Before they could get back to their own territory, however, the Chickasaws—armed with rifles and pistols—overtook them. Possessing only bows and arrows, the Comanches were severely beaten. Many of them, including a chief, were killed. But no report was ever made of the fight. Recovering their horses, the Chickasaws took no prisoners and permitted the Comanches to go home.

At 207.4 *m.*, back on State 99, is the junction (R) with graveled State 7.

Right on State 7 to BALLARD'S PARK (*swimming, cabins, boats, recreational facilities*), 3.0 *m.*, a private resort on the site of former Chickasaw summer gatherings for sport and amusement. It lies in a wooded area threaded by small streams. Adjoining the park is Oklahoma's only U.S. Fish Hatchery.

At 215.0 *m.* is the junction with an improved road.

Right here to a natural park called DEVIL'S DEN (*private; adm. $1 per car; fishing, camping*), 2.0 *m.*, through which Pennington Creek flows in a series of rapids, cataracts, and falls. "Oklahoma's Scenic Wonderland" is a rugged, boulder-strewn area, in which the Devil's Den proper—a cavelike recess—is formed by the overhead joining of two enormous rocks. Other features of the park are a great balanced rock known as the Devil's Chair; Dead Man's Cave, a cavern in the rocks containing grotesque formations; and high up on one of the canyon walls, a curiously shaped rock known both as the Devil's Coffin and the Witch's Tomb. One and one-half miles down Pennington Creek is the old site of Harley's Institute, Chickasaw Boys' Boarding School, now the site of the Tishomingo Golf Club. The name Devil's Den came from the Indians, who saw early-day outlaws use the area as a virtually inaccessible hideout. One mile to the west is Bullet Prairie, where legend has it that a famous Spanish explorer fought a battle with the Indians. The legend comes complete with the inevitable buried treasure.

TISHOMINGO, 216.8 *m.* (670 alt., 2,325 pop.), seat of Johnston County, was named for a beloved Chickasaw leader and served as capital of the Chickasaw Nation from its formation as an independent nation in 1856 until statehood. It is now a trade center for a productive farming region lying along the bends of Pennington Creek and the Washita River, and for the ranch country to the north and northwest. It is also a sportsmen's center for fishing and hunting on near-by Lake Texoma (*see Tour 6*).

After the Chickasaws effected their formal separation from the

Choctaws by treaty in 1855, their own government was organized and the tribal capitol installed in a small log building, which still stands in the northwestern part of the town. The second capitol was built of brick hauled from Paris, Texas. After being gutted by fire, this building was torn down and replaced by a two-story structure of native granite, which has been used as the JOHNSTON COUNTY COURTHOUSE since 1907.

Before the Chickasaw capital was located here, the place was known by the Indians as a fine camp site and was called Good Springs. In 1850, a residence was built near the springs by Jackson Frazier, an Indian, and soon afterwards two stores began business. Tishomingo received its name in 1856, and its post office in 1857. One of Oklahoma's governors, the late William H. ("Alfalfa Bill") Murray (*see History*), came to the town when a young man, married the niece of a Chickasaw governor, Douglas Johnston (for whom the county was named), and started his career as a lawyer-politician. He presided over the Constitutional Convention in 1906–07. Murray died in 1956 at the age of eighty-six, having lived to see his son Johnston also serve as Oklahoma governor, 1951–55.

The first Oklahoma state legislature, in 1908, authorized the establishment at Tishomingo of the MURRAY STATE AGRICULTURAL COLLEGE, which attained junior college rank in 1924. The two-year college course emphasizes agriculture, dairying, animal husbandry, science, mechanical arts, home economics, and education.

On a twenty-acre campus at the southern corner of the city, and on approximately one thousand acres of farm land owned by the school, the 580 students receive practical instruction and experience. With the planting of trees and shrubs, the campus has become a pleasant setting for eighteen wide-spaced buildings, including a LIBRARY AND SCIENCE BUILDING and a new FIELD HOUSE, both built since World War II. There are two men's dormitories—LUCAS and POE HALLS—the latter, built in 1919, a three-story brick and stucco structure of attractive southern mansion design. Lucas, the newer hall, was opened for the 1941–42 school year.

BETTY FULTON HALL, a solid brick building erected in 1924, houses eighty women students. A two-story brick building at the center of the campus provides a RECREATION CENTER. The three-story brick ADMINISTRATION BUILDING is used mainly for academic classwork, although it also houses business offices and the college auditorium. Located at the north entrance to the campus is a GRANITE MEMORIAL honoring the late former governor William H. Murray, for whom the school was named.

When Lake Texoma is at normal level, the shore line comes to within a quarter of a mile of Tishomingo's southern limit, with one arm reaching up Pennington Creek through the city.

MADILL, 229.5 *m.* (775 alt., 2,791 pop.) (*see Tour 6*), is at the junction with US 70 (*see Tour 6*), with which State 99 unites for its last 7.8 miles.

State 99 and this tour end at KINGSTON, 237.3 *m.* (791 alt., 677 pop.), in the heart of the Lake Texoma playground *(see Tours 6 and 8)*.

TOUR 15

Junction US 60–66–69—Grove—Jay—Westville—Sallisaw—Heavener —(Mena, Ark.); US 59, 187.5 m.

Roadbed paved throughout.
The Kansas City Southern Ry. roughly parallels the highway between Watts and the Arkansas Line.
Accommodations in the larger towns.

The eye-appeal of US 59 ranges picturesquely from the ancient to the modern. This lake and forest region of the Sooner State (where the Ozark-Ouachita play areas of Missouri and Arkansas lap over into Oklahoma) is, in effect, a visual summary of more than a century of Cherokee Indian history and old Choctaw backgrounds. Except for a few cultivated fields and occasional short stretches across timber-encircled grassland areas—which the Indians used to call "old fields"—US 59 in Oklahoma threads the narrow valleys and winds across the ridges of one of the most highly scenic sections of the state. Here and there are ruins and old buildings of the first missions established in the West. And the route itself is an ageless, one-hundred-mile April trail of dogwood, wild plum blossoms, and redbud.

US 59 has its modern touches, too—the concrete wedges that have dammed eastern Oklahoma's many streams and backed sprawling reservoirs of water into countless coves and inlets. And it is around these huge man-made lakes—Grand, Upper and Lower Spavinaw, Tenkiller, Fort Gibson, Wister, and others still unfinished—that Oklahoma's recently awakened recreation interests have centered. Strangely enough, with so much talk of drought in connection with Oklahoma, the Sooner State ranks no lower than seventh among the forty-eight states in the amount of its impounded lake and pond water. An estimated eight hundred thousand acres in Oklahoma are now covered by its 188 man-made lakes, its 100 natural lakes, its 102,000 farm and ranch ponds, its 225 creeks and 30 rivers. Along no other route will the motorist find so many water attractions.

It is a comparatively poor region, so far as farms and commercial timber are concerned. But almost from end to end, US 59 provides for the fisherman, the boatsman, the squirrel and deer hunter, the history scout, or the folklore collector. The plain vacationist has access here to beautifully clear streams, well-developed lakes, rugged hills, excellent modern accommodations, and comfortable camp sites. Toward its southern end, the tour penetrates the northern border of the Winding Stair and Kiamichi Mountains (*see Tour 15A*), where an expanding road system is opening up yet another relatively untouched vacationland.

The section of US 59 covered in this tour trends south and east from the junction with US 60–66–69 (*see Tour 1*), 0 *m.*, and runs across a brief stretch of prairie farms and ranches. At 8.9 *m.* the highway arches high above the main Grand River arm of Grand Lake on Sailboat Bridge. Beyond, the road threads a narrow neck of wooded land between Wolf Creek Bay (L) and Carey Bay (R), both of which are dotted with resorts.

GROVE, 13.9 *m.* (757 alt., 1,928 pop.), at roughly the northern end of the old Cherokee Nation, is the resort center for the eastern shore of Grand Lake (*see Tour 1*). Although still a trade center for scattered farms, orchards, and berry patches, the town's biggest industry by far is providing goods and services for vacationists.

Eight miles northeast of Grove are the ruins of a town called Cayuga, promoted and almost entirely built by a Wyandotte Indian named Mathias Splitlog. The site of Kansas City, Kansas, and other land near by, was in possession of the Wyandottes before they were moved to the small reservation they now occupy in northeastern Oklahoma. While still in Kansas, Splitlog, born in Canada in 1813, developed a keen business sense and acquired considerable wealth as a flour miller, builder, and real estate dealer. After coming to Indian Territory, he resumed his building operations on the banks of Cowskin Creek, and Cayuga became the first town in Delaware County. Extending his operation into Missouri, he built a railroad (*see below*) to serve his own flour industries and sawmills, his wagon-building works, and his mines.

Splitlog died in 1893, and his creations have practically disappeared. Only the ruins of a three-story millhouse mark the site of Cayuga. That and Splitlog Street in Kansas City, Kansas, and a small Missouri town named Splitlog are the only reminders of this pioneer Indian tycoon.

Immediately south of Grove, on either side of the Honey Creek arm of Grand Lake, is another area of vacation development. Accommodations range from fine motels to economical fishing cabins. Here is the home berth of the Southern Belle excursion boat, one of two operating on the lake. And here, too, are more than a half-dozen varieties of that Grand Lake innovation, the heated fishing dock (*see Tour 3*), inaugurated here quite recently and now spreading to eastern Oklahoma's other lakes.

Southward US 59 leaves the vacation scene momentarily and loops over flint-rock hills covered with matted oak forests. At 18.8 *m.* is the junction with a graveled road.

Left on this road to POLSON CEMETERY, 6 *m.*, where the Cherokee Confederate Brigadier General Stand Watie is buried. In Cherokee history, this Indian loomed large as one among the insignificant minority of the tribe who signed the spurious "treaty" under which the federal government acted in removing them from Georgia and Tennessee in 1838. Three other signers—Elias Boudinot, Watie's brother; Major Ridge; and his son, John—were killed after the removal by Cherokees who regarded them as traitors. From that time on Stand Watie became a bitter opponent of Chief John Ross, titular head of the tribe for almost forty years, whom he accused (on no better evidence than unfriendly gossip) of instigating the killings. Many other killings followed, and at one time Watie gathered a force together to overthrow the Ross government.

Committing himself and his adherents to the Confederate cause at the outbreak of the Civil War, Watie recruited a regiment of Cherokees, took part in the battle of Pea Ridge (*see Arkansas Guide*), was made brigadier general and put in command of an Indian brigade. According to local history, he was the last Confederate officer to surrender—more than two months after Appomattox. At one time during the Civil War he laid claim to the office of chief of the Cherokees, but his right to the office was recognized only by his own limited following.

Immediately north of the STAND WATIE GRAVE are those of members of the Ridge family, including Major Ridge.

JAY, 26.7 *m.* (1,035 alt., 697 pop.), is yet another eastern Oklahoma town where serving the area's farmers and fruit and berry growers has taken a back seat to vacationist trade. Its population has doubled since 1950, largely on the strength of its strategic location between three of the state's most dependable fishing lakes.

Named for Jay Washburn, a nephew of Stand Watie, Jay is the seat of Delaware County, having won that distinction from Grove in a special county-seat election on December 8, 1908. The actual removal of the county seat to Jay, however, was followed by a comic-opera war between two factions of the little town's promoters, each of whom fought to have the county records stored in its own courthouse. From their sketchy entrenchments, the forces of old and new Jay faced each other for several days. Some wild firing was indulged in (the only casualty: a stray mule) before the "war" was finally called off. Jay is one of three county seats in Oklahoma which have never been served by a railroad.

In the timbered Spavinaw Hills, some five miles east of Jay, is the Oak Hills Indian Center (*visitors welcome*). Here Cherokee artisans weave blankets, shawls, and other articles on their hand looms. Finished handicraft items are on sale, and special orders can be made.

At 26.3 *m.* is the junction with paved State 20.

Right on this road, past numerous developed resort areas (L) on the northern shore of both Upper and Lower Spavinaw lakes, is SPAVINAW, 14.9 *m.* (688 alt., 213 pop.), once one of the northern towns of the Cherokee Nation. It lies in the center of a region broken by flint-rock (chert) hills and gorges through which clear streams plunge. The original town was purchased by the city of Tulsa in 1922, when Spavinaw Creek was dammed to provide a water supply for that city, and moved to higher ground. Lake Spavinaw (*rental boats, motors*) now covers the old site, where once a five-story gristmill and a sawmill served the needs of the Indians. Completed in 1923, the lake has a surface area of 1,650 acres. The town of Spavinaw is strictly a vacation and recreation center.

Farther south on State 20 is the junction, 18.2 *m.*, with State 20B.

Left on this paved road to Spavinaw Hills Park, 1.5 *m.* Extending along the southern and western banks of Lower Spavinaw, this 1,600-acre tract was acquired by Tulsa to protect the lake from pollution and to provide a wildlife refuge. If he is lucky, the visitor who tramps the scenic trails may see wild turkeys (*no open season*) and he is almost sure to see deer, squirrels, rabbits, and quail. Periodic restocking assures generally excellent fishing.

SALINA, 29.2 *m.* (618 alt., 905 pop.) (*see Tour 8*).

At 31.3 *m.* is the house (R) which, it is said, was occupied by Stand Watie's family during the Civil War. Behind it is a steep-walled ravine which, some three hundred yards below, is spanned by a natural bridge.

At 32.5 *m.* is the long bridge over Upper Spavinaw Lake. Created in 1952, it is eight and one-half miles long, little more than half a mile wide, and has a shore line of fifty miles. Not only does it have approximately twice as much surface area (3,192 acres) as the older Lower Spavinaw, but it also has more tourist accommodations, most of which are grouped at either end of the bridge. Officially, Upper Spavinaw is now Lake Eucha, for the small Cherokee Indian village of Eucha, which was inundated by the lake's waters.

Approximately ten miles east of here, on the north bank of Spavinaw Creek, almost at the Arkansas Line, is the Site of Fort Wayne. Although hardly a trace of this border outpost can now be found, it played an interesting role in early-day Indian history. Established in 1832, it was the headquarters from which Captain Nathan Boone, a son of Daniel Boone, conducted early Indian Territory boundary surveys. From 1842, when the garrison was removed, until 1846 the fort stood unoccupied. Then the old buildings became the rendezvous for a force of malcontents whom Stand Watie gathered and proposed to lead against John Ross (*see above*), chief of the Cherokees. Watie again used Fort Wayne in 1861 as a recruiting base for his Confederate Indian troops.

Beyond Upper Spavinaw, US 59 winds over heavily wooded hills past the KENWOOD INDIAN RESERVATION.

At 45.5 *m.* is the junction with paved State 33.

Right on State 33 to KANSAS, 1.4 *m.* (1,000 alt., 250 pop.), a trading point for a restricted farming area, and to the junction with a graveled road, 4 *m.*

Left here is OAKS, 6.6 *m.* (800 alt., 104 pop.), a Cherokee settlement that grew out of the establishment of a Danish Lutheran school in 1902. Right from Oaks on an unimproved dirt road is the SITE OF NEW SPRINGPLACE MORAVIAN MISSION, 7.1 *m.* Here, in 1842, Moravian missionaries to the Cherokees erected a combination log schoolhouse and church. Situated at a ford on the beautifully clear Spring Creek, crossed by a branch of the old military road from Fort Gibson (*see Tour 3*) to Jefferson Barracks (at St. Louis, Missouri), the mission grew and prospered until the fierce sectional strife of the Civil War compelled its closing. After the war, the Moravians reopened the school and mission and continued the work until 1898, when the allotment of the Cherokee Nation deprived them of the land they had used. Only a stone chimney and the foundation sills remain.

At its junction with State 33, US 59 makes a right-angle turn (L) and proceeds eastward. The two highways are joined for the next 12.4 miles.

FLINT, 49.5 *m.* (1,197 alt., 25 pop.), now only a tiny settlement, was important in the first years following the Cherokee removal to this area. Here in 1838 a water-wheel gristmill and a sawmill were set up. Millstones for the gristmill were sent from France, coming by water to Van Buren, Arkansas, and from that landing on the Arkansas River by ox team. The mill was long ago removed from its original site.

In 1872, Polly Chesterton, wife of the miller, was killed by an Indian named Ezekiel Proctor, who meant the shot for her husband. Proctor's trial led to the so-called Goingsnake District Courthouse Massacre (*see Tour 3*).

At the summit of a hill, 50.7 *m.*, is a fine view of some thirty miles of timbered hills and fertile, farm-dotted valleys.

DRIPPING SPRINGS, 53.9 *m.*, is a private resort (*cabins*) that features one of Oklahoma's few waterfalls. It can best be appreciated in early spring. Then, when water is more abundant, the small stream makes an initial drop of seventy-five feet, followed by another of thirty feet, and finally a cascade of fifteen feet. A swinging footbridge some 175 feet in length and a steep path enable the visitor to descend to the pools at the bottom of the gorge.

US 59 leaves State 33 at 57.9 *m.*, near Siloam Springs, Arkansas (*see Arkansas Guide*), turning sharply southward to the junction with a graveled road, 63.5 *m.*

Left on this road is LAKE FRANCIS (*boats, float trips down the Illinois River*) (*see Tour 16*), 0.3 *m.*, a seven-hundred-acre municipal reservoir (for Siloam Springs, Arkansas) extending southward along the border between Oklahoma and Arkansas.

South of the Illinois River, US 59 skirts WATTS, 63.8 *m.* Perched against the side of a wooded hill (R), the little town serves as a rendezvous for hunters and fishermen, many of whom hire boats and guides here for Illinois River float trips (*see Tour 16*).

At 68.6 *m.* is the junction with a graveled road.

Right on this road is the SITE OF CHEROKEE BAPTIST MISSION ("Breadtown"), 0.9 *m.*, established in 1839 by Rev. Evan Jones, a missionary who had been active among the Cherokees of North Carolina for years before their removal. So closely had Jones become identified with the tribe that he was chosen by Chief John Ross in 1838 to lead one contingent of emigrants to the new home of the Cherokees in Indian Territory. With the help of another leader, the Cherokee Bushyhead, who was afterwards chief justice of the Cherokee Nation, he established the new Baptist Mission. The mission was called "Breadtown" because it was one of the places where rations were issued to the newly arrived exiles.

Known for years simply as "Baptist," this mission, under the vigorous and militant Evan Jones and his son, John B. Jones, became an important center of education and Christianization. At one time the six Baptist churches and four branches in the Cherokee Nation had a membership of twelve hundred, practically all of them full bloods. Close rivals were Methodists, who also maintained six missions.

The second printing press set up in the Cherokee Nation was at "Baptist," and here in 1844 appeared the first issue of *The Cherokee Messenger*—printed, of course, in the Cherokee characters invented by Sequoyah (*see below, see Newspapers and History*). An aggressive Unionist, Evan Jones was driven out of the Cherokee country during the Civil War by Stand Watie's Confederate forces.

At the southwest corner of WESTVILLE, 72.1 *m.* (1,128 alt., 781 pop.) (*see Tour 3*), is the junction with US 62 (*see Tour 3*).

A charcoal-burning kiln at BARON, 77.1 *m.* (904 alt., 80 pop.), is the largest of several in the state. Near-by Baron Fork Creek provides fine fishing, as it did in the old days when the Cherokees sometimes took great numbers of fish from the creek by stupefying them with the juice of certain roots. The roots were bruised and thrown into the water. The drugged fish were then caught with the hands, with gigs, or shot with arrows. Those not taken soon recovered completely from the effects of the juice.

At 84.4 *m.* is the junction with State 51, an asphalt road.

Right on this road and a graveled road that branches off to the left at approximately 4 *m.* (*follow signs*) is BITTING WATER MILL, 12.4 *m.*, one of the country's few remaining gristmills run by water power. The first mill here, with a crude undershot wheel, was built in the late 1830's or early 1840's by the Worley family. Dr.

Nicholas Bitting acquiring the springs soon afterward and the mill remained in his family's possession for almost a century. A modern overshot wheel of steel was installed which still turns out packaged stone-ground corn meal. Visitors are taken on a conducted tour of the old mill (*adm. 25c*) and given a sample of the corn meal. The name Bitting, applied to the mill, is frequently corrupted to Bidding, after Bidding Springs, the spelling used by U. S. postal authorities for the tiny settlement when it still possessed a post office.

STILWELL, 85.1 *m.*, (1,108 alt., 1,813 pop.), is the seat of Adair County, which claims a higher percentage of Indian population than any other county in the United States. Here is, in fact, the heart of the district first settled by the immigrant Cherokees in the 1830's, and two active churches are still maintained near Stilwell by Cherokees.

Farming, fruit growing, and lumbering have long maintained the town, but in recent years the strawberry has become a one-million-dollar industry. In 1956 some 1,200 acres of strawberries were grown in the Stilwell area. The local cannery (the state's largest food freezing and processing plant) employed from 275 to 300 men and women during the rush period and handled eight thousand crates of berries a day. At other seasons it both cans and freezes other fruits and vegetables. Stilwell's biggest annual event is its mid-May strawberry festival.

Along this eastern fringe of Oklahoma—especially from Stilwell south through the Cookson Hills to Sallisaw—US 59 is called "The Dogwood Trail." It should, if possible, be traveled in the last three weeks of April. Not only can the white blaze of the large-petaled dogwood be seen at this time under the tall oaks, but the pink of the redbud trees and the fragrant wild plum blossoms along the small streams are also at their best. Recently civic groups throughout the Cookson and Cherokee Hills have pooled their efforts to stage a Dogwood Week. Organized tours are arranged and signs put up to direct motorists to the most beautiful spots.

At 111.2 *m.* is the junction with paved State 101.

Left on this road is SEQUOYAH'S CABIN STATE MONUMENT, 7.6 *m.* Inside the stone fence (*adm. free*) is a simple log cabin (L). Built in 1855, it was originally attached to the Sequoyah Cabin, using the same fireplace. A path leads a hundred yards, past the caretaker's house (R), to a large stone building. Inside this is now preserved the original Sequoyah Cabin, built by Sequoyah himself in 1829, along with an old organ, a hymn book, and other relics and documents relating to Sequoyah's life and to the Cherokee Nation.

Sequoyah, whose English name was George Gist, was a half-blood Cherokee. A silversmith, soldier, and manufacturer of salt at various times during his life, he is better known throughout America as an influential tribal statesman and an educator who bestowed upon the Cherokees the greatest addition ever made to the culture of a primitive people. When Sequoyah first conceived the idea of his syllabary he was thought to be possessed of evil spirits, and his fellow tribesmen picked a group of warriors to try him. After a week of trial, all of the jury had learned to read and write by Sequoyah's system. Needless to say, he was vindicated.

As a leading man of the "Old Settler" Cherokees, who migrated west before the forced removal, Sequoyah signed the Act of Union with the "Newcomers" on July 12, 1839. The Cherokee Nation awarded him, shortly before his death, an income of $500 a year, to be derived from the working of a salt bed near Sallisaw (*see Tour 2*). According to ethnologist Alice Marriott, this was the first (and probably the only) purely literary pension ever awarded within the history and boundaries of the United States. The Cherokee Nation also presented him with a medal, which he wore on a chain around his neck for the rest of his life. It appears in the portrait of him by the artist, Charles Bird King, now in the Smithsonian Institution. The giant Sequoyah trees of California were also named for him, and his statue—by George Julian Zolnay—stands in Statuary Hall in the national Capitol at Washington, D.C. Fittingly, Sequoyah was chosen as one of the world's twelve alphabet inventors to be reproduced in bronze on the great doors of the Library of Congress Annex. It is interesting to note that ten of the other characters chosen are mythological: T'sang Chieh, Nabu, Brahma, Cadmus, Tahmurah, Hermes, Odin, Ogma, Itzamna, and Quetzalcoatl.

SALLISAW, 114.7 *m.* (513 alt., 2,885 pop.) (*see Tour 2*), is at the junction with US 64 (*see Tour 2*). The two highways are united west through the town to 115.9 *m.*, where US 59 turns south (L).

At the ARKANSAS RIVER, 126.6 *m.*, US 59 enters the old Choctaw Nation. At 137.2 *m.* the highway joins with US 271 (*see Tour 7*) for the next 17.0 miles.

POTEAU, 151.3 *m.* (483 alt., 4,776 pop.) (*see Tour 7*).

US 59 leaves US 271 at 154.2 *m.*, proceeds south along the fertile valley of the Poteau River to its junction with US 270, 165.0 *m.* (*see Tour 5*). The two routes are united for the next 22.5 miles to the Arkansas Line.

HEAVENER, 167.7 *m.* (561 alt., 2,103 pop.), lies at the northern limit of the Ouachita mountain range in an area of good farms and pastures, and there are virtually unlimited opportunities for sports and recreation. The immediate area was known to the Choctaws as the Prairie of the Tall Grass. The town was named for Joe Heavener, a white man who lived among the Choctaws and owned the land on which it was laid out. So well liked by the Indians was Heavener that at times he served as arbitrator of disputes among them.

In 1910 the town was made a division point on the Kansas City Southern Railway, a part of which was built by the wealthy Wyandotte Indian, Mathias Splitlog (*see above*). For some years the road was known as "The Splitlog." Looming some twelve hundred feet over Heavener to the northeast is the mass of a hogback ridge called POTEAU

MOUNTAIN. Under it lie undeveloped veins of coal, and on its slopes are fine stands of hardwood timber.

South of Heavener, at 172.9 *m.*, is another of Oklahoma's six state fish hatcheries. A dam across Black Fork River, 250 feet long and 80 feet high, provides water for the culture ponds. Bass, bluegill, and channel catfish have been propagated here in recent years. The hatchery occupies a 344-acre tract.

At 175.5 *m.* is the junction with a natural-gravel road, the eastern end of the highly scenic Holson Valley Road (*see Tour* 7).

Right here (*following signs*) to CEDAR LAKE (*fishing, camping*) 3.9 *m.*, a ninety-three-acre reservoir that offers excellent fishing and unexcelled scenery. It is one of the few lakes in this area under the supervision of the United States Forest Service.

At 179.3 *m.* is the junction (R) with State 103 (*see Tour* 15A).

This last stretch of US 59 cuts through the Oklahoma section of the vast OUACHITA NATIONAL FOREST, a 181,000-acre playground of heavily timbered mountains and well-watered valleys. (The entire forest, most of which lies in Arkansas, includes nearly 1,500,000 acres.) Hunting and fishing resources here are among the finest offered anywhere in the state. Forest-service trails lead to a number of developed campgrounds, and fire towers offer the visitor, at the end of a brisk climb, unsurpassed panoramas of the entire area. For complete information on the Ouachita playground, the visitor should go to the district ranger's office in Heavener.

PAGE, 183.2 *m.* (922 alt., 90 pop.), lies in the heart of the Ouachita National Forest, which includes parts of the Winding Stair Mountains to the west and the Kiamichi Mountains to the south. It serves as a convenient outfitting point for sportsmen and vacationers.

The 2,900-foot summit (R) of RICH MOUNTAIN, 185.8 *m.*, is on the Oklahoma-Arkansas Line. In an area just one mile square atop this mountain, naturalists and timber experts say, one can find forty-seven varieties of trees, twenty-seven varieties of wild fruits, seventeen kinds of medicinal plants, and more than one hundred different flowers, plus many mosses and ferns, some of which are subtropical. At the top of the mountain—the most convenient access is from Arkansas (*see Arkansas Guide*)—at an elevation of two thousand feet above the surrounding valleys, are the picturesque ruins of the WILHELMINA CASTLE (*see Arkansas Guide*).

US 59 crosses the ARKANSAS LINE, 187.5 *m.*, fifteen miles northwest of Mena, Arkansas (*see Arkansas Guide*).

TOUR 15A

Junction US 59—Big Cedar—Bethel—Broken Bow—Junction US 70; State 103, Unnumbered road, State 21, 73.4 m.

Roadbed natural gravel, except the last six miles, which are paved. After flooding rain in the Kiamichi Mountains, it is advisable to wait a few hours for water to run off.
Accommodations limited to Smithville, Beavers Bend State Park, and Broken Bow.

Perhaps Oklahoma's most scenic byway, this route crosses the southern half of the Ouachita National Forest, then cuts through extensive privately owned forests under the supervision of the state's Division of Forestry. This means that the whole region is under special care by either the federal or the state government, that the roads, if not turnpikes, are adequately maintained, that the game is properly protected, that the streams are stocked with fish, and that the visitor is provided with at least a minimum of facilities for his convenience and enjoyment. In return, the hunter, fisherman, camper, or passing tourist is urged to co-operate, particularly in the prevention of fire. From strategically placed lookout towers (to which visitors are always welcome) rangers keep the entire area under observation at all times.

Progress is gradually being made in the long-time struggle to change the status of this mountain route from byway to highway. Latest step forward was the recent rebuilding of the 15.5-mile stretch at the beginning of the route now known as State 103. Although the roadbed has only a gravel surface at present, it is a first-class road in every other respect, for this will eventually be the route followed by US 59, which is now forced to make a dog-leg into Arkansas before continuing its southern course through Texas.

Tour 15A is essentially a route for sportsmen, experienced campers, and those motorists who are willing to sacrifice ease in driving for beauty of setting. It penetrates the best hunting and fishing region in the state. In the woods and valleys of the Winding Stair and Kiamichi mountains are deer, ducks, quail, and squirrels. Here, too, an occasional flock of wild turkeys may be seen, though this once-plentiful game bird is not yet common enough to afford, with the others, an open hunting season. From such streams as the Kiamichi, Mountain Fork, Glover, Eagle, Boktukolo, and countless smaller creeks fishermen take largemouthed, smallmouthed, and rock bass, channel catfish, and goggle-eyed perch. (The largest bass and the largest flathead ever caught in Oklahoma were taken from the Kiamichi River.) Fishermen trail down shadowed canyons, scramble through cliffside underbrush, and climb over high-piled rocks that give a distinctive character to this southeastern corner of the state.

The timber resources of the area are still considerable, and lumbering is a principal industry, although far less important than it once was. The operations of lumber companies and the destruction from fires over the years have almost exhausted the former fine stands of pine and seriously depleted the supply of such hardwoods as oak, hickory, elm, and walnut. But federal and state authorities, as well as far-sighted lumbering interests, are now co-operating intelligently and wholeheartedly on fire protection and on long-range reforestation programs. In the valleys are farms whose owners supplement their generally meager crop income by working in the logging camps and at the "groundhog" (small local) sawmills which turn out sizable amounts of crossties, telephone poles, and fence posts.

Southwestward from its junction with US 59, 0 *m.* (*see Tour 15*), four miles northwest of PAGE (922 alt., 90 pop.) (*see Tour 15*), State 103 cuts through the Ouachita National Forest to the junction with a second gravel road, 4.5 *m.*

West (R) on this road is the WINDING STAIR TOWER (*visitors welcome*), 1.5 *m.*, one of the forest's lookout towers. It affords a long, impressive view of the northern reaches of the Ouachita preserve, and the many crags and ridges of the Ouachita and Winding Stair ranges.

State 103 veers south here, skirting the western edge of the Rich Mountain hogback (*see Tour 15*), a part of the Ouachita system.

BIG CEDAR, 9.3 *m.* (964 alt., 13 pop.), is a tiny mountain crossroads village from which the motorist can get a minimum of necessary supplies, but a maximum of advice and useful information, so far as the region's sport and recreational facilities are concerned.

At Big Cedar is the junction with State 63, which leads westward along the southern boundary of Ouachita National Forest twenty-six miles to Talihina (*see Tour 7*). Eastward, State 63 cuts through the forest thirteen miles to the Arkansas Line and then, via Arkansas 8, to Mena, Arkansas (*see Arkansas Guide*).

The KIAMICHI RIVER, 11.3 *m.* is the most important stream of the southeastern Oklahoma mountain region. South of the river, the route climbs up into the main range of the Kiamichi, reaching its highest elevation, 1,600 feet, on the side of Kiamichi Mountain itself, 13.3 *m.* From this point the motorist gets perhaps his finest panorama of timbered ridges and stream-cut valleys.

At 13.7 *m.* is the junction with a CCC-built skyline drive.

Left on this road to Crow's Nest, 7 *m.*, another Forest Service lookout tower, from which one gets an excellent view of Lynn, Blue Bouncer, Pine, Rich, and Walnut mountains, Turkey Snout Ridge, and some of the Arkansas Ouachita range.

At 15.5 *m.* is the southern boundary of Ouachita National Forest. State 103 ends here. The fairly primitive mountain road extending southward to Smithville provides safe, but relatively slow going. Dropping down off the crest of the mountains, the road enters the valley through which flows Cucumber Creek, and a second valley drained by the united Big Eagle and Eagle Fork creeks. Here in the old Choctaw Nashoba (Wolf) County, the Kiamichis are at their wildest and most beautiful. Deer are plentiful. Squirrels, quail, and ducks are always close at hand. And in the deep pools of the clear-water rivers and creeks the big fish lie waiting for the angler.

Cucumber Creek, crossed at 18.6 *m.*, is one of the area's dependable fishing streams. The name comes from the curiously curved and thickened branch-ends of the magnolia trees along its banks.

SMITHVILLE, 28.6 *m.* (700 alt., 256 pop.), is an isolated village in the heart of a sportsman's paradise. Several fishing camps provide accommodations for vacationists and serve as outfitters for those wishing to make "float" trips down the Mountain Fork River. Too many portages prevent this river from rivaling the Illinois (*see Tour 16*) in float-trip popularity, but a boat is a virtual necessity in reaching the stream's largest and deepest holes. According to pioneers, it was in this region that the Choctaws found game and fish most plentiful in the old days. Here they could fish when "the rabbit hollers" or "the Peter bird sang," using as bait anything from bread dough to foot-long fishworms—one of which was judged ample for catching twenty fish.

It was the Indian squirrel-shooter, too, who established the vogue of the "still hunt," still popular in the Kiamichis. With the idea of obtaining game with the least amount of effort, the still hunter goes out at daybreak when there is no breeze to ruffle the leaves of the trees. Taking his stand in a likely spot, he waits motionless, scanning the treetops for the first telltale movement of a squirrel. When it comes, the shot must be quick and true. But in pleasant contrast to most sports, failure in the still hunt is generally unaccompanied by physical exhaustion.

At Smithville is the junction with State 21, graveled for the most part, over which the tour continues. The highway veers southwestward from Smithville, following the north bank of Mountain Fork River (L) and serving a number of picturesquely located fishing camps.

At 35.4 *m.* the route crosses Boktukolo Creek, another of the region's fine fishing streams. Below the bridge, on the east bank of the creek, which flows into Mountain Fork immediately to the south, the motorist can see the cut of an old horseback trail used before the Civil War. During the early 1870's, this pass was often traveled by prospectors searching for silver and copper in the mountains to the north. Part of the picturesque route through "The Narrows" can now be used by adventurous fishermen.

On the bank of a branch of Glover River, BETHEL, 44.9 *m.* (750 alt., 150 pop.), is a trading point for scattered farm families and timber workers, and a favorite rendezvous for deer hunters during the brief open season in the fall. For the past few years a state-wide deer season has been proclaimed for the first time, but the seven southeastern counties continue to provide the bulk of the kill. In 1955 some 23,000 hunters bagged 1,344 deer.

At 49.8 *m.* is the community of MT. HERMAN.

Left from Mt. Herman on an improved CCC-built road is the OKLAHOMA STATE GAME PRESERVE, 8.1 *m.*, comprising some 16,000 acres of densely wooded land lying astride Mountain Fork River. It is Oklahoma's only virgin-timber park (mostly pine, with oak, gum, cypress, sycamore, and a dozen other native trees in sizable numbers), and although facilities for visitors are virtually nonexistent, it offers a concentration of wildflowers and native birds of such variety as to made the trip more than worth while.

In this section the route twists and turns, dips downhill and rises abruptly. In places the roadbed has been improved, but the motorist should drive slowly and carefully.

Topping the highest peak (L) of the southern Kiamichis, CARTER MOUNTAIN TOWER (*visitors welcome*), 54.2 *m.*, is another fire lookout. At the end of the tower's stairs the visitor will have reached an altitude of 1,320 feet, with a view of more than fifteen miles in every direction.

GOVERNMENT SPRINGS, 62.0 *m.*, marks the camp site of the government crews that made the original surveys in this area. Immediately beyond is the Opah Trail, one of many which crisscross the surrounding forests.

At 64.2 *m.* is the junction with a natural-gravel road.

Left (east) on this road to MOUNTAIN FORK RIVER, 4.0 *m.*, where it is feasible to launch a boat for float-trip fishing. Across the river at HOCHATOWN is a country school, representing all that remains of an old Choctaw settlement.

At 66.7 *m.* is the junction with paved State 21A.

Left on this rolling, forest-lined road is BEAVERS BEND STATE PARK (*cabins, store, fishing, swimming, boating, hiking trails, picnic and play areas*),

7.6 *m.*, a 1,300-acre preserve of rough, primitive beauty. Clear, fast-flowing Mountain Fork River bisects the park, running between high and rugged banks. Cold, spring-fed streams cascade down the mountain slopes. Squirrels, deer, quail, and wild turkeys, and what is said to be the greatest variety of birds found anywhere in Oklahoma live in game-preserve security among the pines and hardwoods. And the boulder-filled deep holes and stony riffles of Mountain Fork teem with game fish. A low water dam in the park provides seven thousand feet of river front for swimming and boating, as well as for fishing. Hiking trails serve the more remote areas, provide the nature lover with his best opportunity for enjoying the park's great variety of wildflowers. Among those usually encountered along the way are bird's-foot and dogtooth violets, wild hyacinth, iris, plum, trillium, bloodroot, honeysuckle, trumpet creeper, and the profusely growing wild rose.

State 21 descends gradually, on pavement, south of the Beavers Bend entrance. At 71.7 *m.* (L) is the Broken Bow district headquarters of the STATE DIVISION OF FORESTRY (*visitors welcome*).

The route ends on the southwest edge of BROKEN BOW, 73.4 *m.* (467 alt., 1,838 pop.) (*see Tour* 6), at the junction with US 70 (*see Tour* 6).

TOUR 16

Lake Francis Dam (Watts)—Tahlequah—Barber—Tenkiller Lake; Illinois River, 69 m. (all mileages are approximate).

Accommodations limited to towns near the river banks; cabins and camping facilities at various points on the river. A state fishing license (nonresident, $5.00 per yr., 10 days $2.25; resident, $2.00 per yr.) may be obtained at Lake Francis Dam, at Tahlequah, or at the larger camps along the river.

This tour is a drifting voyage down the Illinois River, a picturesque stream that twists its way in a southerly and slightly westerly direction through the hills of the old Cherokee country at the eastern edge of Oklahoma. The river penetrates a region known as the last retreat of the full bloods. At places it is broken by portages that vary from a few feet to a few yards, but none is difficult under ordinary conditions. Throughout almost the length of the tour, the river runs between rugged, rocky bluffs that range in height from 50 to 150 feet. The water is generally deep, and the stream bed either rock or coarse gravel, though occasionally it is covered with silt washed in from upland farms. Those who choose the fall for their "float" trip will find the Illinois rich in color from the trees and shrubs that cling to the steep bluffs and crowd to the water's edge. Brilliant reds and yellows predominate.

Fishermen may make the tour at any time, but it is least advisable at the midsummer low-water stage. The best seasons are early spring and late fall. The river and its tributaries are stocked annually by the State Game and Fish Department, which has also constructed more than three hundred low-water dams in feeder streams to regulate the volume of the Illinois and to provide year-round fishing.

The Illinois is free of rapids, whirlpools, and undertows. It flows swiftly, but always smoothly, except for brief periods following heavy rains. The entire "float" may occupy the leisurely fisherman for eight or nine days. But for one with fewer days to spend on the water, it can be done easily in four. And the hurried floater can always arrange to take only the upper section from Lake Francis to Tahlequah, or many shorter trips between those two points. At most of the camps from Watts to Tahlequah arrangements can be made to float any part of the river. The boat will be hauled to the desired launching site, from which one may drift for one to seven days. A one-day trip will cost two people from $20.00 to $25.00, which includes the boat, guide, and food. On longer floats, where camping gear as well as food are provided, the cost goes up to as much as $18.00 a day per person.

At the western end, 0 *m.*, of LAKE FRANCIS DAM, 1.6 miles north of WATTS (958 alt., 267 pop.) (*see Tour 15*), the voyager gets into his fishing clothes—not forgetting an old coat to wear in the cool of the evening—and climbs aboard his boat. Necessary equipment includes blankets or bedrolls and changes of clothing, as well as such camping items as frying pan, coffee pot, tin plates, and a large all-purpose knife. Luxury equipment on the river might include such things as a tent, wading boots, and rifles. Dry-fly fishermen and plug casters are outnumbered two to one by those who cut willow switches and bait their hooks with live bait which is readily obtainable along the stream.

Most commonly taken in the Illinois are crappie, largemouthed and spotted bass, blue channel catfish (which sometimes attain enormous size), and mountain and black perch. Red horse—tasty, hard-fighting fish that vary in size from three to eight pounds—are seldom taken except during "shoalings." At this time, about one week before the dogwood blooms in early April, the red horse are laying eggs in shallow stretches of the water. Then the local fishermen descend on them, using baitless hooks on a heavy line from twelve to eighteen feet long. Usually two or three grab hooks are placed about three feet apart and the line is weighted with a heavy sinker. As the line, thrown into the water in a big loop, is dragged across the shoal, the red horse either take the hooks or are caught by the gills when the line is pulled in.

During almost the entire trip the fly caster will stick to his boat, for the banks are generally too rugged and overgrown to permit fishing from shore. Recommended to the bass fishermen are dark flies and live minnows. The water is so clear that brilliantly colored flies and spinners are not required. Good flies on the Illinois are black gnat, Nez Perces, black hackle, black spider, a fly known locally as "yellow Sally," and other small yellow or brown varieties. For casting, experienced fishermen choose the small dark Chugger Spook, the Al Foos, or similar shimmy wigglers.

At 25 *m.*, downstream, are cabins and ample camping space. A store here is stocked with fishing equipment and groceries. Adjoining the camp on the south is a RECREATION GROUND (*free water, picnic facilities*), maintained by the State Game and Fish Department.

Northwest of the camp are the buildings and grounds of the NORTHEAST OUTING CLUB (*private*).

At 27 *m.* is HANGING ROCK CAMP (*cabins, store*). Near it (R) is a ROADSIDE PARK (*open to tourists*) extending from the west bank of the river to State 10.

NORTHEASTERN TEACHERS CAMP, 39 *m.*, is privately owned, but floaters are usually permitted to camp here. Downstream is MARTIN'S CAMP (*open to the public*), at 41 *m.* In this section the river banks offer good camp sites and supplies can often be bought at near-by farmhouses.

At 54 *m.* is the BRIDGE over which US 62 (*see Tour 3*) crosses the river. TAHLEQUAH (864 alt., 4,750 pop.) (*see Tour 3*) is 3.2 miles to the west. South of the bridge, at the highway, is RIVERSIDE PARK, owned and maintained by the city of Tahlequah.

For the floater who wishes to vary his voyage by leaving the river to hunt (*state license, $2.00; the land owner's permission is required*), the Cookson Hills south of Tahlequah offer the best opportunity. Cottontail rabbits (*no closed season*) and red and gray squirrels (*closed season Jan. 1 to May 1*) are fairly plentiful in the woods. The country is too thickly wooded to tempt the quail hunter. And the only wild ducks seen are occasional teal that linger for a time after early October.

On this section of the river it is unprofitable for the fisherman to explore the small tributary streams. They are uniformly shallow, clear, and devoid of large rocks or sunken logs needed to provide hiding places for the fish.

BARON FORK CREEK, 59 *m.*, however, is a good fishing stream (L) accessible by boat for some twenty miles. Besides the varieties found in the Illinois, the fisherman in this beautiful, canyon-locked stream may take excellent miniature brown bass, a game fish that prefers the cold spring-fed creek to the warmer expanses of the river. The creek, varying in width and depth, has cut its way through rugged hills. Its rock-and-gravel bottom is shaded most of the day by high, steep cliffs that rise on either side.

At 66 *m.* the river makes a wide horseshoe bend, flowing rather swiftly under the shadow of a limestone bluff (L) that rises some one hundred feet above the water. At the middle of the bend is a similar cliff (R), its sheer surface bare and deeply eroded. Trees at the top of the cliffs grow so near the edge that their shadows are cast upon the water below.

At 69 *m.* the bluff slopes so gradually that near-by farmers have cut a road down to the lake over which they haul water for livestock.

Left on this road is BARBER, 2.5 *m.*, a tiny country settlement grouped about a small church in which services are still conducted in the Cherokee language. For many years the Sunday sermon has usually been preached by Jackson Standing Deer Larvin, a North Carolina–born Cherokee who came to Indian Territory at the age of nine.

The CHEROKEE CEMETERY, 3 *m.*, is worth a visit on Decoration Day. Indians begin to arrive the evening before on foot, on horseback, by wagon, and by automobile, camping near the cemetery. The evening is spent singing songs in Cherokee. In the morning they march in procession to the burying ground and hold a service, after which they re-form to march slowly through the cemetery, scattering flowers indiscriminately upon all graves. Most of the flowers are made of crepe paper, but some are gathered from roadsides and pastures. At noon a communal meal is spread on plank trestle tables. Here are served such characteristic Cherokee dishes as *conutchie* (a hominy made of corn and nuts), bean bread, and lye-treated hominy.

Many white residents of Barber and the surrounding neighborhood belong to a religious sect called the True Followers of Christ. They have no church building and no ordained minister, but meet on Sunday afternoons at the home of a member, where services are conducted by various members. The True Followers' faith teaches them to rely upon "the power of the word," and to refuse all medical aid when ill. Instead, the elders of the congregation assemble at the home of the patient and pray for his recovery.

Members of the sect habitually greet one another with the "holy kiss" and observe the foot-washing ritual at Sunday services. Women members are forbidden to cut their hair, use cosmetics, or wear beads, rings, or other ornaments. Severe simplicity of dress is demanded, though no uniform has been adopted. They profess to be in constant communication with God and declare that messages come from Him directing each small detail of their lives.

The Illinois River floating tour ends at Horseshoe Bend, where the river flows into the upper reaches of Tenkiller Lake (*see Tour 2*), at approximately 79 miles.

PART IV: *Appendices*

CHRONOLOGY

1541 Francisco Vásquez de Coronado crosses western Oklahoma in search of the golden city of Quivira; claims land for Spain but makes no permanent settlement.
Hernando de Soto explores along present eastern border of Oklahoma.

1650 Don Diego de Castillo spends six months in the Wichita Mountains prospecting for gold and silver.

1682 René Robert Cavelier, Sieur de la Salle, claims for the King of France all lands drained by the Mississippi River (including Oklahoma) under the name of Louisiana.

1719 Bernard de la Harpe crosses southeastern Oklahoma from the Red River to the vicinity of the present Muskogee.
Charles Claude du Tisné visits Pawnee villages near the present site of Chelsea.

1762 Louisiana (including Oklahoma) is ceded to Spain by France.

1800 Louisiana is retroceded to France by Spain.

1802 United States makes a compact with Georgia to remove the Creeks and Cherokees from the state as soon as it can be done "peaceably and on favorable terms."
Pierre Chouteau induces some of the Osages to remove from Missouri to northeastern Oklahoma and opens up a profitable trade with them.

1803 United States purchases Louisiana from France.
President Thomas Jefferson draws up a proposal for exchanging land occupied by Indians in the eastern states for "equivalent portions" in Louisiana.

1804 All of Louisiana north of the thirty-third parallel is designated as the District of Louisiana and placed under the administration of Indiana Territory; William Henry Harrison thus becomes the first American governor of Oklahoma.

1805 District of Louisiana is organized as the Territory of Louisiana with the seat of government at St. Louis.

1806 Lieutenant James B. Wilkinson descends the Arkansas River crossing northeastern Oklahoma.

1808 Several Cherokee chiefs and headmen inform President Jefferson that a portion of the tribe wishes to emigrate to the West.

1812 Territory of Louisiana is organized as the Territory of Missouri.
George C. Sibley, United States Indian agent, explores the Great Salt Plains near the present Cherokee.

1817 Cherokees sign the first removal treaty obtaining land in the present state of Arkansas, and the movement of one-third of the tribe to the new location begins.
Fort Smith is established on the present border of Oklahoma to protect the immigrant Indians.

1819 That portion of the Territory of Missouri south of 36°30′ is organized as the Territory of Arkansas, including all of Oklahoma except a strip along the present northern boundary.
Thomas Nuttall, English naturalist, visits Oklahoma studying flora and fauna.
Boundary between the United States and the Spanish possessions is fixed at the Red River and the one-hundredth meridian, thus establishing the southern and western limits of Oklahoma.

1820 Choctaws purchase the area south of the Canadian and Arkansas rivers—the first eastern Indian tribe to acquire land in Oklahoma—but few remove to the new location.
Arkansas legislature passes an act creating Miller County in southeastern Oklahoma and establishing the Miller Courthouse, the first court within the present state.

1821 Rev. Epaphras Chapman founds Union Mission on Grand River among the Osages—the first Protestant mission in Oklahoma.
Sequoyah completes the Cherokee alphabet.

1824 First post office in Oklahoma is opened at Miller Courthouse.
Fort Gibson—the first fort in Oklahoma—is established on the Grand River; Fort Towson is established on the Red River near the mouth of the Kiamichi.

1825 Treaty with the Choctaws fixes the present eastern boundary of Oklahoma from Fort Smith to the Red River.

1826 Creeks purchase a tract of land in Oklahoma, and a portion of the tribe prepares to emigrate.
Military road is constructed from Fort Gibson to Fort Smith, the first road established in Oklahoma.

1828 First immigrant Creeks arrive in Oklahoma and begin to lay out farms in the Arkansas valley.
Cherokees in Arkansas exchange their land for a tract in Okla-

homa; the boundary established by this treaty fixes the remainder of the present eastern boundary of the state.

1829 Arkansas Cherokees begin their removal to Oklahoma; Sequoyah settles in the present Sequoyah County; Dwight Mission, established by the Presbyterians for the Arkansas Cherokees, is removed to Oklahoma. Sam Houston, after resigning as governor of Tennessee, settles near Fort Gibson and is granted full citizenship rights by the Cherokee Council.

President Andrew Jackson in his message to Congress advises removal of all Indians remaining in the East.

1830 Indian Removal Act is passed by Congress.

Choctaws cede the remainder of their land in Mississippi and prepare to remove to Oklahoma, the main removals taking place during the succeeding three years.

A Presbyterian church is organized among the Creeks in the Arkansas valley.

1832 Cherokee Council provides for the opening of five schools, the first school law enacted in the present state of Oklahoma.

Washington Irving accompanies United States rangers on an expedition from Fort Gibson to the present site of Norman, recording his experiences in *A Tour on the Prairies*.

Creeks cede the remainder of their land in the East, thus paving the way for the removal of the succeeding four years.

A Presbyterian church is organized among the immigrant Choctaws at Wheelock, and a Baptist church among the Creeks.

1833 Seminoles are tricked into signing a removal treaty, which is followed by the long and exhausting Seminole War and the final colonization of the tribe in Oklahoma.

1834 United States Commissioners draw up a territorial form of government for the immigrant Indians, the first of many futile attempts to create an Indian state of Oklahoma.

Leavenworth-Dodge Expedition from Fort Gibson visits southwestern Oklahoma and establishes friendly relations with the wild tribes.

1835 Comanche and Wichita Indians enter into treaty relations with the United States at a council near the present site of Lexington.

Criminal jurisdiction of the federal courts of Arkansas is extended over Oklahoma.

Cherokees remaining in the East cede their land to the United States, thus paving the way for the removals of the succeeding three years.

Samuel A. Worcester installs a printing press at Union Mission and publishes the first book printed in Oklahoma.

1837 Chickasaws surrender their lands in the East and begin their removal to Oklahoma.

1838 Choctaws complete a council house of hewn logs near the present site of Tuskahoma, the first capitol built in Oklahoma.

1839 Newly arrived Cherokees and "Old Settler Cherokees" adopt a new constitution and establish a council ground at Tahlequah.

1842 Fort Washita is established to protect the Chickasaw settlements from the wild tribes of the Southwest.

Choctaw congregation at Wheelock builds a stone church, which still stands as the oldest church building in Oklahoma.

1843 A great council of eighteen Indian tribes is held at Tahlequah, and a code of intertribal law is drawn up and adopted by the Cherokees, Creeks, and Osages.

1844 *The Cherokee Messenger*—the first newspaper published in Oklahoma—is issued at a Baptist missionary station north of the present Westville; it is followed a month later by *The Cherokee Advocate,* published at Tahlequah.

First cotton gin in the Cherokee Nation—probably the first in Oklahoma—is constructed on the Arkansas fifteen miles above Fort Smith.

1849 First Masonic Lodge established in an Indian tribe is organized at Tahlequah.

Hordes of California gold-seekers follow a well-defined trail across Oklahoma.

1850 Texas relinquishes the land north of 36°30′, thus forming the southern boundary of the Oklahoma Panhandle.

1851 Fort Arbuckle is established.

1852 Tahlequah is incorporated under Cherokee law—the first incorporated town in Oklahoma.

1854 Kansas-Nebraska Act defines the southern boundary of Kansas at 37°, thus fixing the northern boundary of Oklahoma.

1856 Seminoles separate from the Creeks and form their own government.

Chickasaws set up a tribal government, adopt a constitution, and establish Tishomingo as their capital.

1858 Butterfield stage and mail route is laid out, crossing Oklahoma from Fort Smith west and south to the Red River.

1859 An intertribal law code is drawn up by the Five Civilized Tribes (Cherokees, Choctaws, Chickasaws, Creeks, and Seminoles) at North Fork Town.

Fort Cobb is established on the western frontier of civilized Indian settlement.

1860 Choctaws adopt the constitution under which their government functions until the end of the tribal period.

1861 United States abandons the forts in Oklahoma; most of the Indian tribes align with the Confederates; thousands of Union Indians flee to Kansas.

1862 A Union military expedition from Kansas penetrates to Fort Gibson.

1863 Union forces defeat the Confederates at Honey Springs, the most important battle fought in Oklahoma during the Civil War.

1865 Confederate Indians surrender to Union forces more than two months after Appomattox; United States officials hold a council with the Indians and lay down terms for the resumption of treaty relations.

1866 Five Civilized Tribes sign treaties with the United States freeing their slaves, ceding the western half of Oklahoma for the settlement of other Indians, and agreeing to a tentative intertribal organization.

The name Oklahoma is first suggested by Allen Wright, member of the Choctaw treaty delegation.

Congress grants franchises for the construction of the first two railroads across Oklahoma.

1867 United States makes the first of a series of treaties, assigning reservations to Indian tribes in the ceded territory.

Creeks adopt their final constitution.

1869 Fort Sill is established as the base of operations against the Plains Indians.

1870 Construction is started on the Missouri-Kansas-Texas Railroad —the first to enter the Oklahoma area.

Federal government begins the survey of the Chickasaw district, establishing the initial point from which all of Oklahoma except the Panhandle is eventually surveyed.

First meeting of the intertribal council is convened at Okmulgee.

1872 First coal mining on a commercial scale begins at McAlester in the Choctaw Nation.

1874 Fort Reno is established.

1875 Resistance of the Plains Indians to white encroachment is finally crushed.

Intertribal council at Okmulgee holds its last session.

1876 Last buffalo herd is reported in Oklahoma.

1879 First telephone in Oklahoma is set up, connecting Fort Sill and Fort Reno.

"Boomers" begin their attempts to settle on the "Oklahoma Lands."

Will Rogers is born in the Cherokee Nation near Oologah.

Population of the Indian Territory is estimated at 81,381; this includes Indians, a few white residents, and former slaves of the Indians.

1882 Isparhecher begins the rebellion against the Creek government known as the Green Peach War.

Atlantic and Pacific Railroad establishes a station in the Creek Nation at a place called "Tulsey Town" by the Indians.

1883 Isparhecher faction makes peace with the constitutional Creek government.

Cherokee Strip Live Stock Association leases the "Outlet" from the Cherokee Nation.

1884 A company of Choctaw citizens drills for oil near Atoka.

1887 Congress passes the Dawes Act, providing for breaking up the Indian reservations into individual allotments and opening the surplus land to white settlement.

1889 First federal court in Oklahoma is established in Muskogee.

Oklahoma's first producing oil well is drilled near Chelsea.

First Run opens an area in Oklahoma to white settlement; Oklahoma City, Guthrie, Norman, and other cities and towns are established.

1890 Congress creates a Territorial government for the settlers in the "Oklahoma Lands"; Guthrie becomes the capital; George W. Steele is appointed governor; the First Territorial Legislature adopts a code of laws and establishes a school system.

Panhandle is joined to the Territory of Oklahoma.

First federal census shows a population of 78,475 in Oklahoma Territory and 180,182 in the area of the Five Civilized Tribes.

1891 First statehood convention is held in Oklahoma City.

First Territorial college—later the Central State College—is opened at Edmond; the Oklahoma Agricultural and Mechanical College is opened at Stillwater.

The Sac and Fox, Iowa, Shawnee, and Potawatomi reservations are opened for settlement, adding two new counties.

1892 University of Oklahoma is opened at Norman.

The Cheyenne and Arapaho country is opened for settlement, adding six new counties.

1893 Dawes Commission is created for the purpose of liquidating the affairs of the Five Civilized Tribes.
Oklahoma Historical Society is founded at Kingfisher.
Cherokee Outlet is opened to white settlement by the greatest of all the Runs in Oklahoma.
1896 Greer County is awarded to the United States by a Supreme Court decision and joined to the Territory of Oklahoma.
1897 Choctaws, Chickasaws, and Seminoles make agreements with the Dawes Commission.
1898 Congress passes the Curtis Act providing for compulsory liquidation of the Five Civilized Tribes.
Many Oklahoma and Indian Territory frontiersmen serve with Roosevelt's Rough Riders in the Spanish-American War.
1899 United States takes over the schools, the Dawes Commission starts allotting the lands, and the first townsites are platted for the Five Civilized Tribes.
1900 First course in geology is taught at the University of Oklahoma.
Federal census shows a population of 398,331 in the Territory of Oklahoma and 392,060 in the Five Civilized Tribes area.
1901 Kiowa-Comanche and Wichita reservations are opened to settlement, the last opening in Oklahoma.
1905 Inhabitants of the Five Tribes area hold a convention and draw up a constitution for a state to be named Seyuoyah.
Glenn Oil Pool is discovered.
1906 Congress passes the Enabling Act providing statehood for Oklahoma; the constitutional convention meets at Guthrie.
1907 November 16, Oklahoma is admitted to the Union, the forty-sixth state; the first election reveals overwhelming Democratic majority; Charles N. Haskell, the first governor, is inaugurated at Guthrie.
Special federal census enumerates a population of 1,414,177 for the new state.
1910 State capital is removed to Oklahoma City.
Population, 1,657,155.
1911 State legislature provides for placing a statue of Sequoyah in Statuary Hall in the national Capitol.
Lee Cruce is inaugurated as governor.
1912 Cushing Oil Pool is discovered.
1913 Healdton Oil Field is discovered.
1915 Robert L. Williams is inaugurated as governor.
1916 Oklahoma National Guard sees service on the Mexican Border.
1917 United States declares war on Germany; in the first draft Okla-

homa registers 173,744; the "Green Corn Rebellion" breaks out against conscription.

1918 End of World War I, for which Oklahoma furnished 88,496 men in uniform and purchased $116,368,045 worth of Liberty Bonds.

1919 J. B. A. Robertson is inaugurated as governor of Oklahoma.

1920 Oklahoma for the first time in its history votes Republican. Oil fields in Osage County begin spectacular production. Population, 2,028,283.

1923 John Calloway (Jack) Walton becomes governor, is impeached and removed from office, and is succeeded by Martin Edwin Trapp.

1926 Greater Seminole Oil Field is developed, bringing serious overproduction in the oil industry.

1927 Henry S. Johnston becomes governor.

1928 Oklahoma City Oil Field is opened.

1929 Governor Johnston is impeached and removed from office; William J. Holloway becomes governor.

1930 Population, 2,396,040.

1931 William H. ("Alfalfa Bill") Murray is inaugurated as governor. Governor Murray closes Oklahoma oil wells in an effort to stabilize prices.
Wiley Post, noted Oklahoma air pilot, completes round-the-world flight of 16,474 miles in 8 days, 15 hours, 51 minutes.

1935 E. W. Marland is inaugurated as governor.
Will Rogers and Wiley Post die in airplane crash in Alaska.

1937 Construction begins on $22,750,000 Grand River Dam in eastern Oklahoma.

1939 Leon C. ("Red") Phillips becomes governor.

1940 Population, 2, 336,434, a loss of 59,606 since census of 1930.

1941 The United States is involved in World War II. Oklahoma adjusts to war conditions.

1943 Robert S. Kerr becomes the twelfth governor, and the first who was born in Oklahoma.

1944 Oklahoma votes for Franklin D. Roosevelt for a fourth term as President.

1945 More than two hundred thousand Oklahomans in armed services of the United States.

1947 Roy J. Turner begins term as governor.
Legislature authorizes turnpike connecting Oklahoma City with Tulsa.

1948 Oklahoma votes for Harry S. Truman for President, over Thomas E. Dewey.
1950 Population, 2,233,351.
1951 Johnston Murray, son of "Alfalfa Bill," inaugurated as governor.
1952 Oklahoma casts its vote for Dwight D. Eisenhower over Adlai E. Stevenson: total vote 948,984, largest in the state's history.
1953 Turner Turnpike, Oklahoma City to Tulsa, completed.
1955 Raymond Gary becomes governor.
Racial segregation in Oklahoma schools in process of abandonment.
Oklahoma City selected as site of National Cowboy Hall of Fame.
1956 Oklahoma again votes for Eisenhower over Stevenson.

SELECTED READING LIST

This list is not designed as an exhaustive or scholarly bibliography, but as a guide to the general reader seeking further information about Oklahoma.

Alford, Thomas Wildcat. *Civilization*. Florence Drake, ed. Norman, University of Oklahoma Press, 1936. Life on the Shawnee reservation as told by a great-grandson of Tecumseh; a first hand account of Indian life and customs and the adjustment to the white man's institutions.

Allen, C. M. *The Sequoyah Convention*. Oklahoma City, Harlow Publishing Company, 1925. A history of the movement which resulted in the formation of the state of Oklahoma.

Alley, John. *City Beginnings in Oklahoma Territory*. Norman, University of Oklahoma Press, 1939. Shows how the cities of Guthrie, Oklahoma City, Kingfisher, El Reno, Norman, and Stillwater sprang up at the time of the first Run.

Ball, Max W. *This Fascinating Oil Business*. Indianapolis and New York, Bobbs-Merrill Company, 1940. A nontechnical book, giving a complete description of the oil industry from prospecting to the finished product; not confined to Oklahoma, but presenting an adequate background of oil development in the state.

Barnard, Evan G. A *Rider of the Cherokee Strip*. Boston and New York, Houghton Mifflin Company, 1936. A firsthand account in vivid, narrative style of ranching and homesteading in Oklahoma.

Bass, Althea. *Cherokee Messenger*. Norman, University of Oklahoma Press, 1936. A readable biography of Samuel Austin Worcester; an account of the missionary work of the Worcester family and the early educational progress of the Cherokees.

Brookings Institution. *Organization and Administration of Oklahoma*. Oklahoma City, Harlow Publishing Company, 1935. A critical study of the functioning of Oklahoma government with recommendations for improvement. Since its publication, of course, much has transpired which could not have been anticipated in the report itself.

Buchanan, James Shannon, and Dale, Edward Everett. A *History of Oklahoma.* New York, Row, Peterson and Company, 1935. Designed for a school textbook and told in simple language; historically sound, and one of the best brief surveys of Oklahoma history.

Buck, Solon J. *The Settlement of Oklahoma.* A reprint from Volume XV, Part II, of the transactions of the Wisconsin Academy of Science, Arts, and Letters, Madison, Wisconsin, 1907. A research project, well annotated.

Campbell, Walter (Stanley Vestal). *The Book Lover's Southwest: A Guide to Good Reading.* Norman, University of Oklahoma Press, 1955. A comprehensive guide for the general readers and specialists alike.

Canton, Frank M. *Frontier Trails.* Edward Everett Dale, ed. Boston and New York, Houghton Mifflin Company, 1930. An autobiography of a colorful Oklahoma pioneer.

Collings, Ellsworth, and England, Alma Miller. *The 101 Ranch.* Norman, University of Oklahoma Press, 1937. An account of the manifold activities of this famous ranch near Ponca City; traces the development from range cattle industry to agriculture, oil production, rodeos, and Wild West shows.

Connelly, W. L. *The Oil Business As I Saw It.* Norman, University of Oklahoma Press, 1954. Fifty years of the oil game, told in factual stories by an old-timer.

Dale, Edward Everett. *Cherokee Cavaliers.* Norman, University of Oklahoma Press, 1939. Forty years of Cherokee history, graphically told in the correspondence of the Ridge-Watie-Boudinot family.

———. *Cow Country.* Norman, University of Oklahoma Press, 1943. The story of the Old West during the period of the great cattle drives from Texas to the railheads in Kansas—or on to states farther west where great baronial ranches were being stocked.

———. *The Range Cattle Industry.* Norman, University of Oklahoma Press, 1930. A vivid and authentic history of ranching on the Great Plains, including the area now comprising the state of Oklahoma.

———, and Rader, Jesse L. *Readings in Oklahoma Hitsory.* New York, Row, Peterson and Company, 1930. A collection of nontechnical source material illustrating phases of Oklahoma history.

Debo, Angie. *And Still the Waters Run.* Princeton, Princeton University Press, 1940. The liquidation of the Five Civilized Tribes in preparation for statehood, and the picture of the Indians as citizens of Oklahoma.

———. *Oklahoma: Foot-loose and Fancy-free.* Norman, University of

Oklahoma Press, 1949. An interpretation of the Sooner State with insight and accuracy, sympathy and truth.

———. *Prairie City*. New York, Knopf, 1944. The story of a typical town in western Oklahoma, authentic and interpretative.

———. *The Rise and Fall of the Choctaw Republic*. Norman, University of Oklahoma Press, 1934. A political, social, and economic history of the Choctaw Indians.

———. *The Road to Disappearance*. Norman, University of Oklahoma Press, 1941. A scholarly study of the Creek Indians to the dissolution of their tribal government in Oklahoma.

———. *Tulsa: From Creek Town to Oil Capital*. Norman, University of Oklahoma Press, 1943. A book-length biography of the city of Tulsa, from the establishment, under a great oak tree still standing near the center of the present city area, of the "chunkey yard," or council square of the emigrant Creek Indians, to the modern city of magnificent skyline and palatial homes.

Ferguson, Mrs. Tom B. *They Carried the Torch*. Kansas City, Burton Publishing Company, 1937. The spirited reminiscences of a pioneer newspaperwoman; almost a social history of the development of Oklahoma Territory.

Forbes, Gerald. *Flush Production: The Epic of Oil in the Gulf-Southwest*. Norman, University of Oklahoma Press, 1942. The story of the world's richest oil fields—the petroleum empire known as the Gulf-Southwest, comprising six states, including Oklahoma.

———. *Guthrie: Oklahoma's First Capital*. Norman, University of Oklahoma Press, 1938. A brief description in pamphlet form of the establishment at Guthrie of the first capital of the newly opened Oklahoma Territory, and its removal to Oklahoma City.

Foreman, Carolyn Thomas. *Indians Abroad*. Norman, University of Oklahoma Press, 1943. The definitive account of the travels abroad of American Indians from the time of Columbus to the present day.

———. *Oklahoma Imprints*. Norman, University of Oklahoma Press, 1936. A comprehensive history of printing in the area forming the present state of Oklahoma, from the establishment of the first press in 1835 to the time of statehood. Useful as a reference book, presenting in its newspaper history a complete cross section of Indian and pioneer life.

Foreman, Grant. *Advancing the Frontier*. Norman, University of Oklahoma Press, 1933. A well-told and documented story of the immigrant Indians and their problems from 1770 to 1830.

———. *Adventure on Red River*. Norman, University of Oklahoma Press, 1937. Report on the exploration of the headwaters of the

Red River by Captain Randolph B. Marcy and Captain G. B. McClellan.

———. *Down the Texas Road.* Norman, University of Oklahoma Press, 1936. A handy little booklet, giving an authentic description of historical places along Highway 69 through Oklahoma.

———. *The Five Civilized Tribes.* Norman, University of Oklahoma Press, 1934. Probably the most interesting of this historian's many books; an authentic picture of life in what is now Oklahoma before the Civil War.

———. *Fort Gibson.* Norman, University of Oklahoma Press, 1936. A readable pamphlet describing the active life that centered around this frontier post.

———. *A History of Oklahoma.* Norman, University of Oklahoma Press, 1942. The first full history of Oklahoma to appear in one volume.

———. *Indian Removal.* Norman, University of Oklahoma Press, 1932. An interesting and authentic account of the emigration of the Five Civilized Tribes.

———. *Indians and Pioneers.* Norman, University of Oklahoma Press, 1936. The story of the American Southwest before 1830.

———. *Marcy and the Gold Seekers.* Norman, University of Oklahoma Press, 1939. The journal of Captain Randolph B. Marcy with an account of the gold rush over the "California Trail" across Oklahoma.

———. *Sequoyah.* Norman, University of Oklahoma Press, 1938. The definitive biography of this Indian genius.

Gard, Wayne. *The Chisholm Trail.* Norman, University of Oklahoma Press, 1954. The story of the greatest migration of domestic animals in world history.

Gipson, Fred. *Fabulous Empire: Colonel Zack Miller's Story.* Boston, Houghton Mifflin, 1946. Story of the 101 Ranch in Oklahoma, told with Southwestern feeling, color, and understanding.

Gittinger, Roy. *The Formation of the State of Oklahoma.* Norman, University of Oklahoma Press, 1939. A scholarly history of events leading to the creation of the state.

———. *The University of Oklahoma: A History of Fifty Years, 1892–1942.* Norman, University of Oklahoma Press, 1942. A human and mellow story of the state university in its first half-century of existence.

Glasscock, C. B. *Then Came Oil.* Indianapolis and New York, Bobbs-Merrill Company, 1938. Oklahoma history as affected by the discovery and development of the oil industry of the state.

Gould, Charles N. *Oklahoma Place Names.* Norman, University of Oklahoma Press, 1933. Explains the origin of numerous names of rivers, cities, towns, and mountains of Oklahoma.

Hill, Luther B. *A History of the State of Oklahoma.* Chicago and New York, Lewis Publishing Company, 1908. An early attempt to tell the story of Oklahoma from the date of the Louisiana Purchase through the formation of the state.

Hitchcock, Ethan Allen. *A Traveler in Indian Territory.* Grant Foreman, ed. Cedar Rapids, Iowa, The Torch Press, 1930. An extremely interesting journal of Hitchcock's visit to the Indian Territory in 1842. It is especially rich in Creek material, showing how that recently transplanted tribe was establishing its institutions upon a remote frontier.

Hollon, W. Eugene. *Beyond the Cross Timbers: The Travels of Randolph B. Marcy, 1812–1887.* Norman, University of Oklahoma Press, 1955. A well-written account of Marcy's explorations.

Irving, Washington. *A Tour on the Prairies.* John Francis McDermott, ed. Norman, University of Oklahoma Press, 1956. A rich and interesting account of Irving's journey across Oklahoma, the real experiences of real people. This is the work of Irving the artist and Irving the factual observer.

Jacobson, Oscar Brousse. *Kiowa Indian Art: Watercolor Paintings by Indians of Oklahoma.* Nice, France, C. Szwedzicki, 1929. A rare collector's item, consisting of the work of three young Kiowa Indian artists who were encouraged to paint in the natural Indian manner.

James, Marquis. *The Cherokee Strip.* New York, Viking, 1945. Excellent Americana concerned with life in Oklahoma before oil was found under the short grass.

Johnson, Vance. *Heaven's Tableland: The Dust Bowl Story.* New York, Farrar, Straus, 1947. History of the dust bowls from the times of the Plains Indian winter calendars.

Kraenzel, Carl Frederick. *The Great Plains in Transition.* Norman, University of Oklahoma Press, 1955. A penetrating analysis of the Great Plains from the standpoints of history, culture, economy, climate, and global perspective.

Lewis, Anna. *Along the Arkansas.* Dallas, The Southwest Press, 1932. Early history of the Arkansas River region in Oklahoma; also the Cimarron and Canadian.

McDermott, John Francis, ed. *The Western Journals of Washington Irving.* Norman, University of Oklahoma Press, 1944. The Irving Journals, fully annotated. These notes, written by Irving during his trip to and through the Osage country of Oklahoma in 1832, provided the basis for his subsequent book, A *Tour on the Prairies.*

McReynolds, Edwin C. *Oklahoma: A History of the Sooner State.* Norman, University of Oklahoma Press, 1954. An up-to-date record of the state's historical development.

Marable, Mary Hays, and Boylan, Elaine. *A Handbook of Oklahoma Writers.* Norman, University of Oklahoma Press, 1939.

Marriott, Alice. *The Ten Grandmothers.* Norman, University of Oklahoma Press, 1945. The history of the Kiowa tribe during its residence in Oklahoma, from 1847 to 1944, told in vivid narrative sketches from the memories of living Kiowas.

Mathews, John Joseph. *Life and Death of an Oilman: The Career of E. W. Marland.* Norman, University of Oklahoma Press, 1951. The story of the millionaire, sportsman, and governor of Oklahoma, told with convincing historical background.

———. *Wah'Kon-Tah.* Norman, University of Oklahoma Press, 1932. A beautifully written interpretation of the Osage spirit, based on notes kept by Laban J. Miles, United States Agent to the tribe.

Moorman, Lewis J., M.D. *Pioneer Doctor.* Norman, University of Oklahoma Press, 1951. The story of half a century of medical practice from the early days of Oklahoma.

Morrison, William Brown. *Military Posts and Camps in Oklahoma.* Oklahoma City, Harlow Publishing Company, 1936. An account of early-day military establishments and activities in Oklahoma.

Nelson, Oliver. *The Cowman's Southwest.* Angie Debo, ed. Glendale, Arthur H. Clark, 1953. Reminiscences of a frontiersman in Oklahoma, Indian Territory, Kansas, and Texas from 1878 to 1893.

Nye, W. S. *Carbine and Lance.* Norman, University of Oklahoma Press, 1937. A popular and accurate account of Indian campaigns in western Oklahoma, centered about the history of Fort Sill.

Oklahoma Historical Society. *Chronicles of Oklahoma.* Oklahoma City 1921— A quarterly publication containing scholarly articles by historians and colorful reminscences by pioneers.

Oklahoma Writers' Program. *Tulsa, a Guide to the Oil Capital.* Tulsa, Mid-West Printing Company, 1938. Contains information about the history, industry, and cultural institutions of Tulsa, with directions to its points of interest. Brief and factual.

Peyton, Green. *America's Heartland: The Southwest.* Norman, University of Oklahoma Press, 1948. An exciting biography of the Southwest and its people.

Rader, Jesse L. *South of Forty.* Norman, University of Oklahoma Press, 1947. A bibliography of books and documents portraying the persons and events that shaped the development of that area between the fortieth parallel and the Gulf of Mexico, and from the Mississippi westward to the Rio Grande. It begins with the era of discovery and continues to July 1, 1939.

Rainey, George. *The Cherokee Strip*. Guthrie, Co-operative Publishing Company, 1933. An intimate, readable history of the Cherokee Outlet from the date of its acquisition by the Cherokees to the opening in 1893.

———. *No Man's Land*. Enid, Oklahoma, 1937. A story of the Oklahoma Panhandle, beginning with the first white man's visit to the region. Contains many human-interest stories peculiar to the section.

Ridings, Sam P. *The Chisholm Trail*. Guthrie, Co-operative Publishing Company, 1936. A comprehensive and entertaining account of the drives, personalities, and places along the trail in the period of its greatest use.

Rister, Carl Coke. *Land Hunger*. Norman, University of Oklahoma Press, 1943. A biography of David L. Payne, as well as the narrative of the "Boomer" movement which attracted thousands to the campaign to open Oklahoma Territory to settlement.

———. *No Man's Land*. Norman, University of Oklahoma Press, 1948. The colorful, dramatic history of that orphaned territory that finally became the Oklahoma Panhandle.

———. *Oil! Titan of the Southwest*. Norman, University of Oklahoma Press, 1949. The history and interpretation of the petroleum industry and its effects on life in the region.

———. *Southern Plainsmen*. Norman, University of Oklahoma Press, 1938. A history of the southern half of the Great Plains, especially noting the characteristics of the short-grass country, which includes western Oklahoma.

Sears, Paul B. *Deserts on the March*. Norman, University of Oklahoma Press, 1935. A brilliant study of soil erosion; not limited to Oklahoma, but inspired by Oklahoma problems.

Seger, John H. *Early Days Among the Cheyenne and Arapahoe Indians*. Stanley Vestal, ed. Norman, University of Oklahoma Press, 1934, 1956. The memoirs of a great educator among Plains Indians; an intimate, informal account written with grace and charm.

Snider, Luther Crocker. *Geography of Oklahoma*. Norman, Oklahoma Geological Survey, 1917. Describes the geology, physical features, mineral resources, plant and animal life, agriculture, and political and social institutions of Oklahoma. Encyclopedic in style but nontechnical. Not seriously outdated.

Starr, Emmett. *History of the Cherokee Indians*. Oklahoma City, The

Warden Company, 1921. In this genealogical history of the Cherokees is included much of the tribe's legends and folklore.

Stewart, Dora Ann. *Government and Development of Oklahoma Territory*. Oklahoma City, Harlow Publishing Company, 1933. An account of the building of a commonwealth in the seventeen years from 1890 to 1907, with special emphasis on the federal government's program of Indian education.

Thoburn, Joseph B., and Wright, Muriel H. *Oklahoma, a History of the State and Its People*, Vols. I–IV. New York, Lewis Historical Publishing Company, 1929. A convenient set that may be found in most public libraries of the state.

Wallace, Ernest, and Hoebel, E. Adamson. *The Comanches: Lords of the South Plains*. Norman, University of Oklahoma Press, 1952. A serious study of a primitive, pragmatic tribe who fought for slaves and loot.

Wardell, Morris L. A *Political History of the Cherokee Nation*. Norman, University of Oklahoma Press, 1938. The political story of the Cherokees from the Removal in 1838 to the breakup of tribal government.

Wright, Muriel H. A *Guide to the Indian Tribes of Oklahoma*. Norman, University of Oklahoma Press, 1951. Miss Wright, an Indian herself, has written an unusually comprehensive treatment of sixty-seven Indian tribes associated with Oklahoma.

———. *Our Oklahoma*. Guthrie, Co-operative Publishing Company, 1939. A school text on Oklahoma history, profusely illustrated. readable, accurate.

PICTURE SOURCES

Between pages 26 and 29: *Fall Plowing,* Bill Sheets; *Washington Oil Pool,* Carter Oil Company; *Tilted Rock Strata, Water Skiing,* Mac McGalliard; *Fort Gibson Lake, Snipe Regatta, Skyline Trail,* Oklahoma Planning and Resources Board; *Fort Gibson Dam,* Muskogee Chamber of Commerce; *Skelly Ranch, Quail Hunting,* Halliburton Oil Well Cementing Company; *Buffalo Wallow, Fort Sill Military Reservation,* Lawton Chamber of Commerce; *Turner Turnpike,* Phillips Petroleum Company.

Between pages 90 and 93: *Will Rogers Memorial,* Oklahoma Planning and Resources Board; *Owen Tah,* Cities Service Company; *Bacone College,* Muskogee Chamber of Commerce.

Between pages 154 and 157: *Capitol Building,* Oklahoma Planning and Resources Board; *Church of Tomorrow,* Duane Conner, architect; *Veterans Administration Hospital,* C. E. Bates; *Thomas Gilcrease Museum, Utica Square,* Tulsa Chamber of Commerce; *National Guard Armory, McMahon Memorial Auditorium,* Lawton Chamber of Commerce; *Price Tower,* Halliburton Oil Well Cementing Company; *Fort Gibson Stockade,* Muskogee Chamber of Commerce; *Cement Kiln,* Baynes McSwain; *Indian Sanatorium,* Shawnee Chamber of Commerce.

Between pages 250 and 253: *Oil Well in the East Lindsay Pool,* Carter Oil Company; *Gasoline Plant, Pressure Maintenance in Oil Sands,* Phillips Petroleum Company; *Oil Pumping Unit,* Sunray Mid-Continent Oil Company; *Spheres for Butane Storage,* Texas Company; *West Tulsa Refinery, Textile Mill,* Tulsa Chamber of Commerce; *Oil Well Cementing Shops,* Halliburton Oil Well Cementing Company; *Lead and Zinc Concentrate Mill,* Miami Chamber of Commerce; *Hauling Saw Logs,* Dierks Forests, Inc.; *Lumber Stacked for Air-Drying,* Oklahoma Planning and Resources Board; *Aero*

Commander, Aero Design and Engineering Company; *Jet Assembly Line*, Douglas Aircraft Company.

Between pages 346 and 349: *Typical Cattle Farm Scenes*, Oklahoma State Board of Agriculture and Oklahoma Planning and Resources Board; *On the Robert Adams Farm*, Tulsa Chamber of Commerce; *Wheat Fields at Harvest Time*, Cities Service Company and Enid Chamber of Commerce; *Modern Farm Homes*, J. Eldon Peek; *"Wildcat" Oil Well*, Sunray Mid-Continent Oil Company; *Cotton Picker, Seedbed Preparation on a Wheat Farm, Farm Irrigation*, Oklahoma Farmer Stockman; *Bales of Cotton*, Muskogee Chamber of Commerce; *Turkeys Ready for Market*, Hallren Products Company.

Between pages 442 and 445: A *Favorite Sport*, Lawton Chamber of Commerce; *Sunday Morning Service, Saturday Night in Town, In the Little Leagues, First-Aid Training*, Cities Service Company; *Oil Well Driller*, Phillips Petroleum Company; *Jet Acrobatics*, Carter Oil Company; *Easter Pageant*, Wichita Mountains Easter Service Association; *Workers in Electric Products Plant*, Shawnee Chamber of Commerce; *Excitement at the Rodeo*, Halliburton Oil Well Cementing Company; *Eighty-Niner Celebration*, Guthrie Chamber of Commerce; *Students*, Tulsa Chamber of Commerce.

INDEX